THEATRE

Fourth Edition

ALSO BY ROBERT COHEN

THEATRE

Fourth Edition

Robert Cohen

University of California, Irvine

MAYFIELD PUBLISHING COMPANY

Mountain View, California
London • Toronto

Library of Congress Cataloging-in-Publication Data

Cohen, Robert
   Theatre / Robert Cohen—4th ed.
     p. cm.
   Includes bibliographical references and index.
   ISBN 1-55934-666-3
   1. Theater. I. Title.
PN2101.C63   1996
792—dc20   96-13608
                          CIP

Manufactured in the United States of America
10 9 8 7 6 5 4 3

Mayfield Publishing Company
1280 Villa Street
Mountain View, CA 94041

Sponsoring editor, Janet M. Beatty; production editor, Julianna Scott Fein; manuscript editor, Margaret Moore; art director, Jeanne M. Schreiber; text designer, Anna George; cover designer, Susan Breitbard; cover photo, Tomoko Ogawa; art manager, Robin Mouat; manufacturing manager, Amy Folden; prepress, H & S Graphics Inc. The text was set in 10/12 Galliard by Thompson Type and printed on acid-free 50# Chromatone Matte by Banta Book Group.

TO MICHAEL COHEN

Preface

I am sitting in a darkened theatre correcting the galley sheets for the book you are about to read. A technical rehearsal for a play I am directing is in progress; I am seated at a makeshift desk in the back of the house, my reading illuminated by a tiny covered gooseneck lamp. On stage stand several actors, silent and motionless, as light plays over their faces and bodies. Above me, unseen and unheard, technicians operate, adjust, and record the settings for another of the play's hundred and fifty light cues. To the outside observer, it is the dullest situation imaginable; nothing observable happens for twenty or thirty minutes at a stretch. A pool of light intensifies and then recedes, muffled conversation crackles over headsets, footsteps clang on steel catwalks lacing the ceiling, and a spotlight is carefully repositioned. This has been going on now since eight in the morning, and it is already past dinnertime.

And yet my eye is continually pulled from these pages to the dance of light upon the stage. The violet and amber hues are rich with color, and the sharp shafts of incandescence dazzle with brilliance. I am fascinated by the patient weariness of the actors, alternately glowing in and then shadowed by the lights, endlessly holding the positions that, in performance, they will occupy for only a few transitory seconds. I gaze with admiration at the followspot operator, his hands gloved, as he handles his instrument with the precision and sensitivity of a surgeon.

The silence, the stasis, is hypnotic. All is quiet but profound with held-back beats, incipient torrents of passion and exhilaration.

The potential is riveting—I am alive with excitement—and I look back to these cold galley sheets with alarm.

How can I have thought to express the thrill of the theatre in these pages? How can I have hoped to make recognizable the joy and awe I feel in theatrical involvement?

The theatre is not merely a collection of crafts, a branch of literature, a collaboration of technique, or even an all-encompassing art form. It is a life. It is people. It is people making art out of themselves. Its full reality transcends by light years anything that could be said or written about it.

What I have tried to do in these pages is not so much to introduce the theatre or to survey it as to *present* the theatre with its liveliness and humanness intact, with its incipient passion and exhilaration always present, with its potential for joy, awe, wisdom, and excitement as clear to the reader as they have been made clear to me.

FEATURES

Integral to the text are the presentations of seven "model plays," drawn from the theatre's history, as the core of the "past" and "present" sections. These seven plays—*Prometheus Bound, Oedipus Tyrannos*, the *York Cycle, Romeo and Juliet, The Bourgeois Gentleman, The Three Sisters*, and *Happy Days*—represent, in combination, the range and magnitude of human theatrical achievement. That is not to say that they are the world's greatest dramatic masterpieces (although some of them surely are), but that they collectively define the major horizons of the drama as well as the theatre's major styles, themes, and expressions of human imagination. However, I do not intend for these model play presentations to substitute for seeing the plays or for reading them. Readers of this fourth edition may gain access to six of these model plays (together with two others) in their entirety through a companion anthology, *Eight Plays for Theatre,* and to twelve more plays, including *Prometheus Bound,* in *Twelve Plays for Theatre.*

With or without the knowledge of the whole plays, however, I believe that the model presentations in this book, along with the excerpts from 25 other plays, will provide outlines for the reader's understanding and springboards for the reader's imagination of drama as it has been created and practiced through the major periods of theatrical history.

To enhance the reader's understanding of drama, I have included more than 200 photos gathered during my recent surveys of stage productions in North America and abroad. Extended captions help readers better appreciate these images of theatre worldwide and make stronger connections to the text examples. Quotes from prominent theatre professionals such as Peter Brook, Edith Head, Tennessee Williams, August Wilson, and others are included in boxed insets throughout the text as another means of bringing the theatre to life.

The text offers a number of pedagogical aids to help students get the most out of a written introduction to a highly visual and aural medium. Terms commonly used in theatre and theatre history are defined in the glossary at the back of the book, and further sources of information for the curious can be found in the selected bibliography. To help students enjoy performances to the fullest, I've included an appendix that offers advice on observing and writing critically about plays.

A Test Bank, written by Marilyn Moriarty, includes 50 multiple choice questions and several short answer or essay questions per chapter. A computerized version of the test bank is available to qualified adopters.

WHAT'S NEW?

Most prominently, this edition includes a wholly new chapter on the theatre of Asia, with a special focus on Japan and the Kabuki theatre. I hope this chapter will provide not only a basic introduction to one of Asia's major dramatic forms, but also a representation of the brilliance and variety of Eastern theatrical creativity and its parallels and contrasts with Western drama.

Chapter 10, "Theatre Today," has been thoroughly updated, with new coverage of American dramatists Terrence McNally and Tony Kushner and expanded coverage of the American musical, including color photos of major new productions such as *Passion* and *Sunset Boulevard* and important revivals such as *Carousel* and *A Funny Thing Happened on the Way to the Forum.*

As part of the updating throughout, I've included more than 60 new color photographs of significant theatre developments in Europe, Asia, and North America. Chapter 13 now includes a section on computer uses in theatre design, and Chapter 15 offers a box with two contemporary reviews of a modern play (*The Sisters Rosensweig*) to illustrate differing modes of current dramatic criticism.

ACKNOWLEDGMENTS

Let me again express my gratitude to the generous and wise scholars and theatre artists who provided me with advice and suggestions on the first three editions of this book, and to the very gracious and perceptive reviewers of the fourth edition manuscript who have helped me shape this text: Jim Billings, New Mexico State University; Tom Bliese, Mankato State University; Chris Jones, Northern Illinois University; Stephen D. Malin, University of Memphis; Kent K. Miller, California State University, Long Beach; Ellis M. Pryce-Jones, University of Nevada, Las Vegas; James E. Shollenberger, University of Mississippi; Leon J. Van Dyke, University of Wisconsin, Parkside; Jeffrey L. Warburton, University of Arizona; and Albert F. C. Wehlburg, University of Florida.

For helping me select the new photographs of the American theatre for this edition, I would like to thank Jeff Fickes and Arvin Brown at the Long Wharf Theatre, Rochelle Franco and Gavin Cameron-Webb at the Studio Arena Theatre of Buffalo, James Seacat and Jon Jory at the Actors Theatre of Louisville, Dresden D. Engle and Howard Millman at the GeVa Theatre of Rochester, Kelli A. Walker and Libby Appel at the Indiana Repertory Theatre, Wendy Bowers and Fred Adams at the Utah Shakespearean Festival, Steve Moyer and Peter Hunt at the Williamstown Theatre Festival, Larry Biederman and Carey Perloff at the American Conservatory Theater, Cristofer Gross at the South Coast Repertory Theatre, Sarah Rowell and Kent Thompson at the Alabama Shakespeare Festival, and James Calleri and Joan Marcus in New York City.

For the new photographs from France: Françoise Paris at the Enguerand Studios in Paris. And for the new photographs of Kabuki drama, Shoshichi Nasu and Ken Lawrence of the Japanese Center of the International Theatre Institute, the Shochiko theatre company, Haiyu Kyokai (Japanese Actors Association), Taichi Suematsu, and, most particularly, Matthew Johnson ("The Kabuki Master") and photographer Tomoko Ogawa.

For their expert counsel on the Kabuki: Akira Mark Oshima, Matthew Johnson, and Shoshichi Nasu in Tokyo; Professor Susan Klein of the University of California at Irvine; and, most particularly, Professor Leonard Pronko of Pomona College.

Contents

THEATRE

Fourth Edition

Introduction

....

It is evening in Manhattan. On Broadway and the streets that cross it—44th, 45th, 46th, 47th, 50th, 52nd—marquees light up, "Performance Tonight" signs materialize in front of double doors, and beneath a few box-office windows placards announce "This Performance Completely Sold Out." At Grand Central Station to the east and Pennsylvania Station to the south, trains disgorge suburbanites from Greenwich, Larchmont, and Trenton, students from New Haven and Philadelphia, daytrippers from Boston and Washington. Up from the Seventh and Eighth Avenue subway stations of Times Square troop denizens of the island city and the neighboring boroughs. At the Times Square "TKTS" Booth, hundreds line up in the deepening chill to buy the half-price tickets that go on sale a few hours before curtain time for undersold shows. Now, converging on these few midtown blocks of America's largest city, come limousines, restaurant buses, private cars, and taxis, whose drivers search for a curbside slot to deposit their riders among the thousands of pedestrians who already throng the streets. Financiers and dowagers, bearded intellectuals, bedraggled bohemians, sleek executives, hip Harlemites, arm-in-arm widows, conventioneers, tourists, honeymooners, out-of-work actors, celebrities, the precocious young—all commingle in this bizarre aggregation that is the Broadway audience. It is as bright, bold, and varied a crowd as is likely to assemble at any one place in America.

It is eight o'clock. In thirty or forty theatres houselights dim, curtains rise, spotlights pick out performers whose lives center on this moment. Here a new musical, here a star-studded revival of an American classic, here a contemporary English comedy from London's West End, here a new play fresh from its electrifying Seattle premiere, here a one-woman show, here an off-Broadway hit moving to larger quarters, here a new avant-garde dance-drama, here a touring production from Eastern Europe, and here the new play everyone expects will capture this year's coveted Pulitzer Prize. The hours pass.

Eleven o'clock. Pandemonium. All the double doors open as at a signal, and once again the thousands pour out into the night. At nearby restaurants, waiters stand by to receive the after-theatre onslaught. In Sardi's private upstairs room, an opening-night cast party gets under way; downstairs, the patrons rehash the evening's entertainment and sneak covert glances at the celebrities around them and at the actors heading for the upstairs sanctuary to await the reviews that will determine whether they will be employed next week or back on the street.

Now turn back the clock.

It is dawn in Athens, the thirteenth day of the month of Elaphebolion in the year 458 B.C. From thousands of low mud-bricked homes in the city, from the central agora, from temples and agricultural outposts, streams of Athenians and visitors converge upon the south slope of the Acropolis. Bundled against the early damp, carrying with them breakfast figs and flagons of wine, they pay their tokens at the entrance to the great Theatre of Dionysus and take their places in the seating spaces allotted them. Each tribe occupies a separate area. They gather for the Festival of the Great Dionysia, celebrating the greening of the land, the rebirth of vegetation, and the long sunny days that stretch ahead. It is a time for revelry, a time for rejoicing at fertility and its fruits. And it is above all a time for the ultimate form of Dionysian worship: the theatre.

The open stone seats carved into the hillside fill up quickly. The crowd of 17,000 people here today comprises not only the majority of Athenian citizens, but thousands of noncitizens as well: women, slaves, tradesmen, foreign visitors, and resident aliens. Even the paupers are in attendance, thanks to the two obols meted out to each of them from a state fund so that they can purchase entry; they sit with the foreigners and latecomers on the extremities of the *theatron*, as this first of theatres is called.

Now as the eastern sky grows pale, a masked and costumed actor appears atop a squat building set in full view of every spectator. A hush falls over the crowd, and the actor, his voice magnified by the wooden mask from which it emanates, booms out this text:

I ask the gods some respite from the
　weariness
of this watchtime measured by years I lie
　awake . . .

And the entranced crowd settles in, secure in the knowledge that today they are in good hands. Today they will hear and see a new version of a familiar story—the story of Agamemnon's homecoming and his murder, the revenge of that murder by his son Orestes, and the final disposition of justice in the case of Orestes' act—as told in the three tragedies that constitute *The Oresteia*. This magnificent trilogy is by Aeschylus, Athens' leading dramatist for more than forty years. The spectators watch closely, admiring but critical. Tomorrow they or their representatives will have to decide by vote whether the festival prize should go to this group of plays or to one of those shown yesterday, whether Aeschylus still reigns supreme or the young Sophocles has better sensed the true pulse of the time.

*The Broadway theatre district. About three dozen theatres line the streets of a mere ten blocks in midtown Manhattan; four of them—the Royale, the Golden, the Imperial (*Les Misérables*), and the Martin Beck (*Guys and Dolls*)—are shown here in a single half-block of 45th Street. Broadway was largely developed at the turn of the century as theatres replaced aging apartment buildings in what was originally a quiet residential district known as Longacre Square. The theatres— mostly designed by one man, Herbert J. Krapp—are relatively intimate (most seat a maximum of 1,000) and are closely situated, making for a bustling concentration of theatres unknown in most other cities.*

Even forty years later the comic playwright Aristophanes will be arguing the merits and demerits of this day's work.

It is noon in London, and the first Queen Elizabeth sits on the throne. Flags fly boldly atop three of the taller buildings in Bankside, across the Thames, announcing performance day at The Globe, The Rose, and The Swan. Boatmen have already begun ferrying theatre-bound Londoners across the river. Meanwhile, north of town, other flocks of Londoners are headed by foot and by carriage up to Finsbury Fields and the theatres of Shoreditch: The Fortune and The Curtain. Public theatres have been banned in the city for some time now by action of the Lords Aldermen; however, an ensemble of trained schoolboys is rehearsing for a private candlelight performance before the Queen.

Now, as the morning sermon concludes at St. Paul's Cathedral, the traffic across the river increases; London Bridge fills with pedestrians hurrying to Bankside, where The Globe players will present a new tragedy by Shakespeare (something called *Hamlet*, supposedly after an old play by Thomas Kyd), and The Rose promises a revival of the late Christopher Marlowe's *Dr. Faustus*. The noisy crowds swarm into the theatres, where the price of admission is a penny; another penny is needed for a pint of beer, and those who wish to go upstairs and take a seat on one of the benches in the gallery—the best place to see the action, both on stage and off—must plunk down yet more pennies.

At The Globe, 2,000 spectators are on hand for the premiere. A trumpet sounds, sounds again, and then builds into a full fanfare. The members of the audience exchange a few last winks with friends old and new, covert and overt invitations to postperformance intimacies of various kinds, and then turn their attention to the pillared, trestled, naked stage. Through one giant door Bernardo bursts forth. "Who's there?" he cries. Then through another door, a voice: "Nay, answer me: stand and unfold yourself," and Francisco enters with lighted lantern in hand. In 2,000 imaginations, the bright afternoon turns to midnight, the Bankside gives way to the outskirts of Elsinore. A shiver from the actors on stage sets up an answering chill among the audience as Francisco proclaims, "'Tis bitter cold, and I am sick at heart." The audience strains forward. The tragedy has begun.

It is evening at Versailles, 1664. King Louis XIV nods graciously as the celebrated actor-playwright bows before him. Jean-Baptiste Poquelin, known throughout France as Molière, has just presented his *Tartuffe*, with its scathingly witty denunciation of the powerful Church extremists. The courtiers, taking Louis's nod, applaud vigorously; in one corner of the glittering hall, however, a bishop glares coldly at the actor. The Archbishop of Paris will hear of this.

It is 5 A.M. in Moscow, 1898. At a café in the shadow of the Kremlin wall, Konstantin Stanislavski and Vladimir Nemirovich-Danchenko hotly discuss the wretched state of the current Russian theatre. It is too declamatory, they agree; it is also too insensitive, too shallow, too inartistic. Out of this all-night session the Moscow Art Theatre will be formed, bringing to the last days of czarist society the complex, gently ironic masterpieces of Chekhov and an acting style so natural as to astonish the world.

It is midnight in a coffeehouse in the East Village, or on the Left Bank, or in the campus rehearsal room. Across one end of the room, a curtain has been drawn across a pole suspended by wires. It has been a long evening, but a play yet remains to be seen. The author is unknown, but rumor says that this new work is brutal, shocking, poetic, strange. The audience, by turns skeptics and enthusiasts, look for the tenth time at their programs. The lights dim. Performers, backed by crudely painted packing crates, begin to act.

There is a common denominator in all of these scenes: they are all theatre.

Theatre is the most natural of the arts. There is no culture that has not had a theatre in some form, for theatre is the art of people acting out—and giving witness to—their most pressing, most illuminating, and most inspiring concerns. Theatre is at once a showcase and a forum, a medium through which a society's ideas, fashions, moralities, and entertainments can be displayed and its conflicts, dilemmas, and struggles can be debated. Theatre has provided a stage for political revolution, for social propaganda, for civil debate, for artistic expression, for religious conversions, for mass education, and even for its own self-criticism. It has been a performance ground for witch doctors and priests, intellectuals, poets, painters, technologists, militarists, philosophers, reformers, evangelists, prime ministers, jugglers, peasants, children, and kings. It has taken place in caves, in fields and forests, in circus tents, in inns and in castles, on street corners, and in public buildings grand and squalid all over the world. And it goes on incessantly in the minds of its authors, its actors, its producers, its designers, and its audiences.

For theatre is, above all, a *living* art form— a *process,* an *event* that is fluid in time, feeling, and experience. It is not simply a matter of "plays," but also of "playing"; and a play is composed not simply of "acts," but also of "acting." As "play" and "act" are both noun and verb, so theatre is both a "thing" and a "happening." It is continually forming, continually present in time. In fact, that very quality of "presentness" (or, in the actor's term, "stage presence") defines great theatrical performance.

Theatre, unlike the more static arts, presents a number of classic paradoxes:

It is unique to the moment, yet it is repeatable.

It is spontaneous, yet it is rehearsed.

It is participatory, yet it is presented.

It is real, yet it is simulated.

It is understandable, yet it is obscure.

The actors are themselves, yet they are characters.

The audience believes, yet it does not believe.

The audience is involved, yet it remains apart.

These paradoxes stem not from any flaw or weakness in the logic of theatrical construction, but from the theatre's essential strength, which resides in its kinship and concern with the ambiguity and irony of human life—our life. It is *we* who are at the same time unique yet conventional, spontaneous yet premeditating, involved yet isolated, candid yet contriving, comprehensible yet fundamentally unknown and unknowable. Theorists of dramatic literature and of dramatic practice often ignore these paradoxes in their attempts to "explain" a play or the art of the stage; in this they do a grave disservice to art as well as to scholarship, for to "explain" the theatre without reference to its ambiguities is to remove its dynamic tension—in other words, to kill it. And although much valuable information can certainly be discovered at an autopsy table, it is information pertinent only to the appearance and behavior of a corpse.

In this book we shall not be overly concerned with corpses. Our task will be the harder one—to discover the theatre in being, *alive* and with all its paradoxes and ambiguities intact. From time to time it will be necessary for us to make some separations— between product and process, for example— but we must bear in mind at all times that these separations are conveniences, not representations or fact. In the end we shall be looking at the theatre as part of the human environment and at the ways in which we fit into that environment—as participants and observers, artists and art critics, role models and role players, actors and persons. So this book about the theatre is also about ourselves.

PART I

THE THEATRE: ITS ELEMENTS

SHAKESPEARE FESTIVAL

When we go to see a play, we see a whole work of art. If it moves us, or makes us laugh, or makes us think, it does so as a whole and complete artistic event; it seems, or should seem, absolutely seamless in its construction.

But it isn't. The theatre is a composite artistic process made up of many elements—acts and scenes, plot and character, art and entertainment—and an analysis of theatre is a study of its multiple elements. We will discuss some of those elements in the following section.

Analysis means the breaking up of something into its parts, from the Greek *ana* (up) plus *lysis* (loosening); the purpose of this breaking up is to study how the parts themselves work and how they are put together to create, in the case of theatre, an art form. Analysis is important work; without it we would find it impossible to direct or design a play, or write effectively about one. We would even find it difficult to act a small part in a play without examining the smaller parts of which that part is made.

As we look carefully and separately at the elements of the theatre, however, let us always bear in mind that we are studying, as it were, the cells and organs of a living creature. They will not stand perfectly still while we look at them, nor will they suffer our scalpels and microscopes gladly.

Theatre is an art we had best capture on the run, and with our eyes wide open, keeping its liveliness always before us as we fix it in our sights.

What Is the Theatre?

• •

What is the theatre?

The word comes from the Greek *theatron,* or "seeing place." It is "a place where something is seen."

And the companion term *drama* comes from the Greek *dran,* "to do." It is "something done."

Theatre: Something is seen, something is done.

We now use the word *theatre* in many ways.

We use it often to describe the *building* where plays are put on: the architecture, the structure, the *space* for dramatic performance—the place where "something is seen." In popular parlance, we also use the term to indicate where films are shown, as in "movie theatre." And we use it metaphorically to refer to where wars and surgeries take place: the theatre of operations and the operating theatre.

But that's just the "hardware" definition of theatre, the merely physical layout. The "software" definition—the theatre *activity* that goes into a theatre—is far more important.

For *theatre* also refers to the *company of players* (and owners, managers, and technicians) that perform in such a space and to the body of plays that such a company produces. This is the "something that is done." When we say "the Guthrie Theatre," we are refer-

THEATRE AND DRAMA

The words *theatre* and *drama* are often used interchangeably, yet they can also have distinct meanings.

While both are very general terms, *theatre* often denotes the elements of the whole theatrical production (architecture, scenery, acting) and *drama*, a more limited term, tends to refer mainly to the plays produced in such a "theatrical" environment. To use a modern metaphor, theatre is the "hardware" of play production, and drama is the "software." This reflects on the words' separate etymologies: theatre is that which "is seen," and drama is that which "is done."

"Theatre" can mean a building; "drama" cannot. "Theatre" is used to include all the theatrical arts—architecture, design, acting, scenery construction, advertising, marketing, and so on—whereas "drama" is often used in a more limited sense to refer to plays and to dramatic texts (or dramatic literature). Therefore, drama-derived terms such as *dramatic* and *dramaturgy* are often used to refer to the verbal aspects of theatre; "theatrical" tends to suggest visual aspects, as well as "effects" that generate audience impact. (Detractors of the theatre sometimes use the word *theatrical* in a pejorative sense, implying gaudiness and sensationalism, as in "mere theatricality.")

In some parts of North America, particularly in Canada, a further distinction is made: *theatre* is used more to denote staged plays (the product), and *drama* refers more to the acting and improvising of situations (the process).

ring not merely to a building on Vineland Place in Minneapolis, but also to the group of stage artists and administrators that work in this building and to the body of plays produced there. We are also referring to a body of ideas—a vision—that animates the artists and integrates them with the body of plays. "Theatre," in this sense, is a combination of people, ideas, and the works of art that emanate from their collaboration.

And, finally, we also use the word *theatre* to summon up an *occupation* that is the professional activity—and often the passion—of thousands of men and women all over the world. It is a vocation, and sometimes a lifetime devotion. *A Life in the Theatre* is the title of one theatre artist's autobiography (Tyrone Guthrie, in fact, for whom the Guthrie Theatre is named), but it is also the informal title for the unwritten biographies of all theatre artists who have dedicated their professional lives to perfecting the special arts of acting, directing, designing, managing, and writing for "the theatre" in *all* the above senses.

A building, a company, an occupation: we should look at all three of these usages more closely.

THE THEATRE BUILDING

Sometimes a theatre is not a building at all, but merely, in Peter Brook's term, an empty space. The most ancient Greek *theatron* was probably nothing but a flat circle where performers chanted and danced before a hillside where people sat watching them. The minimal requirement for a theatre "building" is nothing but a place to act and a place to watch.

And when there is a text for the performance, it is a place to *hear* as well as to watch. Hence the word *audience,* from the Latin "those who hear."

The empty space needs some definition, then. This includes some attention to a large number of people seeing the performers, hence the hillside presenting a bank of seats, each

Sometimes there is no theatre building at all. This original production of The Mahabharata, *adapted from the ancient Sanskrit epic, was first staged by director Peter Brook in a limestone quarry outside of Avignon, France. Subsequently, it was performed around the world. (Photo: Gilles Abegg.)*

with a good view. It also includes some attention to *acoustics* (from the Greek *acoustos,* "heard") so that the sound is protected from the wind and directed (or reflected) toward the hearers.

Often these "places"—for performing and for seeing and hearing—can be casually defined: the audience up there, the actors down there. Occasionally, the spaces are even merged together, with the actors mingling with—and sometimes interacting with—the watchers and listeners. When tickets began to be sold and actors began to be paid (both practices are more than twenty-five hundred years old), rigid physical separation of the spaces began to be employed.

Theatre buildings may also be very elaborate structures. Greek theatres of the fourth century B.C.—the period immediately following the "Golden Age" of Greek playwrights—were gigantic stone edifices, capable of holding upwards of 17,000 spectators at a time. Magnificent, three-story Roman theatres, complete with gilded columns, canvas awnings, and intricate marble carvings, were often erected for dramatic festivals in the time of Nero and Caligula—only to be dismantled when the festivities ended. Grandly free-standing Elizabethan theatres dominated the London skyline in the illustrated sixteenth-century pictorial maps of the town. Opulent proscenium theatres were built throughout

The Guthrie Theatre in Minneapolis was founded in 1963 by celebrated British director Tyrone Guthrie, who oversaw the architectural design which—like sixteenth-century Shakespearean playhouses—"thrusts" the actors in the midst of the audience. Shown here is Chekhov's Three Sisters, *directed by Mr. Guthrie and designed by Tanya Moiseiwitsch for the theatre's initial season. (Photo: Courtesy Guthrie Theatre.)*

Europe and in the major cities of the United States in the eighteenth and nineteenth centuries, and many are in full operation today—where they compete with splendid new stagehouses of every description, serving as the urban focus for metropolitan areas around the world. Theatres (the buildings) are central to modern urban architecture, just as theatre (the art) is central to contemporary life.

THE COMPANY, OR "TROUPE," OF PLAYERS

Theatre is a collaborative art, usually involving dozens, even hundreds, of people for a single performance. Historically, therefore, theatre practitioners have worked together in long-standing companies, or "troupes," of such theatre artists. Since the third century B.C., troupes of "players" (actors or, more generally, play-makers) have toured the countrysides and settled in cities to present a repertory (or repertoire) of plays as a means of earning their livelihood. Generally these players have included actor-playwrights and actor-technicians as well so that the company becomes a self-contained production unit, capable of writing, preparing, and presenting whole theatrical works that tend to define the "theatre" named after it. Some of these troupes—and the works produced by them—

Environmental staging, as pioneered by American director/theorist Richard Schechner, intermixes the audience and the actors, as seen here in Schechner's celebrated production of Commune *at the Performing Garage in New York. (Photo: Elizabeth Le Compte.)*

have become legendary: the Lord Chamberlain's Men of London, which counted actor-playwright William Shakespeare as a member; the Kabuki Theatre of Edo (now Tokyo), which was the artistic home of the great Japanese writer Chikamatsu; various *commedia dell'arte* troupes that toured Italy during the Renaissance; and the "Illustrious Theatre" of Paris, founded and headed by the great actor-writer Molière. These companies and their works will be remembered as long as civilization endures. And mid-twentieth-century American theatre troupes, such as the Living Theatre of Julian Beck and Judith Malina, the Open Theatre headed by Joseph Chaikin, and the Story Theatre ensemble gathered around Paul Sills, have enjoyed a vibrant history in relatively recent times, with, in many cases,

the company members sharing living quarters as well as theatrical duties. A theatre troupe is something more than a purely professional association; it inevitably includes at least a notion of an artistic "family."

These "theatres"—these companies of players—have proven more long-lasting than the buildings that in some cases survived them; they represent the genius and creativity of theatre in a way that stone and steel alone cannot.

In a more general sense, we may also treat theatre practitioners as theatre "families" linked by geography, era, aesthetics, or ideology. In this way, the term *theatre* may also be used to indicate a category of associated works, such as the American theatre, the Elizabethan theatre, dance theatre, musical the-

THEATRE AND *THEATER*

You may have noticed that the word used for the title of this book has two English spellings. *Theatre* is the French (and British) spelling; *theater* is the German. Both have been incorporated into American usage. There is no consensus as to which spelling is preferred, and pronunciation is identical.

atre, the theatre of the absurd, the theatre of Neil Simon, and black theatre: any or all of these terms may serve to represent a specifically defined grouping of plays, players, authors, and buildings that form a broad identity in the minds of theatre students, critics, and enthusiasts.

THE OCCUPATION OF THEATRE

And, finally, theatre is a principal occupation of its practitioners—a vocation for professionals, an avocation for amateurs. In either case, theatre is *work*. Specifically, it is that body of artistic work in which actors impersonate characters in a live performance of a play. Each of these terms deserves some attention in this chapter designed to address the question "What is theatre?"

Work

The "work" of the theatre is indeed hard work. An original play—as distinct from a revival—usually takes about one year to produce and often five years or more from con-

Improvisational theatre is sheer performance—performance without script. Here the Paul Sills company is seen in a presentation of "Story Theatre," which consists of children's stories improvised and acted out by versatile adult performers. Originally produced at the Mark Taper Forum Theatre in Los Angeles, Sills's Story Theatre proved immensely popular and subsequently enjoyed a considerable run on Broadway. (Photo: Courtesy Mark Taper Forum.)

ception to presentation. Rehearsal alone accounts for a minimum of four weeks, and for most effective productions it goes on a good deal longer. The labors of theatre artists in the final weeks before an opening are legendary: the ninety-hour week becomes commonplace, expenditures of money and spirit are intense, and even the unions relax their regulations to allow for an almost unbridled invasion of the hours the ordinary world spends sleeping, eating, and unwinding. The theatre enterprise may involve hundreds of people in scores of different efforts—many more backstage than onstage—and the mobilization and coordination of these efforts is in itself a giant task. So, when we think of the "work" embodied in the plays of Shakespeare or Neil Simon, for example, we must think of work in the sense of physical toil as well as in the loftier sense of *oeuvre,* by which the French designate the sum of an artist's creative endeavor.

The work of the theatre is generally divisible into a number of crafts:

Acting, in which actors perform the roles of characters in a play

Designing, in which designers map out the visual and audio elements of a production, including the scenery, properties, costumes and wigs, make-up, lighting, sound concepts, programs, advertising, and general ambience of the premises

Building, in which carpenters, costumers, wigmakers, electricians, make-up artists, recording and sound engineers, painters, and a host of other specially designated craftspeople translate the design into reality by constructing and finishing in detail the "hardware" of a show

Running, in which technicians execute in proper sequence, and with carefully rehearsed timing, the light and sound cues, the shifting of scenery, the placement and return of properties, and the assignment, laundering, repair, and changes of costumes

Producing, which includes securing all necessary personnel, space, and financing, supervising all production and promotion efforts, fielding all legal matters, and distributing all proceeds derived from receipts

Directing, which includes controlling and developing the artistic product and providing it with a unified vision, coordinating all its components, and supervising all rehearsals

Stage managing, which includes the responsibility for "running" a play production in all its complexity in performance after performance

House managing, which includes the responsibility for admitting, seating, and providing for the general comfort of the audience

And finally, there is *playwriting,* which is in a class by itself. It is the one craft of the theatre that is usually executed away from the theatre building and its associated shops—that may indeed take place continents and centuries away from the production it inspires.

Of course, the work of the theatre need not be apportioned precisely as the preceding list indicates. In any production, some people will perform more than one kind of work; for example, many of the "builders" will also be "runners." Moreover, many a play has been produced with the actors directing themselves, or the director handling production duties, or the dialogue improvised by the actors and director. On occasion most, if not all, of the craft functions have been performed by the same person: Aeschylus not only wrote, directed, and designed his Greek tragedies, but he probably also performed the leading parts.

Although there is nothing inevitable or necessary about the allocation of craft functions of the theatre's work, the functions themselves have remained fairly constant over the theatre's history. In virtually every era we can look back and see the same sorts of work going on—and the same kinds of efforts being expended—as we see in the work of the theatre today, be it professional or amateur, American or European, commercial or academic. Later on in this book we shall take a closer look at the various craft and managerial functions that go into the creation of a theatrical event.

Theatre is also work in the sense that it is not "play." This is a more subtle distinction than we might at once imagine. First, of course, recall that we ordinarily use the word *play* in describing the main product of theatre work. This is not merely a peculiarity of the English tongue; for we find that the French *jeu*, the German *Spiel,* and the Latin *ludi* all share the double meaning of the English *play,* referring both to plays and playing in the theatrical sense and to sports activities or games. This association points to a relationship that is fundamental to the understanding of theatre: theatre *is* a kind of game, and it is useful for us to see how and why this is so.

The theatre and games have a shared history. Both were developed to a high level of sophistication in Greek festivals: the Dionysian festivals for theatre and the Olympian festivals for sport were the two great cultural events of ancient Greece at which the legendary Greek competition for excellence was most profoundly engaged. The Romans merged sports and theatre in their circuses, where the two were performed side by side and in competition with each other. In much the same fashion, the Elizabethan Londoners built playhouses to accommodate both dramatic productions and animal-baiting spectacles somewhat akin to the modern bullfight; the stage that was set up for the plays was simply removed for "play." Today, sports and dramatizations dominate the television fare that absorbs so much leisure time not only in America but also in most of the Western world. Moreover, professional athletes and entertainers are among the foremost celebrities of the modern age—and many a retired sports hero has found a second career in act-

ing. Thus it is not extraordinary that sports and the theatre still share in the compound use of the word *play.*

For the individual, a link between games and theatre is formed early in life, in "child's play," which usually manifests both gamelike and dramalike aspects. The game of hide-and-seek, for example, is a playful competition between children that can be repeated over and over, a harmless but engrossing activity involving counting, hiding, searching, and at last the triumph of finding. It is also an acting out of one of childhood's greatest fears—the fear of separation from the parent, or "separation anxiety," as psychologists term it. Hide-and-seek affords the child a way of dealing with that fear by confronting it over and over "in play" until it loses much of its power. Play is *often* grounded in serious concerns, and through play the individual gradually develops means of coping with life's challenges and uncertainties.

Drama and sports are different but related adult forms of the same "play." One of the aspects of adult play—in both its forms—is that it attracts a tremendous amateur following; as child's play is engaged in without prompting or reward, so adult sports and theatre commonly yield no remuneration beyond sheer personal satisfaction. Both sports and theatricals offer splendid opportunities for intense physical involvement, competition, self-expression, and emotional engagement—and all within limits set by precise and sensible rules. What is more, both can generate an audience because the energies and passions they project are rarely expressed so openly in daily life beyond the playgrounds of childhood. It is little wonder that people who spend a lifetime in the theatre or in athletics are often regarded as childlike—or, more pejoratively, as immature and irresponsible—for their "playing" evokes myriad memories of youth.

But the theatre must finally be distinguished from child's play, and from sports as well, because theatre is by its nature a calculated act from beginning to end. Unlike adult games, which are open-ended, every theatre performance has a preordained conclusion. The Yankees may not win the World Series this year, but Hamlet definitely will die in the fifth act. The *work* of the theatre, indeed, consists in keeping Hamlet alive up to that point—brilliantly alive—to make of that fore-ordained end a profoundly moving, enno-bling, even surprising climax to the whole experience.

We might say, finally, that *theatre is the art of making play into work—specifically, into a work of art.* It is exhilarating work, to be sure, and it usually inspires and invigorates the en-ergies and imaginations of all who partici-pate; it transcends more prosaic forms of labor as song transcends grunts and groans. But it is work: that is its challenge, and the great accomplishments of the theatre are always at-tended by prodigious effort.

Art

As we have suggested, the work of the theatre goes beyond the mere perfecting of skills, which is after all a goal of professionals in every field of endeavor. The theatre is *artistic* work. The word *art* brings to mind a host of intangibles: creativity, imagination, elegance, power, aesthetic harmony, and fineness of form; in addition, we expect a work of art to capture something of the human spirit and to touch upon sensed, but intellectually elusive, meanings in life. Certainly great theatre never fails to bring together many of these intangi-bles. In great theatre we glimpse not only the physical and emotional exuberance of play, but also the deep yearnings that propel hu-manity's search for purpose, meaning, and the life well lived.

Art, of course, is one of the most supreme pursuits of humanity, integrating, in a unique fashion, our emotions with our intellects and our aesthetics with our revelations. Art is em-powering, to both those who make it and those who appreciate it. Art sharpens thought and focuses feeling; it brings reality up against imagination and presses creativity to the ever-expanding limits of human potential. Al-though life may be fragmented, inconclusive, and finally frustrating, art can provide integra-tion, synthesis, and lasting satisfaction. One might, of course, find similar values in religion or philosophy as well; but art, lacking a formal dogma, is accessible without catechism: it is an ecumenical and open-ended response—and a refreshingly civil approach—to life's unending puzzles. It is for this very reason that all great religions—Eastern and Western, ancient and modern—have expansively em-ployed art and artworks (including great ex-emplars of dramatic art) in their liturgies, structures, and services from the earliest of times.

The art of the theatre is never "pure" art in the sense that it represents the personal vi-sion of a solitary artist. Indeed, many "pure" artists consider theatrical art a bastard form, combining as it does the several arts of acting, writing, designing, directing, and architec-ture. It is significant, however, that such great individual artists as Shelley, Beethoven, Pira-nesi, Tolstoy, Eliot, Palladio, and Yeats have achieved only moderate success when they turned their efforts to this impure art; the the-atre seems to reserve its greatest rewards for those whose artistic lives are first and foremost theatrical. The creative work of the theatre is in its essence collaborative and interdiscipli-nary, and thus its art can be judged only on its own merits.

The opulent interior of Booth's Theatre, New York, at its 1869 opening. This grand "temple of theatre" was built by America's finest actor of the time, Edwin Booth (the brother of Lincoln's assassin). Booth staged and performed in a classical repertory of Shakespearean plays at his theatre for four years. The side "boxes," similar to those that still exist in older Broadway theatres today, had poor sight lines: spectators electing to sit there were more interested in being seen than in seeing the play. The luxurious seating in the orchestra made this a particularly comfortable as well as an elegant way to see classic theatre. This watercolor was painted by Charles Witham, Booth's original stage designer; part of Witham's scenery (a street scene) is shown on stage. (Courtesy Museum of the City of New York. Photo: Judy Davis.)

Exciting theatre today is not always comfortable; audiences often have to "work" as well. Here, at dawn in Central Park, producer Joseph Papp addresses the audience after the New York Shakespeare Festival's all-night production of the "Wars of the Roses" (the three parts of Shakespeare's Henry VI plus Richard III). Papp, who founded the Festival and headed it until his death in 1991, continually challenged—as well as entertained—a vast public. (Photo: © George E. Joseph.)

The Adams Theatre in Cedar City, Utah, is an open-air structure employing many features thought to exist in outdoor London theatres of Shakespeare's time: a platform jutting well into the audience, a balconied and pillared stage with relatively neutral scenery, and stage doors that provide entrances from—and exits into—a backstage dressing area, or tiring house. *Seen at the 1993 Utah Shakespearean Festival production of Shakespeare's* Timon of Athens; *setting by Ann Gibson, costumes by Janet Swenson. (Photo: Bruce Lee.)*

The audience gathers at a matinee performance at the ornate Kabuki-za Theatre in Tokyo, principal home of Japan's Kabuki drama. Matinees begin at eleven o'clock here and last until four o'clock, with the audience enjoying snacks or full meals during the play's several intermissions. (Photo: Robert Cohen.)

Impersonation

The theatrical art involves actors impersonating characters. This feature is unique to the theatre and separates it from other art forms such as poetry, painting, sculpture, music, performance art, and the like. Further, impersonation is the single most important aspect of the theatre; it is its very foundation.

Try to imagine what extreme conceptual difficulties the ancient creators of the theatre encountered in laying down the ground rules for dramatic impersonation. For how was the audience to distinguish the "real person" from the "character" portrayed, the actor-as-himself from the actor-as-character? And when the playwright was also an actor, how could onlookers distinguish between the thoughts of playwright-as-himself and those of the playwright-as-character? Questions such as these are often asked by children today as they watch a play; and it is inevitable that when a public press conference is arranged by the producer of a television soap opera, some fans will address the actors by the names of the characters they play and ask them questions

In Jean Genet's The Blacks, *black actors wear white make-up or white masks as shown here in the American premiere of the play directed by Gene Frankel. This bitterly ironic play deals with the social masks an individual wears and with the way racial accommodation is determined by skin color. (Photo: Martha Swope and Associates.)*

The masked chorus cringes in awe, in a modern (1992) production of Euripides' Iphigeneia at Aulis, *directed by Garland Wright, with costumes and masks by Susan Hilfterty. (Photo: Courtesy the Guthrie Theatre, Minneapolis.)*

pertinent only to their stage lives. Given this confusion in what we like to think of as a sophisticated age, it is easy to see why the ancients had to resolve the problem of actor-character separation before the theatre could become a firmly established institution.

The solution the ancient world found was the mask. Western theatre had its true beginning that day in ancient Greece when an actor first stepped out of the chorus, placed an unpainted mask over his face, and thereby signaled that the lines he was about to speak were "in character." The Nō Drama in Japan and many of the ritual dance-dramas of Africa, Asia, and native America have used the mask to similar effect. Basically, the mask is the tool of impersonation, at once hiding the face of the performer and projecting that of the "character" demanded by the play. Although today the mask is rarely seen in the dramas of the Western world, it remains the symbol of the theatre—usually in the form of the double masks of Comedy and Tragedy that adorn the prosceniums of numerous playhouses and the letterheads of various theatrical organizations.

The mask provides a physical as well as symbolic separation between the impersonator and the impersonated, thus aiding the literal-minded onlooker to suspend awareness of the real world of the former and to accept in its place the stage world of the latter. In a

Audiences are first captivated by the sheer exuberance of August Wilson's characters and then drawn into the tragedies and broken dreams that confront at least some of them. Wilson's plays, such as The Piano Lesson *shown here, provoke laughter and tears, entertainment and profound realizations. The play, under the sympathetic direction of Lloyd Richards, won the 1990 Pulitzer Prize. The talented ensemble of actors includes, left to right, Lou Myers, Rocky Carroll, Samuel L. Jackson, and Carl Gordon. From the world premiere production at the Yale Repertory Theatre. (Photo: Gerry Goodstein.)*

play, it must be the "characters" who have apparent life; the actors themselves are expected to disappear into the shadows, along with their personal preoccupations, anxieties, and career ambitions. This convention gives rise to one of the great paradoxes of the theatre, what the eighteenth-century French encyclopedist Denis Diderot called "the paradox of the actor": when the actor has perfected his or her art it is the *simulated* character, the mask, which seems to live before our eyes, while the *real* person has no apparent life at all. The strength of such an illusion still echoes in our use of the word *person*, which derives from the Latin word for mask.

But of course we know that the actor does not die behind the mask, and herein lies an even greater paradox. We believe in the character, but at the end of the play we applaud the actor. Not only that—but as we watch good theatre we are always, somewhere in the back of our mind, applauding the actor. Our appreciation of theatre rests largely on our dual awareness of actor and character and our understanding that they live inside the same skin.

Actors, of course, are aware of the same duality. For them, the art of acting is a sublime combination of the freedom that comes with anonymity (since they are hidden in their roles) and the ego gratification that comes with exhibitionism. Thus actors commonly report that they both "lose themselves" and "find themselves" in theatrical performances and indeed that these phenomena sometimes happen simultaneously. The sense of liberation and heightened self-awareness that comes with an intense, creative effort within a standardized, formalized structure is one of the functions of all play, including sport.

The act of impersonation, with or without an actual mask, depends on an implicit agreement or set of agreements between actor and audience. In essence, the agreement is that the actor will pretend to "be" a character and the audience will pretend to "see" him or her as that character. This agreement does not at all mean that the actor must perform the role in a lifelike manner. On the contrary, the agreement concerning mutual pretense allows the acceptance on both sides of certain conditions, such as that the character will wear a mask, or speak into a microphone, or perform a dance when angered, or employ any of the scores of other devices and actions that have found acceptance in the theatre over time. In this century, particularly since the rise of motion pictures and television, much attention has been paid to the desirability of the actor's "use of self" in creating the characters he or she plays; this emphasis reflects a trend, but not a fundamental shift, in the art of theatrical impersonation. Remember that impersonation itself remains a constant in the theatre despite changing modes and styles of theatrical presentation.

Throughout history actors have often been accused of flirting with a suspect morality in impersonating characters. Audiences too have been castigated for applauding this impiety. The Greek word for actor was *hypokrites*, a term that originally meant "answerer" (the actor "answered" the odes of a chorus), but it came to mean "pretender" as well. The more negative connotation has come down to us as "one who dissembles." Indeed, the oldest recorded anecdote in theatrical history

portrays the ancient lawmaker Solon chiding Thespis, the first actor, for "telling so many lies before such a number of people." When Thespis replies that there is no harm in lying "in play," Solon answers, "Ah, if we honor and commend such 'play' as this, we shall find it some day in our business." At least since Solon's day, actors have had to contend with varying degrees of social skepticism, and the same notoriety that has given them celebrity status has occasioned intense and often disapproving curiosity about their private affairs.

The impersonation that underlies the acting art is not, however, aimed at imposture; its goal is artistic. The actor does not pretend to "be someone else," for a dramatic character is not a person but an abstraction, no more human than paint on a canvas or words on a page. It is true that the dramatic character is represented by a living person who goes through the motions of the character's acts and in many cases experiences them fully as well. It is also true that some characters are drawn from life, and their dialogue may be taken from the actual transcripts of a historical event. Nonetheless, the character is not a "somebody else"; it is an artistic fabrication—a shaped presence—that gains acceptance as a real person only by virtue of the implicit agreement of actors and audience alike. Actors deserve no moral disgrace for engaging in impersonation, nor should they feel hypocritical about engaging in impersonated acts and feelings; they are "honest hypocrites," in William Hazlitt's words, and their pretending is simply part of the artistic work of an old and endlessly creative profession.

Nowadays, as we have seen, the art of impersonation rarely calls for use of a mask that conceals the actor's face; instead, costume, make-up, dialogue, accent, movement, gesture, and a variety of acting methods and techniques support the delineation of character formerly expressed by mask and voice alone. Owing to a twentieth-century emphasis on verisimilitude, most American and European actors favor, in whole or in part, the

Actors don't impersonate only human beings; in this experimental contemporary production by the KOM Theater of Helsinki, Finland, actress Marja Packa-lèn, though not disguising her face, plays a bear in the mythic and erotic dance-drama Karhunainen (The Bearwoman). *(Photo: Rauno Träskelin.)*

concepts of Konstantin Stanislavsky, the Russian actor-director and acting teacher who proclaimed that the actor should "live the life of the character onstage." This view has fostered the development of a number of techniques and training methods to aid the actor not only in performing a character's actions in minute physiological detail, but also in experiencing the character's feelings to such a degree that occasionally even the presence of the audience is forgotten. If this movement of modern times has its fervent supporters, however, it also has its equally aroused critics. It is probably fairest to say that the question of the proper relationship between the actor and the role—or of the degree to which the actor ought to "identify with" the part—remains

as perplexing today as it was two hundred years ago when Diderot defined the paradox of acting.

Performance

Theatre is performance; but what, exactly, does "performance" mean? Performance is an action or series of actions taken for the ultimate benefit (attention, entertainment, enlightenment, or involvement) of someone else. We call that someone else the audience.

If two people engage in a strictly private conversation, that is a simple communication between them. If, however, their conversation is undertaken in order to impress or involve a third person whom they know is in a position to overhear it, the "communication" becomes a performance and the third person becomes its audience.

Obviously, performance is a part of everyday life; indeed, it has been analyzed as such in a number of psychological and sociological works. When two teenage boys wrestle on the schoolground, they may well be "performing" their physical prowess for the benefit of their peers. The student who asks a question in the lecture hall is frequently "performing" for the other students—and the professor "performs" for the same audience in providing a response. Trial lawyers examining witnesses invariably "perform," often drawing on a considerable repertoire of grunts, snorts, shrugs, raised eyebrows, and disbelieving sighs for the benefit of that ultimate courtroom audience, the jury. Politicians kiss babies for the benefit of parents (and others) in search of a kindly candidate. Even stony silence can be a performance—if, for example, it is the treatment a woman metes out to an offensive admirer. We are all performers, and the theatre only makes an art out of something we all do every day. The theatre reflects our everyday performances and expands those performances into a formal mode of artistic expression.

Direct performance: the characters of Robert Schenkkan's Pulitzer Prize–winning play, The Kentucky Cycle, *share the play's political and social concerns directly with the audience, in the 1993 Broadway production directed by Warner Shook. (Photo: Joan Marcus.)*

The theatre makes use of two general modes of performance: direct and indirect. Direct performance is the basic nightclub mode. Nightclub performers continuously acknowledge the presence of the audience: they sing to them, dance for them, joke at them, and respond overtly to their applause, laughter, requests, and heckling. Dramatic forms of all ages have employed these techniques and a variety of other direct presentational methods as well, including asides, soliloquies, direct address, plays-within-plays, and curtain calls.

Indirect performance, however, is probably the more fundamental mode in drama; it is certainly the one that makes drama "dramatic" as opposed to simply "theatrical." For indirect performance is the mode whereby the audience watches interactions that are staged as if no audience were present at all. As a result the audience is encouraged to concentrate on the events that are being staged, not on their presentation. In other words, the members of the audience "believe in" the play and allow themselves to forget that the characters are really actors and that the apparently spontaneous events taking place before their eyes are really a series of scripted scenes. This belief—or, to borrow Coleridge's famous double negative, this "suspension of disbelief"—engenders audience participation via the psychological mechanism of *empathy*. In other words, the audience is likely to feel kinship with certain (or all) of the characters, to identify with their aspirations, sympathize with their plights, exult in their victories—to care deeply about what happens to them. When that happens, the audience experiences the

Indirect performance: the characters of Wendy Wasserstein's The Sisters Rosensweig *seem to be performing only for each other, but as we watch their interactions, the themes of sibling affection (and rivalry), romantic longings (and resentments), cultural identification (and alienation), and sexual orientations (and disorientations) are deeply, and often amusingly, driven home. From the 1995 Alabama Shakespeare Festival: appearing clockwise from the top are Lucy Martin, Greta Lambert, and Linda Bansavage. (Photo: Courtesy Alabama Shakespeare Festival.)*

"magic" of the theatre. Well-written and well-staged dramas make people *feel;* they draw in the spectator emotionally and leave him or her in some measure a changed person. This is as much magic as the modern world provides anywhere, and its effect is the same all over the world.

Occasionally either the direct or the indirect mode of performance is taken to an extreme. For examples of the former, look at the plays of Bertolt Brecht, the twentieth-century German author who deliberately set out to repudiate the "magic" of the theatre by direct appeals to the audience on a variety of social and political issues. Brecht's plays featured songs, signs, chalk talks, arguments addressed directly to the house, and slide projections; he specifically avoided use of concealed stage trickery or "effects." Brecht wanted his audience distanced from the story of the play; he also wanted them to consider his actors as performer-illustrators rather than as specific characters with specific involvements, so that the political and social themes of the play would dominate the viewer's awareness.

In this effort, Brecht was specifically attacking the realist movement of the turn of the century, a movement that afforded many cases of the other extreme. It propounded a style of performance in which the actors behaved exactly as they did in life, in settings made as lifelike as possible (in one notable example, a celebrated New York restaurant was disassembled and reconstructed on stage, complete with its original moldings, wallpaper, furniture, silverware, and linens). At times the indirect mode so dominated in the realist productions that actors spoke with their backs to audiences, directors allowed interminable pauses and inaudible whispers, playwrights culled their dialogue from random fragments of overheard conversations, and house managers timed intermissions to the presumed time elapsing in the play's story. The realistic theatre of that time was sometimes called "the theatre of the fourth wall removed" because its goal typically was to re-create life inside a room, and the sole departure from complete verisimilitude that was allowed was the removal of one wall to let the audience peer in—much as the lab scientist peers at a slide through a microscope.

The two modes of performance, however, can never be entirely separated. The fact is that the Brechtian theatre, despite all the best efforts of Brecht himself and all the resources he had at his disposal, never managed to eliminate audience empathy with the leading characters; and even the most resolutely realistic theatres have never escaped the ultimate audience recognition that the actors are, indeed, performing. As it turns out, theatrical performance is always *both* direct and indirect, and it is always both simultaneously.

Moreover, the audience inevitably demands two things of a theatrical performance: it demands characters it can care about, and it demands actors it can admire. In other words, the audience wants to see the characters struggle and the actors sweat. In watching a performance, therefore, audience members intuitively look for two things: they look for a well-crafted dramatic story that holds implications for their own lives, and they look for extraordinary individual acting performances. One of these elements may predominate— as when a cast of brilliant actors submerge themselves in a masterpiece by Chekhov or, conversely, when a relatively trivial script be-

August Wilson's great plays exemplify the adventure—comprising joy, anguish, and bitter struggle—of African Americans in the twentieth century; each of Wilson's plays is set in a different decade. Wilson's latest work, Seven Guitars, *portrays the last days of a blues guitarist in the 1940s; seen here with Keith David and Viola Davis in the 1995 Hartford Stage production, directed by Lloyd Richards. (Photo: Joan Marcus.)*

comes the vehicle for a "star's" bravura performance. Both elements are always present in a successful production; and when they are, the viewer experiences a complex and deeply satisfying sense of inner expansion.

Two other aspects of performance distinguish theatre from certain other forms: theatre is *live* performance, and it is in most cases a *scripted* and *rehearsed* event.

The medieval trestle stage—a few planks on trestles—was a standard perfor-mance space for more than a thousand years. Portable, serviceable, and inexpen-sive, it could be set up almost anywhere and could be dismantled in an instant if the actors chanced to be chased out of town—as they often were. Such trestle stages may still be seen at many summertime European festivals. (Drawing: John von Szeliski.)

Live Performance Unlike video and cinema (although sometimes employing elements of them), the theatre is a living, real-time event, with performers and audience mutually interacting, each fully aware of the other's immediate presence.

This turns out to be an extremely important distinction. Actors who are accomplished in both "live" and filmed performance invariably report a strong preference for the former, despite the usually greater financial rewards of the latter. In explaining this preference, they often mention the applause of the crowd, the sensation of "presence," and a special tingle of excitement. Beyond question, some fundamental forces are at work in live theatre.

The first of these forces consists of a rap-port between actor and audience. Both are breathing the same air. Both are involved, at the same time and in the same space, with the stage life depicted by the play, and sometimes their mutual fascination is almost palpable. A collective gasp from the audience at a climactic moment in a play can be the spark that evokes a transcendent performance from an actor. Every actor's performance is affected in some measure, for better or for worse, by the way the audience yields up or withholds its responses—its laughter, its sighs, its applause, its silences. Thus live theatrical performance is always a two-way communication between stage and "house."

A second major element in live theatre has to do with the relationship between the members of the audience who, having arrived at

Live performance: one of the excitements of theatregoing is seeing plays of the past come vividly to life in our own times. The job of the contemporary theatre artist is to make the genius of the past speak persuasively in the present. In Andrei Serban's radically contemporized production of Shakespeare's Twelfth Night, *the Duke Orsino arrives, with his bodyguards, by helicopter. (Photo: Richard Feldman.)*

the theatre locked inside their own personalities and predilections, quickly find themselves fused into a common enterprise with total strangers. This particular sort of intra-audience relationship is never developed by television drama, which is directed chiefly to solitary watchers or to small audiences of viewers known to each other—two to four people in each of a million different living rooms. Nor is it likely to happen in motion picture houses, where audiences find themselves in essentially a one-to-one relationship with the screen and rarely break out in any *collective* response. Live theatrical presentations foster the kinds of audience behaviors that are demonstrably *social* in nature: everyone arrives at the theatre at about the same time and all depart together; intermissions

allow for an exchange of ideas; theatre programs afford material for conversation. Further, audience responses to the entertainment are social in nature. Laughter and applause build upon themselves and gain strength from the recognition that others are laughing and applauding. The ovation—unique to live performance—inevitably involves the audience applauding itself, as well as the performers, for its own understanding and appreciation of theatrical excellence. Plays with social themes can be particularly effective in creating a feeling of audience participation and oneness. In a celebrated example in the 1930s, the American play *Waiting for Lefty* was set up to treat the audience as a group of union members at a meeting, and by the play's end the whole audience was yelling "Strike! Strike!" Obviously, only a live performance could evoke such a response.

Finally, live performance inevitably has the quality of immediacy. The action of the play is taking place *right now* as it is being watched, and anything can happen. Although in most professional productions the changes that occur in performance from one night to another are so subtle that only an expert would notice, the fact is that each night's presentation is unique and everyone present—in the audience, in the cast, and behind the scenes—knows it. This awareness lends an excitement that is not present in theatrical events that are wholly "in the can." One reason for the excitement, of course, is that in live performance mistakes can happen; this possibility occasions a certain abiding tension, perhaps even an edge of stage fright, which some people say creates the ultimate thrill of the theatre. But if disaster can come without warning, so can splendor. On any given night, each actor is trying to better her or his previous performance, and no one knows when this collective effort will coalesce into something sublime. The actors' constant striving toward self-transcendence gives the theatre a vitality that is missing from performances fixed unalterably on tape or celluloid. But perhaps most appropriately, the immediacy of live performance creates a "present-ness" or "presence" that embodies the fundamental uncertainty of life itself. One prime function of theatre is to address the uncertainties of human existence, and the very format of live performance presents a moment-to-moment uncertainty right before our eyes. Ultimately this "immediate theatre" helps us to define the questions and confusions of our lives and lets us grapple, in the present, with their implications.

Scripted and Rehearsed Performance

Theatre events ordinarily differ from certain "happenings" and other forms of performance art by the fact that they are largely derived from written and rehearsed texts, or, in

---

A SCRIPT IS NOT A PLAY

A play in a book is only the shadow of a play and not even a clear shadow of it. . . . The printed script of a play is hardly more than an architect's blueprint of a house not yet built or [a house] built and destroyed. The color, the grace and levitation, the structural pattern in motion, the quick interplay of live beings, suspended like fitful lightning in a cloud, these things are the play, not words on paper nor thoughts and ideas of an author.

Tennessee Williams

---

theatrical parlance, scripts. While improvisation and ad-libbing may play a role in the preparation process, and even in certain actual performances, most theatre events proceed according to a set "plan" that is established before—and modified during—the play's rehearsal period. Most plays are then rehearsed and polished to such a dependable level of regularity as the actors and staff can sustain. Mainstream professional play productions, therefore, appear virtually the same night after night: barring major cast changes, the Broadway production of *Miss Saigon* that you see on Thursday will be almost identical to the show your friend saw on Wednesday or that your mother saw last fall. And when you read the published text, you will see on the page the same words you heard spoken or sung on the stage.

But the text of a play is not, by any means, the play itself. The play fully exists only in its performance: the script is merely the record the play leaves behind after the audience has gone home. The script, therefore, is to the play it represents only what a shadowpainting is to the face it silhouettes: it outlines the principal features, but conveys only the outer margins of the spirit, the complexity, the color, the smell, and the nuance of the living actuality.

Let us now look closer at the relations between playscript and play production. First, we should be aware that the finished playscript does not necessarily precede the finished performance. In fact, virtually all important playscripts available to us today were published *following* their initial performance, and the versions we read reflect not only the staging decisions of a director and the portrayal choices of many actors, but also the changes in dialogue that took place during the play's rehearsal period and frequently in its performance period as well. While most original play productions are begun with a script in hand (usually it is called the "working script"), that script is rarely treated as a sacred document. The evolution and "doctoring" of new playscripts during rehearsal took place in past times as well as in the present, as historical accounts amply attest. For revivals, of course, a "fixed" script generally dictates the dialogue in fairly strict manner, but that script was itself fixed by the one or more productions which intervened between the play's first drafting and its eventual publication.

Second, even a fixed script is in some ways as notable for what it lacks as for what it contains. Apart from the odd stage-set description or acting note (for example, "through her tears," "crossing to the bannister," or "softly"), a written playscript usually tells almost nothing about a play's nonverbal components. For how can it describe the degrees of expression within the range of even the beginning actor? How can it capture the bead of sweat that forms on Hamlet's brow as he stabs Polonius or Romeo's nervous laugh as he tries to part dueling adversaries? Written stage descriptions (which hardly ever appear in playscripts that antedate the present century) serve mainly to delineate the outer form of a play and do little to convey its inner life. As for the words of dialogue, although they are probably the most important single element of a play, they are not in any way the whole experience. Words on a page do not resound in the mind in the same way as do words spoken aloud; and even spoken words do not encompass the facial expressions, the color and sweep of costumes, the play of light, the movement of form in space—and the audience response—that conspire to support a living production.

The chief value of playscripts, then, is that they generate theatrical production and they provide an invaluable, albeit imperfect, record of performances past. Two and a half millennia of play productions have left us a repository of thousands upon thousands of scripts, some awful, many ordinary, a few magnificent. This rich store puts us in touch with theatre history in the making and allows us to glimpse the nature of the originals in production. It also suggests ways in which the plays of yesterday can serve as blueprints for vital theatre today.

This, then, is the theatre: buildings, companies, and plays; work, art, impersonation, and performance; living performers and written, rehearsed scripts.

It is a production, an assemblage of actions, sights, sounds, ideas, feelings, words, light, and, above all, people.

It consists of playing and—of course—plays.

But what is a play? That question deserves a separate chapter.

2

What Is a Play?

A play is, essentially, the basic unit of theatre. It is not a "thing" but an event, taking place in real time and occupying real space. It is a "drama"—remember its origin from the Greek *dran,* "something done." It is *action,* not just words in a book.

Action is not merely movement, of course: it is argument, struggle, persuasion, threats, seduction, sound, music, dance, speech, and passion. It comprises all forms of human energy, including language, spatial dynamics, light, color, sonic shocks, aesthetic harmonies, and "remarkable things happening" from moment to moment. It is *live* action, ordinarily unmediated by video electronics or cinematic celluloid.

And yet a play does not merely produce (or reproduce) live action, but also frames and focuses it. Life may be, as Shakespeare's Macbeth says, "a tale told by an idiot, full of sound and fury, signifying nothing"; but drama, which is also full of sound and fury, signifies all sorts of things: if not answers, then at least perspectives, vocabularies, and aesthetic illuminations. Plays give us stories against which we can judge our own struggles; they present characters that can serve us as positive and negative role models; they offer up themes, ideas, and revelations that we can accept, scorn, or store away for further contemplation. A play is a piece of life—

animated, shaped, and framed to become a work of art. It provides a structured synthesis—sometimes a critique and sometimes a celebration—of both life's glories and life's confusions.

Of course, a play is also a piece of literature. There has been a reading audience for plays at least since the time of the ancient Greeks, and play collections—such as Shakespeare's works—have been published since the Renaissance. Today, plays are often printed in literary anthologies, intermixed with poems, short stories, and even novels. But drama should not be thought of as merely a "branch" or "genre" of literature; it is a live performance, some of whose repeatable aspects (chiefly, the words) may be captured in a written and published text.[1]

Finally, "a play" is "playing" and those who create plays are "players." The theatrical play contains root notions of "child's play" in its acting-out and adventurism, of "dressing up" in its costumes and props, and of the thrill of sportive competition in its energy and abandon. Like all play, drama is an exhibition, and its players are, in a real sense, willingly exhibitionistic. These are not fundamentally literary characteristics.

CLASSIFYING PLAYS

Plays may be volatile, but they are also contained. They are framed, with a beginning

---

[1]If the arboreal metaphor is insisted upon, drama would have to be considered the "trunk" of the literary tree, not merely a branch. Certainly no other literary form—the novel, the epic poem, the lyric poem, the short story—has the sustained level of literary excellence over twenty-five centuries as does the written dramatic work of Aeschylus, Sophocles, Euripides, Aristophanes, Marlowe, Shakespeare, Jonson, Chikamatsu, Webster, Racine, Corneille, Lope de Vega, Calderón, Molière, Congreve, Dryden, Farquhar, Fielding, Goethe, Schiller, Ibsen, Wilde, Yeats, Chekhov, Shaw, O'Casey, O'Neill, Pirandello, Giraudoux, Sartre, Brecht, Beckett, Williams, Churchill, Wilson, and so on.

and an end, and, no matter how original or unique, they can be seen to fall into a variety of classifications. Two of these are duration and genre. Although these classifications have been emphasized more in the past than they are today, they still play a part in our understanding of drama.

Duration

"How long is a play?" American playwright Arthur Miller admitted that when he first thought of writing for the theatre, "How long should it be?" was his most pressing question. The answer is far from obvious.

Historically, in Western drama, a "full-length" play has usually lasted somewhere between two and four hours. This is not an entirely arbitrary period of time; it represents roughly the hours between lunch and dinner (for a matinee), or between dinner and bedtime. The Jacobean playwright John Webster wrote that the actor "entertains us in the best leisure of our life, that is between meals, the most unfit time either for study or bodily exercise." Webster was thinking of the afternoon performances in the outdoor theatres of his day (c. 1615). A few years earlier, speaking of candlelit evening performances at court, Shakespeare's Theseus (*A Midsummer Night's Dream*) asks for a play "to wear away this long age of three hours between our after-supper and bed-time." Inasmuch as eating and sleeping habits have remained fairly constant over the millennia, we should not be too surprised that the two- to four-hour standard has been common to the drama since ancient times.

But plays may be much shorter or longer. "One-act" plays of an hour or less, often combined in a "bill" with other short works, are often presented as full theatre programs; on other occasions such short plays are presented in nontraditional settings, such as lunchtime theatres, dramatic festivals, school assemblies, social gatherings, street entertain-

The basic action of many plays is a seemingly ordinary conversation, in which, however, the stakes turn out to be much higher than usual. An ordinary bench in New York's Central Park is the setting for many recent American plays, including Richard Greenberg's The Extra Man, *shown here in its 1992 South Coast Repertory Theatre premiere. (Photo: Cristofer Gross.)*

ments, or cabaret performances. Very short plays are known from ancient times; the Greek satyr plays, for example, could be performed in a half-hour and were presented following a day-long series of three tragedies. Nobel Prize winner Samuel Beckett probably holds the minimalist record in drama, with his sixty-second play, *Breath,* initially presented in a fanciful "erotic entertainment" (*O, Calcutta!*) that consisted of more than a dozen short works, some written by celebrities (like John Lennon), as compiled by critic Kenneth Tynan in 1969.

The very long play has also been a recurring anomaly and, in the Eastern world, a standard. Chinese theatre usually lasts all day (spectators bring their meals), as did the Japanese Kabuki in its classical seventeenth-century period (modern Kabuki is somewhat more contained). In English-language theatre of the 1920s, Eugene O'Neill's *Strange Interlude* and George Bernard Shaw's *Back to Methuselah* were each performed with dinner breaks between two sessions of more than three hours, and in the 1980s and 1990s a number of six- to nine-hour dramatic epics were celebrated internationally: Trevor Nunn's *Nicholas Nickleby* in London and New York, Peter Brook's *The Mahabharata* in Paris and Los Angeles, Peter Stein's *Oresteia* in Berlin, and Ariane Mnouchkine's *Les Atrides* (which includes the *Oresteia* and then some) in Paris,

Montreal, and New York. In 1992 the Pulitzer Prize for Drama was awarded to Robert Schenkkan's nine-play, six-hour cycle, *The Kentucky Cycle,* which was performed in Seattle and Los Angeles, requiring viewing on two successive nights or during one long afternoon and evening "marathon" divided by dinner. The same schedule was employed for Tony Kushner's extraordinary *Angels in America,* which was commissioned by the Eureka Theatre of San Francisco and subsequently performed in Los Angeles and New York in 1992–93.

The American actor-director Robert Wilson probably holds the absolute duration record, however, first with his twelve-hour, overnight, *The Life and Times of Joseph Stalin,* and subsequently with his *Ka Mountain,* which has been performed for anywhere between 24 and 168 continuous hours. These extremes, however, demand such drastic accommodation on the part of audiences, actors, and behind-the-scenes personnel that it is highly doubtful they ever will be commonplace.

Genre

Genre is a more subjective means of classifying plays than is duration, and the term brings with it certain critical perspectives. *Genre* is directly derived from the Old French word for "kind" (this is also our root word for "gender"); thus to define a play's genre is to categorize it—to say "what kind of play" it is. Editors and publishers of playtexts have often sought to identify genres as a shorthand description: early publications of Shakespeare's plays bore generic classifications on the title pages (for example, *The Most Excellent Conceited Tragedy of Romeo and Juliet*); and when the first collection of his plays was published (the First Folio of 1623), his plays were divided into three genre classifications: "Comedies," "Tragedies," and "Histories."

Considerations of genre in some periods, however, degenerated into a pseudoscientific

taxonomy, with absolute rules defining what would constitute, say, a "tragedy." Because of this, many critics, and even more authors, ridicule the notion of genre altogether (see box). But an identification of genres can generate useful distinctions—not only for the student but also for the practitioner. The great Russian playwright Anton Chekhov certainly guided the principal director of his works, Konstantin Stanislavski, by pointing out that his plays were intended as "comedies," thereby agreeably blunting what he thought was Stanislavski's excess of directorial naturalism. And many an actor, hamstrung by considerations of psychological realism, has been freed to find a more vigorous theatricality when given to understand that the author meant the play as "farce," thereby encouraging a rampaging and "over-the-top" comic style.

Two genres have dominated dramatic criticism since ancient times: *tragedy* and *comedy.* To Aristotle, the Greek philosopher generally recognized as the father of dramatic criticism, tragedy and comedy were not genres, but wholly separate art forms, derived from entirely unrelated sources. Tragedy, to Aristotle, was an outgrowth of certain prehistoric religious rituals, whereas comedy was a secular entertainment developed out of bawdy skits and popular revels. Aristotle strove to create a poetics (poetic theory) that would define

Tragedy is the oldest form of recorded drama, probing fundamental problems in the human condition. Aeschylus, Sophocles, and Euripides—the great Greek tragedians of the fifth century B.C.—each developed plays about the Royal House (family) of Atreus, revealing ancient Greek thought (and disagreement) about the crucial issues of justice, revenge, and the often conflicting obligations of family, state, religion, and personal/sexual fulfillment. Contemporary French director Ariane Mnouchkine's compilation and reworking of several of these ancient plays, collectively retitled Les Atrides, *toured Europe and North America in the late 1980s, demonstrating the permanence of these themes and the power of tragedy to animate and illuminate them for modern times. (Photo: Marc Enguerand.)*

these dramatic forms and create standards for their perfection. Unfortunately, only his poetics for tragedy has survived.

Today, aestheticians and scholars recognize a number of generic classifications. In addition to the original tragedy and comedy (now more narrowly defined than in Aristotle's day), the interlude, cycle play, history play, tragicomedy, dark comedy, melodrama, farce, documentary, and the musical have been iden-

tified as major genres into which modern plays (and, retroactively, older plays) can be classified.

A *tragedy* is a serious play (although not necessarily devoid of humorous episodes) with a topic of universal human import as its theme. Traditionally, the central character, often called the *protagonist*, is a person of high rank or stature. During the play, the protagonist undergoes a decline of fortune, leading to suffering and death. Integral to tragedy is the protagonist's period of insightful recognition or understanding. The effect of a tragedy, Aristotle claimed, was to elicit both pity and terror in the audience, which were resolved in a *catharsis,* or purging, of those aroused emotions.

The insightful recognition of the protagonist, his or her struggle against decline, and the consequent catharsis of the audience's aroused feelings are central to the tragic experience, which is not to be confused with a merely sad or pathetic experience. Tragedy is neither pathetic nor sentimental; it describes a bold, aggressive, human attack against huge, perhaps insurmountable odds. Tragic protagonists are often flawed in some way (indeed, classical tragic theory insists that they must be flawed or at least acting in ignorance), but they are leaders, not victims, of the play's events. Indeed, their leadership of the play's action and their discoveries during the course of that action bring the audience to deep emotional and intellectual involvement.

The notion of *protagonist* (Greek: "carrier of the action") is complemented by a notion of *antagonist* ("opposer of the action"), which gives tragedy its fundamental conflict and character struggle. The protagonists of tragedy often go forth against superhuman antagonists: gods, ghosts, "fate," or else the hardest of human realities. Such protagonists are *heroes*—or tragic heroes—because their supreme struggle, although perhaps a doomed effort, takes on larger-than-life proportions. Then, through the heat of supreme conflict, the tragic heroes themselves assume a superhuman force and draw us into the full magnitude of their thoughts and actions. Thus tragedy offers us a link with the divine and puts us at the apex of human destiny.

A tragedy should ennoble, not sadden, us. Characters that we admire may fall, but not before heroically challenging the elements, divinity, and death. Tragic heroes carry us to the brink of disaster—but, finally, it is their disaster and not ours, or at least not ours yet.

Seeing a tragedy is to contemplate and perhaps rehearse in our minds the great conflicts we may still have ahead of us.

There are only a few universally acknowledged tragedies of this sort. Sophocles' *Oedipus Tyrannos* was Aristotle's model of a great tragedy; most critics also class that author's *Electra* and *Antigone;* Aeschylus' *Oresteia* and *Prometheus Bound;* Euripides' *The Trojan Women, Medea,* and *The Bacchae;* Racine's *Phèdre;* and Shakespeare's *Hamlet, King Lear, Othello,* and *Macbeth* as among a dozen or so true tragic masterpieces. The question is often raised as to whether or not a modern play can be such a tragedy. Arthur Miller's *Death of a Salesman* (1947) is often the play for which this question is posed, for Miller deliberately challenged the traditional notion of a high-ranking protagonist by naming his principal character "Willy Loman" (that is, low man). Further, the antagonists Willy challenges are faceless bureaucrats, insensitive children, and an impersonal capitalistic economic system—not gods, fates, or ghosts. Most critics today, if they approach this question at all, deny Miller's play the tragic dimension on the grounds that the struggle is human, not superhuman, and that tragedy demands a larger-than-life context. If that is the case, tragedy probably belongs to an earlier world, a world in which audiences could be expected to accept without dissent the presence of divine forces mixing in with everyday human affairs.

Comedy began, according to Aristotle, as an improvised entertainment that combined satirical skits, bawdy jokes, erotic singing and dancing, and uninhibited revelry. The first known written comedies were those of Aristophanes, a playwright of brilliantly funny wit and savagely penetrating political acumen. Writing in Athens in the late fifth century B.C., Aristophanes set the general pattern, although not the structure, for comedies to come: interpersonal conflicts, topical issues, witty dialogue, physical buffoonery, verbal and sexual playfulness.

"Comedy Tonight" is the apt title of the opening song from A Funny Thing Happened on the Way to the Forum, *a Broadway musical by Stephen Sondheim,
based primarily on a 2,000-year-old Roman play by Plautus. Brilliant colors,
wildly exaggerated expressions, and tightly choreographed staging characterize
both classical and musical comedies. The 1995 Utah Shakespearean Festival production features costumes by Bill Black. (Photo: Wilkes & Bernard.)*

Comedy is not a simple amusement, however, nor is comedy simply entertaining; comedy is always about a serious human conflict.
The passionate pursuit of love, ambition,
social status, and money are age-old comic
themes. Indeed, the themes of many comedies
are often hard to distinguish from those of
tragedies; the plot and the style of comedies,
not the theme, ensure that the dramatic experience will avoid sustained pity or terror and
will elicit more laughter than cathartic shock.

The comic plot requires a generally happy
ending; the comic style includes characters
drawn on human scale, often in an exaggerated manner, who face the kinds of everyday
problems we know well in our own lives.
Gods, fate, suffering, and death rarely figure
significantly in comedies, and the problems of
the characters are social rather than cosmic,
interpersonal rather than metaphysical.

The best comedies are often those in which
characters foolishly overreach themselves and

are hilariously shown up for their foolishness. Not only are Aristophanes' plays (*The Birds, The Frogs, The Clouds, The Acharnians,* for example) masterpieces of this format, but so are the great comedies of Shakespeare (*As You Like It, Twelfth Night, A Midsummer Night's Dream*) and Molière (*The Miser, The Bourgeois Gentleman, The School for Wives*). In these plays, excesses of romantic love, intellectual pretension, physical braggadocio, or financial greed are wittily shown up, to the delight of the spectators in the audience—who can also recognize the germs of such behaviors in themselves. In this fashion, comedy seeks to advise as well as to entertain. The Roman poet Horace coined the term *utile dulce,* or "sweet instruction," to denote this deeper purpose of the comic drama.

There are many modern authors of dramatic comedy: George Bernard Shaw, George S. Kaufman, Simon Gray, Alan Ayckbourne, and Neil Simon are only a few of the twentieth-century playwrights who have succeeded in this genre. Because they are topical, comedies are usually less long-lasting than tragedies. Because they generally probe less profoundly into the matter of human destiny, they offer less fertile ground to academic scholarship. Hence, relative to tragedies, comedies are usually less frequently published in play anthologies, less frequently examined in critical literature, and less frequently studied in most academic institutions. Nevertheless, comedy's place in the theatre is every bit as secure as is tragedy, and its impact on audiences is no less strong now than it was in Aristophanes' day.

Comedy and tragedy remained the two "official" dramatic genres through the seventeenth century, when neoclassic French critics attempted to formalize them into absolutely rigid classifications. But from the Renaissance onward, playwrights and critics began to develop new dramatic genres or to dispense with genres altogether.

The medieval theatre, for example, brought to the stage *interludes,* comic entertainments presented between courses at state banquets

Shakespeare's history plays treat the real personages—kings, queens, nobles, and peasants—of the late medieval period in England. Eight of these plays treat the Wars of the Roses: the internecine battles between the royal families of York and Lancaster, each struggling for the English crown. Today, the plays are often combined in production, as in the Guthrie Theatre's version of the two parts of Henry IV (1990), directed by Guthrie Artistic Director, Garland Wright. (Photo: Michal Daniel.)

(from *inter* = between and *ludus* = play), and *cycle* plays, short biblical plays performed in a series (cycle), often in procession through a town.

Shakespeare's editors divided his plays into the traditional genres of tragedy and comedy, plus a newly defined genre, the *history,* which is a play purporting to dramatize the key events in the life of a king or head of state. Shakespeare seems to have invented this genre; and his great series of nine history plays, covering English royal history from 1377 to 1547 (inaccurate as they may be as historical documents) provides the bulk of what most people ever remember of the English kings Richard II, Henry IV, Henry V, Henry VI, and Richard III. Shakespeare's histories combine serious scenes, brilliant poetry, battlefield pageants, and hilarious comic moments. None of the plays, however, seeks to attain the classical catharsis of tragedy or the sustained humor of comedy. The history play thus seems to have been a mixed genre whose only successful proponent was its originator, Shakespeare himself.

More long-lived are two other mixed genres, *tragicomedy* and *dark comedy,* which also have both tragic and comic components.

Tragicomedy, as the name implies, is a form that deliberately attempts to bridge the two original genres. It maintains a serious theme throughout but varies the approach from serious to humorous and relaxes tragedy's larger-than-life scale. The problems of tragicomedy are solvable, and the antagonists are not divinely insuperable; tragicomedies, despite their rousing speeches and sentiments, conclude without the violent catharsis that their audience has been led to expect. Tragicomedy has been called "tragedy that ends happily." *Amphitryon,* by the Roman playwright Plautus, is generally considered the first tragicomedy (the play has been revised by subsequent authors into both tragic and comic versions). Many of Shakespeare's tragedies were in fact turned into tragicomedies by rewrite men in the tragicomedy-prone seventeenth century: Nahum Tate's 1687 revision of *King Lear,* for example, concludes with Lear and Gloucester retiring to "calm reflections on our fortunes past" and with Cordelia installed as Queen of England; all are dead at the close of Shakespeare's original.

Dark comedy is the obverse: an often comic but finally disturbing play that ends darkly (or ironically), leaving the impression of an unresolved universe surrounding the play's characters—and perhaps surrounding the audience as well. Dark comedies are usually funny, at least at the beginning, but they don't aim to leave us laughing. There are dark themes and ironic endings to many of Shakespeare's later plays, including *The Tempest, The Winter's Tale,* and *Pericles* (these are

Melodrama, an exaggerated seriousness, is evident in this moment from the American Conservatory Theatre production of The Tavern, *an early twentieth-century theatrical piece by showman George M. Cohan. (Photo: William Ganslen, ACT.)*

also often classed as romances), and to many of the late nineteenth- and early twentieth-century plays of Anton Chekhov, Bertolt Brecht, George Bernard Shaw, Luigi Pirandello, and Jean Giraudoux. In modern (post–World War II) times, the dark comedy has come to dominate the theatre, particularly in the work of playwrights such as Harold Pinter, Samuel Beckett, Edward Albee, Joe Orton, Beth Henley, August Wilson, Wendy Wasserstein, John Guare, Christopher Durang, Terence McNally, and Caryl Churchill.

If histories, tragicomedies, and dark comedies are mixed genres, then *melodramas* and *farces* are pure extremes, carrying the notion of dramatic genre as far as it can be taken.

Melodramas are plays that purport to be serious but are in fact trivial entertainments, often embellished with spectacular stagings, sententious dialogue, and highly suspenseful—and contrived—plotting. Melodrama

The essence of farce is captured in this production photograph from Georges Feydeau's Hotel Paradiso, as presented by the American Conservatory Theatre. Actors' exaggerated expressions and postures, as well as multiple-door setting, are standard features of farcical plays. The actors, left to right, are Sydney Walker, Raye Birk, Elizabeth Huddle, Michael Winters, and Ruth Kobart. (Photo: William Ganslen, ACT.)

Andre Gregory and Joyce Van Patten are dinner guests forced by bizarre circumstances to cook and serve their own meal in Neil Simon's Rumors (1990), the author's only self-proclaimed farce. The Old Globe Theatre of San Diego produced the world premiere production, shown here, which was directed by Gene Saks. (Photo: Martha Swope and Associates.)

presents a simple and finite confrontation between good and evil rather than a complex exposition of universal human aspirations and sufferings. Plays in this genre cannot sustain unpleasant endings or generate catharsis, but can indeed provoke a deeply emotional outpouring of audience sentiment—always a powerful theatrical response. A pure creation of the theatre, melodramas employ every possible theatrical device to generate audience emotion (the name "melo-drama" reveals the function music originally played in the melodramatic experience) and tend to reflect reality, or real human issues, only on the most superficial and sentimental level. Melodrama in its pure form rarely exists today—the melodramas that are occasionally produced these days are parodies, played for laughs—

but melodramatic elements frequently find their way into dramas of every sort.

Farces are similarly pure creations of the theatre. In farce, one finds a wildly hilarious treatment of a trivial theme, ordinarily one of the various stock themes—mistaken identity, illicit infatuation, physical dissolution, monetary scheming—that have come down from ancient times. Plot components of farces are also drawn from a set of stock situations and events; identical twins, lovers in closets or under tables, full-stage chases, switched potions, switched costumes (often involving transsexual dressing), misheard instructions, and

Documentary plays dramatize actual events, using real names, dates, places, and even transcribed statements where possible. Richard Greenberg's Night and Her Stars, *shown here in its 1993 South Coast Repertory Theatre (California) premiere, portrays the TV quiz show scandals of the mid-1950s. At center, Dylan Baker plays Charles Van Doren, the cheating quiz show contestant who had been secretly provided answers. (Photo: Cristofer Gross.)*

various disrobings, discoveries, and disappearances characterize this age-old and perennially durable dramatic genre. Elements of farce exist in almost all comedies, but pure farce makes no pretense toward Horace's *utile dulce;* the motto instead is "laugh 'til you cry," and in a well-written, well-staged farce the audience does just that. Michael Frayn's *Noises Off,* a pure farce set in a provincial English theatre, had audiences collapsed in hysteria on both sides of the Atlantic in the 1980s; every couple of years a new "laugh-riot" tends to appear—just as we are beginning to lament the demise of this popular dramatic genre.

Many minor genres have been usefully described in the contemporary theatre; the *documentary* and the *musical* are of particular importance.

The *documentary* is a genre of fairly recent development, in which a great deal of authentic evidence is used as a basis for portraying relatively recent historical events. Trial transcripts, news reports and pictures, personal and official records are marshaled as documentation to bring alive a particular issue and point of view. Famous court trials—those of J. Robert Oppenheimer, John C. Scopes, Adolph Eichmann, the "Zoot Suit" gangs, and Leopold and Loeb, for example—have been a prime source of material for documentary dramatizations.

Musicals are often dismissed as simply light entertainment, but modern musicals often have serious themes and thought-provoking dramatic action. Grand Hotel, *staged by Tommy Tune on Broadway in 1989, was set in 1930s Germany and convincingly re-created the savagely decadent atmosphere in which fascist mentalities and anti-Semitism could flourish. (Photo: Martha Swope and Associates.)*

The *musical* genre is defined by its extensive musical score, particularly by its vocal score. Operas and operettas are, of course, examples of musical theatre but are generally considered more music than theatre. The musical exists as a dramatic genre, however, in such popular and stage-oriented forms as musical comedy (a comedy with songs and dances, such as *Crazy for You*), musical drama (a serious play with songs and dances, like *Fiddler On The Roof*), musical documentary

(such as the World War I–inspired *Oh, What a Lovely War!*), or a musical melodrama (Stephen Sondheim's *Sweeney Todd, the Demon Barber of Fleet Street*). The musical play has often been considered America's greatest contribution to the theatre, particularly owing to the great post–World War II musicals by Cole Porter (*Kiss Me Kate*), Frank Loesser (*Guys and Dolls*), Alan Jay Lerner and Frederick Loewe (*Brigadoon, My Fair Lady*) and Richard Rodgers and Oscar Hammerstein (*Oklahoma, South Pacific, The Sound of Music, The King and I*). Today, however, the musical is at least a multinational dramatic genre, with much of the newest work originating from Stephen Sondheim in America (*Follies, A Little Night Music, Sunday in the Park with George, Passion*); Andrew Lloyd Webber in England (*Cats, Evita, Phantom of the Opera, Sunset Boulevard*), and Alain Boublil/Claude-Michel Schönberg in France (*Les Misérables, Miss Saigon, Martin Guerre*). The musical is considered more fully in the discussion of modern theatre.

Potentially, of course, there are as many theatrical genres as the diligent critic wishes to define. No system of classification should obscure the fact that each play is unique, and the grouping of any two or more plays into a common genre is only a convenience for purposes of comparison and analysis. We in the twentieth century have learned that past formulations of tragedy and farce have had little bearing on the long-range assessment of the importance, quality, or worth—on the staying power—of any individual play; and critics who today dwell inordinately on such questions as "Is *Death of a Salesman* a true tragedy?" are doubtless spending too much time deciding what box to put the artistic work in and too little time examining and revealing the work itself.

On the other hand, genre distinctions can be useful if we keep their limitations in mind. They can help us to comprehend the broad spectrum of purposes to which plays may be put and to perceive important similarities and differences. For the theatre artist, an awareness of the possibilities inherent in each genre—together with a knowledge of the achievements that have been made in each—stimulates the imagination and aids in setting work standards and ambitions.

STRUCTURE

Plays can be analyzed structurally in two ways: by their components (that is, plot, character, theme, etc.) and by their order of organization (exposition, development, climax, etc.). Both methods are used by most people who find it worthwhile to analyze dramatic art, and both will be used in this book. However, it must be clear from the outset that a drama which is taken apart in the classroom inevitably loses something. The individual components and the sequential aspects of any given play are never in fact isolated in the theatrical experience, and any truly useful dramatic analysis must end with a resynthesis of the studied portions into a living whole. The complexity of the theatrical experience and its multisensual impact decree that we see it always as greater than the sum of its parts.

The Components of a Play

The division of plays into components is an ancient analytical practice. Aristotle in his *Poetics* (325 B.C.) described the components of a tragedy (by which he meant a serious play) as plot, characters, theme, diction, music, and spectacle—in that order. Aristotle's list, with some modification and elaboration, still serves as a pretty fair breakdown of what theatre is all about, although the relative importance of each component has been a matter of continuing controversy.

Plot While we may colloquially think of "plot" as synonymous with "story," the two words are quite different: plot refers to the *mechanics* of storytelling, including the se-

Singing and dancing, often allied to romantic themes, are the traditional distinguishing arts of the American musical play. One of the classic American musicals was the 1930 Girl Crazy, by the late Gershwin Brothers, George (who wrote the music) and Ira (lyrics). With a new script (by Ken Ludwig), a new title—Crazy for You—and some additional Gershwin songs, this show became a new Broadway hit in 1992. Pictured are Harry Groener and Jody Benson as the "Embraceable You" romantic leads. (Photo: Joan Marcus.)

THE WELL-MADE PLAY

The *pièce bien faite* ("well-made play") was a term used to describe certain dramatic works, known for their complex and elegant plots, written by the popular French dramatists Eugène Scribe and Victorien Sardou (among others) during the latter part of the nineteenth century. The expression was originally complimentary but soon became a derisive reference to plays that were seen as merely mechanical, plot-heavy contrivances, holding their audience solely by a series of calculated dramatic effects. Arguing that drama should also be the vehicle for grand ideas and deep passions, playwright George Bernard Shaw coined the term "Sardoodledom" to express his contempt for Sardou's well-made, but shallowly felt, plays.

quence of comings and goings of the characters; the timetable of the play's events; and the specific order of revelations, reversals, quarrels, discoveries, and actions that take place on stage, as in "furthering the plot." (In London theatres of the sixteenth century, a written "platte" or "plotte" was hung on the wall backstage, reminding the actors of the play's order of major events, entrances, and exits.) Plot is a *structure of actions*: both outer actions (such as Romeo stabbing Tybalt) and inner ones (such as Romeo falling in love with Juliet). The specific sequence and arrangement of these actions is essentially what we take away from the play; it is usually the way we *describe* the play to someone who has not yet seen it. This is undoubtedly why Aristotle describes "plot" first in his list of the elements of tragedy (drama). Creating a dramatically compelling plot is one of the most difficult and demanding tests of a playwright's skill.

Traditionally, the primary demands of plot are logic and suspense. To satisfy the demand for logic, the actions portrayed must be plausible, and events must follow one upon another in an organic rather than arbitrary fashion. To sustain suspense, the actions portrayed must set up expectations for further actions, drawing the audience along in a story that seems to move inexorably toward an ending that may be sensed but is never wholly predictable. Melodramas and farces tend to rely heavily on intricate and suspenseful plots. The "well-made plays" of the late nineteenth century reflect an attempt to elevate plot construction to the highest level of theatrical art; today, murder mysteries and "whodunits" are likely to be the most plot-intensive works to be seen on the stage.

Characters The *characters* of a play are the human figures—the impersonated presences—who undertake the actions of the plot. Their potency in the theatre is measured by our interest in them *as people*. The most brilliant plotting in the world cannot redeem a play if the audience remains indifferent to its characters; therefore, the fundamental demand of a play's characters is that they make the audience *care*. To this end, characters cannot be mere stick figures, no matter how elaborately detailed. The great dramatic characters of the past—Hamlet, Masha, Amanda, Iago, Vladimir, Peer Gynt, Phaedra, to name a few—bring to an experienced theatregoer's or playreader's mind personalities as vivid and memorable as those of good friends (and hated enemies); they are whole images, indelibly human, alive with the attributes, feelings, and expectations of real people. We can identify with them; we can sympathize with them.

Character depth is what gives a play its psychological complexity, its sensuality, and its warmth. Without it, we cannot experience love, hate, fear, joy, hope, despair—any of the emotions we expect to derive from theatre; and a theatre devoid of those emotions that stem from the humanness of the characters portrayed would be a theatre without an audience in a matter of days. For this reason many playwrights have scoffed at the notion of primacy of plot and at the often mechanical

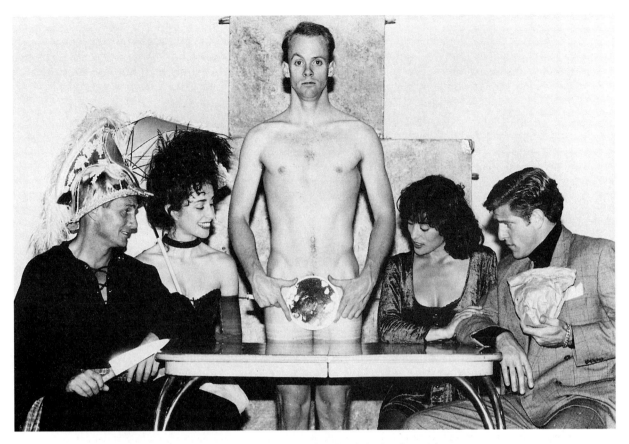

The theme of Patrick Shanley's The Big Funk *is stated explicitly by the playwright: "The only means to a clear picture of what life is, is to approach another human being and be naked." The 1993 production by the Zephyr Theatre, Hollywood, illustrates this explicitly. Directed by Jules Aaron, with Matt Walker in the central (naked) role. (Photo: Garrett W. Ellwood.)*

contrivances of the well-made play. Indeed, several playwrights have fashioned plays that were arbitrarily plotted, with the story line designed simply to show various aspects of a fascinating character.

Theme The *theme* of a play is its abstracted intellectual content. It may be described as the play's overall statement: its topic, central idea, or message, as the case may be. Some plays have obvious themes, such as Euripides' *The Trojan Women* (the horrors of war) or Molière's *The Bourgeois Gentleman* (the foolishness of social pretense). Other plays have

less clearly defined themes, and the most provocative of these have given rise to much scholarly controversy. *Hamlet, Oedipus Tyrannos,* and *Waiting for Godot* all suggest many themes, and each has spawned a great many debates among adherents arguing fiercely about which theme is central.

Nothing demands that a play have a single theme, of course, or even that it be at all reducible to straightforward intellectual generalization. Indeed, plays that are too obviously theme-intensive are usually considered too propagandistic or too somberly academic for theatrical success: "If you want to send a message," one Broadway saying goes, "use a fax machine." Moreover, although the themes of plays address the central questions of society and humanity, a play's theatrical impact hinges always on audience engagement in plot and characterization.

The importance of theme is that a play must have something to say, and that something must seem *pertinent* to the audience. Further, the play must be sufficiently focused and limited to give the audience at least some insight into that something within its two- to four-hour framework. Plays that try to say nothing or, conversely, plays that try to say everything, rarely have even a modest impact, no matter how entertaining or well plotted they may be. Thus, from the beginning, playwrights working in every genre, be it tragedy, comedy, melodrama, or farce, have recognized the merit of narrowing their field of intellectual investigation when crafting a play.

Diction Aristotle's fourth component, *diction,* relates to the pronunciation of spoken dialogue and also to the literary character of a play's text, including its tone, imagery, cadence, and articulation, as well as its use of literary forms and figures such as verse, rhyme, metaphor, apostrophe, jest, and epigram.

The theatrical value of poetry has been well established from the beginning; until fairly recent times, as a matter of fact, most serious plays were written largely in verse. Today, comedies as well as more serious plays still make liberal use of carefully crafted dialogue, although the verse form is relatively rare. Many plays succeed on the basis of brilliant repartee, stunning epigrams, poetic lyricism, witty arguments, and dazzling tirades. Other, quite different, sorts of plays feature a poetry of silences and inarticulate mutterings: these, as fashioned by Anton Chekhov or Harold Pinter, for example, can create a diction no less effective than the more ostentatiously crafted verbal pyrotechnics of a Bernard Shaw or a Tom Stoppard (see the chapters on modern drama).

The diction of a play is by no means the creation of the playwright alone. It is very much the product of the actor as well, and for that reason throughout the history of Western theatre an effective stage voice has been considered the prime asset of the actor. Even today, the study of voice is a primary and continuous obligation at most schools and conservatories of classical acting. The chief aim of these schools is to create an acting voice capable of dealing in spectacular fashion with the broad palette of dramatic diction demanded by the works of the world's most noted playwrights.

Music Any discussion of *music,* Aristotle's fifth component of theatre, forces us to remember that in Aristotle's time plays were sung or chanted, not simply spoken. That mode of presentation has all but disappeared, and yet the musical component remains directly present in most plays performed today, indirectly present in the rest.

Music is *directly* present in a large number of plays, taking many forms. Songs are common in the plays of Shakespeare, as well as in the works of modern writers, such as Bertolt Brecht, who feature "direct" performance techniques. Many naturalistic writers work familiar songs into their scripts, sometimes by having characters play recordings on stage. Chekhov and Tennessee Williams both make extensive use in their plays of offstage music—for example, a military marching band can be heard in Chekhov's *The Three Sisters;* and Williams provides for music from a nearby dance hall in *A Streetcar Named Desire* and from a cantina in *Night of the Iguana.* Directors also frequently add incidental music to play productions—sometimes to set a mood during intermissions or before the play begins, sometimes to underscore the play's action itself. The power of music directly present in the theatre is well known, and its effectiveness in moving an audience to ever-deeper feeling is one that few playwrights or directors wish to ignore.

Lavish spectacle is both the subject and style of the Andrew Lloyd Webber musical, Sunset Boulevard, *which is extravagant in every way: scenery, costuming, and over-the-top acting. Glenn Close stars in the 1994 Broadway production. (Photo: Joan Marcus.)*

"Spectacle" need not be pretty as much as visually penetrating and evocative. In Henrik Ibsen's Peer Gynt, *the author's stage direction merely says "A Madhouse"; in this Berlin production directed by the celebrated Peter Stein, the madhouse is created by hanging and writhing bodies, mostly naked, and an immense sculpture. (Photo: Courtesy German Information Center.)*

Indirectly, music is present in every play. It is in the rhythm of sounds that, while not specifically tuneful, combine to create a play's "score," its orchestration of sound. Vocal tones, footsteps, sighs, shouts, offstage railroad whistles, the shrilling of a telephone, muffled drumbeats, gunshots, animal cries, conversations in the next room, and amplified special effects (heartbeats, respiration, otherworldly noises, for instance) are frequently employed by authors and directors to create a symphony of the theatre apart from, though supportive of, the plot, characters, dialogue, and theme. Moreover, the spoken word creates, in addition to its semantic impact (its meaning and connotation), an aural impact: it is an integer of pure sound, and it can be appreciated as pure musical vibration. Under the guidance of a skilled director, all of a play's sounds can be orchestrated to produce a performance of such dramatic force that it can thrill even persons wholly unacquainted with the language of the dialogue.

Spectacle Aristotle's last component, *spectacle,* encompasses the visual aspects of production: scenery, costumes, lighting, make-up, properties, and the overall *look* of the theatre and stage. It would be wrong to infer that "spectacle" is synonymous with "spectacular," for some productions are quite restrained in their visual artistry. Rather, it is spectacle in the sense that it is something seen. If this point seems obvious, it is also crucial. Theatre is a visual experience as much as it is an aural, emotional, or intellectual experience: the ancient Greeks clearly had this in mind when they chose the name "seeing place" to designate the site of their performances.

Much as the cinema has been called the art of "moving pictures," so the theatre might be called the art of fluid sculpture. This sculpture is fashioned in part from the human body in motion and in part from still or moving scenery and props, natural and manufactured items of both dramatic and decorative importance, all illuminated by natural or artificially modulated light. It is a sculpture that moves in time as well as in space; and although it is generally considered to be primarily a support for the plot, characters, and theme of a play, it has an artistic appeal and an artistic heritage all its own. Certainly some ardent patrons of the theatre pay more attention to settings and costumes than to any other aspect of a play, and in many a successful production dramatic visual effects have virtually carried the play.

Memorable visual elements can be both grand and prosaic, imposing and subtle. Nineteenth-century romanticism, which survives today primarily in the form of grand opera, tends to favor mammoth stagings featuring processions, crowd scenes, palaces, animals, triumphal arches, and lavish costumes. Twentieth-century movements are more likely to go in for domestic environments and archetypal images: Jimmy and Cliff reading newspapers while Alison irons a shirt in John Osborne's *Look Back in Anger* and Laura playing with her glass animals in Tennessee Williams's *The Glass Menagerie;* or Mother Courage pulling her wagon in Brecht's *Mother Courage* and Nagg and Nell in the ashcans of Samuel Beckett's *Endgame.* In the long run, conceptual richness and precision in a play's visual presentation are far more telling than grandeur for its own sake.

Convention To these six components of every play we should add a seventh that Aristotle apparently never saw reason to consider as a discrete component: theatrical *convention*. The agreement between audience and actor includes a set of tacit understandings that form the context of playwatching—conventions that make us understand, for example, that when the stage lights fade out, the play (or the act) has ended. Over the years, other common conventions of the European-American stage have included the following:

- When one actor turns directly from the others and speaks to us, the other characters are presumed not to hear him. This is the convention of the *aside* (to the audience).
- When the actors all leave the stage, and then they or others reenter (particularly when the lights change), time has elapsed, and the locale may be changed.
- When the actors onstage freeze, we are seeing some sort of "dream state" (of one of the characters, presumably), and the words we hear are to be considered his or her thoughts, not anyone's speech.

The conventions of the theatre permit a sort of shorthand communication with the audience, without the encumbrance of extensive physical elaboration or acting out. If the locale can effectively be changed by the convention of a simple light shift, instead of by moving a half ton of scenery, the theatre saves money and the audience saves time. Stage violence is usually executed conventionally (that is, with little physical mayhem) rather than with lifelike (or cinematographic) verisimilitude, since the difficulty in realistically portraying severed torsos, rupturing intestines, and bleeding limbs on stage ordinarily outweighs any dramatic advantage in doing so;

and the theatrical convention ("stab, grab, scream, collapse, and die") can be accepted fully if performed with emotional and psychological (although not physical) authenticity.

Many of our stage conventions are so embedded in the fabric of the theatregoing experience that we tend to forget about them unless something happens that casts them into relief. Our theatre conventions are most visible when we see them from afar—in contrast to the practices of theatres of other cultures. For example, the conventions of the Japanese Nō Drama decree that major characters enter on a gangway, that choruses sing the lines of characters who are dancing, that hand-held fans are used in certain ways to indicate wind, water, rain, or the rising moon. Patrons of the Nō Drama accept these conventions as unquestioningly as we accept the convention that, when the stage lights dim, we are to ignore the scurrying about of actors and stagehands during a scene change.

Each play sets up its own system of conventions, but in most cases they accord with the traditions of their times and therefore go largely unnoticed (doubtless that is why Aristotle, familiar with no drama other than his own, made no specific mention of them). In modern times, with playwrights and directors becoming increasingly aware of other traditions and possibilities, more and more play productions seek to employ conventions of ancient times or foreign cultures and even to establish new ones. Peter Shaffer's *Black Comedy,* which supposedly takes place in the dark, utilizes a convention that Shaffer attributes to the Chinese: when the lights are on they are "off," and when they are off they are "on." Eugene O'Neill's *Strange Interlude* and Steven Berkoff's *Kvetch* give us to understand that when the actors freeze and speak, we in the audience—but not the other characters in the play—hear their thoughts. Jean Anouilh's *Antigone* uses a variation on the Greek device of the chorus: a single man speaks with the author's voice as the characters on stage freeze in silence. Lanford Wilson, in *The Rimers of Eldritch,* presents a story in more than a hundred tiny scenes that jump back and forth in time, and only at the play's end do we get any real sense of story line. Arthur Miller's *After the Fall* places an imaginary psychiatrist in the midst of the audience, and the play's protagonist repeatedly interrupts the action of the drama to address his analyst in highly theatrical "therapy" sessions. And so it goes. There is no formal requirement for the establishment of theatrical conventions, except that the audience must "agree" (which it does, of course, unconsciously) to accept them.

These seven components of every play—with the seventh framing Aristotle's six—are the raw material of drama. All are important, and certainly the theatre could not afford to dispense with any one. Some plays are intensive in one or more components; most great productions show artistry in all. The *balancing* of these components in theatrical presentation is one of the primary challenges facing the director, who on one occasion may be called upon mainly to clarify and elaborate a theme, on another to find the visual mode of presentation that best supports the action, on another to develop and "flesh out" the characterizations in order to give strength and meaning to the plot, on another to heighten a musical tone in order to enhance sensual effect, on another to develop the precise convention—the relationship between play and audience—that will maximize the play's artistic impact. For as important as each of these components is to the theatrical experience, it is their combination and interaction, not their individual splendor, that is crucial to a production's success.

The Order of a Play

Plays can also be looked at in terms of their temporal (time) structure. Here again, Aristotle affords some help. He tells us that drama has "a beginning, a middle, and an end," and here and there in his *Poetics* he proffers a little detail about the nature of each of these elements. We can expand Aristotle's list somewhat, for by now some fairly consistent features can be distinguished in the orderly sequencing of a theatrical experience. These individual features can be divided into three major groupings: the preplay, the play proper, and the postplay.

The events that take place before the play proper begins are referred to as the *preplay*.

The Gathering of the Audience   Dramatic theorists often either ignore the audience in considering the crucial elements of the theatre or dismiss it as a "paratheatrical" (*para* meaning "only somewhat") concern. The gathering of the audience is, however, an important consideration in the presentation of a play, entailing a process that is not without its artistic and cultural significance. The chief concerns in that process have to do with publicity, admission, and seating. Each of these concerns has given theatre producers much food for thought since ancient times.

For how does the theatre attract its audience in the first place? Theatregoing, after all, is not a need of mankind in the same way that eating is a need; the population of a society does not spend half its waking hours trying to supply itself with theatre in the way it strives to secure food, shelter, and physical security. Rather, the theatre, if it is to survive, must go out and recruit attention; in every era, theatre has had the responsibility of gathering its audience.

Therefore, the goal of every theatre producer is to make his or her theatre accessible, inviting, and favorably known to the widest possible public—and also, in many eras, to the *richest* possible public—and to make theatre as an art form as thrilling and spiritually *necessary* as it can possibly be.

One of the oldest known ways of publicizing the theatre is by means of a procession. The circus parade, which still takes place in some of the smaller towns of Europe and the United States, is a remnant of a once universal form of advertisement for the performing arts that probably began well in advance of recorded history.

The Greeks of ancient Athens opened their great dramatic festivals with a *proagon* (literally, "pre-action") in which both playwrights and actors were introduced at a huge public meeting and given a chance to speak about the plays they were to present on subsequent days. Today, similar conclaves—usually via television talk shows in this global village of ours—are often used to promote theatrical events to the public at large. The Elizabethans flew flags atop their playhouses on performance days, and the flags could be seen across the Thames in "downtown" London, enticing hundreds away from their commercial and religious activities. The lighted marquees of Broadway theatres around Times Square and of London theatres in the West End are a modern-day equivalent of the flags that waved over those first great English public theatres.

Developments in the printing and broadcast media have spurred the growth of theatre advertising until it is today a major theatrical craft in its own right. Splendid posters, illustrated programs, multicolor subscription brochures, full-page newspaper advertisements, staged media events, articulate press releases, and flashy thirty-second television commercials have been employed to summon us out of the comfort of our homes and into the theatre. For premieres or for openings of new playhouses, giant searchlights are often used to beckon the public to the theatrical location. Far from being an inconsequential aspect of theatre, publicity today occupies a place of fundamental importance in the thinking of theatrical producers and commands a major share of the budget for commercial theatrical ventures.

Procedures for admitting and seating the audience are usually straightforward and conventional; however, they can have important—

and occasionally decisive—effects on the overall theatrical presentation.

Ordinarily, theatre is supported at least in part by fees charged the audience. These fees make up what is called the "box office revenue." For commercial theatres, box office revenue provides the sole means of meeting production costs and providing a profit to investors. The admission charge dates from ancient Greek days, and since then only a few amateur or civic productions (such as the religious pageants of medieval England or the free Shakespeare performances in contemporary New York City) have managed to survive without it.

Seating is frequently determined by the price of admission: the best seats cost the most. What determines "best" and "poorest" seating, however, depends on many things. In modern Broadway and West End theatres, the most costly seats are in the orchestra (known in the West End as "the stalls"), which is the ground-level seating area; balcony seats ordinarily cost less, and the higher the balcony, the smaller the price. In the public theatres of Elizabethan London, however, the ground level (which was standing room) provided the cheapest space, and the "gentlemen's rooms" in the balcony—where one could be seen and visited—commanded up to twelve times as much. In the Restoration period, seats on the stage itself brought the highest prices of all, assuring their purchasers the widest possible personal recognition (but affording a ridiculously poor view of the play's action).

Seating is not always scaled according to price, however. In the Greek drama festivals of ancient Athens, the front-row seats were reserved for priests, and members of the lay audience sat in sections of the *theatron* reserved for their particular tribe. In many noncommercial theatres today, the best seats go to those patrons willing to wait longest in line to get them. The National Theatre of England has experimented with a seating system designed to reward the most eager of its fans, not the richest; this practice is common in

East European countries. In racially divided countries, audiences are segregated according to the color of their skin. This regrettable practice persisted well into the twentieth century in the United States, and indeed in the 1960s was occasionally revived by "Black Theatre" companies. Perhaps the most radical seating experiments occurred in the "New Theatre" movement of the early 1970s, in which audiences were often led one by one to seats determined in an impromptu interview with one or another of the cast members acting as ushers. What is more, patrons were sometimes ordered to leave their assigned seats in midperformance to make room for actors!

The Transition Gathered, admitted, and seated, the audience remains a collection of individuals preoccupied with their daily concerns. Now the theatre must transform them into a community devoted to the concerns of the play and enmeshed in the actions of imaginary characters. The theatre, in other words, must effect in the audience's awareness a transition from real life to stage life, and it must do so in a smooth and agreeable fashion.

The written program is one modern device (modern in the sense that it dates from the eighteenth century) that helps to prepare the audience for the fiction they are about to see. It gives them the locale and time of the action, the names of the characters and of the actors who impersonate them; in these ways it allows the audience to preview the general scope of the play's environment—spatial, temporal, and personal—and to accept the actors as valid impersonators of the play's characters. Having read that Kevin Kline is playing Hamlet, for example, we don't spend playwatching time trying to figure who the lead actor is.

Often music is used, in the contemporary theatre, to set the mood or tone of a play, particularly when the action is set in a certain period in the past. For a musical production, an entire orchestral piece—called the overture—sometimes precedes the action on stage.

Lobby displays are sometimes used to supplement the written programs, featuring either pictures of the actors or other pictures and documents relevant to the play, its period, its author, and its critical reception. Occasionally the seating area is altered to aid in this transition, sometimes by the addition of wall posters, sometimes by other ornamentation. When no curtain is used, the scenery may be "warmed" by preshow lighting that eases the audience into an expectation of the performance to follow—in some productions that "scenery" includes actors sitting, standing, or lying motionless on the set or engaging in quiet, understated movement. Sometimes slide presentations, songs, or improvised activities take place on stage before the play begins, and the patrons may be asked to participate in some way as they find their way to their seats. Many of these methods date from ancient times; all of them have been used to introduce modern plays to an audience and to prepare the audience to enter the world of the stage.

Finally, a swift new transition to stage life occurs: the play proper begins. Most often this is a shared moment. The houselights dim and a curtain rises or stage lights come up to reveal a scene. Occasionally this transition is more subtle, and each member of the audience glides into the play at her or his own moment of discovery; a preshow improvisation begins to take on a more pronounced, attention-demanding character, or perhaps some small but seemingly significant alteration galvanizes the consciousness to full attention. Either way, the transition is complete. The thinking of the audience shifts from workaday concerns to the characters of the play and their story. This, to use a familiar theatrical term, is "magic time."

Almost all plays (as compared to most happenings, improvisations, and performance art pieces) contain a structured sequence of these four identifiable dramatic elements in the *play proper:* exposition, conflict, climax,

and denouement. Alternative dramatic structures will be discussed in Chapters 9 and 10.

The Exposition   No important play has ever begun with a character dashing onstage and shouting, "The house is on fire!" At best, such a beginning could only confuse the audience, and at worst it could cause them to flee in panic. At that point they would have no way of knowing what house, or why they should care about it. Most plays, whatever their style or genre, begin with dialogue or action calculated to ease us, not shock us, into the concerns of the characters with whom we are to spend the next two hours or so.

Exposition is a word not much in favor now, coming as it does from an age when play structure was considered more scientific than it is today. But it is still a useful term, referring to the background information the audience must have in order to understand what's going on in the action of a play.

In the rather mechanical plotting of the "well-made" plays, the exposition is handled with little fanfare, with a few characters, often servants (minor figures in the action to follow), discussing something that is about to happen and enlightening each other (and, of course, the audience) about certain details around which the plot will turn. Consider these lines from the opening scene of Henrik Ibsen's 1884 classic, *The Wild Duck:*

PETTERSEN, *in livery, and* JENSEN, *the hired waiter, in black, are putting the study in order. From the dining room, the hum of conversation and laughter is heard.*

PETTERSEN: Listen to them, Jensen; the old man's got to his feet—he's giving a toast to Mrs. Sorby.

JENSEN: (*pushing forward an armchair*) Do you think it's true, then, what they've been saying, that there's something going on between them?

PETTERSEN: God knows.

JENSEN: He used to be quite the lady's man, I understand.

Only the exposition has made clear to the astonished Mortimer (standing) that Mr. Gibbs (at right) is about to drink a cocktail poisoned by Mortimer's delightfully dotty aunts. The Long Wharf Theatre production of Joseph Kesselring's classic American comedy, Arsenic and Old Lace, *featured Joyce Ebert (left) and Joanne Woodward as the comically murderous ladies. (Photo: T. Charles Erickson.)*

PETTERSEN: I suppose.

JENSEN: And he's giving this party in honor of his son, they say.

PETTERSEN: That's right. His son came home yesterday.

JENSEN: I never even knew old Werle had a son.

PETTERSEN: Oh, he has a son all right. But he's completely tied up at the Hoidal works. In all the years I've been here he's never come into town.

A WAITER: (*in the doorway of the other room*) Pettersen, there's an old fellow here . . .

PETTERSEN: (*mutters*) Damn. Who'd show up at this time of night?

After a few more lines, Pettersen, Jensen, and the waiter make their exits and are seen no more. Their function is purely expository—to pave the way for the principal characters. The conversation they are having is a contrivance intended simply to give us a framework for the action—and the information they impart is presented by means of a conversation among servants only because a convention of realism decrees that words spoken in a play be addressed to characters, not to the audience.

The exposition of nonrealistic plays can be handled more directly. It was the Greek custom to begin a play with a prologue preceding the entrance of the chorus and the major play episodes; the prologue was sometimes a scene and sometimes a simple speech to the audience. Shakespeare also used prologues in some of his plays. In one particularly interesting example, Shakespeare's *Henry V,* each of the five acts begins with a character called Chorus directly addressing the audience and setting the scene for the act:

CHORUS: O for a Muse of fire, that would ascend
  The brightest heaven of invention!
  A kingdom for a stage, princes to act,
  And monarchs to behold the swelling scene!
  Then should the warlike Harry, like himself,
  Assume the port of Mars, and at his heels
  (Leash'd in, like hounds) should famine, sword, and fire
  Crouch for employment. But pardon, gentles all,
  The flat unraised spirits that hath dar'd
  On this unworthy scaffold to bring forth
  So great an object. Can this cockpit hold
  The vasty fields of France? Or may we cram
  Within this wooden O the very casques
  That did affright the air at Agincourt?
  O, pardon! since a crooked figure may
  Attest in little place a million,
  And let us, ciphers to this great accompt,
  On your imaginary forces work.
  Suppose within the girdle of these walls
  Are now confin'd two mighty monarchies,
  Whose high, upreared, and abutting fronts
  The perilous narrow ocean parts asunder.
  Piece out our imperfections with your thoughts;
  Into a thousand parts divide one man,
  And make imaginary puissance;
  Think, when we talk of horses, that you see them
  Printing their proud hoofs i' th' receiving earth;

For 'tis your thoughts that now must deck our kings,
  Carry them here and there, jumping o'er times,
  Turning th' accomplishment of many years
  Into an hour-glass: for the which supply,
  Admit me Chorus to this history;
  Who, Prologue-like, your humble patience pray,
  Gently to hear, kindly to judge, our play.

This famous prologue establishes setting, characters, and audience expectation of plot in a straightforward manner, and it begs the audience's indulgence for the theatrical conventions they will be called upon to entertain.

The Conflict   Now is the time for the character to enter shouting, "The house is on fire!"

It is a truism that drama requires conflict; in fact, the word *drama,* when used in daily life, implies a situation fraught with conflict. No one writes plays about characters who live every day in unimpaired serenity; no one would ever choose to watch such a play. Conflict and confrontation are the mechanisms by which a situation becomes dramatic.

Why is this so? Why are conflict situations so theatrically interesting? The reasons have to do with plot, theme, and character. Plot can hold suspense only when it involves alternatives and choices: Macbeth has strong reasons to murder King Duncan and strong reasons not to; if he had only the former or only the latter, he would project no real conflict and we should not consider him such an interesting character. We are fascinated by a character's actions largely in light of the actions she rejects and the stresses she has to endure in making her decisions. In other words, plot entails not only the actions of a play but also the inactions—the things that are narrowly rejected and do *not* happen. A character's decision must proceed from powerfully conflicting alternatives if we are to watch this behavior with empathy instead of mere curiosity. In watching a character act, the audience must also watch him *think;* a playwright gets him to think by putting him into conflict.

Conflict can be set up between characters as well as within them; it may be reducible to one central situation, or it may evolve out of many. Whatever the case, conflict throws characters into relief and permits the audience to see deeply into the human personality. To see a character at war with herself or in confrontation with another is to see how that character *works,* and this is the key to our caring.

The theme of a play is ordinarily a simple abstraction of its central conflict. In Sopho-

(Photo: Courtesy Alabama Shakespeare Festival.)

(Photo: Tod Martens.)

Conflict is fundamental to drama but appears in a great many guises: direct confrontation, as Joan (Rebecca Waxman, right) faces her accusers in George Bernard Shaw's St. Joan, *Alabama Shakespeare Festival, 1995 (facing page, top); playful, as Beatrice and Benedick (Patricia Hodges and Marco Barricelli) negotiate the "merry war" of their courtship in Shakespeare's* Much Ado About Nothing, *in the 1994 Indiana Repertory Theatre production directed by Libby Appel (facing page, bottom); violent: Karina Arroyave and V. Craig Heidenrich in José Rivera's* Marisol; *Actors Theatre of Louisville, 1992 premiere (below, left); and conspiratorial, as Cassius and Brutus (Delroy Lindow and Dakin Matthews) confront each other as to the roles each should play in the Roman succession, in Shakespeare's* Julius Caesar *at the Mark Taper Forum Theatre in Los Angeles, 1991 (below, right).*

(Photo: Richard Trigg.)

(Photo: Jay Thompson.)

cles' *Antigone,* for example, the theme is the conflict between divine law and civil law; in *Death of a Salesman,* it is the conflict between Willy's reality and his dreams. Conflicts are plentiful in farces and comedies as well; the conflicts inherent in the "eternal triangle," for example, have provided comic material for dramatists for the past two millennia. Many of the more abstract philosophical conflicts—independence versus duty, individuality versus conformity, idealism versus pragmatism, integrity versus efficiency, pleasure versus propriety, progress versus tradition, to name a few—suggest inexhaustible thematic conflicts that appear in various guises in both ancient and contemporary plays.

The playwright introduces conflict early in a play, often by means of an "inciting incident" in which one character poses a conflict or confrontation either to another character or to himself. For example:

FIRST WITCH: All hail, Macbeth, hail to thee,
    Thane of Glamis!
SECOND WITCH: All hail, Macbeth, hail to
    thee, Thane of Cawdor!
THIRD WITCH: All hail, Macbeth, that shalt
    be King hereafter!
BANQUO: Good sir, why do you start, and
    seem to fear
    Things that do sound so fair?

In this, the inciting incident of Shakespeare's *Macbeth* (which follows two brief expository scenes), a witch confronts Macbeth with the prediction that he will be king, thereby posing an alternative that Macbeth has apparently already considered, judging from the startled response that elicits Banquo's comment.

Once established, conflict is intensified to crisis, usually by a series of incidents, investigations, revelations, and confrontations that the playwright creates. Sometimes even non-events serve to intensify a conflict, as in the modern classic *Waiting for Godot,* in which two characters simply wait, through two hour-long acts, for the arrival of a third who never comes. Indeed, with this play, Samuel Beckett virtually rewrote the book on playwriting technique by showing how time alone, when properly managed, can do the job of heightening and developing conflict in a dramatic situation.

The Climax Conflict cannot be intensified indefinitely. In a play, as in life, when conflict becomes insupportable, something has to give. Thus every play, be it comic, tragic, farcical, or melodramatic, culminates in some sort of dramatic explosion.

Aristotle described that dramatic explosion, in tragedy, as a *catharsis,* or purification. Aristotle's conception is susceptible to various interpretations, but it has been widely accepted and broadly influential for centuries. According to Aristotle's system, the catharsis is the crucial axis in the structure of tragedy, evolving out of the tragic hero's recognition (*anagnorisis*) of some fundamental truth and his consequent reversal (*peripeteia*) of some former ignorance, such as a horrific deed unknowingly performed (*pathos*). The catharsis releases the audience's pity and thereby permits the fullest experience of tragic pleasure, washing away the terror that has been mounting steadily during the play's tragic course. Such catharsis as accompanies Oedipus' gouging out his own eyes as he recognizes his true self illustrates the extreme theatrical explosion of which the classical Greek tragic form is capable.

For any dramatic form, the climax is the conflict of a play taken to its most extreme; it is the moment of maximum tension. At the climax, a continuation of the conflict becomes unbearable, impossible: some sort of change is mandated. Climaxes in modern plays do not as a rule involve death or disfiguration (although there are exceptions: Peter Shaffer's celebrated *Equus* reaches its climax with the blinding of six horses, and Edward Albee's *The Zoo Story* climaxes with one character impaling himself on a knife held by another). However, climaxes inevitably contain ele-

Ray Reinhardt, as Gloucester, waits to be blinded by Cornwall and his thugs in the horrifying third-act climax of Shakespeare's King Lear. *Reinhardt, a veteran professional, was a guest artist in this student production at the University of California at Irvine. (Photo: Philip Channing.)*

ments of recognition and reversal if not of catharsis, and usually the major conflicts of the play are resolved by one or more of these elements.

The Denouement   The climax is followed by and the play concluded by a denouement, or resolution, in which a final action or speech or even a single word or gesture indicates that the passions aroused by the play's action are now stilled and a new harmony or understanding has been reached.

The tenor of the denouement tends to change with the times. In the American theatre of the 1950s and 1960s, for example, the sentimental and message-laden denouement was the rule: in Robert Anderson's *Tea and Sympathy,* a teacher's wife prepares to prove to a sensitive boy that he is not homosexual; in Dore Schary's *Sunrise at Campobello,* a future American president makes his way on crippled legs to a convention platform. In the current theatre, in this existential age that looks with suspicion on tidy virtues and happy endings, more ironic and ambiguous denouements are to be expected. The current theatre also provides less in the way of purgation than do more classical modes; that is doubtless because the conflicts raised by the best of contemporary drama are not amenable to wholesale relief. But a denouement still must provide at least some lucidity concerning the problems raised by the play, some vision or metaphor of a deeper and more permanent understanding. Perhaps the final lines of *Waiting for Godot* best represent the denouement of the current age:

ESTRAGON: Well, shall we go?
VLADIMIR: Yes, let's go.
   They do not move.

Events that take place after the play ends are referred to as the *postplay.*

The Curtain Call   The last staged element of a theatrical presentation is the curtain call, in which the actors bow and the audience applauds. This convention, which has been customary in the theatre at least since the time of the Romans, plays an important but often overlooked role in the overall scope of theatrical presentation.

The curtain call is *not* simply a time for the actors to receive congratulations from the audience, although many actors today seem to think it is. Historically, it is a time in which the actors show their respect for the audience that patronizes them. And aesthetically, it is a time in which the audience allows itself to see the other side of the "paradox of acting." The curtain call liberates the audience from the

The exuberant curtain call for this American Conservatory Theatre production of
The Bourgeois Gentleman *presents the entire cast to the audience for a rousing*
final bow. (Photo: William Ganslen, ACT.)

world of the play, and when there is no curtain call audiences are palpably distressed and often disgruntled. For it fulfulls the last provision, so to speak, in the mutual agreement that characterizes the theatre itself—the agreement by which the audience agrees to view the actors as the characters the actors have agreed to impersonate. It is at the curtain call that actors and audience can acknowledge their mutual belonging in the human society, can look each other in the eye and say, in effect, "We all know what it is to experience these things we've just seen performed, we must all try to understand life a little better, we have enjoyed coming this far together, we are with you, we like you." In the best theatre, this communication is a powerful experience.

The Aftermath: Criticism What follows the curtain call? The audience disperses, of course; but the individual audience members do not die, and through them the production enjoys an extended afterlife both in talk and in print—in late-night postmortems at the theatre bar; in probing conversations and published reviews over the next few days; and sometimes in formal classroom discussions, television talk shows, letters to the editor in the local newspaper, and scholarly articles and books seen weeks, months, or years later. For the theatre is a place of public stimulation, both intellectual and emotional, and it should be expected that the stimulation provided by a provocative production would generate both animated discussions and illuminating commentaries.

Both of these we may call *dramatic criticism,* which is the audience's contribution to the theatre. Criticism is as ancient as Aristotle and as contemporary as the essays and lectures that are presented daily in newspapers, journals, books, and academies all over the world. But criticism is not solely an expert enterprise; criticism—which combines analysis and evaluation—is everybody's job. We shall look further at this key aspect of the theatre's art in the final chapter of the book.

PART II

THE PAST

SHAKESPEARE FESTIVAL

Why include in a study of the theatre an examination of its past?

Because today's theatre rests solidly on that past, which extends back at least five thousand years and is filled with grand experiments, great traditions, and superb achievements.

Because, moreover, the theatre's past still lives. It lives in the revival of great plays that continue to thrill audiences around the world; and it lives in the hearts, minds, and everyday experiences of all whose lives are engaged in the production of contemporary theatrical art.

The theatre is a conservative art. It hangs on to its past, perennially scavenging for material, for effects, for dramatic structures, for great conflicts, great characters, and great events.

Each new theatre form develops out of the discoveries of its predecessors, and often that development is consciously cultivated. A classic comedy by Plautus serves as the basis for a Shakespearean play seventeen hundred years later, which in turn becomes an American musical comedy four hundred years after that. A Roman tragedy of the first century becomes a Molière comedy in the seventeenth and then a French fantasy in the twentieth. Every year, hundreds of plays are directly inspired by hundreds of predecessors.

More indirectly, separate moments, patterns, and components of contemporary theatre develop—mostly unconsciously—from past models. The climax of Sophocles' tragedy *Oedipus Tyrannos,* in which the protagonist blinds himself, is echoed in the equally horrific climax of Peter Shaffer's contemporary play *Equus;* the stunning *parabasis* of Greek comedy, in which the chorus suspends the play's action to speak directly to the audience about political matters, becomes an important dramaturgical device in the "alienated" theatre of Bertolt Brecht. More and more, the conventions of the theatre's past are coming forth to freshen and vivify the present; and often those who most avidly look backward for direction are the most avant-garde theatre artists of our time.

Like a tree, the theatre draws much of its nourishment through its roots for all that is manifest above. In studying the past, then, we are not investigating dead things—antiques and oddities and moldering bones—but rather we are seeking to understand the vitality of the theatre in every age.

The theatre had its beginnings well before recorded history. For whole millennia in the ancient world of Egypt and Mesopotamia, Babylonia and Mycenae, however, we have no texts, no pictures, no records other than cryptic references to seasonal rituals carried out by priests in honor of worshipped gods. It is the more "immediate" twenty-five hundred years, the years from the sixth century B.C. to the nineteenth century of our present era, which provide us with the body of known drama and reported theatrical activity that we call the theatre's past. This epoch is detailed in the next five chapters; the theatre of our present century (since about 1875) will be dealt with in Part III.

It is not our purpose in these five chapters to give a comprehensive survey of the many periods of past theatrical achievement, much less to name the hundreds of authors and thousands of plays known to have contributed to that achievement. Nor shall we undertake to discuss the hundreds of controversies that scholars continue to wage over details of theatrical production in the periods under study.

Our concern here is simply to present a speculative reconstruction of five particularly splendid and interesting times and places from the theatre's past—classical Greece, York of the Middle Ages, England in the Renaissance, the Edo era of Japan, and France at the court of Louis XIV—and to make mention of certain other related developments that took place at about the same times. "Speculative" is, of course, a necessary qualification, for although some of the playtexts of each of these eras have come down to us reasonably intact, the details of performance were rarely recorded. Hence, any historical reconstruction must rest on fragmentary and often-contradictory evidence.

In the coming pages, you should strive primarily to get a *feeling* of what it meant to pro-

duce theatre and to go to the theatre in those times, rather than to discern precisely who did what and when and where and how the curtain fell. We don't quite know the reality, and we almost certainly never shall; but we *can* develop a general understanding of the theatrical effort and the theatrical spirit of those times and places, and we can certainly explore the *possibilities* of theatre as they have variously been attempted throughout the ages. These understandings—of the theatre's aims and its spirit and its possibilities—are the choicest fruits of theatrical research, for they bring us close to the sources of the theatre's enduring vitality.

3

The Greeks

The known history of the Western theatre begins in ancient Greece; that fact alone should compel our interest. Even more compelling, however, is the fact that the theatre of classical Greece still stands as a monumental artistic achievement—indeed, in many estimations, as an achievement that has never been surpassed.

THE GREEK THEATRE

When theatre historians speak of the "Greek theatre," they are speaking specifically of the theatre of just one locale, Athens, and of just one century, the fifth century B.C. For that span of one hundred years, in a city-state of no more than 150,000 persons, the Athenian population was treated to a theatrical life unparalleled in its social importance and aesthetic majesty. Among the contributors to this art form were four of the most brilliant playwrights of all time: Aeschylus, Sophocles, Euripides, and Aristophanes. The theatre they helped to create featured a magnificent and vigorous blend of myth, legend, philosophy, social commentary, poetry, dance, music, public participation, and visual splendor. The heroes of Greek drama have become archetypes in the modern mind, and their actions and examples occupy a major place in our collective cultural endowment. Surviving from the period are forty-three intact plays, plus many play fragments and titles of other works, one great piece of criticism (Aristotle's *Poetics,* written in the following century), the archeological remnants of several theatres (also of somewhat later date, but built on the foundations of fifth-century theatres), and numerous anecdotes and commentaries. Taken together, these treasures constitute a record that lets us envision and comprehend the basic experience of the Greek theatre, a theatre at once vastly different from our own and yet seminal to contemporary developments.

In order to best capture the spirit of the Greeks, we must first rid ourselves of a body of misperceptions that have cluttered our knowledge of the Greek theatre at least since the nineteenth century. Victorian revivals of Greek drama suggest a theatre in which white-robed actors strutted ceremonially through white marble buildings uttering sonorous and sententious speeches about morality. This false vision of Greek civilization and art was doubtless inspired in part by the pristine color of Greek ruins, whose original brilliant colors have completely washed away with centuries of weathering. But why several generations of neoclassicists and scholars contributed to the deception is somewhat of a mystery. The theatre of the ancient Greeks was in fact as far from that pallid, stiff Victorian model as could possibly be imagined. It was a spectacle of loud music, vivid colors, and vigorous dancing; it was regularly bawdy, frequently obscene, and often blasphemous, hilarious, scandalous, and carnal; it was always passionate and controversial. Although, in the surviving plays, acts of violence always occur offstage, there is reason to believe that this is less a result of rigid convention than a reflection of the sensibilities of later librarians, many of them medieval monks, who determined which plays would survive and which would not. In any event, both the comic and tragic Greek theatres were firmly rooted in the violence of life, and both persistently and intensely examined the social and ethical aspects of war, murder, lust, and betrayal.

Origins and Evolution

The Greek theatre had its origins in religion, but the Greek religion bore little similarity to the religions of the Western world today. It was a polytheistic religion, and its deities were much more inclined to be belligerent than benevolent. When they were not at war with mortals—which they often were—they were doing battle with one another. Unlike the modern worshipper who looks to a higher power for succor and salvation, the ancient Greek thought of his gods as meddlers and disrupters; and the "prayer" of the ancient world was basically an attempt at appeasement rather than a plea for aid. "May the eye inescapable of the mighty gods not look on me" is the great choral cry of Aeschylus' *Prometheus Bound.* It echoes the dread of the gods that underlay all ritual in Greek religion.

The theatre at Athens was dedicated to one god in particular: Dionysus, the god of fertility (hence also the god of wine, agriculture, and sexuality). It was at the annual festival of Dionysus that new dramas were first publicly performed. Apart from drama, the festival of Dionysus featured a week of public wine drinking and phallus worshipping that would today be considered a religious orgy. Something of the sort is portrayed in the last known Greek tragedy, Euripides' *The Bacchae,* and it is a terrifying event in which human bodies are torn asunder (a fantasy much in keeping with celebrations of Dionysus, who is himself torn asunder in Greek legend). The early ties between the theatre and this extraordinary celebration of fertility provide a crucial insight into the basic forces at work in the theatrical experience.

The advance of the Greeks over other known civilizations of that time has been attributed in part to the Greek conception that the gods had human form; that is, unlike the Egyptian or Babylonian gods, they were not giant birds or turtles (although they apparently could assume such forms at will). As a corollary to this concept, the Greeks, like most of the monotheists who came later, considered themselves to be created in the image of gods. This notion invited human impersonation of the gods, and it was not long before the impersonator came to be seen as a creature halfway between the divine and earthly realms. Anthropologists call one who enjoys that halfway status a *shaman*—a religious leader who is accredited with an understanding of the superhuman and who has the authority to reveal it to the masses.

The Birth of the Dithyramb

A Greek version of shamanism developed, around the ninth and eighth centuries B.C., with the *dithyrambos:* an ancient, drunken, dance-chant fertility ritual that celebrated the birth of the wine god, Dionysus, and the vaunted fruit of the vine. The *dithyrambos* was performed yearly at four tribal festivals (called *orgia,* from which comes our word *orgy*), including the three-day Anthesteria (the "Festival of the Wine Jugs," also known as the "Old Dionysia") as well as the shorter Agrionia and Rustic festivals. These Dionysian revels were held outside town, probably in and around broad, earthen threshing circles, where, at harvest time, sheaves were pounded to separate grains from the chaff. Such circles can still be found in rural Greece today. For the Anthesteria, a sixteen-foot *phallos* (penis) was erected in the center of the circle as a focal point for the orgiastic festivities.

Befitting its patron deity, all the Dionysian festivals involved drinking enormous quantities of wine; at the Anthesteria, each participating man, woman, and child began the festivities by tossing down a two-liter jug at a single sitting. Wine drinking continued throughout

Euripides' tragedy The Bacchae *is often seen as a link between ancient dithyramb and tragedy because it harks back in many ways to the origins of tragedy. It is the only surviving tragedy from the Greek classic period in which Dionysus appears as a character, and it ends with a ghastly sequence in which a young man (Pentheus) is torn to pieces by his mother (Agave), who acts under the spell of Dionysus. The tearing apart, or* sparagmos, *recalls the dismemberment of Dionysus in legend. Here, Agave holds the head of her murdered son in a contemporary production of the play by Théâtre National de l'Odéon in Paris, directed by Michael Cacoyannis. (Photo: Courtesy French Cultural Services.)*

the three days of this festival, which also included bull sacrifices and dismemberments, the consuming of hallucinogenic mushrooms, and the ecstatic dithyrambic dance-chants, led by a group of goatskin-covered, *phallos*-bearing priests. The *dithyrambos* concluded with a sacred marriage ritual, in which drunken women danced around the *phallos,* adorned with a bearded mask, after which the tribal Queen was "given" to "Dionysus." Although we don't know exactly how this gift was accomplished, historians believe that real sexual intercourse took place, accompanied by the cheers of the rhapsodic throng.

Other Dionysian festivals were equally, if not more, raucous. At the Agrionia festival, dissolution, inversion, madness, and ecstatic cannibalism were celebrated. The Rustic festival included a mass phallic procession. As one historian notes, "In the Dionysus cult, ecstasy plays a quite unique role. . . . Since the god himself is the Frenzied One, the madness is at the same time divine experience, fulfillment, and an end in itself; the madness is then admittedly almost inseparably fused with alcoholic intoxication."[1] Amazingly (but crucially), this tribal frenzy lies at the origin of drama. Though theatre has obviously become more refined and "civilized" since these ritual beginnings, the "Dionysian ecstasy" certainly remains at drama's very roots.

By the end of the seventh century (that is, by about 600 B.C.), written versions of the *dithyrambos,* or dithyramb, appeared, with authorship attributed to, among others, one Archilocus of Paros and one Arion of Corinth. These written dithyrambs were milder and more literary dance-chants than their predecessors; they were in formal verse (trochaic tetrameter) and in cultivated speech. Fragments of several such dithyrambs survive today. Already, a sort of formalism had begun to restrain and channel the anarchy of Dionysian rapture: Athens was now becoming part of a larger Mediterranean economy, and tribal rituals were consequently evolving into secular events for a multicultural audience. Ritual ecstasy had begun to give way, in public at least, to rational storytelling and quasi-dramatic representation. Nonetheless, the persistence of drunkenness as part of the dithyramb performance is made clear by a statement of Archilocus: "I know how to lead the fair song of Dionysus, the dithyramb, only when my wits are fused with wine." Long after the Greek theatre had developed the extraordinary sophistication that commands our admiration today, drunken, choral dithyrambs were being produced in the theatre at Athens, with animal sacrifices preceding them; at the same dramatic festivals, the noble tragedies of Aeschylus and Sophocles and the scintillating modern comedies of Aristophanes were on display.

What did these "orgies"—with their ritual drunken phallic dances, performed by goat-skinned cultists—have to do with the magnificently civilized classic Greek theatre? Aristotle tells us only that "tragedy . . . which was at first mere improvisation . . . originating with the dithyramb . . . advanced by slow degrees. Each new element that showed itself was in turn developed. Having passed through many changes, it found its natural form and there it stopped." Aristotle further explains that comedy originated in "phallic songs which are still in use in many of our cities." Aristotle's brevity on the subject of this evolution indicates he knew little about the steps or processes it involved, and indeed many scholars have questioned his entire premise. But the similarities between dithyramb and tragedy (as well as between phallic song, as we can imagine it, and comedy) seem clear enough and are both suggestive and illuminating.

Certainly, by the late sixth century B.C., Athenians had developed a need for "mod-

---

[1]Walter Burkert, *Greek Religion* (Oxford: Basil Blackwell, 1985), pp. 240, 110.

THE SATYR PLAY

The satyr play is one of the most puzzling dramatic forms ever to come down to us through history. Its lifetime in the theatre of ancient Greece was as long as that of tragedy, but its origins, aims, and ultimate significance all remain somewhat obscure. Unquestionably comic in tone and entertaining to the audiences of its time, it attracted little attention from manuscript preservers: only one fairly complete satyr play remains—the *Cyclops* of Euripides—together with a long fragment of *The Bloodhounds* by Sophocles. A sample of the dialogue from the latter makes clear the generally ribald, jocular tone of the satyr plays:

FIRST SEMICHORUS:
1. Hey, satyrs, what can this be?
2. So big and brown?

3. It's stinking terribly! You can smell it all around!

SECOND SEMICHORUS:
1. Here, just take it in your hand!
2. Do you see what we've got?
3. Oh, we've really had it. It's cattle turds, that's what!

And then, according to the dialogue, the ordure is thrown about the stage—at the god Apollo, at a nymph named Cyllene, and among the chorus of satyrs themselves. Numerous graphic illustrations of satyr plays, including those found on a magnificent painted vase now in the Naples Museum, amply convey the spirit of satyric drama.

---

ern" and "safe" secular entertainment, suitable for foreign visitors and potential trading partners and with a more distinct separation between performer and spectator than ecstatic ritual allows. Greek drama sprang from a disciplined regularization of these Attic tribal rites. In the nineteenth century, the German philosopher Friedrich Nietzsche postulated that tragedy was born in Greece as a synthesis—a coming together—of Dionysian ecstasy (chaos, passion, emotion) and Apollonian rationality (order, art, discipline: the attributes of Apollo), and no more elegant explanation of theatre has ever been put forth.

The Classic Period

By the time the historical record grows sharper, which is at the beginning of the fifth century

B.C., Greek drama consists of two dissimilar forms: the ever-popular comedy and the *tetralogy* (four-play sequence), which is now central to the theatrical and spiritual culture. It is this tetralogy which will attract the greatest attention in later times, for it includes the great works of Greek tragedy and best reveals the peculiar genius of the Greek literary mind.

Originally, the tetralogy consisted of a *trilogy*—three *tragedies,* which were serious, interrelated plays concerning a cast of gods, demigods, and great historical figures—followed by a *satyr play,* which was a grotesque travesty of the same preceding trilogy. This format remains uniquely Greek, for no subsequent playwright has ever sought to revive it. Indeed, by the end of the classic Greek period, the Greeks themselves seem to have

The chorus is a link between the dithyramb and the drama. Initially celebrants at the Dionysian rituals, the chorus was formalized into a group of fifty chanting dancers in the dithyrambs of the sixth century B.C. Sometime after Thespis emerged from the chorus as an actor, creating tragedy (and drama as we know it), Aeschylus reduced the chorus to twelve members. The chorus retained its dance-chant role throughout the history of Greek drama. Sometimes it mainly commented on the action, representing the "elders" of the village; sometimes, as in The Trojan Women, *it represented full participants in a play's struggle. Although Sophocles increased the chorus to fifteen dancers later in the fifth century, the chorus became less and less crucial to the play's action by the end of the era. Here the chorus dances around a circular "orchestra" in Euripides'* Iphigeneia at Aulis, *as directed by Garland Wright at the Guthrie Theatre, 1992. Set design, employing traditional elements, is by Douglas Stein. (Photo: Courtesy the Guthrie Theatre, Minneapolis.)*

abandoned all but the outer form of the tetralogy by presenting trilogies comprising unrelated tragedies, followed by a relatively independent satyr play. Unfortunately, no complete tetralogies have survived, and only Aeschylus' Oresteian trilogy has come down to us intact; still, we have enough of the separate elements, tragedies and satyr plays, to understand and admire the general format.

The satyr play, which in the classic period featured satyrs dressed in goatskins—followers of Dionysus—was perhaps the closest of all the components of the tetralogy to the dithyrambic form of previous centuries. It has been suggested that by the time of Aeschylus and Sophocles the satyr play was retained as a favor (or appeasement) to the sponsor, Dionysus—much as "The Star-Spangled Banner" is played today at sporting events in the United States or as "God Save the Queen" was played, until recently, prior to theatrical performances in Great Britain. Although Greek tragedy is less obviously related to Dionysian worship, links can be seen today in its name (the Greek word for "tragedy" is *tragōidia,* meaning "goat song") and its use of singing and dancing choral practices that had counterparts in the performance of the dithyramb.

The greatest difference between the dithyramb and the tragedy-satyr plays was, of course, the appearance in the latter of the actor. This development is attributed to Thespis, an Icarian of whom little is known save that he is said to have been the first to move out of the dithyrambic chorus and assume the role of "answerer," or *hypokrites* (the first word for "actor"). Thespis' bold move introduced into the old singing, dancing, chanting performance the crucial elements of impersonation and enactment. Thespis is also credited with the invention of the mask: this simple device—and the early masks were indeed simple, made plainly of undyed linen—enabled Thespis to portray not one but a number of "characters," in series, engaged in discussions and debates with the chorus. Now a whole story could unfold through the revelation of numerous points of view, in action and dialogue instead of in recitation. The theatre as we know it was born. In the year 534 B.C., the ancient chroniclers tell us, it was Thespis who walked off with the first prize in the first tragedy contest in the City Dionysia of Athens.

We have none of the plays of Thespis; in fact, we have little writing of any kind from the theatre of the sixth century B.C.—only scraps, most of anonymous origin. But we know that except for a few seemingly modest but significant changes, the sixth-century format of the Greek tragedy-satyr tetralogy remained intact. Aeschylus made a significant innovation in the fifth century when he increased the number of actors to two, allowing for dialogue between characters; Sophocles later added a third actor, allowing for "overheard" dialogue situations and more subtle and complex character interactions. By the time of Aeschylus, the dithyrambic chorus was reduced to twelve; Sophocles increased it to fifteen. The bawdiness, drunkenness, and scatological motifs that pervaded the early rituals probably increased in the satyr plays as they were removed from the tragedies. And of course the internal structure of the tragedies changed enormously during the fifth century as the grand mythic retellings of Aeschylus gave way to the tightly plotted character dramas of Sophocles and the savagely fascinating complexities of Euripides. Still, the tragedy-satyr tetralogy established in the mid-sixth century remained essentially unchanged in form: a limited number of masked characters, a singing and dancing chorus, and a triad of tragedies followed by a satyr piece. Apparently no later "reforms" in the classic period affected these essential elements, and yet the entire format disappeared with the end of the Greek era.

The form of *comedy* that prevailed in the Greek theatre of the fifth century seems to have developed somewhat later than the tragedy-satyr form and seems to reflect little if any religious origin; moreover, unlike the tragedy-satyr format, the comedy seems amazingly contemporary. Now called Old Comedy to distinguish it from developments of later centuries, it appears to us audacious, sexy, and unabashedly political. It is also astonishingly scatological, so much so that until recent times few of the surviving plays—all by Aristophanes—were considered fit material for translation or publication. The Greek comedy was presented at the City Dionysia from 486 B.C. onward, sometimes following the performance of a tetralogy, sometimes on separate days. It was presented at many other festivals as well, including the *Lenaea,* or feast of the wine vats, held in Athens in midwinter during the dormant trade season.

Two early phases of Greek theatre development. The orchestra, *a circular playing space, was the major feature of the physical Greek theatre. (Drawing: John von Szeliski.)*

The *Theatron*

The physical features of Athenian theatres in the classic age derived directly from the dithyrambic ceremonies of earlier times. The staging area was essentially a large cleared space on the ground, known as the *orchestra* (from the Greek word for dancing, itself from a Sanskrit word for raving, raging, and trembling), with the audience area (*theatron*) the hillside overlooking it. We have long assumed that the orchestra was circular, like the dithyramb's threshing circles, particularly since some major surviving theatres (notably the Theatre of Epidaurus) still show circular orchestras; however, persuasive current research suggests that at least some (and possibly most) early orchestras were in fact rectangular. The *phallos* of the dithyrambic rituals was replaced, for drama, with an altar, or *thymele,* which was probably at the periphery of the orchestra, where it would be visible to all spectators, but out of the way of the principal dramatic action. In most theatres, the orchestra was placed south of the hillside so that the audi-

ence could bask in the sun from dawn to dusk, but not have to contend with blinding low-angle rays at sunup or sunset. Wooden (and eventually stone) gradations were set into and onto the hillside, providing comfortable seating for the entire city, with special front-row seating for the city priests.

A wooden changing room, called a *skene,* was located on the other side of the orchestra, opposite the hillside, and actors (but not the chorus) could enter the orchestra through its door or perhaps doors. Since the word *skene* originally meant something like "hut" or "tent," we must imagine this structure was originally small and unimposing in appearance; however, it eventually was enlarged sufficiently to permit some scenes to take place on its roof. Many scholars today conjecture that a slightly raised forestage also was added to the front of the skene, together with a few steps leading down to the orchestra below, to enhance the acting area.

And that was it for the theatre "building" of the classic period. The elaborate stone and marble structures that survive at several Med-

THE EARLY SCENE BUILDING WAS MADE OF WOOD AND WAS BRIGHTLY PAINTED & DECORATED... PARTLY DUE TO A GREAT INTEREST IN PAINTING OF LANDSCAPE and PERSPECTIVE...

DOORWAYS AT THE REAR ALLOWED ENTRANCES and EXITS AT VARIOUS "HOUSES" OR LOCALES...

OPEN AREAS of the COLONNADE WERE EVENTUALLY FILLED IN IN VARIOUS WAYS TO SUGGEST CERTAIN "SCENIC BACKGROUNDS"

A conjectural reconstruction of the fifth-century skene. *No longer a "hut" but not yet a marble building (that was to come a century later), this structure served as a basic background area for all productions. Later versions of the* skene *were constructed with two levels. (Drawing: John von Szeliski.)*

iterranean sites today all date from later periods; and none of our grand reconstructions, such as the Hearst Theatre in Berkeley and the Greek Theatre in Los Angeles, bears significant resemblance to what was seen in Greece in the classic period. There was, of course, no representational scenery, no curtain, no fly gallery, no lighting apparatus. There were some stage "machines," but they were of a rudimentary sort, consisting of rolling platforms apparently used to display corpses and immobile tableaux and cranes to hoist visiting and departing "gods." We know that there were also pivoting prisms, called *periaktoi,* and that Sophocles introduced panels of abstractly painted scenery called *pinakes;* but the precise appearance and function of both of these features is unclear, and their importance to the overall staging is generally assumed to be incidental rather than fundamental.

The Spectacle

The true spectacle of Greek theatre consisted of what we today would call its costuming and its acting, dancing, and music. The Greek tragic actors—always male—were costumed in brilliantly colored full-length robes, called *chitons,* which were often supplemented by tunics (either the long *himation* or the shorter *chlamys*) used primarily for character differ-

THE CHITON was the basic dress, worn long by women, short by men...

Ties

extra fold sewn-in

A large patterned cloak: the HIMATION was draped over the shoulder

Representative costumes. Paid for by the choregus, *Greek costumes were lavish, ornate, and colorful. (Drawing: John von Szeliski.)*

entiation. Realism was never the controlling aspect of the Greek tragic costume. Masks, which were of carved wood during the classic era, were full faced, richly painted, and highly stylized, extending up to fanciful wiggings called *onkoi*. Both *onkoi* and the actors' footwear, called *kothurnoi*, eventually were exaggerated in scale to give the actor the appearance of considerable height. In later ages, the *onkos* and *kothurnus* together became symbols of the tragedian's art.

Comic and satyric costume differed substantially from the tragic dress, being at once more realistic (in comedy) and more obscene (in both). Simulated partial nudity was a nota-

ble feature of both comic and satyric costuming—and much of this simulation would be considered shocking to audiences even today. The *phallos* (representing both penis and testicles) was blatantly displayed in costumes for both dramatic forms, and a tail seems to have adorned the goatskin garb of the satyric actors. The masks for comedy performers, as one might expect, were designed to amuse, often representing absurdly deformed human faces, occasionally representing animals, birds, or insects, and sometimes caricaturing celebrities such as Socrates and Euripides.

The costumes and masks of the classic drama are portrayed in numerous surviving

THE GREEK TRAGIC MASK PROJECTED A STRONG FACIAL EXPRESSION... SUITED TO A LARGE THEATRICAL SPACE...

THE MASK WAS BUILT OF WOOD PLASTER, AND PAINTED LINEN...

A Greek mask from the fifth century B.C. *(Drawing: John von Szeliski.)*

illustrations, mainly from vase paintings made in the fourth century. Though these illustrations are not entirely accurate—the vase paintings are themselves stylizations—they give ample evidence of a vigorous aesthetic and a striking theatrical splendor in the staging elements of the fifth-century drama in Athens.

We are on much shakier ground when we try to reconstruct the music, dancing, and acting that were equally crucial to the spectacle, for no records can help us recover the process of an Athenian performance. The music is entirely lost; however, we know the names of its various modes—Dorian, Lydian, Ionian, Aeolian, and Phrygian—and many of the emotional qualities with which these modes were associated (heroic, lyric, elegiac, and so forth). The dances were equally varied. There were grave dances, exalted ones, ecstatic ones, and hugely comic ones—each separately designated and each obviously demanding great artistry in execution. Taken all together, the evidence suggests a musical and choreographic sophistication beyond that generally expected today for scripted, text-intensive drama.

The sensual impact of the acting in these spectacular productions, particularly in the tragedies, can only be imagined as a combination of the known elements: flowing robes, singing male voices emanating from mouth-holes in wooden masks, steady dancing movements, and the famed pure light of Greece ever present over all. The resulting theatrical style indeed must have been unlike any that has been seen since.

The Greek plays were presented at festivals, most of which lasted several days. The City Dionysia of Athens in the Golden Age, which succeeded the Anthesteria of more primitive times, was a week-long springtime festival, featuring dithyrambic rituals and dramatic competitions in honor of Dionysus. Three playwrights competed annually, each contributing a tragedy-satyr tetralogy. The three tetralogies to be performed each year were chosen in advance by civic authorities (primarily by the *archon,* or mayor), and each playwright whose work was selected was then assigned a wealthy producer (the *choregus*) who was required to provide funds for costumes, instruction (rehearsal), and any other necessaries of production.

Most business came to a halt during the Dionysia to allow virtually every citizen to attend the spectacle. On the first day (the *pro-agon,* or "before-action," this day was called), introductory ceremonies were held; at these ceremonies, each playwright introduced his cast and announced the theme of his work.

A Greek dancer. Dance was an essential element of religious worship as well as of theatrical presentation. (Drawing: John von Szeliski.)

A CITIZENS' THEATRE

There is one vital difference between the Greek conception of theatre . . . and ours. In the Greek situation, the audience was totally visible. . . . The players could see the audience, and, more important, the audience could see itself. It was conscious of its own presence. Thus we see operating in the theatre the same factors that governed the conduct of public worship or the workings of Athenian democracy. The Greek concept of worship was not that of an active priest preaching to a passive multitude, nor was democratic government interpreted as meaning the handing down of edicts from the governing body (albeit popularly elected) to the governed. In both activities the entire public was spiritedly involved. Nor did the Greek theatrical concept envisage a passive audience. In all three spheres—less distinct, in any case, than in our world—the public was an active partner, free to comment, assist, and intervene. The very form of the theatre was reminiscent of the places of public assembly and induced the same responses. We observe, in consequence, that many Greek plays are little more than staged debates, with the audience hearing each side in turn as the Athenian audience was accustomed to listen to rival orators on the Pnyx, across the valley from the theatre, where the assembly met.

Peter D. Arnott

The second day featured processions, sacrifices, and the presentation of ten dithyrambs; on the third day, five comedies were played. On the fourth, fifth, and sixth days the three selected playwrights presented their tetralogies; on the seventh day, judging was conducted (by an intricate tribal voting procedure) and prizes were granted to the most popular playwrights and actors.

The City Dionysia was a giant outdoor religious and civic celebration, a cultural affair in the fullest sense, at which a society gathered en masse to recall the deeds of its heroes and to engage in the various modes of storytelling—epic, ritual, mocking, and comic—that came to be known as drama. The stories were traditional, contemporary, mythic, domestic, profound, absurd; in short, they spanned virtually the whole range of cultural experience, and religious activities were directly or indirectly present everywhere in the proceedings. Certainly nothing in the theatre that has followed has even begun to approximate this massive open-air intellectual, cultural, and spiritual convocation that allowed a community to celebrate itself for several days each year in words, music, dance, dress, and action. Perhaps the only event in our time that bore a remote resemblance to the spirit of the Greek Dionysia was the famous rock concert at Woodstock, New York, in 1969.

THE GREEK PLAYS

There were probably thousands of Greek tragedies, comedies, and satyr plays written and performed in classical times. We know the names of hundreds of these plays, but only forty-three playscripts remain in complete form. If this number seems disappointing, we must be aware that we are incredibly fortunate that any still exist—considering that they were written two thousand years before the invention of movable type. The surviving plays comprise thirty-one tragedies, eleven comedies, and one satyr play; in addition, we have numerous fragments from other works, mostly culled from later citations. Though not all the remaining plays are indisputable masterpieces, they are all from authors who were the most celebrated of their times: Aeschylus, Sophocles, Euripides, and the comic author Aristophanes.

Ever since Aristotle wrote his *Poetics,* theatre critics and historians have labored to deduce common structural characteristics in the dramatic works of the Greek authors. Over the centuries they have come up with these labels for various recurring aspects of dramatic construction: the *prologue* for the opening speech, usually delivered by one or two actors; the *parodos* for the ode subsequently sung by the chorus as it enters the *orchestra;* the *agon* (action) or *episode* (inter-ode) and the *stasimon* (choral ode) for the elements that alternate between actors and chorus as the dramatic story develops; and the *exodos* for the departure ode that concludes the play. Critics

have also defined a *parabasis* in Greek comedy, in which, about halfway through the play, the chorus, representing the author, directly addresses the audience in a long speech not necessarily relevant to the immediate action.

The existence of such a complete and historically important nomenclature should not, however, lead us to suppose that Greek plays were written with any distinct formula in mind; nor should we conclude from the critics' analyses that any single controlling concept—such as fate, pride, or tragic flaw—necessarily provides the fundamental thematic line for every Greek play. The themes, styles, conclusions, and manners of the four known playwrights are vastly dissimilar, and each of these playwrights exhibits considerable structural and thematic versatility from one play to the next. In looking at the body of Greek drama, then, we must be wary of oversimplifications that tend to amalgamate highly individual works into a "Greek style."

The Three Greek Tragedians

Aeschylus, Sophocles, and Euripides were not only the great masters of Greek tragedy, but they also remain among the handful of great tragedians that have ever lived. Indeed, it might be said that at least half of the world's great tragedies were written by these three men within a brief two generations—twenty-five centuries ago.

Their lives overlapped; they knew each other, and they profoundly influenced each other. But they had very different ways of thinking and writing; and, apart from superficial resemblances, their tragic styles are remarkably unlike. In the two plays we look at in the balance of this chapter, we see two different approaches to the theatre: approaches that set many of the standards playwrights have aspired to—and been inspired by—for the centuries and millennia that have followed.

AN ARISTOPHANIC PARABASIS

In the parabasis, or author's address to the audience, in his comedy *The Acharnians,* Aristophanes delightfully explains what he believes is his own worth to the state:

CHORUS LEADER: And now, the customary Choral Interlude.
Places, men! It's time for the ANAPESTS.
Off with the cloaks—let's get this atrophied ritual on the road!
Gentlemen, our Playwright is a modest man. Never in his career
has he written his ego into the script, or prostituted his Parabasis
to declare his genius. But now that genius is under attack.
Before the people of Athens (so notorious for their snap decisions),
his enemies charge that he degrades the City and insults the Populace.
And thus our Poet requests this time to defend his Art
before the people of Athens (so illustrious for their reasoned revisions of their snap decisions).
    Our Poet gives his accusers the lie.
He protests that he is a Public Benefactor, instilling in the Body
Politic a healthy resistance to rhetoric. No longer, Gentlemen,
are you ceaselessly victimized by foreign oratory, willingly wallowing,
unthinking and blissful, in flattering unction—wearing a wide-eyed,
slack-jawed gawk as your National Mien.
   . . .
[T]his is all past, thanks to our Poet—our Public Benefactor.
Consider a second benefit, Gentlemen. Why do you think
that the Allies keep flocking to town to pay the tribute you exact?
Because they love you? Because they hate money? Not in the least.
Because last year, in *The Babylonians,* a Certain Comic Poet*

ripped the lid off the relations between Athens and the rest of the Federation,
exposing how we democratically democratize our Allies into Complete Equality—
with each other, like slaves. So now these Allies are wild to see
this Nonpareil among poets with the Courage to Tell the Truth in Athens.
And they come—and you get the money.
    This Courage, in fact, is famous
throughout the world, as witness a recent report from Persia:
It seems that the Great King was sounding out a delegation from Sparta,
and asked about the relative strength of their side and ours.
First, of course, he wanted to know which State had the larger
Navy; but *then* he turned to the question of the famous Poet
who criticized his own city without mercy. Which side had *him?*
"The men who have been guided by that adviser," he said,
"are necessarily far superior; their decisive victory in the War
is only a matter of time." And *there* is the reason for the Spartans'
recent suit for Peace . . .
your Fearless, Peerless Poet, ARISTOPHANES. I urge you, Friends,
don't give him up! Don't discard the Voice of Justice!
Hear now the pledge of the Poet as Teacher: his subtle stagecraft
will bear you along to perfect happiness, public and private.
His integrity remains absolute. He will not knuckle, truckle,
hoax, or coax his way into favor. He will not adulterate
the pure matter of his plays with soft soap, bunkum, or grease,
simply to win a prize. His aim is not your applause, or votes,
but your *Edification.* ONWARD AND UPWARD WITH HIS ART!

---

*Aristophanes, of course; unfortunately, the play does not survive.

PROMETHEUS BOUND

Aeschylus' *Prometheus Bound* was long thought to be the oldest of the surviving Greek tragedies. In fact that honor probably belongs to Aeschylus' *The Persians,* written in 472 B.C., but it is easy to see the reason for the mistake. Compared to the plays of Sophocles and even others by Aeschylus himself, *Prometheus* seems structurally primitive, with its series of two-character scenes and its epical narrative speeches. Moreover, *Prometheus* is a play that looks back to the beginning of time, as though the playwright himself were consciously dwelling on his own culture's recent emergence from barbarism and trying to peer into the shrouded past. Yet *Prometheus* is, in fact, a late play for this first of playwrights, probably written within a year of Aeschylus' death in 457–6. It may even be—as some recent scholars suggest—a post-Aeschylean play, written by a later, unknown poet. But however "late" this tragedy was actually created, it speaks to us with a deliberately ancient, or "old fashioned," voice.

The story line of the play is simple, as is characteristic of the early plays of Aeschylus. It is a play about gods. Two Olympians, Zeus and Prometheus, have been on the winning side of a war with the Titans, and Zeus, as the leader of the victorious Olympians, has become king of the gods. The two victors have had a falling out, however, after Prometheus gave humankind the gift of fire (and with it, knowledge). Zeus has exiled Prometheus to the outer reaches of the known world, and there has ordered him chained to a cliff. It is at this point that Aeschylus begins his drama,

Hephaestus and Might head off on a motorcycle in the contemporized 1978 Geneva production. Masks by Werner Strub. (Photo: Daniel Vittet.)

with Might, a demon in service of Zeus, and Hephaestus, Zeus' blacksmith, arguing about the propriety of Prometheus' punishment as they seek to execute it:

MIGHT: This is the world's limit that we have come to; this is the Scythian country, an untrodden desolation. Hephaestus, it is you that must heed the commands the Father laid upon you to nail this malefactor to the high craggy rocks in fetters unbreakable of adamantine chain. For it was your flower, the brightness of fire that devises all, that he stole and gave to mortal men; this is the sin for which he must pay the Gods the penalty—that he may learn to endure and like the sovereignty of Zeus and quit his man-loving disposition.

HEPHAESTUS: Might . . . , in you the command of Zeus has its perfect fulfillment: in you there is nothing to stand in its way. But, for myself, I have not the heart to bind violently a God who is my kin here on this wintry cliff. Yet there is constraint upon me to have the heart for just that, for it is a dangerous thing to treat the Father's words lightly.

(to PROMETHEUS) High-contriving Son of Themis of Straight Counsel: this is not of your will nor of mine. . . . Such is the reward you reap of your man-loving disposition. For you, a God, feared not the anger of the Gods, but gave honors to mortals beyond what was just. . . .

MIGHT: Come, why are you holding back? Why are you pitying in vain? Why is it that you do not hate a God whom the Gods hate most of all? . . .

HEPHAESTUS: You are always pitiless, always full of ruthlessness.

MIGHT: There is no good singing dirges over him. . . . Hurry now. Throw the chain around him that the Father may not look upon your tarrying.

HEPHAESTUS: There are the fetters, there: you can see them.

MIGHT: Put them on his hands: strong, now with the hammer: strike. Nail him to the rock. . . .

HEPHAESTUS: Look now, his arm is fixed immovably!

MIGHT: Nail the other safe, that he may learn, for all his cleverness, that he is duller witted than Zeus.

Prometheus is silent during this first scene of the play, but we find out all we need to know not only about the reason for his plight, but also about the tone of the argument that surrounds it. For Zeus is portrayed as a monster-god inimical not only to the virtue of Prometheus but also to humankind, for whom Prometheus has made this sacrifice. There is much already in this scene to remind us of two figures from the Judeo-Christian tradition: the exiled demigod Lucifer (which means "bringer of light"), who induced Adam and Eve to eat of the tree of knowledge, and the crucified Jesus Christ, who sacrificed his life on behalf of humanity and who, at least for a critical moment, believed himself abandoned by God the Father. But if the God of the Bible (or at any rate, the Yahweh of the Old Testament) is a jealous god, the Zeus of the Aeschylean *Prometheus* is a vicious, egotistical, and indecently lustful one—a god who insists on being called "the Father" like some modern-day Mafia warlord and whose goal is not so much to secure the allegiance of Prometheus as to effect his abject abasement ("that he may learn . . . that he is duller witted than Zeus"). This god hates not only mortals but also those gods who help mortals, and his only motivating principle seems to be vanity. This portrayal brilliantly sets up the introduction of Prometheus, Aeschylus' heroic protagonist.

MIGHT: (to PROMETHEUS) Now, play the insolent; now, plunder the Gods' privileges and give them to creatures of a day. What drop of your sufferings can mortals spare

Alone onstage, Prometheus speaks. (Photo: Daniel Vittet.)

you? The Gods named you wrongly when they called you Forethought; you yourself *need* Forethought to extricate yourself from this contrivance.

(PROMETHEUS *is left alone on the rock.*)

PROMETHEUS: Bright light, swift-winged winds, springs of the rivers, number-less laughter of the sea's waves, earth, mother of all, and the all-seeing

circle of the sun: I call upon you to see what I, a God, suffer

at the hands of Gods—

see with what kind of torture

worn down I shall wrestle ten thousand years of time. . . .

You see me a wretched God in chains,

the enemy of Zeus, hated of all the Gods that enter Zeus's palace hall, because of my excessive love for Man.

What of course distinguishes Prometheus in his opening speech in the play is that, unlike Might and Hephaestus, Prometheus is revealed as a poet! Here Aeschylus produces (and translator David Grene emphasizes) a dramaturgical weapon that has since been wielded to great effect by generations of playwrights: the emotional power of poetry. When Might sarcastically tells Prometheus to "play the insolent," he does not know what power he invokes, for he thereby gives Prometheus the opportunity to *perform* in a medium—the theatre—where performance is everything. In the course of *Prometheus Bound,* Prometheus will win by his words what he loses by his chains as he pleads his cause before an audience composed of the very group on whose behalf he is being made to suffer. Obviously, there is no place that Prometheus would rather be, and he loses no time in telling the audience how he is suffering for his love of them.

Now into this setting comes the first of a series of visitors. It is a winged chorus, the daughters of Oceanus, the sea king. This chorus will remain with Prometheus until the very end of the play, sympathizing with him and offering counsel, hearing his woes and serving as a sounding board for his plans. The chorus of the Greek theatre stood both metaphorically and physically between the principal characters and the audience, and for this reason it served a vital function. It allowed playwrights to bridge the narrative and the dramatic forms, permitting the insertion of internal monologues (thinking-out-loud speeches) as well as incendiary public addresses—both used extensively in this play—that would otherwise be difficult to incorporate in the drama.

PROMETHEUS: What is that? The rustle
  of birds' wings near? The air whispers
  with the gentle strokes of wings.
  Everything that comes toward me is occa-
    sion for fear.
CHORUS: Fear not: this is a company of friends
  That comes to your mountain with swift
  rivalry of wings. . . .
PROMETHEUS: Alas . . . ,
  look, see with what chains
  I am nailed on the craggy heights
  of this gully to keep a watch
  that none would envy me. . . .
CHORUS: I see, Prometheus: and a mist of fear
    and tears
  besets my eyes as I see your form
  wasting away. . . .
  Who of the Gods is so hard of heart
  that he finds joy in this?

Who is that that does not feel
  sorrow answering your pain—
  save only Zeus? For he malignantly,
  always cherishing a mind
  that bends not, has subdued the breed
  of Uranos. . . .
PROMETHEUS: . . . there shall come a day for
    me
  when he shall need me, me that now am
    tortured
  in bonds and fetters—he shall need me
    then,
  this president of the Blessed. . . .
  Then not with honeyed tongues
  of persuasion shall he enchant me;
  he shall not cow me with his threats
  to tell him what I know,
  until he free me from my cruel chains
  and pay me recompense for what I suffer.
CHORUS: You are stout of heart, unyielding
  to the bitterness of pain.
  You are free of tongue, too free. . . .
PROMETHEUS: I know that he is savage: and
    his justice
  a thing he keeps by his own standard: still
  that will of his shall melt to softness
      yet. . . .

Prometheus uses the chorus as a companion, receiving their sympathy and letting them in on his great secret: that many generations hence, "a man renowned for archery" (Hercules) will free him and force Zeus to take him back into the Olympian fold, a story that Aeschylus was to treat in his next two plays, which, unfortunately, do not survive. But Prometheus also rebuffs the chorus for their assessment of him as "too free of tongue." Freedom in all things defines Prometheus' character. While his ultimate strength may be said to come from his knowledge that eventually he will be restored to Zeus' favor, his greater dramatic force proceeds from his absolute refusal to compromise his inner freedom: this stubborn resolve, so distressing to the chorus, is the source of Prometheus' courage and his heroism. The contrast between Prometheus' will to freedom and the chains that pin him to the rock provides the basic dramatic tension of the play and also its central metaphor: rebellious humanity straining against the shackles of oppressive authority. It is a metaphor applicable throughout civilization wherever freedom of thought is considered to be threatened by intellectual or spiritual restraints. Prometheus is the archetypical rebel, a model for the teenager rebelling against parental control (Zeus, of course, is "the Father" in this play), as well as for the romantic spirit struggling to burst free of tradition or the artistic sensibility at war with the bureaucratism, egomania, and arbitrary rule-making of dictatorships the world over.

Apart from the chorus, Prometheus has three single visitors in his rocky exile, all of whom Aeschylus uses to point up the differences between his hero and the common run of humanity. The first, Oceanus, father to the chorus, is brought on primarily so that his advice can be rejected:

OCEANUS: . . . My poor friend, give up
    this angry mood of yours and look for means
    of getting yourself free of trouble. Maybe
    what I say seems to you both old and commonplace;
    but this is what you pay, Prometheus, for
    that tongue of yours which talked so high and haughty:
    you are not yet humble, still you do not yield
    to your misfortunes, and you wish, indeed,
    to add some more to them; now, if you follow
    me as a schoolmaster you will not kick
    against the pricks, seeing that he, the King,
    that rules alone, is harsh and sends accounts
    to no one's audit for the deeds he does.
    Now I will go and try if I can free you:
    do you be quiet, do not talk so much. . . .
    [I]t is a profitable thing, if one is wise, to seem foolish.

It is interesting to consider Oceanus' advice in "real world" terms, for obviously not one person in a thousand would finally refuse to take it, given the consequences. The facts of human intercourse—which certainly have not changed from Greek times to our own—are that human beings learn to adapt to power struggles by the very tactics Oceanus advises: compromise, tact, realistic appreciation of the strengths of one's adversaries, and prudent silence. The beauty of drama, however, is that it can examine the extreme case, the one in a thousand who chooses to test the universe by confronting its laws directly. Often the playwright has to go into the realm of fantasy or the divine to make a credible illustration of universal principles, but the important thing to realize in this play is that, despite the antiquity of the script or the divinity of the characters, Aeschylus is talking about human courage, human rebellion, and human compromise. The story is applicable in its entire import to the ordinary affairs of humankind.

Prometheus, of course, will have none of Oceanus' suggestions: he rejects them outright and sets himself to wait out his torture defiantly. He challenges the universe, and he is a hero. Even today we use the term *Promethean* to describe a character whose actions, by their extreme courage and recklessness, seem to redefine the human possibility. In drama, particularly in tragedy, some of the great actions are refusals: refusal to compromise, to modify one's demands, to sacrifice one's ideals. *Prometheus Bound* is essentially a play of refusals, with Prometheus receiving a series of offers that he indignantly rejects.

Prometheus' next visitor is Io, a mortal woman who, having unintentionally attracted the lust of Zeus, has been set upon by the jealous Hera and forced to wander eternally through the world pursued by the savage gadfly. Io's transcontinental punishment, so vividly contrasted to Prometheus' immobility, serves both to increase the audience's antipathy toward Zeus and to further ennoble the patiently suffering hero on the rock. It also gives Aeschylus an opportunity to indicate the epic scale of this drama and the international consequences that are focused on the activities here at the world's edge, as he has Prometheus "predict" the travels of Io country by country until he has provided his audience with a breathtaking account of Aegean geography.

And finally to the mountain prison comes Zeus' personal messenger, the "lackey of the gods," Hermes, whose mission is to demand from Prometheus the secret he has earlier hinted to the chorus.

HERMES: [Y]ou thief of fire:
　　the Father has commanded you to say
　　what marriage of his is this you brag about
　　that shall drive him from power. . . .

Prometheus' response is the climax of the play: a rhetorical barrage that mocks the strength of the chains that hold him and the gods who have imprisoned him:

　　. . . Do you think I will crouch before your
　　　　Gods,
　　—so new—and tremble? I am far from
　　　　that. . . .
　　There is not
　　a torture or an engine wherewithal
　　Zeus can induce me to declare these things,
　　'till he has loosed me from these cruel
　　　　shackles.
　　So let him hurl his smoky lightning flame,
　　and throw in turmoil all things in the world
　　with white-winged snowflakes and deep
　　　　bellowing
　　thunder beneath the earth: me he shall not
　　bend by all this to tell him who is fated
　　to drive him from his tyranny.

HERMES: Think, here and now, if this seems
　　　　to your interest.
PROMETHEUS: I have already thought—and
　　　　laid my plans.

Io arrives. (Photo: Daniel Vittet.)

HERMES: Bring your proud heart to know a true discretion—

O foolish spirit—in the face of ruin.

PROMETHEUS: You vex me by these senseless adjurations,

senseless as if you were to advise the waves.

Let it not cross your mind that I will turn

womanish-minded from my fixed decision

or that I shall entreat the one I hate

so greatly, with a woman's upturned hands,

to loose me from my chains: I am far from that.

HERMES: I have said too much already—so I think—

and said it to no purpose: you are not softened:

your purpose is not dented by my prayers.

You are a colt new broken, with the bit

clenched in its teeth, fighting against the reins,

and bolting. . . .

Think what a storm, a triple wave of ruin

will rise against you, if you will not hear me,

and no escape for you. First this rough crag

with thunder and the lightning bolt the Father

shall cleave asunder, and shall hide your body

wrapped in a rocky clasp within its depth; . . .

Then Zeus's winged hound, the eagle red,

shall tear great shreds of flesh from you, a feaster

coming unbidden, every day: your liver

bloodied to blackness will be his repast. . . .

This is no feigned boast

but spoken with too much truth. The mouth of Zeus

does not know how to lie, but every word

brings to fulfilment. Look, you, and reflect

and never think that obstinacy is better

than prudent counsel.

CHORUS: Hermes seems to us

to speak not altogether out of season.

He bids you leave your obstinacy and seek

a wise good counsel. Hearken to him. Shame

it were for one so wise to fall in error.

PROMETHEUS: Before he told it me I knew this message:

but there is no disgrace in suffering

at an enemy's hand, when you hate mutually.

So let the curling tendril of the fire

from the lightning bolt be sent against me: let

the air be stirred with thunderclaps, the winds

in savage blasts convulsing all the world.

Let earth to her foundations shake, yes to her root,

before the quivering storm: let it confuse

the paths of heavenly stars and the sea's waves

in a wild surging torrent: this my body

let Him raise up on high and dash it down

into black Tartarus with rigorous

compulsive eddies: death he cannot give me.

Aeschylus here concludes the play with the same dramatic ingredient with which he introduced his hero: poetic magnificence. The heroics of Prometheus are literary in nature; and the theatre, a noble home for the spoken word, now resounds with his eloquence. Nothing Hermes can threaten, and nothing the chorus can plead, can match the fire of Prometheus' language—the fire that was in fact *Aeschylus'* gift to humanity.

In the end, the chorus is won over by Prometheus, not he by them. As he refuses to turn "womanish-minded" from his rebellion, so they finally become disgusted with the blandishments of Hermes.

HERMES: (*to* CHORUS) [Y]ou, who are so sympathetic with his troubles,

away with you from here, quickly away!

lest you should find your wits stunned by the thunder

and its hard defending roar.

CHORUS: Say something else
     different from this . . . this word of yours
     for all its instancy is not for us.
     How dare you bid us practice baseness? We
     will bear along with him what we must
         bear.
     I have learned to hate all traitors: there is
         no
     disease I spit on more than treachery.

This, the last line spoken by the chorus, expresses the final *public* judgment of the play—that traitors must be hated, that treachery must not be borne. In using the chorus to pronounce this final judgment, Aeschylus draws the audience further into the world of his play: it is the *audience*, finally, who will remain with Prometheus at the play's conclusion and who will have made the final moral decision concerning Prometheus' plight. It is to both chorus and audience that Hermes speaks at the end of the play:

HERMES: Remember then my warning before
         the act:
     when you are trapped by ruin don't blame
         fortune:
     don't say that Zeus has brought you to
         calamity
     that you could not foresee: do not do this:
     but blame yourselves: now you know what
         you're doing. . . .

Hermes brings the chorus—and with them the audience—into the full flush of human responsibility. It is not Zeus or fate that runs our lives; it is we ourselves, with our knowledge, our shared sympathy with the heroic, the persecuted, the noble in spirit. Prometheus who brought knowledge to mortals now brings them—to us, actually—the awareness of our responsibility for that knowledge. We cannot turn back and pretend ignorance: we are the masters of our fate, and we must bear the consequences of our actions. Aeschylus transforms the audience members into heroes along with Prometheus, making us reckon

Prometheus on the rock, as staged at the Théâtre de l'Est Parisien in 1982. Although the technology is modern, the setting uses real earth and stone to reflect ancient times. (Photo: Marc Enguerand.)

with both his suffering and his exaltation. Therefore, as Prometheus concludes the play with his last magnificent speech, we shudder with him:

PROMETHEUS: Now it is words no longer:
         now in very truth
     the earth is staggered: in its depths the
         thunder
     bellows resoundingly, the fiery tendrils
     of the lightning flash light up, and whirling
         clouds
     carry the dust along: all the winds' blasts
     dance in a fury one against the other
     in violent confusion: earth and sea
     are one, confused together: such is the
         storm
     that comes against me manifestly from
         Zeus

that the author is struggling to transcend the
literary format. But it is with words, of course,
that he paints the cataclysm that is building as
this play ends, words which when they were
first sung, danced, and passionately enacted
must have provided a supremely thrilling moment in that classical theatre on the hillside at
Athens.

Prometheus is a direct play, linear in structure, that probes deeply into a single theme—
freedom of thought—and makes use of poetry, staging, and performance to create the
Greek tragic hero. The rhetorical heroics of
Prometheus are not merely devices to entertain the audience or to display Aeschylus' verbal skills; they are employed to illustrate the
transcendent human spirit. The dramaturgy
therefore serves the theme of the play; it is the
vehicle that delivers the author's points. *Prometheus* is a play that enjoyed great popularity
in the romantic era—when Shelley wrote a
poetic sequel titled *Prometheus Unbound*—
and not surprisingly, it experienced a new
wave of popularity in the socially rebellious
1960s. Indeed, as a clear model of defiance in
the face of force, it has few equals in the
known literatures of the world.

to work its terrors. O Holy mother mine,
O Sky that circling brings the light to all,
you see me, how I suffer, how unjustly.

No one can tell us precisely how this final
scene was to be played; Greek manuscripts,
we must sadly note, include no stage directions. It almost seems that Aeschylus himself
is rebelling against the restraints of dramaturgy here; Prometheus' declaration that it is
"words no longer: now in very truth" suggest

OEDIPUS TYRANNOS

Oedipus Tyrannos (also known by the Latin
title *Oedipus Rex* and the English title *Oedipus
the King*) was written in about 425 B.C., a
long generation after the first presentation of
Aeschylus' *Prometheus Bound*. The author was
Sophocles, who succeeded Aeschylus as Athens' leading writer of tragedies. The contrast

between the plays, as well as the contrast between the authors of the plays, well illustrates
a significant development in the nature of
Greek tragedy and in theatre.

Oedipus Tyrannos tells the story of an ancient (and almost certainly legendary) *tyrannos* (absolute ruler) of Thebes who, seeking

the murderer of his predecessor, discovers that he is the murderer and, worse, that his predecessor was in fact his own father and the widow whom he has married is his mother. Utterly appalled at these findings, he goes into his palace and finds that his mother/wife has made the same discovery and has killed herself. He thereupon gouges out his eyes so that he may seek no more. This gory, shocking tale was well known to the audiences of Sophocles' time, but Sophocles' skill in recounting it ensured it a permanent place in Western literature. Even today, his play retains the suspense, majesty, and irony that led Aristotle and two millennia of critics after him to adjudge it the greatest tragedy ever written.

Both *Oedipus* and *Prometheus* are plays that treat the audience to a series of revelations—revelations about the past, which are known dramaturgically as *exposition*, as well as revelations about the future, often called *prophecy*. In one way or another, these sorts of revelations are common to all drama, since they establish the events of the play in a framework of time. What distinguishes the revelations in *Oedipus* from those of the earlier plays, however, is a seemingly simple thing that in fact marks a crucial step in the development of drama. Whereas in *Prometheus* the revelations are made *by* the principal character, in *Oedipus* they are made *to* the principal character, and thus the events of the play are placed beyond the awareness and control of that character. Unlike Prometheus, Oedipus does not know of his own tragic plight as the play's action begins; hence he is powerless in the context of events he himself has unwittingly set in motion. He thus shares one vital characteristic with all of humankind: ignorance. He is one of us; and because we know of his ignorance in the face of tragic circumstances, we sympathize.

What Sophocles develops in *Oedipus* is a *human* tragedy; indeed, this concentration on the human individual is a hallmark of his plays. Whereas Aeschylus dealt with abstract themes that he illustrated and embodied by means of articulate spokesmen, Sophocles created finite dilemmas and characters who must struggle to deal with them. Moreover, Sophocles created *personal* drama. For whereas Prometheus' battle must be waged against a force outside himself (Zeus), Oedipus' struggle is self-motivated: he seeks understanding. This dramaturgical development helped to solve one of the great logical problems in creating tragedy—which is, quite simply, how to keep the protagonist on stage. Given insuperable circumstances, why would not the reasonable protagonist walk away? Aeschylus' solution in *Prometheus* was to chain the protagonist to the stage; Sophocles created circumstances that make Oedipus *want*—despite horrifying revelations—to remain on stage to the play's bitter end, where he will at last discover and confront his allotted fate. This dramaturgical creation, more than any other, brought to the fore the human and sympathetic tragic hero, who was made accessible to audiences for all time.

The manner of Sophocles' evocation of the Oedipus story is vastly illuminating. This is a play of questions. Whereas *Prometheus* begins with Hephaestus' declarations, *Oedipus* begins with an investigation: why is a plague ravaging Thebes? As the play opens, Oedipus addresses a gathering of citizens and their priest:

OEDIPUS: What is it, children, sons of the ancient house of Cadmus? Why do you sit as suppliants crowned with laurel branches? What is the meaning of the incense which fills the city? The pleas to end pain? The cries of sorrow?

Oedipus' investigation is quickly developed as Creon, Oedipus' brother-in-law, returns from the Oracle at Delphi with the revelation that it is the yet unsolved and unavenged murder of Laius, the previous *tyrannos*, that has occasioned this plague. Oedipus, always the conscientious ruler, sees his duty and invokes his curse:

The chorus and Teiresias in Timberlake Wertenbaker's translation of Oedipus, *directed by Adrian Noble for the Royal Shakespeare Theatre in England. (Photo: Mark Douet.)*

OEDIPUS: I will serve the god and the dead. On the assassin or assassins, I call down the most vile damnation—for this vicious act, may the brand of shame be theirs to wear forever. And if I knowingly harbor their guilt within my own walls, I shall not exempt myself from the curse that I have called upon them. . . . I will avenge him [Laius] as I would avenge my own father.

Thus damning himself, although he does not know it, Oedipus embarks on his second and more difficult investigation: who killed Laius?

In pursuing this second investigation, Oedipus consults with five people; each gives him (and the audience) a piece of the answer, but until the fifth person speaks, the information is always conveyed in such a way that Oedipus fails to apprehend the whole. He is like a man picking up pieces of a jigsaw puzzle and trying to fit them together without any notion of what the final picture will disclose. For the observer, therefore, the process is as suspenseful as it is pathetic.

The first to give information is Creon. The second, at Creon's suggestion, is the ancient, all-knowing blind seer Teiresias, who reveals information that seems so strange, so incomprehensible, to Oedipus that it only bewilders and enrages him and goads him on in his searching:

OEDIPUS: . . . My lord Teiresias, we turn to you as our only hope. . . . We must find Laius' murderers and deal with them . . . only then will we find release from our suffering.

TEIRESIAS: . . . I should not have come. . . .

OEDIPUS: . . . For God's sake, if you know, don't turn away from us! We are pleading. We are begging you.

TEIRESIAS: Because you are blind! No! I shall not reveal my secrets. I shall not reveal yours.

OEDIPUS: What? You know, and yet you refuse to speak? . . .

TEIRESIAS: . . . Stop asking me to tell; I will tell you nothing.

OEDIPUS: You will not tell? You monster! You could stir the stones of earth to a burning rage! You will never tell? What will it take?

TEIRESIAS: Know yourself, Oedipus. You denounce me, but you do not yet know yourself. . . . I shall say no more. Rage, if you wish.

OEDIPUS: I *am* enraged. And now I will tell you what *I* think. I think this was *your* doing. *You* plotted the crime, *you* saw it carried out. It was *your* doing. All but the actual killing. And had you not been blind, you would have done *that* too!

TEIRESIAS: Do you believe what you have said? Then accept your own decree! From this day on, deny yourself the right to speak to anyone. You, Oedipus, are the desecrator, the polluter of this land. . . . I say that you, Oedipus Tyrannos, are the murderer you seek. . . .

OEDIPUS: You—you cripple! Your ears are deaf, your eyes are blind, your mind—your *mind* is crippled! . . . You live in night, Teiresias, in night that never turns to day. And so you cannot hurt me—or any man who sees the light. . . .

TEIRESIAS: You have eyes, Oedipus, and do not see your own destruction. You have eyes and do not see what lives with you. Do you not know whose son you are?

What is particularly impressive about the exchange between Oedipus and Teiresias is the excessive vigor with which Oedipus errs! That misplaced rage he expresses so vividly becomes especially ironic in light of what happens later—and what the audience knows will happen—and the irony of this and other of Oedipus' proclamations is something for which the play and its author are well known. Indeed, *dramatic irony* is the term given to precisely this sort of theatrical contrivance that allows the audience to see the characters' situation better than the characters do themselves. *Oedipus Tyrannos* is a virtual textbook of dramatic irony. All the accusations Oedipus hurls against Teiresias are to be turned back against himself by the play's end; the audience, knowing this, follows Oedipus' utterances with a dread fascination. Dramatic irony is one of the surest techniques for encouraging the audience to participate emotionally and sympathetically in the action of a play. Sophocles was a master of this technique; in fact, he is often considered to have been its inventor.

Having rejected the report of Teiresias,

who in fact knows all, Oedipus struggles doggedly in the ensuing episodes to narrow his investigation through a series of confrontations in which he challenges, taunts, berates, and interrogates other characters until he finally amasses the information that lays bare his own disgrace. But now—and this is the cleverness of Sophocles—all his information comes indirectly and by inference, from the views expressed by people whose ignorance equals his own. Thus Jocasta, his wife, tries to allay his suspicions and only succeeds in giving him fresh ones:

JOCASTA: In the name of Heaven, my Lord, tell me the reason for your bitterness.

OEDIPUS: I will—because you mean more to me than anyone. The reason is Creon and his plot against my throne.

JOCASTA: But can you *prove* a plot?

OEDIPUS: He says that I—Oedipus—bear the guilt of Laius' death.

JOCASTA: How does he justify this charge?

OEDIPUS: He does not stain his own lips by saying it. No. He uses that false prophet to speak for him.

JOCASTA: Then you can exonerate yourself because no mortal has the power of divination. And I can prove it. An oracle came to Laius once . . . that he would die at the hands of his own child, his child and mine. Yet the story which *we* heard was that robbers murdered Laius in a place where three roads meet. . . .

OEDIPUS: Jocasta—my heart is troubled at your words. . . . Where is this place where three roads meet?

JOCASTA: In the land called Phocis where the roads from Delphi and from Daulia converge.

OEDIPUS: How long a time has passed since then?

JOCASTA: We heard it shortly before you came. . . . What is it, Oedipus? What frightens you?

OEDIPUS: Do not ask me. . . . Just tell me—what was Laius like? . . .

JOCASTA: He was tall and his hair was lightly cast with silver tones, the contour of his body much like yours.

OEDIPUS: O God! Am I cursed and cannot see it?

Here, remembering an incident in which he killed a rude stranger and his entourage at a crossroads, Oedipus begins to suspect that Teiresias has spoken truth because of the very information Jocasta gives to prove Teiresias lied. To find out more, he calls for the shepherd who witnessed the incident.

The same pattern is followed in the succeeding episode, in which a messenger from Corinth arrives to announce the natural death of Oedipus' presumed father, Polybus. This news seems at first to disprove the prophecy that Oedipus would kill his father; however, the messenger "dis-disproves" the prophecy with subsequent information:

OEDIPUS: There was an oracle—a dreadful oracle sent by the gods . . . that I would take my mother for my bride and murder my father with my own hands. That is the reason I left Corinth long ago. . . .

MESSENGER: Is this the fear that drove you away from Corinth? . . . Then you must realize that this fear is groundless.

OEDIPUS: How can that be—if I am their son?

MESSENGER: Because Polybus was no relative of yours.

And the messenger explains that the infant Oedipus had been left to die on the mountainside, his ankles pierced with rivets, when a shepherd found him and gave him to the messenger, who in turn gave him to the *tyrannos* Polybus to raise as a son. Here Sophocles shows well the great possibilities of the three-character scene (it was Sophocles, we remember, who introduced the third actor for just these occasions), for now Jocasta, who remembers the piercing of her infant son's ankles, listens with growing horror to the exchange between Oedipus and the Corin-

thian—and the audience sees that she now grasps the picture better than either of the men.

MESSENGER: . . . [I]t was the swelling in your ankles that caused your name: Oedipus—"Clubfoot."[2]

OEDIPUS: . . . Who did this to me? . . .

MESSENGER: You will have to ask the man who handed you to me . . . he was of the house of Laius . . . a shepherd. . . .

OEDIPUS: (*addressing the* CHORUS) Do any of you know this shepherd? Have you seen him in the fields? Here in Thebes? Tell me now! . . .

CHORUS: I think it is the shepherd you have asked to see before. But the queen will know.

OEDIPUS: Jocasta, is that the man he means? Is it the shepherd we have sent for? Is *he* the one?

JOCASTA: Why? What difference does it make? Don't think about it. . . . It makes no difference.

OEDIPUS: No difference? . . .

JOCASTA: In the name of God, if you care at all for your own life, you must not go on with this. . . .

OEDIPUS: Do not worry, Jocasta. Even if I am a slave—a third-generation slave, it is no stain on your nobility.

JOCASTA: Oedipus! I beg you—don't do this!

OEDIPUS: I can't grant you that. I cannot leave the truth unknown. . . .

JOCASTA: God help you! May you never know what you are!

OEDIPUS: Go, someone, and bring the shepherd to me. Leave the queen to exult in her noble birth.

What we have here is a plot line intricately assembled out of Oedipus' erroneous as-

---

[2]A translator's liberty. Literally, the name means "swollen foot."

Oedipus (Douglas Campbell) addresses the chorus in a celebrated production at the Stratford (Ontario) Shakespeare Festival, directed by the late Tyrone Guthrie. The masks, by Tanya Moisewitsch, are contemporary versions of myth-making proportions. (Courtesy of the Stratford Festival, Canada. Photo: Donald McKague.)

sumptions, Jocasta's evasive pleadings, and the messenger's naive partiality. Almost imperceptibly, the investigation begun by Oedipus has shifted to its third and deepest level: from "Who killed Laius?" to "Who am I?" For now the combined prophecies, memories, revelations, and long-suppressed fears are beginning to circle closer and closer around one horrible truth. In the narrowing spiral of plot construction—a foreshortening in which the action gets more and more intense as the climax nears—Sophocles makes one character serve the work of two: the shepherd who witnessed the assassination at the crossroads is also the shepherd who had been entrusted with leaving the infant, ankle-pierced son of Laius, on the mountainside to die. And when the shepherd enters, the play's central fact comes to light in perhaps the most gripping scene of ancient drama:

MESSENGER: . . . Do you remember a child you gave me to bring up as my own?
SHEPHERD: What are you saying? Why are you asking me this?
MESSENGER: This, my friend, this—is that child.

SHEPHERD: Damn you! Will you keep your mouth shut!

OEDIPUS: Save your reproaches, old man. . . .

SHEPHERD: . . . He's crazy.

OEDIPUS: If you don't answer of your own accord, we'll make you talk.

SHEPHERD: No! My Lord, please! Don't hurt an old man.

OEDIPUS: (*to the* CHORUS) One of you—twist his hands behind his back! . . . Did you or did you not give him that child?

SHEPHERD: I did. I gave it to him—and I wish that I had died that day.

OEDIPUS: You tell the truth, or you'll have your wish now.

SHEPHERD: If I tell, it will be worse.

OEDIPUS: Still he puts it off!

SHEPHERD: I said that I gave him the child! . . .

OEDIPUS: Whose? . . . Whose house?

SHEPHERD: O God, master! Don't ask me any more.

OEDIPUS: This is the last time that I ask you.

SHEPHERD: It was a child—of the house of Laius.

OEDIPUS: A slave! Or of his own line?

SHEPHERD: Ah, master, do I *have* to speak?

OEDIPUS: You have to. And I *have* to hear.

SHEPHERD: They said—it was his child. But the queen could tell you best.

OEDIPUS: Why? Did *she* give you the child?

SHEPHERD: Yes, my Lord.

OEDIPUS: Why?

SHEPHERD: To—kill!

OEDIPUS: Her own child!

SHEPHERD: Yes. . . . My Lord, if you are the man he says you are—O God—you were born to suffering!

OEDIPUS: O God! O no! I see it now! All clear! O Light! I will never look on you again! Sin! Sin in my birth! Sin in my marriage! Sin in blood!

And Oedipus goes into the palace, next to emerge with his eyes gouged from his head by his own hand, a stage effect enhanced by the audience's foreknowledge—ensured by a pal-ace messenger's report—of what has taken place within. As Oedipus retreats from the scene at the end of the play, victim of his own curse and denied the comfort of his own children, the chorus intones the final words of the tragedy:

There goes Oedipus . . .
now he is drowning in waves of dread and
  despair.
Look at Oedipus—
proof that none of us mortals
can truly be thought of as happy
until he is granted deliverance from life,
until he is dead
and must suffer no more.

What was Sophocles' purpose in writing this play? Why, despite its gruesome and bitter conclusion, does it continue to offer some sort of "entertainment" for generations far removed from oracles, seers, mysterious plagues, and ancient tribal superstitions? There are several answers, not mutually exclusive, each illustrating a different attribute of tragedy as well as of *Oedipus.*

The view of Aristotle is that tragedy offers an audience the gift of *catharsis,* a term whose literary meaning, as far as we can tell, Aristotle coined, and one which he used *Oedipus* to exemplify. In the Aristotelian construct, tragedy concerns a great hero who has a flaw, or *hamartia* (the word has also been translated as "error" and "frailty"). The flaw brings him down so that he experiences a reversal of fortunes (*peripeteia*) and a recognition of higher truth (*anagnorisis*). This process stimulates in the audience feelings of terror and great pity for the hero, feelings that mount during the development of the action until they undergo a complete purgation, or *catharsis,* at the climax of the play. In Aristotle's view, Oedipus' tearing out of his eyes—a rending asunder that is akin to the dismemberment of Dionysus in primitive legend—exorcises the audience's anxieties and cleanses their emotions, essentially leaving them with the courage and serenity to face their own mortality. To Aristotle, and to many critics who have followed his formulation, this is the goal of tragedy: to ritualize suffering and, by ritualizing it, to give us perspective on our fears of what lies ahead. Tragedy, in this view, is a sort of sacrifice, in which the hero takes away our own dread by an act of self-immolation. A somewhat similar ritual effect can be seen in the modern-day Spanish bullfight, in which a noble animal with a "tragic flaw" (pride, lack of intelligence), after a series of violent attacks on his tormentors, is finally brought down in the "moment of truth" and then dismem-

Oedipus returns to stage with bloodied eye sockets: a horrific use of make-up replacing more stately masks of ancient tradition. American Conservatory Theatre production, with the late Paul Shenar in title role, flanked by Ellis Rabb (Creon) and Ken Ruta (Teiresias). (Photo: William Ganslen, ACT.)

THE OEDIPUS COMPLEX

Oedipus' destiny moves us only because it might have been ours—because the oracle laid the same curse upon us before our birth as upon him. It is the fate of all of us [males], perhaps, to direct our first sexual impulse towards our mother and our first hatred and our first murderous wish against our father. Our dreams convince us that this is so. Oedipus . . . merely shows us the fulfillment of our own childhood wishes. But, more fortunate than he, we have meanwhile succeeded, in so far as we have not become psychoneurotics, in detaching our sexual impulses from our mothers and in forgetting our jealousy of our fathers. Here is one in whom these primeval wishes of our childhood have been fulfilled, and we shrink back from him with the whole force of the repression by which these wishes have since that time been held down within us. While the poet, as he unravels the past, brings to light the guilt of Oedipus, he is at the same time compelling us to recognize our own inner minds, in which those same impulses, though suppressed, are still to be found.

Sigmund Freud

bered to the great ovation of the emboldened crowd. The aim of catharsis is well established in primitive rituals of exorcism; and the concept has been used in some contemporary psychotherapies, most notably in "catharsis therapy," in which patients are encouraged to act out primal urges and fantasies and to purge themselves with "primal screams" at the climax of their treatment.

The view of Sigmund Freud, the Viennese psychiatrist who formulated the theory of the "Oedipus complex," is that dramatic tragedy touches upon universal aspects of the human psyche which are repressed in adult life and therefore obstructive to self-realization until they can be liberated from the unconscious. High art affords one means of effecting this liberation. Freud contends that the Oedipus myth springs from the universal desire of the male child to unite sexually with his mother and from his corollary desire, necessary for the fulfillment of the first, to murder his father. According to Freud, these desires are most intense between the ages of three and five years; as the child matures and comes to understand that they cannot be realized and are, moreover, horrifying to contemplate, they are repressed and "go underground" into the unconscious, where they fester and cause anxiety, displaced rage, and neurosis. A performance of *Oedipus* has the effect of freeing us from the control of these unconscious desires, by illuminating and "punishing" them in the central character. To Freud, it is the (male) audience's unconscious recognition of the similarity between Oedipus' plight and their own repressed desires that makes the production moving, thrilling, and profound. Other tragedies, Freud suggests, tap other fundamental aspects of the human psyche and so stir the unconscious to similar response.

OEDIPUS: THE EXISTENTIAL VIEWPOINT

Oedipus demonstrates that the urge to know might in itself be an awful thing, a terrible gift of man's which can lead to pain rather than joy. . . . Given man's *daimon* that he must know, and the irrationality that lies at the heart of things, it is not any particular human act but human existence itself that is tragic, and the fault lies not in Oedipus as this particular man but in Oedipus as man living in a world which is ultimately not made for man the knower.

Laszlo Versenyi

Yet a third view advanced to explain the sustained popular success of *Oedipus* on stage is that it echoes humanity's existential quest for meaning and identity in a universe that confirms neither and indeed, in the case of

EURIPIDES

Euripides was the youngest of the three great Greek tragedians and by far the most modern looking: his style made enormous departures in the direction of realism and political activism, and his concerns were revolutionary. *The Trojan Women*, often considered his masterpiece, treats the Trojan War—the greatest event in Athenian mythic history—from the astonishing viewpoint of Athens' victims: it is as though an American playwright were to write about World War II from the sympathetic vantage of the Japanese empress and her suffering ladies-in-waiting. But *The Trojan Women* is not simply concerned about rewriting history: Euripides' real interest was a recent Athenian massacre of innocent citizens on the island of Melos. When, in the play, the

god Poseidon cries, "That mortal who sacks fallen cities is a fool, / His own turn must come," no one in the audience could have been unaware that Euripides was pointing his remarks at Athens' current military leaders. A passionate pacifist, feminist, and agnostic, Euripides often reviled his fellow citizens and even ridiculed his nationally revered predecessors, Sophocles and Aeschylus, for what he considered their old-fashioned views and stodgy dramaturgy. Though not beloved in his own time (he won the first prize only four times in his life and died in exile), more of Euripides' plays survive than of any other Greek playwright, and his realistic approach found great favor with later Roman dramatists.

Eliza Ward, as Queen Hecuba, cries bitterly from her chains in the Royal Shake-speare Company version of The Trojan Women, *directed by John Barton. (Photo: Donald Cooper.)*

Oedipus, repudiates both. *Oedipus* is seen as the archetypical human being striving to contend with blind circumstance, with what one critic calls "the terror of coincidence." By this view, his quest for self-knowledge is as futile as it is heroic. Further, it is dangerous. "I *have* to hear" he shouts to the terror-stricken shepherd in a rage for self-discovery; and of course what he learns is that *Oedipus tyrannos* and the infant *Clubfoot* are one: as if to find oneself is to destroy oneself, a terrifying but eternally fascinating dramatic theme.

These viewpoints in no way exhaust the interpretations and perspectives that have been put forth concerning this most discussed of all ancient tragedies. They do, however, represent three sorts of approaches—dramaturgical, psychological, philosophical—that can be applied to any play dealing with the human condition. The play itself is neither summed nor stilled by such analyses. It remains accessible to all who are similarly questing in the struggle for personal, social, and spiritual clarity.

THE ROMAN THEATRE

Roman civilization lasted a thousand years and dominated intellectual and cultural life in most of what we now call Europe and the Middle East from the end of the Greek classic age well through the beginnings of the Christian era. And Rome had an active theatre for most of this time, leaving us with magnificent theatre buildings that are among the most impressive ruins of antiquity. Roman theatre practice also has given us a wealth of theatrical terminology: *auditorium* ("hearing place"), *vomitorium* (a tunnel leading through the audience and onto the stage), and *persona* (mask, or character represented by the mask).

It is also Roman drama, not Greek, which was first known to the poets and scholars of the Renaissance and to the Elizabethan and Jacobean playwrights, up through and even beyond the time of William Shakespeare.

However, the Roman theatres and the dramas that played in them were not highly original creations; rather, they were usually adaptations of earlier Greek models. Indeed, right to the end of the Roman era, most Roman plays were about Greek characters, wearing Greek costumes and acting out Greek legends.

Roman drama consisted mainly of comedies, generally provided by the ruling class at harvest festivals, mass birthday celebrations, and eventually at circuses—where plays competed for audience attention with gladiatorial contests and animal combats. An aggressively entertaining style seems to have predominated, not surprising under these circumstances. Roman plays were relatively free of cultural rituals, religious odes, serious politics, or Dionysian revelry.

What mainly survives of Roman theatre—in addition to the glorious archeological ruins of great stages at Orange (France) and Aspendos (Asia Minor)—are the wonderfully comic plays of Plautus and Terence, plus some closet dramas (plays intended to be read, not performed) attributed to Seneca.

Titus Maccius Plautus (c. 254–184 B.C.) is certainly the most popular of the Roman playwrights; his twenty-one known plays, all adapted from late (New) Greek comedies, are fast-paced, joke-filled, lusty stage romps, filled with songs, puns, topical satire, trickery, schemings, and general debauchery. Plautus's plays, while they are occasionally performed today, have proven to be especially long-lasting through their subsequent adaptations: *Miles Gloriosus,* the story of a braggart soldier, became the prototype for later English plays (the early Elizabethan *Ralph Roister Doister*) and Shakespeare's great creation of Sir John Falstaff. Similarly, Plautus's *The Menachmi Twins* became Shakespeare's source for *The Comedy of Errors;* his *Aulularia,* a study of miserliness, became the source play for Molière's *The Miser;* and his *Pseudolus* became one of several Plautine sources for the Stephen Sondheim musical *A Funny Thing Happened on the Way to the Forum.* The comic gags of Plautus often move into these adaptations unchanged; modern audiences laughing at *Henry IV* or *A Funny Thing . . .* are usually responding to the same lines that had Roman crowds in stitches two thousand years ago.

Publius Terentius Afer, or Terence (c. 190–159 B.C.), was a freed African slave whose six comedies, all based on Greek models, are substantially less roughshod and farcical than those of Plautus and correspondingly more elegant and refined; indeed, Terence's plays became even more highly regarded in the Middle Ages and the Renaissance, where they were prized for their rhetorical excellence and their philosophical depth.

Lucius Annaeus Seneca (c. 4 B.C.–65 A.D.), the tutor of Emperor Nero, wrote nine tragedies adapted from the Greek, none of which seems to have been performed on (or written for) the stage. Still, these plays had a vast influence on the Renaissance theatre that followed, mainly from the beauty of many of his choral passages and the horrific power of his gruesome, highly charged scenes of passion and violence. Senecan influences can be seen

John Gielgud as the blinded Oedipus in the Roman version by Seneca (first century A.D.). Actors wore modern dress in this production of the National Theatre (London), directed by Peter Brook. Seneca's nine surviving tragedies, which were probably meant for chamber reading rather than public performance, feature elaborate rhetoric, sententious moralizing, and grisly (although only reported) violence; his works were highly influential in the Renaissance and served as models for plays such as Thomas Kyd's The Spanish Tragedy *and Shakespeare's* Titus Andronicus. *(Photo: © Morris Newcombe.)*

in the first Elizabethan plays and are present in some of Shakespeare's masterpieces, including *Hamlet;* occasionally Seneca's works are staged today with relative success, as, for example, Peter Brook's London production of Seneca's *Oedipus.*

The Roman theatre building, like the Greek, was a vast outdoor structure built to accommodate many thousands of spectators. Freestanding, the Roman theatre building was semicircular; the audience sat in a series of forty or more rows, rising in an arc that surrounded a semicircular orchestra. A long narrow stage backed the orchestra and was itself backed by an elaborately decorated wall, known as the *frons scaenae*. Doorways in the *frons scaenae* provided entrances to the stage and exits to the dressing rooms behind. The Romans also experimented with various stage devices: front curtains (which fell into a pit at the beginning of a play) and extravagant stage machines; it was the fashion for later Roman producers to indulge their audiences with spectacular stage effects, such as quick scene changes and fully staged sea battles fought in a water-filled orchestra.

Roman theatre withered in the decadence and extravagance of the end of the Roman Empire (Nero ordered Seneca to commit suicide, which he did), and it finally collapsed under the stern condemnation of the early Christian Church—which in late Roman times excommunicated all actors and forbade the faithful from attending theatrical performances of any kind. The end of Roman theatre ushered in a dark age of the drama; not a single play was written or performed anywhere in Europe for nearly five hundred years. But when theatre was reborn in the High Middle Ages, it led to an era of dramatic creativity not known since the days of the ancient Greeks.

Greek Tragedy in the 1990s: Above: Olympia Du-
kakis is Hecuba, in the Euripides play of that name,
produced by the American Conservatory Theatre in
San Francisco in 1995. The antiwar theme, carried
over from the same author's The Trojan Women,
has never been more urgently sounded, before or
since. With Ken Ruta as Odysseus. (Photo: Tom
Chargin.) Right: The chorus in Matthias Langh-
off's 1992 radically contemporary production of
Oedipus Tyrannos *in Lausanne, Switzerland.*
Langhoff is one of Europe's great twentieth-century
directors, creating astonishing yet deeply relevant
images in his productions of classical texts; he was
also the codirector of the Geneva Prometheus *pro-*
duction pictured earlier in the chapter. (Photo:
Marc Enguerand.)

4

The Middle Ages

The "Middle Ages" is the label historians have given to those years of European history between the fall of Rome (476 A.D.) and the coming of the Renaissance; it is a curiously colorless designation for one of the most diversely creative periods in the annals of Western civilization. It embraces a thousand years that were dominated by a feudal political and economic system of bishoprics and dukedoms, a chivalric order of knights, and a sharp differentiation between nobility and peasants. This was a cultural empire without an emperor, and it was held together by a common language, Latin, and a common piety, Christianity.

We tend to think of the Middle Ages as a transitional time and also as a primitive one. It is certainly true that the civilization of the period was essentially rural, that the literature was mostly doctrinaire, and that the physical and social technology—roads, sewers, and political institutions—lacked the sophistication of either the preceding epoch or the succeeding one. It is also true that the first five centuries of the Middle Ages—the centuries known to historians as the "Dark Ages"—are mostly lost to history, and few of the human accomplishments of those years survived the deaths of their creators. Yet none of this should obscure the fact that the years we do know well—the so-called High Middle Ages from the tenth and eleventh centuries on—were as active and productive of lasting accomplishment as any comparable time span in recorded civilization. If we think of the great cathedrals of Chartres and Salisbury and the magnificent abbeys of Cluny and St. Denis, if we reflect upon the incalculable social energy that produced crusades, kingdoms, religious revolutions, and the bursting forth of modern languages and literatures, we recognize a medieval civilization of sublime creativity and daring, wholly in command of its own intellectual, artistic, and material resources. The Middle Ages were neither transitional nor primitive; and in truth some of the achievements of that day, including the theatrical ones, have never been surpassed in magnitude or in popular appeal.

The great theatre of the Middle Ages was a religious one—a profoundly religious one. Upon examination, it reveals many important parallels with the Greek theatre. Like the Greek theatre, the medieval theatre began as a springtime religious observance ritualizing the resurrection of a divine figure—in this case, Jesus Christ—and, by analogous extension, the rebirth of vegetation in the fields. Also like the Greek theatre, the medieval one was intensely public and communal, attracting a mass audience for the celebration and illustration of a common mythos (the Old and New Testaments of the Christian Bible). Finally, once again like the Greek theatre, the medieval theatre became a function of the evolving civic government—that is, a part of the political and social life of the community as well as a vehicle for its religious expression.

It is true that the drama of the Middle Ages never produced a body of work demonstrating great individual literary genius—no Sophocles speaks to us from the 1400s. Nonetheless, if we expand our criteria for measuring dramatic effectiveness to include sheer scale and public response, we must appreciate and wonder at this theatre that was the ancestor to much of what has followed it.

THE *QUEM QUERITIS:* FROM TROPE TO DRAMA

The medieval theatre was born in the liturgy of the Christian Church of the early tenth century, when a series of liturgical elaborations, known as *tropes* (from the Latin *tropus,* meaning "added melody"), expanded the offices (services) of the Mass. The most significant of these tropes, the *Quem Queritis* (Whom seek ye), appeared in the Easter Mass. It celebrates, in responsive chanting, the visit of the three Marys to the tomb of the crucified Christ: they are met by an angel who tells them that Christ has risen, and their grief turns to joy. The text comes straight from the New Testament:

ANGEL: *Quem queritis in sepulchro, O Christicole?*
[Whom seek ye in the sepulchre, O Christian women?]
MARYS: *Jesum Nazarenum crucifixum, O caelicolae.*
[Jesus of Nazareth, the crucified, O heavenly one.]
ANGEL: *Non est hic, surrexit sicut praedixerat. Ite, nuntiate quia surrexit de sepulchro.*
[He is not here; He is risen, as He foretold.
Go, announce that He has risen from the sepulchre.]

This was not yet drama—there was no impersonation attempted—but it was dialogue, and it apparently proved a popular and meaningful addition to the Easter Mass. A similar trope was added to the Christmas Mass; it concerns shepherds seeking the infant Jesus.

The step from trope to full-fledged drama occurred late in the century. By a rare stroke of fortune, one of the earliest manuscripts for this drama, complete with full stage directions, exists today as part of a major medieval document, the *Concordia Regularis,* prepared in about 980 by St. Ethelwold, Bishop of

Winchester (and therefore of England). In the *Concordia,* which governed all English church procedures for centuries to follow, were the following instructions for the enactment of the *Quem Queritis* in English Easter masses:

While the third lesson is being chanted, let four brethren vest themselves. Let one of these, vested in an alb, enter as though to take part in the service, and let him approach the sepulchre without attracting attention and sit there quietly with a palm in his hand. While the third respond is chanted, let the remaining three follow, and let them all, vested in copes, bearing in their hands thuribles with incense, and stepping delicately as those who seek something, approach the sepulchre. These things are done in imitation of the angel sitting in the monument, and the women with spices coming to anoint the body of Jesus. When therefore he who sits there beholds the three approach him like folk lost and seeking something, let him begin in a dulcet voice of medium pitch to sing *Quem queritis?* And when he has sung it to the end, let the three reply in unison *Jesum Nazarenum.* So he, *Non est hic, surrexit sicut praedixerat. Ite, nuntiate quia surrexit a mortuis.* At the word of his bidding let those three turn to the choir and say *Alleluia! Resurrexit Dominus!* [Hallelujah! The Lord is risen!] This said, let the one, still sitting there and as if recalling them, say the anthem *Venite et videte locum* [Come and see the place]. And saying this, let him rise, and lift the veil, and show them the place bare of the cross, but only the cloths laid there in which the cross was wrapped. And when they have seen this, let them set down the thuribles which they bore in that same sepulchre, and take the cloth, and hold it up in the face of the clergy, and as if to demonstrate that the Lord has risen and is no longer wrapped therein, let them sing the anthem *Surrexit Dominus de sepulchro* [The Lord is risen from the sepulchre], and lay the cloth upon the altar. When the anthem is done, let the prior, sharing in their gladness at the triumph of our King, in that, having vanquished death, He rose again, begin the hymn *Te Deum laudamus* [We praise Thee, O God]. And this begun, all the bells chime out together.

The *completeness* of this wholly satisfying liturgical mini-opera is apparent. Structurally, it contains all the classical requirements of serious drama, including exposition, conflict, recognition, reversal, and even a minicatharsis attendant on the singing of the *Alleluia.* Theatrically, it presents its viewers with dramatic demonstration (the showing of the empty cloth), ritualization (the laying of the cloth on the altar), and celebration (the singing of the *Te Deum*). It is, moreover, a drama wholly impersonated; for, although the priest-performers are not to be thought of as naturalistic actors, they seek to embody the characters they perform through costume (copes for the Marys and an alb for the angel), vocal modulation ("a dulcet voice of medium pitch"), carefully staged movements ("stepping delicately"), and, in general, what we call "acting" ("like folk lost and seeking something"). The staging of this drama includes furniture (something on which the angel sits), a set piece of some sort (the sepulchre), props (the palm, the thuribles, the cloth), pantomime (showing the cloth and making clear what is *not* there), singing, and a concluding orchestral effect ("the bells chime out together"). There is even a suggestion of stage trickery in the preplay entrance of the priest who plays the angel and who, lacking scenery or a proscenium to lurk behind, must enter the staging area "as though to take part in the service . . . without attracting attention [and] sit there quietly." It is as if the whole of theatrical possibility—the sacred and the sham—were compressed into this tiny, seminal playlet from the first millennium A.D.

What is further significant about this playlet is its centrality to the Christian religion: it concerns the single most crucial episode of the Christian mythos—Christ's resurrection, which both "proved" His divinity and signified, by analogy, the redemptive power of God. Thus drama used as a part of the Easter Mass was not relegated to a decorative or subsidiary function, but rather was accorded the highest function of the liturgical office: to ritualize and bring life to this most important moment in the story of Christ. Obviously, any expansion of dramatization beyond the *Quem Queritis* episode would of necessity be in the direction of the "less-holy."

And indeed that is the direction that Christian drama took. The *Quem Queritis* grew longer as additional dialogue and then story lines were added to the central episode. Soon there were additional playlets showing the events leading up to the Resurrection and following it. More and more the dialogue departed from holy writ and was developed simply by surmise and increasingly with an eye to theatricality. The language was "vulgarized," both in the literal sense—that is, it was translated from Latin into the "vulgar" or "common" languages of English, French, Flemish, German, and so forth—and in the figurative sense. The dramas became, in short, grander, funnier, and more theatrical. By the middle of the twelfth century, these additions to the Easter service had evolved into a full-fledged "liturgical drama" consisting of playlets tracing the history of humankind from Creation to Judgment Day. Expanding from the cathedral altar into the apse and transepts of the church, the plays began to attract hundreds of curious strangers in addition to the faithful parishioners. As time passed, the increasingly elaborate costumes and scenery, and the growing virtuosity of the performers, seemed less tied to the sacred office of the Mass that had given them birth and more aimed at sheer art and entertainment. The next step was perhaps inevitable: the medieval liturgical theatre outgrew the Mass, outgrew the liturgy, outgrew the production capabilities of the clergy, outgrew the cathedral itself—and burst forth upon the medieval marketplace.

OUT OF THE CHURCH

Drama left the Church during the thirteenth century, in part because it had grown too large for presentation in the cathedrals and in part because Church officers began to rebel against the growing secular theatricality of the plays. The clergy may also have feared that the popularity of the dramatic format would supplant more traditional means of worship and devotion. In any event, in 1240, Pope Innocent II decreed that drama be removed from the Church.

But the move proved a good one for the drama, adding to the ever-present religious core of medieval theatre a social and aesthetic dimension that could never be wholly achieved within the confines of liturgical works. For the medieval theatre was becoming an immensely popular meeting ground, with the annual springtime performances attracting crowds from neighboring towns and countryside alike. Both civic pride and commercial interest stood to benefit from such gatherings. And so it was that the civic community took over the production of the expanded devotional plays. It was a community that included guilds, brotherhoods, municipal governments, and religious associations, all united in a concept of congruity between faith and commerce, ritual and entertainment, devotion and artistry, salvation and society. As a result of this mingling of interests and opportunities, an immense flowering of the medieval theatre occurred all over Europe from about 1250 until well into the sixteenth century. This theatre, conceived on a scale that we can hardly even imagine today, was devoted above all to the dramatic glorification of Christ; in pursuit of that aim, it proved a powerful force for the moral instruction of an illiterate but ethically receptive populace, the ritualization of the two Testaments of biblical mythos, the urbanization of a rural society—and the festive amusement and entertainment of the European community after a long winter locked in against the cold.

What was this flowering medieval theatre like? We can cite no single "typical" example, because it evolved over the course of more than two hundred years of annual productions performed in hundreds of towns in more than a dozen different languages and cultures. The plays have been given numerous names (mystery plays, passion plays, cycle plays, pageant plays, miracle plays, Corpus Christi plays), but basically their pattern was always the same: a series of playlets inspired by stories in the Bible, written in a common language of the populace, presented in sequence, performed in, on, and/or around a stage or series of stages. Some stages were rolled about from one location to another; others were stationary. The total production told the story of humankind as it was understood in the Christian thought of the day.

Scale and duration were two of the most imposing features of medieval plays. Virtually all of them lasted a number of days. One passion play lasted forty days and had three hundred actors playing five hundred roles. Playlets were performed on elaborately crafted temporary stages (sometimes called *mansions* in France) that were set up in public squares and moved about from day to day (or, in some cases, from playlet to playlet). Convenience rather than aesthetic convention governed the methods of production: medieval directors produced their works wherever it seemed most practical—in earthen amphitheatres of contemporary construction, in the ruins of Roman arenas, in marketplaces and public squares, and in processions through village streets.

The "stations" of a passion play, set up in a public square much as the play would originally have been staged inside the church. The action of the play flowed from one area to the next. (Drawing: John von Szeliski.)

The two-day festival at Lucerne, Switzerland, took place in the Wine Market Square, which survives today much in its original form; the stage plans and directions for the 1583 production at Lucerne reveal that the performance utilized, in addition to *mansion* stages erected in the square, the doors, windows, facades, and balconies of fronting buildings. The 1509 performance at Romans, France, took place in the garden of a monastery, where temporary bleachers were set up for audience seating and scaffolding was erected for the staging area and *mansions.*

The English plays of the Middle Ages hold particular interest for the English-speaking reader and theatregoer, not only because they are among the first literary works written in the English language, but also because they used one of the most astonishing staging practices of all time, the rolling procession. At least 125 English towns produced mystery plays, generally called "cycle plays" because of their peculiar staging format, or "Corpus Christi plays" because they were commonly performed at the time of the church festival of Corpus Christi (literally, "body of Christ"). This festival occurred in spring sometime between late May and late June (on the Thursday following Trinity Sunday) and, as the name implies, it celebrated the mystery of divinity in the body of Jesus Christ: it was therefore seen as an appropriate holy day for reaffirming the spiritual aspects of human existence by means of humanly enacted drama. Of the surviving English medieval plays, most come from Corpus Christi dramas performed at Chester, Wakefield, and York; we now turn to the York festival for specific illumination and a reconstruction of the excitement of medieval theatre.

THE CORPUS CHRISTI PLAYS AT YORK

Corpus Christi plays are known to have been produced at York, in northeast England, from at least the year 1378; they were probably go-

ing on long before that. Historical records tell us that King Richard II attended the York festival in 1397, and actual playtexts survive from the early fifteenth century. These, along with court records, other documents, and information from other festivals, permit a fairly clear reconstruction of the content and staging of the plays and convey a vivid sense of the dramatic vitality of the times.

In York, as in most of England, the town corporation, or governing body, was charged with the overall coordination of Corpus Christi plays. The individual playlets (at York there were forty-eight of these) were allocated by the corporation to various craft guilds, which were somewhat akin to modern-day craft unions; each guild assumed responsibility for casting, funding, rehearsing, and producing its assigned playlet. This association of government, guild, and theatre could have come about only with the universal rise in the late Middle Ages of a civic and commercial bourgeoisie—a middle class that, while properly obedient to Church and king, depended on neither clergy nor royalty for lifeblood support. Indeed, it was a time when urban and commercial interests were growing at the expense of the landed aristocracy. The theatre of the High Middle Ages was resolutely middle class. It was also "professional," not in the sense that we speak of professional theatre today, but in the sense that it was created and supported by highly motivated professional craftspeople and artisans who employed their skills to the fullest in the service of their dramatic assignments. Perhaps a comparison to a later age can be made with respect to El Teatro Campesino in California, which allied with the Farm Workers Union in the 1970s to produce a series of plays that did much to dignify not only the union's cause but also the social aspirations of migrant farm workers and Mexican Americans in the western United States.

The York plays, like all surviving English plays of the Middle Ages, are of unknown authorship. Anonymous creativity was characteristic of the Middle Ages, which were in general devoted more to piety than to self-celebration; even the great Gothic cathedrals of the times were "unsigned." And, though some scholars detect the consistent hand of a "York realist" through the surviving manuscripts, the York plays were revised and refined frequently as they were handed down from generation to generation, and reveal a great diversity of writing styles from play to play.

There were, at the peak of the Age, forty-eight plays in the York Cycle (see box). The numerological features of this sequence certainly would have attracted the medieval mind, addicted as it was to discerning patterns in the universe. The number of plays not only is twice the number of hours in the day (the Chester cycle, more perfectly, contained twenty-four plays), but also effects what was taken to be a sacred geometric balance: the annunciation of Christ's coming occurs one-quarter of the way through the overall drama, and the Crucifixion-Resurrection (covered in four plays) falls at the three-quarter point, giving the whole a mathematical order that achieved, in the view of its spectators, an echo of divine organization.

The means of presentation at York, as in other parts of England, was astonishing, even for medieval times. It was a procession through town in which each of the entire series of playlets was "toured" on its own rolling stage (known as a "pageant" or "pageant wagon") to ten, twelve, sometimes even sixteen different locales ("stations") throughout the city for as many separate performances as there were stations. This resulted in a daylong procession, beginning at four-thirty in the morning and apparently lasting until late at night, until each of the forty-eight playlets had been performed at every station! In trying to imagine the sheer magnitude of this enterprise, some modern-day theatre historians have come to suspect that we may have erred in our interpretation of the records (see bibliographical note for this chapter); however, it seems possible that a society possessed

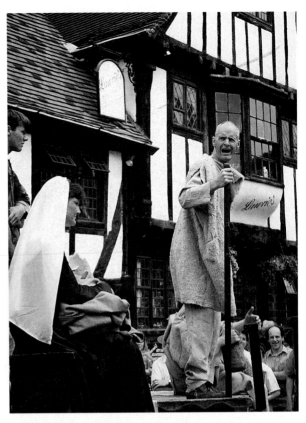

In July 1994, for the first time in 335 years, the City of York mounted a procession of medieval wagon performances through city streets. Nine cycle plays, each on its own wagon, were presented sequentially at five different "stations," under the overall direction of Jane Oakshott. Shown here is the play of the Annunciation and Visitation, performed in front of a restaurant on Jubbergate. (Photo: Robert Cohen.)

of the energy and exuberance to build grandiose cathedrals and to pursue ambitious and costly crusades would not shrink from the hard work and spiritual dedication implicit in the York Cycle processional.

What the rolling pageant wagon looked like we cannot say for certain. A reference from the early seventeenth century describes it as a four- or six-wheeled two-story cart with a curtained dressing room below and an acting area above. All wagons had at least two

Pageant wagons in a town square; a conjectural reconstruction. (Drawing: John von Szeliski.)

vertical levels, possibly more, and all afforded some means of access to the street. Scaffolding might have been erected at each station to afford additional acting space, or more than one wagon might have been used for playlets requiring more staging facilities than a single wagon could accommodate. Some such arrangement would seem necessary, for exam-

ple, for the staging of the last of the York sequence, the Judgment Day.

We do know that the wagons were elaborate and expensive structures: guilds that did not own them had to rent them for the enormous sum of five shillings (about $1,000 today), and guilds that did own them had to rent buildings to store them from one Corpus Christi day to the next. The skills of the guild members were frequently employed in building the wagons and their attendant scenic elements—it was no coincidence that the Shipwrights were allocated the "Noah" pageant and the Goldsmiths the "Adoration." And if the York craftspeople lent anything like as much artistry to the making of pageant wag-

THE PLAYS AND PRODUCERS OF THE YORK CYCLE

These were the forty-eight plays, and the forty-eight producers, of the York Cycle plays. These plays comprise, to the medieval mind, the history of the cosmos, from the beginning to the end of time.

1. The Creation and the Fall of Lucifer—Barkers
2. From the Creation to the Fifth Day—Plasterers
3. God Creates Adam and Eve—Cardmakers
4. Adam and Eve in the Garden of Eden—Fullers
5. Man's Disobedience and Fall—Coopers
6. Adam and Eve Driven from Eden—Armorers
7. Sacrifice of Cain and Abel—Glovers
8. Building of the Ark—Shipwrights
9. Noah and the Flood—Fishers and Mariners
10. Abraham's Sacrifice—Parchmenters and Bookbinders
11. The Israelites in Egypt, the Ten Plagues, and Passage of the Red Sea—Hosiers
12. Annunciation and Visitation—Spicers
13. Joseph's Trouble About Mary—Pewterers and Founders
14. Journey to Bethlehem, Birth of Jesus—Tile Thatchers
15. The Angels and the Shepherds—Candlemakers
16. Coming of the Three Kings to Herod—Masons
17. Coming of the Three Kings, the Adoration—Goldsmiths
18. Flight into Egypt—Marshals (i.e., horse grooms)
19. Massacre of the Innocents—Girdlers and Nailers
20. Christ with the Doctors in the Temple—Spurmakers and Bitmakers
21. Baptism of Jesus—Barbers
22. Temptation of Jesus—Blacksmiths
23. The Transfiguration—Curriers
24. Women Taken in Adultery, Raising of Lazarus—Capmakers

ons as they did to the construction of York Minster, their magnificent cathedral, those wagons must have been splendid structures indeed.

The great majority of actors in the York plays were local guild members and their friends. Hundreds of actors were required, and for most the play was doubtless viewed primarily as a major annual social activity. However, performers received some wages, and premium wages were paid to those with special abilities. Although the secular theatre had died with the fall of Rome, its tradition of miming, juggling, "mumming," and min-

streling had never been wholly extinguished during the Dark Ages; and in the pageant plays of the High Middle Ages the inheritors of this performing tradition found an opportunity to combine their skills with dramatic performance. Some roles—chiefly those of the grand villains of the Bible (Herod, Pilate, Satan) and the most eloquent deities (God and Jesus)—demanded considerable acting skill to fulfill the expectations of the medieval audience. Other roles, more playful and rustic, became vehicles for highly entertaining comedic performances.

To envision the ultimate effect of the York

25. Christ's Entry into Jerusalem—Skinners
26. Conspiracy to Take Jesus—Cutlers
27. The Last Supper—Bakers
28. The Agony and Betrayal—Cordwainers
29. Peter Denies Jesus, Jesus Examined by Caiaphas—Bowyers and Fletchers (i.e., bow and arrow makers)
30. Dream of Pilate's Wife, Jesus Before Pilate—Tapiters and Couchers (i.e., makers of tapestry and carpets)
31. Trial Before Herod—Litsters (i.e., dyers)
32. Second Accusation Before Pilate, Remorse of Judas, Purchase of Field of Blood—Cooks and Waterleaders
33. Second Trial Continued, Judgment on Jesus—Tilemakers
34. Christ Led up to Calvary—Shearmen
35. The Crucifixion—Pinners and Painters
36. Mortification of Christ—Butchers
37. The Harrowing of Hell—Saddlers
38. The Resurrection, Fright of the Jews—Carpenters
39. Christ's Appearance to Mary Magdalen—Winedrawers
40. Travelers to Emmaus—Sledmen
41. Purification of Mary; Simeon and Anna Prophesy—Hatmakers, Masons, and Laborers
42. Incredulity of Thomas—Scriveners
43. Ascension—Tailors
44. Descent of the Holy Spirit—Potters
45. The Death of Mary—Drapers
46. Appearance of Our Lady to Thomas—Weavers
47. Assumption and Coronation of the Virgin—Ostlers (i.e., stablemen)
48. Judgment Day—Mercers (i.e., dealers in cloth)

processional drama, we might compare it to the Rose Bowl Parade currently held each New Year's Day in Pasadena. This annual outdoor holiday procession (staged in the eternal springtime of Southern California) features a number of floats, each sponsored, funded, and prepared by a civic or community group, each dedicated to an overall theme chosen by the parade's governing body, and each stopping by a reviewing stand for a "living tableau" with amateur "performers" waving, smiling, and conveying an idea or a topic. Just as the floats are advertisements for their sponsors, so the pageant wagons at York attested to the professional and commercial merits of the guilds that built them; and as the Pasadena floats have grown in technological sophistication over the years, so we might expect that the medieval wagons became increasingly splendid and elaborate over the course of their more than two-hundred-year history. The cycle plays outdid the Pasadena parades, of course, by being dramatic as well as theatrical and processional and by stopping at numerous stations instead of a single reviewing stand; nonetheless, the parallel may bring into focus the extraordinary public spectacle of York theatre five and six centuries ago.

THE YORK CYCLE

Of the forty-eight playlets that constituted the York sequence, we shall look at four, none of which consumed more than fifteen or twenty minutes in playing time. In combination—which is the only way we can fairly look at them—they give a general picture of the main themes and theatrical practices of the entire cycle.

The Creation and the Fall of Lucifer

The first playlet in the York sequence was, naturally, the Creation. It is one of the shorter texts—only 166 lines—and, when delivered with a great deal of action, could be expected to provide a snappy opening for the entire forty-eight-play marathon. It is staged alternately in Heaven and Hell and therefore requires (as do most of the playlets) at least two acting areas, probably at different vertical levels.

The action begins in Heaven. God appears, announcing himself to a host of angels and, by extension, to the audience gathering in the early morning streets of York.

GOD: I am Alpha and Omega, the Life, the Way, the Truth,

the First and the Last.
I am gracious and great, God without beginning;
I am maker unmade, all might is in me;
I am life and way unto wealth-winning;
I am foremost and first; as I bid shall it be.
On blessing my blee shall be blending,
And hielding from harm to be hiding,
My body in bliss ay abiding,
Unending without any ending.[1]

Here we can see at a glance the distance between medieval verse and our own and the remarkable directness and simplicity of the dramaturgy. The exposition is absolutely straightforward, as of course it must be in this short dramatic form. The writer cannot waste time on subtle or clever story development, and he has no need to introduce characters as familiar as God (and, later, Adam, Eve, Jesus, and Pilate). As for the language, not only is it remote in time, but it is also written in a verse form that is often (incorrectly) called doggerel, a form somewhat irregular in meter and rhyme and alliterative to an extraordinary degree ("foremost and first," "hielding from harm," "gracious and great," "on blessing my blee shall be blending"). Shakespeare was to subsequently satirize this form of seemingly primitive versifying (see box on page 114), and today we have to look into it closely to discern the source of its impact in its own time.

The verse of the medieval theatre was aimed first and foremost at conveying a sense of spiritual majesty comparable to that attained by the use of Latin in the earlier liturgical plays:

---

[1]The spelling in this speech has been modernized, but the passage is otherwise unedited to show the characteristics of Middle English verse. Passages that appear later have been lightly edited for this text. "Blee" is a meaningless word, utilized solely for its poetic sound. "Hielding" means hiding; the verse features abundant repetition.

The play of Noah at York in 1994. (Photo: Robert Cohen.)

the play was to be perceived as a message of divine origin, of scriptural import. The use of verses that fit into subtle mathematical metric and rhyme schemes—as many of the verses in these plays do—was intended to elevate the medieval drama beyond the ordinary and into the mystical and to give a sense that the anonymous authors of the verses were not ordinary mortals at all, but scribes of the divine. Thus, fundamentally, the verse of the medieval theatre was created for purposes of religious instruction, not for aesthetic reasons; its whole justification was to support the notion of divine intent behind the play's messages and themes. To the medieval mind, then, the stylization of the verse was perceived not as a literary decoration, but as a proper means of communicating spiritual *truth;* thus verse was thought to create a greater sense of "reality"

than could be achieved in the ordinary language of the day.

Let us now return to our playlet. God, having announced himself, then creates the world:

GOD: Here underneath me an island I neven [name],
Which island shall be Earth. Now there be Earth, wholly, and Hell; this—highest Heaven,
And all that wealth wields, here give I to ye.
This grant I you, ministers mine,
As long as y'are stable in thought.
As far as those that are nought—
They in my prison shall pine.

Then, turning to his archangel Lucifer, God appoints him second in command and intro-

MEDIEVAL THEATRE: A SATIRICAL VIEW

The conventions and verse forms of medieval theatre lend themselves readily to satire, as Shakespeare made clear in a clever parody woven into his *A Midsummer Night's Dream* (c. 1594). There a group of village crafts-men produce the "play" of "Pyramus and Thisbe," and we are privileged, in the course of *Dream,* to watch the casting, rehearsing, and finally the presentation of this play-within-a-play.

"Pyramus" is described as a "most lamen-table comedy," and lamentable indeed is its production by these well-meaning amateurs. Afraid that the "audience" will mistake a character's stage death for a real murder, the actors demand a prologue that will explain "that I Pyramus am not Pyramus, but Bot-tom the Weaver: this will put them out of fear." Lest the ladies in the audience be terri-fied of the lion, the actor who plays "Lion" insists that half his face "must be seen through the lion's neck," and that he must say, during the course of the play, "Fair ladies . . . I would entreat you not to fear, not to trem-ble. . . . If you think I come hither as a lion, it were pity of my life: no, I am no such thing; I am a man as other men are . . . Snug the Joiner." Since the story of the "play" calls for Pyramus and Thisbe to meet by moonlight, one actor is required to play the moon—that is, to hold a lantern above him and to "disfig-ure, or to present, the person of moonshine." Because the "play" calls for a wall, and a crack within it, another actor "must present wall: and let him have some plaster, or some loam, or some roughcast about him, to signify wall; and let him hold his fingers thus, and through that cranny shall Pyramus and Thisbe whisper."

The versification of "Pyramus" is reminis-cent of medieval stanzas—over-alliterative, short-footed, and tortured into rhymes:

PYRAMUS: Sweet moon, I thank thee for
    thy sunny beams;
I thank thee, moon, for shining now so
    bright;
For, by thy gracious, golden, glittering
    gleams,
I trust to take of truest Thisbe sight.
      But stay, O spite!
      But mark, poor knight,
    What dreadful dole is here!
      Eyes, do you see?
      How can it be?
    O dainty duck! O dear!
      Thy mantle good,
      What, stain'd with blood!
    Approach, ye Furies fell!
    O fates, come, come,
    Cut thread and thrum,
    Quail, crush, conclude, and quell!

Shakespeare encases this parody within one of his most lyrical and elegant comedies; indeed, the juxtaposition of crude verse and elementary stage devices with the complexity of Shakespeare's poetic dramaturgy empha-sizes both the professional sophistication of the later writer and the experimental ama-teurism of the medieval stage. In laughing at the "rude mechanicals" who present this playlet, the characters in Shakespeare's larger drama share with the audience an indulgent superiority over preceding generations and, by implication, exult in the presumed prog-ress of civilization since the days of such ru-dimentary theatricals.

duces the playlet's central conflict and the great division of the universe into two worlds: good and evil.

GOD: Of all the mights I have made most next after me,
  I make thee as master and mirror of my might;
  I bield [protect] thee here bainly [now], in bliss for to be,
  And I name thee Lucifer—bearer of light.

Next the angels sing a hymn, "Holy, Holy, Holy, Lord God of Hosts," and praise this act of God:

ANGELS: Ah, merciful Maker, full mickle [powerful] is thy might,
  That all this work at a word worthily has wrought.
  Ay, praised be that lovely Lord of his light,
  That us mighty has made, that before were but nought.

The scene bears some uncanny resemblances to the Greek *Prometheus*. Like Prometheus, Lucifer is a close ally of God (Zeus) and is the bearer (and namesake) of light, the beloved benefactor of lesser demigods and, as it turns out, one who will eventually be spurned by God for too great a prideful exploitation of his gifts. But despite the parallels, what a world of difference! For this light-bearer occasions no sympathy in the audience. Whatever majesty the medieval author had to command was expended on the higher character, the one who began the play with the splendid, metaphorical "I am the Alpha and Omega, the Life. . . ." This was no struggle between coequals in the divine realm, but a simple confrontation between right and wrong in the moral arena.

God leaves the stage, and Lucifer rants. Ranting was apparently considered a particularly effective means of character portrayal by medieval authors and directors; it allowed villainous characters to strut and storm about on the stage and in the audience in colorful exhibitions of bragging, posturing, and rage—doubtless to the delight of all concerned. (Later, Shakespeare was to refer to one of the great villains of medieval plays when he had Hamlet warn his actors not to "tear a passion to tatters . . . it out-herods Herod!") A sample of Lucifer's boasting illustrates how the medieval villain was portrayed:

LUCIFER: All the mirth that is made is marked in me!
  The beams of my brightness are burning so bright,
  And so seemly in sight myself now I see,
  For like a lord I am left to live in this light
  More fairer by far than my feers [friends],
  In me is no point to impair,
  I feel me so famous and fair,
  My power is passing my peers!

Certainly Prometheus also had a high opinion of himself, but the unabashed rantings of Lucifer are comic in their exaggeration; they are neither terrifying nor touching. Nonetheless, Lucifer continues until he takes the unsupportable step of likening himself to God. Again, however, his challenge is foolish rather than frightening:

LUCIFER: In glorious glamour my glittering gleams!
  I shall bide in bliss through my brightness of beams!
  In Heaven I'll set myself, full seemly to sight,
  To receive all reverence, through my right of renown.
  I shall be like unto him that is highest on hight,
  Oh! How I am deft—Oh!!! Deuce!!! All goes down!!
  My might and my main have stopped calling!
  Help, Fellows! In faith, I am FAALLLL-INGGG!

And with that, Lucifer, with his angel admirers, falls into the lower staging area—into "Hell."

The staging of Hell was one of the medieval masterpieces. In continental Europe, where stationary *mansions* were commonly used, the "Hellmouth" was a vividly horrifying stage piece designed to swallow "sinners." The presence of Hell in the cycle—it is portrayed in both the first and the last playlets—reflects its pervasive influence in medieval life. Hell was the supreme terror that both religion and drama sought to explain and to exorcise. It seems unlikely that there would be anything truly frightening about this Yorkshire Hellmouth, which was carted through the village streets on a wagon, but it must have generated the kind of visceral excitement that was needed to get the attention of an early-rising audience and to put them in an active mood of participation on a springtime morning.

As Lucifer and his cohorts land in Hell, the angels (now devils) fight with each other in a roustabout scene of frenzied denunciation:

LUCIFER: Out! Out! Torment! Helpless! HOT it is here!
   This is a dungeon of dole into which I am dight [put]!
   I, Lucifer, once so comely and clear,
   Now am I loathest that ever was light!
   My brightness is black and blue now!
A DEVIL: Out! Out! I wail in woe! My wit is all went now!
   Our food is but filth we find us beforn [before]!
   We that were bathed in bliss, in bogs are we burnt now,
   Out on thee, Lucifer! Lummox! Our light thou has lorn [stolen]!
LUCIFER: Out! Away! Woe is me now—it is worse than it was!
   Don't bother to chide me, I said but a thought.
DEVIL: Out, Lummox! Thou lost us!
LUCIFER: You lie! Out! Alas!

While the medieval "Hellmouth" was an enormous stage prop, constructed to resemble a whale with yawning jaws and sharp teeth, a more modern staging device, shown here, uses simply light, smoke, and fiercely growling devils. From The Plaie Called Corpus Christi, *an integrated series of medieval plays presented by the Focused Research Program in Medieval Drama at the University of California, Irvine. (Photo: Philip Channing.)*

God, above, creates Adam, Eve, the animals, and the tree of knowledge in The Plaie Called Corpus Christi. *Scenery by Douglas-Scott Goheen and costumes by Patricia Goheen employ both modern and medieval elements. Edgar Schell, arranger of the texts in this version, plays God; Mary Workman is Eve (in a painted bodysuit); and Ron Richards is Adam. (Photo: Philip Channing.)*

I wished not this woe should be wrought.
Out on you, lummoxes! You smother me
    in smoke.
DEVIL: This woe you have wrought us!
LUCIFER: You lie! You lie!
DEVIL: YOU lie, and now you will cry.
    Out, lummox! Have at you! Come devils,
    let's poke!

A general battle ensues in the street, much, one must presume, to the merriment of enchanted spectators.

The play concludes with a final scene in Heaven, where God, reappearing, draws the moral in typically unequivocal fashion:

GOD: Those fools from their fairness into fantasy fell,
    And made moan of might that marked
    them and made them.
So passing of power they thought them,
They would not me worship that wrought
    them.

Therefore my wrath shall over go with them.

And then God proceeds with creation, deciding first to create humanity ("Mankind of mould [earth] will I make") and then to create night for the devils ("In Hell shall never murkiness be missing, / The murkiness which I name the night") and daylight for humankind:

> The day, that call I this light,
> My afterworks shall they be guiding.
> And now in my blessing I divide them in two,
> The night from the day, so that they shall meet never.
> But rather to separate gates go they to,
> Both night-time and day, different duties forever.
> (*To the audience*) To you I'll give guidance unceasing.
> This day's work is done—ring the bell,
> For all this work likes me right well,
> And now I give it my blessing.

With that, the wagon rolls off to the next station, leaving God's benediction behind.

It was a brilliant stroke to end this playlet with the creation of daylight, for as timed by the play's producers, that action occurred simultaneously with the first slanting of the sun's rays over the Yorkshire dales. The goal of the medieval theatre was to show the harmony between Heaven and nature as revealed in the cycles of history, the cycles of life, and the cycles of the day. The play was timed to set all three in motion simultaneously.

In comparing this simple, short playlet with the thematically similar *Prometheus,* we can see both shared characteristics and important differences. On the one hand, we feel compelled to ask how it was that two wholly different cultures, unknown to each other and separated in time by two thousand years and in space by two thousand miles, each came to create a drama of a light-god second in command to a more omnipotent deity, and to show in these dramas how the presumption of the light-god caused his fall into a sort of eternal imprisonment whence he battled on against his antagonist. Moreover, we must wonder what caused both cultures to feature this drama at an outdoor springtime festival associated with religious worship and celebration. The answers perhaps lie in the need for both cultures, coming out of their separate dark ages of primitivism and religious monasticism, to come to grips with growing pressures toward individuality and general enlightenment. Both dramas imply an awareness of humanity's potential to defy the laws laid down by religious revelation and to seek out answers to life's perplexities through personal investigation and imagination. Both deal with the struggle of one character to break free from the restraints imposed by a higher authority, and both examine the possibilities of an individual's failure to conform in an otherwise spiritually rigid community. The sin of Lucifer is essentially that of Prometheus: the Greeks called it *hubris,* which means wanton arrogance or outrageous presumption. Moreover, the medieval author, in using a demigod for his challenger, capitalized on the same structure used by Aeschylus to make the challenge to the high god seem possible and credible.

On the other hand, of course, the differences between these plays are amply apparent even on the superficial level. The story told in the York playlet is a simple one based on an uncomplicated theme. It features a good god rather than a rapacious one and a foolish challenger rather than a magnificent one; its climaxes come in simple fights and benedictions rather than in philosophically complex and poetically powerful odes; and its staging is always more entertaining than awesome, more comic than piteous, and more spontaneous than stylistically formalized. The medieval theatre was not yet ready to deal with outsized heroics; this was still an age of the deepest popular piety, and indeed probably more than one would-be rebel decided to toe the mark

Eve is tempted by Satan (Ken Jensen) in the University of California at Irvine's The Plaie Called Corpus Christie. *(Photo: Philip Channing.)*

after seeing the fate of Lucifer and others like him. The emergence and acclaim of individual genius was to come with the Renaissance.

The Fall of Man

The playlet concerning the Fall of Man, the fifth in the York Cycle, expands upon this special topic of ancient drama—man's knowledge and the balance of despair and pride which that knowledge demands—in a manner touchingly realistic and rural for such a profound theological issue. Its action is set in Hell, Earth, and Heaven; it portrays Satan donning the disguise of a serpent (or a

"wicked worm," in the alliterative language of the play) and seducing Eve, who then persuades Adam to eat of the forbidden fruit from the tree of knowledge. The temptation is intellectual, not sensual:

SATAN: Eve . . . thou wilt see
    Who eats the fruit of good and ill
    Shall have knowing as well as He.
EVE: Why, what kind of thing art thou
    That tells this tale to me?
SATAN: A worm, that knowest how
    That ye may worshipped be.
EVE: What worship should we win thereby?
    To eat thereof we needeth nought.
    We have lordship to make mastery
    Of all things that on earth are wrought.
SATAN: Woman, do way! (*Giving her the fruit*)
    To greater state may ye be brought!
EVE: To do that would make us loath
    That should our God mispay.
SATAN: It surely is no wothe [harm];
    Eat it safely, ye may.
    For peril right none therein lies,
    But worship, and great winning.
    For just as God shall ye be wise,
    Equal to him in everything.
    Ay, gods shall ye be,
    Of ill and good to have knowing,
    And you will be as wise as He.
EVE: Is this sooth that thou says?
SATAN: Yea, why trust you not me?
    I would by no ways
    Tell but truth to thee.

Here we see that *knowledge* is the fruit forbidden to man, particularly the knowledge of "good and ill," which up to that time, according to the myth, had been the sole prerogative of God. The Bible suggests that the reason for God's subsequent harsh punishment of Adam and Eve was that He regarded them as potential rivals. Surely priests and others charged with transmitting and interpreting the divine intent have always shared this concern with respect to human knowledge. And just as surely, their concern has been justified.

As the Greek *mythos* had once struggled with (and lost out to) the *logos* of Greek scientific reasoning, so now the medieval authors perceived in man's quest for individual knowledge a threat to religious and revealed truth. Indeed, this quest would become one of the main themes of medieval drama, and the reason is twofold: first, the society was emerging from medieval absolutism and moving toward the spirit of questioning that was soon to inspire the Renaissance and the Reformation; and second, the theatre itself was (and is) particularly well designed to portray such a quest and to celebrate the seeker. We get little of the Reformationist or Renaissance questioning here, of course, and none of the heroics of the free thinker; the medieval theatre was doggedly conservative—even anti-intellectual—and it unfailingly reflected a bias in favor of unthinking obedience. But we do get the topic, and with it a hint of the longing for intellectual independence latent in late medieval culture and literature.

God's visit to Adam after the eating of the fruit is as artless an interrogation scene as the drama provides. It conjures a vision of two Yorkshiremen meeting in a field to talk over a problem of poaching. However, the penalty is appropriately biblical:

GOD: Adam! Adam!
ADAM: Lord?
GOD: Where art thou?
     Yare! [Speak up!]
ADAM: I hear thee, Lord, and see thee nought.
GOD: Say, whereon is it long? [What's going
     on here?]
     This work—why has thou wrought?
ADAM: Lord, Eve made me do wrong.
     And to that breach me brought.
GOD: Say, Eve, why hast thou caused thy mate
     Eat fruit I told thee should hang there still,
     And commanded none of it to take?
EVE: A worm, Lord, enticed me theretill.
     Alas, that ever I did that deed so dill.

And God commands that the snake shall henceforth glide on its "womb" and that Adam and Eve shall henceforth "sweat and swink and travail" (sweat and toil and labor) for their food. Adam and Eve depart from Paradise, wringing their hands ("our hands may we wring") as the wagon rolls away.

The Fall of Man playlet requires three areas of action, presumably on three different levels—one where Satan dresses himself in a worm costume below Paradise; one where God enters; and finally, one to show a middle ground where God orders his angels to drive Adam and Eve after the Fall. There is also a tree in Paradise, from which Eve plucks the fruit. All of this indicates a staging of some complexity, if not grandeur. In no way should the visual effect of this staging be thought of as realistic, however. The visual elements of the medieval stage were highly symbolic—or "iconographic," as historians would say—and they were standardized in both meaning and appearance, with an economy of detail. The tree of knowledge, for example, was seen as a precursor of the cross on which Christ died, and the symbolic parallel was carried through in the staging as well as in the conceptualization of these plays. The importance of the cycle was in its totality and in the harmony of its elements, which focused always on the conclusion to which the cycle led—the passion of Christ, the harrowing of Hell, and the final judgment. The independent playlets were considered important only as they fit into the grand design of the total production and, implicitly, as they fit into the grand design of the Divine Source Himself.

In addition to its use of familiar symbols in the props and scenery, the medieval theatre clothed its actors in familiar dress (those playing Adam and Eve in The Fall playlet wore "naked suits" of flesh-colored, stockinglike material; later, in the Cain and Abel playlet, Adam and Eve were dressed in ordinary Yorkshire peasant garb), and the lines were spoken in the rural dialect that was the common vernacular of the audience. These features served to bring the world of the Bible into the here and now of medieval life. It was the *message* of the play that was important, not the artistry or historical accuracy of its presentation; thus, though elegance may have been desirable insofar as it represented hard work dedicated to God, the plays never aimed for verisimilitude. The Fall of Man playlet was not meant to create a remote or exotic mood; indeed, had it done so its content might have been overwhelmed. Rather, it was constructed to communicate a message, and whatever other information it conveyed was distinctly subordinate to that message.

The Crucifixion

The Crucifixion playlet was the pivotal one in all the cycle plays because it portrayed the central visual image of Christianity—Christ on the cross, as He appeared above the altar in every medieval church and cathedral in Europe—and at the same time dealt with the physical agony of Christ—the "Passion"—which bespoke the extent of His sacrifice for humanity. So central was this episode, in fact, that the name "passion plays" became a popular designation for the entire medieval religious theatre. The Crucifixion scene is the most intense moment of the one surviving passion play (inspired by the medieval cycle plays, but of later vintage), which is performed every ten years at Oberammergau in southern Germany; and indeed, many isolated Crucifixion plays are still performed at Eastertime in various parts of the world, including the United States. (These performances are often illegal, owing to the tendency of the actors to pursue undue realism, occasionally with calamitous results.)

The York Crucifixion playlet, thirty-fifth in the cycle, was performed in late afternoon and was staged on a wagon representing Calvary. It showed the torture of Christ by four soldiers, who both tied and nailed Him to the Cross, then lifted it into an erect position. The tying of the actor to the Cross was, of course, a sheer practical necessity, but the medieval author ingeniously made it part of the torture—in fact, the worst part:

FIRST SOLDIER: Put on that cord,
    And tug him to, by top and tail. . . .
    These cords have evil increased his
        pains. . . .
SECOND SOLDIER: Yea, asunder are both sinews and veins. . . .

This scene once again calls to mind the opening scene of *Prometheus,* in which the divine hero is chained to his place of torture by baser, more dull-witted attendants; and as in *Prometheus,* the majesty of Christ is conveyed primarily by His silence in the face of these terrible abuses. Only twice does Jesus speak: in two short, lovely, eloquent prayers that soar above the brutish exchange of the torturers to plead for all humankind. The dramatic achievement of this playlet is that it communicates the transcendence that is the essence of religious experience; Jesus, in less than twenty-five lines out of the playlet's three hundred, convincingly rises above evil, pain, intolerance, and the sheer wickedness of intentional indifference:

JESUS: Almighty God, my Father free,
    Let these matters be marked in mind;
    Thou bade that I should ready be
    For Adam's fall to be thus pined [tortured].
    Here to death I offer me,
    From Adam's sin to save mankind,
    And, my God, beseech I thee
    That man for me may favor find.
    God, from the fiend mankind defend,
    And give them wealth without an end,
    For I have naught else to crave.

Mark McManus is the crucified Jesus in this 1985 Royal National Theatre production of The Mysteries, *a somewhat modernized version (by Tony Harrison) of the cycle plays that retained the medieval language but employed contemporary costumes and music. It was staged environmentally in London's Cottlesoe Theatre with the audience at the foot of the cross, as well as above and around the action. (Photo: Michael Mayhew.)*

audience, for whose sake He suffers. It is a spiritual appeal that gains in eloquence by its simplicity and by its contrast to the bickering and fierce selfishness of the four tormentors:

SECOND SOLDIER: Give me this wedge; I shall it in drive.
FOURTH SOLDIER: Here is another yet on hand.
THIRD SOLDIER: Give it to me—look alive!
FIRST SOLDIER: Lay on then fast!
THIRD SOLDIER: Yes, I warrant
    There, now I'll thrive
    Now will this cross full stably stand
    And if he rave—it will not rive [tear apart].
FIRST SOLDIER: (*to* CHRIST) Say, sir, how likes you now
    This work that we have wrought?
FOURTH SOLDIER: We pray you tell us how
    You feel, if you faint not!
JESUS: All men that walk by way or street,
    Look well you see this body mine
    Behold my head, my hands, my feet,
    And fully feel now, while you're still fine,
    If any mourning may be meet,
    Or any misery marked as mine.
    My Father, that all bales may beet [ills may cure],
    Forgive these men that do me pine.
    What they work, know they nought.
    Therefore, my Father, I crave,
    Let not their sins be sought,
    But see their souls to save.
FIRST SOLDIER: Well! Hark! He jangles like a jay!
SECOND SOLDIER: Methink he patters like a pie [magpie]!
THIRD SOLDIER: He has been doing so all day,
    And made great moving of mercy.
FOURTH SOLDIER: Is this the same that did us say
    That he was God's Son almighty?

Then, wrangling over the disposition of Jesus' garments, the soldiers speak of moving off as the pageant wagon rolls away.

    The centrality of this playlet is temporal as

• In this, Jesus' first speech, He harks back to
• the tale of Adam and reveals that His own
• death will atone for the sins of this (bibli-
• cal and dramaturgical) predecessor. Also, like
• Aeschylus' Prometheus, He makes clear that
• He is the friend of humanity, the patron of the

well as spiritual. Temporally, it links the sin of presumption that is brought out in earlier playlets—in the Fall of Lucifer story and the story of Adam and Eve—with the salvation offered by Christ. And spiritually, it personifies forgiveness and redemption in the suffering Christ—that is, in the actual body of Christ, or Corpus Christi, as portrayed by a medieval performer assuming a priestlike function. Moreover, if the playlets that precede the Crucifixion are overwhelmingly cautionary in their moral messages, those that follow the Crucifixion resoundingly repudiate despair, thus setting the positive theme the complete cycle is intended to convey. For the medieval pageant was, above all else, a joyous celebration of faith and salvation and of the wholeness and purposefulness of temporal and spiritual life.

The personage of Christ in the medieval playlet is structurally similar to that of Prometheus in Aeschylus' play, but emotionally and spiritually the two are poles apart. Whereas Prometheus' heroism is expressed in pride, recklessness, and defiance, Jesus is portrayed by his medieval authors as a wholly gentle, beatific, and accessible individual. Moreover, whereas the Greek Prometheus suffers for a principle, the medieval Jesus suffers out of the purest *love*. One could hardly expect the anonymous and untrained authors of the medieval world to rival the verbal magnificence of Aeschylus. Nonetheless, the simple, kind, and exquisitely human words they gave to Jesus in the York Cycle leave a powerful impression even on modern audiences; and, when coupled with the staggering imagery and physicality of the Crucifixion's staging, they must have created a theatrical experience that the medieval visitor to York would remember for a lifetime.

The Judgment

The last playlet in the York Cycle portrayed Judgment Day, and almost certainly was performed very late in the day. One scholar has concluded that it could not possibly have begun earlier than 2:30 A.M.; if that is the case, some sort of artificial lighting must have been used. One can imagine how a pious audience must have looked forward to the final "deliverance" promised by this playlet after the long series of moral messages that led up to it.

As befits the conclusion of a Christian drama, it is Jesus who plays the central role in this playlet. After a long prologue in which God reviews the major events in the history of the universe (as illustrated by the preceding forty-seven playlets), Christ returns to earth in bodily form (again the Corpus Christi) to "deem dooms," that is, to pronounce judgments:

JESUS: This woeful world is brought to an
    end.
  My Father of Heaven, He wills it be.
  Therefore to earth now will I wend
  Myself to sit in majesty.
  To deem my dooms I will descend.
  This body will I bear with me.
  How it was tortured, man's Fall to mend,
  All mankind there shall it see.

Christ's vow that "all mankind" shall see his wounds in this final action of the play serves notice that what is to follow is a message intended for every member of the audience, an affirmation for the faithful and a warning for any souls who lurk about unconverted or who are dallying with impious ideas. It was no coincidence that the last station of the York procession, where this last of the hundreds of performances in the complete cycle took place, was situated on York's own judgment square, a public area known as "the Pavement," where York's real villains and criminals were publicly tried, sentenced, and hanged for their transgressions. Here the staged suffering of Christ, the "Passion" of God's only begotten Son, was to be held up for final evaluation by humanity—and for humanity's ultimate acknowledgment and support.

JESUS: Here may ye see my wounds wide,
The which I suffered for your misdeed,
Through heart and head, foot, hand, and
    hide,
Not for my guilt, but for your need.
Behold both body, back, and side,
How dear I bought your brotherhead!
These bitter pains did I abide
To buy you bliss, thus did I bleed.
My body was scourged without any skill.
As a thief cruelly did they me treat.
On a cross they hanged me on a hill,
Bloody and red, so I was beat
With a crown of thorns, and thrust full ill
This spear into my side was set;
My heart's blood spared they not to spill.
Man, for thy love would I not let [stop
    them].
Man, sure ought thee to quake,
This dreadful day this sight to see.
All this I suffered for thy sake:
Say, man, what suffered thou for me?

Here the action turns outward from the stage and onto the audience. "Man," as here addressed, is not a character in the play but the spectator who watches the production. The audience is asked to examine its own behavior and to measure its own actions against those of the "good souls" and the "bad souls" who appear in this staged judgment. Moreover, the audience is now asked to reckon its own standing in terms of the lessons conveyed in all the preceding playlets of the cycle.

Jesus offers salvation to the good souls, praising them with the words "when I was hungry, ye me fed," and explaining that any good deed done anywhere, to "any that need," is in fact a tribute to God and a token of the doer's salvation. Similarly, he attacks the bad souls:

JESUS: When I was sick and sorriest,

Ye visited me not, for I was poor;
When I in prison hard was stressed,
None of you looked how I did fare.
When I knew never where to rest,
With darts you drove me from your door.
But ever proudful then you pressed;
My flesh, my blood, ye oft forswore.
Clotheless when I was oft, and cold,
In need of you, went I full naked.
Nor house nor harbor, help nor hold
Had I from you, although I quaked.
My misery saw ye manifold;
And none of you my sorrow slaked,
But ever forsook me, young and old.
Therefore shall ye now be forsaked.

When the bad souls argue that they did no such things, that they never saw Jesus naked or harborless, Jesus responds substantially as he did to the good souls:

JESUS: Caitiffs, as oft as it betid [happened]
That needy folks asked in my name,
You heard them not, your ears ye hid,
Your help to them was not at home.
To me was that unkindness kid [shown].
Therefore ye bear this bitter blame;
To least or most, when it ye did
To me ye did the self and same.

Therefore, according to this conclusion at York, Christ is everywhere in human life, and goodness to other people is rewarded by divine salvation. The forty-eight pageants have added up to medieval life's great moral lesson, and as the final wagon departs and we hear and see (according to a final stage direction) "the melody of angels crossing from place to place," we are left with an indelible instruction concerning the realities of eternal life and the ordering of the human and divine cosmos of the Middle Ages.

Oberammergau passion play. *When an outbreak of plague devastated the Bavarian town of Oberammergau in 1633, the town citizens prayed to God for intervention, vowing to present a passion play every ten years if the dying would cease. It did, and the play has been performed in the village every tenth summer since, employing much of the local population and, in modern times, attracting a worldwide audience. The text, originally adapted from a fifteenth-century manuscript, has been revised often, most recently to eliminate anti-Semitic references. This photo is from the 1980 performance. (Photo: Courtesy German Information Center.)*

The York Cycle plays are not generally counted among the masterpieces of medieval dramatic literature—the *Second Shepherd's Play,* which has been performed at Wakefield, and the morality play *Everyman* are usually considered more prominently in English literary surveys. Nevertheless, in their total theatrical impact, the cycle plays well represent the most astonishing aspects of the medieval contribution to theatrical history. The integration of forty-eight separate plays (produced by at least as many separate guilds) into a harmonious whole was in itself an enormous achievement. Even more impressive is the fact that the story line, albeit traditional, was highly selective in achieving a sharp focus on a central, pivotal plot event; and the entire production was contrived to deliver a final, overarching ethical message. The sensational mode of production, with its combination of rolling carts, ambulatory casts of actors, multilevel staging effects, and extremely close audience-actor interplay, has never been duplicated to any significant degree in modern times—nor has the production organization, which drew upon every element of the social and theological order.

Something of the sheer joy of the enterprise reaches down to us across the centuries as we read the rustic texts and imagine the crowds and the bright wagons rolling through the springtime streets. For the medieval participants, this annual retelling of mythic history that so imaginatively combined literature and entertainment and religion and art must have been a transcendent experience.

. . . THE LARGER ECONOMIC AND POLITICAL VALUES . . .

If the Wakefield Cycle is examined as a medieval restatement of certain Bible stories, as primarily a religious event that took place once a year, then both the . . . meaning of the plays and their . . . human purposes are obscured. . . . Instead these plays must be seen as late-feudal articulations of temporally bound beliefs and institutions only secondarily touching on eternal themes. The Christianity of the Cycle is partisan conservative, a Christianity profoundly caught up in the larger economic and political values of a declining land-based society. The Wakefield Cycle demonstrates once again the genius of Christianity in making use of contemporary materials for a conservative statement as to the nature of men and women, people in general, and therefore, of course, late-medieval persons (in whose idiom and for whose pleasure the plays are written), in order to retain control over the largest possible number of people.

George H. Szanto

5

The
Shakespearean
Era

To many of us, the word *Renaissance* immediately summons images of Italian painting
and sculpture, but the Renaissance involved
all of Western Europe. In Spain the Renaissance was a time of exploration and conquest;
in France the Renaissance brought unparalleled developments in social organization
and philosophy; in England the Renaissance
gave us, above all, the theatre of William
Shakespeare.

THE RENAISSANCE

What exactly was the Renaissance? Literally,
the word means "rebirth," and, strictly speaking, it refers to the renewed interest in classical (Greek and Roman) civilization that bur-
geoned throughout Western Europe in the
fifteenth and sixteenth centuries. That definition, however, is too technical. More to the
point, the Renaissance was a grand revolution
in thinking, a new awareness of the individual's potential as a reasoning, creative, and
possibly heroic being. It was also a process of
mind expansion that grew out of medieval
times and has continued right up to the present day. The Renaissance is part of our lives—
in many ways, still coloring our behavior and
our judgments.

The emergence of a Renaissance was first celebrated in southern Europe, most notably in Italy, during the 1400s. At its center was humanism, which is the belief that was first expressed by the Greek philosopher Protagoras when he said, "Man is the measure of all things." *Man*—humanity—not God.

The Renaissance was not at all an atheistic era; in fact, it gave birth to some of the most wonderfully successful religious art and philosophy the Western world has ever seen. But the Renaissance also brought an end to capitulation to dogma and to humility concerning the human role in the universe. Perhaps the most apt visual symbol for the Renaissance is the drawing by Leonardo da Vinci that shows the human body as the basis for geometry; the human being embodied reason, order, and form—was, in short, the modern Apollo. And it was in Shakespeare's plays, more than in any other literature of the time, that this Apollo came to life.

SHAKESPEARE

Shakespeare. The name all but leaps up off the page. He is almost universally acclaimed as the greatest writer in the English language, the most famous Englishman who ever lived, and the greatest playwright, sonneteer, and dramatic poet in the separate histories of all those literary forms. He is now virtually deified in England, where his birthplace is a national shrine; his life has inspired innumerable biographies, novels, and plays, and his works constitute the basic repertoire of dozens of full-time professional theatres. He is the most frequently produced playwright in the world today, not only in England and America but also in Germany, Russia, and many other countries where his works are known only in translation. Actor, producer, director, commentator, and author—his consummate achievement as "man of the theatre" has set the standard for every dramatic artist since his time.

The New York Shakespeare Festival has, for many years, been able to attract some of the nation's best-known actors for its free summer Shakespeare performances in Central Park. Here Meryl Streep plays Katherine, and the late Raul Julia is Petruchio, in an NYSF production of The Taming of the Shrew. *(Photo: © George E. Joseph.)*

And yet, although Shakespeare towers above his age, the fifty-odd years of English drama his lifetime encompassed would have been a celebrated theatrical era even had he never existed. One playwright, Christopher Marlowe, born the same year as Shakespeare (1564), was equally as accomplished as the Bard of Avon at the moment of his tragic and untimely death in 1593. Ben Jonson, John Webster, and John Ford—all playwrights more or less contemporary with Shakespeare—

were also complementary to him, and their works are still presented with considerable regularity. But the list does not end there. Thomas Kyd, John Lyly, Robert Greene, George Chapman, John Marston, Thomas Dekker, Thomas Middleton, Cyril Tourneur, Francis Beaumont, John Fletcher, Philip Massinger, James Shirley—every one of these dramatists contributed works of lasting significance and enhanced the glory of that startlingly productive time in theatre history.

Sometimes it is called the Elizabethan Age, that period of drama in which Shakespeare played the central role. However, that term is misleading, since technically it refers only to the reign of Elizabeth I (1558–1603), whereas Shakespeare and his contemporaries flourished equally under the subsequent rule of King James I, in the so-called Jacobean era (1603–1625). Indeed, their heyday did not end until the Puritan revolution of 1642, when the theatres they built were burned to the ground and the theatrical tradition they had fostered was abruptly terminated. It seems most appropriate for our purposes, therefore, to forget about the names of the regal tenants and call this age for Shakespeare himself—for it is certain that "the Shakespearean era" betokens something of far more lasting significance than the skirmishes of princes, kings, armies, and religious despots.

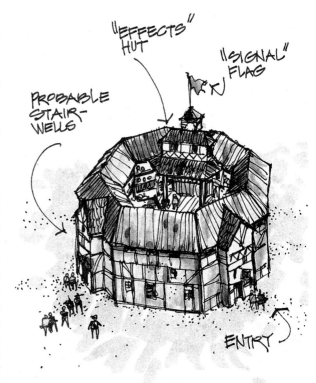

The first Globe Theatre. This conjectural view assumes The Globe to have been an octagonal structure. Inside, a corridor allowed access to various sections of the galleries. (Drawing: John von Szeliski.)

The Theatres

In Shakespeare's time there were almost a dozen London playhouses, most of them presenting plays regularly to large paying audiences, and at the same time providing a livelihood for dozens of professional acting companies and dramatic poets. It was a level of theatrical activity that was not to be duplicated in scope for more than two hundred years anywhere, and then only after London and the other capitals of Europe had increased their population by tenfold and more. The London playhouses of the sixteenth and seventeenth centuries were of two major types: outdoor "public" theatres and more intimate, indoor, "private" ones. Less is known about either type than we would wish, but enough documents have survived from those centuries to provide us with a general idea of how these theatres were constructed and a fairly good idea of what kind of experience awaited the Londoner who set out to attend a Shakespearean play in the early 1600s.

The big public theatres were among the greatest attractions of Elizabethan London. There were nine of them: Shakespeare's Globe, plus The Swan, The Rose, The Theater, The Fortune, The Curtain, and The Hope. All were located outside the city limits, for the

Puritan city officials forbade the public presentation within the city of "unchaste fables, lascivious devices, shifts of cozenage & matters of like sort" which allegedly served as meeting places for "horse stealers, whoremongers, cozeners, conny-catching persons, practicers of treason & such." These theatre buildings were impressive wooden structures that towered over the residences in London's northern and southern suburbs and displayed a brilliance of theatrical architecture that has never been surpassed. Each was built on three levels, enclosed on all sides but only partially roofed to leave a large central expanse open to the sky. The walls surrounded a "yard," at one end of which the players performed on a raised stage. The stage was for the most part backed by a *tiring house* (literally, "attiring house," or dressing room), which provided actors a variety of entries to the stage: windows, balconies, and two or more large doors. Below the stage was a "cellarage," with access via a 4-by-4-foot trap door; above was the gilded "heavens"—a projected semicanopy from which, occasionally, actors descended via pulleys. Virtually all areas not occupied by the stage and tiring house were used to accommodate spectators, as many as three thousand of them, according to one account. They sat in the galleries, stood in the yard (where they were called "groundlings"), and sometimes even perched on the stage itself.

There has been a great deal of conjecture as to the exact size, appearance, and use of these public playhouses; hence, any reconstruction—including that presented here—must be regarded as hypothetical. The documentary and archeological evidence is distressingly skimpy: a single contemporary drawing—indeed, a foreigner's *re*drawing of a friend's lost illustration—of the Swan Theatre's presumed interior; some postage-stamp-sized engravings of the exteriors of the Rose, Globe, and Hope theatres on illustrated maps of London at the time; recently (1989) uncovered foundation fragments of The Rose and The Globe; and two surviving building contracts, one for The

The Globe reconstructed. This 1996 photograph shows the in-progress reconstruction of Shakespeare's Globe Theatre of 1600. Built very near the original Globe's foundations in London's Bankside district, the theatre and adjoining Shakespeare Centre is scheduled to host, by 1997, annual summer seasons of Shakespearean performances, plus a year-round schedule of lectures and conferences. A smaller, indoor theatre named for Jacobean designer Inigo Jones is also part of the project, which was initiated, with extraordinary fervor and persistence, by the late Sam Wanamaker, American actor and Shakespeare enthusiast. (Photo: Robert Cohen.)

Fortune and one for The Hope. The Fortune contract is particularly frustrating in that it refers to an "attached diagram" which has never been found, and it further informs the builder that the stage proportions should be "contrived and fashioned like unto the Stage of the playhouse called the Globe." Of the construction of The Globe, unfortunately, we know virtually nothing except that it was built at least in part from the timbers of the dismantled theater.

The 1989 excavations, limited as they were (both sites remain partly underneath modern office buildings), have stimulated a renewed interest in perfecting our understanding of both The Rose and The Globe theatres. Enough of The Rose's perimeter wall was revealed to make an educated guess as to its exterior shape and size (polygonal, about 74 feet in diameter) and as to the shape and size of the stage (an "elongated hexagon," tapering from 36 feet 9 inches at the rear, to 26 feet 10 inches at the front, with a depth of 15 feet 6 inches).[1] It also appears that the yard of The Rose was enlarged at some point, with the stage and tiring house moved back to accommodate more "groundlings." Less has been found, however, at The Globe excavation, although foundations for a stair turret have been revealed—which might provide further evidence as to how and where the audience was admitted to the yard and to the gallery seats above. As to the exterior size and shape of The Globe, estimates range anywhere from a 64-by-80-foot rectangle to a 100-foot-diameter polygon. Further excavations, although not possible with the current constructions on the site, might someday refine these estimates.

We can, however, add to our knowledge of these theatres with some well-established presumptions. We can presume, for example, that the public playhouse capitalized on three pre-existing architectural or staging elements: the medieval innyard, the trestle stage, and the pageant wagon. Inns were a common sight all over medieval England, both on the rural roadways and in the towns and villages; even London had its inns that, in addition to providing wayfarers with food and lodging, were local gathering places and centers of public activity and entertainment. The typical English inn was U-shaped and stood two or three stories high; the semi-enclosed yard was a perfect place for traveling players to set up their stage and perform, and the balconies that extended from the upper stories afforded a perfect vantage from which to view their performance.

Putting on a play in an innyard meant little more than arriving and setting up a stage,

A portable trestle stage of the kind that might be set up in an Elizabethan innyard. (Drawing: John von Szeliski.)

which itself would consist of little more than a series of boards mounted and secured upon trestles or sawhorses ("the boards," of course, has since become a metaphor for the theatre itself). The inn doors probably served as stage entrances, the inn windows as stage balconies. The combination of three-storied inn, yard, and platform stage was doubtless carried forth in the permanent public theatre (in fact, we know that at least two public theatres had removable trestle stages instead of permanent ones, to allow bear-baiting entertainments to alternate with play productions on a daily basis). Also carried over from the earlier time was the general procedure for audience

[1]Dimensions from Franklin J. Hildy, ed., *New Issues in the Reconstruction of Shakespeare's Theatre* (New York: Peter Lang, 1990), p. 63.

accommodation, with some patrons free to wander in the yard during the performance and others taking more privileged (and higher priced) gallery seats above.

However, the simple trestle stage clearly would have been insufficient for the staging of Shakespeare's plays and for those of many of his contemporaries. Thus the public playhouse was developed beyond the innyard staging. One addition, we know, was the tiring house; another was apparently some sort of balconied and draped architectural unit that has long baffled (but not silenced!) the historians as to its placement and function. Most of the evidence available to us today leads to the supposition that it was a structure—usually called a pavilion—that stood at the rear of the Shakespearean platform, butting against the facade of the tiring house and permitting entrances through curtains or other openings located in it. This pavilion seems to have been modeled on the pageant wagon, and apparently it served much the same purpose: it created upper-level acting areas and gave the director the option of closing off interior spaces by drapery, allowing sudden and dramatic "reveals" when a curtain was drawn open before a tableau of actors.

To these three medieval influences that can be seen in the Elizabethan public playhouse— the innyard, the trestle stage, and the wheelless pageant wagon, or pavilion—we should perhaps add one more architectural carryover: the Roman amphitheatre. At least that is how The Swan was described by the Dutchman whose illustration of that theatre survives. This Dutchman, Johannes de Witt by name, explained that The Swan's columns were "painted in such excellent imitation of marble that it is able to deceive even the most cunning," and he went on to say that in form, scale, and splendor the theatre resembled a "Roman work," an "amphitheatre of noteable beauty . . . magnificent." This disclosure is not so surprising when we recall that this, of course, was the time of the Renaissance, when it was not thought sufficient merely to de-

> ## MORE FOR OUR MONEY
>
> Shakespeare seems better in performance than anyone else because he gives us more, moment for moment, for our money. This is due to his genius, but also to his technique. The possibilities of free verse on an open stage enabled him to cut the inessential detail and the irrelevant realistic action: in their place he could cram sounds and ideas, thoughts and images which make each instant into a stunning mobile.
>
> Peter Brook

velop and exceed the standards of the Middle Ages—it was necessary to reach back to antiquity and outshine the Caesars themselves.

That we know more of the spirit than of the precise details of these public theatres is not a catastrophe, for it is the spirit rather than the theatre measurements that most clearly distinguishes the dramatic art of Shakespeare and his contemporaries. The fact is that in the Shakespearean era there was no formal aesthetic which demanded that plays be written or staged in a certain way, and Shakespeare's own plays were performed in many types of theatres, often in rapid rotation. In addition to using the three public theatres operated at various times by his company—The Theater, The Curtain, and The Globe—Shakespeare produced his works at "private theatres" and at court. The so-called private theatres, like the public theatres, were open to the general public; however, because they charged a considerably higher admission price, they attracted a more elite audience. Also, they were indoor theatres, rectangular and candlelit, quite different from the round, octagonal, or square public theatres open to the sky. The court theatre, of course, was private. Shakespeare was often called upon to provide entertainment to Queen Elizabeth (*A Midsummer*

Modern dress is common in contemporary productions of Shakespeare, demonstrating both the immediacy and universality of his plays. Adrian Hall's 1990 staging of King Lear, *American Repertory Theatre; scenery by Eugene Lee, costumes by Catherine Zuber. (Photo: Richard Feldman.)*

Night's Dream is thought to have been written upon her commission), and his plays were frequently remounted on the shortest of notice in royal palaces, particularly at Whitehall for the annual Twelfth Night Revels. A queen's officer, the Master of Revels, was charged specifically with overseeing these royal entertainments, to which all theatrical companies in London sought invitation.

Finally, Shakespeare's theatre was also a touring company, and few seasons passed without travels to entertain at the Inns of Court, at college halls at Oxford and Cambridge, and at various castles, manor houses, and palaces in the country. During times of plague, the entire theatrical season was "on the road," for public gatherings in or about the city were forbidden by law. For these rea-

sons, Shakespearean stagecraft is marked by flexibility rather than rigidity; plays were written to be staged and restaged in a variety of locales and settings, and no particular stage architecture or staging practice could be considered fixed in the drama of the times, except insofar as it promoted a bold, fluid, vigorous theatre centering on the actor and the spoken text.

The Players

Traveling players were commonly seen throughout Europe as the religious drama of the Middle Ages gave way to the dramatic entertainments of the Renaissance. These were the players (actors) who performed on hastily

erected trestle stages in the medieval innyards, in the public streets and squares, and in the castles and country manors of the nobility. Their performances were made exceptionally hasty when local authorities from time to time outlawed dramatic exhibitions, whether religious or secular. Often, to protect themselves against the whims of provincial aldermen and to guarantee winter employment, these troupes sought and received patronage from celebrated nobles of the realm. By 1486 the Earls of Essex had become patrons to such a company, known as Essex's Men, and not long thereafter Henry VII himself extended his sovereignty over a troupe of four players who were specifically commissioned to provide the royal entertainment.

The troupes of players that came together in England during the sixteenth century were talented and skilled performers, fully as adept as their more famous Italian counterparts, the performers of the *commedia dell'arte*, at singing, dancing, juggling, acrobatics, poetic recitation, and grand rhetorical set speeches (see the discussion at the end of this chapter). They carried their plays with them in their heads, owning them as magicians own their rabbits. The "players" portrayed in *Hamlet*—that is, the characters within that play who come to perform at the Danish court—aptly represent the English traveling actors of that time: men able to spin out speeches from a number of plays, to present any given play at a moment's notice, and even to alter plays to suit a patron's desire (as when Hamlet asks the players to revise "The Murder of Gonzago" for his own purposes).

The troupes were all male. Women never appeared on the English stage during Shakespeare's lifetime nor, indeed, for some fifty years thereafter. The female parts were played by boys who were apprenticed to the troupe. The whole group traveled as a family, rarely staying long in any one location, but shifting between court and city and country as economic, social, and legal conditions dictated. For although they could hole up for a time in

Boys played the female parts in all the plays of Shakespeare's era, which lent a special irony to those Shakespearean comedies where women characters, played by boys, pretended to be men. Now, of course, women's parts are (customarily) played by women, as in Andrei Serban's 1989 production of Twelfth Night, *where Cherry Jones plays the Lady Viola (who is pretending to be the male Cesario) and Diane Lane plays Lady Olivia. American Repertory Theatre, with postmodern scenery by Derek McLane and costumes by Catherine Zuber. (Photo: Richard Feldman.)*

a London inn, such as the Boar's Head in Cheapside (Falstaff's famous tavern), sooner or later the plague or the city aldermen or declining audiences would drive them out. Eventually these troupes became known all over England and even on the Continent. Certainly many troupes visited Shakespeare's birthplace, Stratford-upon-Avon, about 100 miles northwest of London; and tradition has it that some time in the 1580s the young Will Shakespeare simply followed one of them out.

There were two particularly celebrated troupes of players in Shakespeare's own time. The first was the Lord Admiral's Men, a group that included an enterprising (if somewhat unscrupulous) manager-producer named Philip Henslowe, a celebrated tragic actor named Edward Alleyn, and the great playwright Christopher Marlowe. The Admiral's Men were generally in residence at one of the theatres managed by Henslowe, principally The Rose and The Fortune. At one time or another, virtually every promising English dramatist of the time either wrote for the Admiral's Men or collaborated in a play that was produced by them. Shakespeare was no exception: two of his early plays (*Titus Andronicus* and one part of *Henry VI*) fell into the hands of the greatly ambitious Henslowe.

The second troupe, to which Shakespeare belonged for all but the earliest portion of his professional career, was unique in Shakespeare's time and has never been duplicated since. This troupe not only owned its own theatre, but its overall acting skills also made it the most accomplished company in the land; and, of course, Shakespeare's plays gave it a superior original repertoire. Known as the Chamberlain's Men under the rule of Queen Elizabeth, this troupe came under the personal patronage of King James I upon his succession in 1603 and was known thereafter as the King's Men. Shakespeare was a member of this company from at least 1594 onward, as actor, playwright, and investor. He consistently gave the group one or two plays a year to produce as the core of its repertoire. More-

THE ZEST FOR LIFE . . .

The key to life is for Shakespeare, as it is for his age, the assertion of individuality. He creates highly individualized characters more abundantly than any other dramatist, and the conflicts in his plays are invariably produced by the exertions of the human will. Man struggles against man, and not against Fate, god, heredity, or glands. Shakespearean drama is drama of the individual will. . . .

The zest for life so abundantly felt in a dynamic age pulsates in every page of his work. Laughter and tears, concentrated ambition and wasted motion, serious employment and the blithe pursuit of pleasure, jostle each other in the same work. Intensity is all! His characters are nearly all active personalities, from the heroes who win crowns or glory to the vagrants who cut purses or revel in the stews, from passionate queens to promiscuous "queans" and nubile girls who dress in boys' clothes to follow the men of their desire.

John Gassner

over, he was a part owner of the troupe itself and of its real estate holdings; his total share in the enterprise varied over the years but was always substantial. The Chamberlain's Men had no need to arrange playing space with an outside producer like Henslowe, for they owned their own space: the first theatre they had was The Theater, built in 1576; subsequently, they owned the famous Globe, which was built in 1599. Further, after The Globe was destroyed by fire in 1613, the company was rich enough to rebuild it entirely, in a form grander than that of any other private building then in London. And finally, in 1623, this company crowned its achievements with the posthumous publication of the collected plays of Shakespeare. It was a

THE BOY COMPANIES

An oddity of the Shakespearean era—odd because it seems to have had no counterpart in any other period—was the presence on the London theatrical scene of several acting companies composed entirely of young boys. These companies began as outgrowths of school programs, but by the 1580s many of them had become partly or wholly professional. And at one point they seemed to pose a serious threat to the adult companies—as Shakespeare himself makes clear in an extended comment in *Hamlet:*

HAMLET: Do [the players] hold the same estimation they did when I was in the city? Are they so follow'd?
ROSENCRANTZ: No indeed are they not.
HAMLET: How comes it? do they grow rusty?
ROSENCRANTZ: Nay, their endeavor keeps in the wonted pace; but there is, sir, an aery [bird's nest] of children, little eyases [nestlings], that cry out on the top of question, and are most tyrannically clapp'd for 't. These are now the fashion, and so berattle the common stages—so they call them—that many wearing rapiers are afraid of goose-quills and dare scarce come thither.

One of these companies operated out of the Chapel Royal (the "Chapel Boys"), another out of St. Paul's ("Paul's Boys"). These and other boy companies performed adult dramas—some of which were written expressly for them—in a variety of indoor theatres, including the Blackfriars before it was taken over by Shakespeare's company in 1608. They were often in trouble with the local authorities and encountered much hostility from adult theatre companies and from rival boy companies; moreover, they were faced with the inevitable problem of their participants' growing up. After 1610 one finds no mention of them; the best of their artists had been absorbed into the adult theatre, and their stages were taken over by the new "private" theatre movement that came into prominence at about that time.

signally productive union of performing and literary artistry and economic self-ownership.

The Plays

And what plays these players of the Shakespearean era carried about with them! Gone, almost without a trace, were the religious playlets of the Middle Ages; for in fact the cycle plays had been legally forbidden by Queen Elizabeth in 1559, and thereafter only one Elizabethan play of any note, George Peele's *The Love of King David and Fair Bethsabe* (1599), was to treat a biblical theme. Gone too were the rural settings, the irregular rhyming verse, and the domestic environments of the medieval shepherd's plays and moral allegories. In their stead, playwrights wrote of exotic locales all over the world, of settings and times befitting the imagination of the new and intellectually emerging Londoner, and of tales calculated to thrill with discovery, perspective, and awe.

Much as the early film directors exploited history and geography in the first cinema epics of the present century, so the Renaissance playwright of sixteenth-century England roamed far and wide in searching for subject matter. The great plays of the years immediately preceding Shakespeare's meteoric rise were set in distant parts of Europe and Asia—

The Spanish Tragedy by Kyd; Marlowe's two-part epic concerning a Scythian hero, *Tamburlaine the Great;* Thomas Preston's antique tragedy (perhaps England's first), *The Life of Cambises, King of Persia*. And Shakespeare's plays also were set in distant times and places—either well back in history, like his magnificent eight-part chronicle of the wars of York and Lancaster, or well beyond England's shores in locales such as Verona, Venice, Cyprus, Rome, Denmark, Navarre, Athens, Egypt, Padua, Sicily, and Bohemia. The Renaissance was not the age to revere the commonplace or the close-to-home; it was the time of Drake and Magellan, of the first explorations and settlements of America, and of Copernicus and Galileo—a time of courage, curiosity, adventure, and discovery.

The Elizabethan reign was a time of international awareness. Nationalism was still freshly minted from the scrap of the Holy Roman Empire; and cultural, political, and economic ties between the European nations were tightly secured and enmeshed. Literature in particular showed a penchant for moving across boundaries; some plays and novellas were translated into foreign languages almost as soon as they were produced. Not only did Shakespeare (and his fellow playwrights) take most of his plots from foreign sources, but he also frequently peppered his dialogue with foreign phrases, which his audience was expected at least partially to comprehend. Indeed, the fact that Shakespeare's *Henry V* remains today the only significant English play to have an entire scene written in a foreign language (French) bespeaks the tremendously cosmopolitan flavor of the theatre of the age.

Thousands of English plays were written and performed between the first production of Preston's *Cambises* in 1561 and the legally mandated closing of the theatres at the onset of civil war in 1642. Philip Henslowe's Admiral's Men produced twenty-one new plays in a single year—and his was but one of many troupes. Henslowe, a man of great pragmatic and commercial sense, if not of demonstrable aesthetic sensitivity, maintained a stable of authors not unlike that of the mid-twentieth-century Hollywood film studio. Most of these men were continually mortgaged to Henslowe's operation by the threat of debtor's prison, and they therefore had strong reasons to make themselves productive. They commonly worked in collaboration—sometimes as many as five to a play—and virtually all the dramatists of the time took part at least occasionally in such joint ventures.

Of those thousands of plays, hundreds survive. History has not always selected with care, of course, and many of the survivors are quite wretched. The best, however, are among the world's masterpieces of dramatic literature. Taken as a whole, the best and the worst, the drama of the Shakespearean era forms a vast pattern of documentation for a period in history that never ceases to amaze us with its vigor, its openness, its lyricism and love of beauty, its intellectual complexity, and, at the best junctures, its profundity.

The original published versions of the plays that survive bear little resemblance to the carefully edited and annotated versions we commonly see today. Dramatic publication in the Shakespearean era tended to be a shabby venture, often bordering on the illegal. Since plays were owned by the companies that commissioned them (or purchased them) and since there was no copyright law to protect the interests of the author, neither author nor producing company stood to gain anything by publication; therefore, it was usually only "stolen and surreptitious" copies of the major plays, including many by Shakespeare, that turned up in single-play "quarto" editions. Some of these copies are believed to have been pure piracies, consisting mainly of remembered and transcribed dialogue gleaned from the recollections of former actors. Others were

Shakespeare virtually invented the genre of history play, which dramatizes—sometimes closely and sometimes freely—crucial periods of history. Right: Shakespeare's Henry V—shown in a 1994 Alabama Shakespeare Festival staging—details England's great warrior king of the early 1400s, almost two hundred years before Shakespeare's time. The play contains some of Shakespeare's most heroic rhetoric and is frequently staged today. Below: Shakespeare's later Henry VIII is more concerned with the intricate diplomacy of Church and State (and the royal family) during the reign of England's most recent king—and the father of Elizabeth I. Though Henry V is considered the better play today, Henry VIII arguably held greater relevance for its initial audience. François Giroday, center, is Cardinal Wolsey in this Utah Shakespearean Festivalstaging of 1995. (Photos: Courtesy Alabama and Utah Shakespeare festivals.)

A DEMOCRATIC AUDIENCE

Despite the richness of its language and the sumptuousness of its costumes, the English theatre of the Shakespearean era charged a remarkably low admission price: it cost a mere penny, which was no more than the price of a quart of beer or an Elizabethan newspaper. The cheapest London dinner cost three times as much, and a quart of Falstaffian sack (sherry) eight times; thus the cost of attending a Shakespearean premiere—and standing up in the pit, to be sure—was roughly the same as the cost of going to a university "workshop" production in America today or seeing an afternoon movie at a second-run house offering early-bird discounts. This brought theatregoing well within the range of virtually all Londoners, with the result that the typical audience was an amazingly diverse collection encompassing every social stratum, as John Davies noted in an epigram in 1595:

> For, as we see at all the playhouse doors,
> When ended is the play, the dance, and
>   song,
> A thousand townsmen, gentlemen, and
>   whores,
> Porters and serving-men together throng.

Much of the breadth and vigor of Shakespeare's art can be accounted for by the nature of the audience he had to please, which included laborers and intelligentsia, merchants and courtiers, farmers' sons and earls. To succeed in the public theatre of Shakespeare's day, every play had to have at least something for the "groundlings" (the standing audience in the pit) as well as something for the "gentlemen's rooms" (the privileged and higher-priced segregated seating in the gallery).

---

probably printed from pilfered manuscripts. Not until the time of Shakespeare's death, in 1616, did an author undertake to supervise a publication of his own collected "Works": this was Ben Jonson, the Bard's younger contemporary. Shakespeare's own "Folio" of collected plays, as edited by two shareholders and fellow actors in his company, followed in 1623.

The plays of the era were of many kinds: tragedies, comedies, tragicomedies, chronicle or "history" plays, city plays, domestic dramas, and elegant court masques. The predominant language structure was verse, most notably the so-called blank verse, which is written in unrhymed iambic pentameter (a ten-syllable line with stress on the second, fourth, sixth, eighth, and tenth syllables). However, some works were written exclusively in prose, and in general there was a movement during the era away from verse and toward prose. Also present in many plays were songs, sonnets, and rhymed couplets. Some writers, including Shakespeare, even made use of the alliterative "doggerel" style of the Middle Ages, particularly in plays written in the Elizabethan era. Throughout the times, dramatic actors were known as "poets," a perhaps significant usage.

The plays were staged boldly and rapidly on the stages of the public theatres (and presumably on indoor stages as well), and except in court masques, there was little scenery as we know it today. Instead, the permanent architectural features of the stages were worked into the action. There was much coming and going—through the tiring-house doors; in, out, around, and above the pavilion; through the trap door on the stage; and, via pulleys, to and from the "heavens" above. Stage properties, however, were apparently in common use. A surviving inventory maintained by Philip Henslowe lists the following properties and set pieces: trees, rocks, mossy banks, stee-

SHAKESPEARE AND MARLOWE

Christopher Marlowe, born in the same year as Shakespeare (1564), was actually the more successful of the two rival playwrights at the time of his death in 1593. His mastery of the blank verse form—which Ben Jonson termed "Marlowe's mighty line"—paved the way for the grandeur of Shakespearean dramatic poetry. Marlowe received a clerical and classical education at Canterbury, where he was born, and at Cambridge University, before he moved on to stun London with his powerful two-part tragedy, *Tamburlaine the Great,* in 1587–88. The exotic theatricality Marlowe imparted to this tale of a barbaric Scythian warlord made it an epic adventure for the stage, especially as enacted by the thunderous tragedian Edward Alleyn. *The Tragedy of Dr. Faustus,* Marlowe's masterpiece, followed in 1588, again with Alleyn in the title role, and soon became one of the most performed plays of the era. Faustus's closing speech, as he yields his soul to the devil Mephistopheles, is one of the supreme creations of English dramatic verse:

(*The clock strikes eleven.*)
FAUSTUS: Ah, Faustus,
Now hast thou but one bare hour to live,
And then thou must be damned
   perpetually!
Stand still, you ever-moving spheres of
   heaven,
That time may cease, and midnight never
   come;

Fair Nature's eye, rise, rise again and
   make
Perpetual day; or let this hour be but
A year, a month, a week, a natural day,
That Faustus may repent and save his
   soul!
O lente, lente, currite noctis equi!
The stars move still, time runs, the clock
   will strike,
The Devil will come, and Faustus must be
   damned.
Oh, I'll leap up to my God! Who pulls me
   down?
See, see where Christ's blood streams in
   the firmament!
One drop would save my soul—half a
   drop: ah, my Christ!
Ah, rend not my heart for naming of my
   Christ!
Yet will I call on him: O, spare me,
   Lucifer!—
Where is it now? 'tis gone; and see where
   God
Stretcheth out his arm, and bends his ire-
   ful brows!
Mountain and hills come, come and fall
   on me,
And hide me from the heavy wrath of
   God!
No! no!
Then will I headlong run into the earth;
Earth gape! O, no, it will not harbor me!
You stars that reigned at my nativity,
Whose influence hath allotted death and
   hell,
Now draw up Faustus like a foggy mist

ples, stairs, and "the city of Rome" (presumably this last was a painted cloth, but possibly it was a sign or a stage piece). Costuming reflected little concern for historical realism; however, it was apparently splendid. Numerous foreign visitors commented admiringly on the opulence of the English costumes, and it is believed that many of the clothes were donated from the wardrobes of noble pa-

trons and supporters. The performers were thoroughgoing professionals—full-time practicers of their art—and many of them developed brilliant rhetorical skills to match the verbal sophistication of the plays.

It is extremely doubtful that the audiences in Shakespeare's time expected much in the way of long, pregnant pauses or studiously projected "moments of truth." Two of the

Into the entrails of yon laboring clouds,
That when you vomit forth into the air,
My limbs may issue from their smoky
   mouths,
So that my soul may but ascend to
   heaven,
      (*The clock strikes the half hour.*)
Ah, half the hour is past! 'twill all be past
   anon!
O God!
If thou wilt not have mercy on my soul,
Yet for Christ's sake whose blood hath
   ransomed me,
Impose some end to my incessant pain;
Let Faustus live in hell a thousand years—
A hundred thousand, and at last be saved!
O, no end is limited to damned souls!
Why wert thou not a creature wanting
   soul?
Or why is this immortal that thou hast?
Ah, Pythagoras' *metempsychosis!* were that
   true,
This soul should fly from me, and I be
   changed
Unto some brutish beast! all beasts are
   happy,
For, when they die,
Their souls are soon dissolved in
   elements;
But mine must live, still to be plagued in
   hell.
Curst be the parents that engendered me!
No, Faustus: curse thyself; curse Lucifer
That deprived thee of the joys of heaven.
      (*The clock strikes twelve.*)
O, it strikes, it strikes! Now, body, turn
to air,
Or Lucifer will bear thee quick to hell.
      (*Thunder and lightning*)
O soul, be changed into little water-
   drops.
And fall into the ocean—ne'er be found.
My God! my God! look not so fierce on
   me!
      Enter DEVILS.
Adders and serpents, let me breathe
   awhile!
Ugly hell, gape not! come not, Lucifer!
I'll burn my books!—Ah
   Mephistopheles!
      Exeunt

Marlowe was active in political life (he apparently engaged in official espionage for Queen Elizabeth), and when he was killed in a tavern brawl there was some suspicion that he had been assassinated. He was twenty-nine years old at the time, the most celebrated writer in London and a highly controversial figure in town. The strange circumstances of his life and death continue to engage researchers today; it has even been suggested, although on only the flimsiest of evidence, that Marlowe's death was fabricated and that he continued to live and write underground, issuing his plays under the name of an otherwise undistinguished actor named William Shakespeare. This speculation, it should be made clear, has been rejected by virtually all serious scholars.

most notable characteristics of the drama of Shakespeare's time—and of the theatre that presented it—were action and boldness: robust activity and vigorous lyricism. The swordplay scene was as common on the English stage as the shoot-out scene is in action films of today; *wordplay* was pervasive. The soliloquy, a speech addressed directly to the audience, was generally an occasion for self-debate or self-prodding rather than for meditation on a theme. Generally speaking, there was little introspection in Elizabethan drama, and it is partly for that reason that when it did appear (as in Macbeth's "To-morrow and to-morrow and to-morrow" soliloquy and in several other plays written by Shakespeare; see box on Shakespeare's soliloquies), it tended to gain a lot of attention for its author. Even

SHAKESPEARE'S SOLILOQUIES

Although the dramatic soliloquy is not unique to Shakespeare or even to the Shakespearean era, it is universally associated with Shakespeare's great tragic heroes. It is one of the principal means by which he created a direct relationship between his characters and his audience, and some of the most famous lines in the English language are contained in these character-to-audience communications.

Typically, Shakespeare's soliloquies deal with major decisions and challenges faced by a character in a time of crisis and change:

> HAMLET: To be, or not to be, that is the
>   question:
> Whether 'tis nobler in the mind to suffer
> The slings and arrows of outrageous
>   fortune,
> Or to take arms against a sea of troubles,
> And by opposing, end them. . . .

This, the most quoted of all soliloquies, is an open debate on the issue of how one ought to respond to dangerous occasions; it epitomizes the challenge of maturity and, in Hamlet's case, manliness.

King Lear's decision to relinquish the prerogatives of power is also eloquently expressed in soliloquy as he looks back with remorse on his long life and vows to seek a greater understanding of his fellow beings:

> KING LEAR: Poor naked wretches, where-
>   soe'er you are,
> That bide the pelting of this pitiless
>   storm,
> How shall your houseless heads and un-
>   fed sides,
> Your loop'd and window'd raggedness,
>   defend you
> From seasons such as these? O, I have
>   ta'en
> Too little care of this! Take physic, pomp,
> Expose thyself to feel what wretches feel,

> That thou mayst shake the superflux to
>   them,
> And show the heavens more just.

And Lear follows his self-directed advice by ripping off his garments, determined to share the suffering of the common poor whom he has carelessly ruled.

Macbeth, at the end of the play in which he is the title character, confronts the meaning of life and death. Told by a messenger of the demise of his wife, his partner in murder, Macbeth turns away to share his bitter grief with us:

> MACBETH: She should have died
>   hereafter;
> There would have been a time for such a
>   word.
> To-morrow, and to-morrow, and to-
>   morrow,
> Creeps in this petty pace from day to day,
> To the last syllable of recorded time;
> And all our yesterdays have lighted fools
> The way to dusty death. Out, out, brief
>   candle!
> Life's but a walking shadow, a poor
>   player,
> That struts and frets his hour upon the
>   stage,
> And then is heard no more. It is a tale
> Told by an idiot, full of sound and fury,
> Signifying nothing.

This is no mere cry of self-pity; it is a poetic commentary on human mortality—a reality that concerns not merely Macbeth and his wife, but Shakespeare and us as well. Through the convention of the soliloquy, Shakespeare steps across four centuries to strike chords in our contemporary consciousness. And inasmuch as a "poor player" is both Shakespeare's metaphor for life and his instrument for delivering that metaphor, this particular soliloquy engages us on several levels simultaneously, thrusting us deeply into infinite regressions in both time and human perception.

melancholy—a favorite Elizabethan theme—was usually pursued with great vigor, as when the lovesick (and melancholic) Duke Orsino begins Shakespeare's *Twelfth Night* with the cry "If music be the food of love, play on. Give me excess of it." Jokes, puns, taunts, challenges, curses, vows, crudities, and ringing declarations fill the Elizabethan drama with a liveliness and an energy of language that knows no equivalent in any other period of English writing.

THE PLAYS OF SHAKESPEARE

Shakespeare himself was the author of some thirty-seven plays, by general count, although some of these may in fact have been collaborations (particularly those written at the very beginning and the end of his career). At the time of the first publication of his collected dramatic works, these plays were divided into three categories: tragedies, comedies, and histories. It now seems obvious that this division served primarily as an editorial convenience that need not be perpetuated. Shakespeare was born, raised, and married in Stratford-upon-Avon, in Warwickshire, and is believed to have gone to London in the late 1580s, as an actor. He is first cited as a playwright in a deprecatory reference from 1592; by 1598 he was being hailed as a poet comparable to Ovid, as the "most excellent" writer of comedy and tragedy in England, as one in whose "fine-filed phrase" the Muses themselves would speak if the Muses were to speak English: the "mellifluous & hony-tongued Shakespeare." In 1610, or thereabouts, he returned to Stratford and to his wife and two surviving children, leaving his great repertoire of *Hamlet, King Lear, Richard III, As You Like It, Othello, Julius Caesar, Much Ado About Nothing*, and the rest, as the mainstay of his company in London. In all, it had taken him about twenty years to create the whole body of works that were to constitute his priceless literary legacy to the world.

ROMEO AND JULIET

Romeo *and Juliet* well exemplifies the special qualities of the English Renaissance drama and of Shakespearean tragedy during the Elizabethan era. It is certainly one of Shakespeare's most famous plays; it seems the world in general agrees with the Prince's conclusion in its closing lines:

> For never was a story of more woe
> Than this of Juliet and her Romeo.

It is indeed woeful, this tragic tale of love that has become virtually a metaphor for adolescent romance and youthful passion; it is also lyrical, bustling, active, and intense. It is one of Shakespeare's early plays, possibly his first tragedy (with the exception, perhaps, of the horrific *Titus Andronicus*). The play is based on an original novella (short story) by the Italian writer Matteo Bandello; Shakespeare probably read the novella in an English verse translation by Arthur Brooke, which was itself based on an intermediate French version. Dozens of other versions, including at least one dramatic one, circulated in England and on the Continent for at least thirty years before Shakespeare got around to writing his play in the early 1590s. The play was first published in 1597, in an inaccurate pirated edition, and thereafter it cropped up in a number of versions. It has long been a staple of Shakespearean repertory groups throughout the world, and it has served as the basis for numerous operas, ballets, and films. Indeed, there can be few persons of moderate education in the Western world who have not at least heard of *Romeo and Juliet* and, in one way or another, measured their own passions against those of these fictional Veronese teenagers.

Let us try to reconstruct, in some detail, the staging of this play as it might have looked and sounded and felt in its first performances. Any reconstruction, of course, must rely primarily on informed conjecture, for there is virtually nothing of the staging about which we can be absolutely certain. There are, however, a few stage directions in the first editions of the play; these and many other specific pieces of evidence and general understandings derived from them can guide us in our task.

Imagine, then, a theatre like the one depicted on page 146. A sizable standing audience crowds about a thrusting platform stage that stands shoulder high and measures about forty feet wide by thirty feet deep. Three tiers of packed galleries line each wall that looks onto the stage. Behind the stage is a tiring house, with two doors slanted toward the center on either side, and a pavilion that is curtained below and balconied above. A flag flies over the playhouse; in the yard and galleries below, patrons gather to drink ale, meet friends, discuss yesterday's sermon at St. Paul's, and gossip about the queen.

A trumpet sounds. The crowd quiets down, and those in the yard jostle to secure good positions—the lucky ones will reach the stage rail and can lean on it for support as the afternoon wears on. Others perch on rain barrels or lean back against the gallery supports. Suddenly, atop the pavilion roof, a black-clad figure appears, bearing a laurel wreath. This is the "Chorus" to the play: a single actor, otherwise uninvolved in the action, who speaks in introduction of the play.

His speech is a sonnet, in the Italianate form at which Shakespeare excels, and its words transform the naked architecture of the theatre into both locale for the play and metaphor for its strife-torn action.

> "Two households . . ." (and he points to the two tiring-house doors from which the warring families will shortly and separately emerge)
> "both alike in dignity . . ." (and his gesture emphasizes that the doors are identical and dignified, as are the positions of their respective families)
> "In fair Verona, where we lay our scene . . ." (and he firmly establishes the locale of the play and the self-awareness of the players as they embark on its presentation)

The Chorus's sonnet now expands the metaphor of the theatre doors: from households, they become the inhabitants of the households, then the children of those households:

> From forth the fatal loins of these two foes
> A pair of star-cross'd lovers take their life;

implying, in alliterative tones, an astrological fatality that is a hallmark of this play, even here at its prologue:

> The fearful passage of their death-mark'd love,
> And the continuance of their parents' rage,
> Which, but their children's end, nought could remove,
> Is now the two hours' traffic of our stage.

We are being set up: we will be here for two hours; we will see two young and star-crossed lovers emerge from these families, these households, these doors; and we will see them die, ending at last their parents' enmity. It is going to be a tragedy of the old kind—of *Prometheus* and *The Trojan Women*—for we know the end before we begin, and we can only watch in dread and pity as the terrible events overtake these splendid young people. And we know we will be home in time for dinner, too; for the youthful Shakespeare was perhaps a shade diffident in his belief that he could not hold his audience much longer. The line reminds us of the taleteller who keeps promising to "make a long story short."

That very diffidence may have stimulated the first scene, which now ensues; it is an extraordinarily exciting beginning, almost overwrought in its energy. First, out of one door, come two servants of the Capulets, speaking generally of the animosity they bear for the Montagues and speaking specifically in the language of puns:

SAMPSON: Gregory, on my word, we'll not carry coals [bear insults].
GREGORY: No, for then we should be colliers [coal dealers].
SAMPSON: I mean, an we be in choler, we'll draw [I mean, if we are made angry, we'll have to fight].
GREGORY: Ay, while you live, draw your neck out of collar [try to avoid hanging].

Virtually incomprehensible to audiences today, this witty banter between the two servants greatly amused the Elizabethan audience, who were well attuned to verbal hijinks. Quickly now, the puns turn sexual, increasing the delight of the bawdry-loving Londoners:

SAMPSON: . . . when I have fought with the men, I will be civil with the maids; I will cut off their heads.
GREGORY: The heads of the maids?
SAMPSON: Ay, the heads of the maids, or their

maidenheads, take it in what sense thou wilt.
GREGORY: They must take it in sense that feel it.
SAMPSON: Me they shall feel while I am able to stand [i.e., able to maintain an erection]; and 'tis known I am a pretty piece of flesh.
GREGORY: 'Tis well thou art not fish. . . . Draw thy tool, here comes two of the house of Montagues.

And out of the other door come two servants of Montague, symmetrically balancing the Capulets who have preceded them. A spirited exchange of insults ensues, with Sampson biting his thumb—the classic Italian gesture of obscene ridicule. Swords are drawn and the four men duel. Next Benvolio, a friend of Romeo, appears at center, from under the pavilion. Stepping forward, he draws his sword and cries:

BENVOLIO: Part, fools!
     Put up your swords, you know not what you do.

His intervention, however, is misinterpreted by the archenemy of all Montagues, Tybalt, who appears at the top of the pavilion and behind the peace-loving Benvolio:

TYBALT: What, art thou drawn among these heartless hinds?
     Turn thee, Benvolio, look upon thy death.

Benvolio slowly turns around and looks up. He pleads:

BENVOLIO: I do but keep the peace. Put up thy sword,
     Or manage it to part these men with me.

But Tybalt will have none of this:

TYBALT: What, drawn and talk of peace? I hate the word

The maskers' dance, as seen from an upper gallery. (Drawing: John von Szeliski.)

As I hate hell, all Montagues, and thee.
Have at thee, coward!

With that, he leaps from the pavilion, this swashbuckling and ill-tempered versifier, and lands on the stage platform to engage Benvolio. Now from both doors pour out the citizens and servants of both sides, armed with clubs and "partisans" (spear-swords). The old patriarchs, Capulet and Montague, follow from their respective doors as their wives and women servants appear above them in balcony "windows" that surmount each door. Scarcely three minutes into the play and the stage is filled with flashing swords, leaping duelists, servants grappling hand to hand, tottering old men and screaming women—all of this right in the midst of two thousand or more spectators, many of them standing mere feet and inches away.

Then, suddenly, Prince Escalus, the ruler of Verona, enters with his train of attendants on the top level of the pavilion. With a tone of immense authority, he freezes the action:

PRINCE: Rebellious subjects, enemies to peace,
Profaners of this neighbor-stained steel—

Capulet and Montague pause briefly, then move as if to resume their futile struggle.

PRINCE: Will they not hear?—What ho, you men, you beasts!
  That quench the fire of your pernicious rage
  With purple fountains issuing from your veins—
  On pain of torture, from those bloody hands
  Throw your mistempered weapons to the ground,
  And hear the sentence of your moved prince.

And, with a clatter of steel, twelve swords are dropped on the stage platform, and the men who held them drop to their knees in a display of submission and supplication.

In but a few minutes of stage time, we have moved from a scene-setting (and metaphor-establishing) sonnet to servant-class punning to Italianate insults to a street brawl to the regal rhetoric of a prince. We have also met several characters who interest us: the gentle Benvolio, the fiery Tybalt, the Prince, and the patriarchs. And we have come to understand fully the world of the play, with its hot-tempered families, its propensity for violence, its love of language, its youth and exuberance. What we have *not* seen is what we came to see—we have not yet seen or even heard of the Montagues' Romeo or the Capulets' Juliet, and we won't for yet a bit longer. It was Shakespeare's general technique to develop the world of his play first and then introduce his principal characters. This allowed him to detail characters of stature with great individuality, by showing how they differed from more ordinary or stereotyped characters who appeared in the opening scene or scenes.

When Romeo first appears, later in the scene, all have departed save Benvolio; now Romeo reveals to his friend (and, through his friend, to us) that he is in love—with a chaste maid called Rosaline! "The all-seeing sun / Ne'er saw her match since first the world begun," he claims:

ROMEO: . . . she hath Dian's wit;
  And in strong proof of chastity well arm'd,
  From Love's weak childish bow she lives unharm'd.
  She will not stay the siege of loving terms,
  Nor bide th'encounter of assailing eyes,
  Nor ope her lap to saint-seducing gold.
  O, she is rich in beauty, only poor
  That when she dies, with beauty dies her store.
BENVOLIO: Then she hath sworn that she will still live chaste?
ROMEO: She hath, and in that sparing makes huge waste;
  For beauty starv'd with her severity
  Cuts beauty off from all posterity.
  She is too fair, too wise, wisely too fair,
  To merit bliss by making me despair.
  She hath forsworn to love, and in that vow
  Do I live dead that live to tell it now.
BENVOLIO: Be rul'd by me, forget to think of her.
ROMEO: O, teach me how I should forget to think.

This is love poetry, of course: blank verse amended with many rhyming end-syllables ("poor . . . store," "chaste . . . waste"), parallel phrasings ("not stay . . . nor bide . . . nor ope . . ."), antipodal constructions ("rich in beauty, only poor that . . ."), oxymorons ("Do I live dead . . ."), alliterations ("stay the siege," "saint-seducing"), and almost too-clever verbal compilations ("too fair, too wise, wisely too fair") that are the hallmarks of romantic lyricism, particularly in the early Elizabethan and Shakespearean drama.

Romeo and Benvolio exit through the Montague door, whereupon old Capulet, a servant, and the County (Count) Paris enter through the door opposite; this denotes a change of scene (but not scenery) and/or the passage of time. The drama of Shakespeare's age was typically divided into scenes of this sort, with perhaps only the most momentary pauses between scenes; each such division, however, could indicate a new locale and/or an advance in the clock or calendar. Shakespeare was particularly adept at "speeding up" the action of his plays: the story of Romeo and Juliet takes place in less than a week's time in this play, but it spanned nine months in the original novel. This time reduction is an aspect of dramatic economy, or tightening, that gives the action a greater sense of urgency and immediacy. Such time lapses and place changes as were required by any story in Shakespeare's time were indicated simply by this convention of emptying the stage. Then, immediately, new characters entered and perhaps a word or two of dialogue was inserted to clarify what changes were to be considered to have taken place.

Capulet and the Count now discuss a young Capulet daughter, yet unnamed, who "hath not seen the change of fourteen years," but whom Paris is suing to marry. A party is announced, and a servant is left behind to invite guests from a list given by old Capulet. The servant is called "clown" in the original stage direction, and this role is known to have been played by the great comedian Will Kempe. Left alone on stage, the clown reveals to the audience that he cannot read—hence he cannot decipher the names on the list. We cannot tell exactly how Kempe played the scene, but when in the later *Hamlet* the prince instructs the players: "Let those that play your clowns speak no more than is set down for them," we get the idea that Kempe was not above embroidering his part, not only with antic behavior but also with words of his own devising. What Shakespeare wrote for him to say is this:

SERVANT: Find them out whose names are
    written here! It is written that the shoe-
    maker should meddle with his yard and the
    tailor with his last, the fisher with his pencil
    and the painter with his nets; but I am sent
    to find those persons whose names are here
    writ, and can never find what names the
    writing person hath here writ. I must to the
    learned.

Perhaps if we imagine these lines as said by one of our contemporary comics—by Robin Williams, Whoopi Goldberg, Roseanne, or Jim Carrey, for example—we shall get the feeling of the delivery better than by trying to imagine a "Shakespearean actor."

Benvolio and Romeo return now via their door. The clown asks them to read the list, and Romeo, agreeing, comes across Rosaline's name. They decide to crash the party. Where is it? they ask. "Up," says the clown: "My master is the great rich Capulet, and if you be not of the house of Montagues, I pray come and crush a cup of wine." Then the two men retreat to the Montague door resolving to go anyway, and the scene changes again.

This time the curtains are quickly drawn (by servants) around the pavilion posts. Out the Capulet door come Capulet's wife (Lady Capulet) and a nurse; but now the setting, for the first time, is indoors—as the placement of the curtains makes clear.

WIFE: Nurse, where's my daughter? Call her
    forth to me.
NURSE: Now by my maidenhead at twelve
    year old,
    I bade her come. What, lamb! What, lady-
    bird!
    God forbid! Where's this girl? What, Juliet!

And the nurse draws the curtains aside to reveal Juliet within the pavilion, seated on the edge of her bed.

JULIET: How now, who calls?
NURSE: Your mother.

Juliet crosses out of the pavilion and descends to her mother. They talk, and the nurse talks—and talks! Three different times we are told that Juliet is thirteen years old, as if Shakespeare feared his audience might fail to take in this bit of information, and both mother and nurse try to persuade Juliet to accept Count Paris's offer of marriage:

The Nurse and Juliet (Julia Fletcher and Anne Lawder) in an American Conservatory Theatre production. (Photo: William Ganslen, ACT.)

WIFE: Well, think of marriage now; younger than you,
Here in Verona, ladies of esteem,
Are made already mothers. By my count,
I was your mother much upon these years
That you are now a maid. Thus then in brief:
The valiant Paris seeks you for his love.
NURSE: A man, young lady! Lady, such a man
As all the world—why, he's a man of wax!
WIFE: Verona's summer hath not such a flower.
NURSE: Nay, he's a flower, in faith, a very flower.
WIFE: What say you? Can you love the gentleman?

What is remarkable in this dialogue is its simplicity, its earthiness, its genuinely human sense of humor. Neither grand nor pedestrian, the language bespeaks characters of remarkable individuality creating great roles for actors and splendidly lifelike personages.

This scene between the three women (all played by boys) was played in and around the pavilion, making use of the bed inside for sitting, rocking, and listening. At the end, Juliet agrees to wait and see: "I'll look to like, if looking liking move"; and she, her mother, and the nurse are summoned by the antic clown:

SERVANT: Madam, the guests are come, supper serv'd up, you call'd, my young lady ask'd for, the nurse curs'd in the pantry, and every thing in extremity. I must hence to wait; I beseech you follow straight.

They do, with the laughter of the audience trailing after them, and the curtains of the pavilion are pulled fully back and out of view: we are going outside again. From the Montague door come Romeo and Benvolio, masked for the Capulet party and accompanied by six or seven other maskers, including one of Shakespeare's most vitally memorable characters, the rakish Mercutio. They are accompanied by torchbearers, Shakespeare's indication that it is now nighttime in Verona and also his symbol for the purity of love:

ROMEO: Give me a torch, I am not for this ambling;
　Being but heavy, I will bear the light.
MERCUTIO: Nay, gentle Romeo, we must have you dance.
ROMEO: Not I, believe me. You have dancing shoes
　With nimble soles, I have a soul of lead
　So stakes me to the ground I cannot move.
MERCUTIO: You are a lover, borrow Cupid's wings,
　And soar with them above a common bound.
ROMEO: I am too sore enpierced with his shaft
　To soar with his light feathers, and so bound
　I cannot bound a pitch above dull woe;
　Under love's heavy burthen do I sink. . . .

A torch for me. Let wantons light of heart
Tickle the senseless rushes with their heels.
For I am proverb'd with a grandsire phrase,
I'll be a candle-holder and look on:
The game was ne'er so fair, and I am done.
MERCUTIO: Tut, . . . we'll draw thee from the mire
　Of this sir-reverence love, wherein thou stickest
　Up to the ears. Come, we burn daylight, ho!
ROMEO: Nay, that's not so.
MERCUTIO: I mean, sir, in delay
　We waste our lights in vain, like lights by day!

Typically, Shakespeare mixes imagery with specifics; he will, in this play, relentlessly pursue the symbol of light (representing purity, love, and life itself) as the antagonist of dark (representing night, evil, and death): this imaginative use of that symbol has antecedents that go back at least as far as Prometheus (the giver of light) and may be considered one of the archetypal images of theatre itself.

Mercutio now regales Romeo with an extraordinary tale of Queen Mab, "the fairies' midwife," as the men hasten to dinner at the Capulets. There is an interesting original stage direction here: "They march about the stage, and Servingmen come forth with napkins." Presumably Romeo, Benvolio, Mercutio, and their train of followers simply parade about the platform while the servingmen appear at the top of the pavilion: the clown, of course, has already established that the Capulet house, where the party will take place, is "up," and in Shakespeare's day the marching about was all that was required to indicate another change of scene—or, in this case, an overlapping of scenes. After the servants engage in a bit of tomfoolery concerning the party preparations, while other servants, below, dress the pavilion curtains in a festive manner, Capulet and his family and guests appear through the central door and come to the pavilion's center:

CAPULET: Welcome, gentlemen! Ladies that have their toes
    Unplagu'd with corns will walk about with you.
    Ah, my mistresses, which of you all
    Will now deny to dance? She that makes dainty,
    She I'll swear hath corns. Am I come near ye now?
    Welcome, gentlemen! I have seen the day
    That I have worn a visor and could tell
    A whispering tale in a fair lady's ear,
    Such as would please; 'tis gone, 'tis gone, 'tis gone.
    You are welcome, gentlemen! Come, musicians, play.

And musicians, seated in a small room in the very top gallery of the theatre itself, play as the masked ladies and gentlemen dance. Capulet and his aged cousin retreat backstage and reappear at the top of the pavilion, where servants have placed benches, there to sit and watch the proceedings.

CAPULET: Nay, sit, nay, sit, good cousin Capulet,
    For you and I are past our dancing days.

It is at this point that Romeo sees Juliet for the first time; clearly it is a moment for which the audience, primed with their great familiarity with this tale, has anxiously waited.

ROMEO: (*to a* SERVANT) What lady's that . . . ?
SERVANT: I know not, sir.
ROMEO: O she doth teach the torches to burn bright!
    It seems she hangs upon the cheek of night
    As a rich jewel in an Ethiop's ear—
    Beauty too rich for use, for earth too dear!
    So shows a snowy dove trooping with crows,
    As yonder lady o'er her fellows shows. . . .
    Did my heart love till now? Forswear it, sight!
    For I ne'er saw true beauty till this night.

Note the lavish use of light imagery in this passage. Juliet is brighter than fire itself, shining brilliantly as a diamond on a black earlobe, against "the cheek of night"; she is above all other women as a snowy dove is whiter than the crows: this imagery vis-à-vis Juliet will remain consistent throughout the rest of the play. Rosaline is forgotten (although presumably she is present at the party, she is not mentioned in the play text; directors usually make an effort to identify her by some action at the beginning of the scene). Thus, out of the background of dueling and antagonism with which the play begins, true love and its celebration emerge to engage the play's development.

Now Tybalt comes on the scene—hate and the threat of death are never long absent from the stage in this play. He enters above with his servant, at the top of the pavilion to the side of Capulet, and he overhears Romeo's words.

TYBALT: This, by his voice, should be a Montague.
    Fetch me my rapier, boy. What, dares the slave
    Come hither . . . ?

But old Capulet stops him: they argue, the old man protecting his well-ordered party and also standing up for common decency and hospitality, and Tybalt raging but finally relenting. Why is this scene played above? Because below, at the stage level, Romeo is approaching Juliet, and Juliet Romeo; as the menacing exchange occurs up on the pavilion, romance is engendered below, a perfect use of the multileveled stage space. By the time Romeo and Juliet first exchange words, they already have made substantial communication with their eyes:

ROMEO: If I profane with my unworthiest hand
    This holy shrine, the gentle sin is this;
    My lips, two blushing pilgrims, ready stand
    To smooth that rough touch with a tender kiss.

JULIET: Good pilgrim, you do wrong your
　　　hand too much.
　　　Which mannerly devotion shows in this;
　　　For saints have hands that pilgrims' hands
　　　　　do touch,
　　　And palm to palm is holy palmer's kiss.
ROMEO: Have not saints lips, and holy palm-
　　　ers too?
JULIET: Ay, pilgrim, lips that they must use in
　　　pray'r.
ROMEO: O then, dear saint, let lips do what
　　　hands do. . . .

They kiss. And only then, following that first
kiss, do they find out:

ROMEO: Is she a Capulet?
　　　O dear account? my life is my foe's debt!

And

NURSE: His name is Romeo, and a Montague,
　　　The only son of your great enemy.
JULIET: My only love spring from my only
　　　hate!
　　　Too early seen unknown, and known too
　　　late!

The party ends, and the tragedy is on. The
stage is empty; at this point it is convenient to
think that "Act I" is over—for so it is indicated in most modern editions of the play—
but there were no intermissions in the theatre
of this time, and the reentrance of the chorus
at this point is not so much a signal for "Act
II" as a recognition that the tragedy now
moves to its next level.

　　　The chorus, from his high pavilion position
as before, again delivers a scene-setting sonnet
to the audience, this time commenting on the
end of Romeo's infatuation with Rosaline and
the difficulties the lovers face in the new alliance; meanwhile, below, stagehands perhaps
erect a simulated stone wall behind the closed
curtains of the pavilion frame. At the chorus's
departure, the curtains open to reveal Romeo:

*Brian Evans and Rebecca Clark are at the balcony
as Romeo and Juliet, in this 1992 University of
California at Irvine production set in the "mondo
nero" period of late-nineteenth-century Italy—like
the Renaissance, a time of "heroic aesthetes" and
lyrical, swashbuckling romanticism. Costumes by
Sandra Sykora. (Photo: Henry DiRocco.)*

ROMEO: Can I go forward when my heart is
　　　here?
　　　Turn back, dull earth, and find thy centre
　　　out.

Upon hearing the shouts of Benvolio ("Romeo! My cousin Romeo! Romeo!"), Romeo
hurdles the wall and hides at its base. Benvolio
and Mercutio come up behind the wall and,
peering beyond, search for their friend:

MERCUTIO: He is wise,
    And, on my life, hath stol'n him home to
      bed.
BENVOLIO: He ran this way and leapt this or-
      chard wall.
    Call, good Mercutio.
MERCUTIO: Nay, I'll conjure, too.
    Romeo! humors! madman! passion! lov-
      er! . . .
    I conjure thee by Rosaline's bright eyes,
    By her high forehead and her scarlet lip,
    By her fine foot, straight leg, and quivering
      thigh,
    And the demesnes that there adjacent lie,
    That in thy likeness thou appear to
      us! . . .
BENVOLIO: Come, he hath hid himself among
      these trees
    To be consorted with the humorous night.
    Blind is his love and best befits the dark.
MERCUTIO: If love be blind, love cannot hit
      the mark. . . .
    Romeo, good night. I'll to my truckle-bed,
    This field-bed is too cold for me to sleep.
    Come, shall we go?

They leave, but much has been established in this little scene: the orchard setting, the darkness and cold of night, Romeo's furtiveness now that he is genuinely in love, the evocation (conjuring) of sexual desire, and, imagistically, the premonition of darkness and blindness that will attend this particular love.

His friends gone, Romeo stands and comes forward, saying of Mercutio:

    He jests at scars that never felt a wound.

It is the beginning of the most famous scene in the play, surely one of the most celebrated love scenes in all literature. Juliet appears on the pavilion roof, and, characteristically, Romeo sees her as light itself:

ROMEO: But soft, what light through yonder
      window breaks?

SHAKESPEARE'S CHARACTERS: KERR

There is something most peculiar about Shakespeare's methods of characterization, something unique about the *manner* in which his fretting shadows acquire life. His characters aren't stylized, as Molière's are. His characters aren't archetypal, as Sophocles' are. Neither are they psychological in the Euripidean sense, with rather schematized idiosyncrasies still not entirely free of the guiding hands of the gods. Shakespeare's men and women *are* free. They are almost free of him. More than any playwright who ever lived, I think, Shakespeare gave his imagined figures his blessing and their liberty, allowing them an individuality that need not be categorized and cannot be readily explained because it is *theirs:* willful, perverse, self-contradictory, electric, mercurial, evanescent, ineffable, inevitable, *there*. Could you prick them, they would bleed. But you cannot prick them any more than you can seize lightning bolts; once you've seen the flash, it's too late. . . . In the very same moment they are present and have passed. Untrappable, unchallengeable.

Walter Kerr

It is the east, and Juliet is the sun.
Arise, fair sun, and kill the envious
    moon. . . .

Is Juliet aware of his presence? To herself (presumably) she speaks:

JULIET: O Romeo, Romeo, wherefore art
      thou Romeo?
    Deny thy father and refuse thy name;
    Or, if thou wilt not, be but sworn my love.

And I'll no longer be a Capulet.

ROMEO: (*aside*) Shall I hear more, or shall I
    speak at this?

JULIET: 'Tis but thy name that is my enemy;
    Thou art thyself, though not a Montague.
    What's Montague? It is nor hand nor foot,
    Nor arm nor face, nor any other part
    Belonging to a man. O be some other
      name!
    What's in a name? That which we call a rose
    By any other word would smell as sweet;
    So Romeo would, were he not Romeo
      call'd,
    Retain that dear perfection which he owes
    Without that title. Romeo, doff thy name,
    And for thy name, which is no part of thee,
    Take all myself.

And Romeo, needing no more than this, declares himself:

ROMEO: I take thee at thy word.
    Call me but love, and I'll be new baptiz'd;
    Henceforth I never will be Romeo.

But is there more to this exchange than meets the eye? It is, of course, one of the conventions of Shakespearean drama that characters can address the audience (as if speaking to themselves) without being overheard by others on stage; this can be even more easily conveyed if, as in the present case, the characters are standing on different levels. Still, there is the suggestion that Juliet would at least like to be overheard by her new-found idol, to whom her words are addressed apostrophically. One of the more subtle variations on this convention—and one at which Shakespeare was particularly adept—is to turn the characters into an audience for each other, that is, to let them overhear each other's thoughts.

And what are we to make of these two young people who express themselves so eloquently? Modern audiences sometimes have difficulty accepting the notion that such brilliantly turned verses could issue from the mouths of a thirteen-year-old girl and her ad-olescent swain. But this, too, reflects a convention of the theatre and should not be analyzed too critically. It is, after all, no more absurd to find Romeo and Juliet speaking in the fine phrases of Shakespearean poetry than to find them speaking in English (for they are Italians) or, for that matter, to find them on a London stage. The theatre is always only a metaphor for life, and the love language of Romeo and Juliet expresses the free flight of the author's imagination as he seeks to exact from his characters an image of star-crossed passion that will register indelibly in the audience's mind. Realism is not the goal, although the play deals with real human emotions. To that end, the language is art, it is expression, and in its own way it is truth.

JULIET: My ears have not yet drunk a hundred
    words
    Of thy tongue's uttering, yet I know the
    sound.
    Art thou not Romeo, and a Montague?

ROMEO: Neither, fair maid, if either thee dislike.

JULIET: How camest thou hither, tell me, and
    wherefore?
    The orchard walls are high and hard to
    climb,
    And the place death, considering who thou
    art,
    If any of my kinsmen find thee here.

ROMEO: With love's light wings did I o'erperch these walls,
    For stony limits cannot hold love out,
    And what love can do, that dares love
    attempt;
    Therefore thy kinsmen are no stop to me.

JULIET: If they do see thee, they will murther
    thee.

ROMEO: Alack, there lies more peril in thine
    eye
    Than twenty of their swords! Look thou
    but sweet,
    And I am proof against their enmity.

JULIET: I would not for the world they saw
    thee here.

ROMEO: I have night's cloak to hide me from
    their eyes,
    And but thou love me [if you do not love
    me], let them find me here;
    My life were better ended by their hate,
    Than death prorogued [postponed], want-
    ing of thy love.

Juliet is called away; she comes back. They
agree to marry. She is again called away; again
she comes back.

JULIET: 'Tis almost morning, I would have
    thee gone—
    And yet no farther than a wanton's bird,
    That lets it hop a little from his hand. . . .
ROMEO: I would I were thy bird.
JULIET: Sweet, so
    would I.
    Yet I should kill thee with much cher-
    ishing.
    Good night, good night! Parting is such
    sweet sorrow,
    That I shall say good night till it be mor-
    row.
ROMEO: Sleep dwell upon thine eyes, peace in
    thy breast!
    Would I were sleep and peace, so sweet to
    rest!
    Hence will I to my ghostly father's cell,
    His help to crave, and my dear hap to tell.

And Romeo leaves to visit his "ghostly father," Friar Lawrence, to ask that he perform
the wedding ceremony the next day.

Although the foregoing is a love scene, it is
filled with the imagery of death: the swords of
the Capulet kinsmen ("My life were better
ended with their hate"), the bird that would
be killed with too much cherishing, and the
"ghostly" confessor, whose well-intentioned
intervention will ultimately cause the double
suicide with which the play ends. This imagery sustains the undertone of pathos, established at the very outset of the play, that is the
foundation for tragedy in this celebration of
light and love.

The play starts to pick up momentum at
this point, with a series of short scenes in different locales accelerating the action. Romeo
leaves by one tiring-house door and Friar
Lawrence, basket in hand, enters from the
other. The position of the curtains tells us that
we are still outdoors. It is the following morning; the words set the scene:

FRIAR: The grey-ey'd morn smiles on the
    frowning night,
    Check'ring the eastern clouds with streaks
    of light. . . .

and Romeo enters and tries to pursuade the
Friar to marry him to Juliet.

FRIAR: Holy Saint Francis, what a change is
    here!
    Is Rosaline, that thou did'st love so dear,
    So soon forsaken? Young men's love then
    lies
    Not truly in their hearts, but in their eyes.
    Jesu Maria! . . .

But he is persuaded, and together they enter
through the curtains into Friar Lawrence's
"cell," as Romeo has called it, which is represented by a curtained area of the lower pavilion. Benvolio and Mercutio enter the stage
from the Montague door:

MERCUTIO: Where the dev'l should this Ro-
    meo be?
    Came he not home to-night?
BENVOLIO: Not to his father's. I spoke with
    his man.
MERCUTIO: Why, that same pale hardhearted
    wench, that Rosaline,
    Torments him so, that he will sure run
    mad.
BENVOLIO: Tybalt, the kinsman to old Cap-
    ulet,
    Hath sent a letter to his father's house.
MERCUTIO: A challenge, on my life.
BENVOLIO: Romeo will answer it.

MERCUTIO: Any man that can write may answer a letter.

BENVOLIO: Nay, he will answer the letter's master, how he dares, being dar'd.

MERCUTIO: Alas, poor Romeo, he is already dead. . . .

And the plot relentlessly advances. Think what we have to contend with at this point, only a third of the way into the play: five young men (Romeo, Benvolio, Tybalt, Mercutio, Paris), two young women (Juliet and the unseen Rosaline), and various assorted elders—a prince, a friar, a nurse, a clown, and four parents—all drawn with a good deal of attention to their individuality, all blended skillfully in a plot of considerable complexity. In addition, we have already seen a full-stage street brawl, an elegant party with music and dancing, an unforgettable love scene, and a sampling of comedy that ranges from the broad tomfoolery of the servant-clown to the sparkling eloquence of Mercutio. And now we are headed into a marriage on the one hand and a duel on the other: love and death, the two most profound themes of art in any age.

Romeo has summoned Juliet to Friar Lawrence's cell: this Juliet learns in a message from the nurse, delivered on the highest pavilion level after a long and anxious wait amusingly described to us in Juliet's soliloquy:

JULIET: The clock struck nine when I did send the nurse;

In half an hour she promised to return.

Perchance she cannot meet him—that's not so.

O, she is lame! . . .

Now is the sun upon the highmost hill

Of this day's journey, and from nine till twelve

Is three long hours, yet she is not come. . . .

But old folks—many feign as they were dead,

Unwieldy, slow, heavy, and pale as lead.

O God, she comes! . . .

And, having at last extracted the good news from the older woman, she leaves her platform as the curtains open below to reveal Romeo and the friar. Shortly, Juliet joins them, "somewhat fast and embraceth Romeo" according to an original stage direction, and the curtain is drawn again around them as they are wedded by Friar Lawrence within the "cell."

Now a variation of the first scene takes place. Benvolio, Mercutio, and several followers come out the Montague door, soon to be met by Tybalt and others from the Capulet door opposite. They meet center; angry words are exchanged. Benvolio, consistent with his character, tries to make peace, but the antagonism escalates between the proud, hot-tempered Tybalt and Mercutio. Romeo, hearing the dispute, enters from the cell, center, and tries to explain to Tybalt; this only inflames Tybalt more and scandalizes Mercutio. Tybalt and Mercutio fight; Romeo tries to intervene; Mercutio is mortally wounded:

MERCUTIO: I am hurt.

A plague a' both houses! I am sped.

Is he gone and hath nothing?

BENVOLIO: What, art thou hurt?

MERCUTIO: Ay, ay, a scratch, a scratch, marry, 'tis enough.

Where is my page? Go, villain, fetch a surgeon.

ROMEO: Courage, man. The hurt cannot be much.

MERCUTIO: No, 'tis not so deep as a well, nor so wide as a church-door, but 'tis enough, 'twill serve. Ask for me tomorrow, and you shall find me a grave man. . . . Why the dev'l came you between us? I was hurt under your arm.

ROMEO: I thought all for the best.

MERCUTIO: Help me into some house, Benvolio,

Or I shall faint. A plague a' both your houses!

They have made worms' meat of me. I have
    it,
And soundly too. Your houses!

And Benvolio helps Mercutio out through
the center pavilion curtains, now no longer
Friar Lawrence's cell, but a neutral "house"
between the two other "houses" left and
right—the same two "households" pointed
out by the chorus in the first line of the play;
upon them both Mercutio hurls his dying
curse, his wit dissolving in desperation in
this deepening moment of the tragic pattern.
Thus does this play move from violence to
love and back again in an alternating fashion,
each time getting closer to the core, in an
inward-spiraling, self-accelerating course.

    Romeo, at the nadir of his life (his "I
thought all for the best" is one of the most
pathetic lines in all drama), reflects on the ambiguity of manliness:

<blockquote>
O sweet Juliet,
Thy beauty hath made me effeminate,
And in my temper soft'ned valor's steel.
</blockquote>

Upon seeing the reentering Tybalt, Romeo
challenges and kills him in impetuous rage.
The stage is filled with people; chaos is come:

BENVOLIO: Romeo, away, be gone!
    The citizens are up, and Tybalt slain.
    Stand not amazed, the prince will doom
      thee death
    If thou art taken. Hence be gone, away!
ROMEO: O, I am fortune's fool!

As Romeo flees, the Prince again appears at
the top level of the pavilion to restore order
and send down his punishment: Romeo is
banished and the families are fined.

    Romeo and Juliet have a final love scene,
"aloft" as the stage directions say, at the top
pavilion level. They have made love (in the
fine film adaptation by Franco Zeffirelli, this
scene is played in the nude, a possibility that
Shakespeare could not even contemplate, given

his boy Juliet) and, as in the balcony scene,
daylight threatens.

JULIET: Wilt thou be gone? It is not yet near
    day.
    It was the nightingale, and not the lark,
    That pierc'd the fearful hollow of thine ear;
    Nightly she sings on yond pomegranate
      tree.
    Believe me, love, it was the nightingale.
ROMEO: It was the lark, the herald of the
    morn,
    No nightingale. Look, love, what envious
      streaks
    Do lace the severing clouds in yonder east.
    Night's candles are burnt out, and jocund
      day
    Stands tiptoe on the misty mountain tops.
    I must be gone and live, or stay and die.
JULIET: Yond light is not day-light, I know
    it, I;
    It is some meteor. . . .
    O now be gone, more light and light it
      grows.
ROMEO: More light and light, more dark and
    dark our woes.

The alternation of imagery between light
and dark begins to accelerate; day and night
come faster on each other's heels as the plot
moves inexorably toward its fatal conclusion.
Romeo descends from the pavilion with his
rope ladder; Juliet's mother then appears and
tells Juliet she is to marry Paris. The curtains
below open to reveal Paris in the midst of
a discussion with Friar Lawrence about the
wedding date:

FRIAR: On Thursday, sir? The time is very
    short.

And the time has been made to appear shorter
by Shakespeare's dramaturgy, which begins
the scene with the friar's response, making us
deduce what Paris's question had been by
inference.

The climax of the play is developed around the friar's plan: alone with Juliet, he gives her a vial containing a "distilling liquor" that will make her appear dead; later, and in secret, he will come with Romeo to take her, freshly revived, from her open tomb, thereby saving her from an unwanted second marriage. Back in her "room" under the pavilion, Juliet draws the vial from her bosom:

JULIET: Farewell! God knows when we shall meet again.
I have a faint cold fear thrills through my veins,
That almost freezes up the heat of life.
I'll call them back again to comfort me.
Nurse!—What should she do here?
My dismal scene I needs must act alone.
Come, vial.

Shakespeare is the most stage-conscious and, in a sense, the most self-conscious, of dramatists; an actor himself, he explicitly uses the stage as a metaphor for life: Juliet, in this scene, sees herself as an actress "acting" a "scene." It is not entirely unlike her apostrophe to Romeo from the balcony: she is aware of her words—they are not mere fragmentary mutterings—and she speaks aloud as if to test her own sincerity and motivation.

Juliet swallows the potion, and, in an original stage direction, "falls upon the bed within the curtains," which are drawn around her. Now much bustle takes place on the platform in front of her. Lord and Lady Capulet enter and command their servants to action: spices are sent for, meats are ordered baked, a cock crows, a curfew bell rings, servants come in bearing logs and are ordered to get drier ones. Carnality is in the air—a marriage is to be held today, music is heard from the Count's commissioned performers, and Lady Capulet accuses her husband of flirting with the help. Paris has arrived. The Nurse goes to the curtains to waken Juliet:

NURSE: Mistress, what, Mistress! Juliet!—
Fast, I warrant her, she.—
Why lamb! why lady! fie, you slug-a-bed!
Why, love, I say! madam! sweet heart! why, bride!
What, not a word? You take your penny-worths now;
Sleep for a week, for the next night, I warrant,
The County Paris hath set up his rest
That you shall rest but little. God forgive me!

She draws aside the curtains. Juliet is dead, apparently. What follows is a scene that is peculiarly Elizabethan and virtually impossible to perform today—a scene of lamentation:

NURSE: O woe! O woeful, woeful, woeful day!
Most lamentable day, most woeful day
That ever, ever, I did yet behold!
O day, O day, O day! O hateful day!
Never was seen so black a day as this.
O woeful day, O woeful day!
PARIS: Beguil'd, divorced, wronged, spited, slain!
Most detestable Death, by thee beguil'd,
By cruel cruel thee quite overthrown!
O love, O life! not life, but love in death!
CAPULET: Despis'd, distressed, hated, martyr'd, kill'd! . . .
(etc.)

The later Shakespeare probably would have considered this scene an embarrassment—he was to satirize just this sort of writing a year or two later in *A Midsummer Night's Dream*. Still, it exemplifies the Elizabethan notion that the use of language had no limits and that every feeling, idea, and emotion could be transcribed into blank verse. The later Shakespeare would write these words for a father looking upon his dead daughter:

KING LEAR: And my poor fool is hang'd! No, no, no life!

Why should a dog, a horse, a rat, have life,
And thou no breath at all? Thoul't come
   no more,
Never, never, never, never, never. . . .

By the time Shakespeare wrote those lines, his own father and son were dead; in *Romeo and Juliet,* he was still speculating on grief, not reporting it.

The final scene of *Romeo and Juliet* takes place in the "monument" where Juliet lies "buried." Romeo, it turns out, has not received word from Friar Lawrence explaining the use of the potion—the messenger was deterred by a quarantine—and instead he learns (falsely) that Juliet is dead. He thereupon buys a poison from an apothecary (possibly played by Shakespeare) and hastens back to Verona. He enters the stage by a tiring-house door and confronts the pavilion once more; it now houses the tombs of Juliet and Tybalt. The curtains are closed. His servant, Balthazar, holds a lantern (once more it is night); Romeo wrests it from him:

ROMEO: Give me the light. Upon thy life I
   charge thee,
   What e'er thou hearest or seest, stand all
      aloof,
   And do not interrupt me in my
      course. . . .
   The time and my intents are savage-wild,
   More fierce and more inexorable far
   Than empty tigers or the roaring sea.

Balthazar leaves. With a crowbar, Romeo attacks the pavilion curtains:

ROMEO: Thou detestable maw, thou womb of
   death,
   Gorg'd with the dearest morsel of the
      earth,
   Thus I enforce thy rotten jaws to open,
   And in despite I'll cram thee with more
      food.

The curtains part; the tombs (biers—such are listed in Henslowe's list of properties for The Rose) are revealed. Paris, who had entered previously and hidden to watch this scene, reappears and challenges Romeo. They duel, Paris is slain, and Romeo drags the body into the tomb, as Paris has requested with his dying breath. Now the alternations between love and violence, savagery and affection, light and darkness, follow upon each other as fast as heartbeats.

ROMEO: . . . [H]ere lies Juliet, and her beauty
   makes
   This vault a feasting presence full of
      light. . . . O my love, my wife,
   Death, that hath suck'd the honey of thy
      breath,
   Hath had no power yet upon thy beauty:
   Thou are not conquer'd, beauty's ensign
      yet
   Is crimson in thy lips and in thy cheeks,
   And death's pale flag is not advanced
      there. . . .
   Forgive me, cousin! Ah, dear Juliet,
   Why art thou yet so fair! Shall I believe
   That unsubstantial Death is amorous,
   And that the lean abhorred monster keeps
   Thee here in dark to be his paramour?
   For fear of that, I still will stay with thee,
   And never from this palace of dim night
   Depart again. Here, here will I remain
   With worms that are thy chambermaids; O
      here
   Will I set up my everlasting rest,
   And shake the yoke of inauspicious stars
   From this world-wearied flesh. . . .

With a last embrace, a swallow of poison, and a final kiss, Romeo falls: "Thus with a kiss I die." Consider the superb ironies of this scene. In seeing that Juliet looks as if alive, Romeo fails to realize that she *is* alive. In thinking to shake off the "yoke" of his "inauspicious stars," he is only fulfilling the astrological prediction made at the play's beginning—this love is indeed star-crossed, and therefore what the stars foretold is true. In his fear that Death will become Juliet's "paramour," he kills himself to guard her from that fate—and in so doing yields her up to Death. Dramatic irony, which is the device of letting the audience in on information unknown to the characters, has rarely been more skillfully exploited than in this scene; the audience, despite their prior knowledge of the denouement, all but stand in their chairs to shout Romeo from his fatal course.

Friar Lawrence enters the tomb, takes in the ghastly scene, and realizes his mistake; no sooner has he done so than Juliet revives. From that moment, neither he nor anyone else can forestall the play's conclusion.

JULIET: O comfortable friar! where is my lord?
 I do remember well where I should be,
 And there I am. Where is my Romeo?
FRIAR: I hear some noise, lady. Come from that nest
 Of death, contagion, and unnatural sleep.
 A greater power than we can contradict
 Hath thwarted our intents. Come, come away.
 Thy husband in thy bosom there lies dead;
 And Paris too. Come I'll dispose of thee
 Among a sisterhood of holy nuns.
 Stay not to question, for the watch is coming.
 Come, go, good Juliet. I dare no longer stay. (*He leaves.*)
JULIET: Go get thee hence, for I will not away.
 What's here? A cup clos'd in my true love's hand?
 Poison, I see, hath been his timeless end.
 O churl, drunk all, and left no friendly drop
 To help me after? I will kiss thy lips,
 Haply some poison yet doth hang on them,
 To make me die with a restorative. (*Kisses him.*)
 Thy lips are warm.

There is noise: a watchman cries.

JULIET: Yea, noise? Then I'll be brief. O happy dagger (*seizes* ROMEO's *dagger*),
 This is thy sheath (*stabs herself*); there rust, and let me die.

And she dies. Finally love and death are fully unified: she dies, as he did, with a kiss, and the final (and somewhat gratuitous) death blow is made with Romeo's dagger, for which she becomes a sheath: a sexual image of mortal intercourse that unites the passions of violence and love that have pursued each other throughout the play.

The play has climaxed, and the climax is towering. It is a development of flowing plot and action, of leaps over walls and from platforms and marches about the stage, of rope ladders, musicians and torchbearers, a ghostly father in his cell, a blabbering nurse, an officious father, a savagely funny friend who almost (but not quite) manages to die laughing. It is empty as narrative alone: when the friar, in the play's final moments of resolution, makes an effort to explain all that has gone on, he can only say

 I will be brief, for my short date of breath
 Is not so long as is a tedious tale.

But the two hours' traffic on the stage has been anything but tedious. What would be little more than sentimental versification in a narrative poem has been made thrillingly dynamic through its embodiment in passionate performances and flowing, immensely varied theatrical staging. The sheer theatrics of Shakespeare's craftsmanship—the rapid and important alternation of daytime and night, indoors and out, lovemaking and street brawling, poetry and prose, humor and pathos, dancing and killing, ecstasy and lamentation, thundering sonority and silken eloquence—has created a richly patterned tale that delivers to its audience a riveting and memorable experience. We pity Prince Escalus at having to hear Friar Lawrence's necessarily lame narration of this tale, for we have seen it all. We have shared in its feelings and we know, *really* know, its people: we see, in them, ourselves.

One can only speculate as to the conversations that took place among Elizabethan theatregoers after their first exposure to Shakespeare's *Romeo and Juliet*. One imagines certain reconsiderations: of the role of parents in the arrangement of marriages, of the age at which infatuation becomes overwhelming, of the function of romantic love in family affairs, of the applicability of Italian passions to English morals. It is inescapable that some lives were changed and some long-held prejudices weakened. Can we also sense a great satisfaction, a profound sympathy, a quiet but irresistible awe?

Romeo and Juliet is not, perhaps, a play of great majesty. The same author's *Hamlet* and *King Lear* are surely more complex, his *Othello* and *Macbeth* more intense, his *Twelfth Night* and *As You Like It* more wittily brilliant, *The Winter's Tale* and *The Tempest* more hauntingly beautiful. But those are all later plays, written in the fullest vision of Shakespeare's maturity. What *Romeo and Juliet* provides its audience is a bold portrayal of the passions and playfulness of youth as seen by an author who was himself barely out of his twenties. With its masterful depiction of first love, *Romeo and Juliet* has leaped the centuries; it is one of those theatrical experiences that liberate us from our own time and free us to share in the sensibility of the ages as we relive this timeless human experience.

ITALY: THE *COMMEDIA DELL'ARTE*

Although Shakespeare's theatre in England was certainly the high-water mark of Renaissance drama, it was by no means the only theatrical activity of the age. Public theatre in Germany was stimulated by traveling English players; and a Spanish public theatre that was somewhat comparable to the Elizabethan flourished under the genius of playwrights Miguel de Cervantes and Lope de Vega. But unquestionably the theatre of greatest and most lasting importance apart from Shakespeare's was the *commedia dell'arte*. This theatre began in Italy and toured throughout Europe, mainly on medieval-type platform stagings in marketplaces, during the sixteenth and seventeenth centuries and beyond.

The Renaissance *commedia* has left us no scripts, for it was a theatre largely improvised on the spot by troupes of masked actors independently responding to audiences in towns all over the Continent. Most of the performances were built around a *scenario*—or rudimentary plot—and made use of set speeches, stock characters, and set physical business, usually (but not always) of a comedic, even farcical nature. But the most outstanding characteristic of the *commedia* was its magnificent energy; the vivacity of its characters, the extraordinary whimsicality of its masks and costumes, and the audacity of its improvisation generated excitement wherever it moved, through towns and countries and across centuries.

Commedia actors were complete professionals, skilled in all the performing arts. Each performer tended to play the same character for many years, sometimes for a lifetime. There were young lovers, *innamorato* and *innamorata* (male and female, for females performed in the *commedia*), the foolishly bragging soldier Capitano, the too-shrewd Venetian merchant Pantalone, the absurdly pompous Bolognese academician Dottore, and the wily Bergamese servant Arlecchino (Harlequin). Each character had his or her standard costume and standard mask (except for the lovers, who were barefaced); each had a standard dialogue or style of speaking. *Commedia* plots revolved around commonplace predicaments: young love thwarted, marital fidelity compromised, social climbing unrewarded, and the presumptions of the rich vis-à-vis the righteous poor. Pantalone, Dottore, and Capitano always came out the losers in this highly pro-plebian drama of the European Renaissance.

The action of the *commedia* was broadly physical. Plot development, such as it was, often was suspended for long periods while comic characters performed stock bits of clownish business, called *lazzi.* Arlecchino's "slapstick"—a wooden sword with a hinged flap that made an exaggerated clap when striking Pantalone's bottom—was a traditional device that was to lend its name to the whole genre of physical farce.

The *commedia* was and remains a somewhat enigmatic phenomenon. Its origins are unknown, and its history mysterious; it seems to have flourished from about the middle of the sixteenth century, but its roots may go back centuries before that. Its impact on the theatre since Renaissance times has been incalculable. Molière was greatly influenced by the *commedia* actors with whom he shared stage space for much of his early career, and the Punch and Judy of English puppet theatre are direct descendants of the *commedia*'s Pulcinello and his fellows. Many companies today seek to carry on the *commedia* tradition, and several are wholly dedicated to this purpose. Current street theatre in Europe and America is rarely without its pretenders to the *commedia* heritage, and *commedia* masks are now standard equipment for actor-training in both scripted and improvisational exercises. Thanks to its prototypical conflicts and characters, its costumes, and its eternal laugh-provoking potential, the *commedia dell'arte* has strong universal appeal and is still very much a vital force in theatre today.

6

Kabuki—and the Theatre of Asia

· ·

What we know as theatre is produced in almost every inhabited area of the world today, and in several thousand different forms, yet virtually all such activity can be divided into two all-encompassing categories: theatre of the West and theatre of the East. The West is Europe and its direct cultural heirs, including most of North and South America, Australia, and various other outposts around the world. The East is Asia, the world's largest continent, plus Asian peripheries in Oceania.

Of these two halves of our planet, the East holds far more people, with Asia claiming two and a half times the population of Europe, Australia, and North, South, and Central America combined. And, though our English words *drama* and *theatre* are of European origin, the theatrical activity of Asia is vastly richer than that of the West, at least in range, profusion, and regional diversity. That fact alone makes Eastern drama a major topic of world cultural inquiry.

Moreover, Eastern and Western theatre arts have such divergent origins and contrasting practices as to make their comparative study enormously revealing of what features—by appearing in both of them—might be universal characteristics of theatrical art itself—for Eastern and Western theatres have largely existed in near-total isolation from each other. Indeed, Eastern and Western *civilizations* have existed in relative isolation until the past two or three centuries. As a result, Western theatre scholarship has, until the past two or three decades, been remarkably thin in its coverage of the East, and most Western theatregoers to this day remain relatively ignorant of Eastern theatrical achievements.

THEATRE IN ASIA

It is deeply misleading to say there is "an" Asian theatre. The world's largest continent and its more than three billion people account for dozens of countries, hundreds of languages, and thousands of identified theatre forms: some highly complex and refined, and some relatively unchanged from Stone Age times. Indian drama, generally considered the taproot of Asian theatre, dates from well before classical Greek times (from about the eighth century B.C.), and the Sanskrit *Natya Sastra,* or Doctrine of Dramatic Art (begun in the second century A.D.), is by far the most comprehensive and detailed theatrical treatise of the ancient world. Indonesia alone, often described as an "anthropologist's paradise," contains more than a thousand distinct genres of dramatic expression, most dating well back into the islands' prehistory. In China the Peking Opera (and its immediate predecessors), with their Tang dynasty costumes, beards to the waist, falsetto recitatives, and flamboyant acrobatics, has entertained audiences for centuries; it was even adapted during the Mao Tse Tung era to promote a powerful military-socialist agenda. Korea, Thailand, Laos, and Burma also draw successfully upon rich and individual theatrical heritages for their profuse modern-day drama and dance-drama performances.

Japan, however, probably holds the greatest interest for the Western theatre student. In this island nation, an astonishingly sophisticated dramatic imagination has created a profusion of unique and brilliant theatrical forms, most of which are professionally performed today. These include the *Kabuki,* the *Nō,* and the *Bunraku,* which will be looked at more closely later in this chapter.

Asian theatre, then, is not a single category of drama, nor a mere variant art form, but a vast range of theatrical endeavor spanning a third of the globe and two-thirds of its people over at least the past three millennia.

GENERAL CHARACTERISTICS OF EASTERN DRAMA

Despite the great diversity of the forms of Eastern drama, there are several general characteristics of most Asian theatre traditions that remain relatively constant from country to country and from century to century.

Asian theatre, to begin with, is almost never just "spoken"; rather, it is danced, chanted, mimed, and very often sung. Mere spoken drama, where it does occur in the East, is always recognized as Western in origin or influence.

Moreover, language in Asian drama is invariably rhythmic and melodic, and it is appreciated for its sound as much as (or more than) for its meaning. Alliteration, imagery, rhyme, and verbal juxtaposition are often as important in Asian dramatic dialogue as logic, persuasive rhetoric, and realism are in Western drama; and sonic value is as valued by an Asian audience as semantic value is by a European or American one.

As this description suggests, Asian theatre is more visual and sensual than literary or intellectual. Though there are Asian dramatists known for their literary gifts—such as Zeami Motokiyo (1363–1443) and Chikamatsu Monzaemon (1653–1724) in Japan and Kalidasa in India (late fourth to early fifth century A.D.)—few Asian plays have been widely circulated for general reading or academic study, and most Asians would consider the act of reading a play—separate from seeing it in performance—an odd pastime. Asian drama is inextricable from the arts of perfor-

Chikamatsu Hanji's Mount Imose *(1771) is a Kabuki tragedy in which, as in* Romeo and Juliet, *children of rival families fall in love. Here Princess Hinadori (at left, played by Nakamura Senjaku III) is in her house, and the nobleman Kaganosuke (Nakamura Baigyoku IV, at right) laments their separation. The houses, backed by blossoming cherry trees, are separated by the Yoshino River, represented by rolling cylinders of wavy stripes. (Photo: Tomoko Ogawa.)*

mance that embody it and bring it to life: dance, song, mime, gesture, acrobatics, puppetry, music, sound, costume, and make-up.

Asian theatre has a strong emphasis on storytelling and myth but is not tightly plotted in the way Western drama normally is, and it rarely leads to escalating incidents, stunning reversals, crescendoing climaxes, or elaborate plot closures. Asian theatre, whose metaphysical roots lie in the timeless meditations on human existence that are at the heart of Indian Hindu and Buddhist cultures, instead seems, to Western tastes, leisurely, aesthetic, and almost wandering; and its dramatic appeal is more continuous and rapturous than cathartic and intellectual.

Asian theatre is also heavily stylized. As one might expect of a dramatic form deeply allied with music and dance, slice-of-life realism is virtually unknown in the Eastern theatre. This is a matter of artistic preference rather than cultural ignorance or artistic limitation: Asian filmmakers, of course, have been among the greatest contemporary innovators in cin-

ematic realism and *cinéma vérité*. However, live Asian drama remains largely a matter of formalized performance, whose forms (*kata* in Japanese) are handed down through the centuries—most often from father (since almost all performers are male) to son—and taught in a highly methodical and imitative manner.

The Asian theatre is deeply traditional. Though there are contemporary avant-garde and political theatre movements in many Asian countries, what is most remarkable about all Eastern theatre is its consonance with folk history, ancient religion, and cultural myth. Traditional folk dramas are performed to this day at rural festivals throughout Asia: the *khon* mask theatre of Thailand, the *wayang wong* dance-drama of Java, and the *kamyonguk* mask-dance theatre of Korea are still presented as part of agricultural rituals throughout the Asian countryside. Ancient aristocratic dramas are likewise maintained: Nō dramas are performed in Tokyo and Kyoto temples and secular theatres today very much as they were performed before provincial Japanese courts five and six hundred years ago.

Virtually all Kabuki actors in modern Japan can trace their lineage—familial and professional—to their actor-fathers and actor-grandfathers and beyond; thus the current Ichikawa Danjuro XII is the twelfth actor in his line and the direct descendant of (and artistic heir to) his great-great-great-great-great-great-great-great-great-grandfather, Ichikawa Danjuro I, born in 1660. Even the most radical contemporary Asian dramatic forms pay homage, in various ways, to their cultural roots.

JAPAN AND THE KABUKI

There is no better way for a Westerner to cross the barrier into Asian drama than via the Japanese theatrical art of Kabuki. Kabuki is one of the world's great historical theatre forms, created in Shakespeare's time and reaching something of a zenith—from which it has never completely descended—during Japan's *shogun*-dominated Edo era (1616–1853). Yet, as with Shakespeare, historical Kabuki continues to be performed today—not merely as a museum reproduction, but as immensely popular entertainment that fills large theatres on a daily basis, both at home and on tour throughout the world. Indeed, Kabuki's generation-to-generation consistency has helped Japan maintain its cultural continuity despite more than most nations' share of ravages: fires, earthquakes, world war, nuclear destruction, and foreign occupation.

Finally, Kabuki is a uniquely pure art form, flowering during a period when Japan was completely isolated from all foreign influence. As an autonomous form, therefore, Kabuki reveals a striking and unique contrast to our own drama: not only does it shine with its own light, but it also brilliantly illuminates Western drama through a vivid apposition.

So let us consider Kabuki as but one example—but an extraordinary one—of the immense creativity contained within the larger framework of Asian theatre.

The History of Kabuki

Kabuki was invented by a Kyoto shrine maiden, Izumo Okuni, around 1600—about the time Shakespeare created *Hamlet*. At its inception, however, kabuki was more an erotic dance and fashion show than a drama. It featured an all-woman cast in short musical skits, in which women played both male and female parts, and was performed for an audience all but given over to drinking, horseplay, and sexual adventurism. Indeed, the word *kabuki* derives from *kabuku*, meaning "tilting" or "askew," and refers to a style of behavior or dress that might today be called "hip" or "punk."

By 1629, however, "Okuni's Kabuki" had become so raucous, and so entwined with prostitution, that the Japanese government outlawed women from the stage. Yet Kabuki would not be stilled: catamites—attractive boy prostitutes—were hired to assume the Kabuki performing assignments—and Kabuki's sexual raucousness continued. By 1652 the Japanese government, not to be so thwarted, outlawed the boy performers as well. Kabuki's survival demanded yet another switch—to adult male performers, who were required to shave their forelocks to demonstrate an elderly (and non-erotic) appearance. This succeeded: in the space of fifty years, Kabuki had switched from an all-female dramatic art to an all-male one, like Shakespeare's. Kabuki remains all-male to this day.

By necessity, then, Kabuki became more sober and dramatic. By the end of the seventeenth century—which was also the beginning of Kabuki's greatest era—Kabuki had become a full-fledged dramatic medium, with multi-act plays, magnificent costumes and scenery, and star performers. Even its name was redefined with a wholly new etymology, employing three Chinese ideographs: *ka* ("song"), *bu* ("dance"), and *ki* ("skill"). Ka-

KABUKI AND BUNRAKU

About half of the Kabuki plays actually originated in the traditional Japanese puppet theatre, now known as Bunraku. First called *jōruri* ("literary delight"—the term is still used for the playscript), Bunraku is derived from medieval storytelling, puppet shows, and lute strumming; by the mid-seventeenth century, the integration of banjo-like *samisen* music and the elegant chanting art of Takemoto Gidayu (1651–1714) had brought this puppet theatre to a high art. During most of the seventeenth and eighteenth centuries, Bunraku rivaled Kabuki in popularity, and each of these sister arts borrowed plays and techniques freely from the other. Chikamatsu Monzaemon, Japan's greatest playwright, wrote for both theatres at various times; his plays can be seen on the stages of both theatres today.

Since 1984 Bunraku has been presented regularly at the National Bunraku Theatre in Osaka, Japan's second largest city. Bunraku puppets are wondrous creations: almost half life-size (they weigh seventy pounds apiece) and crafted with realistically movable eyes, eyebrows, mouths, and fingers. Each principal puppet requires three skilled operators (one for the head and right hand, one for the left hand, one for the feet). The puppeteers operate in plain view of the audience and are often hooded in black so as to keep the audience's attention on their puppets—the play's "characters." Operators are required to work with such perfect coordination that they must breathe in unison.

Although the characters are wooden, and the dialogue and narration are delivered from reciters kneeling in fixed positions beside the stage, each Bunraku performance is a deeply emotional experience. The recitation is a virtuoso performance in *gidayu* style, named after Takemoto, who invented it, and is fervidly chanted over a multi-octave range: the *gidayu* performer sighs, sobs, shouts, pants, screams, whispers, and emotes passionately as he delivers his text—to the stirring, frequently violent strumming of the *samisen*. It is said that it takes nineteen years for a *gidayu* performer simply to master the various types of weeping that Bunraku requires. And often the narration is punctuated with additional shouts or cries from the *samisen* players or even the lead puppeteer.

Scenery and costume in Bunraku are lavish, as in Kabuki, but it is the dramatic text, not the spectacle, that is always paramount in Bunraku, and the *gidayu* reciter respectfully hoists his script above his head at the beginning of each performance. It may be for this reason that Chikamatsu returned to the Bunraku for the last years of his career: it is a dramatic art that takes pains to honor—and illuminate—the written text.

buki had arrived at the theatrical forefront, where it has remained.

Visualizing Kabuki Today

In the same way that it is impossible to visualize what happens in an opera simply from reading its libretto, it is hard to get much sense of Kabuki by just reading its plays. Indeed, Kabuki plays are seen by the Japanese mainly as production vehicles, not literary texts, and such scripts are not widely read, even in Japan. Nor are the scripts normally considered fixed documents; most Kabuki plays have multiple authors, some of them anonymous, and almost all the working scripts incorporate improvisations and alterations that actors have interpolated over the years. Kabuki, in short, is a performance, not a text.

The Plays

Most Kabuki plays are in one of three categories: history plays (*jidaimono,* or "period

Kabuki is not spectacle alone: Kaganosuke's seppuku, *or ritual self-emboweling, witnessed and aided by his father, Daihanji, follows the ceremonial beheading of Princess Hinadori by her mother, creating a deeply emotional conclusion to the final scene of* Mount Imose. *This play, entitled* Imoseyama Onna Teikin *in Japanese, is one of Kabuki's most famous* jidaimono, *or history plays. Ichikawa Danjuro XII plays Daihanji in this performance; the role of Koganosuke is played by Nakamura Tokizo V. (Photo: Tomoko Ogawa.)*

things"), domestic plays (*sewamono*, or "trouble things"), or dance-dramas (*shosagoto*). History plays dramatize—usually in spectacular fashion—major political events of the remote past, with plots usually drawn from the Heian (9th–11th centuries), Kamakura (12th–13th centuries), or civil war (15th century) eras. Often, however, the historical distance is little more than a protective cover for playwrights and actors who were in fact reflecting—under the guise of an apparently historical depiction—upon various controversial issues of nobles and political officials of their own time.

Domestic Kabuki plays, by contrast, deal with the affairs of the townspeople, merchants, lovers, and courtesans of the playwright's own era, often focusing on the conflict—intense throughout Japanese culture—between affairs of the heart and the stern call

Shosagoto *plays are dance-dramas, the most famous of which is the 1753* Musume Dojoji *(The Maiden at Dojo Temple) in which the wronged, fire-breathing serpent Kiyohime, masquerading as the beautiful young lady Hanako, dances for the monks of Dojo Temple only in order to seize the temple's new gong and melt it down in vengeance. Nakamura Jakuemon IV plays the* onnagata *("women-type") role of Kiyohime/Hanako; the kneeling chanters and musicians upstage perform the* shosagoto*-accompanying* nagauta, *or "long song" music. (Photo: Tomoko Ogawa.)*

of duty. It was in such plays that Kabuki's greatest playwright, Chikamatsu Monzaemon excelled. A great many domestic plays end in suicide; many, in fact, end in double suicides, with the lovers vowing to meet again in the world to come. Such plays have been the subject of attempts to ban them, as they have led to real suicides in consequence, but the plays have remained popular and have continued to be performed.

Dance-dramas are among the most popular Kabuki works today and often deal with the world of spirits and animals, such as *Kagami Jishi,* "The Lion Dance." Other dance-dramas derive from ancient Nō dramas—most notably *Kanjincho,* which was the first play adapted from Nō to Kabuki (by Ichikawa Danjuro VII in 1840), and *Musume Dojoji.*

Kabuki Theatres

Kabuki theatres today are grand edifices in major Japanese cities: the Kabuki-za Theatre in Tokyo, the Minami-za in Kyoto, and the Shinkabuki-za in Osaka are all eye-catching Japanese baroque structures, with curved gables and undulating tile roofs. Decorated on the outside with Japanese lanterns, splashy posters, and bold vertical banners that indicate the current attraction and stars, each of these theatres is an important city tourist site, as well as a dramatic house. But Kabuki is regularly performed in contemporary, international-styled buildings built for it as well, such as the National Theatre (1966) and the Shimbashi Embujō (1983), both in Tokyo.

In Kabuki's famous shosagoto, Kagami Jishi *(The lion dance), the lion (played by Nakamura Kankuro V) is teased by butterflies (played by his sons Nakamura Kantaro II and Nakamura Schichinosuke II). (Photo: Tomoko Ogawa.)*

The Kabuki has always essentially been a dinner theatre. In previous centuries, Kabuki was an all-day affair that started at dawn, with the audience shuttling back and forth between tea houses and the stagehouse until the play's end late in the day. Today, at the Kabuki-za, matinee performances begin at 11:00 A.M. and evening performances at 4:30 P.M.; the audience is expected to take its meals during—not before or after—the performance. Thus the modern Kabuki theatre lobby contains *sushi* bars, box-lunch stands, restaurants, snack bars, and drink machines, and each Kabuki performance includes two or three breaks for meals, which are either eaten in the lobby or taken back into the auditorium for consumption during the next act. Kabuki is therefore not simply a drama, it is a consuming event.

The Kabuki auditorium is large—the Kabuki-za seats 2,600—and it is for the most part Western-styled, with seating in theatre chair rows that fill both the main hall and the two balconies. Reminiscent of older Kabuki, however, are a few traditional audience boxes at the sides, where spectators may kneel on *tatami* mats and sip tea while watching the performance. In past centuries, all Kabuki spectators knelt on such mats or on straw rushes simply strewn in front of the stage.

The Kabuki stage is vast: it includes a proscenium approximately ninety feet wide (twice

The geisha Agemaki and her followers enter the stage on the raised gangway known as hanamichi, *in a performance of the Kabuki play* Sukeroku *at the Japanese National Theatre in Tokyo. (Photo: Tomoko Ogawa.)*

the width of a standard Broadway stage) and an acting area thirty feet deep. And, in an invention wholly unique to Kabuki, the stage is abutted at stage right by a perpendicular runway that extends back through the audience. Known as the *hanamichi,* deriving from characters meaning "flower way" (perhaps because actors were offered flowers when they traveled down it), the *hanamichi* is used for many of Kabuki's most important entrances, exits, and confrontations. It also provides an intimacy between the actors and the audience within the large hall. Traditionally, a point known as the *shichi-san* (seven-three), which is seven-tenths of the distance toward the stage, becomes the "hot" spot on the *han-*

amichi for major speeches and tableaux; there is also an elevator underneath this point that is used for the entrances and exits of supernatural characters. For some plays a "temporary" *hanamichi* is also erected, parallel to the main one at stage left; some of the greatest Kabuki scenes feature actors speaking to each other, over the heads of the audience, from the *shichi-san* positions of the two *hanamichi.*

The Kabuki curtain (*hikimaku*)—a famous symbol of Kabuki art—is a lightweight cloth that has been used since the seventeenth century. Comprised of alternating black, green, and rust-colored vertical stripes, the *hikimaku* billows fetchingly in the slightest air currents and creates—for Kabuki devotees—a vibrant anticipation of the drama to come. The Kabuki performance begins with a few claps from wooden blocks, known as *ki,* which build into a furiously accelerating crescendo as the *hikimaku* suddenly is whipped across the stage by a stagehand hidden in its folds. It is a truly thrilling beginning to the Kabuki Drama.

Scenery

Kabuki is a visual spectacle from beginning to end. It employs three-story "buildings," dazzling costumes, lavishly painted backdrops, and elaborate stage machinery; indeed, Kabuki was the first theatre anywhere to make regular use of revolving stages (a Kabuki invention in 1758), stage elevators (dating from 1727), and rolling stage wagons. Kabuki scenery is stylized but not abstract. Flat, painted scenery provides illustrative backgrounds and indicates a locale but does not attempt to create realistic dimension, shadowing, or detail.

Conventions abound in the scenic picture. A stage-wide black backdrop indicates night; when it drops suddenly to the floor we are instantly shifted to day. A blue groundcloth represents ocean waves; a *tatami* floormat indicates an interior. Hanging strings of painted blossoms stand for cherry boughs in spring; these have a special and almost mystical meaning in Japanese culture, representing the brief and fragile existence of earthly life and romantic love. A river is sometimes depicted by a series of forward-rolling cylinders, painted with wavy blue, black, white, and gray lines; in the play called *Mount Imose,* which is sort of a Japanese *Romeo and Juliet,* such a river flows between the houses of the two warring families and symbolizes their antagonism and the lovers' estrangement. Kabuki scenery provides a highly aesthetic and symbolic support for the play's narrative; it does not attempt to create realistic stage illusion.

Music

At the extreme stage right of the proscenium opening is a raised music room, called the *geza,* with a slatted front wall; it is here that the play's orchestra performs. The chief instrument in that orchestra is a three-stringed banjo-like plucked instrument, known as a *samisen.* Made in a variety of sizes, and plucked vigorously with an ivory plectrum, the *samisen* can be subtly melodic or abrasively jarring; several *samisen* are ordinarily played in the *geza,* along with the *ki* clappers and various flutes, drums, gongs, and bells. The *geza* is almost continuously alive with music and sound effects, for in addition to its melodic strains, *geza* musicians are responsible for beating out rhythms, building the tension, creating the clamor of rain, wind, waves, and thunder, and indicating supernatural activity.

Nor is the musical accompaniment restricted to the *geza.* In the performance of many plays, visible musicians also accompany the action. Formally costumed *samisen* players, and special singer-chanters known as *gidayu,* appear onstage in many Kabuki plays, underscoring the action and often taking part in it.

KABUKI ACTING

Actor Families

Kabuki is a tightly controlled family business. Every leading Kabuki actor is a male member of one of only a dozen historic Kabuki families, a few of whose names—Nakamura, Onoe, Ichikawa, and Bando—are even more celebrated than the rest. An acting student not from one of these Kabuki families can no more become a major Kabuki actor than he could become emperor of Japan. A rigid system, known as *iemoto,* ensures the orderly succession of the family's actors, with fathers

The hikinuki *is an instant costume change performed—with the help of black-garbed* koken *(stage assistants)—right in front of the audience. Here the celebrated* onnagata *star Nakamura Jakuemon, playing the beautiful Hanako in* Musume Dojoji, *is changed in a matter of seconds from a red kimono to a white one. (Photo: Tomoko Ogawa.)*

The gidayu *reciter (left) chants an onstage commentary to many Kabuki dramas; he is always accompanied by a* samisen *player (right), who plucks his three-stringed banjo-like instrument with a heavy ivory plectrum. (Photo: Tomoko Ogawa.)*

passing on their skills, roles, and even their earned stage names to favored sons at elaborate public rituals.

Acting Style

That all the actors are male presents special challenges and opportunities to Kabuki art. So-called *onnagata* ("women-type") roles—particularly those of young courtesans and princesses—are assumed only by actors who have devoted years of study to their performance. Such "transvestized" acting is funda-

mental to Kabuki; it is said that if the Kabuki were to employ actresses, they would have to imitate the current, male *onnagata* performances.

But the *onnagata* style is not so much a realistic depiction of female behavior as it is a depiction—stylized and to a certain degree estranged—of a female "ideal" that Japanese men have developed over the centuries. *Onnagata* performance must include a deferential tilt of the head, pinched-back shoulders, and a silky gait with the knees bent and held together and the toes pointing inward and padding rapidly and silently. The style also features a high-pitched and sweetly demure voice; an extravagantly styled geisha-like appearance, with chalk-white make-up, tight and brightly reddened lips, and eye liner; a magnificently brocaded kimono; an elaborate wig and headdress. Certain movement patterns are also proscribed for *onnagata*, who, for example, may not step in front of male actors but must instead walk half a step behind.

It has often been said that the greatest *onnagata* performers create such an example of traditional Japanese femininity—in appearance, movement, and deferentiality—that they may serve as role models for real-world Tokyo and Osaka brides. It is doubtful that young Japanese women today set as much store in this maxim as their mothers did, but it is also clear that the Kabuki *onnagata* continues to represent an exquisitely refined version of what remains perceived in Japan as a cultural icon of traditional female beauty, grace, and modesty.

Actors playing principal male parts perform in two main styles. The "wild" *aragoto* is an outlandish exaggeration of the samurai warrior, an outrageous caricature of machismo, appearing mainly in the Kabuki history plays. *Aragoto* is comprised of a thunderous deep voice, capable of a back-of-the-house resonance in several registers; a high-stepping, arms-flailing deportment; and an enormous costume with billowing sleeves, elevator clogs, two long swords, and a red, purple, and black striped facial war-paint make-up known as *kumadori*. The *aragoto* style—associated in the Japanese mind with the military city of Edo (Tokyo)—was first developed by the great eighteenth-century star Ichikawa Danjuro I and is principally carried forth by his descendants in the Ichikawa family today.

Wagoto, or "soft style" acting, by contrast, is associated with the court city of Kyoto, where it originated and was perfected by the actor Sakata Tojuro, principally for use in domestic Kabuki. More realistic in his speech and movements, and gentler of disposition, the *wagoto* character wears whitened make-up and moves with refined delicacy and grace. *Wagoto* characters can be romantic but are often effeminate, petulant, and—to the audience—amusing.

Costumes and Wigs

Costumes in Kabuki are based on the history of the period described, and for domestic plays they are nominally realistic versions of appropriate period wear. It is with the principal players in history plays that Kabuki extends itself into extravagantly exaggerated versions of formal Edo-era (1616–1853) dress: elegant *kimono* (gowns, which are worn by both men and women), often covered by heavily brocaded stiff tunics and wrapped with sashes (*obi*), are the basic garments. White socks and *zori* (thong-like sandals) are the basic footwear, replaced by high wooden clogs for many *aragoto* characters. All Kabuki actors are elaborately wigged as well, often with grand headdresses and hair ornaments as added adornments. The combination of wigs and clogs can elevate a character to unusual heights, both physically and aesthetically.

In a unique Kabuki invention, both costumes and wigs are often changed instantaneously onstage with a quick yank of some threads by special assistants, called *koken,* who are clothed in black and stand behind the actors. Sometimes the change indicates a character transformation (as in *Musume Dojoji,* where a priestess metamorphoses into a serpent), and sometimes it is intended merely to delight the audience with Kabuki's theatrical dexterity.

Actor Training and Rehearsals

Professional Kabuki actors train for much of their lives. If they are talented enough, they will work up from smaller parts to larger ones, inheriting the major roles when they reach their forties and sometimes later. It is said that an actor does not develop a "Kabuki face" until he is in his fifties. All Kabuki actors must study the various forms of Kabuki music and dance, and they must learn to play the *samisen* and other instruments. All must also memorize the principal Kabuki repertoire, for there are few rehearsals—in the Western sense—except for the rare revivals of long-forgotten plays. Most Kabuki programs—consisting of separate four-hour matinee and evening performances—are rehearsed in just three or four days, which are devoted to working out new additions and the details of fight scenes. As one actor has noted, "With a standard play, . . . there isn't a single actor in the kabuki world that does not know every line. . . . Even at the first reading the actors are assumed to have memorized all their lines. An actor who does not know his lines will be embarrassed, and be ridiculed or scolded by the other actors."[1]

Actors' Assistants

The Kabuki actor is aided by various onstage assistants, known as *koken*, who are dressed wholly in black and sometimes veiled in black as well. Such shadowy figures may scurry onstage to help the actor through an on-stage costume change, as we have seen, and may also hand the actor his props, provide the actor with a stool to sit on (and take it away when no longer needed), straighten the actor's wig or costume after a dance, and even bring the actor a cup of tea after a big speech. *Koken* are also the apprentices of—and often the understudies for—the actors they serve, and are in these cases expected to finish the scenes of actors who become ill during performance.

---

[1]Nakamura, 1990, p. 105.

Acting Moments

Most of the individual "moments" of Kabuki performance have been stylized in ways set down years in advance—by the fathers, grandfathers, and elder ancestors of the men performing them today. As a group, these moments of stylized behavior—and there are a near-infinity of them—are known as *kata*, or "forms," and in many ways they are what the Kabuki audience specifically comes to see. Kabuki actors rarely walk; they sashay, they swagger, and they bound about in a variety of well-established and often electrifying moves.

No moment in a Kabuki performance is more astonishing than the *mie*, a sudden, grotesquely contorted "freeze" with which a male character, ordinarily in an *aragoto* role, concludes a violently accelerating dance movement coming at a key moment in the play. Classic *mie* posture requires the actor's eyes to cross, his head to sharply turn forward with the chin tucked in, and a big toe to point skyward. The *mie* is scored to the furious crescendo of special clappers, called *tsuke*, which are beaten by a formally garbed musician who kneels at the opposite side of the stage. The *mie* expresses, to the Kabuki audience, the emotional climax of a scene or a play, and the pause during the *mie* freeze is usually accompanied by shouts of approval and applause from the audience.

Fight scenes, or *tachimawari*, are group *kata* much beloved of Kabuki audiences; these are stylized to the point that there is no contact between actors or between weapons, or even any appearance of contact; rather, each actor waves his sword back and forth, to the left and right of his opponent, until one fighter either flees or falls, which ordinarily takes place in a matter of seconds. And when a defeated character falls, the actor merely tumbles into a somersault and runs offstage, the character's death being presumed and the actor's life preserved to "fight" (or represent fighting) again. Victory, on the other hand, is

One of Kabuki's most celebrated moments is Tomomori's suicide, which centers the
1747 jidaimono *(history play)*, Yoshitsune Sembon Zakura *(Yoshitsune and the
thousand cherry trees). Tomomori, a defeated Heike warlord, ties a ship's anchor
to his waist and throws it back over his head, following it overboard to a watery
death. The role is performed here by Ichikawa Danjuro XII in the blustery
aragoto *style his family has made famous. (Photo: Tomoko Ogawa.)*

A classically violent two-actor mie *freeze from Chikamatsu's* Nihon Furisode Hajime. *Nakamura Shikan VII is Orochi, a multi-headed serpent (a stage assistant's feet in the air represent his hooked tail), and Nakamura Hashinosuke III is the god, Susa no-o, with whom Orochi is locked in battle. (Photo: Tomoko Ogawa.)*

represented by a victory *mie*. All the battle sounds—sword blows and footfalls—come from the onstage *tsuke* beater at left, who has again entered for this sole purpose, and who times his beats to the action as it occurs and exits as soon as the fight is completed.

THE KABUKI AUDIENCE

The Kabuki audience has always enjoyed a participatory role in Kabuki's performance. As noted earlier, shouts of approval and disapproval for individual actors have been a feature of Kabuki since its earliest days, with

the insulting cry of "*Daikon!*" ("radish") being somewhat the Japanese equivalent to the mocking English cry of "Ham!" But a more common, and wholly unique, Kabuki feature is the specific vocal encouragement known as *kakegoe*, which is given to favored actors by certain fans, who, located in the topmost balcony of the theatre, boldly cry out approval at key moments during the play. These cries are formalized expressions, such as Japanese idioms for "You're the best!" and "This is what we've been waiting for!" But the most common *kakegoe* cry is the actor's *yago*, a traditional "shop name" taken by each actor (in addition to his stage name, family name, and legal name). The *yago* traditionally represents the town and shop his family may (or may not) have owned several generations ago. The shop name for the current star, Ichikawa Danjuro XII, for example, is Narita-ya, meaning "shop from Narita," a town near Tokyo. It is therefore customary for members of the gallery to cry out "Narita-ya!" when Danjuro enters the stage. They may also cry out "The Twelfth!" (in Japanese, of course) for the same purpose, as generational numbers are appropriate subjects for *kakegoe*. All Kabuki actors learn how to anticipate the *kakegoe*, and to time their speeches accordingly, so that the shouts from the audience actually add to rather than detract from the integrity of the performance. When Kabuki is performed abroad on tour, the absence of the *kakegoe* (as well as the absence of a *hanamichi*) can seriously unsettle the performers.

KABUKI AND ARTISTIC CREATIVITY

Kabuki changes slowly. An actor's *kata*—the word can be used to describe anything an actor does or wears—is handed down from father to son. When an actor first assumes a role, he is expected to perform the role precisely as it was handed down to him. Later, however, he is expected to add variations on his own—after, however, first requesting permission to do so from his father-teacher.

With all the rigidity of handed-down Kabuki performance *kata*, can acting in Kabuki be considered a creative art? Kabuki performers insist that it can and that Kabuki is always "in the moment" in the actor's head. In an eighteenth-century volume on Kabuki acting, the actor Sakata Tojuro says, "If you wish to be praised, the best way to set about it is to forget the audience and to concentrate upon playing the play as if it were really happening." In the same volume, another actor complains that when a contemporary (i.e., eighteenth-century) actor "turns his sword

round and threatens his enemy, it is but show, and his heart is not in his sword play [but in] the thought of the praise the audience will give him. . . . Therefore, his performance shows only weakness."[2] It seems that even the highly stylized Kabuki actor must—in part—be able to concentrate on the action more than the audience and to throw his "heart" into his "play" rather than just seek out public approval.

MODERN KABUKI

Although most Kabuki performances are of plays dating from the eighteenth century, the Kabuki has changed in some measure with the times. Theatre buildings became largely Westernized by the end of the nineteenth century, with lobbies, prosceniums, modern theatre seating, air conditioning, box offices, public address systems, and other theatrical paraphernalia refreshingly (or dismayingly) similar to their Western counterparts. Kabuki lighting is also Westernized, except that the audience area is fully lit during the performance. And Kabuki plays continue to be written, often in somewhat modern and Westernized forms. A "New Kabuki" was attempted when Japan was opened to the West, in the 1860s, and a particularly glittery "Super-Kabuki," with contemporary music and state-of-the-art lighting technology, is currently in vogue. Despite all of these influences and variations, however, it is the classic Edo repertoire that remains the standard in all Kabuki theatres, as it is this repertoire that, year after year, brings in the vast Japanese as well as worldwide audience.

KABUKI AND THE WEST

In conclusion, Kabuki is a brilliant dramatic form that, developing wholly independently of Western drama, both illuminates certain

---

[2]Dunn and Torigoe, 1969, p. 31.

A Kyōgen performance on the ancient Nō stage at the Mibu-dera (Mibu Temple) in Kyoto, Japan. These pantomime plays—with amateur actors, and costumes and masks dating from centuries past—have been given at this temple every spring for the past seven hundred years. (Photo: Robert Cohen.)

universals in the theatrical experience and defines hundreds of radical alternatives to Western practices. It has proven enormously influential to a growing number of Western theatre artists who have been captured by its appeal, but, more important, thrives today both as magnificent classic tragedy and as an overwhelmingly popular modern entertainment. Its survival through the centuries is a blessing, for Kabuki is a creation of artistic genius and unequaled theatrical marvels. And it is but one form of a huge repertoire of dramatic activity that has flourished—and in many cases continues to flourish—throughout the vast Asian continent.

NŌ DRAMA AND KYŌGEN

Nō is Japan's most revered and cerebral theatre. Kyōgen is a coarsely hilarious Japanese folk drama. Oddly, these two highly contrasting forms, collectively known as Nōgaku, have developed in tandem and have been performed together for centuries, with Nō as the high art and Kyōgen as the comic relief.

Nō is an exquisite, highly ceremonial, music and dance drama; it is mysterious, tragic, and usually supernatural. Most of the performers—all of whom are male—are masked. Nō texts—about 240 are performed today, most of them written by members of a single

Matsubame-mono *means "pine-tree setting" and is used to refer to Kabuki plays derived from the Nō, where a single painted pine tree is the sole pictorial backdrop. Such plays in Kabuki feature one or more painted pine trees plus a formal on-stage orchestra of samisen, flutes, drums, and chanters. (Photo: Tomoko Ogawa.)*

family about five hundred years ago—are richly poetic and are sung or chanted rather than spoken. And Nōgaku theatre design— used for both Nō and Kyōgen—is unique in every aspect of production: masks, wigs, costumes, and the theatre building itself.

In former times, Nōgaku took place outdoors, in a roofed, free-standing structure with the audience seated in a separate building overlooking it; white gravel separated the "stage" from the "house." Some such stages survive (see accompanying photo), but even today, when Nō theatres are wholly enclosed in larger buildings, the stage roof and white-gravel separation of stage and house are retained. The stage proper is eighteen feet square, with highly polished, Japanese cypress flooring, supported by large earthenware jars underneath which resonate with the actors' foot-stompings during certain dances. A bridge-like runway, called the *hashigakari,* angles away from stage right; it is used for entrances and exits. An ornate curved roof covers the stage; it is supported by four wooden pillars, each with its own name and historic dramatic function. And a wooden "mirror wall" at the rear of the stage bounces back the sounds of music and singing to the audience. A painted *yōgō* pine tree on this wall, gnarled but delicate, provides the only scenery used in Nō Drama, but the tree is not representational of anything—other than Nō itself. A four-man orchestra—flute, small and large hand drums, and stick drum—provides continuous musical accompaniment at the rear of the stage, and a chorus of six to ten singer-chanters is on a platform addition at stage left.

All Nō plays center on a single character known as the *shite,* who is interrogated, prompted, and challenged by a secondary character called the *waki.* Nō actors train only for one of these role-types and normally perform it throughout their careers. Whereas *waki* characters are always living male humans— usually ministers, commoners, or priests—

shite characters may be gods, ghosts, women, animals, or warriors and are played, unlike the *waki*, in masks.

Nō is hardly a drama of mass entertainment, and first-time viewers—including many Japanese—often find it bewildering. Plotting is weak or nonexistent. The language is medieval, elliptical, and often profoundly obscure. The cast is normally small, the action static and solemn, and the pace glacial. The basic Nō walk, said to be derived from tramping through rice paddies, is a slip-slide shuffle, with the feet barely leaving the ground. Even when unmasked, the actors are trained to keep their faces immobile and expressionless at all times. George Bernard Shaw's (possibly apocryphal) comment, that "Nō drama is no drama" is surely echoed by many Western theatregoers. Certainly Nō is produced today more for enthusiasts than for the general public, but it is of interest that the number of such enthusiasts—at least in Japan—is currently growing, not falling. Adherents of Nō are often passionate devotees. Nō productions, mounted mainly by amateurs but also by a growing group of professionals, are now presented regularly in major cities and at festivals throughout Japan, and the formal study of Nō performance techniques has become—like the studies of martial arts, flower arranging, and the tea ceremony—a Japanese national pastime. Nō's sublime mystery and serenity, reflective of deep Buddhist and Shinto values, resonates profoundly in contemporary Japanese life and has proven increasingly influential to Japanese as well as Western dramatists of the current era.

7

The Royal Theatre

The Renaissance exploded upon the Western world in a tumult of upheaval and exaltation, carrying with it an extravagance of feeling and a burst of creative energy. It was to be followed by a period of consolidation, refinement, and the imposition of rational sensibility and order.

Historians today call this maturation period the Enlightenment, this time in the eighteenth century when the fires of the Renaissance were banked and channeled into a general social and philosophical illumination. The Enlightenment became an age of intellectual classifications and structures: it brought forth the physical laws of Isaac Newton; the political and social analysis of the Baron de Montesquieu; the rational philosophies of René Descartes, John Locke, Immanuel Kant, and David Hume; and the comprehensive encyclopedias of Denis Diderot. It was an age that saw the establishment of great scientific and literary academies that worked to regularize wisdom and codify knowledge; it was also an age of politesse and social decorum, of powdered wigs, gilded snuffboxes, fine laces, and carved walking sticks. Elegance was the order of the day in that era governed by aristocratic tastes and the complex niceties inherent in an emerging code of precisely modulated social behavior.

EARLY COURT THEATRICALS: MASQUES

The Royal theatre of the courts of Charles II and Louis XIV did not simply materialize out of thin air, for the performance of plays and entertainments at court was customary from the fifteenth century onward. Classic Roman comedies were performed in the Italian court as early as 1485, and both Henry VII and Henry VIII in England maintained acting troupes for holiday theatricals in the sixteenth century. With the accession of Elizabeth to the English throne in 1558, court theatre became a major enterprise under the direct administration of a court officer known as the Master of Revels. It was his duty not only to supervise court productions but also to license plays and players for public theatre appearances.

The early European presentations at court included neoclassic comedies modeled on the works of Roman authors and "interludes," which were short comic pieces that carried a moral message. Restagings of public theatre plays were also presented, particularly during the Shakespearean era: at Christmas time in 1612, Shakespeare's *Henry IV Part One, Julius Caesar, Much Ado About Nothing, Othello, The Winter's Tale,* and *The Tempest* were presented at the court of James I, along with Beaumont and Fletcher's *Philaster, The Maid's Tragedy,* and *A King and No King,* Ben Jonson's *The Alchemist,* and sixteen other plays.

But the most notable form of court presentation of the sixteenth and early seventeenth century was the *masque,* which origi-nated in Italy and became a great favorite first of Henry VIII in England and then of James I. The masque was a musical dance-drama, performed by a mix of professional actors (who did the singing and speaking) and talented courtiers (who danced). The masque also featured extravagant scenery and staging that served as inspiration for much of the set design of succeeding centuries. Inigo Jones, an Italian-schooled Londoner who was court architect to James I, became England's foremost scene designer on the basis of his magnificent settings for the masques performed for the Stuart court and for the court of Charles I. The elaborate and costly settings that Jones created within the masque form from about 1605 to 1640 were to have a profound impact on English design for several generations.

For all its scenic splendor, the masque was undistinguished as literature. The texts were limited by a simplistic allegorical structure that allowed for only the most superficial treatment even when written by as skilled a dramatist as Ben Jonson, who wrote several. Shakespeare never attempted a masque, and Jonson abandoned the form after a humiliating dispute with Inigo Jones. The theatrical importance of the court masque was always acknowledged to be scenic rather than literary. This curiosity of the late Renaissance, however, was a significant precursor to the brilliant Royal theatre of the late seventeenth century.

It was not the first time such a consolidation had occurred, nor would it be the last. There seems to be a pattern in the history of civilizations whereby great bursts of creative energy—Dionysian, religious, omnisensual, and rhapsodic—are followed by intellectual structurings and forms—Apollonian, rational, synthesizing, and constrained. Great theatre art—that is, art that encompasses what is widely perceived as truth and beauty—tends to appear between the peaks in this pattern, at those transitional moments in history when *mythos* is turning into *logos* and the raw creative forces brought forth into a culture are just on the verge of coming into rational focus. Pure rawness, as of the Greek dithyramb, creates a theatre that is ultimately anarchic and publicly uncommunicative; pure form and focus, on the other hand, create a theatre that is stultified by its own discipline. And so it was that right between the Renaissance and the Enlightenment—in a brilliantly creative half century after the one era and before the other—the theatre experienced another of its great periods: the "Royal theatre" of the European court. The time was the last half of the seventeenth century; the locale was London, Madrid, and, particularly, Paris.

A THEATRE FOR COURTS AND KINGS

We choose to call this theatre the Royal theatre because of its fundamental association with the courts of kings. In Spain, at the court of King Philip IV, the plays of Pedro Calderón de la Barca provided light entertainment and philosophical food for thought for audiences at the palace and at the royal hunting lodge, La Zarzuela. In France, under the spectacular reign of Louis XIV, the "Sun King," the stirring tragedies of Pierre Corneille and Jean Racine and the scintillating, pointed comedies of Jean Baptiste Poquelin (known as Molière) flourished at a variety of theatres in and around Paris and at the country residences of king and court. And in England, there had been a dramatic Restoration of the Crown: after eighteen years of civil war and Puritan rule (1642–60), English royalty had returned to London and Westminster triumphant—in the person of the "Merry Monarch," King Charles II. Although the Shakespearean theatre had been literally destroyed (the Puritans had outlawed drama when they seized power and had burned the playhouses to the ground), a new and vigorous "Restoration drama" soon flourished under the new regime, featuring the brilliantly acidulous comedies of William Wycherley, William Congreve, John Vanbrugh, and George Farquhar and the elegant neoclassic tragedies of John Dryden.

There were also court theatres in Sweden (a Royal Swedish Theatre was opened in 1737), Denmark (the Royal Danish Theatre dates from 1772), czarist Russia, and in many of the dukedoms and principalities of Germany and Italy. The major kings and nobles of Europe were the prime patrons of these theatres, and the theatres—both the public ones in the cities and the private stagings in the palaces and chateaux—occupied a central position not only in royal society but also in the affairs of state.

Never in history has a body of theatre been so directly and so deliberately associated with national rule. Whether performances were public or private—and at different times they were both—the voice of the court and the voice of the king ultimately decreed what should happen in the theatre and what should not. "The great test of all your plays," said Molière, "is the judgment of the Court: it is the Court's taste which you must study if you want to find the secret of success."

What was the court? It was an aristocracy, in each country numbering in the thousands, a landed nobility drawn into the social circle of the king and sometimes into the king's very household. Manners and decorum became paramount political tools; splendid appearance, verbal dexterity, intellectual dispassion, social grace, and an abiding sense of whimsy and irony became the most prized personal gift in the Royal court of the seventeenth century. The king's authority, which was absolute, extended well beyond politics to encompass art, religion, literature, dress, deportment, and morality. The king's every activity became national gossip, the king's every expressed opinion had the effect of a verdict. When, in the theatre, the king applauded, a general ovation surrounded him; when he was silent, the courtiers rolled their eyes heavenward and reached for their fans and snuffboxes with an ostentatious show of despairing condescension.

All the European courts had much in common. France's Louis XIV was, after all, the son-in-law of Spain's Philip IV, and England's Charles II had spent his enforced exile in

Paris, learning kingship at the French court while he waited out the time until the Restoration would call him home to rule. The theatres of these European courts, naturally, had much in common as well. They were fundamentally elitist theatres, playing to highly restricted audiences. They were often housed in royal palaces and chateaux—and when they went into public buildings, these were intimate, indoor, candlelit spaces that accommodated mere hundreds, not thousands, of spectators.

The Audiences

The courtly audience was a cliquish one: a wealthy and urbane intelligentsia consisting of titled and untitled courtiers, members of the emerging professional class of civil servants and lawyers, and a few representatives of the upper crust of the emerging bourgeoisie. Needless to say, every audience also included a complement of social pretenders of every variety.

The theatre served as a veritable clubhouse for its audience. Seated in their boxes, gathering in the loges, milling about in the aisles and even perching upon the skirts of the stage, the courtly audience came to the theatre to see one another and to be seen, to make contacts and conduct business, to dally and contrive assignations. It was an audience always at least as interested in itself as in any goings-on on stage; it was an audience dressed to kill, anxious to be noticed, and blatantly on the prowl. The diaries of the English government official Samuel Pepys give us a delightful description of such an audience: in one account of a visit to the theatre, Pepys reported that he saw nothing of the play, so diverted was he by the ladies of the gallery. When the king was present, the audience's attention was particularly susceptible to distraction; hence, dramatic authors and actors alike were sorely challenged in the Royal theatre era to find effective means of capturing and keeping the audience's attention.

The Dramaturgy

The dramas of the Royal theatre were governed by critical standards that began to develop during the Renaissance and had since been expanded and refined by classical scholars and aestheticians who professed to take their lead from Aristotle: thus the term *neoclassicism* ("new classicism") is used to describe the accepted dramaturgy of the Royal era. Primary among the critical foundations of dramatic neoclassicism was the avoidance of stage violence and vigorous physical action: the ideal play was one in which the characters spent most of their time simply posing, gesturing, and talking. The brawling, swashbuckling, rough action of the Elizabethans was banished; even Shakespeare was considered somewhat primitive in the late seventeenth century, and his plays were "purified" by courtly writers to make them more acceptable to the new sensibilities.

Central to the dramatic standards of the era were the "Rules" of playwriting. These consisted of a set of ideas, purportedly derived from Aristotle, which had been codified into principles to be applied in writing plays. They covered everything from dividing a play into acts and scenes to structuring the plot and applying the proper metrics to the verse. The most famous section of the Rules dealt with the so-called Unities: the unities of place, time, and action (see box) and the unity of tone, which dictated that no tragedy was to contain comic relief, no comedy was to harbor sustained moments of pathos, and a verse pattern could not be altered in the course of a play. Tonal "irregularities" were deemed offensive to the sensibility of the court. So fiercely were the "Rules" propounded that they became virtually mandatory; playwrights who were said to have violated them often spent the bulk of their time thereafter defending themselves, and many finally gave up writing altogether.

The Royal theatre was one in which its principals consciously wrote for posterity as

THE RULES

Nothing is more perplexing about French neoclassic drama than the "Rules" formulated by critics of the time to define the requirements of play construction. For tragedy in particular, the formal structure dictated by the Rules was imposed almost as if by civil law. The observance of certain "Unities" was deemed to be essential. Among other things, a play was required to concern a single action, which must be conceived to take place in a single locale and within a single day's time. As a result of these restrictions, sprawling stories were sometimes muscled into strangling time confines: Corneille's great classic *The Cid,* for example, packs two duels, a proposal of marriage, a war, and dozens of crisis points into one day's action.

The Rules also dictated an avoidance of onstage violence, a five-act structure—with the stage clear at the end of each act—and, for poetic dramas, the most elaborate verse form known to the theatre: a fixed quatrain of six-foot iambic lines, each couplet rhyming in an alternating pattern of masculine and feminine (stressed and extended stress) endings, each line having a momentary break (*caesura*) after the sixth syllable. In effect, every play was also a word puzzle.

Not surprisingly, few dramatists succeeded in satisfying all the requirements. It is arguable, however, that when the Rules were addressed by a playwright of the genius of Racine or Molière, they fostered such a compression and focus of creative talent that the result shone incandescently from the friction between tight form and imaginative impulse.

---

well as for the moment; as a result, our records of the period are replete with documents: hundreds of plays with prefaces and whole volumes of contemporary criticism, theatre anecdotes, and descriptions of performances. It was in this period that dramatic criticism first came into its own and came to exercise a significant influence over its subject. It was said that a critic who had the king's ear could singlehandedly "reform" the stage, and many critics set out to do just that. Some of the most fascinating works of the times are plays that criticize other plays; their mere existence attests to the potential dramatic impact of criticism and the extent to which the "shop talk" of dramatists could engage contemporary audiences.

Staging Practices

The staging practices of the Royal theatre derived from practices that had been in use in Italy since the Renaissance. Italian Renaissance theatres were the first to make use of the proscenium and, with that, to establish a clear frontal relationship of audience to actors. The original proscenium was an arch that divided the theatre in half, sharply defining the house and stage areas: this design was adopted by theatres of the Royal era. It made way for a liberal use of painted, illusionistic scenery and, in some cases, the use of hoisting machinery. Later, in the Baroque period, designers would use the proscenium itself to create spectacular effects, but the major plays of the Royal theatre were staged fairly simply, with the scenery placed well back of the actors. There was little movement on stage—no dueling, of course—and courtiers who wanted to receive special attention from the audience could feel safe in purchasing seating on the stage itself.

The most important theatrical development of the Royal theatre era, however, occurred not in the area of dramatic structure or scenery and staging, but in the expanded admission of women into the acting profession.

WOMEN AND THE RESTORATION

Women were largely excluded from the theatre in ancient times; it is not even certain that they were permitted as spectators in the Greek Golden Age. Certainly all Greek and Roman actors were male, as were the priests who played the three Marys in the medieval *Quem Queritis* and, of course, all actors of Shakespeare's era. True, one Hrosvitha of Gandersheim, a tenth-century Benedictine abbess, had written six plays in the style of Terence (none, apparently, were produced), and there were actresses in some medieval pageants and European Renaissance plays, but theatre remained largely a male bastion, particularly in England, until the Royal era.

It was a proclamation of King Charles II in 1660 that first permitted women on the English stage, and Charles's reasoning was remarkably curious: it was to prevent the "immorality" of men playing "scurrilous" roles in women's costume:

> And for as much as many plays formerly acted do contain several prophane, obscene and scurrilous passages, and the womens' part[s] therein have been acted by men in the habit of women, at which some have taken offence, for the preventing of these abuses for the future we do hereby strictly command and enjoin that from henceforth no new play shall be acted . . . containing any passages offensive to pity or good manners . . . , and we do likewise permit and give leave that all the womens' part[s] . . . be performed by women so long as their recreations . . . be esteemed not only harmless delight but useful and instructive representations of human life.

Since King Charles was shortly to take up with the actress Nell Gwynne, his motives were probably not as pristine as he described them; given that actresses were much in demand as courtesan-mistresses to the Restoration nobility, there is clearly a tongue-in-cheek implication in these couplets from *The Conquest of China* (Elkanah Settle, 1675):

> Did not the Boys act Women's parts last Age?

Aphra Behn was the first woman in history to make a living as a dramatist, and her Restoration comedy, The Rover, *has had many modern productions, like this Williamstown Festival staging, featuring, from left to right, Edward Herrmann, Harry Groener, Christopher Reeve, and Stephen Collins. (Photo: Nina Krieger.)*

> Till we in pity to the barren stage
> Came to reform your eyes that went
>   astray
> And taught you Passion the true English
>   way.

Not only did women break into the acting profession in England at this time, but one woman became a popular playwright as well. Aphra Behn (1640–1689) was the first Englishwoman to earn her living as a dramatist, and, except for John Dryden, wrote more plays than any other Restoration author. There has recently been a renewal of interest in Behn's work, and, among her many comedies and serious dramas, *The Rover* and *The Emperor of the Moon* are constantly revived today.

The French theatre of the Royal era produced what most critics consider the finest tragedies since Shakespeare: specifically in the work of Pierre Corneille and Jean Racine. Shown here: Racine's Bérénice, *in a 1986 staging by France's first national theatre, the Comédie Française. (Photo: Marc Enguerand.)*

This development had begun in Italy more than a century before, during the 1540s, and had spread to Spain and France before being decreed by Royal charter in England in 1660. The widespread introduction of actresses brought a fundamental and irreversible change in the level of abstraction that had characterized Western theatre since its inception more than two thousand years earlier. The appearance of real women on the European stage—particularly of women clad in the revealing décolletage of the times—introduced a sensual realism that invigorated even the most turgid productions. No longer were romance, marital infidelity, sexual lust, and sexual jealousy portrayed in the abstract by men and boys "in drag"; the chemistry of heterosexual attraction could be created live, on stage, simultaneously with the play—by the simple expedient of having men play male roles and women play female roles. The impact of this development on theatrical life—both onstage and off—has been overwhelming.

THE FRENCH THEATRE

Unquestionably the most splendid theatre of the Royal era was the French theatre of the 1660s and 1670s. This was the theatre that brought together the brilliantly humane comedies of Molière, the exquisite verse tragedies of Racine, and the incomparably talented court of King Louis XIV. In turning to this apex of monarchal civilization, we are immediately struck by the dual location of dramatic presentation: at palaces and at playgrounds.

Royal Court and Tennis Court

It is not surprising, of course, that the king should choose to make his palaces places of entertainment for his court; that practice had been common in royal circles for centuries. During the reign of Louis XIV, the Louvre, Versailles, the Tuileries, the Palais Royale, Fontainbleau, Saint-Germaine-en-Laye, and the hunting chateau of Chambord were premiere sites for the plays of Molière and many another *grand siècle* playwright.

But the association of the French public theatre with a once popular tennis game is perhaps more surprising; certainly it is intriguing. We have noted already, in Chapter 1, how sports and the theatre have been intertwined since ancient times: the Romans staged plays in the intervals between gladiatorial contests, the Shakespearean theatre was at times alternated with bear-baiting bouts, and the overall functions and development of theatre and sports display some significant parallels. Now that theme surfaces anew. The Royal theatre in France, however, was associated with tennis, not bear-baiting, and indeed this association points up some of the fundamental cultural dissimilarities between Elizabethan England and the France of Louis XIV.

The public theatre building in seventeenth-century France was for the most part an adaptation—and a rather modest adaptation at that—of a type of structure that was first built to accommodate a game called *jeu de paume,* a forerunner of modern-day tennis. *Jeu de paume,* or "palm game," was originally a simple handball sport that, with the addition of racquets much like contemporary ones, became the favorite game of the French King Henry IV (r. 1589–1610). It is estimated that by the end of the sixteenth century there were a thousand or more *jeu de paume* courts in Paris alone, many more in the countryside.

The *jeu de paume* (the name refers to the building as well as the sport) was a rectangular structure with spectator galleries on the two long sides and an open or windowed area running around the building below the roof. Because they were free of partitions and provided for both daylight (the windows) and the seating of spectators (the galleries), the *jeux de paume* lent themselves well to theatrical conversion—particularly to the frontal, proscenium-type theatre that became the order of the day. It was only natural, as the tennis game waned in popularity and the theatre grew, that this conversion would take place. Even the theatres that were not converted tennis courts—and the most famous one, the Hotel de Bourgogne, was not—were designed almost as if in imitation of them, for the rectangular, galleried shape became the dominant form of theatre architecture for the entire period.

The public theatre that developed from this *jeu de paume* configuration also bore a certain resemblance to the public theatre of

A jeu de paume *court with game in progress.* (Drawing: John von Szeliski.)

A jeu de paume *court after conversion to theatre. The conversion consisted mainly in the addition of a simple stage at one end of the building and the creation of spaces where actors could enter and leave the stage. (Drawing: John von Szeliski.)*

the room itself as scenery...

STEEP HORSESHOE SEATING surrounding the main space.

THE MAIN PORTION of THE AUDITORIUM was a COURTLY ARENA ...

▲

The "picture frame" theatre of the Royal theatre era gave physical form to the sense of theatre as a decorative diversion, an elegant and courtly meeting place. The proscenium divided audience and stage, elaborately framing the action of the play for those who wanted to look at it. Painted scenery, often in the form of receding "wings" delineated in strict perspective, was a notable feature of Royal era staging. (Drawing: John von Szeliski.)

Modern productions of foreign plays are often translated into contemporary language—which you cannot do so easily in English language works. A 1991 Alabama Shakespeare Festival production of Molière's The Misanthrope (right) is translated into modern American by Neil Bartlett and set in the show-biz environs of Southern California. Funda Duyal is Celimène. (Photo: Alabama Shakespeare Festival.) A 1989 production of Molière's The Miser (below), directed by Andrei Serban at the American Repertory Theatre, plays similarly fast and loose with its original setting and language. (Photo: Richard Feldman.)

Shakespeare's London in that it featured a large standing-room area (the *parterre,* or pit) and surrounding, costlier *loges,* or galleries.

The Public Theatre Audience

It was a varied audience that attended the Parisian public theatres of the seventeenth century, a mixture of old nobility and newer bourgeoisie. The Parisian audience has never been shy or aloof, but this audience was particularly notable for its audacious appearance and its vociferous voicing of opinion. The seventeenth-century parterre was a bazaar of ideas, fashions, philosophies, and political intrigues.

Many of the spectators were already on hand when the theatre doors opened at one o'clock, a full two hours before the performance was to begin. They crowded inside and filled the intervening time with activity: political and romantic assignations; brawls at the door as flippant cavaliers tried to enter without paying and ran up against stalwart doorkeepers; and the continual hawking and peddling of "refreshing drinkables: lemonades, lemon sherbert, strawberry, currant, and cherry waters, dried confitures, lemons, Chinese oranges, and, in winter, drinks which warm the stomach, such as rose liquors and Spanish wines." Unlike the pit of the Elizabethan theatre, which was sought out mainly because of its low price, the Parisian parterre was regarded as a splendid place to be noticed, second only to the more costly stage seating as a place to display one's fine dress and deportment. Gossip, gawking, and gallivanting—not to mention the possibility of actually rubbing elbows with the king—were fully as much motivation for this Parisian theatrical crowd as was the prospect of seeing a play.

MOLIÈRE

No one, certainly, better typifies the Royal theatre age than Molière.

Born Jean-Baptiste Poquelin (it is hazarded that he changed his name to protect his family from being dunned for his early debts), Molière was to become the most produced French playwright of all time. He personifies the wit, the charm, the ebullience, and above all the genius of his era; he was, as well, one of its most fascinating and complex individuals. An actor, producer, critic, and comic playwright, he was what the French call *un homme du théâtre,* a complete "man of the theatre," whose gifts and achievements radiated into every aspect of theatrical culture. He is today the best loved foreign-language playwright on the English-speaking stage. In France he is a national hero comparable to Shakespeare in England, and his theatre company still remains the core and the source of France's great national theatre, the *Comédie Française,* which has now performed continuously for more than three hundred years following its creation seven years after his death.

Molière is known primarily as an author of comic plays: his *Tartuffe, The Misanthrope, The Miser,* and *The Doctor in Spite of Himself,* for example, have found such favor with audiences around the world that they are now essential pieces of repertoire in many companies. He was also, however, a theatrical manager of singular capability: he was not only the leader of his own celebrated troupe but also the producer of dozens of plays by other writers, including Pierre Corneille, with whom he once collaborated, and France's premiere tragedian, Jean Racine, whom Molière actually discovered and first produced. In addition, Molière was a fine actor who played the leading roles in most of his productions—to the great delight of his audiences and patrons. And he was a critic—for although he often railed against excessive critical strictures, his works themselves embody some of the most incisive dramatic criticism of his time.

Nor was France the only country on which Molière's genius had impact in his own time: English Restoration drama owes an incalculable debt to Molière. William Wycherley's *The*

Plain Dealer, one of the outstanding Restoration comedies, is in part an adaptation of Molière's *The Misanthrope,* and the general influence of Molière's style and structure can be felt throughout the English comedy of the era.

Molière's theatrical career ran the gamut from abject failure to dizzying success. He was born in Paris in 1622, the son of the Royal Upholsterer to King Louis XIII; thanks to his father's position, he gained an early exposure to the court. After receiving a superior classical education at the College of Clermont and a degree in law at Orléans, Molière renounced both his academic training and his father's business in order to enter the theatre, shortly before his twenty-first birthday, in 1643.

His first enterprise—the Illustre Théâtre in Paris—failed within two years, and he was imprisoned for the theatre's debts. Following his release, Molière and his troupe headed south, where for the next twelve years they entertained public and gentry alike in the street theatres and private homes of the French provinces. During this time Molière became the principal director of his troupe and, for the first time, an author of comedies in the troupe's repertoire. When finally the company was invited to Paris to play before the king—now Louis XIV—it was one of Molière's own plays, an afterpiece to the main work of the evening, that secured the royal favor and led to Molière's installation, at the king's direction, at the Théâtre du Petit Bourbon in the French capital. An odd arrangement faced Molière at that theatre—at first his company could perform only on the "off" days; a popular *commedia dell'arte* troupe had all the most prestigious afternoons already booked. But as Molière's brilliant plays began drawing ever-greater attention, his company moved to the "on" days—and soon to the more elegant Palais Royale, where they received from Louis the official name of "King's Comedians." Thus, Molière's return to Paris had become a triumph, and for the rest of his

---

MOLIÈRE ON THE "RULES"

You are most amusing with your rules of Art, with which you embarrass the ignorant, and deafen us perpetually. To hear you talk, one would suppose that those rules of Art were the greatest mysteries in the world; and yet they are but a few simple observations which good sense has made, the same good sense which in former days made observations every day without resorting to Horace and Aristotle. I should like to know whether the great rule of all rules is not to please, and whether a play which attains this has not followed a good method? Can the public be mistaken in these matters, and cannot every one judge what pleases him? Let us laugh at the sophistry with which the critics would trammel public taste, and let us judge a play only by the effect which it produces upon ourselves. Let us give ourselves up honestly to whatever stirs us deeply, and never hunt for arguments to mar our pleasure.

Molière

---

life he was one of the most celebrated and controversial figures in the French court and in Parisian literary life.

It was a glittering life. At the theatre, Molière continued to share a bohemian and rather notorious existence with his intimate company family. In the days of his Illustre Théâtre, he had acquired as his mistress the actress Madeleine Béjart, with whom he had lived throughout the twelve years of provincial touring. Once in Paris, however, he married the mysterious Armande Béjart, said to be Madeleine's sister, but openly rumored to be Madeleine's (and Molière's) daughter instead. Both Béjarts continued to perform with Molière for years, providing endless fodder for the popular press. In the literary world, Molière was active in a circle of writers who gathered regularly at the Mouton Blanc, a Parisian café; included in that group were the tragedian Jean Racine, the critic Nicolas Boileau, and the fabulist Jean de La Fontaine.

But perhaps the most remarkable aspect of Molière's life was his relationship with the Sun King himself, the *Grand Roi* of that *grand siècle*. Louis XIV provided Molière with his theatre and his title. He granted Molière an annual pension and was godfather to his first child. In finally permitting the public presentation of Molière's controversial *Tartuffe,* King Louis overrode the violent objections not only of the Archbishop of Paris and the established deaconry of France, but also of his own mother, Queen Anne of Austria. Louis further commissioned plays from Molière annually and bade Molière to premiere virtually all of his other plays at court before their public debuts; he even *performed* in two Molière comedies at their court presentations. Finally, toward the close of his life and with Molière long dead, King Louis paid final tribute to his erstwhile protégé by staging private productions of several of Molière's comedies for his own personal enjoyment.

The court was not the sole audience to Molière's theatre, of course, nor was it his sole source of inspiration. The influence of the boisterous *commedia* is as evident in his plays as is the neoclassic style that he fashioned after Terence (whose works Molière knew by heart in the original Latin). Indeed, the fact that Molière's theatre still gloriously survives two hundred years after the French monarchy was toppled by revolution indicates how well his vision transcended courtly preciosity. Molière bespoke the best impulses of his age. His works glorify sensibility, rational temperament, personal freedom, and common justice. They deplore pompousness, greed, artifice, and humbuggery. In so artfully exposing the foibles of his own time, Molière hit at man's timeless ingenuity at contriving disguises for ambition, exploitation, and lust. A complex man himself—and his life seems to have been

AN ELEGANT ROUGHNESS

There is in Molière's writing a colloquial, rough quality and there is also an elegance: on the one side humor, which shows the characters as unintentionally funny; on the other side wit, by means of which the characters are deliberately funny. . . . The sources of the dualism are not difficult to determine. The colloquial elements, especially the naturalness of his language, whether in prose or verse, were shaped by his experience as a traveling performer and fortified by his knack for clothing dramatic ideas in what look suspiciously like everyday sentences. The elegance comes partly from the strained, even stilted, literary mannerisms of his time, partly from the nature of the Court audiences to whom he played in the later years of his career, partly from his striving for a new and elevated style in the writing of comedy.

Albert Bermel

riddled with conflict and despair, even in his most successful years—he well understood the difficulty of arriving at sensible, simple solutions to many of life's problems. His comedies repeatedly explore irreconcilable human conflicts: common sense versus implacable desire, hard reality versus galloping irrationality, personal integrity versus political and social ambition. Certainly an element of self-therapy is suggested in Molière's best work—particularly when we consider that his plays were written to be performed by him, his often-estranged wife, his best friends, and his past and present mistresses. Indeed, it seems likely that Molière drew heavily upon his own predicaments to help his audiences laugh at the human comedy. At all events, it is certain that he knew whereof he wrote. For that reason, his plays constitute a "humane comedy" of universal applicability.

THE BOURGEOIS GENTLEMAN

The Bourgeois Gentleman is characteristic of most of Molière's work in two respects: it is a social satire, and it pleased court and public alike with its rare combination of wit, romance, sharp-edged social commentary, and farcical hijinks. A comedy-ballet in five acts (the ballet, with music by Jean-Baptiste Lully, separates the acts and also works into the main action), it is structured as a typical royal *divertissement:* a frothy entertainment of simple format designed solely for the diversion of the court, to be savored with relish and quickly forgotten. Owing to Molière's comic genius, however, this play escaped the fate of most of its kind and became one of the best loved and most admired comedies of all time. Commissioned by Louis XIV for a 1670 premiere at the Royal Chateau of Chambord (a palatial hunting lodge in the Valley of the Sologne, about one hundred miles south of Paris), *The Bourgeois Gentleman* achieved great initial acclaim; and after several repeat performances it was brought north to Paris, first to play at the suburban Palace of Saint-Germain-en-Laye, then in the public theatre of the Palais Royale. Ever since that time it has continued to attract public favor. It is today a staple of the Comédie Française, and it is regularly translated, produced, and enjoyed around the world.

The Bourgeois Gentleman is a comedy of character, and it deals with a phenomenon as familiar in our day as it was in the seventeenth century: social climbing. Its central character, one Monsieur Jourdain, is a merchant of the bourgeois (middle) class who aspires to gentility and the status of nobility; his attempts to improve his standing are at first amusing, finally ridiculous and hilarious as he sacrifices family obligations, common sense, and his own welfare in pursuit of his goal. It is not merely ambition that Molière satirizes here, but foolish perceptions as well: what Jourdain takes for "gentle" elegance is mere foppery, what he takes for "gentle" admiration is mere flattery. Molière himself was no stranger to ambition—he the upholsterer's son turned court favorite—and he knew well the tortuous path of social ascent. As both author of the play and original performer of the role of Monsieur Jourdain, Molière had his subject well in hand.

Our imaginary reconstruction of the Palais Royale production of *The Bourgeois Gentleman* is based on incomplete evidence, but from the time of Molière onward we do begin to have a fair body of written and pictorial documentation of theatrical production.

The theatre of the Palais Royale, which was Molière's public home for most of his career, was the most elegant theatre in Paris at that time. Built in 1641 for Cardinal Richelieu, the theatre was a tennis-court-sized structure that measured about 108 by 36 feet and was equipped with a handsome proscenium arch. It was a lavish work of theatre architecture that showed strong signs of Italian influence. Although its galleries were set up in the fashion of the *jeu de paume*, it differed from other Parisian theatres in that it originally contained a curious "amphitheatre" arrangement of stone steps that rose in the parterre across from the stage and supported twenty-

It is likely that formal staging for most of Molière's works—except for the ballets—was kept to a minimum by Molière the director. This conclusion is suggested by several bits of evidence. First, we know that the stage of his theatre was relatively small and apparently did not have an upper level, that courtier-spectators were often seated on the periphery of the stage itself, and that Molière was regularly called upon to restage works at court. Add to that the highly verbal nature of the plays themselves and his troupe's twelve years of ensemble touring with its *commedia* associations. All of these factors indicate a staging pattern that could be improvised by the actors on the spot. Molière portrays precisely that sort of situation in his play *The Versailles Rehearsals,* in which he has the director saying to some actors, "You there—arrange yourselves about, these aren't the sort of people who crowd each other," and telling two others to jump up and sit down as they wish, according to their "natural anxiety" in the scene.

seven rows of wooden bleachers. This arrangement ultimately proved unsuccessful. The bleachers were uncomfortable and somewhat treacherous—Queen Anne of Austria, the stern mother of Louis XIV, is said to have toppled backward on one of the rows while watching a play, exposing her undergarments for several hilarious minutes as she tried to right herself—and someone, probably Molière, had the seats removed, returning the parterre to its more familiar function as a standing and ambling space. Situated conveniently close to court, splendidly equipped with machinery, ornate in its interior design and fittings, the Palais Royale theatre held many attractions for distinguished audiences.

And beyond question it presented magnificent plays, performed by one of the greatest acting troupes ever.

The Bourgeois Gentleman is set in the home of Monsieur Jourdain; in Molière's day the interior setting was created by two angle wings, representing interior sidewalls, and by a shuttered backdrop called a *ferme.* The angle wings were realistically painted and in perspective; seemingly three-dimensional bays were skillfully painted onto the flat surface, and the realistic appearance was heightened by the addition of actual moldings and sconces. A ceiling cloth enhanced the general illusion. Yet there was no effort at realism in the contemporary sense at all. For example, no actual doorways were provided: the angle wings did not connect with the painted *ferme* at the rear, and performers simply made their entrances and exits in the space between these two elements or else downstage of the entire setting.

How was Monsieur Jourdain's house decorated? We have a rare glimpse of it in a frontispiece to the published edition: this shows, in addition to tapestries, a set of wall sconces that take the excruciating form of a cherub's severed arm, mounted somewhat like stags' heads on the angle wings. It is an element of decor meant to represent Jourdain's lack of taste, one of the first known examples of background scenery used for a specific satiric effect.

The Bourgeois Gentleman opens with a musical overture, played by a "great assemblage of instruments" located in front of the stage. This overture, composed by Jean-Baptiste Lully—the "other Jean Baptiste," who was later to become Molière's rival for the King's attentions—foretokens the *divertissement* format that this play follows: a theatrical combination of scenes, songs, and dances. This is the precursor of the musical comedy mode of modern times.

As the overture proceeds, the candles of the onstage candelabra are lit and slowly hoisted to positions above and to the sides of

The tailor presents a ridiculously pretentious gown—with mismatched fabrics and upside-down flowers—to a startled but foolishly impressed Monsieur Jourdain (Charles Hallahan) in a dazzling production of The Bourgeois Gentleman, *produced by the American Conservatory Theatre. (Photo: William Ganslen, ACT.)*

the action. The costs of tallow were not insignificant, and producers always waited until the last moment to light the stage, letting the afternoon sunshine from the upper windows provide illumination insofar as possible.

A chair and table are seen at the middle of the stage; on the chair sits a "music student," at work composing a song that will figure into the ensuing dialogue. It would be a simple matter for the furniture to be preset and the actor likewise, but it is also possible that chair, table, and "music student" rose mechanically through the floor; machinery for that very purpose existed in the Palais Royale at the time, and the effect would have bridged overture and story in a fine bit of musical stagecraft.

The overture ends. From rear wings on either side come two groups—a music master and his musicians, and a dancing master and his dancers. After the music master checks his "student's" composition, the two masters are left on stage to discuss the absent hero:

MUSIC MASTER: (*grinning broadly*) We have found here just the man we need: our "ticket to ride," this (*sniffs loudly*) Monsieur Jourdain—with his visions of gallantry and *noblesse oblige* flitting about his head. (*Chortles pompously*) A true "pay-trone of the ahts," this "Monsewer"—I only wish there were more where he came from!

DANCING MASTER: (*mincing, with a flourish of his walking stick*) Well, I suppose, but I certainly wish he knew something about the arts he patronizes!

MUSIC MASTER: He knows nothing, doesn't he? (*They both laugh.*) But he pays through the nose, and that's what counts: that's what the arts need these days, my dancing friend, money!

DANCING MASTER: But to PLAY for these fools! (*He crosses down toward the audience, studying them while talking to the* MUSIC MASTER.) For me, I confess I hunger more for the applause of those who can tell good work from bad, who can sense the refinements and delicacies of art, who know beauty when they see it (*he poses prettily, clasping his hands upon his stick*)—and who can reward an artist with the honor of their favor and praise. (*He smiles.*)

MUSIC MASTER: (*following him: enthusiastically*) Of course, of course; nothing is better than that—but we also must live! Praise must be mixed with something solid if we are to pay our rent: tell your people of refinement to put their money where their mouth is! (*They face each other.*) This Jourdain, it's true, is somewhat unenlightened

(*the* DANCING MASTER *snorts agreement*)—he speaks backwards and forwards at the same time (*the* DANCING MASTER *chuckles approvingly*)—and he applauds only when he's not supposed to (*the* DANCING MASTER *breaks out in a burst of laughter*)—but his money makes up for everything: he has great wisdom in his purse, and his praise comes in the coinage of the realm. (*The* MUSIC MASTER *ambles away, jingling his purse full of coins.*)

DANCING MASTER: (*scowling*) Well, you're right, as usual, but I don't like it; you're just too money-minded, my friend.

MUSIC MASTER: And you? You take what he gives out, just as I do!

DANCING MASTER: (*self-righteously*) Yes, but it hurts me to do so! (*The* MUSIC MASTER *clutches his heart in mock pain.*) I only can wish for a more tasteful benefactor!

MUSIC MASTER: (*realistically*) Well, of course, so would we all—but that's life, my friend. In any event, Monsieur Jourdain is giving us the chance to make names for ourselves at court—and if you will take my advice, you'll let him pay us what the court won't, and let the court praise us as this imbecile can't!

DANCING MASTER: (*quickly*) Shhhhh! Here he comes.

Like Hephaestus and Might in the opening scene of *Prometheus,* these masters argue in order to give us a foretaste of the central character and his basic predicament; here, however, the setup of the hero is clearly comic and devoid of awe. Molière, of course, must tread a fine line in his satire in this scene; he cannot afford to alienate true patrons of the arts: his own fortunes rest on the sustained approval of often less-than-tasteful followers.

Monsieur Jourdain's "prepared" entrance follows Molière's own direction, as explained by him in his "rehearsal play," *The Versailles Rehearsal,* as that of the "ridiculous marquis" always "guaranteed to get laughs":

MOLIÈRE: Now remember to come in as I've instructed you, with that put-on pomposity that is called grandness, combing your wig, and humming a little tune between your teeth, like this: la la la la la la la.

Jourdain is a sight to behold. He is followed by two lackeys, and at his entrance the singers and dancers, who had earlier retired from the scene, again emerge from the wings. He is a model of outrageous foppery:

M. JOURDAIN: (*crossing to the two masters and nodding grandly*) Well, gentlemen? And what do we have here? You have made for me, I presume, some little drollery for the afternoon?

DANCING MASTER: (*confused*) Drollery?

M. JOURDAIN: (*delighted*) Ah, yes! (*Then, fearful he has said something wrong*) Ah, no! (*Desperate*) But how do you call it? (*To each of them, in turn*) Your prologue? Your, um, dialogue? Your singing and dancing?

DANCING MASTER: (*relieved*) Ah, yes!

MUSIC MASTER: (*overly hearty*) At your service!

M. JOURDAIN: (*thrilled*) I know I've made you wait a bit, but it is only because I have decided today to dress in the fashion of quality folk, and my tailor has sent me (*he raises the hem of his gown*) these stockings—(*confidentially*) silk, of course—which (*angrily, to his lackeys*) take forever to get on! (*He hastily lowers his gown.*)

MUSIC MASTER: (*embarrassed*) We are here to attend your convenience.

M. JOURDAIN: (*hastily*) Well, then, you mustn't go—they are bringing my new suit, and you must see me in it!

DANCING MASTER: (*obsequiously*) Whatever pleases you.

M. JOURDAIN: (*proudly*) Then you will see me in the height of fashion—from toe to head!

MUSIC MASTER: (*trying not to laugh*) We don't doubt it.

M. JOURDAIN: (*turning about*) My dressing gown *à la indienne;* do you like it?

DANCING MASTER: (*smiling, through gritted teeth*) Très, très chic!

M. JOURDAIN: (*gesturing grandly with the folds of the garment*) My tailor tells me it's the morning fashion of quality folk!

MUSIC MASTER: (*with an ironic wink to the* DANCING MASTER) Suits you perfectly!

M. JOURDAIN: (*suddenly and imperiously*) Lackeys! I say, LACKEYS!

THE LACKEYS: (*springing forward in terror*) Yes, Monsieur?

M. JOURDAIN: (*turning to look at them*) Oh, nothing, nothing. (*As though it were obvious*) Just checking! (*The lackeys return to their position, puzzled.* JOURDAIN *admires them and turns, beaming, to the masters.*) How do you like their liveries?

DANCING MASTER: Magnificent.

M. JOURDAIN: (*as one bestowing a precious gift, opens his gown, revealing red velvet tights and a hideous green velvet jacket*) My little underdress outfit for the morning exercises!

MUSIC MASTER: (*grinning through his revulsion*) Oh, très gallant, très gallant indeed.

This scene is classic comic fun in the spirit of a theatrical tradition that goes back as far as Aristophanes: funny clothes, funny manners, and funny speeches. With that combination, common social pretensions can be taken to outlandish extremes. Here, the foppery and foibles of Jourdain are wonderfully satirized by his absurd dress and behavior and the slickly comic repartee.

The first two acts of *The Bourgeois Gentleman* provide a series of variations on this opening scene. Successively, a fencing master, a philosophy master, and finally a tailor visit Jourdain, each offering advice and instruction on the art of being a gentleman.

The scene with the fencing master is pure physical farce that owes its effect to inventive stage business interspersed with brisk commands; imagine it played, say, by Bill Murray and Chevy Chase:

FENCING MASTER: (*giving* JOURDAIN *a sword*) Come, sir, your bow! (JOURDAIN *bows deeply and stiffens; his back has gone out.*) Up! (FENCING MASTER *playfully points his sword at* JOURDAIN's *belly;* JOURDAIN *quickly straightens up.*) Body erect! More to your left! Not so far apart, those legs! Square your feet! Your wrist opposite your hip! (JOURDAIN *grows confused as the* FENCING MASTER *barks his orders faster and faster.*) The tip of your sword across from your shoulder. Relax your arm! Your left hand at eye level! Your left shoulder—square it! Head up! (JOURDAIN *is now twisted like a pretzel.*) Look fierce! (JOURDAIN *makes a ludicrous attempt to look warlike.*) Advance! (JOURDAIN *advances and stumbles.*) Body firm! (JOURDAIN *sighs;* FENCING MASTER *slashes at* JOURDAIN's *sword;* JOURDAIN *screams as his sword vibrates out of control.*) Touché! One, two, retreat! (JOURDAIN *retreats, still trying to gain control of his vibrating sword.*) Again: stand firm! (JOURDAIN *tries to resume his warlike mien.*) Jump back! (JOURDAIN *does so.*) The sword forward and the body back. One! Two! (FENCING MASTER *hits* JOURDAIN's *sword again,* JOURDAIN *yelps.*) Touché! Keep coming! Advance! (JOURDAIN *begins to whimper.*) Body firm! Advance! (JOURDAIN *is crying.*) From there! One! Two! Retreat! (JOURDAIN *starts to run away;* FENCING MASTER *"spanks" him with his sword.*) Again! Jump back! *En garde*, sir, *en garde*!

M. JOURDAIN: (*in a paroxysm of terror; contorted, but still trying to look his best*) Owwwwww!

MUSIC MASTER: (*grinning*) You're doing fine!

FENCING MASTER: (*didactically, illustrating each point with a flourish of his foil*) It is as I said before, the whole secret of fencing lies simply in hitting (*swats* JOURDAIN) and not being hit. Do you understand? It is more blessed to give blows (*swats again*) than to receive them—did I not explain that sufficiently the other day? All you need concentrate on is that little outward movement of the wrist—(*stops for a moment, afraid of having contradicted himself*) or is it a little inward movement . . .

M. JOURDAIN: (*overjoyed*) You mean if I could learn that, I could be certain of killing my opponent—without myself being killed?

FENCING MASTER: (*fiercely*) Of course! Isn't that what I just showed you?

M. JOURDAIN: (*trying to put the best face on it*) Oh! Yes, of course.

The fencing scene is a classic rendition of the comic tradition of poking fun at physical braggadocio; this tradition can be traced through a long line of comic swordsmen in theatrical history, including Aristophanes' Lamachos, Plautus's Miles Gloriosus, and Shakespeare's Falstaff. The satire of the braggart soldier derives from a fundamental human fear—the fear of armed physical assault—and gains in hilarity precisely as it touches unconscious terrors.

The next scene portrays yet another familiar predicament—intellectual intimidation—and another character—the pedant—with theatrical antecedents dating back to the time when Aristophanes caricatured Socrates on the Athenian stage.

MASTER OF PHILOSOPHY: (*with grave sonority*) There are five vowels, A, E, I, O, and U!

M. JOURDAIN: (*nodding sagely*) Yes, I know.

MASTER OF PHILOSOPHY: (*studiously*) The sound "A" is formed by opening the mouth wide. (*He does so, saying*) "A."

M. JOURDAIN: (*imitating*) "A" . . . "A" (*Smiling*) Yes!

MASTER OF PHILOSOPHY: The sound "E" is made by closing the jaws. (*Opening his mouth*) "A" (*Closing it*) "E."

M. JOURDAIN: (*opens and closes his mouth, mechanically*) "A"–"E" "A"–"E." (*Beams*) My god! You're right! How wonderful learning is!

MASTER OF PHILOSOPHY: (*grimly*) And to make an "I" you close your jaws even further, and spread your cheeks to your ears: "A"–"E"–"I."

M. JOURDAIN: (*with exaggerated movement*) "A"–"E"–"I." "I." (*Spreads his cheeks as wide as he can with his fingers*) "I!" "I!" It's true! Magnificent! Long live science!

MASTER OF PHILOSOPHY: (*stalwartly*) Now, to make an "O" you must open your jaw and bring together the corners of your lips: "O."

M. JOURDAIN: (*does as told*) "O." "O." Nothing could be more wonderful than this! (*Moving his face in absurdly exaggerated configurations*) "A"–"E"–"I"–"O." "I"–"O"! Splendid! "I"–"O"! "I–O"!

MASTER OF PHILOSOPHY: (*as to a four-year-old, making a circle with his finger*) The shape of your mouth, you see, is a little round "o."

M. JOURDAIN: (*astounded, making the same circle with his finger and then tracing his lips in an "o"*) "O"–"O"–"O"—you're sooooooooo right. Oooooooooo. Ah, what a beautiful thing to knooooooooow something. (*Beams at his own cleverness*)

MASTER OF PHILOSOPHY: (*relentlessly continuing*) The sound "U" is made by bringing the teeth together, by spreading the lips, and then making them come together without quite touching: "U."

M. JOURDAIN: "U." "U"—nothing could be truer: "U"!

MASTER OF PHILOSOPHY: (*suddenly making a grotesque face at* JOURDAIN, *who recoils in shocked surprise*) It's like making a face at someone: if you want to make fun of somebody, just say "U" at them.

M. JOURDAIN: "U"–"U"! Oh, it's jtruuuuuuuue! Oh, why didn't I take up education earlier, I would have known all this!

Jourdain then asks the Master of Philosophy for a great favor:

M. JOURDAIN: (*crossing to him and looking about before he speaks*) Now I must be very confidential with you. I am in love with a grand lady of quality, and I want you to help me write a little love note (*he giggles*) that I can drop at her feet. (*Giggles again*)

MASTER OF PHILOSOPHY: (*trying to hide his disdain*) Very well.

M. JOURDAIN: (*with a comradely wink*) Something *très gallant*, yes?

MASTER OF PHILOSOPHY: (*grimacing*) Of course. Some verses?

M. JOURDAIN: (*horrified*) No, no. No verses.

MASTER OF PHILOSOPHY: (*relieved*) Ahah! Entirely in prose, then.

M. JOURDAIN: (*equally horrified*) No, no, no—no prose either.

MASTER OF PHILOSOPHY: (*beginning to weary, despite himself*) Well, it must be one or the other.

M. JOURDAIN: (*suddenly confused*) Why?

MASTER OF PHILOSOPHY: (*as if to a child*) Because, Monsieur, there are only the two: prose—and verse.

M. JOURDAIN: (*bewildered*) There is only prose—and verse?

MASTER OF PHILOSOPHY: Only. Whatever is not prose—is verse; and whatever is not verse—is prose.

M. JOURDAIN: (*beginning to understand*) And talking, what is that?

MASTER OF PHILOSOPHY: (*with great patience*) That is prose.

M. JOURDAIN: (*on the verge of a great discovery, his eyes widening all the time*) It is? When I say, "Nicole, bring me my slippers and my nightcap," that's—(*almost unwilling to believe it*) prose?!

MASTER OF PHILOSOPHY: (*as in benediction*) That's prose.

M. JOURDAIN: My God! (*starts dancing about*) For forty years I've been speaking PROSE without knowing it! Oh, thank you, THANK YOU, thank you, thank you.

Finally, the scene with the tailor completes Jourdain's lessons in social deportment, bringing the world of costume fashion into the theatre in both hilarious and provocative ways. The tailor arrives with garments and assistants, and in short order the scene becomes a comic ballet of both movement and language:

MASTER TAILOR: (*entering, trailed by assistants, and carrying an elaborate gown*) Here—this is the most beautiful new suit ever fashioned for the court, serious but colorful, a masterpiece no one in Paris could even touch. (*With a flourish, he and his assistants hold the gown up for general examination.* JOURDAIN *gasps.*)

M. JOURDAIN: (*unbelieving*) But—my good man—the flowers are upside down!

MASTER TAILOR: (*stunned, looks at his mistake, but immediately recovers and takes the offensive*) Well—you never told me you wanted them rightside up!

M. JOURDAIN: (*dismayed*) You mean I'm supposed to tell you?

MASTER TAILOR: (*vastly relieved, he boldly continues*) Of course! Persons of quality like them like this!

M. JOURDAIN: (*utterly perplexed*) Persons of quality like their flowers upside down?

MASTER TAILOR: Yes, of course.

M. JOURDAIN: (*making the best of it*) Oh. Well, it's all right then.

MASTER TAILOR: (*pressing advantage*) If you wish, I'll redo them.

M. JOURDAIN: (*frightened*) Oh, no, no.

MASTER TAILOR: (*wickedly*) Just say the word—

M. JOURDAIN: (*urgently*) No, no, I tell you, they're PERFECT. . . . Here, give it to me, I'll put it on.

MASTER TAILOR: Wait, wait. That's just not DONE, Monsieur. I've brought my people to dress you properly—(*his eyes lofting heavenward*) in RHYTHM! (*Reverentially*) Clothing like this must be put on with ceremony—BOYS! (*The orchestra strikes up a minuet: four tailoring assistants dance forward and* JOURDAIN *whirls around.*) Dress Monsieur as a Man of Quality!

A ballet ensues, with the assistants undressing Jourdain and redressing him in his new suit, to the light strains of Lully's orchestral rendition. Jourdain parades gaily around in his new garments as the dancers pretend to admire him.

MASTER TAILOR: (*as the dance concludes, to* JOURDAIN, *gracefully*) My dear gentleman, you may now give my boys their gratuity.

M. JOURDAIN: What did you call me?

MASTER TAILOR: (*a little frightened*) My dear gentleman?

M. JOURDAIN: (*overjoyed*) Gentleman! That's what happens when you dress in quality, they call you gentleman! No one calls you that if you dress like a petty bourgeois! Here (*giving money to the tailor*) this is from your "dear gentleman"!

MASTER TAILOR: (*pleased with himself*) My lord, we are all obliged to you.

M. JOURDAIN: (*stunned*) My lord! Oh! Oh! My lord! Wait, HEY! wait, my friend, "My Lord" means something more. "My Lord," why that's not just a little thing: here, here's what "My Lord" will give you. (*He gives more money to the tailor.*)

MASTER TAILOR: Well, well, we drink the health of Your Excellency, don't we, boys?

M. JOURDAIN: Your Excellency! Oh, oh oh! Wait, wait! Me, Your Excellency! (*Turns away from them, to the audience*) My god, if he goes up to "your Highness," my purse is his. (*Turns back to the tailor*) Here, here's from "Your Excellency." (*Gives yet more money*)

MASTER TAILOR: (*who now would rather leave than milk* JOURDAIN *further*) My lord, we thank you humbly. (*He bows and turns away.*)

M. JOURDAIN: (*turning again to the audience, confidentially*) Thank God. I was just about to give him all I had!

With this, the second act ends. Another ballet follows, danced by the tailor's assistants, and costumed attendants come onto the stage and into the auditorium, trimming the wicks of the candles which by now have begun to sputter and smoke.

The first two acts are virtually plotless: a series of "lessons" around a theme, their frivolous tomfoolery contrived of verbal wit, visual gags, costume and prop humor, traditional and novel whimsicality. Jourdain, the focal point for all this comedic revelry, is seen to be foolish but not malicious; as will be true in the rest of the play as well, he is continually delighted throughout his dupedom, and his gaiety is as infectious as his taste is deplorable. His last line in Act II ("Thank God. I was just about to give him all I had!") even suggests that he may not be wholly without perspective and that he may indeed share a certain amusement at his comic condition.

Act III introduces a whole new set of characters around Jourdain: his wife, his intended mistress (Dorimène, the intended recipient of the love note he discusses with the philosophy master), her lover (Dorante), Jourdain's daughter (Lucile), her suitor (Cléonte), Jourdain's valet (Covielle), and a housemaid to the Jourdains (Nicole). The masters and tailors of the first two acts will not return to the play—their function, to establish the character of the *bourgeois* who would be a *gentilhomme,* is completed. The intrigue of Act III is traditional: Jourdain seeks to woo Dorimène, to marry Lucile to a marquis, and to deceive his wife; he is instead duped by Dorante and evaded by Lucile, and the tough and commonsensical Madame Jourdain sees through him completely, as does the saucy Nicole:

M. JOURDAIN: (*summoning the maid imperiously*) Nicole!

NICOLE: (*rushes in and, seeing* JOURDAIN'*s costume with its upside-down flowers, curt-*

seys *in an effort to keep from laughing out loud*) Yes?

M. JOURDAIN: Listen to me!

NICOLE: (*bursting into giggles*) Hee hee hee hee hee hee hee hee!

M. JOURDAIN: (*infuriated*) What are you laughing at?

NICOLE: (*swallows her laughter, then breaks out again, even louder*) Hee hee hee hee hee hee hee hee!

M. JOURDAIN: (*exasperated*) What's that supposed to mean?

NICOLE: (*trying to get it out*) Hee hee hee. The way you're dressed. Hee hee hee.

M. JOURDAIN: Dressed? How am I dressed?

NICOLE: Ahh, well, My God! Hee hee hee hee!

The bourgeois emperor's new clothes have failed their very first test; not even his housemaid finds them impressive. Jourdain's efforts to justify his dress only mire him deeper in mortification as his wife enters the scene:

M. JOURDAIN: (*turning away in fury*) Nicole, you jabber pretty well for a peasant.

MME. JOURDAIN: (*patting* NICOLE *on the back as the housemaid struggles to recover her composure*) Nicole's right, and she has better sense than you do. (*Crossing over to her husband and shaking her finger at him*) What are you doing with a dancing master at your age, I'd like to know?

NICOLE: (*stifling more giggles*) And a foot-clomping swordsman who's going to tear the house apart with his "lessons"?

M. JOURDAIN: (*rising to his full height—or as high as his high heels can bring him*) Shut up, both of you. . . . You are both stupid and I am ashamed of your ignorance. (*Wickedly*) Do either of you know, for example, what it is you are talking right now?

MME. JOURDAIN: (*in no-nonsense tone*) Talking? I'm talking good common sense, and you better think about reforming your behavior pretty fast.

M. JOURDAIN: (*in pursuit*) That's not what I'm asking—I'm asking you what are these WORDS you're speaking?

MME. JOURDAIN: Sensible ones, unlike yours!

M. JOURDAIN: I'm not speaking of that! I'm asking you (*fumbling about to express himself*) what we're saying, what we have been speaking, what is it?

MME. JOURDAIN: (*humoring him*) Drivel?

M. JOURDAIN: (*thundering*) No! (*Triumphant*) It's prose, you imbecile!

MME. JOURDAIN: (*amused*) Prose?

M. JOURDAIN: (*as if announcing a new religion*) Yes, prose! (*Sonorously*) Everything that is not verse is prose! Everything that is not prose is verse! And that's education for you! (*Turns away*) How infuriating it is to deal with ignorant women!

Jourdain thereupon decides to teach Nicole how to fence, and she ends up beating the daylights out of him.

Jourdain's education in manners has taught him nothing about economics, and in subsequent developments Jourdain lends the rakish Count Dorante a large sum of money—with no assurance or collateral beyond Dorante's all too obvious flattery and lies.

DORANTE: (*pretending to admire* JOURDAIN*'s costume*) Why, Monsieur Jourdain, how magnificent you look!

M. JOURDAIN: (*pleased*) Ah, you like it?

DORANTE: The suit is—well it's—(*he searches for the right description*) it gives you a splendid appearance—(*and, finding the perfect ambiguous compliment*) none of the young men at court could possibly come up with anything like it!

M. JOURDAIN: (*ecstatic*) Ay yi! Ay yi!

MME. JOURDAIN: (*to the audience*) It's you scratch my back, and I'll . . .

DORANTE: (*interrupting her, afraid that* JOURDAIN *will overhear*) Turn around. . . . (JOURDAIN *does so.*) Ah, how gallant, how. . . .

MME. JOURDAIN: (*still to the audience*) It's as stupid in the be-hind as in the front. . . .

DORANTE: (*hurrying to interrupt*) In faith, Monsieur Jourdain (*walking* JOURDAIN *away from his wife, his hand on* JOURDAIN*'s back*) I could hardly wait to get here this morning, for I esteem you far above all other men. Why this very morning I— (*whispers confidentially in* JOURDAIN*'s ear*) I found myself speaking of you, once again, right in the King's Chamber!

M. JOURDAIN: (*stunned, suddenly doffs his hat and bows clumsily, obsequiously to* DORANTE; *with true humility*) You do me too much honor, Monsieur! (*Crosses to his wife*) Did you hear that? In the King's Chamber!

DORANTE: (*crossing to him*) Ah, Monsieur, please, put on your . . .

M. JOURDAIN: (*turns to* DORANTE, *still clutching his hat in his hand*) I am overcome with respect, Monsieur.

DORANTE: (*with ingratiating sincerity*) My God, please, put on your hat, I beg you, there must be no artificial ceremony between us.

M. JOURDAIN: (*utterly overawed at* DORANTE*'s kindness*) Monsieur!

DORANTE: (*with oily charm, taking off his own hat*) Put it back on, I tell you, you are my FRIEND.

M. JOURDAIN: (*almost falling to his knees, his legs trembling*) Monsieur, I am your servant.

DORANTE: (*with sudden mock anger*) I will not put on my hat unless you do!

M. JOURDAIN: (*quickly, with mustered dignity, puts on his hat*) If you insist. (*His hand trembles with anxiety as he lets go of the brim;* DORANTE *puts his hat back on also.*)

DORANTE: (*coming to his true subject, now that* JOURDAIN *has been primed*) I am your debtor, as you know.

M. Jourdain's dinner party gets out of hand, in Jerôme Savary's staging at the Théâtre de l'Est Parisien in 1983. (Photo: Brigitte Enguerand.)

MME. JOURDAIN: (*throwing up her hands and walking away, to the audience again*) Oh yes, we know all right!

And Dorante begins to total up his 18,000-franc debt—and then to borrow 200 pistoles more.

Many of Molière's plays involve issues of money; one of his greatest plays, *The Miser*, centers on the subject. Money, in the developing commercial world of the seventeenth century, is pure existential reality; when weighed against words and postures and posings, it highlights the difference between feigned values and intrinsic ones, between hollow presumption and solid worth. Flattery, Molière implies, is cheap; words are freely used and equally freely abused, and only coin has lasting value: on a coin, it matters not if the crowned head smiles or frowns. Years of dealing in the provinces with the promises and flattery of noble patrons had doubtless taught Molière a great deal about the difference between verbal and fiscal support and about the final impoverishment of those who seek to dine on eloquence. As a fashioner of words himself and as the manager of a thriving enterprise, it is equally probable that Molière was not above a few Dorante-like capers of his own. There is, in any event, nothing remote in this comedy, nothing more than a mask's breadth from human experience.

The third act culminates in a giant dinner party that Dorante has persuaded Jourdain to give on behalf of Dorimène, Dorante's own intended, who remains delightfully ignorant of Jourdain's pursuit of her. The occasion allows Molière some fun on a classic comedy subject, one often treated by him: the foolish older man pursuing a younger woman. This topic has a certain piquancy here, since Molière himself had married a woman half his age (Armande Molière played the daughter, Lucile, in the original production of *The Bourgeois Gentleman*) and was generally known as a much-cuckolded husband. Certainly there could be no better model for the futile lover than Jourdain:

M. JOURDAIN: (*with increasing desperation*) Madame, it is a great honor for me to see myself so blessed as to be able to be so happy as to have the great and good fortune of having your good will to grant me the grace of doing you the honor of honoring me with the favor of your presence— and if I also could have the merit of meriting a merit such as you provide, and that heaven . . . envious of my great fortune . . . has granted me . . . (*breaking into a nervous sweat*) the advantage of making me worthy . . . of . . .

DORANTE: (*enjoying this spectacle, but finally cutting it short*) That's quite all right, Monsieur Jourdain. She doesn't like compliments, actually, and she knows a man of spirit when she sees one. (*To* DORIMÈNE) Ridiculous, isn't he?

DORIMÈNE: (*to* DORANTE, *with great sarcasm*) How clever of you to say so.

Having given Dorante a diamond to pass on to Dorimène (which of course Dorante has presented as his own gift), Jourdain is now informed by the count: "To be a true gallant, you must act as though it wasn't you who gave it to her!" And so Jourdain does as he is advised:

M. JOURDAIN: (*taking her hands*) Ah, what beautiful hands you have!

DORIMÈNE: (*radiantly*) My hands are only hands, Monsieur Jourdain; perhaps you are speaking of this beautiful diamond?

M. JOURDAIN: (*despairingly*) I, Madam? God forbid I should speak of it; no gallant man would call attention to that trifle.

DORIMÈNE: (*greatly amused*) How weird.

M. JOURDAIN: (*relieved*) Ah, you are too kind, Madame, too kind.

Madame Jourdain, tipped off by Nicole, bursts in upon the dinner scene to foil her husband's plans vis-à-vis Dorimène, which would have come to naught in any case. This intervention hardly matters to the plot, however, because by then, true to the fashion of the *divertissement*, Molière has jumped adroitly into other topics. We are now concerned, in the last two acts of the play, with Jourdain's plan to marry off his daughter to a marquis and with the honest Cléonte's attempt to win her hand: this situation also is a typical Molière theme, one which he pursued on a far more serious level in the dark comedy of *Tartuffe*. Here, however, there is just foolery. Jourdain has no specific marquis in mind for his daughter; hence there is no one to contest the action to follow when Jourdain's hopes are thwarted by the traditional "wily servant," in this instance Covielle, a direct descendant of the *commedia* character of Arlecchino. It is Covielle's plan that Cléonte will disguise himself and participate in a little comedy masquerade designed to induce Jourdain to yield his daughter. Thus the last two acts of *The Bourgeois Gentleman* turn on that hoary metatheatrical device, the play-within-the-play:

COVIELLE: (*sprightly*) All this seems a little like a comedy, but with Jourdain there's no reason to be subtle; he's the kind of man who will play his role to the hilt. . . . I'll get the actors and the costumes, leave it to me.

Covielle's play-within-the-play is the final gulling of Jourdain, who is led on by nothing but his own fantastical desires:

COVIELLE: (*disguised, to* M. JOURDAIN) Do you know that the son of the Grand Turk is in town?

M. JOURDAIN: (*confused*) Me? No.

COVIELLE: (*his hand on* JOURDAIN's *shoulder, confidentially*) Really? He has a most magnificent retinue—the whole town has come

to see him; he's being received as a *grand seigneur*.

M. JOURDAIN: (*amazed*) My word. I had no idea.

COVIELLE: (*conspiratorially*) And what's more, he's in love with your daughter.

M. JOURDAIN: (*astonished*) The son of the Grand Turk?

COVIELLE: (*triumphantly*) Yes indeed, he wants to be your son.

M. JOURDAIN: (*overwhelmed*) My son? The son of the Grand Turk?

COVIELLE: (*grandly*) The son of the Grand Turk! Your son-in-law! Indeed, he was just telling me that. We had hardly begun our conversation when he said to me (*in heroic mock-Turkish*), "*Acciam croc coler ouch alla moustaph gidelum amanahem varahini oussere carbulath.*" That is, "Do you know the pretty young girl who's the daughter of Monsieur Jourdain, the Parisian gentleman?"

M. JOURDAIN: (*utterly intrigued*) The son of the Grand Turk said that of me? A Parisian gentleman?

COVIELLE: (*pouring it on*) Yes, he did. And I told him I knew you well, and that I knew Lucile. "Ah," he said to me, "*Marababa sahem.*" "How I love her."

M. JOURDAIN: (*figuring it out*) *Marababa sahem* means "how I love her"?

COVIELLE: Yes.

M. JOURDAIN: Lordy, thanks for telling me. I never would have thought *marababa sahem* meant "how I love her." (*Exalted*) What a magnificent language, Turkish!

Covielle further announces that it is the desire of the Grand Turk's son to make Jourdain a *Mamamouchi*: "there are no persons in the world more noble than the *Mamamouchi*—you will be the equal of the greatest *seigneurs* on earth!" Now Cléonte, disguised as the Grand Turk's son himself, enters to complete the masquerade:

CLÉONTE: (*grandly*) *Ambousahim oqui boraf, Iordina salamalequi.*

COVIELLE: (*translating*) That means: "Monsieur Jourdain, may your heart flourish like a year-round rose." (*Whispers*) They go in big for compliments in Turkey.

M. JOURDAIN: (*responding through* COVIELLE, *with a bow*) I am the very humble servant of his Turkish Highness.

COVIELLE: *Carigar camboto outsin moraf.*

CLÉONTE: *Outsin yoc catamelequi basum base alla moran.*

COVIELLE: He says, "Let heaven give you the strength of the lion and the wisdom of the serpent."

M. JOURDAIN: His Turkish Highness honors me too much, and I wish him all sorts of prosperity.

COVIELLE: *Ossa binamen sadoc babally oracaf ouram.*

CLÉONTE: *Bel men.*

COVIELLE: (*excitedly*) He says you must go right away with him and prepare yourself for the ceremony, and bring your daughter so that he and she can get married.

M. JOURDAIN: (*puzzled*) All that in two words?

COVIELLE: (*reassuring*) O yes, Turkish is like that: few words suffice. Go quickly!

And Jourdain goes off as Covielle remarks, "He couldn't have played his role better if he had learned it by heart." The little metatheatrical joke here cannot fail to be subtly amusing, for Molière, as the original Jourdain, not only had learned the role by heart, he had written it—and Covielle's role too! This kind of playing with playing, of theatre about "acting," is as typical of Molière as it is of Shakespeare; both of these actor-playwrights took much inspiration from, and provided much illumination on, the complex relationship between the drama and the "great stage of fools" called life.

The *Mamamouchi* ceremony, in which Jourdain is vested in the gown and turban of

---

MACHINE PLAYS

Stage machinery was unnecessary in most neoclassic drama, but was nonetheless developed to an extraordinary degree for the staging of opera, ballets, and so-called machine plays in the Royal era. Giacomo Torelli, an Italian stage designer, brought Italian skills and technologies to Paris in 1645, converting the Petit Bourbon and the Palais Royale to mechanically sophisticated theatres suitable for hugely elaborate stagings, which proved quite popular. Fifteen years later another Italian designer, Gaspare Vigarani, came to Paris at the request of Cardinal Mazarin and there created his *Salle des Machines,* a theatre specifically intended for spectacular stage effects, in the Tuileries Palace; this "Machine Hall" opened in 1662. Both Torelli's and Vigarani's theatres featured ornate prosceniums, deep stages (the *Salle des Machines* had a stage depth of 140 feet— vis-à-vis an auditorium depth of only 92 feet), wing and drop scenery elaborately painted in careful perspective, and impressive flying and hoisting machinery. Some of Molière's later plays, including *Amphitryon* and *Psyché,* were "machine plays" that Molière had written so that they could be staged in such theatres.

---

a Turkish prince, is the true highlight of this comedy-ballet. With music by Lully, who also choreographed and played the role of the Mufti (high priest), the ceremony is the ballet that divides Act IV from Act V. Indeed, it is apparently the scene that inspired the play's entire commission, for it is recorded that King Louis had requested a play on a Turkish theme owing to the excitement occasioned at court that winter by a visit from the Sultan's ambassador.

A Turkish ceremony he got. Majestically, the *ferme* at the rear of the stage parts: behind it is a grand arch—and behind that, a splendid

Oriental vista. We are suddenly plunged into a fantastical extravaganza, for the house of Jourdain simply disappears into the larger setting of Jourdain's imagination. The audience is not fooled—the domestic angle wings, with their bizarre sconces, remain to show where we "really" are—but Covielle's play within the play calls forth a stage setting within a stage setting: a metatheatrical vision for which Jourdain's house has become the proscenium.

The stage has been enlarged at least by half to accommodate this vision, and we are thrust into the world of grand comic ballet. Jourdain is brought in in a Turkish gown, his head completely shaven, and guided to a position on his hands and knees; his back, bedecked by a dusty copy of the Koran, becomes the pulpit for the Mufti, whose turban is illuminated by four or five concentric rings of lighted candles. Around and about dance dervishes and Turkish lords, chanting in a mixture of Molière's French, Lully's Italian, and pseudo-Turkish mumbo-jumbo:

TURKS: (*singing and dancing*) Hi valla. Hi valla.

THE MUFTI: (*chanting grotesquely*) Ha la ba, ba la chou, ba la ba, ba la da.

THE TURKS: Ha la ba, ba la chou, ba la ba, ba la da.

M. JOURDAIN: (*cringing, as* THE TURKS *beat upon the Koran placed on his back*) Ouf!

THE MUFTI: (*invoking unseen gods*) *Ti non star furba?*

THE TURKS: (*in mock horror*) No, no, no.

THE MUFTI: *Non star forfanta?*

THE TURKS: No, no, no.

THE MUFTI: (*furiously—the start of an incantation*) *Donar turbanta!*

And the Turks dance about Monsieur Jourdain, dressing him in the grand turban of the *Mamamouchi* and beating him soundly with their Turkish swords.

After this grand musical masterpiece, the fifth act of the play is mere wrap-up and resolution. Dorante will marry Dorimène, Cléonte will marry Lucile, and even Covielle will marry, with the servant Nicole. As for Jourdain, he will return to his practical Mme. Jourdain, being none the wiser for his follies and delighted, as ever, to watch—along with the real audience—the ballet with which the play concludes.

For that, indeed, is *The Bourgeois Gentleman* from beginning to end: a *divertissement* for audience and actors alike, for the king and for Molière's own company. Everything in it is calculated to entertain: the music, the dancing, the characters, the human foibles, the dialogue, the costumes, the scenery, and the delightfully bogus *Mamamouchi* ceremony contrived to enchant a court faddishly fascinated with the Orient. The play radiates good fun and good humor; and despite some potentially weighty themes (the aristocrat's fleecing of the bourgeois, the bourgeois's willingness to sacrifice his daughter's future to his own social pretensions). Molière's manner is to skirt the real issues by trivializing their consequences—and by giving way to song and dance at the least provocation.

The Bourgeois Gentleman was Molière's last great success. Louis told Molière at the time it premiered that he had never done better, yet in just a couple of years the king was to give over Molière's monopoly on the Palais Royale to Lully, who had successfully maneuvered himself above Molière in the royal favor. Thus it seems the scene in which Lully, as the Mufti, preached over Molière's (Jourdain's) back during the Turkish ballet sequence was remarkably prophetic and indeed, quite probably, not wholly accidental.

In 1673 Molière produced his last work, *The Imaginary Invalid;* it was his first play in more than a decade not to premiere at court. In its fourth public performance, Molière, who was by that time something of a true invalid, not an imaginary one, had a convulsion while performing the title role; he finished the performance, but within a few hours he was dead. He had remarked earlier the same day that it was about time for him to "*quitter la partie*"; with his death, and that of Racine six years later, the party itself came to an end. The great age of French neoclassic drama was over.

Although Molière's troupe persisted and soon amalgamated with the rival Marais and Hotel de Bourgogne companies to form the royally chartered Comédie Française, the king thereafter was drawn increasingly into international politics and spent less and less time with theatricals and literary entertainments. So it was that the glittering theatre world that begot *The Bourgeois Gentleman* dissolved into a harsher reality; the play was one of the last efflorescences of a brief but brilliant age.

ENGLAND: THE RESTORATION THEATRE

The theatre of England during the reign of King Charles II (1660–1685) and for about fifteen years thereafter was the Royal theatre of our own English language. Today it is known as the Restoration theatre because it came into being with the restoration of the English monarchy, in 1660, following a period of revolution and Puritan domination. The Restoration theatre never achieved quite the breadth or brilliance of its French model and counterpart; but it is every bit as fascinating historically, and it produced the finest English comedy since the time of Shakespeare and Ben Jonson.

The Restoration theatre was by no means a continuation of the Elizabethan and Jacobean theatres that preceded it. Civil war broke out in England in 1642, leading to the trial and beheading of King Charles I in 1649 and the succession of republican rule that in 1652 became the Protectorate headed by the Puritan Oliver Cromwell. Theatres were outlawed at the very beginning of this period; actors were jailed as rogues, and the playhouses were burned to the ground.

Most of the English courtiers who survived the upheaval escaped to France, where they were royally received by Louis XIV. When the English monarchy was restored in 1660 and Charles II ascended the throne, the theatre he commissioned into existence owed far more to the French neoclassicists, especially to Molière, than it did to Shakespeare and the theatre managers of the time of Queen Elizabeth.

The English Restoration playhouses had little in common with the "wooden O's" of Shakespeare's day; rather, they followed the French fashion wholly and unequivocally: the first two theatres chartered by Charles II were converted tennis courts. One was under the directorship of the king's friend Thomas Killigrew; the other was managed by a long-time London producer named William Davenant. Both of these men first converted tennis courts into temporary stages and then modeled new theatre buildings—Killigrew's Theatre Royal in Drury Lane, designed by Christopher Wren, and Davenant's Lincoln's Inn Fields Theatre—after the *jeu de paume* style.

The Restoration theatres each featured a rectangular hall divided in two by a proscenium arch, with a pit surrounded by two or (usually) three galleries. There were a few clear improvements over the French model, however. The Restoration pit was raked to slope toward the stage and lined with rows of backless benches; standing room thereby became a thing of the past, and sightlines were much improved. The stage also was raked, enhancing the perspective of flat "wing and border" scenery that moved in and out on

A Restoration theatre, with two proscenium doors on each side of the stage. Some theatres had just one door on each side. (Drawing: John von Szeliski.)

grooves; and the French *ferme* was replaced with a shutter at the rear of the stage. Peculiar innovations of the Restoration stage were a large "apron" built to project into the audience and a set of doors in the proscenium itself that opened onto that apron, or forestage, providing entrances and exits for the actors well in front of the scenery. These "proscenium doors," which were surmounted by windows, recall the tiring-house doors of Shakespeare's day and may indeed represent a vestigial carryover from that time.

The acting apron, the small, raked auditorium, the elegant decor, and the official patronage of king and court created in the Restoration theatre much the same atmosphere of intimacy and sophistication as that which prevailed in the Royal theatre in France. Also as in France, the English Restoration audience was largely a self-selected club of self-celebrating luminaries. Afternoon performances began at three o'clock, but, again as in Paris, the doors opened well before then to allow the patrons a few hours of preperformance frivolity and social intercourse. The performers' splendid satin and silk costumes, high heels (for both men and women), towering "perukes" (wigs), handkerchiefs that draped almost to the floor, and elocutionary acting styles created a spectacle well suited to the tastes of a court conspicuously preoccupied with sexual assignation and dalliance. Indeed, the whole mood of the Restoration theatre was one of blatant sexual provocation. Samuel Pepys's candid diaries make clear that the addition of women to the acting companies had given rise to a backstage social scene as lively as that on stage, and he tells us that during and after performances the king's voice was frequently heard in the actresses' dressing rooms. Nell Gwynne, a celebrated Restoration actress, was even more celebrated for her offstage role as mistress of Charles II; and for the benefit of those young "sparks" (gallants) not so favored by theatre personalities, elegant prostitutes wearing *vizard* (face)

masks were always in bold attendance in the audience, competing with the play for general attention. One such charmer is described by dramatic poet John Dryden in these lines:

> But stay: methinks some vizard masque I
>   see,
> Cast out her lure from the mid gallery:
> About her all the flutt'ring sparks are
>   rang'd;
> The noise continues though the scene is
>   changed.

The adoption of the mask by select members of the audience must have added a piquant note of audience participation to the Restoration stagings, for of course the mask was the very symbol of the actor. And in truth these were performances in which actors and audience alike played parts, and a good deal of the "acting" took place backstage and "in the house."

The dramas of the Restoration included heroic and neoclassic tragedies, tragicomedies, and a range of musical entertainments. But certainly the greatest glory of the era was achieved in the exquisite comedies of William Wycherley (*The Country Wife*), Sir George Etherege (*The Man of Mode*), and William Congreve (*The Way of the World*). The scintillating wit, ribaldry, topicality, and invective that these writers brought to the stage faithfully mirrored the age and its dominant values. Their plays portray in detail the snuff-snorting pomposity of the men, the wily coquetry of the women, and the aristocratic snobbery of a court intoxicated with its newfound power. Many of the scenes are set right in London—sometimes just streets away from the theatres where the comedies first played—and many of the characters are drawn from the sparks, the fops, the rakes, the lords and the ladies who sat in the audience.

The Puritans, of course, despised such plays. According to Anglican clergyman Jeremy Collier, they were "faulty to a scandalous degree of nauseousness and aggravation . . . viz. their smuttiness of expression; their swearing, profaneness, and lewd application of Scripture; their abuse of the clergy; their making their top characters libertines, and giving them success in their debauchery." But, as a character in a Wycherley play would reply, "'Tis a pleasant, well-bred, complaisant, free, frolic, good-natured, pretty age; and if you do not like it, leave it to us that do."

THE WAY OF THE WORLD

Perhaps the greatest masterpiece of Restoration comedy is Congreve's *The Way of the World,* which premiered near the end of the era, in 1700. Although the plot is rather typical for the time, revolving as it does about love and money, sexual freedom and security, marriage and social standing, *The Way of the World* transcends its genre by virtue of its perfectly honed dialogue, its brilliant epithets and ripostes, and its incisive portrayal of the manners and values of the Restoration aristocracy.

The wooing scene between the two chief characters, the rakish bachelor Mirabell and the capricious and captivating Mistress Millamant, illustrates Congreve's genius at balancing playful banter with penetrating wit; one must imagine the characters elegantly dressed, artfully posed, and flawlessly articulate:

MIRABELL: (*unlocking the door and surprising her in the salon*) Do you lock yourself up from me to make my search more curious? Or is this pretty artifice contrived to signify that here the chase must end and my pursuit be crowned, for you can fly no further?

MISTRESS MILLAMANT: (*points at him with her closed fan*) Vanity! (*Pirouettes playfully and turns from him, opening her fan to shield her face*) No, I'll fly and be followed to the last moment. Though I am upon the very verge of matrimony, I expect you should solicit me as much as if I were wavering at the gate of a monastery, with one foot over the threshold. I'll be solicited to the very last, nay, and afterwards!

MIRABELL: (*raising his eyebrows*) What, after the last?

MISTRESS MILLAMANT: (*assuredly*) Oh, I should think I was poor and had nothing to bestow if I were reduced to an inglorious ease and freed from the agreeable fatigues of solicitation. (*Walks away from him*)

MIRABELL: (*following*) But do not you know that when favors are conferred upon instant and tedious solicitation, they dimin-

Production of The Way of the World, *National Theatre, England, 1978. Beryl Reid as Lady Wishfort, Nickolas Grace as Witwoud, and Bob Peck as Sir Wilfull Witwoud (on floor). (Photo: Donald Cooper.)*

ish in their value, and that both the giver loses the grace, and the receiver lessens his pleasure . . . ?

MISTRESS MILLAMANT: (*stopping his question with her upraised hand*) It may be in things of common application; but never sure in love. (*With one hand at her breast, staring at him directly and advancing on him*) Oh, I HATE a lover that can dare to think he draws a moment's air independent of the bounty of his mistress. There is not so impudent a thing in nature as the saucy look of an assured man, confident of success. The pedantic arrogance of a husband has not so pragmatical an air. (*Turning, coquettishly, to the audience*) Ah! I'll never marry, unless I am first made sure of my will and pleasure.

MIRABELL: (*slyly seizing upon her last word*) Would you have them BOTH before marriage? Or will you be contented with the first now, and stay for the other till after grace?

MISTRESS MILLAMANT: Ah! Don't be impertinent! (*Holds her fan across her breast, in mock-heroic apostrophe to her soon-to-be former freedom*) My dear liberty, shall I leave thee? My faithful solitude, my darling contemplation, must I bid you then adieu? Ah, adieu, my morning thoughts, agreeable wakings, indolent slumbers, all ye *douceurs,* ye *sommeils du matin* [i.e., sweetnesses and morning naps]! (*With renewed insistence, firmly*) I can't do't, 'tis more than impossible. Positively, Mirabell, I'll lie abed in a morning as long as I please. (*Turns and walks away, snapping her fan closed*)

MIRABELL: (*brightly*) Then I'll get up in a morning as early as I please.

MISTRESS MILLAMANT: Ah! Idle creature, get up when you will. (*Turns back on him, pointing her fan wickedly*) And, d'ye hear, I won't be called names after I'm married; positively I won't be called NAMES.

MIRABELL: Names?

MISTRESS MIRAMANT: (*choosing her words with delicious disdain*): Aye, as Wife, Spouse, My Dear, Joy, Jewel, Love, SWEETHEART, and the rest of that nauseous cant, in which men and their wives are so fulsomely familiar; I shall never bear that. Good Mirabell, don't let us become familiar or fond, nor kiss before folks, like my Lady Fadler and Sir Francis; nor go to Hyde Park together the first Sunday in a new chariot, to provoke eyes and whispers and then never be seen there again, as if we were proud of one another the first week, and ashamed of one another ever after. Let us NEVER visit together, nor go to a play together. But let us be very strange and well-bred; let us be as strange as if we had been married a great while, and as well-bred as if we were not married at all!

MIRABELL: (*beneficently*) Have you any more conditions to offer? Hitherto your demands are pretty reasonable.

MISTRESS MILLAMANT: (*triumphant in her victory, walking confidently in circles about him and gesturing as she speaks*) Trifles!— As liberty to pay and receive visits to and from whom I please; to write and receive letters without interrogatories or wry faces on your part; to wear what I please, and choose conversation with regard only to my own taste; to have no obligation upon me to converse with wits that I don't like because they are your acquaintance, or to be intimate with fools because they may be your relations! Come to dinner when I please; dine in my dressing room when I'm out of humor, without giving a reason. To have my closest inviolate; to be sole empress of my tea-table, which you must never presume to approach without first asking leave. And lastly, wherever I am, you shall always knock at the door before you come in. (*Coming to a stop beside him, grandly*) These articles subscribed, if I continue to endure you a little longer, I may by degrees dwindle into a wife.

Surely the women's movement of the nineteenth and twentieth centuries has never framed an appeal for female freedom in marriage with more articulate bravado. Congreve's verbal mastery spans the centuries with its lively engagement of fundamental marital issues and consequences. It is to just this kind of approach that the best of Restoration drama owes its continuing appeal.

PART III

THE PRESENT

The heritage of the theatre—a past stretching back more than two millennia—is luminous with masterworks that will serve as inspiration to theatrical creativity for uncountable generations to come.

But the past, of course, is not the whole of theatre. What we see in the theatre today is the visible edge of an age every bit as exciting as any in the past: the age of modern theatre. No period of theatrical activity has been more varied, more rich in experimentation, more controversial, or more socially influential than this modern age.

The modern theatre can be said to date from about 1875; thus it is now well into its second century. Its recognizable origins, however, lie deep in the social and political upheavals that developed out of the Enlightenment and dominated European and American culture in the nineteenth century.

Revolution characterizes those times. Political revolution in the United States (1776) and France (1789) irrevocably changed the political structure of the Western world, and industrial-technological revolution cataclysmically overhauled the economic and social systems of most of the world. In the wake of these developments came an explosion of public communication and transportation, a tremendous expansion of literacy, democracy, and public and private wealth, and a universal demographic shift from country to town. These forces combined to create in Europe and the United States mass urban populations hungering for social communion and stimulation: a fertile ground for the citified and civilized theatre of our times.

Simultaneously, an intellectual revolution—in philosophy, in science, in social understanding, and in religion—was altering human consciousness in ways far transcending the effects of revolutionary muskets and industrial consolidation. The intellectual certainty of a Louis XIV, ruling by divine right, appeared ludicrous in an age of Enlightenment governed by secular scientific investigation; the clearsightedness of Molière seemed simplistic in an age of existentialism signaled by the soul-searching, self-doubting analyses of Søren Kierkegaard.

The intellectual revolution was an exceedingly complex phenomenon that occurred in many spheres of thought and was to gain momentum with each passing decade. It continues to this day.

The Copernican theory had already made clear that human beings do not stand at the geographic center of the universe, but rather that our world, indeed our universe, is swept up in a multiplicity of interstellar movements. Later scientists would press much farther than that, until eventually the revelations of Einstein, Heisenberg, and others would remove all our "hitching posts in space" and establish the human animal as little more than a transformation of kinetic energy, wobbling shiftily in a multigravitational atomic field marked by galaxies and black holes, neutrinos and quarks, matter and antimatter, all in a vast dance of inexplicable origin and doubtful destiny.

Nor was that "human animal" so vastly privileged over other species, it would seem. Darwin would argue that we *homo sapiens* are directly linked to other mammals—descended not from Adam and Eve, nor pre-Hellenic demigods, but from primal apes and prehistoric orangutans. Our morals and religions, anthropologist Ruth Benedict would argue, were not handed down to all humanity from a single source, but are instead a ranging complex of laws and traditions, wholly relative to the climes and cultures we inhabit. The work of Freud would disclose the existence of the Unconscious: a dark and lurking inner self aswarm with infantile urges, primordial fantasies, and suppressed fears and rages. The writings of Karl Marx would contend that all social behavior has its basis in economic greed, class struggle, and primal amorality. "Everlasting uncertainty and agitation" is the na-

ture of human intercourse, according to Marx, and society comprises "two great hostile camps" continually engaged in civil war.

These and scores of other serious challenges to previous thinking were accompanied everywhere by public debate and dispute. By the turn of the present century, an investigative ferment had seized European and American civilization: data were being collected on every conceivable topic, and scientific questioning and testing replaced intuition and dogma as the accepted avenue to truth. Experimentation, exploration, documentation, and challenge became the marching orders of artist and intellectual alike.

The modern theatre has its roots in these political, social, and intellectual revolutions. Ever since its outset it has been a theatre of challenge, a theatre of experimentation. It has never been a theatre of rules or simple messages, nor has it been a theatre of demigods or of absolute heroes and villains. It has reflected, to a certain degree, the confusions of its times, but it has also struggled to clarify and to illuminate, to document and explore human destiny in a complex and uneasy universe.

8

The Modern Theatre: Realism

The movement toward a realistic theatre began as a revolt against the intentional artifice of neoclassic form. Theatre ought to hold up a mirror to nature, the antineoclassicists asserted, and why must the five-act structure and the Alexandrine couplet intervene to distort the image? Rebellion against contrived manners and elitist snobbery also fueled the attack—and thus the European theatre that followed the seventeenth century was to develop a distinctly democratic, anti-Royalist air.

The first efforts at a more natural theatre took the form of sentimental comedies and pathetic tragedies featuring admirable characters and noble (if prosaic) sentiments. Richard Steele's *The Conscious Lovers* (1722) and Joseph Addison's *Cato* (1713) still stand as landmarks of this minor period of the theatre's history in England; the eighteenth-century plays and essays of Voltaire (François Marie Arouet) and Denis Diderot exemplify the same trends in France.

The first significant result of this artistic rebellion, however, was *romanticism,* a movement that spread through Europe in the very late eighteenth century and gained widespread acceptance in all the arts in the first half of the nineteenth century. Romanticism in the theatre took the form of a florid attempt to reactivate passion, which the romanticists contended had been dormant since the time of Shakespeare. Works inspired by the romantic movement include Friedrich Schiller's *The Robbers* (1782), Johann Wolfgang von Goethe's *Faust* (Part I, 1808; Part II, 1832), Victor Hugo's *Hernani* (1830), Alexandre Dumas's dramatization of his novel *The Three Musketeers,* and Edmond Rostand's *Cyrano de Bergerac* (1898). With its emphasis on freeform, picaresque stories, exotic locales, grotesque heroes, and sprawling dramatic structure, romanticism gave rise to a liberated and awesome theatricality that survives today primarily in the form of grand opera and Batman films. "Grand" is indeed the proper appellation for romantic theatre, for it strove mightily—and self-consciously—to free dramaturgy from the strictures of neoclassic formulas by means of flamboyant verse, boisterous action, epic adventure, passionate feeling, and majestic style. Unappalled by sentiment and unafraid of crackling rhetoric, the romantic authors searched deeply into the theatre's possibilities for moving, dazzling, and enthralling an audience; and many of the discoveries they made are subtly reflected in the drama of today.

It is to the romantic period that we owe the virtually universal adoption, in Europe and America, of the proscenium theatre building, which remains today the most common form of indoor theatre architecture in the Western world. Built to accommodate rapid changes of painted scenery—most notably the intricately realized scenic flats and backdrops greatly favored by romantic authors—the proscenium theatre of the nineteenth century featured an immense stage, of which only a relatively small fraction was used for playing; the rest served solely for the display or storage of illusionistic scenery. Only in the past four decades has this design been seriously challenged in the construction of new theatrical facilities, for the bulk of existing theatres today either date from the romantic era or were constructed in at least partial imitation of the theatres of that time.

With respect to dramatic achievement, however, the aims of romanticism proved more influential than lasting. The romanticists succeeded in laying bare the possibilities of theatre in an age of rapid change. They also succeeded in wooing a democratic audience into the theatres, and they removed the edge of academic pretension that had threatened to destroy the theatrical experience in the neoclassic era by inhibiting its liveliness. By appealing to the emotions as well as to the mind, the credos and works of romanticism also stimulated a popular taste for rapture, adventure, and discovery in the theatre, and for rebelliousness in both politics and art.

REALISM

Thus far, the movement that has had the most pervasive and long-lived effect on modern theatre is, beyond question, realism.

Realism has sought to create a drama without conventions or abstractions, in simple consonance with life itself. *Likeness to life* is realism's goal; and in pursuit of that goal it has renounced, among other things, idealized or prettified settings, versifications, contrived endings, and stylized costumes and performances.

Realism is a beguiling aesthetic philosophy, since the theatre has *always* taken "real life" as its fundamental subject; and so realism seems at first glance to be an appropriate style with which to approach the reality of existence. Instead of having actors represent characters, the realists would say, let us have the actors *be* those characters; instead of having dialogue stand for conversation, let us have dialogue that *is* conversation; instead of scenery and costumes that convey a sense of time and place and atmosphere, let us have scenery that is genuinely inhabitable and costumes that are real clothes.

But, of course, realism is no more free from contrivance or convention than is any other form of drama: realism is simply another dramatic style, not an absence of style. No matter

Camille (La Dame aux Camélias), *by Alexandre Dumas, is one of the masterpieces of nineteenth-century French romanticism. This classic story of a love story transcending class difference, social antagonism, and fatal illness was first written as a novel, then dramatized by its author, and has subsequently served as the basis for Verdi's* La Traviata *and various modern films. The original play is shown here as performed by the Actors Theatre of Louisville, with Richard McWilliams and Susan Wands as the appealingly doomed lovers. (Photo: Richard Trigg.)*

The romantic spirit encompasses more than romance: it is also swashbuckling swordplay, picaresque characters, poetic elaborations, and period costumes—all of which come together in the famous duelling-rhyming scene between the long-nosed Gascon poet-soldier Cyrano and his aristocratic rival, the Compte de Guiche, in Edmond Rostand's Cyrano de Bergerac *(1898), produced here by the Utah Shakespearean Festival in 1992. (Photo: Sue Bennett.)*

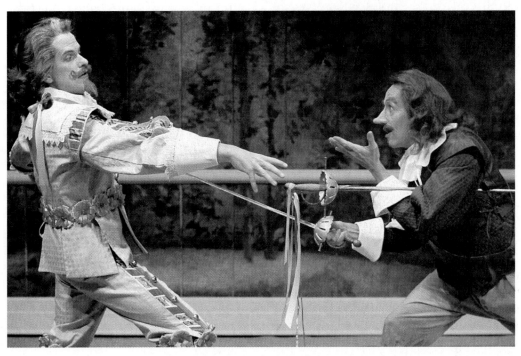

how lifelike the dialogue or action, a "realistic" play stays safely behind the proscenium, ending when the curtain comes down (or the lights go out); and "realistic" actors speak, as did actors in the Royal era, so that their words are heard in the back row of the audience—even though their characters are presumed to be whispering romantic proposals to their paramours. Realism may have rewritten some of the conventions of the theatre, but it did not, nor could not, simply dispose of them.

What the realistic theatre movement *did* accomplish was a wholesale review of every aspect of stage production—from playwriting and acting to directing and design—with an eye to exploring in detail the *complexities*—social, political, and psychological—of human life. Thus genres were blended, climaxes were flattened, and certainties derided. Scenery depicted ordinary living environments that were just as messy and ill-kept as their real-life counterparts; and dramatic characters were likewise drawn from everyday life: not kings and princes but farm widows, merchant seamen, office clerks, low-level bureaucrats, anxious husbands, abused wives, the unwashed, the uneducated, the unemployed. Doubts, muddles, and confusions became the principal actions of realistic plays, just as they infiltrate day-to-day decisions in real life, and a strong tone of nervous uncertainty marked the performances of a new breed of realistic actors. The ringing rhetoric of Aeschylus, Shakespeare, and Racine all but disappeared—or was displayed as hollow posturing and empty rant—and the new hero, as likely as not, was seen as perplexed and inarticulate in the face of myriad forces fighting for control of his or her soul. The simplistic moral judgments of melodrama or farce were likewise junked and replaced with thought-provoking moral and social questions: inquiries into the fundamental values underlying everyday social intercourse. Playwrights openly sought to disrupt complacency with the status quo and

to comment directly on immediate day-to-day issues. Realism, as a movement, was a powerful political as well as aesthetic force in the late nineteenth century and early twentieth centuries, and it remains today, particularly in America, an extraordinarily powerful and significant theatrical style.

A Laboratory

In essence, the realistic theatre is conceived to be a laboratory in which the nature of relationships, or the ills of society, or the symptoms of a dysfunctional family are "objectively" set down for the final judgment of an audience of impartial observers. Every aspect of realistic theatre should strictly adhere to the "scientific method" of the laboratory; nothing must ring false. The setting is to resemble the prescribed locale of the play as closely as possible; indeed, it is not unusual for much of the scenery to be acquired from a real-life environment and transported to the theatre (in one famous instance, American producer David Belasco went so far as to purchase a New York restaurant, dismantle it, and rebuild it within the confines of his Broadway stage). Costumes worn by characters in the realistic theatre follow the dress of "real" people of similar societal status; dialogue is prized as it re-creates the cadences and expressions of daily life.

Early on in the realist movement, the proscenium stage of the romantic era was modified to accommodate scenery constructed in box sets, with the walls given full dimension and with real bookcases, windows, fireplaces, swinging doors, and so forth built into the walls just as they are in a house interior. In the same vein, the acting of the realists was judged effective insofar as it was drawn from the behavior of life and insofar as the actors seemed to be genuinely speaking to each other instead of playing to the audience. A new aesthetic principle was spawned: "the theatre of the fourth wall," in which the life on stage was conceived to be the same as life in a real-world setting, except that, in the case of the stage, one wall—the proscenium opening—had been removed. Thus the "fourth wall" theatre was like a laboratory microscope and the stage like a biologist's slide: a living environment set up for judicious inspection by neutral observers.

And so realism presents its audience with an abundance of seemingly real-life "evidence" and permits each spectator to arrive at her or his own conclusions. There is some shaping of this evidence by author and performer alike, to be sure, but much of the excitement of the realistic theatre is occasioned by the genuine interpretive freedom it allows the audience and by the accessibility of its characters, whose behaviors are familiar enough to the average spectator that they may be easily assimilated and identified.

Moreover, in presenting its evidence from the surface of life, realism encourages us to delve into the mystery that lies beneath—for the exploration of life's mystery is the true, if unspoken, purpose of every realistic play. Realism's characters, like people in life, are defined by detail rather than by symbol or abstract idealization: like people we know, they are ultimately unpredictable, humanly complex rather than ideologically absolute.

The success of realism is well established; indeed, realism remains one of the dominant modes of drama to this day. At its most profound, when crafted and performed by consummately skilled artists, the realistic theatre can generate extremely powerful audience empathy by virtue of the insight and clarity it brings to real-world moments. In giving us characters, the realist playwright gives us *friends:* fellow travelers on the voyage of human discovery with whom we can compare thoughts and feelings. In the uncertainties and trepidations, the wistfulness, the halting eloquence and conversational syntax of these characters, we recognize ourselves; and in that recognition we gain an understanding of our own struggles and a compassion for all human endeavors.

Pioneers of Realism

The realistic theatre had its beginnings in the four-year period that saw the premieres of *A Doll's House* (1879), *Ghosts* (1881), and *An Enemy of the People* (1882) by the Norwegian author Henrik Ibsen. With these three plays, which dealt, respectively, with the issues of women's role in society, hereditary disease and mercy killing, and political hypocrisy, Ibsen revolutionized the drama. Ordinary people populate Ibsen's realistic world, and the issues addressed in these dramas affect ordinary husband-wife, mother-son, and brother-brother relationships, played out in the interiors of ordinary homes. Controversial beyond measure in their own time, these plays retain their edge of pertinence even today and still have the power to inform, to move, and even to shock. The reason for their lasting impact lies in Ibsen's choice of issues and his skill at showing both sides through brilliantly captured psychological detail.

The realistic theatre spread rapidly throughout Europe as the controversy surrounding Ibsen's plays and themes stimulated other writers to follow suit. The result was a proliferation of "problem plays," as they were sometimes called, which focused genuine social concern through realistic dramatic portrayal. In Germany, Gerhart Hauptmann explored the plight of the middle and proletarian classes in several works, most notably in his masterpiece *The Weavers* (1892). In England, Irish-born George Bernard Shaw created a comedic realism through which he addressed such issues as slum landlordism (in *Widowers' Houses,* 1892), prostitution (in *Mrs. Warren's Pro-*

HENRIK IBSEN (1828–1906)

"This mass of vulgarity, egotism, coarseness, and absurdity. . . . This disgusting representation. . . . An open drain; a loathsome sore unbandaged; a dirty act done publicly. . . . Absolutely loathsome and fetid. . . . Crapulous stuff." These were the *London Daily Telegraph*'s comments on the 1891 English premiere of what it described as "Ibsen's positively abominable play entitled *Ghosts*."

The *Telegraph* was hardly alone. "Unutterably offensive. . . . Abominable. . . . Scandalous," said the *Standard*. "Naked loathsomeness. . . . Most dismal and repulsive," said the *Daily News*. "Revoltingly suggestive and blasphemous," said the *Daily Chronicle*. "Morbid, unhealthy, unwholesome, and disgusting," said *Lloyds*. "Most loathsome of Ibsen's plays. . . . Garbage and offal," said *Truth*. "Putrid," said *Academy*. "A wicked nightmare," said *Gentlewoman*. "As foul and filthy a concoction as has ever been allowed to disgrace the boards of an English theatre," said *Era*.

Why such outrage? What offense, precisely, did *Ghosts* commit? This is a play without a single obscene word, without a single undraped bosom, without a single sexual act, a single double entendre.

What *Ghosts* does is to explore ruthlessly, honestly, and *realistically* the fullest implications of a hypocritical Victorian marriage, behind whose seeming serenity exists a chaotic history of promiscuity, incest, disease, and deceit. In the play, Mrs. Alving maintains the outward shell of her marriage, thought by society to be an "ideal" one, despite the profligacy of her husband. When her son, Oswald, loses his mind at the end of the play—a mind destroyed by the syphilitic spirochetes (the literal "ghosts" of the play) inherited from his father's sins—the high spirit of European romanticism was forcibly retired in favor of a more searching, more demanding, ground-

Ibsen's Peer Gynt, *with its mixture of folk fantasy, humor, intellectual skepticism, and epic adventure, is perhaps the greatest of all Scandinavian dramas. This 1981 production was directed by Ralf Langbacka at the Helsinki City Theatre in Finland. (Photo: Kari Hakli.)*

level analysis of contemporary life in a post-industrial age.

Because of their harsh subject matter, their commitment to rigorous investigation, and their unsentimental, almost-scientific analysis, Ibsen's realistic plays shocked and dazzled all of Europe during the 1890s, creating, for the first time in theatre history, a multinational dramatic forum. New "club" theatres—groups of amateur theatre artists committed to the realistic mode—sprang up in major European capitals: the *Théâtre Libre* in Paris (founded by André Antoine, 1887), the *Freie Bühne* in Berlin (founded by Otto Brahm, 1889—both *Théâtre Libre* and *Freie Bühne* translate as "Free Theatre"), and the Independent Theatre in London (founded by J. T. [Jack Thomas] Grein, 1891). Each of these theatres produced *Ghosts* (the latter opened with it), to the wide consternation of later Victorian audiences and to the unanimous disapproval of conservative critics. The controversy extended to virtually every country in Europe and to America. The realistic movement, however, once started, was not to be stilled or slowed; the issues that *Ghosts* and other of Ibsen's plays brought up to public consciousness could not be reburied by the disdain of propriety-minded drama critics. The theatre soon became a forum for the exposure of contemporary ills and not just a medium for entertainment and aesthetics.

Ibsen's skill as a dramatic craftsman, together with his penetrating artistic vision, underlaid the shock value of his dramas, making them indelible works of literature as well as momentous documents of current culture. Ibsen himself was in his sixties when he became the center of international controversy, by which time he had already been an established playwright and theatre director for more than forty years. His early life was spent in his native Norway, where he served both as playwright-in-residence and as artistic director of theatres in Bergen and Christiana (now Oslo). During this period Ibsen had a hand in writing and directing more than a hundred plays; by his mid-thirties, though still a provincial author-director, he had fully mastered the conventional structure of the well-made play as well as the fundamental principles of effective dramaturgy.

In 1864 Ibsen received a modest travel grant to study theatres in Germany and Italy; he spent the next twenty-seven years in self-imposed exile from his homeland. During this period of expatriation Ibsen wrote his great works—first the two poetic dramas, *Brand* and *Peer Gynt,* that gave him a wide reputation (as well as an income), then the stunning realistic plays that revolutionized the theatre, *A Doll's House* (1879), *Ghosts* (1881), *An Enemy of the People* (1882), and *The Wild Duck* (1884). By the time he wrote *The Wild Duck,* Ibsen was already moving beyond realism, into a more philosophical drama in which the universals of human struggle, expressed through symbolism, filtered the realistic investigation. *Rosmersholm* (1886), *Hedda Gabler* (1890), and *The Master Builder* (1892) are the most important works of this period in his life. By the time of this last-named play, Ibsen was back in Norway, where, like his Peer Gynt, he had returned for his final years and reflections. By this time, however, he was no longer obscure; he was the most important theatre artist in Europe and soon to be considered the "father of modern drama," a title he is often (if not universally) accorded today.

Ibsen's remarkable collection of talents, achieved during a long life of relentless craft development and uninhibited artistic exploration, combined to create a drama that cannot be categorized simply by its style or subject; we do the man considerable wrong merely to remember his role in the development of realistic drama. His *Peer Gynt* is one of the most exquisite verse plays ever written, perhaps the finest verse play since Shakespeare. His *Hedda Gabler* is a probing psychological study that creates one of the best acting roles ever written. His dramatic structure, first learned in the nineteenth-century theatre where structure was everything, is still put forward as a model for aspiring playwrights and television scriptwriters; *An Enemy of the People* has provided the firm plot structure for countless plays and films, including the popular film *Jaws.* Ibsen's plays are constantly translated and revived today, purely on their dramatic merits, not because of their importance in the history of the modern theatre.

fession, 1902), and urban poverty (in *Major Barbara*, 1905). In France, under the encouragement of innovative director André Antoine, Eugène Brieux wrote a series of realistic problem plays that included *Damaged Goods* (1902), which deals with syphilis, and *Maternity* (1903), which deals with birth control. By the turn of the century realism was the standard dramatic form in Europe.

Naturalism

Naturalism, a movement whose development paralleled that of realism but was essentially independent of it, represents an even more extreme attempt to dramatize human reality without the appearance of dramaturgical shaping. The naturalists, who flourished primarily in France during the late nineteenth century (Émile Zola was their chief theoretician), based their aesthetics on nature and particularly on humanity's place in the natural (Darwinian) environment. To the naturalist, the human being was merely a biological phenomenon whose behavior was determined entirely by genetic and social circumstances. To portray a character as a hero, or even as a credible force for change in society, was anathema to the naturalist, who similarly eschewed dramatic conclusions or climaxes. Whereas realist plays at that time tended to deal with well-defined social issues—women's rights, inheritance laws, workers' pensions, and the like—naturalist plays offered nothing more than a "slice of life" in which the characters of the play were the play's entire subject; any topical issues that were brought in served merely to facilitate the interplay of personalities and highlight their situations, frustrations, and hopes.

The naturalists sought to eliminate every vestige of dramatic convention: "All the great successes of the stage are triumphs over convention," declared Zola. Their efforts in this direction are exemplified by August Strindberg's elimination of the time-passing intermission in *Miss Julie* (instead, a group of peasants, otherwise irrelevant to the plot, enter the kitchen setting between acts and dance to fill the time Miss Julie is spending in Jean's offstage bedroom), and by Arthur Schnitzler's elimination of conventional scene beginnings, endings, and climaxes in the interlocking series of cyclical love affairs that constitute the action of *La Ronde*.

Inasmuch as sheer verisimilitude, presented as "artlessly" as humanly possible, is the primary goal of the naturalist, the term *naturalism* is often applied to those realistic plays that seem most effectively lifelike. This is not a particularly felicitous use of the term, however, because it ignores the fundamental precept of naturalism—that the human being is a mere figure in the natural environment. Naturalism is not merely a matter of style; it is a philosophical concept concerning the nature of the human animal. And naturalist theatre represents a purposeful attempt to explore that concept, using extreme realism as its basic dramaturgy.

CHEKHOV

If the realistic theatre came to prominence with the plays of Henrik Ibsen, it attained its stylistic apogee in the major works of Anton Chekhov. Chekhov was a physician by training and a writer of fiction by vocation; toward the end of his career, in association with realist director Konstantin Stanislavsky and the Moscow Art Theatre, he also achieved success as a playwright through a set of plays that portray the end of the czarist era in Russia with astonishing force and subtlety: *The Seagull* (1896), *Uncle Vanya* (1899), *The Three Sisters* (1901), and *The Cherry Orchard* (1904). The intricate craftsmanship of these plays has never been surpassed; even the minor characters seem to breathe the same air we do.

STANISLAVSKY (1863–1938) AND CHEKHOV (1860–1904)

Konstantin Stanislavsky and Anton Chekhov were the two towering figures of Russian realism, the first as actor-director and the second as playwright. Their collaboration in the Moscow Art Theatre productions of *The Seagull* (1898), *Uncle Vanya* (1899), *The Three Sisters* (1901), and *The Cherry Orchard* (1904) still rank among the most magnificent achievements of the realist stage. "It was Chekhov who suggested to me the line of intuition and feeling," said Stanislavsky; and Chekhov, for his part, had to admit that his first great success in the theatre was achieved only after he put *The Seagull* into Stanislavsky's hands—the play had excited little enthusiasm in an earlier production in St. Petersburg.

Relations between these two titans were never placid, however. Chekhov often contended that Stanislavsky ignored the poetry of his dramaturgy and did not fully understand the complexity of his characters. At one point Chekhov threatened to withdraw *The Seagull* from the Moscow Art Theatre unless one important role was recast; Stanislavsky refused to recast it.

But there can be little doubt that Stanislavsky recognized the difficulty in creating a Chekhovian theatrical style. In the following passages from his autobiography, *My Life In Art* (Moscow, 1925), Stanislavsky looks back on the exhausting rehearsals for *The Three Sisters* and recalls how one apparent impasse was resolved.

> The actors worked with spirit. We rehearsed the play, everything was clear, understandable, true, but the play was not lively, it was hollow, it seemed tiresome and long. There was *something* missing. How torturing it is to seek this *something* without knowing what it is. All was ready, it was necessary to advertise the production, but if it were to be staged in the form we had achieved, we were faced with certain failure. Yet, we felt that there were elements that augured great success, that everything with the exception of that magic *something* was there. We met daily, we rehearsed to a point of despair, we parted company, and next day we would meet again and reach despair once more. . . .
>
> One evening at one of our agonizing rehearsals, the actors stopped in the middle of the play, ceased to act, seeing no sense in their work. They no longer had any trust in the stage director or in each other. Such a breakdown usually leads to demoralization. Two or three electric lights were burning dimly. We sat in the corners, crestfallen. We felt anxious and helpless. Someone was nervously scratching the bench. The sound was like that of a mouse. It reminded me of home: I felt warm inside, I saw the truth, life, and my intuition set to work. Or, maybe, the sound of the scratching mouse and the darkness and helplessness had some meaning for me in life, a meaning I myself do not understand. Who can trace the path of creative superconsciousness?
>
> I came to life and knew what it was I had to show the actors. It became cosy on the stage. Chekhov's men revived. They do not bathe in their own sorrow. On the contrary, they seek joy, laughter and cheerfulness. They want to live and not vegetate. I felt the truth in Chekhov's heroes, this encouraged me and I guessed what had to be done.

Chekhov's technique is to create deeply complex relationships among his characters and to develop his plots and themes more or less between the lines. Every Chekhovian character is filled with secrets, none of which is ever fully revealed by the dialogue.

In Russia today, Chekhov is revered as a literary hero, and his plays are continually revived with all details of their original production by the Moscow Art Theatre intact. Audiences return to see them, as if to visit dear friends and to understand them better.

Director Libby Appel's beautiful production of Chekhov's The Cherry Orchard, *at the Indiana Repertory Theatre in 1993–1994, captures the faded elegance of Russian society before the revolution. With Frank Raiter as Gayev and Patricia Hodges as Mme. Renyevskaya. (Courtesy of the Indiana Repertory Theatre.)*

THE THREE SISTERS

Chekhov's *The Three Sisters* epitomizes the realistic theatre; in addition to being one of the finest plays of the genre, it is perhaps the most widely known of all Russian plays. Written for Stanislavsky's company in 1901, *The Three Sisters* is a play immensely rich in characterization. It is also immensely rich in its potential for profoundly moving performances; hence it is a favorite of actors wherever the world's great repertory is performed.

There are ten major characters in *The Three Sisters* and, true to the realistic format, no one of them can be regarded as the principal character or protagonist. The play focuses primarily on the network of relations among these characters and, to a lesser extent, on their interactions with the four minor characters.

Three of the characters do stand apart from the rest, however, as the title indicates. These are three young women, sisters, in whose family home the action takes place. As the play begins, Olga, the elder sister, is a provincial schoolteacher; Masha, the middle sister, is the wife of a provincial schoolteacher; and Irina, the youngest, is vocationally and maritally uncommitted. They are all in their twenties (Act I takes place on Irina's twentieth birthday), they are orphans, and they have but one dream: to leave their remote village and move back to Moscow. It is a dream that both haunts and inspires them, and it provides the motivating force for the play.

Provincial dreamers the sisters may be, but they do not lack family or friends or admirers—and each of the play's four acts, which all together span about three and a half years, is built around some kind of occasion for which virtually the entire cast gathers. A brother to the three sisters, Andrei, and his fiancée, Natasha (later his wife), are permanent members of the household. Kulygin, Masha's husband, is a constant visitor. And a nearby military base—the focal point of the town's social life—provides the sisters with admirers and suitors: the elderly Doctor Tchebutykin, who is billeted in the sisters' house, and the youngish officers Vershinin, Baron Tusenbach, and Solyony. These ten characters, plus two younger officers (Fedotik and Roday) and two aged servants (Anfisa and Ferapont), interweave their lives and fortunes for the four acts of the play, until by the final curtain every life has been touched by every other.

The play begins in the drawing room of the sisters' fine old house. A table is being set in the room beyond: the occasion is an open house for Irina's birthday, and the whole town is expected. The sun streams in through

The three sisters and their nurse, at the beginning of the play in the Stratford Festival production (Ontario, Canada) directed by Robin Phillips. Maggie Smith, in black, plays Masha; Marti Maraden, in white, is Irina, and Martha Henry is Olga. Amelia Hall plays the nurse, Anfisa. (Courtesy of the Stratford Festival, Canada. Photo: Robert C. Ragsdale.)

the windows; the sisters await their guests. Each is individualized: Olga is correcting lessons; Masha is reading a book of poetry; Irina, in a white dress, stands lost in thought, planning her future.

OLGA: Father died just a year ago, on this very day—the fifth of May, your birthday, Irina. It was very cold, snow was falling. I felt as though I should not live through it; you lay fainting as though you were dead. But now a year has passed and we can think of it calmly; you are already in a white dress, your face is radiant. . . . It is warm today, we can have the windows open, but the birches are not in leaf yet. Father was given his brigade and came here with us from Moscow eleven years ago and I remember distinctly that in Moscow at this time, at the beginning of May, everything was already in flower; it was warm, and everything was bathed in sunshine. It's eleven years ago, and yet I remember it as though we had left it yesterday. Oh, dear! I woke up this morning, I saw a blaze of sunshine. I saw the spring and joy stirred in my heart. I had a passionate longing to be back at home again! . . . Being all day in school and then at my lessons till the evening gives me a perpetual headache and thoughts as gloomy as though I were old. And really, these four years that I have been at the high school I have felt my strength and my youth oozing away from me every day. And only one yearning grows stronger and stronger—

IRINA: To go back to Moscow. To sell the house, to make an end of everything here, and off to Moscow—

OLGA: Yes! To Moscow, and quickly!

Olga, an unwilling spinster by accident of fate, is the leader of the sisters; she is the family historian, the repository of confidences, the strong hand that holds the household on an even keel. Irina represents the future and the hope of the family. The doctor enters, and Irina addresses him:

IRINA: Tell me, why is it I am so happy today? As though I were sailing with the great blue sky above me and big white birds flying over it. Why is it? Why? . . . When I woke up this morning, got up and washed, it suddenly seemed to me as though everything in the world was clear to me and that I knew how one ought to live. Dear doctor, I know all about it. A man ought to work, to toil in the sweat of his brow, however he may be, and all the purpose and meaning of his life, his happiness, his ecstasies lie in that alone. How delightful to be a workman who gets up before dawn and breaks stones on the road, or a shepherd, or a schoolmaster teaching children or an engine driver—oh dear! to say nothing of human beings, it would be better to be an ox, better to be a humble horse and work than a young woman who wakes at twelve o'clock, then has coffee in bed, then spends two hours dressing—Oh, how awful that is! Just as one has a craving for water in hot weather I have a craving for work. And if I don't get up early and work, give me up as a friend, dear doctor!

TCHEBUTYKIN: (*tenderly*) I'll give you up, I'll give you up—

Chekhov's way is gentle irony; it suffuses the dialogue until almost every word expressed seems to contradict the underlying sentiment of the speaker. Olga speaks of radiance and warmth and flowers and sunshine and joy, but her tones are of unmistakable melancholy, heartache, longing, and despair. Irina's inexperience and her idealism are betrayed a thousand times in her artless "Why is it I am so happy today?" speech as she expounds upon her discovery of the verities of life. Does she really believe it would be "delightful to be a workman who gets up before dawn and breaks stones on the road?" That is the life of a convict in Siberia! Irina's enthusiasm is fervid enough to be engaging, but too shallow to be inspiring; neither pathetic nor Promethean, it is typically human and typically Chekhovian.

When Masha, the third sister, speaks, we find she is given not to prolonged discourses but to apparently idle quotations and cryptic comments.

MASHA: (*quoting from a poem by Pushkin*) "By the sea-strand an oak-tree green—upon that oak a chain of gold—upon that oak a chain of gold—" (*Gets up, humming softly*)

OLGA: You are not very cheerful today, Masha. (MASHA, *humming, puts on her hat.*)

OLGA: Where are you going?

MASHA: Home.

IRINA: How queer!—

OLGA: To go away from a birthday party!

MASHA: Never mind—I'll come in the evening. Goodbye, my darling— (*Kisses IRINA*) Once again I wish you, be well and happy. In the old days, when father was alive, we always had thirty or forty officers here on birthdays; it was noisy, but today there is only a man and a half, and it is as still as the desert.—I'll go—I am in the blues today, I am feeling glum, so don't you mind what I say. (*Laughing through her tears*) We'll talk some other time, and so for now goodbye, darling, I am going—

IRINA: (*discontentedly*) Oh, how tiresome you are—

OLGA: (*with tears*) I understand you, Masha.

The pauses (indicated in this playtext by dashes), the repetitions, and the vagueness are typical of realistic writing and are aimed at demonstrating the rhythms and muddled inanities of natural speech more than the focus of theatrical phrasing. The impact is gradual and imprecise. Masha twice says goodbye, twice says she's going, makes every gesture of departure, but in fact does not go. She twice cautions her sisters not to mind what she says—but she goes on saying it. She laughs but she cries. Indeed, "laughing through tears," which is virtually a Chekhovian trademark, epitomizes the emotional complexity conveyed through realism: the happiest memories are seen to evoke the most painful realizations, and feelings are shown to be most confused when they are most sharply encountered.

A series of brief exchanges during this birthday celebration establishes the expository mode of this play; they are encounters that seem obvious in their lifelike simplicity, and yet their ultimate "meaning" is obscure. Inappropriateness is characteristic of all of them: inappropriate words, dress, actions, or conclusions.

For example, Tchebutykin, the doctor, presents a birthday gift to Irina—a silver samovar:

OLGA: (*putting her hands over her face*) A samovar! How awful! (*Goes out to the table in the dining room*)

IRINA: My dear doctor, what are you thinking about!

TUSENBACH: (*laughs*) I warned you!

MASHA: Doctor, you really have no conscience!

TCHEBUTYKIN: My dear girls, my darlings, you are all that I have, you are the most precious treasures I have on earth. I shall soon be sixty, I am an old man, alone in the world, a useless old man.—There is nothing good in me except my love for you, and if it were not for you, I should have been dead long ago— (*To IRINA*) My dear, my little girl, I've known you from a baby— I've carried you in my arms—I loved your dear mother—

IRINA: But why such expensive presents?

TCHEBUTYKIN: (*angry and tearful*) Expensive presents.—Get along with you! (*To the orderly*) Take the samovar in there— (*Mimicking*) Expensive presents—

But it is not just that the gift is unwarrantedly expensive; it is also a social gaffe: as every member of a Russian audience would know, a silver samovar was a traditional silver anniversary present, an utterly inappropriate gift for a young lady's twentieth birthday. The confusion of emotion is wonderfully theatrical on stage, what with Olga's embarrassment and anger, tinged with spinsterish envy, and her abrupt departure; Irina's charmed consternation; and, most particularly, the doctor's fussy, semicoherent explanations and deprecations, all centering on a splendidly silvered prop samovar glittering in the midst of these ill-at-ease adults: a classic moment of pure realist theatre. What we do not know yet—and in-

Kitty Winn, as Irina, places the silver samovar on the dining table in an American Conservatory Theatre production of The Three Sisters, *directed by William Ball. Notice realism of costumes, furniture, and properties in this production (including real flowers and real candles in the chandelier) and the contrasting stylization of background. (Photo: William Ganslen, ACT.)*

deed will never be sure of—is Tchebutykin's entire motivation in giving this gift; for what indeed was his relationship with Irina's mother? As the play goes on, the suspicion grows on us (although not on Irina) that possibly the doctor is Irina's real father; however, true to realistic playwriting, this suspicion is never confirmed or denied by the author or his characters. Thus the samovar might or might not be as inappropriate as Olga and we at first suppose. This ambiguity is but one of many that the audience will be challenged to explore as the play's actions unfold.

Now the handsome, married, middle-aged Colonel Alexander Vershinin arrives on the scene. He announces that he dimly remembers the sisters from many years past, in Moscow:

VERSHININ: I have the honor to introduce myself, my name is Vershinin. I am very, very glad to be in your house at last. How you have grown up! Aie-aie!

IRINA: Please sit down. We are delighted to see you.

VERSHININ: (*with animation*) How glad I am, how glad I am! But there are three of you sisters. I remember—three little girls. I don't remember your faces, but that your father, Colonel Prozorov, had three little girls I remember perfectly. How time passes! Hey-ho, how it passes!

TUSENBACH: Alexander Vershinin has come from Moscow.

IRINA: From Moscow? You have come from Moscow?

VERSHININ: Yes. Your father was in command of a battery there, and I was an officer in the same brigade. (*To* MASHA) Your face, now, I seem to remember.

MASHA: I don't remember you.

VERSHININ: So you are Olga, the eldest—and you are Masha—and you are Irina, the youngest—

OLGA: You come from Moscow?

VERSHININ: Yes. I studied in Moscow. . . . I used to visit you in Moscow.

Masha and Vershinin are destined to become lovers; their deepening, largely unspoken communion will provide one of the most haunting strains in the play. And how lifelike is the awkwardness of their first encounter! Vershinin's enthusiastic clichés ("how time passes") and interjections ("Aie-aie!") are the stuff of everyday discourse, and the news that he comes from Moscow is repeated to the extent that it becomes amusing rather than informative, a revelation of character rather than of plot.

Masha's first exchange with Vershinin gives no direct indication of the future of their relationship; it is a crossed communication in which one character refuses to share in the other's memory. Is this a personal repudiation or is it a teasing provocation? The acting, not simply the text, must establish their developing rapport. The love between Vershinin and Masha will tax to the maximum the capabilities of the actors who play their parts to express deep feeling through subtle nuance, through the gestures, the glances, the tones of voice, and the shared understandings and sympathetic rhythms that distinguish lovers everywhere: it is a theme that strongly affects the mood of the play but is rarely explicit in the dialogue.

Inasmuch as both Masha and Vershinin are married to others, their relationship is necessarily furtive; this circumstance contributes to a general obliqueness in the play's dialogue, as is evident even in the early exchanges between Masha and her husband, Kulygin:

KULYGIN: (*to the assembled guests, his hand around* MASHA's *waist, laughing*) Masha loves me. My wife loves me.—These window curtains should be put away with the carpets—Today I feel cheerful and in the best of spirits. Masha, at four o'clock this afternoon we have to be at the headmaster's. An excursion has been arranged for the teachers and their families.

MASHA: I am not going.

KULYGIN: Dear Masha, why not?

MASHA: We'll talk about it afterwards. (*Angrily*) Very well, I will go, only let me alone please— (*Walks away*)

KULYGIN: And then we shall spend the evening at the headmaster's. In spite of the delicate state of his health, that man tries before all things to be sociable. He is an excellent, noble personality. A splendid man. Yesterday, after the meeting, he said to me: "I am tired, Fyodor Ilyitch, I am tired." (*Looks at the clock, then at his watch*) Your clock is seven minutes fast. "Yes," he said, "I am tired."

Social awkwardness can be a source of daily anxiety for many an ordinary person; certainly the bumbling good will of Kulygin echoes many of our own mundane disasters. Intended pleasantries that strike unexpected notes of discord, anecdotes that disintegrate in the retelling, idle observations that impart an excruciating dullness to spoken discourse: these conversational features are by no means indigenous only to Russia at the turn of the century, and Chekhov inserts them into this play with characteristic accuracy and wit. Neither wicked enough to merit our scorn nor ridiculous enough to generate our laughter, they serve rather to stimulate our understanding of and our compassion for a wholly recognizable character whose ineptness is not unlike our own.

Two more feasible love affairs are broached in the first act—more feasible in the sense that they involve unmarried young adults. The first involves Tusenbach, an idealistic "baron" of German descent, and the youngest sister, Irina. Tusenbach expresses his adoration for her; she, however, shows no inclination to reciprocate:

TUSENBACH: What are you thinking of? (*Pause*) You are twenty, I am not yet thirty. How many years have we got before us, a long, long, chain of days full of my love for you—

IRINA: Nikolai Lvovich, don't talk to me of love.

TUSENBACH: (*not listening*) I have a passionate craving for life, for struggle, for work, and that craving is mingled in my soul with my love for you, Irina, and just because you are beautiful it seems to me that life too is beautiful! What are you thinking of?

IRINA: You say life is beautiful—Yes, but what if it only seems so! Life for us three sisters has not been beautiful yet, we have been stifled by it as plants are choked by weeds. I am shedding tears—I mustn't do that. (*Wipes her eyes and smiles*) I must work, I must work. The reason we are depressed and take such a gloomy view of life is that we know nothing of work.

Irina and Tusenbach are perfectly suited to each other—but she does not love him! No amount of rational rapport can outweigh that consideration. Irina will barely listen to Tusenbach's declarations; and Tusenbach, for his part, refuses to acknowledge Irina's dissatisfactions. This one-sided love will provide another line of tension in the play, jangling gently until the baron's suicidal duel at the play's conclusion.

And at the very end of Act I, Andrei, brother to the three sisters, is seen to fall in love with the peasant girl Natasha. Unlike the other relationships in the play, that of Andrei and Natasha will result in marriage—but it will be a union that undermines the family rather than enhances it. Shy, ridiculed at her first entrance for gauchely wearing a green sash with a pink dress, Natasha seduces Andrei from the family gathering and wrings from him a promise of marriage as the Act I curtain falls. Her motives are obscure, but Andrei's fumbling vulnerability foretells the direction of their lives:

NATASHA *runs from the dining room, followed by* ANDREI.

ANDREI: Stop, I entreat you—

NATASHA: I am ashamed—I don't know what's the matter with me and they make fun of me. I know it's improper for me to leave the table like this, but I can't help it—I can't. (*Covers her face with her hands*)

ANDREI: My dear girl, I entreat you, I implore you, don't be upset. I assure you they are only joking, they do it in all kindness. My dear, my sweet, they are all kind, warmhearted people and they are fond of me and of you. Come here to the window so they can't see us— (*Looks around*)

NATASHA: I am so unaccustomed to society!—

ANDREI: Oh youth, lovely, marvelous youth! My dear, my sweet, don't be so distressed! Believe me, believe me—I feel so happy, my soul is full of love and rapture—Oh, they can't see us, they can't see us! Why, why, I love you, when I first loved you— oh, I don't know. My dear, my sweet, pure one, be my wife! I love you, I love you—as I have never loved anyone— (*A kiss*)

Two officers come in and, seeing the pair kissing, stop in amazement.

Curtain

This is a scene of physical seduction. Natasha plays first upon Andrei's pity and then upon his lust; hence her tears and her use of her hands are more crucial to this scene than any words can be. Andrei's confusion and desire make him a poor match for Natasha's manipulations, and we watch with a mixture of amusement and chagrin as he ineloquently stammers out his infatuation. As we find so often in this play, Andrei's protestations of happiness, love, and rapture are undermined by his obvious sense of personal inadequacy; his failure to avoid public scrutiny (he indeed pulls Natasha right into the path of the amazed officers) is but a symbol of the greater failure that will mark the course of this ill-founded union.

Acts II and III, which are set approximately one and two years after the first, introduce no new characters and no new plot lines; rather, these acts serve to show the developing relationships between the various characters, the subtle changes that mark the passage of time and the shifting of interpersonal dominances. Both acts, like the first, are social gatherings of sorts: Act II, occurring in the same drawing room as Act I, is an evening tea party preparatory to a carnival dance; Act III takes place in the bedroom of Olga and Irina, where, at three o'clock in the morning, the family and friends organize emergency relief efforts for victims of a neighborhood fire. One must look and listen closely to grasp what is happening and what has happened. Natasha has given birth: to son Bobik by Act II, to daughter Sophie by Act III; the children's presence by turns silences the revelry of the carnival dancers and drives the adults out of the main portion of the house (thus forcing Olga and Irina to share a bedroom in Act III). Servants are dismissed, illicit affairs are somewhat meanly pursued, the unwed sisters become more noticeably unwed, and everyone quite subtly grows older. The doctor becomes more drunkenly morose, the baron becomes more ardent in his hapless romancing, Andrei becomes wearier and more helpless, and Kulygin becomes even more of a bore. The love between Vershinin and Masha deepens and thus becomes more poignant in its futility. Natasha takes a lover, one Protopopov, whose spiritual presence, like that of her children (the latter of whom is probably his), becomes more and more oppressive in the play.

And yet none of this is explicitly stated. Unlike the television soap opera—which is a realistic form superficially Chekhovian in structure—this play presents growth and change and even the definition of relationships in an infinitely complex and humanly obscure manner: nothing is analyzed and nothing is resolved. To discuss the plot of *The Three Sisters* is to *interpret* the play, for Chekhov has simply drawn the action and left it to the audience to draw the consequences. Masha and Vershinin do not exchange a single word in Act III, but when they hum a song together and laugh we know all—or at least all that we will know. Olga rages at the doctor for his drunkenness, but we know that Natasha is the real cause for her anger; Olga simply does not have the courage to confront her sister-in-law face to face. Kulygin never directly addresses his wife's infidelity, but when he says to her, "I am content, I am content, I am content," we feel she gets the message—as do we.

The fourth and final act, in which the story lines are concluded, if not resolved, remains subtle, oblique, and suffused with ironic indirection.

Matthais Langhoff's production of The Three Sisters *at the Théâtre de Ville in Paris in 1994 employed a larger-than-lifesize pictorial backdrop showing the army leaving town, heightening the poignancy of the sisters' increasing isolation downstage. (Photo: Brigitte Enguerand.)*

It is noon on a summer day; for the first time we are outdoors, on the verandah of the family house. The familiar world of the sisters has come to a sudden end; the military garrison is being evacuated to Poland, far away; the soldiers are preparing to depart. Only Baron Tusenbach will remain behind, for he has resigned his commission to marry Irina, who has finally relented to his pursuit. The rest will embark that day, and a farewell champagne party, given by the saddened sisters, has just concluded; it is now time for leave-taking. Whereas most playwrights reserve the final act for tying up loose ends, Chekhov in *The Three Sisters* portrays an unraveling of such slight fabric as has been woven in the first three acts.

Tusenbach and Irina's marriage is not to be. We learn, although Irina does not, that Tusenbach has a rival: the foolish Solyony contests his right to marry Irina and has challenged him to a duel. Before the act is over Tusenbach will be dead. Therefore, ironically, Tusenbach's will be the truest leave-taking in the play.

IRINA: Our town will be empty now.

TUSENBACH: Dear, I'll be back directly.

IRINA: Where are you going?

TUSENBACH: I must go into the town, and then—to see my comrades off.

IRINA: That's not true—Nikolai, why are you so absent-minded today? (*A pause*) What happened yesterday near the theatre?

TUSENBACH: (*impatiently*) I'll be here in an hour and with you again. (*Kisses her hands*) My beautiful one— (*Looks into her face*) For five years now I have loved you and still I can't get used to it, and you seem to me more and more lovely. What wonderful, exquisite hair! What eyes! I shall carry you off tomorrow, we will work, we will be rich, my dreams will come true. You shall be happy. There is only one thing, one thing: you don't love me!

IRINA: That's not in my power! I'll be your wife and be faithful and obedient, but there is no love, I can't help it. (*Weeps*) I've never been in love in my life! Oh, I have so dreamed of love, I've been dreaming of it for years, day and night, but my soul is like a wonderful piano of which the key has been lost. (*A pause*) You look uneasy.

TUSENBACH: I have not slept all night. There has never been anything in my life so dreadful that it could frighten me, and only that lost key frets at my heart and won't let me sleep—Say something to me— (*A pause*) Say something to me—

IRINA: What? What am I to say to you? What??

TUSENBACH: Anything.

IRINA: There, there! (*A pause*)

TUSENBACH: What trifles, what little things suddenly *a propos* of nothing acquire importance in life! One laughs at them as before, thinks them as nonsense, but still one goes on and feels that one has not the power to stop. Don't let us talk about it! I am happy. I feel as though I were seeing these pines, these maples, these birch trees for the first time in my life, and they all seem to be looking at me with curiosity and waiting. What beautiful trees, and, really, how beautiful life ought to be under them! (*A shout offstage of "Halloo!" calling him to the forest and his duel*) I must be off; it's time—See, that tree is dead, but it waves in the wind with the others. And so it seems to me that if I die I shall still have part in life, one way or another. Goodbye my darling— (*Kisses her hands*) Those papers of yours you gave me are lying under the calendar on my table.

IRINA: I am coming with you.

TUSENBACH: (*in alarm*) No, no! (*Goes off quickly, stops*) Irina!

IRINA: What is it?

TUSENBACH: (*not knowing what to say*) I didn't have any coffee this morning. Ask them to make me some. (*Goes out quickly*)

This, one of the saddest scenes imaginable, achieves its almost monumental pathos by what is *not* said rather than by what is. Tusenbach's groping for direction, for confirmation, for love and meaning in his life, is epitomized by his desperate stammer "Say something to me—Say something to me—" and by Irina's agonized inability to respond except in kind. Unable to achieve the rapport he so desires, he speaks of trees, of papers, and finally of morning coffee. The life-and-death confrontation that looms but minutes away remains an unspoken terror, against which Tusenbach can only utter his mirthless, absurdly noble cry of "I am happy!"

Eloquence, which is a characteristic of rhetorical playwrights since Aeschylus, is equally characteristic of the best work of the realists. However, the eloquence of realism, as Chekhov magnificently demonstrates, consists in details of dialogue and action rather than in cogent declamation. Tusenbach's "I didn't have any coffee this morning" stands as one of the great exit lines in theatre, but the key to its greatness lies in its profound understatement. It is a line out of context, out of the morning office break; juxtaposed against the passion of the dramatized moment, however, it reveals a depth of feeling and layers of character beyond the reach of direct verbalization.

Chekhov's poetry is of actions as well as words, and its rhythm is fashioned out of the silences, self-deceptions, petty boasts, unguarded responses, and empty promises of his characters. Even their attempts at lyricism—as when Tusenbach tries to liken himself to a dead tree—are touching more for their clumsiness than for their majesty. It is human fallibility—in expression as well as in act—that is the basic stuff of realism.

The farewell between Masha and Vershinin is the centerpiece of the final act, and it affords us the only fully explicit information we are to have concerning the depth of passion to which this relationship has led. But this too is to be a scene without rhetoric, for the pair are vouchsafed neither the time nor the privacy to voice their feelings. Vershinin's speeches are mere time-filling commonplaces addressed to Olga while he waits for Masha to arrive; and Masha's words, when they finally come out, are a mad reiteration of the Pushkin poem she recited in the play's beginning, chanted to ward off the sympathy of her sister and husband—the latter of whom absurdly tries to distract her from her misery by donning false whiskers. All Masha and Vershinin can exchange is a kiss, but that kiss outweighs volumes of poetry and rational explanation. Here is the scene:

VERSHININ: (*to* OLGA) Everything comes to an end. Here we are parting. (*Looks at his watch*) . . . Well—Thank you for everything—Forgive me if anything was amiss—I have talked a great deal: forgive me for that too—don't remember evil against me.

OLGA: (*wipes her eyes*) Why doesn't Masha come?

VERSHININ: What else am I to say to you at parting? What am I to theorize about—(*Laughs*) Life is hard. It seems to many of us blank and hopeless; but yet we must admit that it goes on getting clearer and easier, and it looks as though the time were not far off when it will be full of happiness. (*Looks at his watch*) It's time for me to go! In old days men were absorbed in wars, filling all their existence with marches, raids, victories, but now all that is a thing of the past, leaving behind it a great void which there is so far nothing to fill: humanity is searching for it passionately, and of course will find it. Ah, if only it could be quickly! (*Pause*) If, don't you know, industry were united with culture and culture with industry— (*Looks at his watch*) But, I say, it's time for me to go—

OLGA: Here she comes!

MASHA *comes in.*

VERSHININ: I have come to say goodbye—

MASHA: (*looking into his face*) Goodbye— (*A prolonged kiss*)

OLGA: (*who has moved away to leave them free*) Come, come—

MASHA *sobs violently.*

VERSHININ: Write to me—Don't forget me! Let me go!—Time is up!—Olga, take her, I must—go—I am late. (*Much moved, he kisses* OLGA'*s hands, then again embraces* MASHA *and quickly goes off.* MASHA *breaks down in hysterical sobs.*)

OLGA: Come, Masha! Leave off, darling—

Enter KULYGIN, MASHA'*s husband.*

KULYGIN: (*embarrassed*) Never mind, let her cry—let her—My good Masha, My dear Masha!—You are my wife, and I am happy, anyway—I don't complain; I don't say a word of blame—Here, Olga is my witness—we'll begin the old life again, and I won't say one word, not a hint—

MASHA: (*restraining her sobs*) By the seastrand, an oak-tree green—Upon that oak a chain of gold—Upon that oak a chain of gold—I am going mad—By the seastrand—an oak-tree green—

OLGA: Calm yourself, Masha—Calm yourself—Give her some water.

MASHA: I am not crying now—

KULYGIN: She is not crying now—she is good—

The dim sound of a faraway shot

THE REALITY OF STANISLAVSKY'S GOODBYE

I remember when Stanislavsky as Vershinin came to say goodbye to Masha in *The Three Sisters*. They had tried not to show their love for each other, but the band was playing, and they looked at each other, and then they grabbed each other. I'll never forget that grabbing. I remember literally holding onto the seat. The simple reality of that goodbye, of the two people holding on as if they wouldn't let go, of both literally clinging to each other, will stay with me always.

Lee Strasberg

MASHA: By the sea strand an oak tree green, upon that oak a chain of gold—the cat is green—the oak is green—I am mixing it up now— (*Drinks water*) My life is a failure. I want nothing now.—I shall be calm directly—It doesn't matter—what does "strand" mean? Why do these words haunt me? My thoughts are in a tangle. *Enter* IRINA.

OLGA: Calm yourself, Masha. Come, that's a good girl. Let us go indoors.

MASHA: (*angrily*) I am not going in. Let me alone! (*Sobs, but at once checks herself*)

IRINA: Let us sit together, even if we don't say anything. I am going away tomorrow, you know— (*A pause*)

KULYGIN: I took a false beard and moustache from a boy in the third grade yesterday, just look. (*Puts on the beard and moustache*) I look like the German teacher. (*Laughs*) Don't I? Funny creatures, those boys.

MASHA: You really do look like the German teacher.

OLGA: (*laughs*) Yes!

MASHA *weeps.*

As elsewhere in this playscript—and in realistic playscripts in general—this scene comes fully alive only insofar as the reader can imagine it being acted. The verbal simplicity of Vershinin and Masha's goodbyes, the inanity of Vershinin's theorizing while looking at his watch, the pathetic attempts of Kulygin to soothe his wife, and Masha's whirlwind of anger and tears—these are the bare outlines of complex reactions that can be captured only through the artistry of actors who are conversant with the psychological intricacies of behavior and are moreover sufficiently liberated to delve into those intricacies on a stage. In the hands of a superb ensemble—which is, of course, what Stanislavsky created for the production of Chekhov's plays—the pattern of details and behaviors in *The Three Sisters* becomes resoundingly meaningful; the inappropriateness of individual words and acts is seen to be integral to a larger and more harmonious vision, in which the portrayal of human fallibility is balanced by a portrayal of human compassion, strength, and endurance.

Masha will not enter the house because Natasha has taken it over; Natasha has also installed her lover, Protopopov, in the residence, and driven even Andrei out of doors, where he walks her latest child (almost certainly not his) in a perambulator. And the distant shot indicated in the script—a shot which is unacknowledged on stage and perhaps not even noticed by the audience—will deprive Irina of her fiancé and her only apparent hope for a worthwhile and independent future. As the fourth act draws to a close, a military band is playing in the distance: the garrison is marching away. The doctor, who will leave tomorrow, has returned to bring the news of Tusenbach's demise. He now sits on a garden bench singing "Tarara-boom-de-ay." And the sisters, arms around each other, speak their final thoughts:

MASHA: Oh, listen to that band! They are going away from us; one has gone altogether, gone forever. We are left alone to begin our life over again—We've got to live—we've got to live—

IRINA: A time will come when everyone will know what all this is for, why there is this misery; there will be no mysteries and, meanwhile, we have got to live—we have got to work, only to work! Tomorrow I shall go alone; I shall teach in the school, and I will give all my life to those to whom it may be of use. Now it's autumn; soon winter will come and cover us with snow, and I will work, I will work.

OLGA: (*embraces both of her sisters*) The music is so gay, so confident, and one longs for life! Oh my god! Time will pass, and we shall go away forever, and we shall be forgotten, our faces will be forgotten, our voices, and how many there were of us; but our sufferings will pass into joy for those who live after us, happiness and peace will be established upon earth, and they will remember kindly and bless those who have lived before. Oh, dear sisters, our life is not ended yet. We shall live! The music is so gay, so joyful, and it seems as though a little more and we shall know what we are living for, why we are suffering—If we only knew—if we only knew!

DOCTOR: (*humming softly*) Tarara-boom-de-ay. (*Reads his paper*) It doesn't matter, it doesn't matter.

OLGA: If we only knew, if we only knew!

Curtain

Here, in the last moments of the play, we find a lyricism of longings that epitomizes Chekhovian theatrical poetry. Counterpointed by the music of the departing regiment and the humming of the doctor as he turns the pages of his newspaper, the sisters' plaints echo their opening monologues in the first act. Thus the dramatist completes a frame around the action of the play that focuses the blended stories and characters and at the same time provides a memorable testament of human courage in adversity.

We have seen how the realists tend to write of human ignorance and failure, and of human confusion in a complicated world and human isolation in an uncaring cosmos. But that perspective would be theatrically unsatisfying were it not for the complementary realist vision of human beings as creatures possessed of a giant will for struggle, survival, and even triumph. The sisters may not get to Moscow, may never love the men they marry or marry the men they love, but one feels certain that they will persist and endure—that

---

STANISLAVSKY ON CHEKHOV

In his plays, Chekhov is master of both outer and inner truth. There is no one who can use lifeless properties, scenery and lighting effects like he does—to make them live. He has shown us the life of things and sounds and lighting which, in the theatre as in life, exert a profound influence on the human soul. Twilight, sunrise and sunset, thunderstorm and rain, the songs of awakening birds, the clatter of horses' hoofs and the rumble of a carriage, the striking of a clock, the stridulation of a cricket, the pealing of bells— Chekhov uses all these not for stage effect, but for the purpose of showing us man's soul. Where is the line dividing us and our feelings from the world of light, sound and things which surround us and on which human psychology so depends?

Konstantin Stanislavsky

they will continue to knock at the door of their desired destiny even if they never get in. Chekhov provides his characters with opportunities; these may be squandered or exploited, but they will never be taken away absolutely. This approach, too, is fundamental to realism, for what could be more true to life than a portrayal of the continual, unending, passionately pursued human quest for a better love and a better world?

The characters of the realists, like people in real life, are neither performers nor object lessons. Kulygin is perhaps as ridiculous in his false moustache and beard as Monsieur Jourdain, in *The Bourgeois Gentleman,* is in his Turkish gown and turban; but Kulygin is one of us in a way that Jourdain never could be, and in the end we cannot but be moved by the kind of intentions beneath his clumsy ministrations. The sisters, by turns foolish and noble, innocent and worldly-wise, shallow and profound, leave us with an admixture of feelings; like members of our own families they are continually shifting figures in our consciousness, impossible to categorize, easy to scorn, easier to forgive. The lovemaking in *The Three Sisters* is as awkward as our own and

the speechmaking as inarticulate, but that never prevents our appreciation of the characters; rather, it provokes our shared sympathy. If Tusenbach, in asking for coffee as he goes off to his death, is less self-possessed than Mercutio crying "Ask for me tomorrow and you shall find me a grave man," we understand him better and, through him, we understand immeasurably better the forces that underlie human reticence.

Realistic acting is the medium of realist drama, and it took the staging breakthroughs achieved by Stanislavsky and his colleagues to accommodate the action of realistic plays such as *The Three Sisters.* The "prolonged kiss" between Masha and Vershinin is representative of a revolution in theatrical performance as great as almost any in the theatre's history, for a kiss is a *biological* act that implies emotional consequences unrealizable through words alone. A prolonged kiss would have been impossible in the Greek or Elizabethan theatre, since it only would call attention to the theatrical conventions separating the play from normal life (that is, the Greek masks and the Elizabethan boy actors in the female roles); and in the Royal theatre such a kiss, like any other robust physical action, was deemed too rude for the stage. Even in the romantic period, kissing was idealized: one showed one's affection in that era by reciting great torrents of verse while displaying physical self-denial. But because the realistic theatre demands the actions of life, lovers in realistic theatre must be seen to kiss—and, in many later works, to do much more than that. Moreover, the sheer physiological reality of Masha and Vershinin's kiss—meaning, of course, the physiological reality of the actors' kiss—is integral to the play's climax in a way that becomes clear when one sees the play performed.

Scenery, costumes, and particularly props and music also figure prominently in the theatrical texture of Chekhovian realism. Vershinin looks at his watch three times during his final conversation with Olga; could we even imagine Prometheus looking at his watch (assuming the Greeks had such a thing as a watch)? The doctor's newspaper, the silver samovar, the faded window curtains Kulygin complains about, Irina's white dress, Masha's hat and her book of poetry, Natasha's green sash, a broken clock, a child's top, a marching band, the offstage sound of masquers playing—these are the mundane elements, artfully selected, from which Chekhov has fashioned a symphony of meaning.

Participation in the realistic theatre is akin to participation in life itself; the realistic theatre makes inroads into our biological and psychological cognition and leaves us *personally* moved and shaken. The characters' situations resonate with the strains of our own. Irina's wistfulness, Masha's desolation, Olga's determination, Tusenbach's compulsiveness, Kulygin's jovial desperation—these are ours too, and their staged reenactments affect us in ways we find difficult to express. We leave the theatre after *The Three Sisters* as we would leave a party given by the sisters themselves:

filled with the contradictory and ambivalent feelings of warmth and sadness, criticism and kindly thoughts, annoyances and admirations, understandings and a wealth of further questions.

The purest form of realism allows no firm conclusions. *The Three Sisters* has given rise to a whole spectrum of evaluations and interpretations, from outright condemnation of the sisters and their social milieu to high praise for their fortitude and gentility. Certainly if they were *our* sisters, there is much we would find to criticize in them, much to admire. The genius of the play resides in the complexity and individuality of the characters and the intricacy of the pattern that links them in a social network. The playwright has given us as much detail as we are likely to observe in reality itself. He has also given us *people:* to laugh at, to gossip about, to analyze, and to sympathize with. He has presented us with all of this evidence and encouraged us to draw our own conclusions. And when it all comes together on a stage, theatrical magic as potent as any in the past can work its spell.

AMERICAN REALISM

There was no "United States of America" in ancient times, of course, nor was such a place known during the Middle Ages or the Renaissance. Nor did the United States enjoy (if that is the correct word) a "Royal era," since the North American continent, during the years of the Royal theatre, went from tribal society to colony to republic. Although theatre activity in what is now the United States dates from the 1500s (in Spanish) and native dramatic writing is known from the late 1700s (Thomas Godfrey's *The Prince of Parthia*),

the first truly important American plays date from the beginning of the current century—not surprising in light of the lack of ancient theatre buildings, royally established acting companies, and traditional dramatic repertories to call upon. The dominant style of American drama at its beginning, and continuing right up to the present day, has been realistic.

Eugene O'Neill (1888–1953), universally considered America's first master dramatist, was the first to develop an international reputation. The son of a famous actor (James O'Neill), the younger O'Neill worked as a

August Wilson is one of the most authentic and effective voices of the African-American experience to have emerged in the 1980s; his play, Fences, *pictured above in the 1986 Goodman Theatre production in Chicago with James Earl Jones (center) and (left to right) Charles Brown, Mary Alice, and Ray Aranha, went on to win the 1987 Pulitzer Prize and Tony Award following its Broadway production. (Photo: Lisa Ebright.)*

merchant sailor and newspaper reporter before studying playwriting at Harvard; soon thereafter, in the 1920s and 1930s, he turned out a remarkable series of realistic dramatic studies: *Anna Christie,* about a prostitute; *All God's Chillun Got Wings,* about interracial marriage; *Desire Under the Elms,* about rural passion and incest; and the extraordinary *Mourning Becomes Electra,* a rewriting of the Oresteian trilogy in a puritanical New England setting, with Freudian motivation replacing the Greek fates. After O'Neill's death, his widow shared with the world his deeply revealing autobiographical work, and undoubted masterpiece, *Long Day's Journey into Night.*

Al Pacino (right) is one of the three low-life hoodlums inhabiting a junk shop in David Mamet's American Buffalo *in the 1981 Long Wharf Theatre production directed by Arvin Brown. Mamet's play initially failed on Broadway when critics found its naturalism formless and oppressive. But Brown's New Haven production was a tremendous success and eventually transferred to New York, giving the play a second chance with the Broadway press. This time,* American Buffalo *succeeded, and it is now considered a contemporary American classic. (Photo: William Carter.)*

Tennessee Williams's heartbreaking The Glass Menagerie *is one of the classics of American realism, as shown here in Emily Mann's 1991 production at the McCarter Theatre in Princeton. (Photo: T. Charles Erickson.)*

O'Neill's influence reigned over the American theatre for the generation that followed, and the principal American dramatists in the post–World War II years worked largely in a realistic vein as well. Arthur Miller (1915–) succeeded O'Neill as America's most "serious" playwright; his plays include *All My Sons,* about wartime profiteering; *Death of a Salesman,* about the broken "American dream" of financial success; *The Crucible,* about the seventeenth-century witch hunts in Massachusetts (and, by analogy, about the anti-communist witch hunts of Joe McCarthy in the 1950s); *A View from the Bridge,* about illegal immigration; and *After the Fall,* a thinly disguised autobiographical drama about his own life and liaisons, including his celebrated marriage to Marilyn Monroe.

Miller, deeply committed to social and political reform, was often paired in the post–World War II years with the more poetic, but still realistic, Tennessee Williams (1911–

Urban American life is David Mamet's subject in Glengarry Glen Ross, *seen here in the original 1984 Goodman Theatre production in Chicago, Mamet's hometown, with Joe Montegna (right) and Mike Nussbaum. The play is set in a Chicago real estate office, and the setting, action, and dialogue are about as close as you could get to what happens in certain such environments. (Photo: Brigitte Lacombe.)*

1983), whose *The Glass Menagerie, A Streetcar Named Desire, Cat on a Hot Tin Roof, Suddenly Last Summer,* and *The Night of the Iguana* were brilliantly evocative and idealized character studies—often of characters psychologically unable to cope with what they viewed as the brutalities of daily American life. An admitted homosexual, Williams in his later years spoke profoundly to the need for a broader human understanding and compassion for those who, like himself, saw themselves as outside the mainstream of American life. Williams's works, which remain enormously popular today, are testimonies to the dignity of all human individuals and to the artistic impulse.

The basis in realism of these major mid-century American playwrights—and of William Inge, Robert Anderson, William Gibson, and Lorraine Hansberry—was abetted by a deep commitment to realistic styles in acting, as perpetuated by Konstantin Stanislavsky in Russia and brought to America by the Actors Studio in New York, which is described in more detail in the chapter on acting. The combination of realistic dramas and realistic acting in what are virtually the formative years of the American drama led to realism's role as a basic language of the American stage today.

9

The Modern Theatre: Antirealism

If realism was the first new movement to make itself strongly felt in the modern theatre, it was not the only one. A counterforce, equal and opposite, was to follow right on its heels.

We may call this counterforce antirealism, for its practitioners, despite their radical dissimilarities, were united by their hatred of realism and their passion to move the theatre beyond what they saw as its narrow confines. Thus the antirealistic theatre was not simply a collection of plays and play stagings, but also an emotionally charged social and cultural movement, marked by scandals, manifestos, counterattacks, and calls to arms.

THE SYMBOLIST BEGINNINGS

The antirealistic counterforce first appeared in the artistic movement known as symbolism, which began in Paris during the 1880s as a joint venture of artists, playwrights, essayists, critics, sculptors, and poets.

If realism was the art of depicting reality as ordinary men and women might see it, symbolism would explore—by means of images and metaphors—the *inner* realities that cannot be directly or literally perceived. "Symbolic" characters, therefore, would not represent real human beings, but would symbolize philosophical ideals or warring internal forces in the human (or the artist's) soul.

Symbolism had another goal as well: to crush what its adherents deemed to be a spiritually bankrupt realism and to replace it with traditional aesthetic values—poetry, imagery, novelty, fantasy, extravagance, profundity, audacity, charm, and superhuman magnitude. United in their hatred for literal detail and for all they considered mundane or ordinary, the symbolists demanded abstraction, enlargement, and innovation; the symbolist spirit soared in poetic encapsulations, outsized dramatic presences, fantastical visual effects, shocking structural departures, and grandiloquent speech. Purity of vision, rather than accuracy of observation, was the symbolists' aim, and self-conscious creative innovation was to be their primary accomplishment.

The first symbolist theatre, founded in 1890 by Parisian poet Paul Fort, was intended as a direct attack on the naturalistic Théâtre Libre of André Antoine, founded three years earlier. Fort's theatre, the Théâtre d'Art, was proposed as "a theatre for Symbolist poets only, where every production would cause a battle." In some ways Antoine's and Fort's theatres had much in common: both were amateur, both gained considerable notoriety, each served as a center for a "school" of artistic ideology that attracted as much attention and controversy as did any of its theatrical offerings.

But the two theatres were openly, deliberately, at war. While Antoine was presenting premieres of naturalistic and realistic dramas by Strindberg, Zola, and Ibsen, Fort presented the staged poems of Rimbaud, Verlaine, Shelley, Milton, Marlowe, Maeterlinck, and Edgar Allen Poe. Whereas Antoine would go to great lengths to create realistic scenery for his plays (for example, he procured sides of real beef and hung them on real meathooks for his presentation of *The Butchers*), Fort would prevail upon leading impressionist easel painters, including Pierre Bonnard, Maurice Denis, and Odilon Redon, to dress his

---

REALISM AS PRISON: YEATS'S VIEW

At the first performance of [Ibsen's realistic play] *Ghosts* I could not escape from an illusion unaccountable to me at the time. All the characters seemed to be less than life-size; the stage, though it was but the little Royalty stage, seemed larger than I had ever seen it. Little whimpering puppets moved here and there in the middle of that great abyss. Why did they not speak out with louder voices or move with freer gestures? What was it that weighed upon their souls perpetually? Certainly they were all in prison, and yet there was no prison. In India there are villages so obedient that all the jailer has to do is draw a circle upon the ground with his staff, and to tell his thief to stand there so many hours; but what law had these people broken that they had to wander round that narrow circle all their lives? . . .

What is there left for us . . . but . . . to rediscover an art of the theatre that shall be joyful, fantastic, extravagant, whimsical, beautiful, resonant, and altogether reckless?

William Butler Yeats

---

stylized stage. Silver angels, translucent veils, and sheets of crumpled wrapping paper were among the decors that backed the symbolist works at the Théâtre d'Art.

Fort's theatre created an immediate sensation in Paris. With the stunning success, in 1890, of *The Intruder,* a mysterious and poetic fantasy by the Belgian symbolist Maurice Maeterlinck, the antirealist movement was fully engaged and, as Fort recalled in his memoirs, "the cries and applause of the students, poets, and artists overwhelmed the huge disapproval of the bourgeoisie."

The movement spread quickly as authors and designers alike awakened to the possibili-

James Barrie's Peter Pan *features the famous flying young man, Peter, who symbolizes eternal youth. The role is usually played by a female actress. The play is most widely known today through a musical adaptation, here staged on Broadway in a revival starring Sandy Duncan as Peter. (Photo: Martha Swope and Associates.)*

ties of a theatre wholly freed from the constraints of verisimilitude. Realism, more and more people concluded, would never raise the commonplace to the level of art; it would only drag art down into the muck of the mundane. It ran counter to all the theatre had stood for in the past; it throttled the potential of artistic creativity. Soon such naturalistic and realistic authors as Ibsen, Strindberg, Hauptmann, and Shaw came under the symbolist influence and abandoned their social preoccupations and environmental exactitude to seek new languages and more universal themes. As an added element, at about this time the research done by Sigmund Freud was being published and discussed, and his theories concerning dream images and the worlds of the Unconscious provided new source material for the stage.

By the turn of the century, the counter-force of theatrical stylization set in motion by the symbolists was established on all fronts; indeed, the half decade on either side of 1900 represents one of the richest periods of experimentation in the history of dramatic writing. Out of that decade came Gerhart Hauptmann's archetypal fairy tale *The Sunken Bell* (Germany, 1896), Alfred Jarry's outrageously cartoonish and scatological *Ubu Roi* (France, 1896), Henrik Ibsen's haunting ode to individualism *When We Dead Awaken* (Norway, 1899), August Strindberg's metaphoric and imagistic *A Dream Play* (Sweden, 1902), William Butler Yeats's evocative poetic fable *Cathleen ni Houlihan* (Ireland, 1903), George Bernard Shaw's philosophical allegory *Man and Superman* (England, 1903), and James Barrie's whimsical, bouyant fantasy *Peter Pan* (England, 1904). Almost every dramatic innovation since then has been at least in part

AUGUST STRINDBERG, REALIST AND ANTIREALIST

Swedish playwright August Strindberg (1849–1912), like Ibsen and German playwright Gerhart Hauptmann (1862–1946), pioneered in writing both realistic and antirealistic plays. Two of his prefaces, in fact, serve as important documents of both movements.

> **Preface to *Miss Julie* (1888):** I do not believe in simplified characters for the stage. An author's summary judgement upon men (this man is a fool; that one brutal, etc.) ought to be challenged and rejected by the Naturalists who are aware of the richness of the human soul and who know that vice has another side to it that is very like virtue. I have depicted my characters as modern characters, living in an age of transition . . . thus I have made them more vacillating, disjointing . . . conglomerates of a past stage of civilization and our present one, scraps from books and newspapers, pieces of humanity, torn off tatters of holiday clothes that have disintegrated and become rags—exactly as the soul is patched together. . . . As far as the dialogue is concerned, I have broken with tradition by not making catechists out of my characters; that is, they do not keep asking silly questions merely for the sake of bringing forth a clever or jocular retort. I have avoided the symmetrical, mathematical construction commonly used by the French in their dialogue. Instead I have had my characters use their brains only intermittently as people do in real life where, during a conversation, one cog in a person's brain may find itself, more or less by chance, geared into another cog; and where no topic is completely exhausted. That is the very reason that the dialogue rambles.

> **Author's Note to *A Dream Play* (1902):** In this dream play, . . . the Author has sought to reproduce the disconnected but apparently logical form of a dream. Anything can happen; everything is possible and probable. Time and space do not exist; on a slight groundwork of reality, imagination spins and weaves new patterns made up of memories, experiences, unfettered fancies, absurdities, and improvisations. The characters are split, double and multiply; they evaporate, crystallise, scatter and converge. But a single consciousness holds sway over them all—that of the dreamer.

prefigured by one or more of these seminal works for the nonrealist theatre.

The realist-versus-symbolist confrontation affected every aspect of theatre production. Symbolist-inspired directors and designers, side by side with the playwrights, were drastically altering the arts of staging and decor to accommodate the new dramaturgies that surged into the theatre. Realist directors like Antoine and Stanislavsky suddenly found themselves challenged by scores of adversaries and renegades: a school of symbolist and poetic directors rose in France, and a former disciple of Stanislavsky, the "constructivist" Vsevolod Meyerhold, broke with the Russian master to create a nonrealist "biomechanical" style of acting and directing in sharp contrast to that established at the Moscow Art Theatre. By 1904 Stanislavsky himself was producing the impressionistic plays of Maurice Maeterlinck at the MAT. With the advent of electrical stage lighting, opportunities for stylizing were vastly expanded: the new technology enabled the modern director to create vivid stage effects, starkly unrealistic in appearance, through the judicious use of spotlighting, shadowing, and shading. Technology, plus trends in post-impressionist art that were well established in Europe by 1900, led to scenery and costume designs that departed radically from realism. Exoticism, fantasy, sheer sensual delight, symbolic meaning,

Strindberg's contrasting styles are immediately evident in these two productions, both directed by Ingmar Bergman for Stockholm's Royal Dramatic Theatre in the winter of 1985–86. LEFT: *Sexual passion and frustration is the subject of* Miss Julie, *realistically performed here by Marie Goranzon and Peter Stormare.* RIGHT: *Costume, make-up, properties, and staging all indicate a dream world in the same author's* A Dream Play. *(Photos: Bengt Wanselius.)*

and aesthetic purity became the prime objectives of designers who joined the antirealist rebellion.

In some respects, the symbolist aim succeeded perhaps beyond the dreams of its originators. Paul Fort's art theatre, although it lasted but a year, now has spiritual descendants in every city in the Western world where theatre is performed.

THE ERA OF "ISMS"

The symbolist movement itself was short-lived, at least under that name. "Symbolism," after all, was coined primarily as a direct contradiction of "realism," and movements named for their oppositional qualities—called for what they are not—are quickly seen as artistically limited, as critiques of art rather than as art itself.

Within months of the symbolist advances, therefore, symbolism *as a movement* was deserted by founders and followers alike. Where did they go? Off to found newer movements: the avant-garde, futurism, dada, idealism, aestheticism, impressionism, expressionism, constructivism, surrealism, formalism, theatricalism, and perhaps a hundred other isms now lost to time.

The first third of this century, indeed, was an era of theatrical isms, an era rich with continued experimentation by movements self-consciously seeking to redefine theatrical art. "Ism" theatres sprang up like mushrooms, each with its own fully articulated credo and manifesto, each promising a better art—if not, indeed, a better world. It was a vibrant era for the theatre; for out of this welter of isms, the aesthetics of dramatic art took on a new social and political significance in the cultural capitals of Europe and America. A successful play was not merely a play, but rather signified a *cause;* and behind that cause was a body of zealous supporters and adherents who shared a deep aesthetic commitment.

THE ERA OF STYLIZATION

The era of isms gave way, in the second third of the century, to an era of dramatic stylization. Antirealism remained the unifying principle, but the artistic movements lost their social character; playwrights could be grouped and labeled by critics, but they did not, as a whole, group and label themselves. Nor did they seek to redefine the essence of theatre or to destroy realism as a viable theatrical mode. Rather, what marks the antirealists of the mid-twentieth century is their effort to expand the potential of the theatre to incorporate an infinite admixture of dramatic styles, each consciously conceived and uniquely created. Thus the antirealistic playwrights (and directors) of modern times not only have created new plays, but they also have created new styles of playing.

Of course, theatre has always had its style, but in the past that style was largely imposed by conventions and by the limitations of theatre technology—as well as by governing social, political, and religious strictures. World War I changed that. The world was suddenly international; Americans, Austrians, English, Italians, Hungarians, French, Russians, and Germans intermixed on European battlefields and in the great theatre cities of the Continent. The conventions that had largely caused the war, after all, were largely destroyed by it. Victorian aesthetics went the way of Victorian sexuality in the ensuing flapper age. And technology soared. Hydraulic stages, electric dimmer boards, and electronically recorded sound opened the theatre's options in all directions.

The antirealistic playwright, director, or designer became, therefore, able to stylize consciously—that is, to choose and create unique styles from a nearly infinite palette. Source material could be ancient or modern, Oriental or Occidental, drawing on futuristic fantasy, Kabuki dance, Haitian ritual, and Aristophanic farce—all at the same time. There is no set format for the modern antirealistic theatre and no absolute set of governing principles. The only limit to what can be put on stage lies in the imagination of the artists and the patience of the spectators.

In general, the stylized theatre does not altogether dispense with reality, but it wields it in often unexpected ways and freely enhances it with symbol and metaphor, striving to elucidate by parable and allegory, to deconstruct and reconstruct by language and scenery and lighting. Further, it makes explicit use of the theatre's very theatricality, frequently reminding its audience, directly or indirectly, that they are watching a performance, not an episode in somebody's daily life. Stylization inevitably reaches for universality. It tends to treat problems of psychology as problems of philosophy, and problems in human relations as problems of the human condition. Stylization reaches for patterns, not particulars; it explores abstractions and aims for sharp thematic focus and bold intellectual impact.

In the stylized theatre, characters usually represent more than individual persons or personality types. Like the medieval allegories, modern stylized plays often involve characters who represent forces of nature, moral positions, human instincts, and the like—entities such as death, fate, idealism, the life force, the earth mother, the tyrant father, and the prodigal son. And the conflicts associated with these forces, unlike the conflicts of realism, are not responsive to any human agency: they are, more often than not, represented as permanent discords inherent in the human condition. The stylized theatre resonates with tension and human frustration in the face of irreconcilable demands.

But that is not to say that the stylized theatre is necessarily grim: to the contrary, it often uses whimsy and mordant wit as its dominant mode. Although the themes of the stylized theatre are anxious ones—for example, the alienation of man, the futility of communication, the loss of innocence, the intransigence of despair—it is not on the whole a theatre of pessimism or of nihilistic outrage. Indeed, the glory of the stylized theatre is that, at its best, it refuses to be swamped by its themes; it transcends frustration; it is the victory of poetry over alienation, comedy over noncommunication, and artistry over despair. The stylized theatre aims at lifting its audience, not saddling them; and if it proffers no solutions to life's inevitable discords, it can provide considerable lucidity concerning the totality of the human adventure.

EARLY ISMS AND STYLIZATIONS: A SAMPLER

Stylized theatre is often classified by critics into various groupings: ritual theatre, poetic theatre, holy theatre, theatre of cruelty, existentialist theatre, art theatre, theatre of the absurd, and theatre of alienation. Although playwrights ordinarily reject these labels (mid- and late-twentieth-century playwrights prefer to think of themselves as unique and individual, not as members of a "school"), the groupings, along with the earlier isms, are often useful indications of shared characteristics of certain plays. Still, diversity remains the mark of the antirealistic theatre—which, finally, is united only by what it is against (realism) rather than by what it is for. To help us understand this diversity, we will examine a sampling of some of the most representative antirealistic plays from the period preceding World War II and the isms or stylizations they help to define.

The French Avant-Garde: *Ubu Roi*

The opening of Alfred Jarry's *Ubu Roi* (*King Ubu*) at the Théâtre Nouveau in Paris, on December 11, 1896, was perhaps the most violent dramatic premiere in theatre history: the audience shouted, whistled, hooted, cheered, threw things, and shook their fists at the stage. Duels were fought after subsequent performances. The *avant-garde* was born.

The term *avant-garde* comes from the military, where it refers to the advance battalion, or the vanguard, or the "shock troops" that initiate a major assault. In France, the term initially described the wave of French playwrights and directors who openly and boldly assaulted realism in the first four decades of the current century. Today, the term is used worldwide to describe any adventurous, experimental, and nontraditional artistic effort.

Jarry, a diminutive iconoclast ("eccentric to the point of mania and lucid to the point of hallucination," says Roger Shattuck), unleashed his radical shock troops from the moment the curtain rose. Jarry had called for an outrageously antirealistic stage—painted scenery depicting a bed, a bare tree at its foot, palm trees, a coiled boa constrictor around one of them, a gallows with a skeleton hanging from it, and snow, falling. Characters entered through a painted fireplace. Costumes, in Jarry's words, were "divorced as far as possible from [realistic] color or chronology." And the title character stepped forward to begin the play with a word that quickly became immortal: "*Merdre!*" or "Shitr!"

This, "*le mot d'Ubu*" ("Ubu's word"), occasioned the scandal more than anything else; for while Ibsen had broken barriers of propriety in subject matter, no one had tested the language barriers of the Victorian age. Vulgar epithets, common enough in Aris-

Ubu (Geoff Hoyle, right) tweaks the nose of Mrs. Ubu (Joe Bellan) in a modern revision of Jarry's Ubu Roi, *titled* Ubu Unchained *and produced by the Eureka Theatre of San Francisco. "The power and importance of Jarry's grotesque couple lies . . . in the boldness and clarity with which they . . . embody the qualities which . . . epitomize . . . our century: greed, violence and stupidity, all expressed with charismatic self-satisfaction," says Oscar Eustis, dramaturge of the 1986 production. (Photo: Courtesy Eureka Theatre.)*

tophanes and Shakespeare, had been pruned from the theatre in the Royal era and abolished entirely in the lofty spirit of romanticism; far from trying to sneak them back in, Jarry simply threw them up, schoolboy-like, in the face of the astonished audience. The added "r" in *"merdre,"* far from "cleansing" the offending obscenity, only called more attention to it and to its deliberate intrusion onto the Parisian stage.

Ubu Roi was, in fact, a schoolboy play; Jarry wrote the first version at the age of fifteen as a satire of his high school physics teacher. Jarry was only twenty-three when the play astounded its Parisian audiences, and the juvenile aspects of the play's origins were everywhere evident in the finished product, which proved to be Jarry's sole masterwork.

Ubu Roi is a savage and often ludicrous satire on the theme of power, in which Father (later King) Ubu—a fat, foul-mouthed, venal, amoral, and pompous Polish assassin—proves one of the stage's greatest creations. The play sprawls; its thirty-three scenes are often just crude skits, barely linked by plot; but the interplay of farce and violence is inspired, as in the famous eating scene:

Father Ubu, Mother Ubu, Captain Bordure and his followers.

MOTHER UBU: Good day, gentlemen; we've been anxiously awaiting you.

CAPTAIN BORDURE: Good day, madam. Where's Father Ubu?

FATHER UBU: Here I am, here I am! Good lord, by my green candle, I'm fat enough, aren't I?

CAPTAIN BORDURE: Good day, Father Ubu. Sit down boys. (*They all sit.*)

FATHER UBU: Oof, a little more, and I'd have bust my chair.

CAPTAIN BORDURE: Well, Mother Ubu! What have you got that's good today?

MOTHER UBU: Here's the menu.

FATHER UBU: Oh! That interests me.

MOTHER UBU: Polish soup, roast ram, veal, chicken, chopped dog's liver, turkey's ass, charlotte russe . . .

FATHER UBU: Hey, that's plenty, I should think. You mean there's more?

MOTHER UBU: (*continuing*) Frozen pudding, salad, fruits, dessert, boiled beef, Jerusalem artichokes, cauliflower à la shitr.

FATHER UBU: Hey! Do you think I'm the Emperor of China, to give all that away?

MOTHER UBU: Don't listen to him, he's feeble-minded.

Mother Ubu pokes her strikingly made-up face through an abstractly colored backdrop in Babette Masson's 1993 French production of Jarry's Ubu Roi. *(Photo: Marc Enguerand.)*

FATHER UBU: Ah! I'll sharpen my teeth on your shanks.

MOTHER UBU: Try this instead, Father Ubu. Here's the Polish soup.

FATHER UBU: Crap, is that lousy!

CAPTAIN BORDURE: Hmm—it isn't very good, at that.

MOTHER UBU: What do you want, you bunch of crooks!

FATHER UBU: (*striking his forehead*) Wait, I've got an idea. I'll be right back. (*He leaves.*)

MOTHER UBU: Let's try the veal now, gentlemen.

CAPTAIN BORDURE: It's very good—I'm through.

MOTHER UBU: To the turkey's ass, next.

CAPTAIN BORDURE: Delicious, delicious! Long live Mother Ubu!

ALL: Long live Mother Ubu!

FATHER UBU: (*returning*) And you will soon be shouting long live Father Ubu. (*He has a toilet brush in his hand, and he throws it on the festive board.*)

MOTHER UBU: Miserable creature, what are you up to now?

FATHER UBU: Try a little. (*Several try it, and fall, poisoned.*) Mother Ubu, pass me the roast ram chops, so that I can serve them.

MOTHER UBU: Here they are.

FATHER UBU: Everyone out! Captain Bordure, I want to talk to you.

THE OTHERS: But we haven't eaten yet.

FATHER UBU: What's that, you haven't eaten yet? Out, out, everyone out! Stay here, Bordure. (*Nobody moves.*) You haven't gone yet? By my green candle, I'll give you your ram chops. (*He begins to throw them.*)

ALL: Oh! Ouch! Help! Woe! Help! Misery! I'm dead!

FATHER UBU: Shitr, shitr, shitr! Outside! I want my way!

ALL: Everyone for himself! Miserable Father Ubu! Traitor! Meanie!

FATHER UBU: Ah! They've gone. I can breathe again—but I've had a rotten dinner. Come on, Bordure.

They go out with Mother Ubu.

The elements of deliberate scatology, toilet humor, juvenile satire, and a full-stage food fight make clear that *Ubu Roi* is a precursor of American teen films such as *Dumb and Dumber*. It is a little more difficult to see the play as a precursor of a serious art and literary movement like surrealism, but such is the case. *Surrealism,* an invented word that means "beyond realism" or "superrealism," was officially inaugurated by André Breton in 1924 but can be said to date from *Ubu Roi*—which, its advocates claim, reaches a superior level of reality by tracing the unconscious processes of the mind rather than the literal depictions of observable life.

Intellectual Comedy: *Man and Superman*

George Bernard Shaw (1856–1950) founded no school of playwrights, for his style was inimitable, his talents unmatchable, and his interests more social and political than dramatic or aesthetic. Social reformer, street orator, public philosopher, and indefatigable essayist and letter writer, Shaw's sixty-odd plays represent only a small fraction of his extraordinary lifetime productivity.

To Shaw, the stage was a vehicle for the discussion and transmission of ideas—ideas that were important only insofar as they had the power to transform social institutions. Thus Shaw's plays featured direct discussions as much as actions; and, in the printed versions of Shaw's plays, those discussions often preceded the plays in lengthy prefaces, extended into the play with voluminous stage directions, and culminated with summarizing "afterwords."

There is nothing inherently antirealistic about Shaw's dramaturgy: discussion is as much a part of everyday life as action is, and Shaw's plays were otherwise rather conventionally plotted. What in Shaw transcends the realistic mode is the elegance and brilliance of his dialogue. No person in life has ever spoken as cleverly, as wittily, as precisely, or as cogently as Shaw's characters do—hour after hour. Shaw's characters frame their arguments instantly, perfectly, and assuredly; there is no Chekhovian stammering, no indecision or confusion. Rather, there are exquisitely turned epithets, brilliantly timed retorts, ascending rhetorical crescendos, and a series of comic climaxes. Virtually all the characters in Shaw's plays are wickedly adept at a nearly superhuman verbal cascading.

Shaw called *Man and Superman* (1903–1905) "A Comedy (And a Philosophy)" on its title page and "a drama of ideas" in its first stage direction. The published version begins, characteristically, with a 30-page dedicatory epistle and concludes with a 54-page "Revolutionist's Handbook" supposedly written by the play's principal character. The play itself, which uncut is more than four hours long, features a cast of English characters, mostly upper class, and their romantic, spiritual, political, and intellectual engagements. In the midst of the third act they fall asleep and reappear as dream characters in Hell; this long scene, often performed alone as a one-act play (with the title *Don Juan in Hell*) is one of drama's most unusual masterpieces: a sparkling series of stylized debates, punctuated with brilliant argumentative speeches of enormous length:

DON JUAN: When I was on earth, and made those proposals to ladies which, though universally condemned, have made me so interesting a hero of legend, I was not infrequently met in some such way as this: The lady would say that she would countenance my advances, provided they were honorable. On inquiring what that proviso meant, I found that it meant that I proposed to get possession of her property if she had any, or to undertake her support for life if she had not; that I desired her continual companionship, counsel, and conversation to the end of my days, and would take a most solemn oath to be always enraptured by them: above all, that I would turn my back on all other women forever for her sake. I did not object to these conditions because they were exorbitant and inhuman: it was their extraordinary irrelevance that prostrated me. I invariably replied with perfect frankness that I had never dreamt of any of these things; that unless the lady's character and intellect were equal or superior to my own, her conversation must degrade and her counsel mislead me;

This 1990 production of George Bernard Shaw's 1903 play, Man and Superman, *employs costumes and props of Shaw's time but has a thoroughly modern (or post-modern) spirit. Directed by Martin Benson and designed by Cliff Faulkner (scenery) and Shigeru Yaji (costumes) at the South Coast Repertory Theatre in Costa Mesa, California. (Photo: Cristofer Gross.)*

that her constant companionship might, for all I knew, become intolerably tedious to me; that I could not answer for my feelings for a week in advance, much less to the end of my life; that to cut me off from all natural and unconstrained intercourse with half my fellow creatures would narrow and warp me if I submitted to it, and, if not, would bring me under the curse of clandestinity; that, finally, my proposals to her were wholly unconnected with any of these matters, and were the outcome of a perfectly simple impulse of my manhood towards her womanhood.

ANA: You mean that it was an immoral impulse.

DON JUAN: Nature, my dear lady, is what you call immoral. I blush for it; but I cannot help it. Nature is a pandar, Time a wrecker, and Death a murderer. I have always preferred to stand up to those facts and build institutions on their recognition. You prefer to propitiate the three devils by proclaiming their chastity, their thrift, and their loving kindness; and to base your institutions on these flatteries. Is it any wonder that the institutions do not work smoothly?

The English stage had not seen such glittering prose and brashly ironic wit since the days of William Congreve two hundred years earlier, and Shaw's plays dominated the London stage for the entire first half of the twentieth century; moreover, his political ideas were part of British intellectual life through two world wars. And while Shaw started no school of playwrights, his witty, unsentimental, and fiercely intelligent verbal style has been regularly echoed in the modern era, particularly by British playwrights Simon Gray, Alan Ayckbourn, Michael Frayn, Tom Stoppard, Christopher Hampton, and Peter Shaffer.

Expressionism: *The Hairy Ape*

Of all the isms, expressionism is the one that has given rise to the most significant body of modern theatre, probably because of its broad definition and its seeming alliance with expressionism in the visual arts. The theatrical expressionism that was much in vogue in Germany during the first decades of the century (particularly in the 1920s) featured shocking and gutty dialogue, boldly exaggerated scenery, piercing sounds, bright lights, an abundance of primary colors, a not very subtle use of symbols, and a structure of short, stark, jabbing scenes that built to a powerful (and usually deafening) climax.

America's first major playwright, Eugene O'Neill, came under the influence of the expressionists after earlier ventures into naturalism; in the 1920s O'Neill wrote a series of explosive plays concerning human nature in an industrial landscape. *The Hairy Ape,* produced in 1921, is almost a textbook case of expressionist writing. Although this play seems clumsy, transparent, and naively ineffective today, it well illustrates the extreme stylization popular with "ism" writers. It is a one-act play featuring eight scenes. Its workingman-hero Yank meets and is rebuffed by the genteel daughter of a captain of industry. Enraged, Yank becomes violent and eventually crazed; he dies at play's end in the monkey cage of a zoo. Scene Three illustrates the tenor of the writing:

Elmer Rice's expressionistic American play, The Adding Machine *(1923), was well ahead of its time in portraying the difficulties in sustaining human values in a labor market increasingly dependent on electronic technology. Ann Bogart directed this production for the Actors Theatre of Louisville, 1995. (Photo: Richard C. Trigg.)*

The stokehole. In the rear, the dimly outlined bulks of the furnaces and boilers. High overhead one hanging electric bulb sheds just enough light through the murky air laden with coal dust to pile up masses of shadows everywhere. A line of men, stripped to the waist, is before the furnace doors. They bend over, looking neither to right nor left, handling their shovels as if they were part of their bodies, with a strange, awkward, swinging rhythm. They use the shovels to throw open the furnace doors. Then from these fiery

Eugene O'Neill's The Hairy Ape *in its original New York production by the Provincetown Playhouse. The setting is of the opening of Scene Three. (Photo: Courtesy Library of the Performing Arts, Lincoln Center, New York.)*

round holes in the black a flood of terrific light and heat pours full upon the men who are outlined in silhouette in the crouching, inhuman attitudes of chained gorillas. The men shovel with a rhythmic motion, swinging as on a pivot from the coal which lies in heaps on the floor behind to hurl it into the flaming mouths before them. There is a tumult of noise—the brazen clang of the furnace doors as they are flung open or slammed shut, the grating, teeth-gritting grind of steel against steel, of crunching coal. This clash of sounds stuns one's ears with its rending dissonance. But there is order in it, rhythm, a mechanical regulated recurrence, a tempo. And rising above all, making the air hum with the quiver of liberated energy, the roar of leaping flames in the furnaces, the monotonous throbbing beat of the engines.

As the curtain rises, the furnace doors are shut. The men are taking a breathing spell. One or two are arranging the coal behind them, pulling it into more accessible heaps. The others can be dimly made out leaning on their shovels in relaxed attitudes of exhaustion.

PADDY: (*from somewhere in the line—plaintively*) Yerra, will this divil's own watch nivir end? Me back is broke. I'm destroyed entirely.

YANK: (*from the center of the line—with exuberant scorn*) Aw, yuh make me sick! Lie down and croak, why don't yuh? Always beefin', dat's you! Say, dis is a cinch! Dis was made for me! It's my meat, get me! (*A whistle is blown—a thin, shrill note from somewhere overhead in the darkness.* YANK *curses without resentment.*) Dere's de damn engineer crackin' de whip. He tinks we're loafin'.

PADDY: (*vindictively*) God stiffen him!

YANK: (*in an exultant tone of command*) Come on, youse guys! Git into de game! She's gettin' hungry! Pile some grub in her. Trow it into her belly! Come on now, all of youse! Open her up! (*At this last all the men, who have followed his movements of getting into position, throw open their furnace doors with a deafening clang. The fiery light floods over their shoulders as they bend round for the coal. Rivulets of sooty sweat have traced maps on their backs. The enlarged muscles form bunches of highlight and shadow.*)

YANK: (*chanting a count as he shovels without seeming effort*) One—two—tree— (*His voice rising exultantly in the joy of battle*) Dat's de stuff! Let her have it! All togedder now! Sling it into her! Let her ride! Shoot de piece now! Call de toin on her! Drive her into it! Feel her move. Watch her smoke! Speed, dat's her middle name! Give her coal, youse guys! Coal, dat's her booze! Drink it up, baby! Let's see yuh sprint! Dig in and gain a lap! Dere she go-o-es.

(*This last in the chanting formula of the galley gods at the six-day bike race. He slams his furnace door shut. The others do likewise with as much unison as their wearied bodies will permit. The effect is of one fiery eye after another being blotted out with a series of accompanying bangs.*)

PADDY: (*groaning*) Me back is broke. I'm bate out—bate— (*There is a pause. Then the inexorable whistle sounds again from the dim regions above the electric light. There is a growl of cursing rage from all sides.*)

YANK: (*shaking his fist upward—contemptuously*) Take it easy dere, you! Who d'yuh tink's runnin' dis game, me or you? When I git ready, we move. Not before! When I git ready, get me!

VOICES: (*approvingly*) That's the stuff!
Yank tal him, py golly!
Yank ain't affeerd.
Goot poy, Yank!
Give him hell!
Tell 'im 'e's a bloody swine
Bloody slave-driver!

YANK: (*contemptuously*) He ain't got no noive. He's yellow, get me? All de engineers is yellow. Dey got streaks a mile wide. Aw, to hell wit him! Let's move, youse guys. We had a rest. Come on, she needs it! Give her pep! It ain't for him. Him and his whistle, dey don't belong. But we belong, see! We gotter feed de baby! Come on! (*He turns and flings his furnace door open. They all follow his lead. At this instant the* SECOND *and* FOURTH ENGINEERS *enter from the darkness on the left with* MILDRED *between them. She starts, turns paler, her pose is crumbling, she shivers with fright in spite of the blazing heat, but forces herself to leave the* ENGINEERS *and take a few steps nearer the men. She is right behind* YANK. *All this happens quickly while the men have their backs turned.*)

YANK: Come on, youse guys! (*He is turning to get coal when the whistle sounds again in a peremptory, irritating note. This drives* YANK *into a sudden fury. While the other men have turned full around and stopped dumbfounded by the spectacle of* MILDRED *standing there in her white dress,* YANK *does not turn far enough to see her. Besides, his head is thrown back, he blinks upward through the murk trying to find the owner of the whistle, he brandishes his shovel murderously over his head in one hand, pounding on his chest, gorilla-like, with the other, shouting.*) Toin off dat whistle! Come down outa dere, yuh yellow, brass-buttoned, Belfast bum, yuh! Come down and I'll knock yer brains out! Yuh lousy, stinkin', yellow mut of a Catholic-moiderin' bastard! Come down and I'll moider yuh! Pullin' dat whistle on me, huh? I'll show yuh! I'll crash yer skull in! I'll drive yer teet' down yer troat! I'll slam yer nose trou de back of yer head! I'll cut yer guts out for a nickel, yuh lousy boob, yuh dirty, crummy, muck-eatin' son of a— (*Suddenly he becomes conscious of all the other men staring at something directly behind his back. He whirls defensively with a snarling, murderous growl, crouching to spring, his lips drawn back over his teeth, his small eyes gleaming ferociously. He sees* MILDRED, *like a white apparition in the full light from the open furnace doors. He glares into her eyes, turned to stone. As for her, during his speech she has listened, paralyzed with horror, terror, her whole personality crushed, beaten in, collapsed, by the terrific impact of this unknown, abysmal brutality, naked and shameless. As she looks at his gorilla face, as his eyes bore into hers, she utters a low, choking cry and shrinks away from him, putting both hands up before her eyes to shut out the sight of her face, to protect her own. This startles* YANK *to a reaction. His mouth falls open, his eyes grow bewildered.*)

MILDRED: (*about to faint—to the* ENGINEERS, *who now have her one by each arm—whimperingly*) Take me away! Oh, the filthy beast! (*She faints. They carry her quickly back, disappearing in the darkness at the left, rear. An iron door clangs shut. Rage and bewildered fury rush back on* YANK. *He feels himself insulted in some unknown fash-*

ion in the very heart of his pride. He roars.) God damn yuh! (*And hurls his shovel after them at the door which has just closed.*

It hits the steel bulkhead with a clang and falls clattering on the steel floor. From overhead the whistle sounds again in a long, angry, insistent command.)

Curtain

O'Neill's forceful combination of visual and auditory effects lends this expressionistic play a crude, almost superhuman power. The use of silhouette in the staging and lighting, the "masses of shadows everywhere," the "tumult of noise," the "monotonous throbbing heat of the engines," the "fiery light," the "rivulets of sooty sweat," the massed chanting and the movements in unison, the "peremptory, irritating note" of the "inexorable whistle," the shouting of curses and bold ejaculations, the animal imagery, and the "horror, terror . . . of . . . unknown, abysmal brutality, naked and shameless," are all typical of the extreme stylization of early-twentieth-century expressionism. The scene also demonstrates how O'Neill and his followers in the American theatre spurned realism and romanticism in their effort to arrive at a direct presentation of social ideology and cultural criticism.

Theatricalism: *Six Characters in Search of an Author*

First produced in 1921, *Six Characters in Search of an Author* expresses from its famous title onward a "theatricalist" motif in which the theatre itself becomes part of the content of play production, not merely the vehicle. "All the world's a stage," said Shakespeare; but in this play Luigi Pirandello explores how the stage is also a world—and how the stage and the world, illusion and reality, relate to each other. In this still stunning play, a family

---

O'NEILL'S EXPRESSIONISM

In the scene [in *The Hairy Ape*] where the bell rings for the stokers to go on duty, you remember that they all stand up, come to attention, then go out in a lockstep file. Some people think even that is an actual custom aboard ship! But it is only symbolic of the regimentation of men who are the slaves of machinery. In a larger sense, it applies to all of us, because we all are more or less the slaves of convention, or of discipline, or of a rigid formula of some sort.

The whole play is expressionistic. The coal shoveling in the furnace room, for instance. Stokers do not really shovel coal that way. But it is done in the play in order to contribute to the rhythm. For rhythm is a powerful factor in making anything expressive. You can actually produce and control emotions by that means alone.

Eugene O'Neill

PIRANDELLO: THE PLANE OF REALITY TRANSFORMED

A stage which accommodates the fantastical reality of these six characters is not, itself, a fixed or immutable space, nor are the events of the play preconceived in a fixed formula. On the contrary, everything in this play is created freshly as it happens; it is fluid, it is improvised. As the story and the characters take shape, so the stage itself evolves, and the plane of reality is organically transformed.

Luigi Pirandello

eternal confusions between appearance and reality:

THE FATHER: What I'm inviting you to do is to quit this foolish playing at art—this acting and pretending—and seriously answer my question: WHO ARE YOU?

THE DIRECTOR: (*amazed but irritated, to his actors*) What extraordinary impudence! This so-called character wants to know who I am?

THE FATHER: (*with calm dignity*) Signore, a character may always ask a "man" who he is. For a character has a true life, defined by his characteristics—he is always, at the

of dramatic "characters"—a father, his stepdaughter, a mother, her children—appear as if by magic on the stage of a provincial theatre where a new play by Pirandello is being rehearsed: the "characters," claiming they have an unfinished play in them, beg the director to stage their lives in order that they may bring a satisfactory climax to their "drama." This fantasy treats the audience to continuingly shifting perceptions, for clearly a "play-within-the-play" is involved, but which is the real play and which the real life? There are actors playing actors, actors playing "characters," and actors playing actors-playing-"characters"; there are also scenes when the actors playing "characters" are making fun of the actors playing actors-playing-"characters." It is no wonder that most audiences give up trying to untangle the planes of reality Pirandello proposes in this play; they are simply too difficult to comprehend except as a dazzle of suggestive theatricality.

Pirandello contrasts the passionate story of the "characters"—whose "drama" concerns a broken family, adultery, and a suggestion of incest—with the artifice of the stage and its simulations; in the course of this exposition Pirandello's performers discuss the theatricality of life, the life of theatricality, and the

The six characters from Luigi Pirandello's Six Characters in Search of an Author, *in William Ball's production at American Conservatory Theatre. The six characters come from a world of fantasy, but as this production photograph well illustrates, their dramatic intensity gives them the appearance of a superior reality. (Photo: William Ganslen, ACT.)*

least, a "somebody." But a man—now, don't take this personally—A man is generalized beyond identity—he's a nobody!

THE DIRECTOR: Ah, but me, me—I am the Director! The Producer! You understand?

THE FATHER: Signore—Think of how you used to feel about yourself, long ago, all the illusions you used to have about the world, and about your place in it: those illusions were real for you then, they were *quite* real—But now, with hindsight, they prove to be nothing, they are nothing to you now but an embarrassment. Well, signore, that is what your present reality is today—just a set of illusions that you will discard tomorrow. Can't you feel it? I'm not speaking of the planks of this stage we stand on, I'm speaking of the very earth under our feet. It's sinking under you—by tomorrow, today's entire reality will have become just one more illusion. You see?

THE DIRECTOR: (*confused but amazed*) Well? So what? What does all that prove?

THE FATHER: Ah, nothing, signore. Only to show that if, beyond our illusions (*indicating the other characters*), we have no ultimate reality, so your reality as well—your reality that touches and feels and breathes today—will be unmasked tomorrow as nothing but yesterday's illusion!

These lines illustrate Pirandello's use of paradox, irony, and the theatre as metaphor to create a whimsical drama about human identity and human destiny. By contrasting the passion of his "characters" and the frequent frivolity of his "actors," Pirandello establishes a provocative juxtaposition of human behavior and its theatricalization—and the whole fantastical style is nothing but an exploitation of the theatrical format itself.

Theatre of Cruelty: *Jet of Blood*

Antonin Artaud (1896–1948) is one of drama's greatest revolutionaries, although his importance lies more in his ideas and influence than in his actual theatrical achievements. A stage and film actor in Paris during the 1920s, he founded the Théâtre Alfred Jarry in 1926, producing, among other works, Strindberg's surrealist *A Dream Play* and, in 1935, an adaptation of Shelley's dramatic poem, *The Cenci*. Artaud's essays, profoundly influential in the theatre today, were collected and published in 1938 in a book titled *The Theatre and Its Double*.

The theatre envisaged by Artaud was a self-declared "theatre of cruelty," for, in his words, "Without an element of cruelty at the root of every performance, the theatre is not possible." The "cruel" theatre would flourish, Artaud predicted, by "providing the spectator with the true sources of his dreams, in which his taste for crime, his erotic obsessions, his savagery, his illusions, his utopian ideals, even his cannibalism, would surge forth."

In Artaud's vision, ordinary plays were to be abolished; there should be, in his words, "no more masterpieces." In place of written plays there should be

cries, groans, apparitions, surprises, theatricalities of all kinds, magic beauty of costumes taken from certain ritual models; resplendent lighting, the incantation of beautiful voices, the charms of harmony, rare notes of music, colors of objects, physical rhythm of movements whose crescendo and decrescendo will accord exactly with the pulsation of familiar movements, concrete appearances of new and surprising objects, masks, effigies yards high, sudden changes of light, the physical action of light which arouses sensations of heat and cold . . . evocative gestures, emotive or arbitrary attitudes, excited pounding out of rhythms and sounds . . . [and] all the abortive attitudes, all the lapses of mind and tongue, by which are revealed what might be called the impotences of speech.

Language in Artaud's theatre was an impotent force, drowned out by the more "sensational" (as in sensory) aspects of sonic vibrations and visual extravagance continuously assaulting all the senses. But this was not to be simply a theatre of stage effects: it was, for Artaud, a theatre of profound meaning.

> Even light can have a precise intellectual meaning, light in waves, in sheets, in fusillades of fiery arrows. . . . Paroxysms will suddenly burst forth, will fire up like fires in different spots. . . . The varied lighting of a performance will fall upon the public as much as upon the actors— and to the several simultaneous actions or several phases of an identical action in which the characters, swarming over each other like bees, will endure all the onslaughts of the situations and the external assaults of the tempestuous elements.

In a famous metaphor, Artaud compared the theatre to the great medieval plague, noting that both plague and theatre had the capacity to liberate human possibilities and illuminate the human potential:

> The theatre is like the plague . . . because like the plague it is the revelation, the bringing forth, the exteriorization of a depth of latent cruelty by means of which all the perverse possibilities of the mind, whether of an individual or a people, are localized. . . .
>
> In the theatre as in the plague there is a kind of strange sun, a light of abnormal intensity by which it seems that the difficult and even the impossible suddenly become our normal element.
>
> One cannot imagine, save in an atmosphere of carnage, torture, and bloodshed, all the magnificent Fables which recount to the multitudes the first sexual division and the first carnage of essences that appeared in creation. The theatre, like the plague, is in the image of this carnage and this essential separation. It releases conflicts, disengages powers, liberates possibilities, and if these possibilities and these powers are dark, it is the fault not of the plague nor of the theatre, but of life.

Artaud's ideas were radical and his essays were incendiary; his power to shock and inspire are undiminished today, and many contemporary theatre artists claim an Artaudian heritage. It is not at all clear, however, what final form the "theatre of cruelty" should actually take in performance, and it is readily apparent even to the casual reader that the theatre Artaud speaks of is much easier to realize on paper than on an actual stage. Artaud's own productions were in fact failures; he was formally "expelled" from the surrealist movement, and he spent most of his later life abroad in mental institutions. His one published play, *Jet of Blood*, illustrates both the radically antirealistic nature of his dramaturgy and the difficulties that would be encountered in its production. This is the opening of the play:

THE YOUNG MAN: I love you, and everything is beautiful.

THE YOUNG GIRL: (*with a strong tremolo in her voice*) You love me, and everything is beautiful.

THE YOUNG MAN: (*in a very deep voice*) I love you, and everything is beautiful.

THE YOUNG GIRL: (*in an even deeper voice than his*) You love me, and everything is beautiful.

THE YOUNG MAN: (*leaving her abruptly*) I love you. (*Pause*) Turn around and face me.

THE YOUNG GIRL: (*she turns to face him*) There!

THE YOUNG MAN: (*in a shrill and exalted voice*) I love you, I am big, I am shining, I am full, I am solid.

THE YOUNG GIRL: (*in the same shrill tone*) We love each other.

THE YOUNG MAN: We are intense. Ah, how well ordered this world is!

A pause. Something that sounds like an immense wheel turning and blowing out air is heard. A hurricane separates the two. At this moment two stars crash into each other, and we see a number of live pieces of human bodies falling down: hands, feet, scalps, masks, colonnades, porches, temples, and alembics, which, however, fall more and more slowly, as if they were falling in a vacuum. Three scorpions fall down, one after the other, and finally a frog and a beetle, which sets itself down with a maddening, vomit-inducing slowness . . .

Enter a knight of the Middle Ages in an enormous suit of armor, followed by a nurse holding her breasts in both hands and puffing and wheezing because they are both very swollen.

Artaud's apocalyptic vision has stimulated many subsequent theatre directors, including Jean Louis Barrault and Roger Blin in France, Peter Brook in England, Jerzy Grotowski in Poland, and André Gregory in America; his influence can also be seen in the plays of Jean Genet and the productions of Robert Wilson. His notion of a theatre of cruelty, while not fully realized on stage in his lifetime, has been more closely approached by each of these artists and may still be achieved.

Philosophical Melodrama: *No Exit*

A one-act fantasy written in 1944, *No Exit* is one of the most compelling short plays ever written. In the play, Jean-Paul Sartre, the well-known French existentialist philosopher, establishes a unique "Hell," which is a room without windows or mirrors. Into it come three people, lately deceased, all condemned to this nether world because of their earthly sins. The three are brilliantly ill matched: Garcin, the sole man, tends toward homosexuality; so does Inez, one of the two women. Estelle, the final occupant of this bizarre inferno, tends toward heterosexual nymphomania: she pursues Garcin, Garcin pursues his fellow spirit Inez, and Inez pursues the beautiful Estelle in a triangle of misdirected affection that, one presumes, will continue maddeningly through all eternity. The infinite bleakness of this play's fantastical situation and the numbing futility of each character's aspirations provoke Garcin to beg for some good old-fashioned torture—but nothing quite so simple is forthcoming. Instead, he is forced to conclude: "Hell is other people." And the play ends with a curtain line that is characteristic of the modern stylized theatre:

"TRUE REALISM": SARTRE

Our new theatre definitely has drawn away from the so-called "realistic theatre" because "realism" has always offered plays made up of stories of defeat, laissez-faire, and drifting; it has always preferred to show how external forces batter a man to pieces, destroy him bit by bit and ultimately make of him a weathervane turning with every change of wind. But we claim for ourselves the true realism because we know it is impossible, in everyday life, to distinguish between fact and right, the real from the ideal, psychology from ethics.

[Our new] theatre . . . seeks to explore the state of man in its entirety, and to present to the modern man a portrait of himself, his problems, his hopes and his struggles. We believe our theatre would betray its mission if it portrayed individual personalities. . . .

Jean-Paul Sartre

GARCIN: Well, well, let's get on with it.

This line suggests that although the play concludes, the situation continues, eternally, behind the drawn curtain.

No Exit is a classic dramatic statement of existentialism, of which Sartre was this century's leading exponent. Remove the fantastical elements—that this is Hell and the characters are ghosts—and we have Sartre's vision of human interaction: every individual forever seeks affirmation and self-realization in the eyes of the Other. Each character in the play carries with him or her a baggage of guilt and expectation, each seeks from another some certification of final personal worth, and each is endlessly thwarted in this quest. We are all condemned to revolve around each other in frustratingly incomplete accord, suggests Sartre; we are all forced to reckon with the impossibility of finding meaning out of the unrelated events that constitute life.

Jean-Paul Sartre's No Exit *is a philosophical study of three characters locked together in "Hell"—which is discovered to be "other people"—in a 1993 Comédie Française production. (Photo: Brigitte Enguerand.)*

One can accept or reject Sartre's view—which is perhaps more than usually pessimistic for having been written during the Nazi Occupation of Sartre's Paris—but there can be little dispute over the assertion that his technique for dramatically stylizing it is brilliant. The fantastical Hell, an amusing "valet" who brings each character onto the stage, and the highly contrived assemblage of mismatched characters all serve to focus the intellectual argument precisely. Sartre's characters are philosophically representative rather than psychologically whole; there is no intention on Sartre's part to portray individual people with interesting idiosyncracies, and there is no feeling on our part that the characters have a personal life beyond what we see in the play. Biographical character analysis would be useless for an actor assigned to play one of these roles, and the interlock of psychological motivation, even in this sexually charged atmosphere, is deliberately ignored by the author. What Sartre presents instead is a general understanding of human affairs: a philosophy of interpersonal relations.

Although these six plays do not begin to demonstrate all the ways in which the theatre was explored stylistically in the first half of the twentieth century, they suggest, in combination, the broad range of newer stylization techniques that were developed; and they give a clue to the capacity of the theatre to express, through bold and direct means, ideas, images, conflicts, and philosophies germane to the times. Each of these plays is independently significant as dramatic literature; taken together, they show a theatre active in redefining itself and its collective possibilities.

EXISTENTIALISM, ABSURDISM, AND WORLD WAR II

Both Sartre's existentialism and Camus's philosophy of the absurd were forged largely in the outrages of World War II, when both men were leading figures in the French Resistance movement. A hellish world that affords "no exit," and in which human activity is as meaningless as Sisyphus' torment, seems perfectly credible during such desperate times, times of national occupation and genocidal slaughter. After the war, Jean-Paul Sartre, who was France's foremost exponent of existentialism and one of that country's leading dramatists in the 1940s and 1950s, spoke eloquently of his first experience as playwright and director, which occurred when he was a prisoner of war:

> My first experience in the theatre was especially fortunate. When I was a prisoner in Germany in 1940, I wrote, staged and acted in a Christmas play which, while pulling the wool over the eyes of the German censor by means of simple symbols, was addressed to my fellow prisoners. This drama, biblical in appearance only, was written and put on by a prisoner, was acted by prisoners in scenery painted by prisoners; it was aimed exclusively at prisoners (so much so that I have

never since then permitted it to be staged or even printed) and it addressed them on the subject of their concerns as prisoners. No doubt it was neither a good play nor well acted: the work of an amateur, the critics would say, a product of special circumstances. Nevertheless, on this occasion, as I addressed my comrades across the footlights, speaking to them of their state as prisoners, when I suddenly saw them so remarkably silent and attentive, I realized what theatre ought to be—a great collective, religious phenomenon.

> To be sure, I was, in this case, favored by special circumstances; it does not happen every day that your public is drawn together by one great common interest, a great loss or a great hope. As a rule, an audience is made up of the most diverse elements: a big business man sits beside a traveling salesman or a professor, a man next to a woman, and each is subject to his own particular preoccupations. Yet this situation is a challenge to the playwright: he must create his public, he must fuse all the disparate elements in the auditorium into a single unity by awakening in the recesses of their spirits the things which all men of a given epoch and community care about.

POSTWAR ABSURDITY AND ALIENATION

In the aftermath of World War II, many of the antirealistic movements dissolved or consolidated; against the awful realities of the concentration camps and the nuclear destructions, aesthetic antirealism seemed a feeble gesture.

Two antirealist movements, however, with strong philosophical cores, emerged to dominate the theatre in the ensuing cold war era. These were the theatre of the absurd, centered in Paris, and the theatre of alienation, centered in Berlin. We shall examine these two forms in some detail.

Theatre of the Absurd

The name *theatre of the absurd* applies to a grouping of plays that can be shown to share certain common structures and styles and to be tied together by a common philosophical thread: the theory of the absurd as formulated by French essayist and playwright Albert Camus. Camus likened the human condition to that of the mythological Corinthian king Sisyphus, who, because of his cruelty, was condemned forever to roll a stone up a hill in Hades only to have it roll down again upon nearing the top. Camus saw the modern individual as similarly engaged in an eternally futile task, the absurdity of searching for some

Romanian-born Eugène Ionesco utterly repudiates realism in his 1952 one-act masterpiece, The Chairs, *in which an aged couple arrange chairs for an audience (which never arrives) to hear an orator (who arrives—but cannot talk). The couple throw themselves out the windows at play's end, with the orator muttering unintelligibly. American Repertory Theatre production directed by Andrei Belgrader; Roberts Blossom and Teresa Wright play the husband and the wife. (Photo: Richard Feldman.)*

ALBEE ON THE ABSURD

As I get it, The Theatre of the Absurd is an absorption-in-art of certain existentialist and post-existentialist philosophical concepts having to do, in the main, with man's attempts to make sense for himself out of his senseless position in a world which makes no sense—which makes no sense because the moral, religious, political, and social structures man has erected to "illusion" himself have collapsed.

Edward Albee

meaning or purpose or order in human life. To Camus, the immutable irrationality of the universe is what makes this task absurd. On the one hand, human beings yearn for a "lost" unity and lasting truth; on the other hand, the world can only be seen as irrecoverably fragmented—chaotic, unsummable, permanently unorganized, and permanently unorganizable.

The plays that constitute the theatre of the absurd are obsessed with the futility of all action and the pointlessness of all direction. These themes are developed theatrically through a deliberate and self-conscious flaunting of the "absurd"—in the sense of the ri-

Didi and Gogo (Vladimir and Estragon) are still waiting for Godot in this eloquent 1993 Paris production at the Théâtre de la Tempête, directed by Philippe Adrien. (Photo: Marc Enguerand.)

diculous. Going beyond the use of symbols and the fantasy and poetry of other nonrealists, the absurdists have distinguished themselves by creating clocks that clang incessantly, characters that eat pap in ashcans, corpses that grow by the minute, and personal interactions that are belligerently noncredible.

The theatre of the absurd can be said to include mid-twentieth-century works by Jean Genet (French), Eugène Ionesco (Romanian), Friedrich Duerrenmatt (Swiss), Arthur Adamov (Russian), Slawomir Mrozek (Polish), Harold Pinter (English), Edward Albee (American), and Fernando Arrabal (Spanish); however, the unquestioned leader of the absurdist writers is Samuel Beckett (Irish). And although Paris is the center of this theatre— so much so that the works of Ionesco, Adamov, Arrabal, and Beckett are all written in

French rather than in their native tongues— its influence is felt worldwide.

Samuel Beckett

Samuel Beckett, poet, playwright, and novelist, is perhaps the foremost explorer of human futility in Western literature. Beckett eschews realism, romanticism, and rationalism to create works that are relentlessly unenlightening, that are indeed committed to a final obscurity. "Art has nothing to do with clarity, does not dabble in the clear, and does not make clear," argues Beckett in one of his earliest works, and his theatre is based on the thesis that man is and will remain ignorant regarding all matters of importance.

Born in Dublin in 1906, Beckett emigrated in 1928 to Paris, where he joined a literary

The American Repertory Theatre 1984 production of Samuel Beckett's Endgame, *directed by JoAnne Akalaitis, caused an enormous scandal: Akalaitis had chosen to set the play in an abandoned subway station, and Beckett responded with a letter fiercely objecting to what he considered a violation of the author's specific staging instructions. The ensuing debate, though inconclusive, crystallized arguments that had been waged for half a century about the roles of directors and designers: are they implementors of playwrights' visions or free and independent creative artists? (Photo: Richard Feldman.)*

circle centered on another Irish emigré, James Joyce. Beckett's life before World War II was an artistic vagabondage, during which he wrote several poems, short stories, and a novel; following the war and his seclusion in the south of France during the Occupation, he produced the masterworks for which he is justly famous: the novels *Molloy, Moran Dies,* and *The Unnamable,* and the plays *Waiting for Godot* and *Endgame.* By the time of his death in 1989, Beckett had received the Nobel Prize in literature, and his works had become the subject of literally hundreds of critical books and essays. *Godot* first brought Beckett to worldwide attention: the play's premiere in Paris in 1953 caused a great stir among French authors and critics, and its sub-sequent openings in London and New York had the same effect.

Waiting for Godot   As the archetypal absurdist play, *Waiting for Godot* is a parable without message. On a small mound at the base of a tree, beside a country road, two elderly men in bowler hats wait for a "Mr. Godot" with whom they have presumably made an appointment. They believe that when Godot comes they will be "saved"; however, they are not at all certain that Godot has agreed to meet with them, or if this is the right place or the right day, or whether they will even recognize him if he comes. During each of the two acts, which seem to be set in late afternoon on two successive days (although nobody can be sure of that), the men are visited by passersby—first by two men calling themselves Pozzo and Lucky, subsequently by a young boy who tells them that Mr. Godot "cannot come today but surely tomorrow." The two old men continue to wait as the curtain falls. Although there is substantial reference in the play to Christian symbols and beliefs, it is not clear whether these imply positive or negative associations. The only development in the play is that the characters seem to undergo a certain loss of adeptness while the setting blossoms in rebirth (the tree sprouts leaves between acts).

What Beckett has drawn here is clearly a paradigm of the human condition: an ongoing life cycle of vegetation serving as background to human decay, hope, and ignorance. Beckett's tone is whimsical: the characters play enchanting word games with each other; they amuse each other with songs, accounts of dreams, exercises, and vaudevillian antics; and in general they make the best of a basically hopeless situation. Beckett's paradigm affords a field day for critical investigators. *Waiting for Godot* has already generated a library of brilliantly evocative discussions, and few plays from any era have been so variously analyzed, interpreted, and explored for symbolic meaning and content. Owing largely to the international critical acceptance of this play and its eventual public success, not only absurdist drama but also the whole of stylized theatre was able to move out of the esoteric "art theatre" of the world capitals and onto the stages of popular theatres everywhere.

Beckett repeatedly conjures up what appear to be terminal situations, and phenomena come into focus in his plays only to reveal their ambiguity. *Endgame,* Beckett's second major play, involves four characters who are seeming survivor-victims of some nuclear holocaust. They live out their last days (two—who reside in the famous ashcans—seemingly die during the play's action, although one cannot be sure of this) in a surrealistic landscape where there is no more painkiller to assuage their physical and mental agony. *Krapp's Last Tape* portrays a solitary man with his tape recorder, dictating what will be—judging from the play's title—the last of his annual birthday memoirs.

And *Happy Days* displays a woman partially buried alive (?) in a mound of earth.

HAPPY DAYS

Happy Days, which was first produced in America (1961), is an appropriate model of absurdist drama and of the stylized theatre in general. It is extreme in its use of symbols, comedic in its tone, devastating in its implications. Because it is also an easy play to visualize, it serves admirably to demonstrate to the reader the impact and tone of a theatre dedicated to delving into the irrationalities of human existence.

The setting for both acts of this two-act play is a small mound, covered with "scorched grass" and bathed in "blazing light." Behind the mound is "unbroken plain and sky receding to meet in far distance," a setting the author describes as having "maximum of simplicity and symmetry."

In the exact center of the mound, embedded up to above her waist, is Winnie, the central character of the play. She is "about fifty, well preserved, blond for preference, plump, arms and shoulders bare, low bodice, big bosom, pearl necklet." Beside her are her props: a big shopping bag, a collapsible parasol. Willie, her husband and the play's only other character, is as yet unseen.

As the plays begins, Winnie is discovered sleeping, her head resting on her arms. There is a long pause; Winnie sleeps on. A bell "rings piercingly" for about ten seconds; still she does not move. The bell rings again; Winnie opens her eyes and the bell stops. Winnie looks forward; there is another long pause, then, slowly, Winnie raises her torso erect. Laying her hands on the ground, Winnie throws her head backward and stares above her. Finally:

WINNIE: (*gazing at zenith*) Another heavenly day.

What's going on here? First-time audiences to theatre of the absurd presentations often react with annoyance or hostility to the sheer peculiarity of the depicted situation. They may even demand realistic explanations; for example, Where are we? Who is she? Why is she buried like that?

The answer is that there are no answers—not even at the end of the play. The situation Beckett creates is insinuative, not realistic: it evokes feelings, intuitions, and flashes of understanding rather than everyday acts with logical consequences. All of stylized theatre is perplexing at its outset; it makes demands on its audience from the rise of the curtain onward. Fortunately, though, when a play is as masterfully constructed as *Happy Days*, audience annoyance and hostility soon give way to rapt involvement.

Happy Days is particularly rich in suggested associations. The mound of scorched earth, bathed in blazing light, may provoke thoughts of nuclear blasts, of holocaust and miraculous survival. Or, as in *Waiting for Godot*, it may stimulate the notion of Calvary, with Winnie, gazing heavenward and speaking of a "heavenly day," perhaps recalling the moment of Christ's presumed forsakenness. The half-burial surely reminds us of human mortality: Winnie—a member of our tribe—appears halfway in (halfway out of?) a metaphoric grave; and we too are locked in the cycle of life, springing from the earth to which we are fated to return. The shopping bag and parasol, rather neat symbols of humanity's worldly preoccupations (a bag to collect material acquisitions, a parasol to protect against the elements), are dwarfed by the desolate surroundings and mocked by the surreal atmosphere: of what use is either shopping bag or parasol in the vast, empty, indifferent universe?

Structurally, *Happy Days* has much in common with *Prometheus Bound,* for in both works the dramatic hero is imprisoned, center stage, for the play's duration; in both, too, the hero uses verbal rhetoric in an effort to surmount the physical oppression of the setting and situation. Both Winnie and Prometheus surge with unflagging positivism and self-theatricalizing bravado that stand in sharp contrast to the bleakness of their stylized environments. Both characters repudiate despair with an astonishing energy that at once inspires and verges on the ridiculous.

But unlike the Aeschylean work, *Happy Days* attempts no explanations: the cause of Winnie's particular entrapment is nowhere even hinted at, much less explained and analyzed. Her situation must simply be viewed as an inexplicable phenomenon in an absurd world, although we may be sure that it is an *analogy* of humanity's permanent condition. Further, unlike her Aeschylean prototype, Winnie's actions betray no heroic revolt, and her rhetoric never achieves the heights of godlike denunciation; rather, her actions consist of mundane behaviors borrowed from the

realistic stage—rummaging in her bag, brush-
ing her teeth, polishing her spectacles—and
her speech is largely inconsequential small talk
directed either to herself or to Willie, who
sleeps behind the mound out of sight of the
audience. Thus the play opens:

WINNIE: (*gazing at zenith*) Another heavenly
day. (*Pause. Head back level, eyes front,
pause. She clasps hands to breast, closes eyes.
Lips move in inaudible prayer, say ten seconds. Lips still. Hands remain clasped. Low.*)
For Jesus Christ sake Amen. (*Eyes open,
hands unclasp, return to mound. Pause. She
clasps hands to breast again, closes eyes, lips
move again in inaudible addendum, say five
seconds. Low.*) World without end Amen.
(*Eyes open, hands unclasp, return to mound.
Pause.*) Begin, Winnie. (*Pause.*) Begin your
day, Winnie. (*Pause. She turns to bag, rummages in it without moving it from its place,
brings out toothbrush, rummages again,
brings out flat tube of toothpaste, turns back
front, unscrews cap of tube, lays cap on
ground, squeezes with difficulty small blob of
paste on brush, holds tube in one hand and
brushes teeth with other. She turns modestly
aside and back to her right to spit out behind mound. In this position her eyes rest on
*WILLIE. She spits out. She cranes a little
further back and down. Loud.*) Hoo-oo!
(*Pause. Louder.*) Hoo-oo! (*Pause. Tender
smile as she turns back front, lays down
brush.*) Poor Willie—(*examines tube, smile
off*)—running out—(*looks for cap*)—ah
well—(*finds cap*)—can't be helped—(*screws
on cap*)—just one of those old things—
(*lays down tube*)—another of those old
things—(*turns towards bag*)—just can't
be cured—(*rummages in bag*)—cannot
be cured—(*brings out small mirror, turns
back front*)—ah yes—(*inspects teeth in
mirror*)—poor dear Willie—(*testing upper front teeth with thumb, indistinctly*)—
good Lord!—(*pulling back upper lip to inspect gums, do.*[1])—good God!—(*pulling
back corner of mouth, mouth open, do.*)—
ah well—(*other corner, do.*)—no worse—
(*abandons inspection, normal speech*)—no
better, no worse—(*lays down mirror*)—no
change—(*wipes fingers on grass*)—no pain—
(*looks for toothbrush*)—hardly any—(*takes
up toothbrush*)—great thing that—(*examines handle of brush*)—nothing like it—(*examines handle, reads*)—pure . . . what?—
(*pause*)—what?—(*lays down brush*)—ah
yes—(*turns towards bag*)—poor Willie—

---

[1]EDITOR'S NOTE: The direction *do.*, which appears in
several places in this playscript, stands for "ditto," or "repeat the action."

(*rummages in bag*)—no zest—(*rummages*)—for anything—(*brings out spectacles in case*)—no interest—(*turns back front*)—in life—(*takes spectacles from case*)—poor dear Willie—(*lays down case*)—sleep for ever—(*opens spectacles*)—marvellous gift—(*puts on spectacles*)—nothing to touch it—(*looks for toothbrush*)—in my opinion—(*takes up toothbrush*)—always said so—(*examines handle of brush*)—wish I had it—(*examines handle, reads*)—genuine . . . pure . . . what?—(*lays down brush*)—blind next—(*takes off spectacles*)—ah well—(*lays down spectacles*)—seen enough—(*feels in bodice for handkerchief*)—I suppose—(*takes out folded handkerchief*)—by now—(*shakes out handkerchief*)—what are those wonderful lines—(*wipes one eye*)—woe woe is me—(*wipes the other*)—to see what I see—(*looks for spectacles*)—ah yes—(*takes up spectacles*)—wouldn't miss it—(*starts polishing spectacles, breathing on lenses*)—or would I?—(*polishes*)—holy light—(*polishes*)—bob up out of dark—(*polishes*)—blaze of hellish light. (*Stops polishing, raises face to sky, pause, head back level, resumes polishing, stops polishing, cranes back to her right and down.*) Hoo-oo! (*Pause. Tender smile as she turns back front and resumes polishing. Smile off.*) Marvellous gift—(*stops polishing, lays down spectacles*)—wish I had it—(*folds handkerchief*)—ah well—(*puts handkerchief back in bodice*)—can't complain—(*looks for spectacles*)—no no—(*takes up spectacles*)—mustn't complain—(*holds up spectacles, looks through lens*)—so much to be thankful for—(*looks through other lens*)—no pain—(*puts on spectacles*)—hardly any—(*looks for toothbrush*)—wonderful thing that—(*takes up toothbrush*)—nothing like it—(*examines handle of brush*)—slight headache sometimes—(*examines handle, reads*)—guaranteed . . . genuine . . . pure . . . what?—(*looks closer*)—genuine pure . . .—(*takes handkerchief from bodice*)—ah yes—(*shakes out handkerchief*)—occasional mild migraine—(*starts wiping handle of brush*)—it comes—(*wipes*)—then goes—(*wiping mechanically*)—ah yes—(*wiping*)—many mercies—(*wiping*)—great mercies—(*stops wiping, fixed lost gaze, brokenly*)—prayers perhaps not for naught—(*pause, do.*)—first thing—(*pause, do.*)—last thing—(*head down, resumes wiping, stops wiping, head up, calmed, wipes eyes, folds handkerchief, puts it back in bodice, examines handle of brush, reads*)—fully guaranteed . . . genuine pure . . . —(*looks closer*)—genuine pure . . . (*Takes off spectacles, lays them and brush down, gazes before her.*) Old things. (*Pause.*) Old eyes. (*Long pause.*) On, Winnie.

This opening speech by Winnie is fairly typical of the play's entire action, which consists in the main of Winnie talking to no one in particular or to a rarely responding, rarely visible Willie. Although the play is thus virtually a monologue—and for that reason a tour de force for the actress who attempts it—the monologue is unusually dynamic in that Winnie addresses multiple audiences: for in addition to Willie, Winnie speaks to us, to her god, and to the universe at large: to whomever it is that rings the piercing bell that wakes her up every day, and who is "looking at me still. (*Pause*) Caring for me still." Although Beckett has provided his actress with a forlorn setting, he has given her a great variety of voices with which to address her thoughts and concerns about it.

The opening speech sets forth Winnie's major quests for the course of the play. She tries to better her appearance, tries to read what is written on the handle of her toothbrush, tries to clean her glasses, tries to make the best of her physical encumbrance, tries to reach out to Willie through her "Hoo-oo"-ing, and tries to reach her god through prayer. She more or less fails at all tasks: the meaning of the words on the toothbrush handle remains obscure, Willie remains almost totally unresponsive to her comments, prayers are "perhaps not for naught" but certainly remain unanswered in our presence, and both her spectacles and her eyes are "old things" that fail her when she needs them.

Would she "bob up out of dark?" she asks? And, if so, would she see a "holy light" or a "hellish light"? She doesn't know and never finds out.

And thus she is reduced to giving herself survival commands, pep talks: "Begin, Winnie. Begin your day." And, speaking to herself as if she were one of Santa's reindeer, "On, Winnie."

Winnie seeks the rhetoric of old: "What are those wonderful lines?" It is a theme that runs throughout the play, as Winnie yearns and pleads "To speak in the old style. The sweet old style. . . ." "What is that unforgettable line . . . ?" "The old style!" In this theme Beckett is not ridiculing the plays and languages of the past; he is merely saying that we can no longer encapsulate our plight in balanced phrases, no longer appeal to our gods in confident, ringing tones. Instead, we must fall back on a determined cheerfulness, a compulsive buoyancy that surmounts resignation and defeatism. "On, Winnie," she cries.

At last the idle Willie stirs himself. From behind the mound, we see the yellow page tops of his newspaper and hear his occasional mutter of a sentence from that paper, such as "Opening for smart youth." Meanwhile, Winnie busies herself, talking all the while. Out of her bag come medicine, lipstick, a magnifying glass, a hat, a mirror, and a revolver. The business of the day begins:

WINNIE: . . . My hair! (*Pause.*) Did I brush and comb my hair? (*Pause.*) I may have done. (*Pause.*) Normally I do. (*Pause.*) There is so little one *can* do. (*Pause.*) One does it all. (*Pause.*) All one can. (*Pause.*) Tis only human (*Pause.*) Human nature. (*She begins to inspect mound, looks up.*) Human weakness. (*She resumes inspection of mound, looks up.*) Natural weakness. (*She resumes inspection of mound.*) I see no comb.

(*Inspects.*) Nor any hairbrush. (*Looks up. Puzzled expression. She turns to bag, rummages in it.*) The comb is here. (*Back front. Puzzled expression. Back to bag. Rummages.*) The brush is here. (*Back front. Puzzled expression.*) Perhaps I put them back, after use. (*Pause. Do.*) But normally I do not put things back, after use, no, I leave them lying about and put them back all together, at the end of the day. (*Smile.*) To speak in the old style. (*Pause.*) The sweet old style. (*Smile off.*) And yet . . . I seem . . . to remember . . . (*Suddenly careless.*) Oh well, what does it matter, that is what I always say, I shall simply brush and comb them later on, purely and simply, I have the whole—(*Pause. Puzzled.*) Them? (*Pause.*) Or it? (*Pause.*) Brush and comb it? (*Pause.*) Sounds improper somehow. (*Pause. Turning a little towards* WILLIE.) What would you say, Willie? (*Pause. Turning a little further.*) What would you say, Willie, speaking of your hair, them or it? (*Pause.*) The hair on your head, I mean. (*Pause. Turning a little further.*) The hair on your head, Willie, what would you say speaking of the hair on your head, them or it?

(*Long pause.*)

WILLIE: It.

WINNIE: (*turning back front, joyful*) Oh you are going to talk to me today, this is going to be a happy day! (*Pause. Joy off.*) Another happy day.

Circular and monotonous, the day's events are so confounded that we can have little recollection of them: Winnie's perplexity extends to whether she did or didn't comb her hair, whether she should or shouldn't comb it, and whether "hair" is a singular or plural noun. On one level, her chatter is simply a satire on domestic conversation. On another level, it is a commentary on the persistence—and futility—of human attempts to communicate. Beckett's dialogue, punctuated by the famous "pauses" which have become his dramatic signature, continually reminds us of the si-

lence that we attempt to surmount by conversation, but that ultimately must prevail over
the dialogue of all living things: each of Winnie's statements, feeble in content as it may
be, is a little victory over nothingness. But
words are not always enough:

WINNIE: . . . Words fail, there are times when
even they fail. (*Pause.*) Is that not so, Willie? (*Pause.*) Is not that so, Willie, that even
words fail, at times? (*Pause.*) What is one
to do then, until they come again? Brush
and comb the hair, if it has not been done,
or if there is some doubt, trim the nails if
they are in need of trimming, these things
tide one over.

If words fail, one is left with physical actions, and in Beckett's theatre the options in
that regard also are notably restricted. What
kind of actions can be sustained by one character buried bosom-deep and another hidden behind a mound? The physical action of
Happy Days is confined but subtle; Beckett's
dramaturgy compels the audience to pay close
attention to physical nuance and demands superior acting performance. In addition, *Happy
Days,* like all of Beckett's plays, is written for
presentation in a relatively small theatre; it
probably could not be performed successfully
in a giant auditorium, since its full impact can
be achieved only if the audience can clearly
perceive the performers' every action and facial expression. Such action as Winnie's opening her parasol, for example, conveys meaning
and importance by a poetry of pauses, turns,
gazes, and shifts of hand positions:

WINNIE: (. . . *Looks at parasol.*) I suppose I
might—(*takes up parasol*)—yes, I suppose
I might . . . hoist this thing now. (*Begins to
unfurl it. Following punctuated by mechanical difficulties overcome.*) One keeps putting
off—putting up—for fear of putting up—
too soon—and the day goes by—quite
by—without one's having put up—at all.
(*Parasol now fully open. Turned to her right

she twirls it idly this way and that.*) Ah yes,
so little to say, so little to do, and the fear
so great, certain days, of finding oneself . . . left, with hours still to run, before
the bell for sleep, and nothing more to say,
nothing more to do, that the days go by,
certain days go by, quite by, the bell goes,
and little or nothing said, little or nothing
done. (*Raising parasol.*) That is the danger.
(*Turning front.*) To be guarded against.
(*She gazes front, holding up parasol with
right hand. Maximum pause.*) I used to
perspire freely. (*Pause.*) Now hardly at all.
(*Pause.*) The heat is much greater. (*Pause.*)
The perspiration much less. (*Pause.*) That
is what I find so wonderful. (*Pause.*) The
way man adapts himself. (*Pause.*) To changing conditions. (*She transfers parasol to left
hand. Long pause.*) Wearies the arm. . . .

Happy Days is built of such business as this:
of words that circle their subjects without
coming to grips with them and physical actions that prove pointless and wearying. Be-

---

BECKETT'S DRAMATURGY

Happy Days is Beckett's furthest move so
far in the direction of absolute stillness,
of a kind of motionless dance in which
the internal agitation and its shaping control are described through language primarily and through the spaces between
words . . . (one of Beckett's chief supports, as well as one of his main themes, is
the tension produced by the struggle between speech and silence and by the double thrust of words towards truth and
lies). . . . From it arises a sense of life ap-
prehended in its utmost degree of noncon-
tingency and existential self-containment,
with all its cross-purposes, vagaries, ago-
nies and waste, its oscillation between hope
and despair, affirmation and denial—a new
enunciation of Beckett's special vision.

Richard Gilman

Irene Worth, as Winnie in Beckett's Happy Days, *is buried up to her chin for the play's second act. NYSF production, 1979. (Photo: © George E. Joseph.)*

fore the end of the first act, Willie recommences his newspaper, Winnie plays a waltz from *The Merry Widow* on her music box, and the parasol inexplicably bursts into flames. Then, with the act nearing its conclusion, Winnie exclaims: "Oh this *is* a happy day! This will have been another happy day!" She pauses, then adds: "After all. (*Pause.*) So far."

The second act conveys the impression of a subsequent day in the existence of these same characters: again the bell rings and Winnie opens her eyes, again Willie is invisible behind the mound. However, in Act II Winnie is embedded all the way up to her neck; her head is rigidly immobilized in the mound of scorched earth and will remain so throughout the balance of the play. Here the dramaturgical challenge Beckett poses for himself—to create dramatic conflict with almost no possibility of physical movement, stage business, or visible interaction—is extraordinary.

Bell rings loudly. [WINNIE] *opens eyes at once. Bell stops. She gazes front. Long pause.*
WINNIE: Hail, holy light. (*Long pause. She closes her eyes. Bell rings loudly. She opens eyes at once. Bell stops. She gazes front. Long smile. Smile off. Long pause.*) Someone is

looking at me still. (*Pause.*) Caring for me still. (*Pause.*) That is what I find so wonderful. (*Pause.*) Eyes on my eyes. (*Pause.*) What is that unforgettable line? (*Pause. Eyes right.*) Willie. (*Pause. Louder.*) Willie. (*Pause. Eyes front.*) May one still speak of time? (*Pause.*) Say it is a long time now, Willie, since I saw you. (*Pause.*) Since I heard you. (*Pause.*) May one? (*Pause.*) One does. (*Smile.*) The old style! (*Smile off.*) There is so little one can speak of. (*Pause.*) One speaks of it all. (*Pause.*) All one can. (*Pause.*) I used to think . . . (*pause*) . . . I say I used to think that I would learn to talk alone. (*Pause.*) By that I mean to myself, the wilderness. (*Smile.*) But no. (*Smile broader.*) No no. (*Smile off.*) Ergo you are there. (*Pause.*) Oh no doubt you are dead, like the others, no doubt you have died, or gone away and left me, like the others, it doesn't matter, you are there. (*Pause. Eyes left.*) The bag too is there, the same as ever, I can see it. (*Pause. Eyes right. Louder.*) The bag is there, Willie, as good as ever, the one you gave me that day . . . to go to market. (*Pause. Eyes front.*) That day. (*Pause.*) What day? (*Pause.*) I used to pray. (*Pause.*) I say I used to pray. (*Pause.*) Yes I must confess I did. (*Smile.*) Not now. (*Smile broader.*) No no. (*Smile off. Pause.*) . . .

Two themes that were broached in the first act combine to form the action and conclusion of the second: these are the themes of Winnie's song and "Brownie," the couple's revolver.

Winnie's song is something which, we are led to understand, she ritually sings at the end of her day: "To sing too soon is a great mistake, I find," says Winnie in Act I, adding, "One cannot sing just to please someone, however much one loves them, no, song must come from the heart, that is what I always say, pour out from the inmost, like a thrush." In Act II the urge to sing one's song—and the timing of the singing—becomes a matter of great importance:

WINNIE: . . . The day is now well advanced. (*Smile. Smile off.*) And yet it is perhaps a little soon for my song. (*Pause.*) To sing too soon is fatal, I always find. (*Pause.*) On the other hand it is possible to leave it too late. (*Pause.*) The bell goes for sleep and one has not sung. (*Pause.*) The whole day has flown—(*smile, smile off*)—flown by, quite by, and no song of any class, kind or description. (*Pause.*) There is a problem here. (*Pause.*) One cannot sing . . . just like that, no. (*Pause.*) It bubbles up, for some unknown reason, the time is ill chosen, one chokes it back. (*Pause.*) One says, Now is the time, it is now or never, and one cannot. (*Pause.*) Simply cannot sing. (*Pause.*) Not a note. (*Pause.*) . . .

Winnie's song, we feel, represents her most exuberant expression: song is surely what passes, in the world of *Happy Days,* as a symbol of the human life force at its fullest flower. Song, of course, is the first medium of the Western theatre, evolving out of the dithyramb to the choral ode of Aeschylus, and the plaintive tune Winnie sings at the end of this play stands in almost grotesque contrast with the harmonies of the classic tragedies of the past.

"Brownie" (for Browning) symbolizes the opposite of song in *Happy Days;* the revolver which Winnie pulls from her bag in the early moments of the play remains to the end as a mark of past contemplations and present potential.

WINNIE: (. . . *plunges hand in bag and brings out revolver. Disgusted.*) You again! (*She . . . brings revolver front and contemplates it. She weighs it in her palm.*) You'd think the weight of this thing would bring it down among the . . . last rounds. But no. It doesn't. Ever uppermost, like Browning. (*Pause.*) Brownie . . . (*Turning a little towards* WILLIE.) Remember Brownie, Willie? (*Pause.*) Remember how you used to keep on at me to take it away from you?

Take it away, Winnie, take it away, before I put myself out of my misery. (*Back front. Derisive.*) *Your* misery! (*To revolver.*) Oh I suppose it's a comfort to know you're there, but I'm tired of you. (*Pause.*) I'll leave you out, that's what I'll do. (*She lays revolver on ground to her right.*) There, that's your home from this day out. . . .

And from then until the end of the play, fully visible and, in the author's stage direction, "conspicuous" at the opening of Act II, the revolver remains to do quickly what the rising earth and blazing sun do slowly: to extinguish Winnie's life. But in Act II Winnie cannot reach it; her hands are in the earth:

WINNIE: (. . . *Eyes open. Pause. Eyes right.*) Brownie of course. (*Pause.*) You remember Brownie, Willie, I can see him. (*Pause.*) Brownie is there, Willie, beside me. (*Pause. Loud.*) Brownie is there, Willie. (*Pause. Eyes front.*) That is all. . . .

Brownie, of course, symbolizes death—and perhaps the brown earth, the earthball, in which Winnie is surely being swallowed up. Perhaps too, we have a parody of those classic lines from Robert Browning, "Grow old along with me! / The best is yet to be," lines which seem almost idiotic in the face of Beckett's austere vision of the realities of aging.

The counterpoint of these two themes, interwoven and contradictory, constitutes the inner action of *Happy Days:* an interplay between the celebration of life and the lure of instant death, played out amidst an encroaching disablement in a landscape blazing with light yet resistant to understanding. Beckett's play ends in a striking *coup de théâtre,* an event unpredicted by anything in the play up to this point, yet wholly consistent with all that has gone before.

WINNIE: . . . I can do no more. (*Pause.*) Say no more. (*Pause.*) But I must say more. (*Pause.*) Problem here. (*Pause.*) No, something must move, in the world, I can't any

Willie appears in tuxedo in the British National Theatre presentation. "Well, this is an unexpected pleasure!" cries Winnie. Note that revolver points directly at Winnie: what will it be used for? (Photo: Courtesy French Cultural Services.)

more. (*Pause.*) A zephyr. (*Pause.*) A breath. (*Pause.*) What are those immortal lines? (*Pause.*) It might be the eternal dark. (*Pause.*) Black night without end. . . . (*Long pause.*) I hear cries. (*Pause.*) Sing. (*Pause.*) Sing your old song, Winnie.

But she does not yet sing her song. Instead, around the mound, comes Willie for the first time. Astonishingly, he is "dressed to kill," in top hat, morning coat, and striped trousers. He sports a "very long bushy white Battle of Britain moustache." And he is crawling on all fours.

WINNIE: Well this is an unexpected pleasure!

The two look at each other, Willie dropping his hat to do so and moving within Winnie's field of vision. It is a ghastly effect: the woman in earth to her chin, staring obliquely; the man in formal attire, on his hands and knees, staring up at her; and, of course, conspicuously between them, Brownie the re-volver. Willie collapses, his head falling to the ground.

WINNIE: . . . Where were you all this time? (*Pause.*) What were you doing all this time? (*Pause.*) Changing? (*Pause.*) Did you not hear me screaming for you? (*Pause.*) Did you get stuck in your hole? (*Pause. He looks up.*) That's right, Willie, look at me. (*Pause.*) Feast your old eyes, Willie. (*Pause.*) Does anything remain? (*Pause.*) Any remains? (*Pause.*) No? (*Pause.*) I haven't been able to look after it, you know. (*He sinks his head.*) You are still recognizable, in a way. (*Pause.*) Are you thinking of coming to live this side now . . . for a bit maybe? (*Pause.*) No? (*Pause.*) Just a brief call? (*Pause.*) Have you gone deaf, Willie? (*Pause.*) Dumb? (*Pause.*) Oh I know you were never one to talk, I worship you Winnie be mine and then nothing from that day forth only titbits from Reynolds' News. (*Eyes front. Pause.*) Ah well, what matter, that's what I always say, it will have been a happy day, after all, another happy day. (*Pause.*) Not long now, Winnie. (*Pause.*) I hear cries. (*Pause.*) Do you ever hear cries, Willie? (*Pause.*) No? (*Eyes back on* WILLIE.) Willie. (*Pause.*) Look at me again, Willie. (*Pause.*) Once more, Willie. (*He looks up. Happily.*) Ah! (*Pause. Shocked.*) What ails you, Willie, I never saw such an expression! (*Pause.*) Put on your hat, dear, it's the sun, don't stand on ceremony, I won't mind. (*He drops hat and gloves and starts to crawl up mound towards her. Gleeful.*) Oh I say, this is terrific! (*He halts, clinging to mound with one hand, reaching up with the other.*) Come on, dear, put a bit of jizz into it, I'll cheer you on. (*Pause.*) Is it me you're after, Willie . . . or is it something else? (*Pause.*) Do you want to touch my face . . . again? (*Pause.*) Is it a kiss you're after, Willie . . . or is it something else? (*Pause.*) There was a time when I could have given you a hand. (*Pause.*) And then a time before that again when I did give you a hand. (*Pause.*) You were always in dire need of a hand, Willie. (*He slithers back to foot of mound and lies with face to ground.*) Brrum! (*Pause. He rises to hands and knees, raises his face towards her.*) Have another go, Willie, I'll cheer you on. (*Pause.*) Don't look at me like that! (*Pause. Vehement.*) Don't look at me like that! (*Pause. Low.*) Have you gone off your head, Willie? (*Pause. Do.*) Out of your poor old wits, Willie? (*Pause.*)

WILLIE: (*just audible*) Win.

(*Pause.* WINNIE's *eyes front. Happy expression appears, grows.*)

WINNIE: Win! (*Pause.*) Oh this *is* a happy day, this will have been another happy day! (*Pause.*) After all. (*Pause.*) So far.

Now Winnie begins her song. It is to the tune of her music box:

Though I say not
What I may not
Let you hear,
Yet the swaying

Dance is saying,
Love me dear!
Every touch of fingers
Tells me what I know,
Says for you,
It's true, it's true,
You love me so!

The bell rings. Winnie smiles. Willie is still on his hands and knees, looking at her. The smile disappears. "*They look at each other. Long pause.* CURTAIN." And the play is over.

Why was Willie climbing the mound? "Is it me you're after, Willie," asks Winnie, "or is it something else?" If it is the revolver, we ask, does he want to kill her, or to kill himself, or to kill them both? Is his "just audible" cry of "Win" simply her nickname, or is the author invoking an association of winning, of victory? And under these circumstances, what are we to make of Winnie's song, with its depiction of a declaration dance of love?

Beckett provides no answers to these questions, and neither should critical analysis. In the theatre of the absurd, and in stylized theatre in general, the elucidation of meaningful questions—not the discovery of practical solutions—is what marks an author's genius and accomplishment. The problems addressed in *Happy Days*—the inevitability of aging and death, the inscrutability of human affection, the obscurity of human motives, and the necessity for arbitrary commitment and action in a universe without final meaning—are inherent conditions of life: they can be diagnosed and epitomized with symbols, but they cannot be remedied. Beckett posits lucid metaphors, intriguing patterns, and evocative images, he does not proffer moral codes or even helpful advice. *Happy Days* stimulates but does not explain; it fascinates but does not presume to lead us out of the dark.

For Beckett and the rest of the absurdists are intent upon portraying humankind as eternally and feebly groping in a darkness that can never be penetrated by the superficial light of human understanding. Reversing the symbolism of Prometheus—who in bringing light brought the hope of knowledge, understanding, joy, and victory over life's mysteries—Beckett suggests that light makes only the inconsequential luminous, thus trivializing the human experience and making human beings oblivious to the greatest grace: total obscurity. Rather in line with the medieval association of light with Lucifer, not enlightenment, Beckett makes the "blazing light" of *Happy Days* a malign symbol of final ignorance, a light that reveals nothing beyond the absurdity of human beings' efforts to "see." Indeed, in the first act, while she can still use her hands, Winnie makes all too clear what the truly "happy day" will be when she finally manages to make out the words on the toothbrush handle:

WINNIE: [*reading*] Fully guaranteed . . . genuine pure . . . hog's . . . setae. (*Pause.*) Hog's setae. (*Pause.*) That is what I find so wonderful, that not a day goes by— (*smile*)—to speak in the old style—(*smile off*)—hardly a day, without some addition

to one's knowledge however trifling, the addition I mean, provided one takes the pains. . . . And if for some strange reason no further pains are possible, why then just close the eyes—(*she does so*)—and wait for the day to come—(*opens eyes*)—the happy day to come when flesh melts at so many degrees and the night of the moon has so many hundred hours. (*Pause.*) That is what I find so comforting when I lose heart and envy the brute beast.

Thus the happy day is to come at the end of these "Happy Days," when the eyes can close, when one takes no further pains to add to one's store of "knowledge," when the blazing light will incinerate Winnie's flesh as it incinerates her parasol, when she can acquire a deeper knowledge illuminated only by the "night of the moon."

Beckett's vision is unique, and the body of theatre he has created is only one small part of the modern drama; other writers associated with the absurd often hold visions less relentlessly severe. Because the extreme situations Beckett creates are unrelieved by sentiment, his work is often called "uncompromising." Yet his plays are undeniably comedies, for they always explore the human condition with irony and a bizarre humor. If the condition of man is terminal, its staged incarnation is hilariously sprightly. Winnie's enthusiasm, although "absurd" in the ordinary sense as well as in the philosophical sense, is infectious: we share in her small triumphs of self-deception and cheer her on in singing against her suspicions and confronting her plight with such unbridled whimsy. Whatever its provocation, whistling in the dark can be agreeable music, and it is this upbeat tone that suffuses Beckett's plays.

Thus, perhaps surprisingly, there is nothing depressing about *Happy Days,* for its uncompromising vision is presented with an always compassionate irony. Nothing is more evident in the works of Samuel Beckett than the author's kindly attitude toward his characters, an attitude that, we feel, also extends across the footlights to us. Beckett is not a prophet of despair; he is simply a reporter of the ineffable and inexplicable: he may not lead us out of the dark, but he *will* hold our hands while we stumble about. Thus, if there is no message in his plays, there is amusement and there is comfort. In the confusion of our times, that is about all any artist or friend can presume to deliver.

Theatre of Alienation

The theatre of the absurd is one of the two main lines of the contemporary stylized theatre; the theatre of alienation, or of *distancing* (the German word is *Verfremdung*), is the other. In contrast to the hermetic, self-contained absurdist plays with their message concerning the essential futility of human endeavors, the sprawling, socially engaged "epic" theatre of Bertolt Brecht and like-minded theatre artists concentrates on humanity's potential for growth and society's capacity to effect change.

Bertolt Brecht's most popular play, in his own time and ours, was one of his first: The Threepenny Opera *(1927), adapted from an eighteenth-century English play (John Gay's* The Beggar's Opera*), with new music by Kurt Weill. Three-penny was a giant popular success in pre-Nazi Berlin, and its Greenwich Village revival with Lotte Lenya was a major factor in beginning New York City's off-Broadway movement in the 1950s. An ironic and satiric romance about thieves, whores, beggars, and the London police, the "opera" established Brecht's reputation as an iconoclastic dramatist. Here directed by equally iconoclastic director Richard Foreman (the wire strung across the stage is a Foreman motif) for the New York Shakespeare Festival production at Lincoln Center. Raul Julia plays the head gangster, Macheath ("Mack the Knife"). (Photo: © George E. Joseph.)*

Bertolt Brecht

The guiding genius of the theatre of aliena-tion is Bertolt Brecht: theorist, dramatist, and director. No single individual has had a greater impact on postwar theatre than Brecht. This impact has been felt in two ways. First, Brecht has introduced theatre practices that are, at least on the surface, utterly at variance with those in use since the time of Aristotle. Second, his accomplishments have invigo-rated the theatre with an abrasive humanism that has reawakened its sense of social respon-

sibility and its awareness of the capacity of theatre to mold public issues and events.

Brecht was born in Germany in 1898 and emerged from World War I a dedicated Marx-ist and pacifist. Using poems, songs, and eventually the theatre to promote his ideals following the German defeat, Brecht vividly portrayed his country during the Weimar Re-public as a country caught in the grips of four giant vises: the military, capitalism, in-dustrialization, and imperialism. His *Rise and Fall of the City of Mahagonny,* for example, an "epic opera" of 1930, proved an immensely popular blending of satire and propaganda, music and expressionist theatricality, social idealism and lyric poetry; it was produced all over Germany and throughout most of Eu-rope in the early 1930s as a depiction of a rapacious international capitalism evolving to-ward fascism.

Brecht was forced to flee his country upon Hitler's accession to the chancellorship. There-after he moved about Europe for a time and then, for much of the 1940s, settled in Amer-ica. Following World War II he returned in triumph to Berlin, where the East German government established for him the Berliner Ensemble Theatre; there Brecht was allowed to consolidate his theories in a body of pro-ductions developed out of his earlier plays and the pieces he had written while in exile.

Brecht's theatre draws upon a potpourri of theatrical conventions, some derived from the ancients, some from Eastern drama, and some from the German expressionist movement in which Brecht himself played a part in his early years. Masks, songs, verse, exotic settings, sat-ire, and direct rhetorical address are funda-mental conventions that Brecht adopted from other theatre forms. In addition, he devel-oped many conventions of his own: lantern-slide projections with printed "captions," asides and invocations directed to the audi-ence to encourage them to develop an objec-tive point of view, and a variety of procedures aimed at demystifying theatrical techniques (for example, lowering the lights so that the

Brecht's Rise and Fall of the City of Mahagonny *in contemporary production of the Berlin Light Opera (Komische Oper). The play satirizes American soci-ety and world capitalism, represented here by giant bottles of American bourbon and Italian vermouth in a fanciful, theatrical, pseudo-Alaskan setting. (Photo: Arvid Lagenpusch.)*

pipes and wires would be displayed) became the characteristics of Brecht's theatre.

Brecht deplored the use of sentimentality and the notion of audience empathy for characters and attempted instead to create a performance style that was openly "didactic": the actor was asked to alienate himself, or distance himself, from the character he played—to "demonstrate" his character rather than to embody that character in a realistic manner. In Brecht's view the ideal actor was one who could establish a *critical objectivity* toward his or her character that would make clear the character's social function and political commitment. In attempting to repudiate the "magic" of the theatre, he demanded that it be made to seem nothing more than a place for workers to present a meaningful "parable" of life, and he in no way wished to disguise the fact that the stage personnel—actors and stagehands—were merely workers who were engaged in doing a job. In every way possible, Brecht attempted to prevent the audience from becoming swept up in an emotional, sentimental bath of feelings: his goal was to keep the audience "alienated" or "distanced" from the literal events depicted by the play so that they would be free to concentrate on the larger social and political issues the play generated and reflected. Brecht considered this theatre to be an "epic" one because it attempted, around the framework of a parable or an archetypical event, to create a whole new perspective on human history and to indicate the direction that political dialogue should take to foster social betterment.

Brecht's theories were to have a staggering impact on the modern theatre. In his wholesale renunciation of Aristotelian catharsis, which depends on audience empathy with a noble character, and his denial of Stanislavsky's basic principles concerning the aims of acting, Brecht provided a new dramaturgy that encouraged playwrights, directors, and designers to tackle social issues directly rather than through the implications of contrived dramatic situations. Combining the technol-

ogies and aesthetics of other media—the lecture hall, the slide show, the public meeting, the cinema, the cabaret, the rehearsal—Brecht fashioned a vastly expanded arena for his *dialectics:* his social arguments that sought to engender truth through the confrontation of conflicting interests. These ideas were played out, in Brecht's own works and in countless other works inspired by him, with a bold theatricality, an open-handed dealing with the audience, a proletarian vigor, and a stridently entertaining, intelligently satirical, and charmingly bawdy theatre. This theatre has proven even more popular in the 1970s and 1980s than it was in Brecht's day, because since then the world seems to have grown even more fragmented, more individualistic, and more suspicious of collective emotions and sentimentality.

The Good Woman of Sezuan   No play better illustrates Brecht's dramatic theory and method than *The Good Woman of Sezuan* (1943). This play, set in western China (of which Brecht knew virtually nothing—thus adding to the "distancing" of the story), tells the story of a kindhearted prostitute, Shen Te, who is astounded to receive a gift of money from three itinerant gods. Elated by her good fortune, Shen Te uses the money to start a tobacco business. She is, however, quickly beset by petty officials seeking to impose local regulations, self-proclaimed creditors demanding payment, and a host of hangers-on who simply prey upon her good nature. At the point of financial ruin, Shen Te leaves her tobacco shop to enlist the aid of her male cousin Shui Ta, who strides imperiously into the tobacco shop and routs the predators, making it safe for Shen Te to return. But the predators come back, and Shen Te again has to call on the tyrannical Shui Ta to save her. A simple story—but Brecht's stroke of genius is to make Shui Ta and Shen Te the same character: Shui Ta is simply Shen Te in disguise! The aim of the play is not to show that there are kindhearted people and tyrannical people, but that people can choose to be one or the other. What kind of society is it, Brecht asks, that forces us to make this sort of choice?

Brecht is no mere propagandist, and his epic theatre is not one of simple messages or easy conclusions. At the end of *The Good Woman of Sezuan*, Shen Te asks the gods for help, but they simply float off into the air reciting inane platitudes as the curtain falls. The gods do not have the answer—so the audience must provide it. In the play's epilogue, a character comes forward and addresses us:

Hey, honorable folks, don't be dismayed
That we can't seem to end this play!
　You've stayed
To see our shining, all-concluding moral,
And what we've given you has been this
　bitter quarrel.
We know, we know—we're angry too,
To see the curtain down and everything
　askew.
We'd love to see you stand and cheer—
　and say
How wonderful you find our charming
　play!
But we won't put our heads into the sand.
We know your wish is ever our command,
We know you ask for *more:* a firm
　conclusion
To this alarming more-than-mass
　confusion.
But what is it? Who knows? Not all your
　cash
Could buy your way—or ours—from this
　mishmash.
Do we need heroes? Dreams? New Gods?
　Or None?
Well, tell us—else we're hopelessly
　undone.
The only thing that we can think to say
Is simply that it's *you* must end this play.
Tell us how our own good woman of
　Sezuan
Can come to a good ending—if she can!
Honorable folks: you search, and we will
　trust

Brecht's Caucasian Chalk Circle *in Slobodan Unkovski's masked production, at the American Repertory Theatre, 1990. (Photo: Richard Feldman.)*

That you will find the way. You must,
　must, must!

Brecht's parables epitomize the conflicts between social classes; they do not presume to solve these conflicts. Indeed, the social problems he addresses are not to be solved on the stage but in the world itself: the audience must find the appropriate balance between morality and greed, between individualism and social responsibility. Brecht's plays reenact the basic intellectual dichotomy posed by Marx's dialectical materialism; thus they are, in a sense, Marxist plays, but they certainly are not Leninist, much less Stalinist. They radiate a faith in the human potential. Yet while they are both socially engaged and theatrically eclectic—qualities not particularly noticeable in the theatre of the absurd—they still resound with the fundamental human uncertainty that pervades all antirealistic theatre.

FUTURE DIRECTIONS IN ANTIREALISTIC THEATRE

Beckett and Brecht represent what are generally considered the two main directions of contemporary antirealistic theatre, directions that Peter Brook, in an influential essay, called the "holy" and "rough" theatres. Beckett's work, the "holy" theatre, ritualizes humanity's permanent condition, whereas Brecht's work undertakes the "rough" approach of grappling with society and changing social situations. Holy and rough, absurd and epic, impressionist and expressionist—these are terms that today occasion much critical contention and many hours of analysis. But it is well to remember that history probably will not accord much notice to the critical lines we now seek so diligently to draw. If the past is any guide to the future, individual genius and individual artistry will determine who will be the lasting voices of our age.

Contemporary antirealist drama appears, as we move closer toward the twenty-first century (and the third millennium), to have edged out realism as the major format of contemporary times. In fact, the term *postmodernism* is sometimes used to indicate that a new era has succeeded the *modern* one, and this new era clearly springs from the absurdist/holy and alienated/epic trends exemplified by Beckett and Brecht, among many others. It is certainly clear that the non-realistic play enjoys a superior academic (if not always a popular) prestige in world theatre of the 1990s.

In an age when reality tends to disappoint, we are looking for more than reality in the theatre. We are looking for radiations of truth rather than observations of detail. We are looking for syntheses and listening for harmonies. In an age when the temporary and the transitional seem everywhere obvious, with human relationships becoming increasingly diversified and short-lived, we are looking for enduring symbols, patterns, and motions, for the subatomic structures of our lives. In an age flooded with propaganda and bewildering masses of data, we are looking for simple elegance, for art.

The modern theatre doubtless will take new turns in the coming decades. We may come to consider distinctions such as realist and antirealist, epic and absurd, to be mere vestigial remains of irrelevant perspectives. The theatre of the future may spurn the acknowledged masters of our immediate past and turn in directions still unforeseeable. But what is certain is that it will reflect the needs and respond to the spiritual inquiries of its time.

Antirealistic theatre did not come about simply because some few persons created it; it derives fundamentally from human needs. No less than the dithyramb of ancient Greece, the stylized theatre of today addresses a mystery and seeks to fill a hollowness in our understanding. Its goal is not merely to add to human pleasure, but also to add to *humanity:* to complete the human consciousness. It gives every indication of pursuing those goals with some success for many years to come.

10

Theatre Today

· ·

The theatre of today exists on stage, not in the pages of this or any other book.

The theatre of today is being performed right now, in the multimillion-dollar theatres of the great cities of the world as well as on the simpler stages of schools and communities, dinner theatres and nightclubs, roadhouses and experimental theatre clubs everywhere.

The theatre of today is all around us, simply waiting to be discovered, seen, heard, felt, and experienced. The easiest and best way to apprehend its fundamental impulse is to go out and see for oneself.

We cannot evaluate our current theatre with the same objectivity as we do that of the past—even the recent past. Theatre is a business as well as an art, and the flurry of promotion, publicity, and puffery that surrounds each current theatrical success makes a cool perspective difficult. Whereas poets and painters are often ignored in their own time, the opposite is more often true of theatre artists: they are frequently lionized in their own time, only to be forgotten just a few years later. A permanent place in the repertory of world theatre is the achievement of very few indeed. Among the playwrights once deemed equal to Shakespeare or better are such now-dimly remembered figures as John Fletcher, Joseph Addison, Edward George Bulwer-

Lytton, August Friedrich Ferdinand von Kotzebue, Eugène Brieux, and Maxwell Anderson. Which of our present-day writers and actors and other theatre artists will achieve more than ephemeral glory? Which, if any, will leave a mark on future generations? No one can answer either question for sure. But there are some directions in today's theatre that show signs of becoming established, and these are worthy of examination.

THE MODERN AND
THE POSTMODERN

From a practical point of view—that is, from the standpoint of theatre practice, as opposed to theory—the theatre is, and probably will always be, a somewhat conservative institution. Almost certainly, theatre companies the world over will continue to present a large number of plays from past eras, including the "modern" one, and will "conserve" many of the theatre's traditional, if not indeed hoary, ways of working. In fact, virtually all the plays mentioned in the previous chapters are being performed somewhere in the world today, while you read these pages, and the vigorous debates among today's actors and directors often repeat, almost verbatim, dialogues current in the days of Aristophanes, Shakespeare, and Stanislavsky.

Yet, as we began to move into the last third of the twentieth century, a new era seemed to be, in William Butler Yeats's remarkable metaphor, "slouching towards Bethlehem to be born." In the defining decades of the 1960s and 70s, triggered by the Vietnam War and the assassinations of Martin Luther King, Jr., John Kennedy, and Robert Kennedy, political and racial turmoil erupted here and abroad. Cold war adventurism in Latin America, Africa, and Asia, and abuses of power at home, led to the unprecedented resignations of an American president and a vice-president. Suddenly, the civilized world rediscovered, and began to confront, a list of past and present horrors: the Nazi Holocaust, the massacres of Native Americans, the formidable hidden oppression of women and minority groups, the vast destruction of the planet's resources. Suddenly (or so it seemed), the potential for world-threatening disasters—nuclear Armageddon, unrestrained pollution, political chaos, environmental collapse—came to the attention of a seemingly helpless populace. Alluring but dangerous drugs proliferated. Crime and terrorism grew exponentially. Famine ravaged populations. Empires began to crumble. And an unknown, sex-linked disease arose from nowhere and began to decimate societies and redefine the pragmatics of lovemaking.

The arts first responded to these social changes with an artistic freedom that was frightening in its extremity—nowhere more so than in the theatre, where Dionysian ecstasy returned to the stage with force almost equal to that of the *dithyrambos*. As play-licensing laws fell in England and legal censorship became locally unenforceable in America, bold profanity, total nudity, open copulation, and direct political accusation—all unknown on the legitimate stage since ancient times—became almost commonplace. Plays popular in America in the 1960s and 70s included one accusing the president (Lyndon Johnson) of murder, one accusing a past Pope (Pius XII) of genocide, one featuring a farm boy copulating with his pig, one showing a scene of mass masturbation, and one concluding with the audience undressing and marching out into the streets. O, Calcutta!, a smarmy, juvenile, all-nude review, played to record box-office receipts in major theatre capitals, including New York's Broadway. Theatre audiences the world over found themselves physically assaulted, hurtled about, handed lit "joints" (of marijuana), and, in at least one case, urinated and defecated upon. In some plays, actors engaged in sexual activity with each other and, in others, with members of the audience. These and other extreme behav-

The Company Theatre of Los Angeles was only one of many theatre companies in the 1960s and 70s experimenting with total nudity and participatory improvisation on stage. This original production, titled The Emergence, *was one of the finest and most visually eloquent productions of the turbulent times. (Courtesy The Company Theatre, Los Angeles.)*

THE CRISIS OF TODAY'S THEATRE

By the late 1970s, this mood of violence was largely spent. The novelty of stage sex and profanity had mostly passed, and the latent voyeurism of the audience had been more than satisfied; an increasingly serious and sober public began demanding a more intelligent and focused response to major issues than the theatre was providing. And by the mid-1980s the AIDS crisis had largely eradicated the public's flirtation with unbridled sex as a cure for social ills ("make love, not war" was replaced with the cry for "safe sex"). Moreover, many artists and critics were beginning to examine the hidden prejudices and privileges that continued to undermine even modernism's putative freedom and fairness.

The fears and confusion of the contemporary age had once again brought the theatre to the fore: as an arena where thoughts, fashions, feelings, morals, and aesthetics could be brought together to bring lucidity and structure to the problems that beset us. Theatre, which brings individual problems to collective attention and collective problems to individual attention, seemed a natural forum to rethink and restudy the crises in contemporary life.

While generalizations about an era wholly upon us and, indeed, just in its early stages, must be tentative, there are clearly three major movements—or themes—in the current theatre: the theatre of the age we increasingly call "postmodern." We might think of these as a theatre of *revival*, a theatre of *postmodern experiment*, and an *open theatre*. (Because these terms are not at all in general use, let us use the indefinite article "a"—rather than the definite "the"—in discussing them.)

A Theatre of Revival

The more extreme theatrical experiments of the 1960s and 70s did not transpire without

iors had become part of the license claimed by a theatre purportedly trying to make itself heard above the societal din of war and corruption. Or were its adherents only clamoring for personal attention? In any event, it was a decade (or more) of this sort of dramaturgical violence and abandon that brought the age of "modernism" to a crisis, if not to a conclusion.

The contemporary sunglasses provide a startling contrast to the eighteenth-century dresses and parasol in this 1991 Alabama Shakespeare Festival production of Richard Brinsley Sheridan's The Rivals. *Costumes by Alan Armstrong; Monica Bell and Suzanne Irving are the performers. (Photo: Scarsbrook/ASF.)*

Romanticism is in full sway in this stage adaptation, reviving Bram Stoker's gothic novel Dracula. *This Broadway production, starring Frank Langella as the fifteenth-century Transylvanian vampire, featured horrifically luscious scenery and costumes by noted artist Edward Gorey. (Photo: Martha Swope and Associates.)*

the expected backlash—indeed, it could be argued that they were created so as to provoke such a backlash. That backlash still continues, leading to fierce battles in the 1990s between artists and the National Endowment for the Arts (NEA), the United States government agency established to "protect" the arts. "What is art?" is now a hot topic for newspaper editorials and presidential debates, as well as on the floor of the U.S. Senate.

The theatre of the past, including the theatre of the "modern" past, has consequently enjoyed an astonishing revival—not only by those revolted at what they considered the excesses of the 1960s, but also by those who were reminded, by the anarchic violence of late modernist art, of the sublime harmonies created by artists of an earlier age. Shakespearean festivals are only one visible national indication of a theatre of revival: at last count, there were 78 theatre companies, in almost every state in the United States, partly or wholly devoted to producing the works of England's great dramatist. Romanticism is also on the theatre of revival's program: the elaborate stage versions of nineteenth-century

romantic novels— *Nicholas Nickleby, Les Misérables,* and *The Phantom of the Opera*—will be seen by hundreds of millions of theatregoers all over the world by the end of the 1990s. And the restagings of great modern plays, both realistic and otherwise, and of American musicals from the "golden era" of the 1940s, 50s, and 60s, constitute, at any given time, roughly half to two-thirds of the offerings along New York's famous Broadway and in America's community and academic theatres. New plays aping these modernist classics—serious dramas as well as comedies—might in any year make up another quarter of the bill.

The theatre of revival—including new plays mimicking those earlier forms—has a broad appeal; for most audiences, such a theatre is familiar, entertaining, and aesthetically satisfying. It is also a theatre capable of addressing, in some complexity, the serious and tangible problems facing humanity around the world. It is even a theatre capable of offering, if not solutions, at least political lucidity and intellectual focus. In avoiding show-offy formalistic innovation (art for art's sake) and gratuitous eroticism and scatology, the theatre of revival is not merely a theatre of nostalgia, but also a forum for insight, information, ideas, empathy, catharsis, wit, rapture, virtuosity, and laugh-till-you-cry humor. Though easily derided by avant-gardists, such a traditional (or derrière-garde) theatre needs no apologists: it is a vital, vibrant, thriving glory of the current stage.

But revivalism by its nature cannot be at the cutting edge of theatrical innovation and creativity.

A Theatre of Postmodern Experiment

The notion of a postmodern era is not as historically centered as the name suggests. As the term has developed since the 1970s, *postmodernism* indicates a way of thinking, or even of nonthinking, more than it defines a particular period in time.

The postmodern defies complete analysis—because postmodernism literally defies (repudiates) the act of analyzing. The postmodern approach essentially dismisses logic and cause-and-effect determinism, replacing both with more random associations and reflections. These reflections are of two sorts: self-reflections, where a work of art pays homage to itself, and reflections of the past, where the art pays homage to past texts and models.

One may see postmodernism, therefore, in the repeated and repainted images by Andy Warhol (of Campbell soup cans, head shots of Marilyn Monroe, and so on), which emphasize the artist's redefining a commercial product as an independent work of "art." One may see it also in Philip Johnson's AT&T building in New York (1984), with its neo-Renaissance

Cliff Faulkner's lighthearted and very postmodern setting for Shaw's Man and Superman *at South Coast Repertory Theatre in 1990 freely juxtaposes classical, Renaissance, and contemporary elements. Production was directed by Martin Benson with costumes by Shigeru Yaji. (Photo: Cristofer Gross.)*

facade and "Chippendale highboy" roofline. Whereas modernism repudiated the past, postmodernism gaily embraces it, "quotes" it, and even recycles it.

A postmodernist work of art, therefore, is not about "something" so much as it is about itself. About "art."

Moreover, a postmodern work might also be said to "deconstruct" itself, so as to make us think about *ourselves*. Indeed, it is about *us* as well as it is about art. How do *we* view art? Are there any hidden assumptions about "what art is" that exclude us from enjoying it? Or that "privilege" other audiences? Inasmuch as a postmodern work is self-referential (refers to itself), it also contains its own critique; it parodies itself; it throws us back, sometimes in amusement and sometimes in irritation, upon our own thoughts.

Postmodern artists—and postmodern critics—are as deeply concerned with the social orders from which art springs, with the *processes* of creating art, and with the open or hidden assumptions that inform art as with the art *products* themselves.

Such definitions of the postmodern are admittedly complex, probably humorous (if not bewildering) to a first-time reader, and themselves subject to parody: which is itself a postmodern approach!

In theatre, which is a practical art, the notion of postmodernism may be concretely understood. Postmodern drama springs directly from the antirealistic theatre; but unlike most antirealistic theatres, it has little, if any, of the modernist's aesthetic or social optimism. Whereas the symbolists and surrealists were working to reveal inner truths, a "higher order" of reality, and where the Brechtian epic theatre was struggling to change (or save) the world and to create a higher level of society, none of these goals is deemed within the reach of the postmodernist—who presupposes no higher levels of reality or social order. Because there is no higher reality to symbolize, the postmodernist abjures symbols (the postmodern is the art, one critic suggests, of the *métaphore manquée,* or missing metaphor). Because social progress is impossible (and social decline is probably inevitable), the postmodernist can only contemplate the future warily, if at all.

The postmodern writer, or director, therefore, is more likely to explore the *discontinuity* of observable reality and information, rather than attempt to find any integrated synthesis or meaning. Postmodern art celebrates the apparent randomness of arbitrary juxtaposition.

Douglas-Scott Goheen's set for Much Ado About Nothing *intermixes outdoors and indoors, putting chandeliers in the "forest" and placing "real" birch trees in front of replicated photos of more birches. The set gives a sense of location, but also, in postmodernist fashion, suggests its own "setting" on the stage. At Theatre 40 in Beverly Hills, California, 1991. (Photo by the designer.)*

Students of the postmodern find its salient features, for example, in the action painting of Jackson Pollock, whose paint was randomly dripped from buckets with holes in their bottoms; in break dancing, which is improvised, haphazard, and disjunctive; and in the music (or, as some say, cacophony) of the late John Cage, which consists of apparently indiscriminate sounds, few of which come from conventional "musical" instruments. Broadcast video, with its night and day agglomeration of new dramatic fragments, intermixed with commercials, promos, newsbreaks, announcements, station identifications, and old film clips, is a perfectly postmodern creation, made all the more discontinuous by picture-in-picture technology that permits the viewing of two agglomerations simultaneously and by remote-control devices permitting the viewer to shuttle between forty-odd channels at lightning speed.

The first great postmodern theatre (although its creators refused to call it "theatre") was the short-lived arts phenomenon called Dada, which flourished in the years immediately following World War I. Dada was begun in 1916 at the Cabaret Voltaire, in Zurich, Switzerland. As critic Mel Gordon describes it, Dada was a "chaotic mix of balalaika music, Wedekind poems, dance numbers, cabaret singing, recitations from Voltaire, and shouting in a kaleidoscopic environment of paintings. . . . Sound poems followed . . . with crazed piano playing and anti-war diatribes . . . [and] chance poetry," the latter created by poet Tristan Tzara, who pulled words at random out of a hat. Writing manifestos that declared themselves "anti-art," the Dadaists—as they came to be called (the name was chosen at random from an unabridged dictionary)—found themselves the artistic darlings of Berlin and Paris in the early 1920s. The movement clearly stimulated some of the experimentalism of the theatre of the absurd, which was its longer-lasting successor, and has, in many respects, been reborn in theatres around the world in the current genre of "performance art" (discussed more fully later in the chapter).

The postmodernism of the current theatre stems from both of the main nonrealistic strains of late modernism: the theatre of the absurd and the theatre of alienation.

It is the very late plays of Samuel Beckett that many feel best exemplify the pessimism and flight from meaning characteristic of the postmodern. For while he was always a proponent of meaninglessness, the stirring vitality of his 1961 *Happy Days* had turned, by the 1980s, to a grim despair, if not a complete

nihilism. In his very short play, *Rockabye* (1981), Beckett's sole visible character is an old lady, with "huge eyes in white expressionless face." On a dark stage, she rocks alone, dimly lit in a rocking chair; during the play she says but one word (it is "More") in what is apparently a beyond-the-grave dialogue with her prerecorded voice. The play ends with the voice saying:

> rock her off
> stop her eyes
> fuck life
> stop her eyes
> rock her off
> rock her off

And the rocking stops as the lights fade out.

If Beckett's theatre stimulates the intellectual pessimism of the postmodern, Brecht's stimulates its parodic and self-referential delight and the theatre's self-deconstruction as it throws issues back to the audience.

Neo-Brechtian authors like Heiner Müller (German), David Henry Hwang (American), Tom Stoppard (English), and Jean Genet (French), plus directors like Ariane Mnouchkine (French), Peter Brook (English), Jerzy Grotowski (Polish), and JoAnne Akalaitis (American), have ransacked the world's cultural history (and, in Grotowski's case, its cultural prehistory) to create contemporary theatre works that make bold associations between ancient models and current icons. Brecht's notion (and he did not, of course, invent it) of calling attention to the theatre itself, and to the means of production, has become almost a cliché of the contemporary theatre: in Robert Schenkkan's Pulitzer Prize–winning *The Kentucky Cycle*, for example, each act begins with the cast coming out to announce its subtitle (and theme); each act ends with the actors picking up their props and leaving the stage; brief interludes are enlivened by members of the cast who gloss the action by singing a relevant song.

It is this post-Brechtian direction—a theatre which, in order to refocus the audience's attention on social issues and values, calls attention to itself and deconstructs and parodies itself—that has led to, in the present day, a newly *open* theatre.

An Open Theatre

As much as we can be sure of anything, we can be sure that the theatre of the twenty-first century will be open to an infinitely wider range of interests, cultures, and individuals than was any period in the theatre's past history.

The deconstruction of the theatre promoted by its most stellar luminaries—Beckett and Brecht among them—made us painfully conscious of the theatre's failure to truly reflect the humanity inside us and the society around us. For most of us in the 1990s, the notion of an all-white, all-male, blank-verse-spouting acting company holding "a mirror up to nature" now seems impossibly limited (if not ludicrous) and makes us look back with some dismay at the theatre of the Shakespearean era, which employed such companies, and also at the so-called modern theatre, which in many respects only reformatted its putatively repudiated ancestors in this regard. How can an exclusively white male company wholly mirror the concerns of nonwhites and nonmales? How many hidden assumptions infiltrate our minds when we find persons of color invariably portrayed as servants, exotics, or "noble" savages and when we see women routinely depicted as brainless playthings, saintly mothers, or simpering helpmeets?

A brilliantly innovative American company named The Open Theatre was created by Joseph Chaikin in 1963 and for a decade combined social improvisation with Brechtian techniques to develop a series of plays in which performers glided into and out of the characters they sometimes played (they also played scenery and props; more often they played themselves) and used story and character merely as vehicles for direct interactions with audiences. Their plays, including Megan Terry's *Viet Rock,* Susan Yankowitz's *Terminal,* and the company-authored *Mutation Show,* were continually evolving workshop performances that addressed immediate audience concerns. The company toured Europe—but also toured prisons. They made fraternal and sororal alliances with the New Lafayette Theatre in Harlem, El Teatro Campesino in California, and the Women's Collective Theatre. The Open Theatre ended its existence in 1973, but its influence has been extraordinary, and its name might very well be lent to the much larger "opening" of the contemporary stage.

For today's newest and most provocative theatre is truly open, or at least opening, to voices heretofore shut out, or severely limited, in the largely Western, white, and male-dominated theatre of yesterday, even of "modern" yesterday. And that opening is occurring on all levels: gender, race, physical condition, and sexual preference.

A Theatre by and about Women

Women, who—save for rare exceptions—were unrepresented in the theatre until the seventeenth century and who from then until the 1950s have been largely relegated to acting and costume construction, are now a major force in playwriting, designing, directing, producing, and technical theatre. Three different American women (Beth Henley, Marsha Norman, Wendy Wasserstein) won Pulitzer Prizes for playwriting during the 1980s, and many critics accord Jane Wagner and Tina Howe similar stature; in England, no dramatic writer of the 1990s is more respected than Caryl Churchill. Women directors are making substantial inroads in the New York theatre, on and off Broadway, and are increasingly assuming artistic directorships at major American repertory companies: fully one-third of the 200-plus regional theatres have recently been headed by women, including Zelda Fitchandler at The (New York) Acting Company, Libby Appel at the Indianapolis Repertory Theatre and the Oregon Shakespeare Festival, Sharon Ott at the Berkeley Repertory Theatre, Irene Lewis at Baltimore's Center Stage, Carey Perloff at the (San Francisco) American Conservatory Theatre, Martha Lavey at the (Chicago) Steppenwolf Theatre, Emily Mann at the (Princeton) McCarter Center, Bonnie Monte at the New Jersey Shakespeare Festival, Mary Robinson at the Philadelphia Drama Guild, and Lynne Meadow at the Manhattan Theatre Club. This is an astounding record of achievement in a field where, until three decades ago, women were largely invisible.

Meanwhile, over one hundred separate feminist theatre groups—groups of women presenting plays by, about, and for women—have been founded in the United States since 1970. The goal of each is to present plays concerning such issues as sex-role stereotyping, abortion, pregnancy, motherhood, rape, the mother-daughter relationship, lesbianism, domestic violence, historically important women, battered women, and women in prison. "The content of almost all feminist drama," says Elizabeth J. Natalle, "comes out of the personal lives of the theatre group members. Feminist theatre groups write their own drama, and the reality they depict comes from their own experience."[1] And from the experience not only of the actors, but of the audience as well, Natalle explains: "In feminist theatre the audience is more than just a passive body viewing the action on stage. . . . Audience members [play] an active role in the creation of a total theatre experience." Na-

Langston Hughes's Mule Bone, *written with Zora Neale Hurston in the "Harlem Renaissance" of the 1930s, did not make it to the Broadway stage until 1990, when the Lincoln Center Theatre company brought it to exuberant stage life. (Photo: Brigitte Lacombe.)*

talle goes on to show how, in a play about rape, for example, the audience is invited "to stop the play at any moment and give witness to their own rapes, both literal and metaphoric."

A Theatre of Color

It is a typically postmodern phenomenon that the leading American playwright of the late 1980s through the mid-1990s has been, without doubt, the African American August Wilson, whose *Ma Rainey's Black Bottom, Fences, The Piano Lesson, Joe Turner's Come and Gone, Two Trains Running,* and *Seven Guitars* are among the most powerful and evocative dramas of our times, concerning, as they do, an entire twentieth-century history of black America. But Wilson's plays have

---

[1]Elizabeth J. Natalle, *Feminist Theatre: A Study in Persuasion* (New York: Scarecrow Press, 1985), p. 21. I am also indebted to this work for the list of subjects covered in feminist theatre.

also been commercial "hits," playing to huge "crossover audiences" of blacks, whites, and members of all races, both on Broadway and in various American regional theatres; Wilson is certainly the most honored playwright of recent years (see discussion of American playwrights later in this chapter), yet he is but one of a number of minority voices that are surfacing in the theatre of the 1990s and beyond.

African-American Theatre An African-American theatre, which had intermittent successes in the earlier years of this century (Langston Hughes's *Mulatto* in the 1930s and Lorraine Hansberry's *A Raisin in the Sun* in the late 1950s), became a revolutionary force on the American stage with Amiri Baraka (then LeRoi Jones) in the early 1960s.

With his boldly defiant plays *Dutchman* and *The Toilet*, Baraka confronted American racism head on and did not shrink from its potentially violent ramifications, to which American society seemed to be potentially subject. In light of the 1965 Watts riots, Baraka's voice proved prophetic; in light of the 1992 Los Angeles uprisings, we can understand how the problems he revealed still have not been solved.

The Negro Ensemble Company, which was created by Douglas Turner Ward, and the New Lafayette Theatre in Harlem, with Ed Bullins as chief playwright-in-residence, soon followed Baraka's successes, inching the African-American experience into the global arts marketplace. In 1970 Charles Gordone's *No Place To Be Somebody,* produced by Joseph

African-American playwright Suzan-Lori Parks won a slot at the 1992 Humana New Play Festival at the Actors Theatre of Louisville, where her Devotees in the Garden of Love *was well received. Esther Scott (left) and Margarette Robinson are the actors. (Photo: Richard C. Trigg.)*

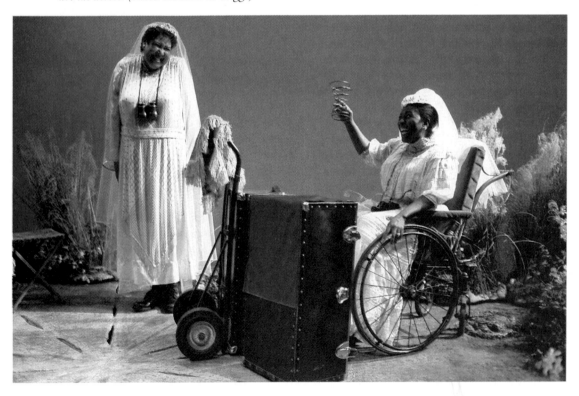

George C. Wolfe's Jelly's Last Jam *brilliantly pairs the "black musical" entertainment format with a serious and avant-garde exploration of African-American life. The play portrays the life and times of Creole jazz composer-performer Jelly Roll Morton. The staging, which is by Wolfe, employs both traditional musical comedy elements and neo-Brechtian stylizations. (Photo: Martha Swope and Associates/William Gibson.)*

Papp at the New York Public Theatre, won the Pulitzer Prize in drama, at once putting black and minority playwrights into the American forefront. Black authors achieving national success in subsequent years included Lonne Elder III (*Ceremonies in Dark Old Men*), Adrienne Kennedy (*Funnyhouse of a Negro*), and Ntozake Shange (*For Colored Girls Who Have Considered Suicide/When the Rainbow is Enuf*). Meanwhile, in Africa, a theatre of color reached another milestone when Nigerian dramatist Wole Soyinka received the Nobel Prize in literature in 1986.

On Broadway the 1970s inaugurated an era of lavishly produced black musicals that,

by the 1990s, included *Purlie, Bubbling Brown Sugar, The Wiz, Ain't Misbehavin', Sophisticated Ladies, Dreamgirls, Timbuktu, Once on This Island,* and *Five Guys Named Moe;* at many times during these years, African-American performers have constituted up to a third of the theatre artists on Broadway. And a merger of the Broadway black musical and more serious African-American theatre was achieved in 1992, with the audacious and remarkable *Jelly's Last Jam,* an exuberant but critical view of the life and career of Jelly Roll Morton, created by the brilliant writer-director George C. Wolfe, author of the previously well-regarded *The Colored Museum.*

With *Jelly's Last Jam,* Wolfe managed to captivate a near-universal audience: black and white, commercial and sophisticated, Broadway and avant-garde.

Many other colors, and other cultural voices, were raised in the postmodernist and experimental theatre of the 1980s and 90s.

Hispanic Theatre A Spanish-speaking theatre has existed in North America since the late sixteenth century; indeed, the first play ever staged in what is now the United States was *Los moros y los cristianos* (The Moors and the Christians) at the San Juan Pueblo outside of Santa Fe, then part of Mexico. By the mid-nineteenth century, serious and talented professional Mexican touring companies had established residence in Los Angeles and San Francisco and were touring to Texas, Arizona, and New Mexico by the century's end. On the East Coast at that time, Hispanic theatre—largely imported from Spain and Cuba—had established permanent beachheads in New York and Tampa, with stable Spanish-language companies presenting the classical plays of Calderón de la Barca and Lope de Vega, mixed with melodramas and *zarzuelas*—light operettas. Spanish-speaking theatre of this time largely served a community function, preserving traditional Hispanic culture in Anglo-dominated environments.

With the founding of El Teatro Campesino by Luis Valdez in 1965, however, a contemporary Chicano theatre, with a powerful creative and political thrust, burst into prominence in California and ultimately won national acclaim. Valdez, a Mexican American, created his Teatro with and for migrant farmworkers in California. "In a Mexican way," wrote Valdez in 1966, "we have discovered what Brecht is all about. If you want unbourgeois theatre, find unbourgeois people to do it." Valdez's short, didactic *actos* of the farmworker's situation have been performed—in English and in Spanish—on farms, in city squares, and, eventually, in theatres all over California, and on national and European tours as well; his full-length plays, *Zoot Suit* and *I Don't Have to Show You No Stinking Badges,* have played to major metropolitan audiences; and his film, *La Bamba,* has brought his Teatro to international acclaim (and some financial stability). "Our theatre work is simple, direct, complex and profound, but it works. In the heart, *el corazon,* of a way of life," Valdez explains.

El Teatro Campesino in one of its early, highly political performances. The stage is one that can quickly be set up in a dining or meeting hall.

Man of the Flesh, *by Octavio Solis, was directed by José Cruz Gonzalez at the South Coast Repertory Theatre, where Gonzalez heads the Hispanic Playwrights Workshop. (Photo: Cristofer Gross.)*

In M. Butterfly, *David Henry Hwang creatively explores Eastern and Western cultural relations and theatrical traditions. Chinese Opera alternates with American realism and the arias of Puccini in this fascinating drama. The Broadway production was directed by John Dexter, with John Lithgow (left) and B. D. Wong. (Photo: Martha Swope and Associates.)*

East-West Theatre The Eastern voice was epitomized in the American drama during the late 1980s by David Henry Hwang, whose *M. Butterfly* strikingly reinterpreted the "Madame Butterfly" myth, effectively exploding (if not completely displacing) the narrow and deprecatory "Orientalism" with which Occidental man stereotypes and misperceives Asian culture as the "Other." Hwang's incorporation of Peking Opera technique into Western drama draws on a tradition that predates postmodernism—Ezra Pound, Bertolt Brecht, W. S. Gilbert, and Antonin Artaud all drew heavily on Asian dramatic styles in their antinaturalistic works of the modernist period. But Hwang, who is of Asian (Chinese) background himself (see discussion later in this chapter), incorporates true Asian performers along with Western ones in this deliberately confrontational play, which poses East against West (and maleness against femaleness) in a continually informing, continually surprising way. Hwang's play brought postmodernism into the American theatre mainstream—as a certified Broadway "hit" spectacle.

In the same way as Hwang, French director Ariane Mnouchkine introduces Japanese Kabuki technique to her production of Shakespeare's *Richard II,* Indian Kathakali technique to her *Twelfth Night,* and Middle Eastern music and dancing to her production of Molière's *Tartuffe,* thereby setting each play's Western orientation in bold relief and universalizing many of the play's themes. Peter Brook's *Mahabharata,* employing an international cast—and performing in Paris and Los Angeles, in French and in English—avoids any hint of "quaintness" or "artsy-craftsy" patronization of this great Sanskrit epic. Instead, it is presented with its origins and contemporary realization precisely juxtaposed. Jerzy Grotowski trains an international group of performers in prehistoric "performance" techniques drawn from around the world, to create an "objective drama" that seeks to dissolve the unconsciously applied linguistic and cultural codes that separate human beings from their true biological (and, some might say, spiritual) selves. (Wilson, Wolfe, Hwang, Mnouchkine, and Brook are each discussed more fully later in this chapter.)

Theatre of Difference

Nor are gender and ethnicity the only bases for the new voices that have entered the mainstream of postmodern theatre. The issue of sexual preference had been buried deeply in the closet during most of the theatre's history, and as late as 1958 the representation of homosexuality was actually illegal in England and widely (if not legally) suppressed in America. The sexual preference that "dared not speak its name" came to the stage in those eras only through authors' implications and audiences' inferences, and gay playwrights such as Tennessee Williams, Gertrude Stein, Edward Albee, William Inge, and Gore Vidal were forced to speak—at certain critical moments in their work—only by innuendo and through oblique code words.

Gay and lesbian life—and gay/lesbian issues—were first directly treated as serious dramatic subjects in the late 1960s, particularly by Mart Crowley in his ground-breaking comedy *The Boys in the Band* (1968). Since that time, sexual-preference issues have become principal or secondary topics in hundreds of plays, including mainstream Broadway musicals (*La Cage Aux Folles, Falsettos, Aspects of Love, Kiss of the Spider Woman*), popular comedies (*Jeffrey, Party, Love! Valour! Compassion!*), and serious dramas (*Bent, M. Butterfly*). In the 1980s, in the wake of a new and terrible illness, a growing genre of AIDS plays (*The Normal Heart, As Is*) addressed the tragic human consequences of this disease, so particularly wrenching to the art and theatre world. And in 1992, Tony Kushner's extraordinary "gay fantasia on national themes," titled *Angels in America*, proved one of the most celebrated stage productions of the decade in both England and the United States. Sexual preference has emerged, in the 1990s, as a defining issue for many theatre groups, theatre festivals, and theatre publications, each seeking to examine the political, cultural, and aesthetic implications of gay- and lesbian-themed drama.

Paul Rudnick's Jeffrey *is a romantic comedy about gay life in (and despite) the age of AIDS. John Michael Higgens and Hank Stratton play the play's central couple. (Photo: William Gibson.)*

Persons differently abled are also represented in new theatre companies created specifically for these voices and for expanding audiences. Theatre By The Blind, in New York, employs sightless actors for all of its productions, and the National Theatre of the Deaf is only one of four American companies (Deaf West, Sign Rise Theatre, and the Fairmount Theater of the Deaf are the other three) that create theatre of and for the hearing-impaired, employing ASL (American Sign Language) as the primary verbal dramatic medium. With Mark Medoff's play *Children of a Lesser God,* the hearing-impaired found a mainstream audience, and a number of hearing-impaired actors and actresses found national recognition.

Theatre By The Blind's production of Lanford Wilson's Talley and Son. *From left: Susan Stevens, George Ashiotis, and Xenophon Thophall; the latter two are legally blind. Directed in New York City by Isaac Schambelain, TBTB's artistic director. (Photo: Martha Swope and Associates/Carol Rosegg.)*

Nontraditional Casting

Across the country, multicultural and cross-gender casting in the classics—once thought of as daring—has become routine, and the casting of differently abled actors in "non-disadvantaged" roles has become equally accepted. African Americans playing roles once "reserved" for whites, and women cast in roles initially "written for" men, have become commonplace. The New York Shakespeare Festival has employed blind interracial casting for years: Morgan Freeman played their most recent Petruchio, and Denzel Washington their most recent Richard III. Both Paris and New York saw female King Lears in the early 1990s, in celebrated productions, and female Hamlets have become almost as customary as male ones in cities at the theatre's cutting edge. At the Los Angeles Mark Taper Forum in 1992, Cassius in *Julius Caesar* was played by an African American, Casca by a woman, and Flavius and Marullus were renamed "Flavia" and "Marulla" to accommodate the actresses who performed them; these practices no longer even raise eyebrows, much less audience objection.

The racial diversification of the American theatre in the current era is not merely anecdotal; it can be measured by powerful statistics: in 1990–91, actors of color received more than 21 percent of the roles in America's regional professional theatre, almost double what had been the case only four years earlier and probably twenty times what it was twenty years ago. Nontraditional and cross-gendered casting may first have surfaced as a novelty; today, however, these practices boldly and routinely serve to echo the needs and interests of increasingly broadly based and multicultural artistic communities of artists and audiences.

Indeed, multiculturalism now reaches to the very center of world theatre. The experiments of Peter Brook and Jerzy Grotowski are among the most admired and most imitated in theatre capitals here and abroad. The theatres of Africa, South America, and the East have become principal topics in widely read international theatre publications, such as *Performing Arts Journal* and *The Drama Review*. The canon of past dramatic works is being exhumed and expanded—to "discover" women and minority voices that had been suppressed or ignored in the past. Revivals to-

Deaf actor Howie Seago signs to Cordelia González in Peter Sellars's staging of Aeschylus' The Persians at the Mark Taper Forum in Los Angeles. (Photo: Jay Thompson.)

day are likely to focus on recently unheralded female authors like Aphra Behn (one of the most prolific Restoration dramatists), Alice Brown, Rachel Crothers, Susan Glaspell, and Zoe Atkins and to demonstrate how women and minorities have often been neglected and marginalized in past cultural undertakings.

Theatres devoted to the exploration of minority voices are but one way to expand the canon with new works. Theatre companies such as the St. Louis Black Repertory Company, the Penumbra Theatre of St. Paul, the New Federal Theatre of New York, the Crossroads Theatre Company of New Brunswick (New Jersey), the Mixed Blood Theatre of Minneapolis, the Latino Chicago Theatre, El Teatro Campesino, the Traveling Jewish Theatre, the East West Players, the INTAR Hispanic American Arts Center in New York, Jomandi Productions of Atlanta, the National Jewish Theatre, the New Federal Theatre (New York), the Pan Asian Repertory Theatre, Repertorio Español, Czechoslovak-American Puppet Theatre, and Yueh Lung Shadow Theatre are only a few of the professional theatre companies seeking to make minority voices competitive in the American theatre world. And for each professional company, there are a dozen amateur and university companies now forming. It is abundantly clear, as we head into the new millennium, that the theatre will never again revert to the protected confines of a privileged elite. Nor can it live successfully in social isolation in some "underprivileged" ghetto. Ghettoization, at the top or bottom, has no place in the postmodern culture. One of the great achievements of the current era has been the relentless (if incomplete) democratization of art and the multiplicity (if not the integration) of struggling, and often competing, voices.

The theatre of today might, in fact, be entering its greatest phase. Certainly, in terms of sheer quantity, there is *more* theatre now than at any time in the past, and there is more interest in theatre. It is odd to think it was only a few decades ago, when developments in cinema and television were much before the public eye, that it became fashionable to consider the theatre a dying art form, a "fabulous invalid" doomed by its technological backwardness and the yoke of tradition. Theatre has not just survived, but it has also thrived. The box-office income just for the Broadway production of *Miss Saigon* during its opening season exceeded the home-ticket income for the New York Yankees and Mets *combined* during the same year. The number of professional plays mounted in the United States every year is vastly greater than the number of professional films made for cinema and television combined, and the number of amateur theatrical events simply boggles the imagination.

Nor is all of this limited to the major theatrical venues: most large cities in the United States and Canada—those with a population of a quarter million or more—have at least one professional theatre, plus at least half a dozen amateur, college, or community theatres. European, South American, and Asian cities are the same; most European countries enjoy a wide range of publicly supported national and municipal theatres, plus, in most cases, commercial theatres and cabaret theatres as well. The Eastern world is no less theatrically active: one expert maintains that there "are more different types of theatre being performed simultaneously in Tokyo than in any other city in the world." The theatre has more than challenged the great boom of electronic media; it has triumphed. And its triumphs are there to be experienced on any given night of the theatrical season.

WHERE IT'S HAPPENING

The current theatre happens all over the world: in rural villages, summer resorts, exurban dinner theatres, festival towns, classrooms, prisons, and civil auditoriums; atop mobile street trestles; within ancient palaces; aboard ocean liners—even, in the case of one recent Russian production, inside an interurban railway car.

The very popular "TKTS booth" in New York's Duffy Square (Broadway at 47th Street—the heart of the New York theatre district) sells unsold tickets at a 25 percent or 50 percent discount for most Broadway and off-Broadway shows on the afternoon of the performance only. (Photo: Robert Cohen.)

But mostly the current theatre is "celebrated" in the cities—in the traditionally great theatrical capitals such as New York, Moscow, London, Paris, Vienna, Tokyo, and Berlin, as well as in cities of more modest theatrical repute, such as Kyoto, Zurich, Hamburg, Edinburgh, Buenos Aires, Helsinki, Mexico City, Cracow, Chicago, San Francisco, Seattle, Minneapolis, New Haven, Louisville, Los Angeles, Hartford, Boston, and Washington, D.C.

In the United States, New York City is without question the center of the nation's theatrical activity. Every year it is the site of more performances, more openings, more revivals, more tours, and more dramatic criticism than any half-dozen other American cities put together. Theatrically, it is the showcase of the nation. In the minds of many

Americans, the "Big Apple" is *the* place to experience theatre; thus the New York theatre is a prime tourist attraction and a major factor in the city's economy. In the minds of theatre artists—actors, directors, playwrights, and designers—New York is the town where the standards are the highest, the challenge is the greatest, and the rewards are the most magnificent. "Will it play in Peoria?" may be the big question in the minds of film and television producers, but "Will it make it in New York?" remains a cardinal issue in the rarefied world of American professional theatre. Therefore the reality of New York is surrounded by a fantasy of New York, and in a "business" as laced with fantasy as is the theatre, New York commands a strategic importance of incomprehensible value in the theatrical world.

Crazy for You is only one of several Broadway musicals set right on Broadway
that are mining the venerable vein of show-business nostalgia. This 1992 adaptation of an older Gershwin show is set in the 1930s, in front of the "Zangler Follies," an obvious reference to the famous Ziegfeld show whose motto was
"Glorifying the American girl." Here, with the chorus of "Zangler girls," is
Harry Groener as Bobby. (Photo: Joan Marcus.)

Broadway

Broadway is the longest street in Manhattan,
slicing diagonally down the entire length of
the island; the world knows it, however,
mainly for its cluster of thirty-some theatres
congregated in the dozen blocks north of
Times Square, at 42nd Street. This has been
the "Great White Way" of the American theatre since the first years of the century: the
place where Eugene O'Neill, Arthur Miller,
Tennessee Williams, William Inge, and Edward Albee all saw their masterpieces first produced; where memories of George M. Cohan,
Ethel Merman, Mary Martin, and Barbra
Streisand—"Broadway Babies" all—sang and
danced; and where John Barrymore, Marlon
Brando, Helen Hayes, Ingrid Bergman, Shirley Booth, Audrey Hepburn, Henry Fonda,

Alfred Lunt, Lynn Fontanne, and thousands
of others acted their way into America's
hearts—and, most of them, into Hollywood's
films.

But these romantic memories must be
set aside with the explosive urban scene that
Broadway is today. There is little that is sentimental or glamorous about Times Square
now: it's the home of sex shops, crack houses,
porno movie theatres, tourist emporia, video-
game parlors, and even more raucously sleazy
enterprises, which vie with each other, and
with the Broadway theatres, for each passer-
by's attention. Urban redevelopment, currently in progress, has promised to tame this
raffish district of its bawdier ways, but Broadway will clearly remain a glitzy, sleazy, allur-
ingly dangerous locale for years to come.
Broadway's lure is its dazzling visual and

THE BROADWAY MUSICAL: A GOLDEN AGE

The Broadway musical, or musical comedy as it used to be called, is often described as America's greatest contribution to the theatre; certainly the hundreds of musical plays that have flourished on Broadway since the 1900 production of *Floradora* have included America's most spectacular stagings and most lucrative commercial successes. Some have also been considered works of true dramatic art.

The musical—a dramatic play with an integrated musical score, often lavishly produced, whose characters both sing and dance—has been a feature of the American stage at least since 1866, when *The Black Crook* was staged at Niblo's Garden in New York City. English imports, including Leslie Stuart's *Floradora* and the operettas of Gilbert and Sullivan (*The Pirates of Penzance, The Mikado,* etc.), as well as light operas from the European continent (Victor Herbert's *Naughty Marietta,* Franz Lehar's *The Merry Widow*) competed with the American product in the years prior to World War I. After that war, however, a particularly American style of musical theatre emerged, and from then until the 1960s Broadway artists created, and all America enjoyed, a golden age of musicals.

There were two distinct phases of this golden age. In the first, "musical comedy" reigned. George Gershwin's *Lady Be Good, Strike Up the Band, Girl Crazy,* and *Of Thee I Sing;* Vincent Youman's *No, No, Nanette;* Jerome Kern's *Sunny;* Cole Porter's *Anything Goes;* and a series of musical comedies by Richard Rodgers (music) and Lorenz Hart (lyrics), including *A Connecticut Yankee, On Your Toes,* and *Babes in Arms,* employed strictly comedic plots and characters, invariably on a trivial theme, all to be enlivened by a lot of singing and dancing, much usually incidental to the play. A growing seriousness, however, plus an increasing integration of plot and musical treatment, enabled the musical form to gain stature and importance. *Of Thee I Sing* received the 1932 Pulitzer Prize

in drama, as much for its political satire as its entertaining cleverness; and Jerome Kern's "Ol' Man River" from *Showboat* became one of the great pieces of acted (as opposed to merely sung) vocal literature in the twentieth century—as did George Gershwin's entire score from the folk opera *Porgy and Bess* (1935).

The second phase of the golden age of musicals is usually dated from Rodgers and Hart's brilliant *Pal Joey* (1939), adapted from some grimly ironic stories by John O'Hara and featuring an amoral gigolo and his often unsavory companions in a musical pastiche of the contemporary urban nightclub scene. Tame by today's standards, *Joey* shocked prewar audiences with its blithely suggestive lyrics about sexual infidelity and shady business ethics and with a show-stopping song belted out by an intellectual stripteaser—who sang out her thoughts while doing her act. Many serious musicals followed, straining the word "comedy" out of the musical's nomenclature. *Lady in the Dark* (1941), with a book by dramatist Moss Hart and with music by Kurt Weill (the Bertolt Brecht colleague who, like Brecht, had fled to America from Nazi rule in Germany) concerned itself with psychoanalysis and dream analysis. *Oklahoma!* (1943), with music by Richard Rodgers and lyrics by Oscar Hammerstein II, dealt with social and sexual tensions in the opening of the western states; the musical featured brilliantly integrated dance choreography by Agnes de Mille and treated its historical subject with romantic passion and a new level of social intensity.

During the late 1940s and 50s, Broadway musicals dominated the commercial American theatre. Rodgers and Hammerstein followed *Oklahoma!* with one success after another: *Carousel, South Pacific, The King and I,* and *The Sound of Music,* all marked with some social (even intercultural) conflict, richly romantic settings and songs, beautiful solo numbers and love duets, and thrilling choral, choreographic, and orchestral ensembles. Frank Loesser's *Guys and Dolls,* based on the idiosyncratic stories of Damon Runyon, also proved immensely popular, as did Cole Porter's *Kiss Me Kate,* based on Shakespeare's *Taming of the Shrew,* and Irving Berlin's *Annie Get Your Gun,* based on the life of American folk heroine Annie Oakley. Leonard Bernstein, one of America's leading orchestral conductors and composers, also left a considerable mark on the musical's golden age with his *On the Town* and *West Side Story.* Alan Jay Lerner (book and lyrics) and Frederick Loewe (music) first successfully collaborated with the fantasy *Brigadoon,* about a mythical Scottish village, and then with their brilliant musical revision of Shaw's *Pygmalion,* which they called *My Fair Lady.*

The Broadway musical during its golden age was broadly influential. Plays ran not for weeks or months, but for years; for the first time, theatre tickets were sold up to six months in advance, and business travelers returning from New York City were expected to provide a full report on "the new musical in town." Touring companies brought the best musicals to the countryside: first-class national tours, with the Broadway stars, and, subsequently, "bus and truck" tours with less well known performers—nonetheless advertising "straight from Broadway!" Perhaps most Americans in these years first experienced live theatre in the form of a road version of a Broadway musical. Songs from the musicals routinely made the "hit parade" (forerunner of the "top ten" or "top forty" listings of today); films of the musical plays were widely popular; and, for a couple of decades, it seemed as if everyone in America was whistling the latest creation from the tunesmiths of Shubert Alley. Performers made famous by the musicals they starred in—performers such as Mary Martin, Alfred Drake, Ethel Merman, Julie Andrews, Rex Harrison, Yul Brynner, Carol Channing, John Raitt—became national celebrities and the pioneer performers on America's new entertainment medium, television. It is certain that the theatre had never played such a central role in American popular culture before; it is questionable if it ever shall again.

Musical drama has continued to develop in the decades since the 1970s, but it is rarely a "Broadway" creation any more and is no longer dominated by American artists; there can be little doubt but that the golden age has fragmented into more sporadic and diverse efforts. Stephen Sondheim is clearly the reigning genius in today's American musical theatre, and his work gets special discussion in this chapter. There have also been some outstanding individual American musicals in the past twenty years: Marvin Hamlisch's *A Chorus Line,* James Lapine and William Finn's *Falsettos,* and George C. Wolfe's *Jelly's Last Jam,* among several others. But the most successful musicals running on Broadway in the 1980s and 90s have, so far, tended to be revivals from the earlier era (full-scale revivals of such American musical classics as *Show Boat, Gypsy, Guys and Dolls, Carousel, Company, Grease, How to Succeed in Business Without Really Trying,* and *Girl Crazy*—retitled *Crazy for You*—were the big hits of the 1990s), and the spectacular British musicals of Andrew Lloyd Webber (*Jesus Christ Superstar, Evita, Cats, Starlight Express, Phantom of the Opera, Aspects of Love, Sunset Boulevard*), plus the French-British musicals of Alain Boublil and Claude-Michel Schönberg (*Les Misérables, Miss Saigon*). Broadway has also seen Polish (*Metro*), South African (*Sarafina*), and various Asian musicals in recent years. American musicals will undoubtedly flourish in the future, but they must now compete on an increasingly international scene.

social excitement; its heady mix of bright lights and famed celebrities; its trend-setting fashions, big-buck entertainments, and high-toned Tony Awards. The stakes are higher on Broadway than anywhere else, and the money is dicier: the gross annual Broadway box-office "take" comes in at over $400,000,000 for the twelve or fourteen city blocks. If you make it here, as the song says, you make it anywhere, and the energy that this lyric connotes—and attracts—makes the Broadway district unforgettably fascinating.

It has been a long time, however, since Broadway passed as a district known for its intellectual or artistic innovation, and few of the theatre's brilliant achievements find their first staging here. Rather, the Broadway theatre has become the place of origin only for spectacular musicals or the occasional star-heavy revival of an American classic (such as Jessica Lange and Alec Baldwin in the 1992 version of Williams's *A Streetcar Named Desire*).

The serious new plays coming to Broadway in the mid-1990s are, almost without exception, works that garnered their first rave reviews and standing ovations at one of America's many regional and/or nonprofit theatres such as the Mark Taper Forum's *Angels in America* (Tony Kushner) and *The Kentucky Cycle* (Robert Schenkkan), the Seattle Repertory Theatre's *The Heidi Chronicles* and *The Sisters Rosensweig* (both Wendy Wasserstein) and *Conversations with My Father* (Herb Gardner), the Goodman Theatre's *Seven Guitars* (August Wilson) and *The Grapes of Wrath* (Frank Galati, adapted from John Steinbeck), and the Manhattan Theatre Club's *Love! Valour! Compassion!* (Terrence McNally). Or the play might be a transfer from England, such as Tom Stoppard's *Arcadia*, J. B. Priestly's *An Inspector Calls*, or *The Buddy Holly Story*. The latter production proved a special embarrassment for the American theatre, because the subject was strictly American rock and roll music. For new drama, Broadway has become the nation's second stage, not its first.

Tony Kushner's brilliant, two-part Angels in America *is thought by many critics to be the finest American play in years or even decades. A complex work of comedy, sagacity, and fantasy, it casts a wicked eye on American politics, religion, economics, medicine, and racial and sexual bigotry—but it is also a moving story of human affection and alienation. Here an angel visits Prior Walter, who is dying of AIDS, in the 1993 Broadway production. (Photo: Joan Marcus.)*

It is quite clear why this is so. Broadway is America's premier *commercial* theatre, and plays mounted there must pay their costs, and make their profits, mainly from box-office income. But the costs of producing on Broadway have grown astronomically over the past three decades. City real estate values, the escalating payroll demands in a labor-intensive, highly unionized business, and the huge expenses of New York advertising have priced even the simplest Broadway production well into seven figures. But the chances of recouping those costs (not to mention making a

The Buddy Holly Story, *a foot-stomping Broadway revue of rock-and-roller Buddy Holly's life and music, was in fact an English import. Paul Hipp, shown here, played Buddy on both sides of the Atlantic. (Photo: Martha Swope and Associates.)*

profit) are, if anything, more slender than ever, particularly with a "straight" (that is, nonmusical) play. Despite ticket prices that in 1996 ascended to upwards of $65 a ticket for straight dramas, and (in one case) $100 for musicals, most new productions on Broadway are, in fact, financial failures. Increasingly, therefore, Broadway producers await the new plays whose worth is first "proven" in the subsidized European (chiefly English) theatre, or on the not-for-profit American regional stage. Only the star-studded revival, or new musical, is likely to be "bankable" and offer sufficient opportunity for commercial success in these financially difficult times. And Broadway, once the flagship of the American theatre, is biding time as its museum. Perhaps new renovations—the restoration, now in process, of three historic theatres on 42nd Street, one under the Disney aegis—will give bold new impetus to America's traditional theatre district. One can hope.

Off-Broadway and Off-Off-Broadway

Not all of New York theatre is performed within the geographic and commercial confines of the Broadway district: distinctly non-Broadway theatres have operated in the nation's largest city for many decades. The symbolic centrality of Broadway, however, is so strong that these theatres are named not for what they are, but for what they are not: they are the *off-Broadway* theatres. "Off-Broadway" is a term that came into theatrical parlance during the 1950s. It refers to professional theatres operating on significantly reduced budgets. They are found primarily in Greenwich Village, in the area south of Houston Street ("SoHo"), and on the upper East and West sides of Manhattan. A few houses in the Broadway geographic area itself fall into this category, but only because they operate under off-Broadway financing structures. Yet another category of theatre is known as *off-off-Broadway,* a term dating from the 1960s. This category consists of semiprofessional or wholly amateur theatres that are located throughout the metropolitan area, often in church basements, YMCAs, coffeehouses, and converted studios or garages.

The off-Broadway and off-off-Broadway theatres generate a great deal of fertile and vigorous activity; leaner and less costly than the Broadway stage, they attract specialized cadres of devotees, some of whom would never allow themselves to be seen in a Broadway house. Much of the original creative work in the American theatre since World War II has been done in these theatres, and their generally low ticket prices have lured successive generations of theatre audiences their way to see original works before they are showcased to the Broadway masses, works still raw with creative energy and radiating the excitement of their ongoing development.

In composite, Broadway and non-Broadway theatres provide almost every conceivable opportunity for theatrical exploration and achievement. Between them, they present in season about fifty professional and one hundred amateur productions *each night;* they also mount close to a thousand new productions each year. Their offerings are a great conglomeration of original scripts, classical revivals, opulent musicals, provocative imports, and a basic collection of workmanlike thrillers, reviews, comedies, and holdover dramas. What is more, thanks to extensive press coverage in the national media—weekly news magazines, monthly journals of opinion, television talk shows and specials, and the annual televising of the Tony Awards ceremonies— the New York theatrical season does not long remain a strictly local phenomenon: it becomes a centerpiece of American cultural activity, and before long the world is privy to its innovations, its successes, its radical ideas, its catastrophes, and its gossip.

The Nonprofit Professional Theatre

But the nonprofit professional theatre is where, in the last decades of the twentieth century, America's theatre is truly happening.

The nonprofit theatre, often called the "regional" or "resident" theatre (because the theatres generally are in "regions" outside of New York, with "resident" staffs and at least some resident company members), is a phenomenon of the last third of the century, an outpouring of theatrical activity that at first diversified the American theatre and has since improved it.

Nonprofit means noncommercial; the nonprofit theatres have in common at least one funding source other than the box office: government grants, foundation or corporate support, private donations, or a combination of these. The nonprofit designation is a legal one: the theatre has no owners, makes no profit, and is exempt from most taxes—and donors to the theatre receive tax deductions for their gifts. But, although noncommercial, these are professional theatres in every sense,

employing professional artists, often exclusively, at every level. There were no such theatres at the end of World War II. There are over two hundred today, and they exist in every major city in America—including New York City. They produce over a thousand productions each year, giving tens of thousands of performances, and provide Americans in every part of the country an opportunity to see professional theatre, often at its best.

Nonprofit theatres vary enormously in character: some concentrate on classics, some on the contemporary international repertoire, others on new American plays. Some operate on tiny stages with tiny budgets and, while engaging professional artists, reduce costs by negotiating salary waivers with the professional unions. Other theatres operate several stages simultaneously and are enormous operations: the New York Shakespeare Festival has an annual budget of more than ten million dollars and often has its productions running all over the city.

Some of the most distinguished of the nonprofit theatre companies in recent years are described in the following paragraphs.

Boston The *American Repertory Theatre,* actually in Cambridge, was founded by Robert Brustein in 1980. Taking some of his colleagues from the Yale Repertory Theatre (discussed later) when he left, Brustein created his award-winning ART in Harvard University's Loeb Drama Center; the company also operates a smaller theatre facility nearby. The ART has been one of America's most experimental companies since its founding and has been known particularly for giving free rein to many of the most experimental directors working in the United States—including Andrei Serban, Peter Sellars, Adrian Hall, Jonathan Miller, Anne Bogart, Susan Sontag, Des McAnuff, JoAnne Akalaitis, and Robert Wilson.

ART won the 1986 Tony Award for its history of ground-breaking, controversial productions, including, in the late 1980s and early 1990s, JoAnne Akalaitis's revisionist version of Samuel Beckett's *Endgame*, Andrei Serban's updated classics (Shakespeare's *Twelfth Night* and Molière's *The Miser*), Adrien Hall's *King Lear,* and Robert Wilson's visually magnificent performance pieces: Euripides' *Alcestis,* Ibsen's *When We Dead Awaken,* and fragments of Wilson's own opus—still unproduced in full—*The CIVIL warS.*

Chicago   The *Goodman Theatre,* which won the 1992 Tony Award for regional companies, is Chicago's oldest and largest nonprofit theatre. Originally founded in 1925 by the Chicago Art Institute, it operates two theatres in a building adjacent to the famous museum and also produces plays elsewhere in the city. The theatre is known for its production of new plays, particularly those of Chicago native David Mamet, who has been an in-residence playwright and whose award-winning *American Buffalo, Glengarry Glen Ross,* and *A Life of the Theatre* were first seen there. The Goodman also premiered David Rabe's *Hurlyburly,* which went on to a major Broadway success, and Scott McPherson's *Marvin's Room,* which was reprised off-Broadway to win the 1992 Drama Desk Award for outstanding new play.

After more than twenty years in a small (211-seat) North Chicago theatre facility, the exceptionally vigorous *Steppenwolf Theatre Company* moved, in the early 1990s, into a 510-seat mainstage theatre. A collective company (seven of the nine founding members remain with the company today), Steppenwolf is known internationally for its intense naturalistic acting and has pioneered in what is frequently called a new "Chicago style" of fervently emotional performances. The actors Gary Sinese, Joan Allen, and John Malkovich are among Steppenwolf's major talents; the Frank Galati adaptation of John Steinbeck's *The Grapes of Wrath,* premiering at Steppenwolf, received the 1990 Tony Award upon its Broadway transfer. In 1995

The Steppenwolf Theatre Company is known for intense acting performances. Here Danny Glover (left) and Francis Guinan enjoy a nervous laugh prior to breaking into a shattering battle in a 1986 production of Athol Fugard's A Lesson from Aloes. *(Photo: Lisa Ebright.)*

Martha Lavey became artistic director of the Steppenwolf Company.

Louisville   *Actors Theatre of Louisville,* founded in 1964, came to national prominence under the artistic leadership of Jon Jory. The ATL national recognition has come from its annual Humana Festival of new plays, in which five to ten new plays are produced simultaneously, attracting an audience of theatre critics from all over the country. Many of these plays, including *The Gin Game, Getting Out, Crimes of the Heart, Agnes of God, Ex-*

tremities, Talking With, and *Execution of Justice,* have enjoyed long subsequent lifetimes in the national repertory, and José Rivera's 1992 *Marisol* has enjoyed subsequent success in New York, Chicago, San Diego, and other regional theatres. Meanwhile, since 1986, an annual ATL "Classics in Context" festival has brought the Moscow Art Theatre, the Berliner Ensemble, and members of Milan's Teatro Piccolo to Louisville, where these artists collaborate with the resident company to re-explore classic theatre works, and historically important acting theories and practices, in the context of contemporary American thinking and culture. The ATL is one of the first American companies to attempt this infusion of scholarship with theatre production, which is more usually observed in the European government-subsidized theatre.

Los Angeles The *Mark Taper Forum* was founded in 1967 by Gordon Davidson, who continues to serve as artistic director. The Forum is celebrated primarily for its production of new American plays, many of which have subsequently received national recognition. These include George C. Wolfe's *Jelly's Last Jam,* Robert Schenkkan's Pulitzer Prize–winning *The Kentucky Cycle* (first created in workshop form at the Taper, then expanded to its present length at Seattle's Intiman Theatre), Mark Medoff's *Children of a Lesser God,* Luis Valdez's *Zoot Suit,* Marsha Norman's *Getting Out,* Michael Christopher's *The Shadow Box,* and Daniel Berrigan's *The Trial of the Catonsville Nine;* these works constitute a remarkable diversity of authorial interests and backgrounds. Located in America's film and television capital, the Taper occasionally attracts internationally prominent actors for its productions, including Jack Lemmon and Walter Matthau, who costarred in Sean O'Casey's *Juno and the Paycock,* as well as well-known television stars available during the springtime hiatus between TV seasons: in 1992 Kelsey Grammer played the title role in the Taper's *Richard II.*

And, forty-five miles south of Los Angeles, the *South Coast Repertory Theatre* vies for attention with its only slightly older rival (the Taper) to the north. SCR was founded by David Emmes and Martin Benson, who are still the company's artistic codirectors, as an amateur touring company in 1964; the then-tiny group enjoyed its first "permanent" home a year later in a small abandoned boat-repair

The Guthrie Theatre's 1990 production of Richard II, *directed by Garland Wright. (Photo: Michael Daniel.)*

shop in Newport Beach and now occupies its own sumptuous, two-stage facility in Costa Mesa. SCR's success story has been built on excellent productions, a devotion to community relations, and, above all, a superb knack at finding (or commissioning) outstanding new plays. Craig Lucas's *Prelude to A Kiss,* commissioned by SCR, went on to become a Broadway success. The company's record for sending new plays to New York expanded mightily in the 1991–92 season, when New York producers mounted no less than three SCR-premiered American plays: Howard Korder's *Search and Destroy,* Donald Margulies's *Sight Unseen,* and Richard Greenberg's *The Extra Man.* South Coast was awarded the Tony for regional theatres in 1988.

Minneapolis The *Guthrie Theatre,* founded by the celebrated English director Tyrone Guthrie in 1963, has gained a distinguished record of classical theatre productions under a variety of managements. Nationally noted early productions included Aeschylus' *Oresteia,* directed by Guthrie in 1967, and Shakespeare's *The Tempest* and *A Midsummer Night's Dream,* directed by the company's second artistic director, the Romanian Liviu Ciulei, in the early 1980s. The Guthrie's third artistic director, Garland Wright, has recently overseen a successful $25 million endowment drive and has created a permanent acting company, permitting the compilation of elaborately coordinated and epic-scale productions of Shakespeare's interrelated histories (*Richard II, Henry IV,* etc.) and the various Clytemnestra plays written by the three ancient Greek tragedians. "We at the Guthrie firmly commit our efforts to artistic excellence at every level, to the greatest plays of the world repertoire, to the actor as the central communicator of the ideas and the poetry within those plays, and to the imagination and its transforming power," says Wright. In 1996 Joe Dowling, formerly artistic director at Dublin's Abbey Theatre, assumed the Guthrie helm.

New Haven The *Long Wharf Theatre,* founded in 1965, has become widely known for its fine, sensitive productions of midcentury American and English classics, often staged by Long Wharf's artistic director, Arvin Brown. Several of these have subsequently moved to New York, including outstanding presentations of Arthur Miller's *A View from the Bridge* and *Broken Glass,* Eugene O'Neill's *Long Day's Journey into Night,* Simon Gray's *Quartermain's Terms,* and Rod Serling's *Requiem for a Heavyweight.*

Frank Langella plays Junius Booth cradling son Edwin in the Long Wharf Theatre 1991 production of Austin Pendleton's historical play, Booth Is Back, *directed by Long Wharf's artistic director, Arvin Brown. The Booths were America's greatest acting family, and Edwin America's greatest Hamlet, until Edwin's brother, John Wilkes, assassinated President Lincoln. (Photo: T. Charles Erickson.)*

Yale Repertory Theatre was founded in 1966 by Robert Brustein as an adjunct to the Yale University School of Drama. New Haven is fortunate to have two world-class professional theatres; YRT is generally more adventurous than the Long Wharf and became known, when Lloyd Richards assumed the artistic leadership in 1979, as the first American home of the widely celebrated plays of South African Athol Fugard (*A Lesson from Aloes, Master Harold . . . And the Boys, The Road to Mecca*), Nigerian Wole Soyinka (*A Play of Giants*), and American playwright August Wilson (*Ma Rainey's Black Bottom, Fences, The Piano Lesson, Joe Turner's Come and Gone,* and *Two Trains Running.*) In 1991–92 Stan Wojewodski, Jr., took over the helm as the YRT's third artistic director, stating as his goal the creation of "a theatre always teeming with ideas, the ripest and readiest of which can then be born to the public view."

New York City The *New York Shakespeare Festival* was founded by Joseph Papp in 1954 with the goal of presenting free Shakespeare productions on trestles in Central Park. By the time Papp died in 1991, the company was operating six performance spaces in its downtown Public Theatre, plus the huge outdoor Delacorte Theatre in Central Park. NYSF has also toured plays around the city and managed full-scale Broadway transfers of several of its successful productions, including *A Chorus Line, The Pirates of Penzance, The Mystery of Edwin Drood, That Championship Season, Much Ado About Nothing,* and *Plenty.* Indeed, the festival has unquestionably been the most important single American theatre-producing agency since the 1970s.

NYSF has spawned, in addition to transferred-to-Broadway successes, a wide variety of new plays, including David Rabe's *The Basic Training of Pavlo Hummel,* Reinaldo Povod's *Cuba and His Teddy Bear,* Eric Bogosian's *Talk Radio,* and Ntozake Shange's *For Colored Girls Who Have Considered Suicide/When the Rainbow is Enuf,* as well as

novel or experimental stagings, such as Gerald Freedman's stunning "Chaplinesque" production of *The Taming of the Shrew* and the John Guare–Mel Shapiro musical version of *Two Gentlemen of Verona;* Richard Foreman's "post-Brechtian" production of *The Threepenny Opera,* starring Raul Julia as Macheath; a well-received *Hamlet,* directed by, and starring, Kevin Kline; the late A. J. Antoon's opulent productions of *A Midsummer Night's Dream* (set in Brazil) and *The Taming of the Shrew* (with Morgan Freeman as Petruchio and Tracey Ullman as Kate); and a thrilling 1992 version of *'Tis Pity She's a Whore,* directed by JoAnne Akalaitis and starring Val Kilmer.

Despite its commercial successes, the Festival retains its goal of producing high-quality professional productions for a broadly based public audience, and it continues to present

Eric Bogosian wrote and starred in Talk Radio, *produced here by the New York Shakespeare Festival at its downtown Public Theatre. The play is a searing, scathing study of an embittered radio host, at war with the world—and with himself. (Photo: © George E. Joseph.)*

its outdoor summer productions, often employing major stars, with no admission charge. The company is also very devoted to interracial and cross-gender casting and to the representation of the widest possible variety of ethnic, racial, and "different" voices. Shortly following Papp's death, one of its leading experimental directors, JoAnne Akalaitis, was appointed artistic director of the company; in 1993 George Wolfe succeeded her.

Seattle With seven theatre companies operating under Actors Equity Association contracts, and an exploding fringe theatre scene, Seattle has arguably become the hottest theatre city on the West Coast. Its major stages include the Intiman Theatre, which mounted the first full-length production of the 1992 Pulitzer Prize–winning *The Kentucky Cycle,* the avant-garde Empty Space (a theatre of "offbeat eclecticism," which is "devoted to the exploration of cutting-edge works and unusual classics"), and A Contemporary Theatre, focusing on playwrights. But the theatre with the largest national reputation is undoubtedly the *Seattle Repertory Theatre,* whose productions of Bill Irwin's *Largely New York,* Wendy Wasserstein's *The Heidi Chronicles* and *The Sisters Rosensweig,* and Herb Gardner's *Conversations with My Father* (the latter three directed by Seattle Rep's artistic director, Daniel Sullivan) went on to notable Broadway successes and, in the case of *Heidi,* the Pulitzer Prize and the Tony Award for best new American drama. In 1991–92, the Seattle Rep joined with New York's Circle Repertory Theatre to create the premiere of Lanford Wilson's *Redwood Curtain* before the New York "reopening." The Seattle Rep is also one of the growing number of American theatres that employs a resident acting company for an entire season, thus permitting actors to enjoy relatively long-term employment in the same city.

San Francisco The *American Conservatory Theatre* was founded as a touring company by William Ball in 1965 and settled in San Francisco shortly thereafter. From the beginning, it set a high standard for brilliantly staged and performed revivals of theatre classics, and for the integration of teaching (through its conservatory) and actual performing. This true "conservatory theatre" also won great admiration for its adoption of a true rotating repertory schedule, where many different plays would alternate in a night-by-night schedule, permitting visitors to San Francisco to see up to half a dozen plays at the same theatre in the space of a week's visit. Sagging income and political infighting, however, plus the resignation of Mr. Ball from the theatre's management in 1986 (he died in 1991), and then the devastating earthquake of 1989, which closed the company's principal facility, the Geary Theatre, have all set ACT scrambling in recent years. Undaunted, the theatre's new director, Carey Perloff, is patiently and vigorously rebuilding the company and its facilities and conservatory to what one hopes will again be world-class levels; happily, the earthquake-rattled Geary Theatre was restored for a triumphant reopening in early 1996.

Washington, D.C. The *Arena Stage* was founded by Zelda Fitchandler in 1950. Fitchandler served as producing director through the 1990–91 season, when, following her resignation, Douglas C. Wager took over the Arena's helm. The Arena retains the novelty of its name, with in-the-round staging (the audience seated on all four sides of the stage) for its primary performance space, "the arena." But the company has also added three non-arena performance facilities to supplement its primary one.

The Arena has had a long history of success. As the leading theatre in the national capital, it has lived up to its particular challenge with a series of outstanding classical and new productions, which include the world or American premieres of several important plays such as William Sackler's *The Great White Hope,* Christopher Durang's *A History of the*

American Film, Michael Weller's *Moonchildren,* and Dario Fo's *Accidental Death of an Anarchist.* The Arena has increasingly been dedicated to echoing the racial and ethnic mix of its hometown and proudly emphasizes its "longstanding commitment to encourage participation by people of color in every aspect of the theatre's life. . . . We seek to create a vibrant emotional and intellectual theatrical landscape that, through storytelling, probes the infinite mystery of the human experience."

This is merely a sampling of important American nonprofit theatres; many others are equally distinctive. The Alliance Theatre of Atlanta, the Cleveland Playhouse, the La Jolla (California) Playhouse, the Alley Theatre of Houston, the Center Theatre of Baltimore, the Wisdom Bridge Theatre of Chicago, the Milwaukee Repertory Theatre, the Denver Theatre Center, the Berkeley Repertory Theatre, the Indiana Repertory Theatre, the Missouri Repertory Theatre, the Philadelphia Drama Guild, and the Alabama Shakespeare Festival are all notable theatre companies that have created excellent productions over the years for their communities and have had substantial influence in the theatre world well beyond their local confines. The Goodspeed Opera House in East Haddam, Connecticut, has pioneered in the production of American musicals (it created the original *Annie*) and particularly the revival of several rarely produced American musicals, including *No, No, Nanette, Very Good Eddie, Fanny,* and a 1991 two-piano revival of Frank Loesser's great *Most Happy Fella,* which, like many of the Goodspeed revivals, went on to great success on Broadway. And there are other nonprofit theatres with focused repertoires—such as El Teatro Campesino, Pan Asian Repertory Theatre, Mixed Blood Theatre Company, National Jewish Theatre, Crossroads Theatre Company, and St. Louis Black Repertory Company, all mentioned earlier—that provide, throughout America's many regions, an extraordinary variety of theatrical art, involvement, and excitement.

The nonprofit professional theatre, which was a "movement" during the 1960s and 70s has become, quite simply, America's theatre: it is the theatre where America's plays are first shaped and first exposed to the American audience. More and more, the national press is attuned to the major theatre happenings in the nonprofit sector; more and more the Broadway audience, while admiring the latest "hit," is aware that they are seeing that hit's second, third, or fourth production. National theatre prizes, once awarded only for New York productions, are now seized by theatres around the country; world-renowned actors, once seen live only on the Broadway stages and on tour, are appearing in the country's two hundred nonprofit regional theatres.

Most important: for the first time in America's history, the vast majority of individuals throughout the country can see first-class professional theatre created in or near their hometowns, and professional theatre artists can live in any major city in the country—not only in New York.

Shakespeare Festivals

In the heyday of Broadway there was also "summer stock," a network of theatres, mainly located in resort areas through the mountains of the Northeast, which provided summer entertainment for tourists and assorted local folks. This "straw hat circuit," as it was called, produced recent and not-so-recent Broadway shows, mainly comedies, with a mix of professional theatre artists from New York and young theatrical hopefuls from around the country; it was both America's vacation theatre and professional training ground.

Summer stock is mostly gone today, but in its place has arisen another phenomenon that, like summer stock, is unique to the United States. This is the vast array of Shakespeare (or

American Shakespeare festivals, which began as rudimentary outdoor, amateur, summertime affairs, are increasingly indoor, professionalized, and year-round these days. The 1995 Utah Shakespearean Festival production of The Tempest *was elegantly staged in the festival's new indoor theatre, with noted Broadway and film/television performer Harold Gould (right) as Prospero. Dean Mogle designed the ravishing costumes. (Utah Shakespearean Festival.)*

Shakespearean) festivals, begun during the Depression era and now flourishing in almost every state in the nation. The Oregon Shakespeare Festival, in rural Ashland, is the much-heralded (and Tony Award–winning) grandparent of this movement. Founded in 1935 by local drama teacher Angus Bowmer, whose three-night production of *The Merchant of Venice* was supplemented by an afternoon boxing match, the OSF now produces—under Libby Appel, who became artistic director in 1996—750 performances of 11 plays each year, employing 40 professional actors and 300 paid staffers and attracting 350,000 spectators during a 10-month season—all in a town of only 17,000.

Characteristic of Ashland and most Shakespeare festivals is a series of summer Shakespearean productions, usually performed outdoors, often supplemented with other plays and sometimes additional indoor stagings. In their varied repertoire the Shakespeare festivals are like Shakespeare's own company, the King's Men, which performed plays of many authors, both at the outdoor Globe and the indoor Blackfriars. A number of American Shakespeare festivals are professional, at least in part: these include the Oregon, Alabama, New Jersey, California, San Diego (Old Globe), and New York Shakespeare festivals. Other distinctive festivals, most of which engage professional artists in key positions, include the Utah, Colorado, Illinois, Texas, Idaho, Virginia, and Santa Cruz Shakespeare festivals.

Shakespeare festivals are a wonderful bridge between amateur and fully professional theatre; most engage, as the old summer stock companies did, a combination of professional artists and advanced students in professional training programs. The repertoire of these theatres is much more varied and serious than is that of the summer stock theatre, however, and the level of theatrical excellence is often outstanding. Many of the Shakespeare festivals, indeed, are moving into fully professional status during the 1990s and are expanding their facilities, their seasons, and their repertoires. In combination, these festivals provide a unique and immensely valuable network of artistic activity and training possibilities for the American theatre.

Summer and Dinner Theatres

There remain, in the United States, some notable professional summer theatres without the word *Shakespeare* in their names. The Williamstown Theatre Festival in Massachusetts is probably the best of these. Founded in 1955 by the charismatic and flamboyant Nikos Psacharapolous, and led by him until his death in 1989, Williamstown employs many of New York's best-known actors, designers, and directors, eager to leave the stifling city in July and August and spend their month or two in this beautiful Berkshire village playing Chekhov (for which the theatre is justly

famous), Brecht, O'Neill, and Tennessee Williams in elegantly mounted productions. Several veteran WTF directors, notably Peter Hunt, have served in the Williamstown artistic directorship since Psacharapolous's death; a new director is to be appointed by summer 1996. The Berkshire Theatre festival in nearby Stockbridge is also a highly accomplished professional summer theatre in this culturally rich area, just two or three hours north of New York (visitors to the Berkshires can also drop in at Tanglewood to see the Boston Symphony Orchestra playing in shirtsleeves).

Several other summer companies in New England and the Mid-Atlantic states have become equally distinguished: theatres such as the Barter Theatre of Abingdon, Virginia (the nation's oldest, founded in 1933); the Theatre at Monmouth (Maine); the Gloucester (Massachusetts) Stage Company (headed by noted playwright Israel Horovitz); and the American Theatre Works (run by author-director Jill Charles, in Dorset, Vermont). These companies and others like them can provide outstanding professional (or semiprofessional) theatre in attractive summer vacation environments, appealing to tourists and local residents alike.

Dinner theatres, which operate year round, were broadly introduced to suburban America in the 1970s, offering a "night on the town" package of dinner and a play in the same facility. The novelty of dinner theatre has worn thin, however, and the acceptable repertory for such packaging—light comedies, mystery melodramas, and pared-down productions of golden-age Broadway musicals—was quickly exhausted; dinner theatre seems to be a declining art in the 1990s. Never high in its artistic aspirations (the format virtually excludes adventurous dramaturgy, challenging themes, or even elaborate staging), dinner theatre has played important roles in bringing the theatre to those otherwise unacquainted with it and in providing employment (and training) to thousands of theatre artists each year.

Amateur Theatre: Academic and Community

Finally, there is an active amateur theatre in America, sometimes operating in conjunction with educational programs.

There are more than one thousand Departments of Drama (or Theatre) offering degrees in the United States, and perhaps an equal number of educational institutions also put on plays or give classes in the various dramatic arts. This is not unique to America. Stage performances in schools have been used worldwide since the Renaissance, not only for the purpose of teaching and exploring dramatic literature (arguably the most important single literary form in history) but also for teaching foreign languages, human behavior, and cultural history, as well as the more personal skills of speech, social development, and self-presentation. For these reasons the putting on of "school plays" has long been a curricular or extracurricular activity, and in the United States this has become a major enterprise.

Long before the development of the nonprofit professional theatre, American universities were providing audiences around the country with the masterworks of the international dramatic repertory, as well as the more serious new works of the American stage. The founding of the Yale Drama Department (now the Yale School of Drama) in 1923 signaled the beginning of a new commitment on

University theatres have as their mission the training of young theatre artists—and also the exploration of important dramatic works that may appear to have little commercial or popular potential. This University of California, Irvine, production of Heiner Müller's Hamletmachine *was directed by Keith Fowler and designed by Douglas-Scott Goheen (scenery) and Elizabeth Novak (costumes); the postmodern approach shows Shakespeare, in a picture on the back wall, glaring at the actors who dare to adapt his work. (Photo: Philip Channing.)*

the part of American higher education: to assume not merely the role of theatre producer, but also that of theatre trainer. Today, the vast majority of American professional theatre artists receive their training in American college and university departments devoted, in whole or in part, to that purpose. As a result, the academic and professional theatres have often grown closer together, with many artists working interchangeably in both kinds of institution. For this reason, the performances at many university theatres often reach extremely sophisticated levels of excellence in many areas and are, on occasion, equal or superior to professional productions of the same dramatic material.

Community theatres are amateur groups who put on plays for their own enjoyment and for the entertainment or edification of their community. There are occasions when these theatres, too, reach levels of excellence; some community theatres acquire substantial funding, handsome facilities, and large subscription audiences. One should always remember that many of the world's great theatres, including Stanislavsky's Moscow Art Theatre and Antoine's Théâtre Libre, began, essentially, as community theatres run by amateurs. One should also remember that the word *amateur* means "lover" and that the artist who creates theatre out of love rather than commercial expedience may in fact be headed for the highest levels of art, not necessarily the lowest. The community theatre has, then, a noble calling: it is the theatre a community makes out of itself and for itself, and it can therefore tell us a lot about who we are and what we want.

Current Theatre in Europe

European theatre has always exerted a keen influence on America—indeed, until well into this century, our theatre was always an import or an imitation of the European—and that influence is no less important today. There

has also been, particularly since the 1970s, a reciprocal influence of American theatre in Europe.

The European theatre is organized quite differently from our own. It is, first of all, highly institutionalized, with state-supported and city-supported theatres the norm rather than the exception. Germany, for example, has more than 200 government-subsidized professional theatres. Finland, whose population is smaller than Philadelphia's, has thirty-five state and city theatres. In most European countries, theatres are as routinely financed by public monies as libraries are in America. These theatres engage artists on annual contracts (unlike show-by-show contracts common in America) and enjoy the luxuries of long rehearsal periods, long-lasting collaborations, and a deeply developed sense of artistic ensemble. Drawbacks of state support include the intransigent threat of bureaucratic

The experimental KOM theatre in Helsinki has helped to make the Finnish theatre one of the most vibrant in Europe. This 1983 production is an adaptation of Russian author Mikhail Bulgakov's novel, The Master and Margarita. *At the time the play was produced, Bulgakov still could not be produced in what was then the Soviet Union. (Photo: Rauno Träskelin.)*

meddling and the imposition—or threatened imposition—of political control over the artistic product; artistic stagnation and complacency are also dangers. However, the generously funded public theatres of Europe are spared a great many financial worries and, when strongly motivated, can undertake the production of a wide variety of classics and experimental plays without an overreliance on box-office success or the distractions of fundraising.

The best European theatre productions are seen increasingly in the United States. International festivals, which have been common in Europe for decades, are growing in popularity in America, particularly since the extraordinarily successful Olympics Theatre Festival in Los Angeles in 1984. Chicago, Denver, Baltimore, New York, and Los Angeles have become sites of international theatre festivals, some recurring; and international tours and theatre exchanges, fostered by the International Theatre Institute and various governments, are greatly on the increase throughout the country.

It is possible that nothing could prove more valuable for the world today than such theatre exchanges, for drama's capacity to serve as a vehicle for international communication—a communication that goes beyond mere rhetoric—is one of culture's greatest potential gifts to humanity. Drama's syntheses of meaning and aesthetics, of intellect and emotions, can coalesce disparate cultures into common understandings; drama can transcend ideologies and make antagonists partners, strangers friends. As drama once served to unite the thirteen tribes of ancient Greece, so it may serve in the coming decades to unite a world too often fractured by prejudice and divided by ignorance. The theatre's virtue is to explore the fullest potential of humankind and to lay before us all the universality of the worldwide human experience: human hopes, fears, feelings, and compassion for the living. Nothing could be more vital in the establishment of a true world peace than a shared, cross-cultural awareness of what it means to be human on this planet.

A trip to a dramatic festival, either in the United States or abroad, is the best way to sample the theatres of several other countries; in Europe the main international theatre festivals are in Avignon (France), Edinburgh (Scotland), Spoleto (Italy), and—although limited to German-language plays—Berlin (Germany). On the other hand, nothing can match a theatre tour abroad, where the adventurous theatregoer can see not only the dramatic productivity of a given culture, but also the "theatre scene" in its own setting. For such adventurers, we shall look at some possible destinations.

England The first and most rewarding stop for American students on a European theatre tour is likely to be England, first because the language is familiar, and second because the English theatre is currently one of the most vigorous in the world. Two subsidized companies are the focus of English theatrical activity: the National Theatre, operating three stages in a fabulous complex overlooking the River Thames on Shakespeare's Bankside, and the Royal Shakespeare Company, which operates theatres both in London (the Barbican) and in Shakespeare's natal town of Stratford-upon-Avon. Each of these companies has several plays in repertory at any given time; and in a week's visit, split between London and Stratford, it would be possible with adroit scheduling to view nearly a dozen different productions.

Commercial theatres in London also are active year round (although as in New York, the most active period is the "season" stretching from October through May), and many fine plays and productions may be seen at the theatres that line Shaftesbury Avenue in the West End, a district comparable to Broadway, and at "fringe" theatres, located elsewhere in the city, that correspond to our off-Broadway and off-off-Broadway ventures. Regional theatre, or "provincial theatre" as it is called in

The Royal Shakespeare Theatre is famous for its namesake playwright, of course, but it produces contemporary plays as well. This 1991 production of Pam Gems's The Blue Angel *was directed by Trevor Nunn; Kelly Hunter and Philip Madoc are the actors. (Photo: Clive Barda.)*

England, is as active there as in the United States, with publicly supported theatres in every major town performing plays in repertory or stock during the seasonal period. Indeed, the "provincial rep" of English towns is the traditional training ground for English actors, who are considered by many to be the most polished and versatile actors in the world.

So esteemed is England in the world of theatre—owing to the past contributions of Shakespeare, Marlowe, Garrick, and Shaw, as well as the splendid contemporary achievements of playwrights such as Tom Stoppard, Edward Bond, Harold Pinter, Simon Gray, Alan Ayckbourn, Pam Gems, Howard Brenton, David Hare, Caryl Churchill, Trevor Griffiths, and Peter Shaffer—that several American colleges have set up summer drama programs to allow their students to experience the riches of English theatre and scholarship at first hand. Flocks of Americans, students and tourists alike, descend every year upon the meccas of London and Stratford and on the summer festivals of Chichester and Edinburgh.

France and Germany   The countries that spawned the theatre of the absurd and the theatre of alienation, respectively, as well as the earlier symbolist and expressionist dramatic movements—France and Germany—remain active theatre centers today. Both countries provide a mix of traditional and strikingly original theatre.

French theatre, headquartered as always in Paris, maintains the traditional Royal theatre style in the Comédie Française, which continues to operate in the French capital much as it has since 1680. But newer state-supported provincial Parisian theatres, including the Théâtre National de Strasbourg, the Comédie de Caen, the National Popular Theatre (T.N.P.) at Villeurbanne, and the Theatre of East Paris (T.E.P.), have complemented the traditional Comédie Française in recent years, and a new "theatre on the hill" (the Théâtre National de la Colline) has taken up the task of presenting new French plays and translations of foreign plays not yet known in France. Another nationally subsidized theatre, the Bobigny MC93 (MC stands for "Maison de la Culture"), brings modern and postmodern performing artists from all over the world to this Paris suburb: artists like Robert Wilson, Peter Sellars, Heiner Müller, David Byrne, and the Kodo drummers of Japan. Meanwhile, two more independent companies—Ariane Mnouchkine's Théâtre de Soleil at the Cartoucherie in Vincennes and Peter Brook's Center of Theatre Research at the Bouffes du Nord in Paris—have created productions of world renown, which are discussed in more detail later in this chapter.

French theatre is not noted only for productions, however: it has been largely French intellectuals—Jean-Paul Sartre, Albert Camus, Roland Barthes, Claude Lévi-Strauss, Jacques Lacan, Jacques Derrida, Jean Baudrillard, and Hélène Cixous—who have been at the forefront first of existentialism (Sartre, Camus) and then of the critical theorizing (structuralism, poststructuralism, deconstruction, feminism) that characterizes all phases of

Jean Genet's The Blacks *was one of the first plays to treat the oppression and exploitation of Africans and their descendants. This French play was given a German staging by Peter Stein in 1983; the production emphasizes the international political reality of contemporary Africa and its peoples. (Photo: Courtesy German Information Center.)*

the postmodern age—and the postmodern drama.

In Paris, comedies of the Broadway type (but entirely Gallic in flavor) are the basic fare at the commercial theatres along the boulevards; indeed, the term *boulevard theatre* in France signifies a light, diverting piece, invariably having to do with marital infidelity. More experimental works can be seen throughout the city and in the suburbs, where warehouses, parks, and abandoned factories are more likely to serve as dramatic venues than are traditional theatres. An annual summer theatre festival at the ancient city of Avignon, in the south of France, brings together the most significant of the avant-garde and popular productions of the preceding year, together with significant productions from overseas, and presents them in a variety of theatres, cloisters, and other settings around the city, including the spectacular and venerable Palace of Popes, thus offering visitors a

The Comédie Française, founded in 1680, presents classic French plays in the traditional manner but also experiments with contemporary stagings. Here, in a production of Molière's Don Juan, *the traditional chandeliers are used in a novel fashion to enhance a sense of decadence. (Photo: Courtesy French Cultural Services.)*

East meets West in this musical production of Jean Giraudoux's French masterpiece, The Madwoman of Chaillot, *set in Chandigarh and performed in Punjabi by an Indian company at the 1995 Avignon Theatre Festival. (Photo: Marc and Brigitte Enguerand.)*

unique opportunity to sample a vast range of contemporary French and foreign dramatic endeavor.

In contrast to France, Germany has no theatre capital; rather, it boasts a myriad of civic theatres—and every year one or more of them does something that causes a national sensation. In recent years, Hamburg, Berlin, Munich, Frankfurt, Cologne, Bochum, Rostock, and Bremen have all been sites of exciting theatrical activity. German theatre, adhering to none of the traditions of its past, is perhaps the most radically innovative in the Western world, particularly in the areas of directing and design; thus a visit to German theatre, particularly in a broad sampling, can be of inestimable value even to the theatre student who has no knowledge of the German language. Richly imaginative and frequently visually astonishing, the German theatre offers a wealth of fresh insights into the possibilities of theatrical aesthetics.

The contemporary German theatre is in part dedicated to an exhaustive re-examination of classic works, with an eye to the possibility of strikingly fresh and unorthodox new theatrical realizations. The result is often starkly, even shockingly, expressive. This production of Euripides' Medea *was directed by Michael Grüber as part of a multi-year "Antiquities Project," funded by the German Government at the Berlin Schaubühne. (Photo: Courtesy German Information Center.)*

Current Theatre in the World

America, England, France, and Germany provide, in combination, a dazzling spectrum of contemporary theatre. But these countries hardly exhaust the theatre of the world today. The International Theatre Institute has official representation in 79 countries around the globe, each of which enjoys a remarkable theatrical history and an active and provocative current theatre. Plays have been staged in *Canada* since the beginning of the seventeenth century; today, theatre flourishes in every Canadian province, with the Stratford (Ontario) Festival Theatre and the Shaw Festival at Niagara-on-the-Lake having international prominence among the country's more than 220 professional theatre groups: Canada now enjoys a virtual flood of new Canadian playwrights, directors, and theatre critics who are developing global reputations.

The sturdy *Russian* theatre has survived revolution, war, purges, foreign occupation, and the astonishing recent political upheavals. Chekhov's three sisters still enchant sold-out houses at the Moscow Art Theatre, while fresh and innovative stagings continue to stimulate huge audiences in St. Petersburg, Moscow, and other cities across this broad land, rife with new artistic—as well as political—fervor. Former USSR-dependent states and nations have exploited their independence both on stage and off in these turbulent recent years. Reenergized theatre companies in *Lithuania, Poland, Hungary,* (ex-Soviet) *Georgia,* and the *Ukraine* are attracting international audiences at home and on international tours. It is hardly coincidental, moreover, that both Czechoslovakia and Hungary elected dissident (and previously jailed) playwrights—Vaclav Havel and Arpád Göncz respectively—as their presidents in the immediate post-Communist period or that the first president of the breakaway Republic of (ex-Soviet) Georgia was also that country's leading Shakespearean translator (Zviad Gamsakhurdia), for the theatre in Eastern Europe has been the primary locus of independent, dissident, and underground expression since the earliest days of the Cold War. When the "Velvet Revolution" in Czechoslovakia overthrew the Communist government in 1989, the revolution was headquartered in the basement of Havel's theatre in Prague. Nor is it entirely coincidental that the presiding pope of this period is himself a former playwright; this is Karol Jozef Wojtyla (John Paul II), a Pole whose commitment to free social and artistic expression has proved seminal during this tumultuous era.

Nor is political-activist playwriting limited to Eastern Europe. The Market Theatre of Johannesburg, *South Africa,* which has won its reputation not only for the outstanding quality of its productions, but also for its courageous and effective confrontation with that country's now-concluded policy of racial apartheid—particularly in productions of Athol Fugard's *Sizwe Banzi is Dead, The Island, Master Harold . . . And the Boys, A Lesson from Aloes, Valley Song, My Children! My Africa!, Playland,* and Mbongeni Ngema's *Woza Albert!* and *Asinamali!* Productions of Fugard and Ngema, which have now toured and been restaged the world over, have proved crucial in shaping world opinion on this tragic issue.

Playwrights Wole Soyinka and Ken Saro-Wiwa of *Nigeria* have played an equally crucial role in the politics and theatre art of their country and the international scene. Nobel laureate Soyinka, who like Havel and Göncz was jailed for his radical political activity, has helped shape his country's destiny since the mid-1960s with plays that both reexamine his country's colonial past (*Death and the King's Horseman*) and savagely parody post-independence African tyranny and corruption (*Opera Wonyosi, A Play of Giants*). Such protest does not come without enormous risk, however, and at the time of writing Soyinka has been forced into political exile. Saro-Wiwa, whose writings have drawn international attention to the environmental pollution ravaging his country, was convicted of murder charges by an obviously biased mili-

Theatregoers study the billboards for upcoming performances at Tokyo's Kabuki-za theatre. (Photo: Robert Cohen.)

tary tribunal operating outside the Nigerian judicial system and was executed—in defiance of worldwide outrage—by his government in 1995.

Japanese theatre is internationally known for its magnificent traditional repertoire of classical Nō, the popular Kabuki, and the Bunraku (puppet) theatre, but *shingeki* ("new drama"), influenced by modernist European realism, has asserted itself since the beginning of the century; and an avant-garde, nonrealistic countermovement called post-*shingeki* has proven even more popular and intellectually exciting to the Japanese theatregoer since the early 1960s. Post-*shingeki*—explosive, violent, sexual, surreal, and often sadistic/masochistic—coalesces present-day Japan with its legendary and mythic past, and often features the metamorphosis of modern characters into ancient gods. While it may be true that traditional rather than avant-garde theatre dominates most of Asia, partly because of political restraints (as in China and the two Koreas), the experimental work of many Japanese artists, such as Tadashi Suzuki (director of SCOT—the Suzuki Troupe of Toga), have proven influential in both staging and theatre training around the world.

Only our own cultural insularity lets us imagine ourselves at the center of the universe, the true and legitimate heirs of those who invented theatre; the truth is that theatre is happening throughout the known world and in forms so diverse as to defy accounting or assimilation. Every component of theatre—from architecture to acting, from dramaturgy to directing—is in the process of change, of learning, of rebelling from convention, of building anew. The theatre's diversity is its very life, and change is the foremost of its vital signs. We must not think to pin it down, but rather to seek it out, to produce it ourselves, and to participate in its growth.

WHAT'S HAPPENING?

No book can tell you what's happening—for by the time you read it in a book, it has already happened.

What we can do is list a few promising artists and artistic trends that should be at the forefront of theatrical life during the last years of the century. Even if the list is less than prophetic, it should give a general picture of the diversity of the theatre of our times and of the sorts of dramatic possibilities that theatre artists and enthusiasts are currently anticipating.

Martha Clarke and Dance-Theatre

Dance-theatre occupies a middle ground between plays and ballet; it is an impressionistic construction of musical, spoken, and choreographic events, ordinarily based on a theme but lacking formal dramatic plot or continuity. The most famous dance-theatre practitioner in Europe, Pina Bausch, defined the form with her *Tanztheater Wuppertal* company in the 1970s; the glorious revival of her *Sacre du Printemps* and *Café Müller* at the 1995 Avignon Theatre Festival added further luster to her legend, maintaining her at the forefront of the avant-garde.

Bausch's American counterpart, Martha Clarke, is likewise extraordinary. Clarke, a veteran of the Pilobolus dance troupe, created two stunning dance-theatre pieces in the late 1980s: *The Garden of Earthly Delights,* based on a painting by Hieronymous Bosch, and *Vienna Lusthaus,* evoking the artistic and sexual ferment of Vienna at the time of Gustave Klimt. Clarke's pieces are in the tradition of

Pina Bausch is one of Europe's great choreographers, and her Tanztheater Wuppertal has made dance-theatre a world-renowned art. Shown here is one of Bausch's early (1975) masterpieces, Sacre du Printemps (Spring's sacrament), *as revived at the 1995 Avignon Theatre Festival; the work, set to music by Stravinsky, celebrates the rapture and terrors of sexual (springtime's) awakening. Costume and scenery by Rolf Borzik. (Photo: Colette Masson/ Enguerand.)*

surrealism and suggest the dream worlds of the later August Strindberg and Antonin Artaud; however, they are highly original in both conception and execution. Her more recent works indicate an increased interest in social, political, and even romantic themes as well. *Miracolo d'Amore,* introduced at the Spoleto (South Carolina) festival in 1988, deals with sexual violence. *Endangered Species,* which premiered in Stockbridge (Massachusetts) in 1990, employs circus animals, a text from Walt Whitman, and eight actors to explore American Civil War themes in the context of contemporary environmental issues. *An Uncertain Hour,* in 1995 (in collaboration with Netherlands Dance Theatre 3), uses four dancers in formal dress, two men and two women, coming together and breaking apart in response to songs by classical composers. Clarke, who received a $285,000 MacArthur Foundation fellowship for her work in 1990, will surely prove a major force in dance-drama for years to come.

The Garden of Earthly Delights, *a highly innovative dance-drama conceived and directed by Martha Clarke, is a brilliantly evocative staging—with music, mime, dance (on the ground and in the air), and stunning stage effects—of the great Hieronymous Bosch painting of the same name (c. 1510). Adam and Eve are seen here in the 1987 New York off-Broadway revival; lighting is by Paul Gallo, costumes by Jane Greenwood, and flying effects by Peter Foy. (Photo: Martha Swope and Associates/Carol Rosegg.)*

The One-Man Show

Although Chekhov wrote a short play for a single actor (*On the Harmfulness of Tobacco,* in which the character is a lecturer addressing his audience), it has only been in recent times that authors have seriously entertained the possibilities of full-length plays employing a single actor. Sometimes, these are little more than star vehicles or extended monologues, often based on historical characters. In recent decades, Hal Holbrook has toured the nation

with his one-man portrayal of America's first great writer in *Mark Twain Tonight,* and James Whitmore has followed with his one-man rendition of America's feisty thirty-third president in *Give 'em Hell, Harry!* But more recent one-person shows have made serious attempts at complex drama and dramaturgy. Spalding Gray's impressionistic and autobiographical storytellings, seemingly casual ruminations that develop a subtly enchanting momentum, became avant-garde classics in the 1980s (*Swimming to Cambodia*) and early 1990s (*Monster in a Box*). Eric Bogosian has created, in a series of intensely and penetrating performances, savage and comic by turns, an indelible cast of American low-life characters—pimps and whores, addicts and agents, executives and rock stars, panhandlers and jocks—in his increasingly amazing *Drinking in America, Sex, Drugs, and Rock & Roll* (1991), *Dog Show* (1992), *Pounding Nails in the Floor with My Forehead* (1994), and *Wake Up and Smell the Coffee* (1996). Patrick Stewart's one-man presentation of Charles Dickens's *A Christmas Carol,* in which the celebrated Shakespearean actor (and "Star Trek" TV star) played all the roles, became a surprise Broadway success in 1991, and has been re-presented on Broadway and around the nation regularly ever since.

Employing a more traditional dramaturgy, Jay Presson Allen, in the ineffably poignant *Tru,* depicts the late author-celebrity Truman Capote alone on stage, shuffling around his New York apartment and making wan jokes to the audience; as played by actor Robert Morse on Broadway (1990), the play probed deeply into serious issues of creativity and social alienation, particularly as Capote is shown against the backdrop of nighttime Manhattan: the thousand lit windows outside his apartment window representing the parties to which he's not invited. Loneliness is also the subtext of Allen's subsequent (coauthored) *The Big Love,* in which Tracey Ullman played Florence Aadland, the mother of Errol Flynn's mistress, and Willy Russell's fictional *Shirley*

Valentine (1990), in which the sole character is presumed to be speaking to her kitchen wall (and, in the second act, to a rock on a Greek island); this play is a wonderful portrayal of an ordinary English woman's despair in a loveless marriage, made all the more touching by her isolation on stage.

The One-Woman Show

In the past two decades, one-woman shows have become a genre of their own. One of the most thrilling of such stagings was Jane Wagner's wondrous *The Search for Signs of Intelligent Life in the Universe,* which Wagner wrote for her friend and colleague, the actress Lily Tomlin, who performed it to rapturous reviews in 1985. Like Bogosian, Wagner creates (and Tomlin performs) a remarkable variety of ragged urban characters, ranging across the breadth of American society: a bag woman, a jaded socialite, a cokehead, a radical feminist, and Agnus Angst, a teenage punk performance artist ("even as a fetus I had womb angst"). But unlike Bogosian's compilations of individual sketches, Wagner's characters interact with each other, and her play comes to a remarkable closure that brings together both characters and audience in a "goose bump" experience: a spirit of theatrical communion. Rarely have there been standing ovations in the recent theatre as spontaneous and warmhearted as at this play—with its amazing solo performance. Indeed, it is such a *theatrical* piece of drama that its subsequent film version proved only the palest of imitations and failed to find an appreciable audience.

Even more recent one-woman shows have had in common an autobiographical exploration of the author-performer's own life, sometimes as narrative, and sometimes lightly translated into dramatic action.

Sherry Glaser's brilliant *Family Secrets,* for example, recounts the author's family story through the lively and racy monologues of five characters: Glaser, her mother, her sister, her father, and her grandmother—all played by Glaser, who transforms herself onstage, often in midsentence, with the necessary costume and make-up changes. Glaser's family secrets—which revolve around sexual identity and ambiguity, religious absorption and assimilation, mental illness and menstruation—are thus theatrically revealed: some hilarious, some painful, and all poignant and provocative. The show, which was directed by Glaser's husband, Greg Howells (who is given coauthor credit), was a great success at the New York Westside Theatre in 1993 and on subsequent tour.

Claudia Shear's *Blown Sideways Through Life* (1993) is even more directly autobiographical: a one-woman show in which Shear (playing herself) describes her sixty-five jobs over the past few years: waitress, chef, model, porn star, whorehouse receptionist, proofreader, and—finally—actress in the show we're watching. "Everyone has at least one story that will stop your heart," says Shear in the play, and Shear delivers a good number of these heart-stoppers—as well as a passel of advice on living in employment-poor urban America of the mid-to-late 1990s.

Lynn Redgrave's *Shakespeare For My Father* (1994) is a celebrity turn in the same genre. Redgrave hails from a famous acting family (the late Michael Redgrave, her father, and Vanessa Redgrave, her sister, are world-renowned performers, as is Lynn Redgrave herself), and her relationship with her family, particularly with her father, is all the more moving as it shows us the personal anxieties that can underlie public achievement. Redgrave's dramatization—which includes her recitation of certain speeches from Shakespeare, in her father's voice as well as her own—begins at the point when the author reads her late father's diary and realizes that the entry on the day of her birth does not mention her arrival. Redgrave's ensuing portrayal of a father who was more a performer

Lynn Redgrave wrote and starred in her one-woman Broadway show, Shakespeare For My Father, *about the relationship—often joyous, more often disappointing—between her and her father, who was, like her, a renowned classical actor.*

than a parent is deeply touching, elegant, and finally ennobling.

Anna Deveare Smith, in two splendid works, *Fires in the Mirror* (published 1993) and *Twilight: Los Angeles 1992* (published 1994), has taken the personal one-woman play to new levels altogether, with performances of the latter play moving from the Mark Taper Forum in Los Angeles (which commissioned it) to the New York Public Theatre and then to Broadway, where it was nominated for two Tony Awards and the Pulitzer Prize, and given top awards from the Drama Desk and the New York Drama Critics Circle. Smith—

who when not performing is a professor at Stanford University—writes of specific urban events that focus on fundamental problems of contemporary American society: particularly racism. *Fires* centers on the many days of rage in Crown Heights, Brooklyn, that followed the violent deaths of Gavin Cato (an African American) and Yankel Rosenbaum (a Hasidic Jew). *Twilight* concerns the massive Los Angeles riots that followed the acquittal of white police officers charged with beating a black motorist, Rodney King. In both pieces, Smith excerpted statements collected from hundreds of personal interviews with individuals who lived through these city-defining events. Using minimal props and costume elements, Smith transforms herself into an entire cast of characters for each social upheaval, creating, in one critic's words, "pure, unbiased, tumultuous symphonies."

Ariane Mnouchkine and the Théâtre de Soleil

Mnouchkine's Paris-based company astounded American audiences in its 1984 appearance at the Los Angeles Olympics with three Asian-inspired Shakespearean productions, particularly *Richard II,* utilizing quasi-Kabuki techniques, and *La Nuit des Rois (Twelfth Night),* which drew on Indian Kathakali dance patterns. But Mnouchkine and the Théâtre de Soleil (Theatre of the Sun) company she heads had been celebrated in Europe since the late 1960s for radically innovative stage productions created collaboratively by the entire theatrical ensemble. The notion of collaborative creation is itself radical, since it dispenses with the ordinary theatrical hierarchy and absolute separation of duties. In Mnouchkine's company, productions come out of improvisations, discussion, and group study; and all members of the group share the various responsibilities of research, scriptwriting, staging, interpretation, design, construction, and even house management. All company members in the Théâtre de Soleil are allocated the same salary—even Mnouchkine herself, who, perhaps alone among artistic directors, has worked to diminish the formal and merely hierarchal superiority of the director in the theatre. (Even today, Mnouchkine herself might be tearing the tickets at the door or clearing away paper plates at the theatre's buffet bar.) The audience, too, is treated as a participant in the Soleil environment; before each show, the actors put on their costumes and make-up in open dressing areas located beneath the audience gallery, where they can and do chat quietly with each other, and with entering spectators, at their own (and the audience's) discretion.

After its initial success with Arnold Wesker's *The Kitchen*, the Théâtre de Soleil moved into a former munitions factory, the Cartoucherie, in the Paris suburb of Vincennes; there, influenced by the French student rebellions and other civil disorders of 1968, the company began to seek a new language of theatre, based in part on Artaudian freedom, in part on Brechtian political commitment, in part on collective improvisation, and in part on a new interculturalism, particularly in blending Eastern with Western performance traditions.

The Théâtre de Soleil also stakes out new ground by working not on single plays, but on groupings of plays linked by time, theme, and methodology. A trilogy of such plays, individually entitled *1789, 1793,* and *The Golden Age,* was the principal result of the company's work in the decade of the 1970s; these company-improvised works, which were concerned with the French Revolution in the light of contemporary French history, proved immediate successes in France and, subsequently, abroad. The company's Kabuki- and Kathakali-inspired Shakespearean productions followed in the early 1980s; then, in the latter part of that decade, Mnouchkine began to mount a series of ancient Greek plays, collectively titled *Les Atrides* (the house of Atreus), consisting of Euripides' *Iphigeneia at Aulis,* followed by the three plays of Aeschylus' *Oresteia.* By 1991, when the entire tetralogy had been assembled and staged, French audiences cheered and international critics raved. "You will be fortunate if you ever see a more exhilarating production of the first great tragedies in European drama," said the *New York Times.* This great compilation was presented in Montreal, Canada, and Brooklyn, New York, in 1992.

More recently, Mnouchkine and her company have turned their attention—for the first time—to classic French drama, and their 1995 production of Molière's *Tartuffe,* which premiered at Vienna and Avignon with an international and interracial cast, is a thrilling revisitation of religious dissonance—seen in the contemporary and pertinent light of North African Islamic fundamentalism.

Mnouchkine's experiments are brilliantly realized—with a group of artists who, over the years, have developed and integrated extraordinary performance skills. Her work has redefined the potential of virtually every theatrical element, from stage movement (characters generally run onstage at full tilt) to staging (mostly full front, facing the audience) to music (live and virtually continuous performance employing more than 140 instruments from many different cultures) to play selection (trilogies and tetralogies) to a devoted intercultural approach to theatrical creativity and convention. The work is profound, yet it is also broadly entertaining; the Théâtre de Soleil is a popular, no less than an intellectual success, and its future work is awaited with the greatest anticipation.

Robert Wilson and Performance Art

The term *performance art,* referring to a largely improvised, nondramatic performance by visual artists, came to prominence in the early 1970s. Performance art differs from theatre to the extent that it recognizes no conventions, ordinarily takes place in nontheatrical facilities (such as art galleries), and normally employs people without theatrical training (although not necessarily without theatrical gifts). Instead, performance art creates a series of visual happenings and audio rhythms, often interwoven with spoken narrative or dialogue. There is generally no plot, no characters (the performers play themselves), and frequently no perceptible theme. There is also little or no dramatic momentum: a provocative association of impressions, rather than suspense, building excitement, or catharsis, provides the aesthetic impact. Dada experiments in the early years of the century (see beginning of this chapter) were certainly forerunners of this provocative art form, which is a pure example of postmodernist ideas and aesthetics.

Lines between the arts are not absolute, however, and many theatre artists may also, in at least some of their work, be regarded as performance artists as well. Or vice versa. Since the early 1970s, Americans Richard Foreman and Robert Wilson have made significant contributions jointly in performance and theatre art. Wilson's achievement, particularly, has enjoyed a high visibility here and overseas.

Wilson, born in Texas, first came to prominence in Germany, where his highly original collages of poetic texts, recited against brilliantly evocative *tableaux vivants* ("living pictures"), gained substantial attention from enthusiasts of the avant-garde. The extraordinary length of these pieces, which Wilson both wrote and directed, earned him some early notoriety for that reason alone: *The Life and Times of Joseph Stalin* (1973) lasted twelve hours; *Ka Mountain* (1972) lasted twenty-three. Wilson was invited to create the central performance work of the 1984 Los Angeles Olympics Arts Festival, for which he composed *The CIVIL warS,* a massive piece that was rehearsed in segments, in several countries around the world; funds could not be raised for the ultimate performance, however, and by the late 1980s, only fragments of the work had been performed.

Wilson's work is not, strictly considered, performance art, for his pieces have a theme, are not improvised, and the performers usually (but not always) play a character other than themselves. Nevertheless, his work is hard to categorize in other ways—incorporating, as it does, all elements of performance and the arts, including dance, music, sculpture, video, painting, lighting, poetry, narrative, and human expressiveness. The sheer time duration of Wilson's work forces a reexamination of the nature of performance and the relationship of audience and art, meaning and aesthetics. Wilson's work makes us question the foundations of dramaturgy: Why do we watch theatre? What are we looking for? What do we care about?

In 1986 Wilson forged a stronger link with drama, by freely adapting a script from the classical theatre repertory (Euripides' *Alcestis*) and by staging it in his own fashion at the American Repertory Theatre in Cambridge, Massachusetts. The result was a visually stunning theatre piece, magically provocative in its imagery, yet contained within the conventional framework of a three-hour performance, staged with professional actors in a normal proscenium theatre. Wilson followed this with a production of Heiner Müller's *Hamletmachine* at the same ART playhouse.

Wilson has turned increasingly to combining his unique aesthetic imagination with at least the rudiments of traditional playtexts, although his cutting, interpretation, and staging of these plays are strictly postmodern and revisionist. Overscale props, intermixing of humans and puppets, exotically nontraditional casting, ideographic and kinetic scenery, interposition of alternate text material, and extreme "slow motion" stage movements characterize Wilson's highly stylized stagings. "I hate ideas," Wilson states, "that's why my theatre is different, noninterpretive. Interpretation is for the audience."

Many of Wilson's recent works, like his initial ones, have premiered in Germany, where he receives more funding than in his native

Robert Wilson is the director, John Conklin the costume designer, and both co-designed the scenery for this dreamlike American Repertory Theatre production of Ibsen's When We Dead Awaken *in 1991. (Photo: Richard Feldman.)*

United States. In 1990 alone, Wilson premiered a *King Lear* in Frankfurt; Chekhov's *Swan Song* in Munich; an adaptation of Virginia Woolf's *Orlando* in Berlin; and a play of his own, *The Black Rider,* in Hamburg. Most of these works have subsequently toured throughout Europe, and more recently Wilson has turned his interest eastward, with a modern adaptation of the Japanese Nō plays, *Hanjo* and *Hagoromo,* produced in Italy. But Wilson produces in the United States as well, as illustrated (see accompanying photo) by his production of Ibsen's *When We Dead Awaken* at the American Repertory Theatre in Cambridge and the Alley Theatre in Houston. And in 1995, Wilson's controversial adaptation of *Hamlet,* performed as a monologue by Wilson himself, playing Hamlet and various other roles, once again redefined the nature of Wilsonian performance. Set in a minimalist construction of black slabs, against a horizon that shifts from white to blue to red according to the Prince's mood, Wilson's *Hamlet* presents the Shakespearean text as a sort of deathbed meditation on the play's confounding events and discoveries.

Stephen Sondheim and the Broadway Musical

No one has changed the face of the American musical more than Sondheim (born in 1930), whose first important work was the composition of lyrics for Leonard Bernstein's 1957 Broadway musical, *West Side Story*. After one more assignment as lyricist (for *Gypsy*), Sondheim turned composer as well, winning high praise and success for both words and music to the songs in the highly novel *A Funny Thing Happened on the Way to the Forum*, drawn from the Roman comedies of Plautus.

Since the 1970s, Sondheim and his collaborators have departed dramatically from the standard Broadway musical format, developing a style marked by a disturbing plot and highly sophisticated and adult lyrics, intricately rhymed and brilliantly integrated with an often-jarring atonal musical score. *Company*, *Follies*, and *A Little Night Music* established Sondheim's supremacy in the American musical form, and Sondheim has gone on to break new boundaries in subsequent works. His *Pacific Overtures* (1975) used Oriental music to trace the modern history of Japan–United States relations, while his *Sweeney Todd* (1979) integrated Brechtian alienation techniques, Italian grand opera, English music hall, and Victorian melodrama, all in a morbid story of a barber's revenge—which takes the form of killing his customers and serving up their flesh in meat pies sold to the public. Conversely, *Sunday in the Park with George* (1984) is an elegant musical play about the pointillist painter Georges Seurat; for this production Sondheim invented a "pointillist" style of music to echo Seurat's style.

Sondheim's most controversial new works are *Assassins* (1991) and *Passion* (1993). The former is a musical review of presidential assassinations (and assassination attempts), which cascades through two centuries portraying the quirks and oddities of John Wilkes Booth, Lee Harvey Oswald, Squeaky Fromm, and John Hinckley, Jr., among other unlikely mu-

"The history of the world, my sweet / Is who gets eaten and who gets to eat!" sings Len Cariou, as Sweeney, to Angela Lansbury, as Mrs. Lovett, in Stephen Sondheim's savagely amusing Broadway musical, Sweeney Todd. *Together, Sweeney and Mrs. Lovett make meat pies out of freshly murdered Londoners of all professions. "The trouble with poet / Is how do you know it / 's deceased? Try the priest!" offers Lovett. "Is that squire / On the fire?" asks Todd. "Mercy no sir," responds Lovett, "Look closer, / You'll notice it's grocer." Sondheim's brilliant, unexpected lyrics, perfectly matched to his innovative tunes, are among Broadway's finest creations. (Photo: Martha Swope and Associates.)*

sical theatre protagonists (if not heroes). *Assassins* was so unconventional and, to some, so alarming that it did not open on Broadway after its limited (and sold-out) off-Broadway premiere, and the show has reached an international audience only through its cast recording and subsequent successful runs in London and Los Angeles. A late Broadway opening, however, is more or less in the (permanent) planning stage.

Passion, on the other hand, opened on Broadway and won four 1994 Tony Awards, including best musical, despite mixed reviews. An intermission-less nineteenth-century gothic tragedy—"one long love song," according to Sondheim—*Passion* tells the strange story of Giorgio, a handsome Italian army officer, who is deeply in love with the beautiful Clara, but

The characters of Sondheim's Sunday in the Park with George *pose as the famous painting by Georges Seurat, whose life this provocative musical dramatizes. South Coast Repertory Theatre production starring Harry Groener as George; directed by Barbara Damashek, with outstanding scenery, costumes, and lighting by Cliff Faulkner, Shigeru Yaji, and Tom Ruzika respectively. (Photo: Cristofer Gross.)*

◄

Sondheim's Passion *is a profound, intense musical examination of irrational sexual attraction, set in a nineteenth-century military camp—and in a woman's bedroom. From the 1994 Broadway production. (Photo: Joan Marcus.)*

relentlessly pursued by his commanding officer's cousin, Fosca, a homely, ailing, and pathetically obsessional woman. The initial attractiveness of Giorgio's and Clara's love—they begin the play in bed together, totally naked, singing in duet, "I'm so happy, / I'm afraid I'll die / Here in your arms"—gradually gives way against its own limitations (Giorgio's assignment to the provinces, Clara's nondivorceable marriage) and to the intensity of Fosca's amorous fixations, to which Giorgio ultimately yields—to Clara's despair and to that of most of the audience as well. As there is little to admire or "root for" in this romantic tangle, *Passion*'s success was somewhat limited, but its achievements and innovations were exhilarating nonetheless.

Sondheim's sheer genius (he also coauthored the classic 1973 film mystery, *The Last of Sheila,* and a 1995 stage mystery titled *The Doctor Is Out,* along with some particularly devilish crossword puzzles) and the creative extravagance of his collaborators, particularly director Hal Prince, have not only kept the Broadway musical alive during the 1980s, but have also provided what many say are its finest masterpieces and have served to forecast the vast potential, still unrealized, of this medium.

Peter Brook and Intercultural Theatre

No director has been more influential in the later half of the twentieth century, and none is more provocative in the current theatre than Peter Brook. Born in 1925, Brook began his directorial career as a teenager during World War II, startling English theatregoers with freshly conceived productions of Shakespeare, Marlowe, Sartre, and Cocteau. In 1945, at the age of twenty, he was engaged to direct at the Shakespeare Memorial Theatre at Stratford-upon-Avon and, shortly thereafter, at Covent Garden Opera House,

Peter Brook's production of The Mahabharata, *India's great epic poem, featured an international cast and toured widely in Europe and America prior to filming. Here seen in Brook's Paris headquarters, the decrepit and long-abandoned Bouffes du Nord theatre, which Brook has resolutely declined to paint or renovate. (Photo: Giles Abegg.)*

the Metropolitan Opera in New York, and on Broadway. His 1955 *Hamlet* at Stratford, with Paul Scofield in the title role, toured to Moscow—the first English company playing there in the Soviet era. Brook's career went into its ascendancy, however, in 1962 when, as the codirector of the new Royal Shakespeare Company at Stratford, he staged *King Lear*, again with Scofield, in a production deeply influenced by the theatre of the absurd. Brook followed this two years later with the English-language premiere of Peter Weiss's *Marat/Sade*, a production influenced in part by the theatre of cruelty. These two productions enjoyed immense international success, both on world tours and in subsequently filmed versions.

Brook's subsequent publication of *The Empty Space* in 1968 established his reputation not merely as a director but as a theorist as well: this long essay puts forth a brilliant analysis of modern drama, which Brook divides into "the deadly theatre, the holy theatre, and the rough theatre" (corresponding, more or less, to the conventional theatre, the theatre of Artaud, and the theatre of Brecht) and culminates with a manifesto on behalf of "the immediate theatre." To Brook, the immediate theatre is not something preplanned by the director, but instead is something developed through an entirely creative and improvisational process, "a harrowing collective experience" rather than a polite collaboration of craft experts.

Brook then astonished the theatre world with his vigorously comic, penetrating, "immediate" production of *A Midsummer Night's Dream*, a production that—staged without sentimentality on a bare white set—combined circus techniques with uninhibited sexual farce and created amazingly fresh interactions between the play's well-known (and often shallowly understood) characters. The *Dream* captivated critics and audiences throughout Europe and America during the early 1970s and established Brook as one of the most cre-

ative and talented theorist/theatrical practitioners of all time.

Brook's current phase began in 1971, as he moved to Paris to create The International Center of Theatre Research. Using a company of actors from all parts of the world and performing in a dilapidated and clay-floored Parisian theatre (the Bouffes du Nord), as well as in various nontheatrical spaces in and out of Europe, Brook has produced a series of intercultural works of extraordinary interest, including *The Iks*, which is about a Northern Ugandan tribe, *The Conference of the Birds*, based on a twelfth-century Persian poem, Jarry's *Ubu*, Bizet's opera *Carmen*, a production of Shakespeare's *The Tempest*, and, most remarkably perhaps, *The Mahabharata*, which opened in Paris in 1986 and which Brook filmed for worldwide audiences in 1991. *The Mahabharata* is the national novel of India, ancient, archetypical, and immense (it is the longest single work of world literature). Brook has adapted it into a nine-hour play, staged with his cast of Asian, American, African, and European actors; it was performed in a rock quarry outside of Avignon and on the clay stage of the Bouffes du Nord. Brook blends the text with a myriad of natural (but not naturalistic) elements: actors wade in pools and rivers of real water, trapped by circles of real fire; chariot wheels are mired in real mud; armies clash by torchlight; candles float in the pond. The multifaceted reality of this Indian epic directed by an Englishman in a French theatre with an international cast creates a universality to the production that leaves the audience fulfilled in ways previously unrealized in the theatre's history.

Brook's most recent work at the time of this writing is *The Man Who*, a 1994 adaptation of Dr. Oliver Sacks's study of neurological illness, *The Man Who Mistook His Wife for a Hat*. Brook's production, staged simply with plain white chairs, two rolling tables, and two TV screens on a square carpeted platform, repeats the minimalism of his *Midsum-*

mer Night's Dream. His interculturalism is perpetuated by his four actors who hail from England, Japan, Mali, and Germany. The play, in which the actors alternately depict mentally aberrant patients and their physicians, is a sensitive, revealing, and theatrical portrayal of extreme human confusion. It is pure Brook: unexpected, unconventional, and deeply illuminating. Brook's notion of an "immediate" theatre is not something that will, in the coming decade, be limited merely to the pages of his book.

AMERICAN PLAYWRIGHTS

In the 1980s and 90s, no playwrights have dominated the American theatre as forcefully as did Tennessee Williams and Arthur Miller in the 1940s and 50s. In part, this is because of the decentralization of the American theatre, which has eliminated the absolute primacy of New York (and the total dominance of New York critics) as America's central locus of theatre production. Today, the new American drama is appearing simultaneously in Los Angeles, Seattle, San Diego, Louisville, Minneapolis, and dozens of other cities around the country. And no single observer, or critic, can hope to track the dozens of new playwrights emerging from the hundreds of theatres throughout the United States now dedicated, in whole or in part, to commissioning and presenting original dramas.

But it is to our benefit that, instead of one or two dominant voices, there are today *dozens* of American playwrights commanding national (and, sometimes, international) attention, both for their existing achievements and for their continuing potential in contemporary drama.

August Wilson

Though none may dominate, one American playwright is clearly foremost: this is August Wilson, who in less than a decade has received five Tony Award nominations and two Pulitzer Prizes and whose work continues to grow and deepen year by year. Wilson, born of an interracial couple in Pittsburgh in 1945, has not merely ascended to the highest rank of importance, but he has also helped to redefine the nature of American theatre.

A little-known poet in the 1970s, Wilson began his remarkable rise as a dramatist when he submitted a manuscript to the Eugene O'Neill Theatre Center in Waterford, Connecticut, in 1981. There it came to the attention of the Center's director, Lloyd Richards. Already a major figure in the American theatre (he had directed the major African-American play of the postwar era, Lorraine Hansberry's *A Raisin in the Sun,* in 1959), Richards quickly saw Wilson's writing potential. In the ensuing ten years (through 1991), he was to encourage and direct an astonishing series of five brilliant August Wilson plays: *Ma Rainey's Black Bottom, Fences, Joe Turner's Come and Gone, The Piano Lesson,* and *Two Trains Running.* Each of these works was first produced at the Yale Repertory Theatre (which Richards also headed at the time); each went on to regional theatre tours and prize-winning Broadway runs.

Together, Wilson's remarkable new canon of plays creates a decade-by-decade history of the lives, accomplishments, and struggles of ordinary twentieth-century African Americans: presenting a lively and evocative depiction of (largely) black home life within the context of a (largely) white political society. Wilson's dramaturgy takes many forms, from mainstream American realism (*Fences* is, in many ways, a black *Death of a Salesman*), to musical/dramatic/satiric commentary (*Ma Rainey,* the story of a black jazz singer), to profoundly emotive family dramas that draw deeply upon black American history and ancient African roots (*Piano Lesson* and *Joe Turner's Come and Gone,* which is his masterpiece, so far). Wilson's most recent play, *Seven*

August Wilson's delicate and imaginative The Piano Lesson *won the Pulitzer Prize in drama in 1990. The world premiere, shown here, was at the Yale Repertory Theatre, directed by Lloyd Richards. The actors are Lou Myers, Rocky Carroll, Samuel L. Jackson, and Carl Gordon. (Photo: Gerry Goodstein.)*

Guitars, is a rapturous, comic, and ultimately eloquent flashback on the life and death of a fictional black singer and guitarist whose business sense fails to match his musical genius. Set in a Pittsburgh alley in the early 1940s, the play opened on Broadway in 1996, after premiering at Chicago's Goodman Theatre.

Wilson's commitment to explore African-American culture is both broadly political and deeply aesthetic, and he is not interested in synthesizing the races or glossing over cultural differences (and cultural glories). "I find in black life a very elegant kind of logical language, based on the logical order of things," he says. "There's the idea of metaphor. For instance, when one character in *The Piano Lesson* asks, 'What time does Berneice get home?' instead of getting a response like 'Berneice gets home at 5 o'clock,' you get: 'You

up there asleep, Berneice leave out of here early in the morning, she out there in Squirrel Hill cleaning house for some big shot down there at the steel mill. They don't like you to come late. You come late they won't give you your carfare. What kind of business you got with Berneice?' When you ask a question, instead of getting an answer to the question, you get this guy's ideas, his opinions about everything, a little explanation. You get all these kinds of things just from one question." A poet still, Wilson blends drama with profound observation and abiding humanity.

And Fourteen More . . .

A remaining dozen-plus American playwrights, here listed in the order of their birthdates (and thereby by the approximate duration of their writing careers), will have at least two or three plays appearing on American professional or academic stages at any given time. At least another dozen playwrights could have been included, but this is a representative sample of the most highly regarded working dramatists in the United States today.

Arthur Miller (born 1915) Although he had for many years abandoned Broadway (and it may be that the feeling was mutual), Miller continues to write plays of great merit and fascination. Thus, in addition to often being considered America's greatest playwright (particularly in England, where his work is constantly revived by leading British theatre companies), he remains a contemporary playwright who cannot be ignored.

In three plays of the 1990s, all dealing with a conflation of twentieth-century social and medical themes, Miller continues to explore—and criticize—the American body politic. *The Ride Down Mount Morgan,* which premiered in London (England) in 1991, is a play that covers almost everything Miller had written about earlier—and then some. Although its principal plot concerns hospitalization and bigamy, the play manages to bring in the warring generations, pleasure, guilt, marriage, money, children, race, sex, death, business, Jewishness, non-Jewishness, socialism, Christianity, suicide, political and sexual betrayal, men versus women, humans versus animals, the Reagan-Bush administration versus Arthur Miller, and, almost as an afterthought, capital-T Truth, delivered in an exquisitely Millerish agony. "Only the truth is sacred, Leah," Miller's protagonist declares to one of his wives at play's end. Miller's *The Last Yankee,* which premiered at the (off-Broadway) Manhattan Theatre Club in 1993, mines many of these same themes in a play also set, in part, in a hospital waiting room, where two middle-aged couples serve as Miller's exemplars of life in America's competitive society. And Miller's newest play, *Broken Glass,* which returned the author to Broadway (briefly) in 1994, bril-

Willy Loman is bent low by his heavy bags in Arthur Miller's Death of a Salesman, *a masterpiece of mid-century (1949) American realism. Willy, a traveling salesman with failing prospects and unhelpful grown sons, has been beaten down by the unending struggle to make a living and be "well liked"; with this play, Miller makes his case that such a "low man" is a modern tragic hero. Actor William Leach plays Willy in this superb 1991 Utah Shakespearean Festival production, directed by Eli Simon. Willy's classic pose is inspired by the original Broadway poster. (Photo: Jess Allen.)*

liantly examines the sexual, social, psychological, and political reactions to Nazism during the 1930s with Miller's typically caustic and lively penetration. No other playwright in the twentieth century has so aggressively called society to task for its failures, nor so passionately told his or her audience to pay attention to the world around them.

Neil Simon (born 1927) It can be argued that Neil Simon is not only America's most successful commercial playwright, but also the most successful playwright in the history of theatre. Initially a TV comic writer in the early 1950s, Simon spun off a phenomenal series of hit Broadway comedies in the following decades, including consistently revived works like *Barefoot in the Park, The Odd Couple, Plaza Suite, The Last of the Red Hot Lovers, The Sunshine Boys,* and *California Suite,* plus the books for musicals such as *Little Me, Sweet Charity,* and *Promises, Promises.* In addition, Simon has written the scripts for dozens of films, some based on the plays, some not. Virtually all of his plays "work," in the sense that they make the audience laugh, and they have made Simon enormously rich. Yet in the late 1980s, Simon turned more serious and philosophical, and his deeply felt trilogy of autobiographical plays, *Brighton Beach Memoirs, Biloxi Blues,* and *Broadway Bound,* have proved astute and compassionate works that have attracted a more sober appreciation of Simon's gifts.

In the 1990s, Simon has continued writing semi-autobiographical works, including the highly unconventional *Jake's Women,* a revisitation of various women in his life—and in his mind; *Laughter on 23rd Street,* which recalls the author and his colleagues as gag writers for the great 1950s TV comic, Sid Caesar; and *Lost in Yonkers,* a profoundly powerful work about a Holocaust survivor and her family, for which Simon has received the Pulitzer Prize and the widespread critical acclaim that, for

Neil Simon's award-winning Lost in Yonkers *(1990) is one of his most serious and moving plays. Here, Irene Worth (seated) plays an embittered Holocaust survivor, and Mercedes Ruehl plays her slightly retarded daughter. (Photo: Martha Swope and Associates.)*

the most part, has previously eluded him. But the prolific Simon has also continued to write straight comedies as well, including the pure farce, *Rumors,* and his most recent play, *London Suite* (1995), which for the first time in Simon's career was premiered off-Broadway rather than on.

Simon is a consummate New York playwright, whose work is also popular in dinner and community theatres; his work is rarely performed in regional theatres, however, and it is almost a mark of pride for regional theatres to say "we don't do Neil Simon" as a short-hand way of saying that they don't produce conventional, or commercial, or well-made comedies. Simon probably has more fans and more detractors than any other living playwright, but his early comedies are unmatchable in their craftsmanship and easygoing humor, and his recent work shows evidence of a deep and lasting theatrical achievement.

Edward Albee (born 1928) *The Zoo Story,* a one-act, two-character play set in New York's Central Park, brought Edward Albee to prominence in 1959. The play concerns a chance meeting between a married publisher (Peter) and a young drifter (Jerry), both male; at play's end Jerry impales himself on a knife he has given to Peter. The odd story, its electrifying dialogue, its gingerly oblique treatment of homosexuality, and, particularly, its initial pairing on a double bill with Samuel Beckett's *Krapp's Last Tape* gave Albee immediate national attention that would be almost impossible to achieve today. And with his first full-length play, *Who's Afraid of Virginia Woolf?,* premiering on Broadway shortly thereafter, Albee quickly assumed the mantle of America's leading new playwright in the early 1960s.

Subsequent Albee plays have had both great success—*A Delicate Balance* (what happens when a married couple mysteriously gets frightened and moves in with their best friends) and *Seascape* (what happens when a pair of lizards pop in on a married couple at the beach) won the Pulitzer Prizes in 1967 and 1975—and failure (*Tiny Alice* provoked outrage along with mild admiration; *The Man With Three Arms* was scathingly attacked by New York critics). But Albee's newest play, the trenchant, autobiographical *Three Tall Women,* thrust the author back in the limelight in 1994, winning him his third Pulitzer and a chance to laugh off his critics once again. This play, a two-act disquisition on Albee's own mother, in person and in spirit, blends anger and compassion as Albee has not previously shown and places its author back in the front ranks of American dramatists.

Lanford Wilson (born 1937) A pioneer playwright in the heady days of New York experimental theatre in the 1960s, Lanford Wilson's first plays, many produced at the Café La Mama and Caffe Cino theatre bars, included evocative and sometimes profound studies of male homosexuality (*The Madness of Lady Bright*), interracial marriage (*The Gingham Dog*), and small-town small-mindedness (*The Rimers of Eldritch*). Joining with director Marshall Mason and other Caffe Cino colleagues, Wilson helped create the Circle Repertory Theatre in New York, which produced his celebrated *The Hot l Baltimore,* about the comings and goings of a down-and-out hotel (the missing "e" in the title indicates the hotel's neon sign with one letter burnt out) and a series of emotionally affecting plays about the fictional midwestern Talley family: *The Fifth of July, Talley's Folly* (which won the 1980 Pulitzer Prize), and *A Tale Told.*

In recent years, the Circle Repertory has coproduced Wilson's newer plays with regional theatres in different parts of the country, developing *Burn This* (1987, with John Malkovich) at the Los Angeles Mark Taper Forum before taking it to New York and its subsequent Broadway success, and *Redwood*

Curtain, which premiered at the Seattle Repertory Theatre before transferring to New York in 1993.

Wilson is a prolific playwright, with more than thirty published plays. His writing for the most part (*Burn This* is an exception) is gentle, poetic, natural, and wise; although he is dramaturgically innovative, his plays do not call attention to their structures or to the author's subtle stylistic departures. Wilson is one of America's most classical native playwrights.

John Guare (born 1938)

Going from graduate school (Yale) also into the Café La Mama–Caffe Cino avant-garde circle in the early 1960s, Guare became widely known with a series of mildly surrealistic and "wacky" plays, such as *Muzeeka* in 1968 and *The House of Blue Leaves* in 1970, laced with social and cultural satire. He continued to mine the same vein, securing a small but loyal New York audience through the 1970s and 80s.

In the 1990s, however, Guare again burst onto the national scene with the masterful satire *Six Degrees of Separation,* which explores, and acidly reveals, racial stereotyping, contemporary parenting and misparenting, and the cultural dissonances in contemporary adult America. *Six Degrees,* which opened at Lincoln Center in 1990, was widely produced by America's regional theatres shortly thereafter. Guare's subsequent *Four Baboons Adoring the Sun,* an even more ambitious allegory, proved more controversial but equally provocative in its 1992 Lincoln Center debut. And his *Moon Under Miami Collides with Chicago! Seer Predicts Audiences Stunned! Outraged! Delighted!,* a tale of political bribery and tropical shenanigans that premiered at the Organic Theatre of Chicago in 1995, is as audacious as its title.

Terrence McNally (born 1939)

McNally's first produced play, the angry and nightmarish . . . *And Things That Go Into The Night,* was virtually booed off its Broadway stage when it premiered in 1965; McNally was viewed as a raging young avant-gardist having little in common with the audiences of his time. Both time and McNally changed. A series of hilarious and provocative comedies, often on sexual themes, followed in the 1970s (*Next* and *The Ritz* became widely popular), yielding to a more deft and delicate comic collection in the 80s and 90s. *The Lisbon Traviata* (1989) explored a gay male couple's relationship in which their passion for opera masked a fundamental void in their capacity for affection. *Lips Together, Teeth Apart* (1992) explored the relationships of and between two married couples, summering in the beach house where a relative of one of them has just died of AIDS; it is a comedy with a poisonous snake under the pretty terrace.

Subsequently, *Kiss of the Spider Woman* (1993) got McNally—who wrote the book—his first Tony Award, and the superb *Love! Valour! Compassion!* (1994) got him his second: the first is a musical about sexual and political betrayal in a South American prison, and the second is a wicked and sensitive portrayal of eight gay men—bright, urban, and urbane—weekending in the country, occasionally in the buff. McNally's most recent play, *Master Class* (1995), about Maria Callas, won him a third Tony in 1996.

McNally has the gift of blending passion with humor and tracking the universal emotions within a variety of lifestyles. No longer just an angry young playwright, McNally has become a superb theatrical craftsman and a powerful innovator of new dramatic idioms.

Sam Shepard (born 1943)

Coming to prominence, like Guare, in the coffeehouses of Greenwich Village in the 1960s, Sam Shepard then received great acclaim in the 70s and 80s with his successful full-length plays *The Tooth of Crime, The Curse of the Starving Class, Buried Child* (which won the Pulitzer Prize), *True West, Fool for Love,* and *A Lie of the Mind.*

Shepard's plays are prose poems; the language is highly musical, and the subject matter, which is generally contemporary and American, suggests modern myth more than everyday reality. His plays, which invariably involve some violence, create arresting (and often inexplicable) images and tantalize the audience with moments of extreme surface realism that ultimately opens into something more abstract. His early plays are wildly surreal and dreamlike, but these qualities have diminished in his more realistic plays of the late 1980s. During this period Shepard became additionally well known for his acting performances in films such as *The Right Stuff* and his own *Fool for Love*. But he continues to write for the theatre and scored a significant success in New York with his *States of Shock* in 1991 and *Simpatico* in 1995.

David Mamet (born 1947) Known as a Chicago playwright because Chicago is his birthplace, his home, the setting of most of his plays, and the city where his plays have most often been premiered, David Mamet served for some time as an associate artistic director of Chicago's Goodman Theatre. Mamet's plays, like some of Shepard's, employ at least fragments of intensely realistic writing and feature rhythmic language patterns that, though brutal, may seem almost musical. Indeed, Mamet's dialogue is often strung out of mere fragments of language: the tortured syntax of everyday speech, rather than the turned phrases of eloquent discourse. Mamet's characters' talk is a series of frustrated stammerings, grunts, curses, repetitions, trail-offs, and the hemmings and hawings of nervous conversation; in all, there might not be but one or two complete sentences in an entire Mamet play. *Sexual Perversity in Chicago* brought him immediate attention in 1974, and *A Life in the Theatre, American Buffalo, Glengarry Glen Ross*, and *Speed-the-Plow* (starring Madonna on Broadway) have solidified his reputation in the ensuing years.

In the 1990s, Mamet (like Shepard) has turned much of his attention to the cinema (with screenplays such as *Hoffa, The Untouch-*

ables, and *House of Games*). But in 1992 he returned to the theatre with the scorching play *Oleanna*, a masterful and intense drama about a charge of sexual (and academic) harassment brought by a college student (female) against her professor (male), and in 1994 he premiered a gripping new autobiographical work, *The Cryptogram*. David Mamet will clearly continue to play a major role in the coming era of American theatre.

Marsha Norman (born 1947) National attention focused on Marsha Norman at the new play festival of the Actors Theatre of Louisville (Kentucky) in 1978 with her first play, *Getting Out:* a driving, biting study of a woman's release from prison—and her even more powerful subsequent "imprisonment" by the forces of economics, male chauvinism, and sexual harassment. Norman's next play, *'night, Mother,* a brutally sad depiction of a young woman's suicide and the helplessness of her mother to stop it, earned Norman the Pulitzer Prize in drama in 1983. Norman's subsequent play, *Traveller in the Dark*, failed to gain critical approval, however, and her career faltered for some time, until she wrote the book for the musical version of *A Secret Garden*, a major Broadway success of 1991. Norman is a strong, committed writer on social and feminist issues, as well as the creator of vivid stage characters and powerful dramatic emotions.

Wendy Wasserstein (born 1950) After graduating from Mount Holyoke College (B.A.) and City College of New York (M.A.), Wendy Wasserstein wrote her first important play, *Uncommon Women and Others,* while a graduate student at the Yale Drama School (1976). Since then she has been highly admired for her successful off-Broadway play, *Isn't It Romantic?*, and then *The Heidi Chronicles,* which was created in workshop format at the Seattle Repertory Theatre before opening on Broadway and capturing both the Tony Award and Pulitzer Prize for 1989.

Marsha Norman's 'night, Mother *is one of the most searing, most touching depictions of the relations between a mother and a daughter ever written. The play is here shown in its 1986 production at the Alliance Theatre of Atlanta, Georgia.*

Wasserstein is deeply concerned with the situation of the American woman, particularly women who struggle with what they see as the dialectics of marriage and career, romance and political struggle, fiery activism and traditionally passive "feminine" roles. Wasserstein's characters mostly come from the upper-middle-class Jewish intelligentsia that the author springs from herself ("Heidi" is an academic and mildly feminist art historian), but her writing is universal and broadly probing. There are no easy answers in Wasserstein's work, but there is a deep level of investigation and a powerful dramatic momentum.

Wasserstein's new play, *The Sisters Rosensweig* (1993), is in some ways her most accomplished: a neo-Chekhovian comedy about three sisters who meet in London, where one of them lives, and compare their in-process lives and loves. Themes of Jewishness, feminism, the career versus the home, and theatricalization in everyday life are melded into a brilliant comic stew. With triumphant performances by Jane Alexander and Madeline Kahn, Wasserstein's play was a Broadway hit and has now moved into the regional theatre with thumping success.

Beth Henley (born 1952)

Crimes of the Heart, Beth Henley's first play, was awarded the Pulitzer Prize in drama in 1981. Initially produced at the Actors Theatre of Louisville new play festival before going to Broadway, *Crimes* is a wildly irreverent comedy about three young Mississippi sisters coming together at the joint crises of their individual lives; the play, while not directly feminist in its themes, was one of the first major mainstream American plays to focus primarily on women's problems and women's issues.

Henley's more recent work has stayed true to this focus: *The Miss Firecracker Contest,* an off-Broadway success in 1984, is another Mississippi family drama in which two cousins vie for top prize in a beauty contest; and *Abundance,* which premiered at South Coast Repertory Theatre in California before moving to off-Broadway, is the story of two mail-order brides in chauvinist nineteenth-century Wyoming. "Henley has an unmistakable talent for making human desperation seem funny, complex and unpredictable," said reviewer Robert Massa in the *Village Voice* of this work.

George C. Wolfe (born 1954)

Widespread attention came to George C. Wolfe with his satirical musical play, *The Colored Museum,* in 1986, and *Spunk,* a musical and dramatic adaptation of tales by Zora Neale Hurston, in 1989. Both were initially produced at the Crossroads Theatre of New Brunswick, New Jersey, and subsequently at the Public Theatre in New York, where Wolfe became artistic director in 1993.

Wolfe, a Kentucky-born African American, uses humor and music as wedges to explore deeply painful subjects; as a result, his plays are hilarious and unsettling—even scathing—at the same time. "Once we reach the desired altitude, the Captain will turn off the 'Fasten Your Shackle' sign," says the stewardess of the "Celebrity Slaveship" at the beginning of *The Colored Museum.*

Wolfe's genius (he is also the director of his plays) is to skewer hoary clichés and persistent stereotypes of the "colored" world that emanate from both white and African-American subgroups—and at the same time to embed his societal critique of racism in a theatricality that is enthusiastic, accessible, and celebratory. With his *Jelly's Last Jam* in 1992, a Broadway musical about the African-American jazz musician Jelly Roll Morton, Wolfe went mainstream—winning Tony nominations for both writing and directing and also winning a worldwide audience of admirers.

Wolfe's most recent achievements have been directorial: a chilling production of a new play by Oliver Meyer, *Blade to the Heat,* at the Public Theatre, mixing a macho sports theme (boxing) with racial and sexual overtones, accompanied by a heart-pounding rhythm and blues score; and a stunningly poetic—but also hot-tempered and political—production of Shakespeare's *The Tempest,* with Patrick Stewart as Prospero, in New York's Central Park. "Dizzying showmanship" said one critic; "awesome" said another of these productions. Other reviews were mixed, but attendance is up at Wolfe's theatres, and multiculturalism is definitely *in* for the rest of the decade.

Tony Kushner (born 1956)

Surely no play has burst upon the contemporary American theatre scene with such thrilling panache as Tony Kushner's seven-hour, two-part *Angels in America.* Initially commissioned by the Eureka Theatre in San Francisco, the play was subsequently developed at the Mark Taper Forum Theatre in Los Angeles and (Part One only) at the Royal National Theatre in London. The two parts had separate openings on Broadway in 1993, under the direction of George C. Wolfe, and received rapturous critical acclaim. Part One, *Millennium Approaches,* took the Tony Award and Pulitzer

Prize in 1993, and Part Two, *Perestroika*, took the Tony in 1994—an unprecedented achievement. By 1995 the play had fully entered the international repertoire and was receiving major productions in theatre capitals and drama festivals throughout the world.

Angels in America fully merits this extraordinary attention: it is a true masterpiece of modern drama; many consider it the finest American play of the present generation. Dealing unstintingly with the AIDS crisis, Kushner has laid bare unsettled issues in the American culture that touch upon race, religion, gender, politics, economics, and sexual orientation. Pairing a heterosexual couple (Joe and Harper Pitt, Mormons from Utah) with a homosexual one (Louis Ironson, a New York Jew, and Prior Walter, afflicted both with AIDS and a lineage that goes back to the *Mayflower*), Kushner interweaves their stories and shakes up their lives within a vast medical/political "America," which is run in Kushner's imagination by Roy Cohn—the (real) self-hating, self-baiting, one-time gay/Jewish lawyer in raging self-denial right up to his awful, AIDS-ravished demise. A black nurse (male) and white angel (female) also play sustained roles in this adventure, which is additionally peopled with another twenty-five characters, real and imagined, and all played by the eight actors in the cast: a rabbi, an Eskimo, a travel agent, a real-estate saleswoman, the ghost of Ethel Rosenberg, various doctors, nurses, angels, and a man we are told is "the world's oldest Bolshevik." What is astonishing about Kushner's work is its explosive humor: this is one of the funniest American plays of the century. But it's also one of the saddest. Not for all audiences, and rejected by many theatre producers in conservative cities (the play includes frontal nudity, grisly depictions of AIDS suffering, savage religious satire, the blatant miming of homosexual acts, and a good deal of in-your-face hurling of loathing invectives), *Angels* has a transporting and transforming effect on spectators who are attuned to its rhythms and subject. Most claim to come out of the seven-hour performance ennobled.

And just who is this Tony Kushner? Born in New York City in 1956 and raised in Louisiana, Kushner had been known, pre-*Angels*, only for one very minor play and an adaptation of Pierre Corneille's French classic, *The Illusion*. Since *Angels* he has been represented with a brilliant short piece on a Russian theme, *Slavs! Thinking About the Longstanding Problems of Virtue and Happiness* (1994), which is comprised mainly of outtakes from *Angels*, including an appearance by the *Angels'* Bolshevik, and he has been devoting his time preparing the screenplay, to be directed (at the time of this writing) by Robert Altman. Is Kushner a one-play dramatist? Time will tell. But even if so, the one play will make him a name to be reckoned with well into the next millennium.

David Henry Hwang (born 1957) Growing up in San Gabriel, California, Hwang began writing—"on a lark" he says—while a Stanford undergraduate; his first play, *FOB* ("Fresh Off the Boat"), is a biting, honest, angry reaction to hidden (and not-so-hidden) American racism; it was first produced by the Stanford University Asian-American Theatre Project. Subsequently, it was accepted and produced at the O'Neill Center in Connecticut and then at the New York Public Theatre in 1980, where it (and its leading actor) both won "Obie" (Off-Broadway) awards.

Hwang's subsequent *M. Butterfly* (1988), his most celebrated work, explores the bizarre relationship between a French diplomat and his Chinese mistress: bizarre because the mistress is revealed, during the play, to be—unbeknown to the diplomat—a man in disguise. Here, Hwang's subject is "Orientalism," or the ingrained sense of deprecation with which Western culture views the Asian East. Hwang, of Chinese heritage, brilliantly interweaves gritty Western realism with Asian theatre and Chinese Opera technique in these two works, lending them both current/political and timeless/mythic proportions; in *M. Butterfly* he inserts portions of the Puccini opera that gives the play its name, creating a wonderfully theatrical East-West confabulation. *M. Butterfly* won Hwang the Tony Award and international fame. Hwang's subsequent *1000 Airplanes on the Roof,* a "science-fiction music-drama" written in collaboration with composer Philip Glass and designer Jerome Sirlin, is a boldly imaginative fantasy monologue, with music and projections, that toured the world following its 1988 premiere in a Vienna airplane hangar. This work is not particularly concerned with East-West themes; Hwang clearly does not intend to be bound to ethnic subject matter in his future work.

CONCLUSIONS ON THE CURRENT THEATRE?

Can there be any conclusions concerning the current theatre? No, there cannot—simply because what is current is never concluded. The current theatre is in process; it is like a book we are just beginning. The plays and playwrights discussed in this chapter may not, in the end, be accorded significant positions in our era of theatre; even the movements they now seem to represent may prove minor and transitory. We are not in a position even to hazard guesses at this point: we can only indicate certain directions in which to look for clues as to where the future will lead us.

Meanwhile the evidence plays nightly on the stages of the theatre world. It is there to apprehend, there to enjoy, there to appreciate, and there, finally, to be refined by opinion and encapsulated into critical theory and aesthetic categorization—if that is our wish.

More than being a play, or a series of plays, or a spectrum of performances, the current theatre is a worldwide event, a *communication* between people and peoples that raises the level of human discourse and artistic appreciation wherever it takes place. The current theatre responds to the impulses of creativity and expression and to the demands of human contact and understanding. It synthesizes the impulses of authors and artists, actors and audiences, to foster a medium of focused interaction that incorporates the human experience and embodies each culture's aspirations and values. No final chapter can be written on this medium, no last analysis or concluding categorization. All that is certain is that the art, and the feeling, of theatrical life will endure.

PART **IV**
THE
PRACTITIONERS

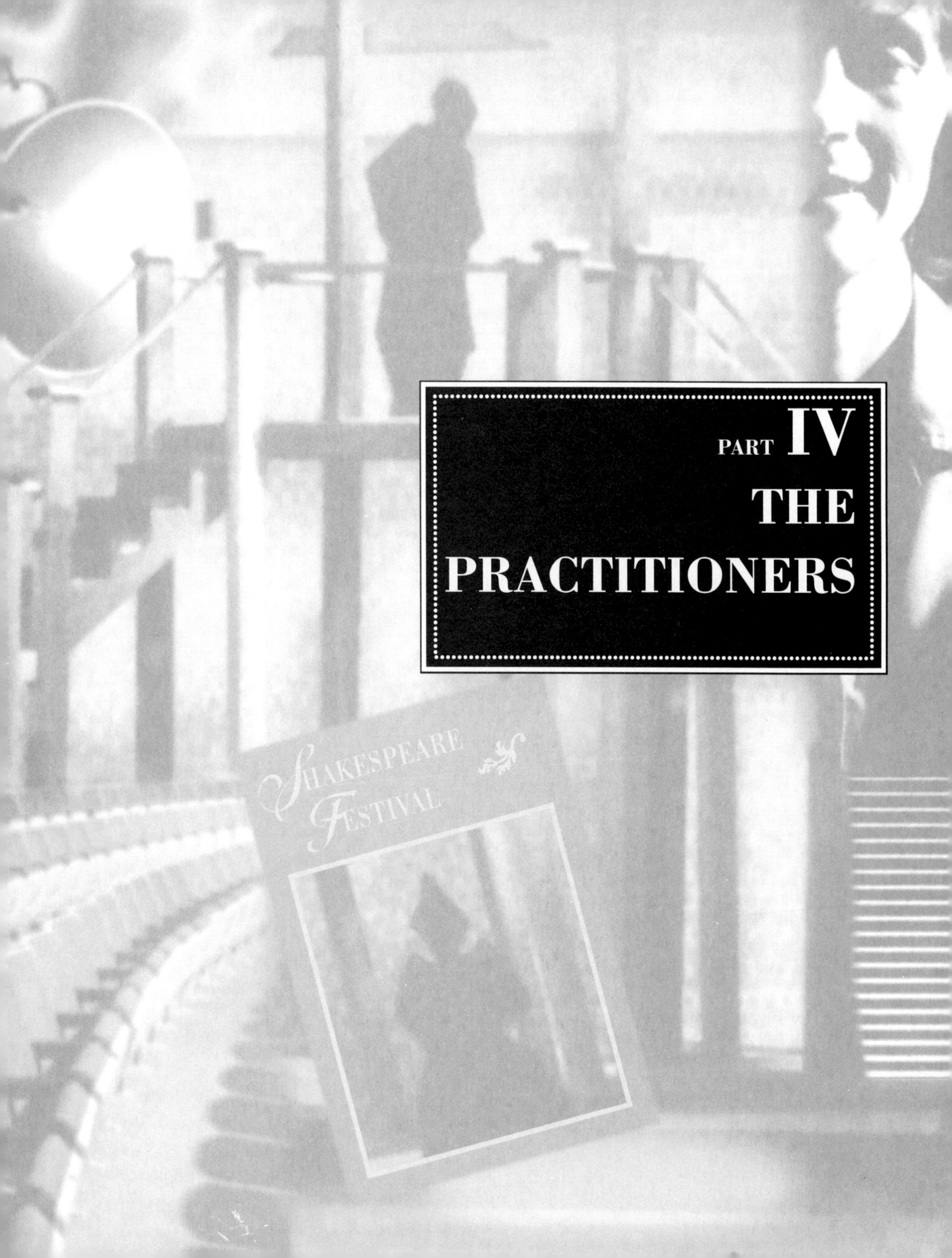

You can read a play by yourself, but it may take dozens of people to bring the play to life in a theatre. These people are the theatre practitioners, and it is through their coordinated efforts that the theatre is created.

These practitioners primarily include the actors, playwrights, directors, designers, and technicians who are directly involved in the writing, staging, and performing of dramatic works—but these job titles do not complete the list. Producers, administrators, poster artists, publicity writers, press agents, box-office staff, secretaries, fund-raisers, photographers, house managers, ushers, and many other individuals also spend much of their time, and perhaps earn much of their living, as vital cocreators of this intricately collaborative art.

To think of "the theatre" simply as a building, or as a series of plays or play productions, is to miss a crucial point: the theatre is, above all, a living artistic process. It is not a thing, but an activity—an activity that, for many men and women, becomes the mainstay of their lives. The theatre basically is people—people who essentially make art out of themselves.

A theatre education should begin, therefore, with a study not merely of the theatre's works, but also of the theatre's workings. Specifically, it should entail a close examination of the many practices that go into theatrical production and of the individual practitioners who must work together in a uniquely collaborative artistic process.

In these ways, "theatre people" create the life of the drama.

11

The Actor

. . . .

She stands alone in the darkness, waiting in the wings, listening with one ear to the insistent rhythms of the dialogue played out upon the stage immediately beyond. Her heart races, and she bounces lightly on the balls of her feet, fighting the welling tension, exhilarated by the sense of something rushing toward her, about to engulf her.

The stage ahead of her is ablaze with light; dazzling colors pour on from all possible directions. The energy on stage is almost tangible: it is there in the eyes of the actors, the pace of the dialogue, the smell of the makeup, the sparkle of sweat and saliva glittering in the lights, the bursts of audience laughter and applause, the sudden silence punctuated by a wild cry or a thundering retort.

She glances backward impatiently. Other actors wait in the backstage gloom. Some perform kneebends and roll their necks against the tension. Some gaze thoughtfully at the action of the play; some stare at the walls. In one corner a stage manager, his head encased in electronic paraphernalia, his body hunched over a dimly lighted copy of the script, whispers commands into an intercom. The backstage shadows pulse with anticipation.

Suddenly the onstage pace quickens: the lines, all at once, take on a greater urgency and familiarity. It is the cue . . . if only there were time to go to the bathroom . . . it is the

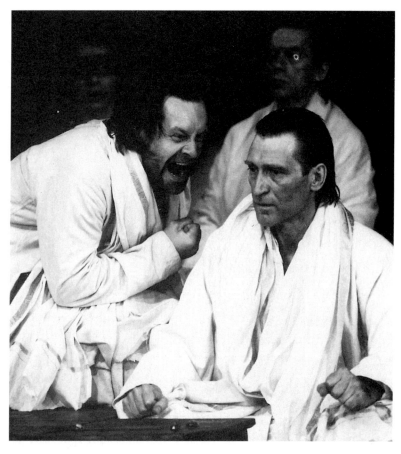

Acting is a flesh-and-blood art: within the lifeless frame of scenery and proscenium, the actors' bodies, minds, feelings, and fantasies are deeply involved, animating the play with vibrant human passion and imagination. The impersonation we call "acting" takes place on every level: physiological, psychological, and spiritual. From the Peter Brook production of The Mahabharata. *(Photo: Gilles Abegg.)*

cue . . . she takes a deep breath, a deeper breath, a gasp . . . it is *the cue* and she bounds from the dimness into the dazzle: she is on stage, she is an actor!

It is perhaps the world's most bewildering profession.

At the top, it can be extraordinarily rewarding. The thrill of delivering a great performance, the roar of validation from an enraptured audience, the glory of getting inside the skin of the likes of Hamlet, Harpagon, and Hecuba: these are excitements and satis-

factions few careers can match. Nor are the rewards purely artistic and intellectual ones: audience appreciation and the producer's eye for profit can catapult some actors to the highest income levels in the world, with salaries in the millions of dollars for actors achieving "star" status in films. And the celebrity that can follow is legendary: the private lives of the most universally admired actors become public property, their innermost thoughts the daily fare of television talk shows and fan magazines.

All actors were male in the Greek and Elizabethan theatre, and in traditional Japanese (Nō and Kabuki) theatre as well; men have played women onstage for more than two thousand years. When they do so in modern plays, it is often as an example of a character's cross-dressing or transvestism; the male actor doing so is said to perform "in drag," as in a skirt that drags on the ground. (Male characters played by females are correspondingly known as "pants roles.") Here, actress Cynthia Mace and actor Stephen Spinella (in "drag") have a gabfest about their respective husbands/boyfriends (among other things) in Tony Kushner's Angels in America, *produced at the Mark Taper Forum in Los Angeles in 1992. This brilliant play, called by its author "a gay fantasia on national themes," explores many social, political, sexual, medical, and even comic aspects of gay American life. (Photo: Jay Thompson.)*

And yet, for all the splendor and glamour, the actor's life is more often than not depressingly anxious, beset by demands for sacrifice from every direction: psychological, financial, and even moral. Stage fright—the actor's nemesis—is an ever-present nightmare that often increases with experience and renown.

Fear of failure, fear of competition, fear of forgetting lines, fear of losing emotional control, fear of losing one's looks, fear of losing one's audience—this combination is endemic to acting as to no other profession.

Nor are the economic rewards in general particularly enticing. The six- and seven-figure salaries of the stars bear little relation to the scale pay for which most actors work: theirs is the lowest union-negotiated wage in the free market economy, and actors often realize less income than the janitors who clean the theatres. And although the stars billed "above the title" may be treated like celebrities or royalty, the common run of actors are freely bullied by directors, bossed about by stage managers, capriciously hired and fired by producers, dangled and deceived by agents, squeezed and corseted by costumers, pinched by wig dressers, poked and powdered by make-up artists, and traduced by press agents. Certainly no profession entails more numbing uncertainties than acting, none demands more sacrifices, and none measures its rewards in such extreme and contradictory dimensions.

WHAT IS ACTING?

But what is acting? The question is not as simple as it might seem.

It is, of course, the oldest of the theatrical arts. Theatre begins with the actor, who improvised his own dialogue. Thespis, the first known actor (from whence our word *thespian*, meaning "actor"), was also the author of the dramas in which he appeared.

It is also the most public art of theatre, and the average theatregoer today can name many more actors than playwrights, designers, and directors put together.

Essentially, the art of acting involves "playing" dramatic roles. This playing, however, involves two somewhat different processes that must be joined together.

Mimesis: Imitation

Superficially, the actor "imitates" a dramatic character. In more technical terms, we can say that the actor presents a "mimesis," or a simulation, of the sort of behavior the author has written about. Part of acting is always mimetic, or imitative. Costume, make-up, and mannerisms may be part of this mimetic activity.

In some cases, imitation is of a real-life person—as when the actor Robert Morse, in the production of Jay Presson Allen's *Tru*, imitated the voice, appearance, and mannerisms of the play's well-known title character, Truman Capote. Richard Burbage, although with more historical distance (and without the advantage—or disadvantage—of photos or videotapes), had much the same task in creating Shakespeare's roles of Richard III and Coriolanus, both based on real individuals.

In other cases, the simulation is of an entirely fictional or even a fantasy character, such as Chekhov's Masha or Barrie's Peter Pan.

Mimesis—imitation—is deeply rooted in child's play, which in all cultures includes "pretending" and "dressing up" as ways of exploring adult roles. We all have a history of imitations; we have all been mimetic "actors" in the "play" of our early lives.

That mimesis is central to theatre was specifically noted by Aristotle, drama's first theorist, who defined tragedy as an "imitation of an action." It is not enough, Aristotle implied, to present the blinding of Oedipus, but the actor has to imitate the action fully as well.

Embodiment: Becoming

Nevertheless, external mimesis is not the whole of acting; and from the earliest times, actors have gone well beyond merely imitating their characters: they have "embodied" them as well, which is to say they have invested them with their own minds and bodies. It is not enough for such actors merely to "put on" Richard III's limp and speak Richard III's lines; they must also—during the moments of performance—think Richard III's thoughts and live Richard III's life.

Of course, much of this embodiment will happen anyway. The actress Jessica Lange may play the role of Blanche du Bois, but it is Lange's arms, legs, face, and eyes we will see; it is Lange's voice we will hear and, indeed, it is Lange's racing pulse and hard breathing that audience members in the first rows can distinctly observe; it is even Lange's perspiration that we may see gathering on her brow. It is Lange, not "Blanche," who sweats. The actor *is* the character in many regards. But how about the actor's personality? Or the actor's feelings?

Most actors, in response to these questions, will say they act their roles "from the inside" as well as from the "outside." These actors believe they "feel" their role's emotions as much as (or more than) they simply imitate feelings artificially. The "pretending" of acting, therefore, goes very deep into the center of the actor's personality. In embodying a role, the actor embodies (puts into his/her body) the feelings as well as the actions of the character.

This embodiment can be literal: one ancient Greek actor, we are told, was so overcome by emotion while playing Atreus that he drew his sword and sliced off the head of an errant stagehand during one performance. Another Greek actor, Polus by name, when playing the role of Electra, brought the ashes of his dead son onstage with him so as to generate the requisite feeling for a cry of lamentation. (In a contemporary variation of

The actor James Whitmore plays Justice Oliver Wendell Holmes in the 1995 Williamstown Theatre Festival production of The Magnificent Yankee, *directed by Peter Hunt. Whitmore's portrayal of a well-known public figure—whose image is remembered by many in the audience—relies on extensive research as well as carefully fashioned costuming (designed by Noel Taylor) and make-up. (Photo: Richard Feldman.)*

We don't know what the real Mark Antony looked like, and we probably don't care. What the actor has to do in playing the role is to convince us of his grief at the death of Caesar, his fury at Caesar's assassins, and his passionate commitment to avenge Caesar's death and fulfill his own ambitions. This calls for attention to the "internal" aspects of acting—that is, playing the character's feelings and acting with (what seems like) the character's level of intensity. Al Pacino in the 1988 Julius Caesar at the New York Shakespeare Festival. John McMartin is the dead Caesar. (Photo: © George E. Joseph.)

that practice, Jessica Lange, performing her Broadway Blanche, wore the scent used by a friend of hers who had died of AIDS; the perfume aided her emotional expression in a speech about Blanche's dead husband.) Embodying a character, as opposed to merely imitating one, requires that the actor's self-expression come from the center. This can elicit a performance that seems—or maybe even *is*—"real" in the sense that the actor's whole physiology performs: pulse, respiration, neural systems, and hormones. (Indeed, the etymology of *emotion* refers to the "out-motion" of presumed "humours" that medieval physicians believed ruled passions and personality—the hormones, in other words.)

The theatre, therefore, has provided the stage not only for character and dramaturgic development, but for actor embodiment and self-expression as well and has done so since the earliest of times. The rituals of the earliest Dionysian dithyrambs and tragedies were improvised out of direct, immediate, ecstatic, and intensely personal demands as much as from a desire to "imitate" anything. Socrates, noting that the rhapsodic poets of his day were overcome by feelings when they recited their work, considered these performances more inspired than rational: "Are you not carried out of yourself, and does not your soul, in ecstasy, seem to be among the persons or the places of which you are speaking?" he asked the poet Ion. Ion agreed that in speaking he was emotionally transported, as was his audience. Horace, in Rome, put this together by stating that orators (and, by implication, actors) could move their audience *only* when, indeed, they were moved themselves; and the vast majority of theatre theorists and critics since—as well as acting teachers—have agreed. Some have even argued that actors should live out their parts in real life. French theatre critic Sainte Albine (1747) proposed that only actors who were truly in love could effectively play lovers onstage, unless they could develop a "happy insanity" that could persuade them they were experiencing exactly what their characters seemed to experience; and for the next two centuries great actors were thought to be either promiscuous—or insane.

Not all have held this view of the actor's emotions, however, and later writers applied Apollonian brakes to some of the Dionysian ecstasies. French encyclopedist Denis Diderot, in his *Paradox of the Actor*, written later in the eighteenth century, argued fervently that the actor should be coldly *un*emotional and should reproduce his part with only rational intelligence and sober aesthetic judgment. "At the moment when [the great actor] touches your heart he is listening to his own voice; his talent depends not, as you think, upon feeling, but upon rendering so exactly the outward signs of feeling that you fall into the trap. . . . The broken voice, the half-uttered words, the stifled or prolonged notes [are all just] . . . magnificent apery," said Diderot. Although a radical statement of a view rarely accepted today, Diderot's words illuminate the issue of what the actor is or is not doing during the moments of actual performance.

Virtually all contemporary acting theories and pedagogies (teaching methods) attempt to integrate the imitative and expressive sides of acting—or to consolidate working from the "outside" and from the "inside," as actors tend to describe these apparently paradoxical demands. Obviously, a performance that fails to fulfill, in its outward (imitative) form, the expectations the text establishes—a performance, for example, that fails to show Prometheus as angry, Falstaff as blustery, or Cleopatra as regally arrogant—will be strikingly unsatisfying. But so will be a performance where the characters' interactions, no matter how boldly or eloquently executed,

Falstaff must be seen as blustery and fat. Actor Lou Zorich creates both characteristics in JoAnne Akalaitis's 1991 production of Henry IV *at the New York Shakespeare Festival. Zorich's grizzled beard and stomach padding (costumes are by Gabriel Berry) help, but the performance finally will be defined by the energy Zorich puts into his depiction. (Photo: © George E. Joseph.)*

seem merely flat and mechanical, or where the passions seem shallowly pasted on, or where no sparks fly and no romance kindles between the persons seemingly represented onstage. Imitation without embodiment rings hollow, and embodiment ("being real") without mimetic definition soon grows tiresome. The best acting synthesizes its expressive and its mimetic aspects and its Dionysian and Apollonian roots.

Beyond these two main lines of the actor's art, there are two other aspects one always finds in the greatest performers: *virtuosity* of technique and the ineffable "magic" that defines the greatest artists in any field.

Virtuosity

Greatness in acting, like greatness in almost any endeavor, demands a superb set of skills.

The characters of drama are rarely mundane; they are exemplary and so must be the actors who portray them. Merely to impersonate—to imitate and embody—the genius of Hamlet, for example, one must deliver that genius oneself. Similar personal resources are needed to project the depth of Lear, the lyricism of Juliet, the fervor of St. Joan, the proud passion of Prometheus, the bravura of Mercutio, or the heroics of Hecuba. Outsized characters demand outsized abilities and the capacity to project them.

Moreover, it is ultimately insufficient for an actor merely to fulfill the audience's preconceptions of his or her character; finally, it is necessary that the actor strive to transcend those preconceptions and to create the character afresh, transporting the audience to an understanding of—and a compassion for—the character that they never would have achieved on their own.

Both of these demands require of the actor a considerable virtuosity of dramatic technique.

Traditionally, the training of actors has concentrated on dramatic technique. Since Roman times (and probably before then), actors have spent most of their lifetime perfecting such performing skills as juggling, dancing, singing, versifying, declaiming, clowning, miming, stage fighting, acrobatics, and sleight of hand. Certainly no actor before the present century had any chance of success without several of these skills, and few actors today reach the top of their profession without fully mastering at least a few of them.

Whatever the individual skills required of an actor over time, the sought-after dramatic technique that is common to history and to our own times can be summed up in just two features: a magnificently expressive voice and a splendidly supple body. These are the tools every actor strives to attain, and when brilliantly honed they are valuable beyond measure.

The actor's voice has received the greatest attention through history. Greek tragic actors were awarded prizes for their vocal abilities alone, and many modern actors, such as James Earl Jones, Patrick Stewart, Glenn Close, and Maggie Smith, are celebrated for their distinctive use of the voice. The potential of the acting voice as an instrument of great theatre is immense. The voice can be thrilling, resonant, mellow, sharp, musical, stinging, poetic, seductive, compelling, lulling, and dominating; and an actor capable of drawing on many such "voices" clearly can command a spectrum of acting roles and lend them a splendor the less gifted actor or the untrained amateur could scarcely imagine. A voice that can articulate, that can explain, that can rivet attention, that can convey the subtlest nuance, that can exult, dazzle, thunder with rage, and flow with compassion—this, when used in the service of dramatic impersonation, can hold an audience spellbound for as long as its owner cares to recite.

The actor's use of his or her body—the capacity for movement—is the other element of fundamental technique, the second basis for dramatic virtuosity. Most of the best actors are strong and supple; all are capable of great physical self-mastery and are artists of body language. The effects that can be achieved through stage movement are as numerous as those that can be achieved through voice. Subtly expressive movement in particular is the mark of the gifted actor, who can accomplish miracles of communication with an arched eyebrow, a toss of the head, a flick of the wrist, a whirl of the hem, or a shuffle of the feet. But bold movements, too, can produce indelible moments in the theatre: Helene Weigel's powerful chest-pounding when, as Mother Courage, she loses her son; Laurence Olivier's breathtaking fall from the tower as Coriolanus—these are sublime theatricalizations accomplished through the actors' sheer physical skill, strength, and dramatic audacity.

Virtuosity for its own sake can be appealing in the cabaret or lecture hall as well as in the theatre, but when coupled with the impersonation of character it can create dramatic performances of consummate depth, complexity, and theatrical power. We are always impressed by skill—it is fascinating, for instance, to watch a skilled cobbler finishing a leather boot—but great skill in the service of dramatic action can be absolutely transporting. Of course, virtuosity is not easy to acquire, and indeed it will always remain beyond the reach of many people. Each of us possesses natural gifts, but not all are gifted to the same degree; some measure of dramatic talent must be inborn or at least early learned. But the training beyond one's gifts, the shaping of talent into craft, is an unending process. "You never stop learning it," said actor James Stewart after nearly fifty years of stage and film successes, and virtually all actors would agree with him.

Traditional notions of virtuosity in acting went into a temporary eclipse in the middle of this century, owing mainly to the rise of realism, which required that acting conform to the behaviors of ordinary people leading ordinary lives. The *cinéma vérité* of the post–World War II era in particular fostered an "artless" acting style, to which virtuosity seemed intrusive rather than supportive. It is certainly true that the virtuosity of one age can seem mere affectation in the next and that modern times require modern skills, a contemporary virtuosity that accords with contemporary dramatic material. Yet even the traditional skills of the theatre have made a great comeback in recent decades: circus techniques, dance, and songs are now a part of many of the most experimental of modern stagings; and multiskilled, multitalented performers are in demand as never before. The performer rich in talent and performing skills, capable not merely of depicting everyday life but of fashioning an artful and exciting theatrical expression of it as well, once again commands the central position in contemporary drama.

Magic

Beyond impersonation and virtuosity, though incorporating them, remains a final acting

Robert DeNiro is surely one of the most charismatic actors of recent years, and his film credits (Jake LaMotta in Raging Bull *won him an Oscar) have made him internationally known. His stage performances are no less noteworthy, however; DeNiro exudes frightening, riveting intensity. Here, he performs with young Ralph Macchio in Reinaldo Povod's powerful play of contemporary urban life,* Cuba and His Teddy Bear, *at the New York Public Theatre. (Photo: © George E. Joseph.)*

ingredient that has been called "presence," "magnetism," "charisma," and many other terms. We shall call it "magic."

It is a quality that is difficult to define but universally felt, a quality we cannot explain except to say we know it when we are under its spell.

We must always remember that the actor began not as a technician of the theatre, but as a priest—and that he embodied not ordinary men, but gods. We may witness this function directly today in certain tribal dramas, in which a shaman or witch doctor is accepted by cocelebrants as the possessor of divine attributes—or as one possessed by them.

The modern secular actor also conveys at least a hint of this transcendent divinity. Ele-

vated upon a stage and bathed in light for all to see, charged with creating an intensity of feeling, a vivid characterization, and a well-articulated eloquence of verbal and physical mastery, the actor at his or her finest becomes an almost extraterrestrial being, a "star," or, in the French expression, a "sacred monster."

The actor's presence, the ability to project an aura of magic—this does not come about as a direct result of skill at impersonation or technical virtuosity. It does, however, depend on the actor's inner confidence, which in turn can be bred from a mastery of the craft. Therefore, though "magic" cannot be directly acquired or produced, it can be approached, and its fundamental requisites can be established. For gifted individuals it might come quickly; for others, despite abundant skills and devoted training, it comes late or not at all and they can never rise above pedestrian performances. It is perhaps frustrating to find that acting greatness depends so heavily on this elusive and inexplicable goal of "magic," but it is also true that every art incorporates elements that must remain as mysteries. The best acting, like any art, ultimately transcends the reach of pure descriptive analysis; it cannot be acquired mechanically. The best acting strikes chords in the nonreasoning parts of our being; it rings with a resonance we do not fully understand, and it evokes a reality we no longer fully remember. We should extol, not lament, this fact.

BECOMING AN ACTOR

How does one become an actor? Many thousands ask this question every year; many thousands, indeed, *act* in one or more theatrical productions every year. The training of actors is now a major activity in hundreds of colleges, universities, conservatories, and private and commercial schools in the United States; and theories of actor training constitute a major branch of artistic pedagogy.

Essentially, actor training entails two distinct phases: development of the actor's instrument and development of the actor's method of approaching a role. There is no general agreement on the order in which these phases should occur, but there is a widespread understanding that both are necessary and that the two are interrelated.

The Actor's Instrument

The actor's instrument is the actor's self—mind, mettle, and metabolism are the materials of an acting performance. An actor's voice is the Stradivarius to be played; an actor's body is the sculpting clay to be molded. An actor is a portrait artist working from inside the self, creating characters with his or her own organs and physiological systems. It is obvious that a great artist requires first-rate equipment: for the actor this means a responsive *self,* disciplined yet uninhibited, capable of rising to the challenges of great roles.

The training of the actor's instrument is both physiological and psychological; for that reason it must be accomplished under the personal supervision of qualified instructors. In the past, acting instructors were invariably master actors who took on younger apprentices; even today, students of classical French and Japanese acting styles learn their art by relentless imitation of the actors they hope to succeed. In America, however, acting instruction has expanded to include a great many educational specialists who may or may not have had extensive professional acting experience themselves; indeed, some of the most celebrated and effective acting teachers today are play directors, theatrical innovators, and academicians.

No one, however, has yet discovered the art of training an actor's instrument simply by reading books or thinking about problems of craft. This point should be borne in mind in reading the rest of this chapter.

The Physiological Instrument

Voice and speech, quite naturally, are the first elements of the actor's physiological instrument to be considered: "Voice, voice, and more voice" was the answer Tommaso Salvini, the famed nineteenth-century Italian tragedian, gave to the question "What are the three most important attributes of acting?" We already have discussed the importance of vocal skills in the acting profession: voice- and speech-training programs are aimed at acquainting the actor with a variety of means to achieve and enhance these skills.

The basic elements of voice (breathing, phonation, resonance) and of speech (articulation, pronunciation, phrasing)—as well as their final combination (projection)—are all

Acting is not something you can do entirely on your own—most acting involves dynamic interaction with other actors. The effectiveness of great acting is usually a factor of the depth, complexity, and intensity of the relationship that two actors can create with each other while performing.

Left: Greta Lambert as Hannah and Greg Thornton as Shannon—verging unsteadily toward a possible relationship—in the 1995 Alabama Shakespeare Festival production of Tennessee Williams's The Night of the Iguana. *(Photo: Scarsbrook.)*

Right: Stephen Spinella and Joe Mantello as a gay couple, torn apart by AIDS but on the verge of a reconciliation, in Tony Kushner's Angels in America. *Mark Taper Forum production, 1992. (Photo: Jay Thompson.)*

separate areas of the integrated instruction a good voice-training program will provide. Such a program ordinarily takes three years or longer, and many actors continue working on their voice and speech all their lives.

As devoted as teachers and scientists have been to the problems of perfecting voice and speech, however, a certain mystery still surrounds much of their work. Even the fundamental question of how the voice actually works is still a subject of fierce dispute among specialists in anatomy and physiology. Moreover, the processes involved in breathing and speaking have acquired a certain mystique; for example, the dual meaning of "inspiration" as both "inhalation" and "spirit stimulus" has given rise to a number of exotic theoretical dictums that border on religiosity. Some of the fundamental practices of vocal and speech instruction, however, are generalized in the box on the components of voice and speech.

THE COMPONENTS OF VOICE AND SPEECH

Breathing pumps air through the vocal tract, providing a carrier for the voice. "Breath support," through expansion of the rib cage and lowering and controlling the diaphragm, is a primary goal, as is natural, deep, free breathing that is sufficient to produce and sustain tone, but not so forced as to create tension or artificial huffing and puffing.

Phonation is the process whereby vocal cord oscillations produce sound, a process that remains something of an anatomical and physiological mystery even today. Vocal warm-ups are essential for the actor to keep his or her vocal cords and other laryngeal (voice box) tissues supple and healthy; they also prevent strain and the growth of "nodes" that may cause raspiness and pain as well as phonic failure (laryngitis).

Resonance is the sympathetic vibration, or "resounding," of the voice as it is amplified in the throat, chest, and head. Resonance gives phonation its *timbre,* or tonal quality, its particular balance of "bass" and "treble" sounds. Open-throatedness—the lowering of the larynx within the neck, as by a yawn—increases the resonance in the pharynx (throat) and is a major goal in voice work. Keeping the mouth open while speaking and raising the soft palate also increase resonance and add to vocal quality.

Articulation is the shaping of vocal sound into recognizable *phonemes,* or language sounds, forty of which are easily distinguishable in the English language. Programs of speech training aim at improving the actor's capacity to articulate these sounds distinctly, naturally, and unaffectedly—that is, without slurring, ambiguous noise, or self-conscious maneuvering of the lip and tongue. A lazy tongue and slovenly speaking habits inhibit articulation and can be overcome only with persistent drill and disciplined attention.

Pronunciation makes words both comprehensible and appropriate to the character and style of the play; clear standard pronunciation, unaffected by regional dialect, is a cru-cial part of the actor's instrument, as is the ability to learn regional dialects and foreign accents when required. Occasionally an actor achieves prominence with the aid of a seemingly permanent dialect—Andy Griffith and Sissy Spacek are two examples—but such actors are likely to find their casting opportunities quite limited unless they can expand their speaking range.

Phrasing makes words meaningful and gives them sound patterns that are both rhythmic and logical. The great classical actors are masters of nuance in phrasing, capable of subtly varying their pitch, intensity, and rate of speech seemingly without effort from one syllable to the next. They rarely phrase consciously; rather, they apparently develop their phrasing through years of experience with classical works and a sustained awareness of the value of spontaneity, naturalness, and a commitment to the dramatized situation. Training programs in speech phrasing aim at enabling actors to expand the pitch range of their normal speech from the normal half-octave to two octaves or three, to double their clear-speaking capacity from 200 words a minute to 400, and to develop their ability to orchestrate prose and verse into effective and persuasive crescendos, diminuendos, sostenutos, and adagios just as if they were responding to a musical score.

Projection, which is the final element in the delivery of voice and speech to the audience, is what ultimately creates dramatic communication; it governs the force with which the character's mind is heard through the character's voice, and it determines the impact of all other components of the actor's voice on the audience. Anxiety and physical tension are the great enemies of projection because they cause shallow breathing, shrill resonance, and timid phrasing; therefore, relaxation and the development of self-confidence become crucial at this final stage of voice and speech development.

An extraordinary degree of movement discipline, including dance and mime technique, is required for the actors in Robert Wilson's theatrical experiments. Wilson's staging relies heavily on dreamlike images, with actors often moving in extreme slow motion through a variety of hard-to-sustain poses and actions. Pictured here is Wilson's startling performance piece, The Forest, *in its 1988 German premiere; Wilson has subsequently restaged the work in the United States. (Photo: Gerhard Kassner; courtesy German Information Center.)*

Movement is the other main factor to be considered in training the actor's physiological instrument, and this factor is developed primarily through exercises and instruction designed to create physical relaxation, muscular control, economy of action, and expressive rhythms and movement patterns. Dance, mime, fencing, and acrobatics are traditional training courses for actors; in addition, circus techniques and masked pantomime have become common courses in recent years.

Sheer physical strength is stressed by some actors. The late Laurence Olivier, for example, accorded it the highest importance because, he contended, it gives the actor the stamina needed to "hold stage" for several hours of performance and the basic resilience

to accomplish the physical and psychological work of acting without strain or fatigue.

An actor's control of the body permits her or him to stand, sit, and move on stage with alertness, energy, and seeming ease. Standing tall, walking boldly, turning on a dime at precisely the right moment, extending the limbs joyously, sobbing violently, springing about uproariously, and occupying a major share of stage space are among the capacities of the actor who has mastered body control, and they can be developed through training and confidence. In the late days of the Greek theatre, known as the Hellenistic period, actors used elevated footwear, giant headdresses, and sweeping robes to take on a larger-than-life appearance; the modern actor has discovered that the same effect can be achieved simply by tapping the residual expansiveness of the body.

Economy of movement, which is taught primarily through the selectivity of mime, permits the conveyance of subtle detail by seemingly inconspicuous movement. The waggle of a finger, the flare of a nostril, the quiver of a lip can communicate volumes in a performance of controlled movement. The beginner is often recognized by uncontrolled behaviors—fidgeting, shuffling, aimless pacing, and fiddling with fingers—which draw unwanted audience attention. The professional understands the value of physical self-control and the explosive potential of a simple movement that follows a carefully prepared stillness. *Surprise,* which is one of the actor's greatest weapons, can be achieved only through the actor's mastery of the body.

The Psychological Instrument *Imagination,* and the willingness and ability to use it in the service of art, is the major *psychological* component of the actor's instrument. At the first level, an actor must use his imagination to make the artifice of the theatre *real enough to himself* to convey that sense of reality to the audience: painted canvas flats must be imagined as brick walls, an offstage jangle must be imagined as a ringing onstage telephone, and an actress no older than the actor himself must be imagined as his mother or grandmother.

At the second, far more important level, the actor must *imagine himself in an interpersonal situation created by the play:* in love with Juliet, in awe of Zeus, in despair of his life. This imagination must be broad and all-encompassing: the successful actor is able to imagine himself performing and relishing the often unspeakable acts of his characters, who may be murderers, despots, or monsters; insane or incestuous lovers; racial bigots, atheists, devils, perverts, or prudes. To the actor, nothing must be unimaginable; the actor's imagination must be a playground for

The scene between Hamlet and his mother, Gertrude, is one of the most unsettling in drama, intermixing deep affection and violent rage. There's a killing, a ghost, and tumultuous feelings of guilt and betrayal. Here, Kevin Kline plays Hamlet (he also directed the play) and Dana Ivey plays Gertrude in a 1990 production at the New York Public Theatre. (Photo: © George E. Joseph.)

expressive fantasy and darkly compelling motivations.

At the third, deepest level, the actor's imagination must become more active; it must go beyond the mere accommodation of an accepted role pattern to become a *creative* force that makes characterization a high art. For each actor creates his or her role uniquely—each Romeo and Juliet are like no others before them, and each role can be uniquely fashioned with the aid of the actor's imaginative power. The final goal of creating a character is to create it freshly, filling it with the pulse of real blood and the animation of real on-the-spot thinking and doing. The actor's imagination, liberated from stage fright and mechanical worries, is the crucial ingredient in allowing the actor to transcend the pedestrian and soar toward the genuinely original.

The liberation of imagination is a continuing process in actor training; exercises and "theatre games" designed for that purpose are part of most beginning classes in acting, and many directors use the same exercises and games at the beginning of play rehearsal periods. Because the human imagination tends to rigidify in the course of maturation—the child's imagination is usually much richer than that of the adult—veteran professional actors often profit from periodic returns to "mind-expanding" or imagination-freeing exercises and games.

Discipline is the fourth and final aspect of an actor's psychological instrument, and to a certain extent it is the one that rules them all.

The imagination of the actor is by no means unlimited, nor should it be. It is restricted by the requirements of the play, by the director's staging and interpretation, and by certain established working conditions of the theatre. The actor's artistic discipline keeps him or her within these bounds and at the same time ensures artistic agility.

The actor is not an independent artist, like a writer or a painter. The actor works in an ensemble and is but one employee (paid or unpaid) in a large enterprise that can succeed only as a collaboration. Therefore, although actors are sometimes thought to be universally temperamental and professionally difficult, the truth is exactly the opposite: actors are among the most disciplined of artists, and the more professional they are, the more disciplined they are.

The actor, after all, leads a vigorous and demanding life. Make-up calls at 5:30 in the morning for film actors, and nightly and back-to-back weekend live performances for stage actors, make for schedules that are difficult to maintain on a regular basis. Further, the physical and emotional demands of the acting process, the need for extreme concentration in rehearsal and performance, the need for physical health and psychological composure, the need for the actor to be both the instrument and the initiator of his or her performance, and the special demands of interacting with fellow performers at a deep level of mutual involvement—these aspects of the actor's life do not permit casual or capricious behavior among the members of a cast or company.

Truly professional actors practice the most rigorous discipline over their work habits. They make all "calls" (for rehearsal, costume fitting, photographs, make-up, audition, and performance) at the stated times, properly warmed up beforehand; they learn lines at or before stipulated deadlines, memorize stage movements as directed, collaborate with the other actors and theatre artists toward a successful and growing performance, and continually study their craft. If they do not do these things, they cease to be actors. Professional theatre producers have little sympathy or forgiveness for undisciplined performers, and this professional attitude now prevails in community and university theatres as well.

Being a disciplined actor does not mean being a slave, nor does it mean foregone capitulation to the director or the management. The disciplined actor is simply one who works rigorously to develop his or her physiological and psychological instrument, who meets all technical obligations unerringly and without reminder, and who works to the utmost to ensure the success of the entire production and the fruitful association of the whole acting ensemble. The disciplined actor asks questions, offers suggestions, invents stage business, and creates characterization in harmony with the directorial pattern and the acting ensemble. When there is a serious disagreement between actor and director (a not uncommon occurrence), the disciplined actor seeks to work it out through discussion and compromise and will finally yield if the director cannot be persuaded otherwise. Persistent, willful disobedience has no place in the serious theatre and is not tolerated by it.

The Actor's Approach: Two Traditional Methods

How does an actor approach a role? How does she or he prepare to simulate a character? to embody a character? to create stage magic in a performance? These questions have been answered in many ways, and they are still shrouded in subjectivity and controversy.

Historically, the answers have generally gravitated toward one or the other of two basic methods, the one often called "external" or "technical" and the other often called "internal" or "truthful." These terms are inexact and even somewhat misleading; nevertheless, their historical importance and wide dissemination demand that we pay them some attention at the outset of this discussion.

The external–internal dichotomy refers back to the basic paradox of the theatre itself and to the fact that the actor both simulates and embodies his role. The external methods of approaching a role have concentrated on the actor's acquisition of technique, on development of virtuoso abilities, and on facility at simulating emotions and behaviors without regard to personal feelings. Diderot, of course, who first articulated the paradox, was an extremist in this position, contending that the best acting was done with cool dispassion and that "the great actor watches appearances . . . he has rehearsed to himself every particle of his despair. He knows exactly when he must . . . shed tears; and you will see him weep at the word, at the syllable, he has chosen, not a second sooner or later. . . . At the very moment when he touches your heart he

is listening to his own voice." Believers in such an external approach treat the actor's performance as an analogue of reality rather than a direct embodiment of it, a calculated *presentation* of a character's life rather than its living representation on stage.

Contrarily, internal methods have focused on an actor's "personal assumption" of her or his character; this includes the "use of one's self" in a dramatized portrayal and an effort to "actually experience" a play's events in the very act of performing them. Internal methods tend to expand the psychological dimensions of acting and to help actors assimilate the psycho-physiological reality of their characters—down to the heartbeats and flushes and hormonal activities their characters would undergo if the dramatized situation were real. Internal methods profess to reach into actors' rationally uncontrollable states and to awaken in them feelings and reflexes that are beyond sheer technical manipulation.

Konstantin Stanislavsky, the founder of the Moscow Art Theatre (1898) and one of the all-time great teachers of acting, is most closely associated with internalized acting. His "System," developed over the last three decades of his life, was based on the maxim "You must live the life of your character on stage." In order to achieve this end, he developed research into the subconscious, vigorously studied the intricacies of the lives of characters he was to play, and demanded that his actors be "in character" not only during intermissions and while waiting for cues in the wings, but for the entire day of the performance. It is the actor's "sense of truth which supervises all of his inner and physical activity," said Stanislavsky. "It is only when his sense of truth is developed that he will . . . express the state of the person he is portraying and . . . not merely serve the purposes of external beauty, as all sorts of conventional gestures and poses do."

The follower of the internal approach is likely to judge the external performance to be "hollow," "shallow," "merely technical,"

Playing "ordinary people" in realistic plays is often the biggest challenge for an actor, since the audience quickly understands the characters—and consequently makes great demands on the performers. Neil Simon's Broadway Bound *is a highly realistic, and even autobiographical, play. Jonathan Silverman is the young writer, shown here with Jason Alexander, who plays his older brother Stanley. (Photo: Martha Swope and Associates.)*

"empty," "unfeeling," or "cold." "I didn't believe it" is the frequent complaint of the Stanislavsky adherent. The externalist's criticisms, by contrast, are usually couched in terms such as "unclear," "muddy," "self-indulgent," "overemotional," "melodramatic," "sentimental," "unfocused," and "confused." Partisans for one or the other position are often more distinguishable by their criticisms of other performances than by significant accomplishments of their own.

Integrated Methods

The two traditional methods have had an extraordinary impact on the theatre of the present century. European acting has been responsive to many of the presentational techniques suggested by Diderot, whereas American acting has been particularly influenced by the teaching of Stanislavsky—and by the acting of several of Stanislavsky's followers who studied at the late Lee Strasberg's celebrated

Actors Studio in the 1950s and 60s. Strasberg's variation of the Stanislavsky System (actually it was a variation of an early version—subsequently discarded—of Stanislavsky's System) soon became widely known in the United States simply as "the Method," or as "Method acting." Though to a lesser extent today than in past years, Strasberg's Method continues to attract adherents. Focusing directly on the problem of how the actor can "make his real feelings expressive on the stage," Strasberg, unlike Stanislavsky, privileged the actor over the dramatic character and generated an acting style that can be highly idiosyncratic to the individual performer, who may be thereby encouraged to bring an entire repertoire of personal behavior into performance. Celebrated midcentury actors like Marlon Brando, James Dean, Paul Newman, and Julie Harris were Strasberg students, as were movie celebrities like Marilyn Monroe; they were perhaps drawn in to the Method by the opportunity to transform their personal idiosyncrasies into recognized art (see box "The Actors Studio").

The division of acting into easily defined, easily opposed "schools" has provided convenient grounds for an oversimplified debate in theatre greenrooms and acting classrooms around the world; all too often, quarrels between Method and technical acting theories obscure rather than clarify the profound—and complicated—art of the actor. Much of the division can now be ruled obsolete: much of what passes for Strasberg-inspired Method acting is little more than intentional shuffling, stumbling, and slurring calculated to convince an audience that the actor is "real." Much of what is called technical acting involves no technique at all beyond the ability to mouth schoolboy rhetoric and look handsome.

The contemporary theatre has come to realize that acting involves *both* simulation and embodiment, *both* impersonation and virtuosity, and that, therefore, *both* external and internal processes are involved; the debate between them is irrelevant. Acting approaches of the present day thus tend to integrate the best of the traditional methods and to combine these with new approaches suggested by recent discoveries in psychology and communications, stressing all the while a contemporary awareness of human identity and of the function of the actor in creating and theatricalizing that identity.

The integrated methods of approach favored by most teachers of acting today encourage the student to study the *situational intentions* of the character, the *variety of tactics* the character can employ in the fulfillment of those intentions, and the specific *mode of performance* demanded by the playwright and/or the director.

By "situational intentions" we mean the goals or desires the characters hope to achieve: the victories they have set ahead for themselves. Romeo's intention, for example, is first to win the love of Juliet, then to marry her—and then to join her in Heaven. Hecuba's intention is to shame the Athenians; Monsieur Jourdain's intention is to awe his family and friends. An actor concentrating as fully as possible on such intentions will focus energy, drive out stage fright, and set up the foundation for the fullest use of his or her instrument.

By "tactics" we refer to those actions by which the character moves through the play, as propelled by personal intentions. Romeo woos Juliet through his expressive use of language, his kisses, and his ardent behavior. Hecuba shames the Athenians by taunting them for their weakness and by defeating their rhetoric with her own more noble recitations. Jourdain awes his family—or tries mightily to do so—by parading in what he considers to be fashionable garments. The point is not that the characters must succeed with their tactics or even that they must fulfill their intentions—for those matters are finally determined by the playwright, not the actor—but that the actor must be fully engaged in the pursuit of the character's intentions and imaginative in employing tactics to get what the

THE ACTORS STUDIO

The most influential school of acting in the United States has been New York's Actors Studio, which was founded by director Elia Kazan and others in 1947 and achieved prominence following the appointment of Lee Strasberg (1901–1982) as artistic director in 1951. Strasberg, an Austrian by birth and a New Yorker by upbringing, proved a magnetic teacher and acting theorist, and his classes revolutionized American acting.

Although the Studio has added commercial acting classes to its activities in 1995, it is not primarily a school, but an association of selected professional actors who gather at weekly sessions to work on acting problems. The methodology of the Studio derives in part from Stanislavsky and in part from the working methods of the Group Theatre—a pre–World War II acting ensemble that included Kazan, Strasberg, and playwright Clifford Odets. But Strasberg himself proved the key inspiration of Studio teaching and of the American love affair with Method acting attributed to the Studio work.

Strasberg's work is not reducible to simple formulas, for the Studio is a working laboratory, and the Studio work is personal rather than theoretical, direct rather than general. Much of the mythology that has arisen about the Studio—that actors are encouraged to mumble their lines and scratch their jaws in the service of naturalness—is fallacious. Strasberg was a fierce exponent of firm performance discipline and well-studied acting technique; insofar as the Studio developed a reputation for producing actors that mumbled and fidgeted, this seems to have been only a response to the personal idiosyncrasies of Marlon Brando, the Studio's first celebrated "graduate."

Strasberg demanded great depths of character relationships from his actors, and he went to almost any length to get them. Explanation was only one of his tools, but it is the only one that can be made available to readers. The following quotes are from Strasberg himself:

> The human being who acts is the human being who lives. That is a terrifying circumstance. Essentially the actor acts a fiction, a dream; in life the stimuli to which we respond are always real. The actor must constantly respond to stimuli that are imaginary. And yet this must happen not only just as it happens in life, but actually more fully and more expressively. Although the actor can do things in life quite easily, when he has to do the same thing on the stage under fictitious conditions he has difficulty because he is not equipped as a human being merely to playact at imitating life. He must somehow believe. He must somehow be able to convince himself of the rightness of what he is doing in order to do things fully on the stage.
>
> When the actor explores fully the reality of any given object, he comes up with greater dramatic possibilities. These are so inherent in reality that we have a common phrase to describe them. We say, "Only in life could such things happen." We mean that those things are so genuinely dramatic that they could never be just made up. . . .
>
> The true meaning of "natural" or "nature" refers to a thing so fully lived and so fully experienced that only rarely does an actor permit himself that kind of experience on the stage. Only great actors do it on the stage, whereas in life every human being to some extent does it. On the stage it takes the peculiar mentality of the actor to give himself to imaginary things with the same kind of fullness that we ordinarily evince only in giving ourselves to real things. The actor has to evoke that reality on the stage in order to live fully in it and with it.[1]

---

[1]Hethmon, 1965, pp. 78, 197–98.

EMOTION IN ACTING

If emotion is a state, the actor should never take cognizance of it. In fact we can never take cognizance of an emotion when we are in its grip, but only when it has passed. Otherwise the emotion disappears. The actor lives uniquely in the present; he is continually jumping from one present to the next. In the course of these successive presents he executes a series of actions which deposit upon him a sort of sweat which is nothing else but the state of emotion. This sweat is to his acting what juice is to fruit. But once he starts perceiving and taking cognizance of his state of emotion, the sweat evaporates forthwith, the emotion disappears and the acting dries up. . . . We cannot think "I am moved" without at once ceasing to be so. [Therefore] . . . no one in a theatre should allude to the fragile phenomenon, emotion. Everyone, both players and audience alike, though under its influence, must concern themselves with actions.

Jean-Louis Barrault

character wants. An actor who is fully and powerfully engaged, who commands the language of the play and the action of the dramatized situation, can create a character who is magnificent even in defeat: he or she can thus transport the audience and deliver a fully theatrical performance.

By "mode of performance" we mean the intended relationship between the play's characters and its audience. For example, the actor must know whether the audience is expected to empathize with the characters, to analyze them, to be socially instructed by them, or merely to be entertained by them. The contemporary theatre has utilized many different performance modes, some entirely realistic, others radically antirealist in tone and structure. We have seen how the theatre of Bertolt

Brecht, for example, theoretically eschews "theatre magic" altogether and demands that the actors simulate their characters without fully embodying them. Other performance modes that have adopted and created distinctive theatrical conventions include improvisational theatre, street theatre, music theatre, and the "holy theatre" of Jerzy Grotowski. All of these modes impose, for the actor, performance requirements beyond the impersonation of character through intentions and tactics.

It is at the junction of tactics, intentions, and performance modes that simulation, embodiment, and virtuosity come together. For they all stand upon the same foundation: the actor's assumption of the character's intentions and the actor's committed pursuit of the character's goals. Forceful tactics derived from that pursuit, such as power and precision in speaking, articulate wit, authoritative bearing, and the implicit threat of pent-up passions, give an acting performance its strength; seductive tactics derived from the same pursuit, such as poetic sensitivity, disarming agreeability, sexual enticement, and evocative nuance, create the magnetism of stage performance.

The aspects of acting, separate in this analysis, come together again in both the actor's mind and in that of the audience. Even Brecht found, despite his theories, that performances under his direction created the very magic he decried and occasioned incontrovertible examples of character embodiment. Great stylized performances are both "felt" by the actors and "believed" by audiences; technical virtuosity, the actor's ability to shift easily and uninhibitedly among a great variety of tactics and to commit fully to a compelling set of character intentions, underlies great acting in any style and any performance motif.

Finally, every actor finds a personal method of approaching a role. Moreover, every actor learns eventually that the process is an everchanging one: every role is different, every role makes different demands on the actor's

"EVERYBODY UNDERSTANDS FRUSTRATION"

One time I had this scene where I was to walk into this actress' dressing room and say something like "I love you; will you marry me?" We managed to make it better by having the girl go into her bathroom and close the door and I had to say those lines to a closed door. I learned to work with counterpoint. To make the material more interesting I would find ways to create obstacles for the character—frustrate him in what he wants to accomplish. That makes the character more sympathetic, because everybody understands frustration.

Jack Lemmon

instrument, and every role strikes different chords within the actor's own psychological experience and understanding. An accomplished actor's method will change with each role, with each director, and to a certain extent with each rehearsal and each performance. The more flexible the actor's approach, the more versatile he can be and the more capable he is of meeting the multiple demands of his art. The more encompassing his method, the more unblinking his self-analysis and the more sophisticated his technique, the more he will be able to apply himself rigorously and creatively, which will lead him further and further into the depth and breadth of his art.

THE ACTOR'S ROUTINE

In essence, the actor's professional routine consists of three stages: auditioning, rehearsal, and performing. The first is the way the actor gets a role, the second is the way the actor learns it, and the last is the way the actor produces it, either night after night on a stage or one time for film or taping. Each of these stages merits independent consideration, for each

imposes certain special demands on the actor's instrument and on his or her approach.

Auditioning

For all but the most established professionals, auditioning is the primary process by which acting roles are awarded. A young actor may audition hundreds of times a year. In the film world, celebrated performers may be required to audition only if their careers are perceived to be declining: two of the more famous (and successful) auditions in American film history were undertaken by Frank Sinatra for *From Here to Eternity* and by Marlon Brando for *The Godfather*. Stage actors are customarily asked to audition no matter how experienced or famous they are.

In an audition the actor has an opportunity to demonstrate to the director (or producer or casting director) how well he or she can fulfill the role sought; in order to show this, the actor presents either a prepared reading (which may be taken from any play) or a "cold reading" from the script whose production is planned.

Every actor who is seriously planning for a career in the theatre will prepare several audition pieces to have at the ready in case an audition opportunity presents itself. For the most part these pieces will be one- or two-minute monologues from plays, although sometimes short narrative cuttings from novels, stories, and poems are used. Each audition piece must be carefully edited for timing and content (some alteration of the text, so as to make a continuous speech out of two or three shorter speeches, is generally permissible); the piece is then memorized and staged. The staging requirements should be flexible to permit adjustments to the size of the audition place (which might be a stage but could just as well be an agent's office) and should not rely on costume or particular pieces of furniture. Most actors prepare a variety of these pieces, for although auditions generally spec-

HOW TO AUDITION

Doubtless many readers of this book will wish to audition for a play at some time in their lives. It is a wonderful experience, provided one is prepared to deal with the chance of rejection, for it energizes the mind and body in a one-to-one relationship that has no exact equal anywhere else.

There can be no consensus as to what sort of audition will be successful in any given circumstance, since directors vary widely in what they are looking for—and what they are *not* looking for—and a certain amount of interpersonal chemistry inevitably influences the final decisions. However, these general points about auditioning might prove useful to the beginner.

Audition pieces should always be selected from material suitable to the actor. For example, an inexperienced young person should not prepare a speech of King Lear's for audition purposes, for this role would almost surely be beyond his grasp; far better that he prepare a piece reasonably in concert with his own age and experience.

Similarly, audition pieces should be suited to the role sought or the play auditioned for. It would be foolish even for a veteran performer to prepare material from *King Lear* if the play being cast were a light comedy; only the most creative casting director could get any idea from the Lear audition of how the actor would come across if given a role in the play under consideration.

Auditions should evoke the actor's most theatrically interesting qualities. They should do something to "grab" the attention of the director; otherwise they fail, no matter how competently performed. An audition, after all, is not a classroom assignment: it is an appeal to the director that should say—should actually *scream*—"Look no farther, you've found what you're looking for!" All auditions, whether of the prepared or the cold-reading variety, should be designed to bring out the actor's ability to concentrate on situational objectives and to employ engaging tactics, thus giving evidence of the actor's range within the required context; only then can the director get a valid idea of the actor's potential contribution to the excitement of his planned theatrical experience.

Auditions should be given with confidence and without extensive preamble, apology, or explanation. Excessive nervousness or slavish deference to the director, though they be occasioned by nothing more than shyness, can freeze the actor and ruin an audition; conversely, the bluster that sometimes is attempted to cover shyness is likely to read as an attitude of superiority or defiance, which is rarely encouraged. Continual auditioning is the best single means of developing calm and powerful auditioning; every actor with professional ambitions should audition as often as possible and under as many sorts of circumstances as present themselves.

Auditions should be short. In some professional situations the actor has no control whatever over the amount of time allotted for auditions, and the audition is routinely cut off after just ten or fifteen seconds. While most directors dislike cutting auditions off in midcourse, they do learn most of what they want to know in a few moments and allow the audition to continue only as a matter of courtesy. Thus the first few moments of an audition count enormously, and the best auditioners learn to get themselves across in a very short time.

Auditions can be practiced; prepared auditions can be coached and rehearsed successfully, and cold-reading techniques can be developed. But nothing demonstrates a fine actor so much, in an audition, as the confidence, control, and authority that come with training and experience. No actor should concentrate exclusively on developing an "audition method," for the audition can afford only a glimpse of the performer's total capabilities. The best preparation an actor can make for auditions is to look to his or her whole development as an actor.

ify two contrasting selections (one verse and one prose, or one serious and one comic, or one classical and one modern), an extra piece that fits a particular casting situation can often come in handy. An actor's audition pieces are as essential as calling cards in the professional theatre world and in many academies as well; they should be carefully developed, coached, and rehearsed, and they should be performed with assurance and poise.

The qualities a director looks for at an audition vary from one situation to another, but generally they include the actor's ease at handling the role; naturalness of delivery; physical, vocal, and emotional suitability for the part; and spontaneity, power, and charm. Most directors also look for an actor who is well trained and disciplined and capable of mastering the technical demands of the part, who will complement the company ensemble, and who can convey that intangible presence that makes for "theatre magic." In short, the audition can show the director that the actor not only knows his or her craft, but also will lend the production a special excitement.

Rehearsing

Plays are ordinarily rehearsed in a matter of weeks: a normal period of rehearsal ranges from ten weeks for complex or experimental productions to just one week for many summer stock operations. Much longer rehearsal periods, however, are not unheard of; indeed, the productions of Stanislavsky and Brecht were frequently rehearsed for a year or more. Three to five weeks is the customary rehearsal period for American professional productions—but these are forty-hour weeks, and they are usually followed by several days (or weeks) of previews and/or out-of-town tryouts, with additional rehearsals between performances.

During the rehearsal period the actor studies and learns the role. Some things investigated in this period are the character's biography; the subtext (the unspoken communications) of the play; the character's thoughts, fears, and fantasies; the character's objectives; and the world envisioned by the play and the playwright. The director will lead discussions, offer opinions, and issue directives with respect to some or all of these matters; the director may also provide reading materials, pictures, and music to aid the actor in his or her research.

The actor must memorize lines, stage movements ("blocking"), and directed stage actions ("business") during the rehearsal period. He or she must also be prepared to re-memorize these if they are changed, as they frequently are: in the rehearsal of new plays it is not unusual for entire acts to be rewritten between rehearsals and for large segments to be changed, added, or written out overnight.

Memorization usually presents no great problem for young actors, to whom it tends to come naturally (children in plays frequently memorize not only their own lines but everyone else's, without even meaning to); however, it seems to become more difficult as one gets older. But at whatever age, memorization of lines remains one of the easier problems the actor is called upon to solve, even though it is the one many naive audience members think would be the most difficult. Adequate memorization merely provides the basis from which the actor learns a part; the important memory goal of the actor is not simply to get the lines down, but to do it *fast* so that most of the rehearsal time can be devoted to concentrating on other things.

The rehearsal period is a time for experimentation and discovery. It is a time for the actor to get close to his character's beliefs and intentions, to steep himself in the internal aspects of characterization that lead to fully engaged physical, intellectual, and emotional performance. It is a time to search the play's text and the director's mind for clues as to how the character behaves and what results the character aims for in the play's situation. And it is a time to experiment, both alone and in rehearsal with other actors, with the possibilities of subtle interactions that these investigations develop.

Externally, rehearsal is a time for the actor to experiment with timing and delivery of both lines and business; to integrate the staged movements, given by the director, with the text, given by the playwright, and to meld these into a fluid series of actions that build and illuminate by the admixture of his own personally initiated behavior. It is a time to suggest movement and "business" possibilities to the director (presuming the director is the sort who accepts suggestions, as virtually all do nowadays) and to work out details of complicated sequences with the other actors. It is also a time to "get secure" in both lines and business by constant repetition—in fact, the French word for "rehearsal" is *répétition*. And it affords an opportunity to explore all the possibilities of the role—to look for ways to improve the actor's original plan for its realization and to test various possibilities with the director.

Thus the rehearsal of a play is an extremely creative time for an actor; it is by no means a routine or boring work assignment—and indeed for this reason some actors enjoy the rehearsal process even more than the performance phase of production. At its best, a rehearsal is both spontaneous and disciplined, a combination of repetition and change, of trying and "setting," of making patterns and breaking them and then making them anew. It is an exciting time, no less so because it invariably includes many moments of distress, frustration, and despair; it is a time, above all, when the actor learns a great deal about acting and, ideally, about human interaction on many levels.

Performing

Performing, finally, is what the theatre is "about," and it is before an audience in a live performance that the actor's mettle is put to the ultimate test.

Sometimes the results are quite startling. The actor who has been brilliant in rehearsal can crumble before an audience and completely lose the "edge" of his performance in the face of stage fright and apprehension. Or—and this is more likely—an actor who seemed fairly unexciting in rehearsal can suddenly take fire in performance and dazzle the audience with unexpected energy, subtlety, and depth: one celebrated example of this phenomenon was achieved by Lee J. Cobb in the original production of Arthur Miller's *Death of a Salesman,* in which Cobb had the title role. Roles rehearsed in all solemnity can suddenly turn comical in performance; conversely, roles developed for comic potential in rehearsal may be received soberly by an audience and lose their comedic aspect entirely.

Sudden and dramatic change, however, is not the norm as the performance phase replaces rehearsal: most actors cross over from final dress rehearsal to opening night with only the slightest shift; indeed, this is generally thought to be the goal of a disciplined and professional rehearsal schedule. "Holding back until opening night," an acting practice occasionally employed in the past century, is universally disavowed today, and opening-night recklessness is viewed as a sure sign of the amateur, who relies primarily on guts and adrenalin to get through the evening. Deliberate revision of a role in performance, in response to the first waves of laughter or applause, is similarly frowned upon in all but the most inartistic of theatres today.

Nevertheless, a fundamental shift does occur in the actor's awareness between rehearsal and performance, and this cannot and should not be denied; indeed, it is essential to the creation of theatre art. The shift is set up by an elementary feedback: the actor is inevitably aware, with at least a portion of her mind, of the audience's reactions to her own performance and that of the other players; there is always, in any acting performance, a subtle adjustment to the audience that sees it. The outward manifestations of this adjustment are

Comedy requires a deep commitment to the passions of the characters; although the action is amusing to the audience, it is dead serious to the characters. Here Jeff Goldblum, as Malvolio, presses his unwanted attentions on Michelle Pfeiffer, Lady Olivia, in Shakespeare's comedy Twelfth Night *at the New York Shakespeare Festival, 1989. This production played at the large, outdoor Delacorte Theatre in Central Park; both actors wear body microphones for electronic sound enhancement. (Photo: © George E. Joseph.)*

Solo performance is perhaps the actor's greatest challenge. For the Broadway production of Jane Wagner's The Search for Intelligent Life in the Universe, *actress Lily Tomlin played all the parts—and won the 1986 Tony Award for best actress of the year.*

usually all but imperceptible: the split-second hold for a laugh to die down, the slight special projection of a certain line to ensure that it reaches the back row, the quick turn of a head to make a characterization or plot transition extra clear.

In addition, the best actors consistently radiate a quality known to the theatre world as "presence." It is a difficult quality to describe, but it has the effect of making both the character whom the actor portrays and the "self" of the actor who represents that character especially vibrant and "in the present" for the audience; it is the quality of an actor who takes the stage and acknowledges, in some inexplicable yet indelible manner, that he or she is there *to be seen*. Performance is not a one-way statement given from the stage to the house; it is a two-way, participatory communication between the actors and the audience, in which the former employ text and movement and the latter employ applause, laughter, silence, and attention.

Even when the audience is silent and invisible—and, owing to the brightness of stage lights, the audience is frequently invisible to the actor—the performer "feels" their presence. There is nothing extrasensory about this: the absence of sound is itself a signal, for when several hundred people sit without shuffling, coughing, or muttering, their silence betokens a level of attention for which the actor customarily strives. Laughter, gasps, sighs, and applause similarly feed back into the actor's consciousness—and unconsciousness—and spur (or sometimes, alas, distract) his efforts. The veteran actor can determine quickly how to ride the crest of audience laughter and how to hold the next line just long enough that it will pierce the lingering chuckles but not be overridden by them; he also knows how to vary his pace and/or redouble his energy when he senses restlessness or boredom on the other side of the curtain line. "Performance technique," or the art of "reading an audience," is more instinctual than learned. It is not dissimilar to the technique achieved by the effective classroom lecturer or TV talk show host or even by the accomplished conversationalist. The timing it requires is of such complexity that no actor could master it rationally; he or she can develop it only out of experience—both on stage and off.

Professional stage actors face a special problem unknown to their film counterparts and seldom experienced by amateurs in the theatre: the problem of maintaining a high level of spontaneity through many, many performances. Some professional play productions perform continuously for years, and actors may find themselves in the position—fortunately for their finances, awkwardly for their art—of performing the same part eight times a week, fifty-two weeks a year, with no end in sight. Of course the routine can vary with vacations and cast substitutions; and in fact very few actors ever play a role continuously for more than a year or two, but the problem becomes intense even after only a few weeks. How, as they say in the trade, does the actor "keep it fresh"?

Each actor has his or her own way of addressing this problem. Some rely on their total immersion in the role and contend that by "living the life of the character" they can keep themselves equally alert from first performance to last. Others turn to technical experiments—reworking their delivery and trying constantly to find better ways of saying their lines, expressing their characters, and achieving their objectives. Still others concentrate on the relationships within the play and try with every performance to "find something new" in each relationship as it unfolds on stage. Some actors, it must be admitted, resort to childish measures, rewriting dialogue as they go or trying to break the concentration of the other actors; this sort of behavior is abhorrent, but it is indicative of the seriousness of the actor's problems of combating boredom in a long-running production and the lengths to which some will go to solve them.

The actor's performance does not end with the play, for it certainly extends into the paratheatrical moments of the curtain call—in which the actor-audience communion is direct and unmistakable—and it can even be said to extend to the dressing-room postmortem, in which the actor reflects upon what was done today and how it might be done better tomorrow. Sometimes the postmortem of a play is handled quite specifically by the director, who may give notes to the cast; more typically, in professional situations, the actor simply relies on self-criticism, often measured against comments from friends and fellow cast members, from the stage manager, and from reviews in the press. For there is no performer who leaves the stage in the spirit of a factory worker leaving the plant. If there has been a shift up from the rehearsal phase to the performance phase, there is now a shift down (or a letdown) that follows the curtain call—a reentry into a world where actions and reactions are likely to be a little more calm. There would be no stage fright if there were nothing to be frightened *about,* and the conquering of one's own anxiety—sometimes translated as conquering of the audience: "I really killed them tonight"—fills the actor at the final curtain with a sense of awe, elation . . . and emptiness. It is perhaps this feeling that draws the actor ever more deeply into the profession, for it is a feeling known to the rankest amateur in a high school pageant as well as to the most experienced professional in a Broadway or West End run. It is the theatre's "high," and because it is a high that accompanies an inexpressible void, it leads to addiction.

THE ACTOR IN LIFE

Acting is an art. It can also be a disease.

Actors are privileged people. They get to live the lives of some of the world's greatest and best-known characters: Romeo, Juliet, Phèdre, Cyrano, St. Joan, and Willy Loman. They get to fight for honor, hunger for salvation, battle for justice, die for love, kill for passion. They get to die many times before their deaths, to duel fabulous enemies, to love magnificent lovers, and to live through an infinite variety of human experiences that, though imaginary, are publicly engaged. They get to reenter the innocence of childhood without suffering its consequences and to participate in every sort of adult villainy without reckoning its responsibility. They get to fantasize freely and be seen doing so—and they get paid for it.

Millions of people want to be actors. It looks easy and, at least for some people, it *is* easy. It looks exciting, and there can be no question that it *is* exciting, *very* exciting; in fact, amateurs act in theatres all over the world without any hope of getting paid merely to experience that excitement. Acting addicts, as a consequence, are common. People who will not wait ten minutes at a supermarket checkout stand will wait ten years to get a role in a Hollywood film or a Broadway play. The acting unions are the only unions in the world that have ever negotiated a *lower* wage for some of their members in order to allow them to perform at substandard salaries. To the true acting addict there is nothing else; acting becomes the sole preoccupation.

The addicted actor—the actor obsessed with acting for its own sake—is probably not a very good actor, for fine acting demands an open mind, a mind capable of taking in stimuli from all sorts of directions, not merely from the theatrical environment. An actor who knows nothing but acting has no range. First and foremost, actors must represent human beings, and to do that they must know something about humankind. Thus the proper study of acting is Life, abetted but not supplanted by the craft of the trade. Common sense, acute powers of observation and perception, tolerance and understanding for all human beings, and a sound general knowledge of one's own society and culture are prime requisites for the actor—as well as training, business acumen, and a realistic vision of one's own potential.

A lifetime professional career in acting is the goal of many but the accomplishment of very few. Statistically, the chances of one's developing a long-standing acting career are quite small; only those individuals possessed of great talent, skill, persistence, and personal fortitude stand any chance of succeeding—and even then it is only a chance. But the excitement of acting is not the exclusive preserve of those who attain lifetime professional careers; on the contrary, it may be argued that the happiest and most artistically fulfilled actors are those for whom performance is only an avocation. The excitement of acting, finally, is not dependent on monetary reward, a billing above the title, or the size of one's roles, but on the actor's engagement with drama and with dramatized situations—in short, on a personal synchronization with the theatre itself, of which acting is the very evanescent but still solid center.

12

The Playwright

....

He is an anomalous figure in the theatre.

In his home he is the master of the stage, the initiator of all theatrical art. Facing his writing paper, he is profoundly in control: actions cascade through his head, characters populate his imagination, great scenes parade across his vision, words and speeches pour from his pen. It is to be *his* play, *his* thoughts, *his* people, and *his* words that will resound through the theatres of the world, that will be praised in the press, immortalized in handsomely bound volumes, and examined diligently in the universities. It is he, the playwright, who will win the Pulitzer Prize and the Critics Circle Award and who perhaps will one day sit next to some contemporary Einstein or Schweitzer when the Nobel laureates are lionized at Stockholm.

In the theatre, however, he is the lonely figure who huddles uncomfortably over a legal pad, in a back row, scarcely noticed by the actors and directors who are rehearsing his play, certain in the back of his mind that the theatre is nothing more than an instrument created for the purpose of diluting his ideas and massacring his manuscript.

Has there ever been such an anomaly? For the playwright is both the most central and the most peripheral figure in the theatrical event.

George C. Wolfe is author and director of Jelly's Last Jam, *a Broadway sensation in 1992. The musical tells the story of a famed musician, Jelly Roll Morton, performed by Gregory Hines (right), shown here being counseled by "The Chimney Man," a ghostly philosopher, played by Keith David. (Photo: Martha Swope and Associates.)*

He is central in the most obvious ways. He provides the point of origin for virtually every play production—the script, which is the rallying point around which the director or producer gathers the troops.

And yet that point of origin is also a point of departure. The days when a Shakespeare or a Molière would gather actors around, read his text to them, and then coach them in its proper execution are long gone, replaced by a more specialized theatrical hierarchy in which the director is interposed as the playwright's representative to the theatrical enterprise and its constituent members. More and more, the playwright's function is to write the play and then disappear, for once the script has been typed, duplicated, and distributed, the playwright's physical participation is relegated mainly to serving as the director's sounding board and rewrite person. Indeed, the playwright's mere physical presence in the rehearsal hall can become an embarrassment, more tolerated than welcomed and sometimes not even tolerated.

Fundamentally, the playwright today is considered an independent artist, whose work, like that of the novelist or poet, is executed primarily, if not exclusively, in isolation. There are exceptions, of course: some playwrights work out of the improvisations of actors, and others participate quite fully in rehearsals, even to the point of serving as the initial director of their plays (as Edward Albee, Sam Shepard, and George C. Wolfe often do) or, more extraordinarily, by acting in them (as Tennessee Williams and Michael Christofer have done).

But the exceptions do not, in this case, disprove the rule; since the age of romanticism, the image of the playwright has turned increasingly from that of theatre coworker and mentor to that of isolated observer and social critic. In the long run, this change should occasion no lamentation; for if theatre production now demands collaboration and compromise, the art of the theatre still requires individuality, clarity of vision, sharpness of approach, original sensitivity, and a devotion to personal truth if it is to challenge the artists who are called upon to fulfill it and the audiences who will pay money to experience it.

It is often said that Shakespeare and Molière wrote great plays because they could tailor their parts to the talents of actors whom they knew well. It seems far more likely that they wrote great plays in spite of this, for at the hands of lesser writers, that sort of enterprise produces sheer hack work that simply combines the limitations of the actors with those of the author. Whether writing from inside an acting company or in submission to one, the playwright strives to give life to a unique vision, to create material that tran-

scends what has gone before, both in writing and in performance.

Therefore, the *independence* of the playwright is perhaps his most important characteristic. Playwrights must seek from life, from their own lives—and not from the theatrical establishment—the material that will translate into exciting and meaningful and entertaining theatre; and their views must be intensely personal, grounded in their own perceptions and philosophy, in order to ring true. We look to the theatre for a measure of leadership, for personal enlightenment derived from another's experience, for fresh perspectives, new visions. In other words, simple mastery of certain conventional techniques will not suffice to enable the playwright to expand our lives.

WE ARE ALL PLAYWRIGHTS

For playwriting is not just something we learn, it's something we already do. All of us. Every day—or night.

Every night, dreams come to us in our sleep. Or, rather, they *seem* to come to us: in fact, we create them. For each of us has our own playwright-in-residence, and designer-in-residence, bringing to our semiconscious minds, often in equal measure, fantasies and realities, imaginary people and real ones, idealized memories and gruesome terrors, mirages and nightmares, delusions of grandeur and depictions of our own demise. The situations and characters of our dreams are our own creations: drawn from our careful observations, colored by our unconscious phobias and fancies, stylized into associations of words, scenes, and "stagings" that ring with deep resonance of our innermost plans, fears, and secrets. We all know what it is to create a play out of our imaginations: we do it every night.

Therefore, there is little conformity among playwrights, nor are there easily identified "schools" of associated writers; nor have

Two of America's leading women playwrights talk about the start of their careers:

> [The women's movement] enabled me to leave New York and give up that whole careerism business—the man's world of career stuff. I was always acting as the woman behind a man anyway, I was giving my energies to male careers. That's what the women's movement freed me from, and it also made me see really clearly that there's a necessity to write about very strong women so women can know that there have been strong women in the past.
>
> Megan Terry
> author of *Viet Rock* with the Open Theatre,
> *Calm Down Mother, Keep Tightly Closed In a Cool Dry Place,* and *Approaching Simone*

In one of my early conversations about writing plays, before I had ever written one, that is, Jon Jory, of Actors Theatre of Louisville, told me, "Go back at least ten years and write about some time when you were really scared."

> *Getting Out*, my first play, was the result of that advice. The scary time was the two years I spent teaching in the children's unit of a state mental hospital. . . . The most frightening thing was the realization that once a violent child got into the system, there was no way out for her. The children were also aware of this, and consequently ran away as often as they could. . . . Later, when I sat down to write, I wondered what would happen if one of our girls ever found herself some place she couldn't get out of. Like solitary confinement in federal prison.
>
> Marsha Norman
> author of *Getting Out, 'night, Mother,* and *The Secret Garden*

"rules" of playwriting been laid down with any demonstrable sustained success. Playwrights may come from anywhere.

THE PLAYWRIGHT'S CAREER

How does a person become a playwright? Writing plays, naturally, is the first (and most important) step. But getting that original play produced is almost as challenging.

There are hundreds of "break in" opportunities for playwrights to develop their scripts in open rehearsals or in developmental workshop productions or staged readings. And sometimes a playwright can realize (or can produce herself or himself) a fully staged production.

Many of these developmental opportunities are available through colleges and universities. David Hwang's *FOB* was first presented at his college dormitory at Stanford University, and Wendy Wasserstein's *Uncommon Women and Others* was first presented at the Yale Drama School.

Virtually all regional professional theatres present new plays from time to time, and many—if not most of them—actively solicit new works, usually presenting them first in script-in-hand readings or special workshops, where the work is presented and critiqued by other writers and company artists. Many prize-winning plays have originated, for example, at the Humana New Play Festival at the Actors Theatre of Louisville or South Coast Repertory Theatre's NewSCRipts and play commission programs. Indeed, most important American plays of the 1980s and beyond have seen their first presentation in readings or workshops at theatres like these, although applicants must realize that the competition for workshop slots at these premier theatres is, naturally, quite fierce. An annual publication, *Dramatists Sourcebook* (published by Theatre Communications Group in New York) lists all theatres that solicit new work and identifies any special areas of interest (such as Hispanic theatre) that these theatres might have.

There are also certain "developmental" theatre companies totally devoted to finding, and developing, new scripts. The National Playwrights Conference (at the Eugene O'Neill Center in Waterford, Connecticut, with year-round offices in New York) receives hundreds of applications each year—and selects nine to twelve plays to present, in staged readings, each summer. August Wilson first came to prominence through his "discovery" at the Playwrights Conference.

Finally, there are dramatic contests, fellowship and grant opportunities, commercial reading and critique services, and literary/dramatic agents that aspiring playwrights may consider as they try to build a career in this field; the *Dramatists Sourcebook* is a useful guide to all of these areas. It should be borne in mind, however, that playwriting is an extraordinarily competitive field and that the quality of the work—not the number of contacts—is far and away the critical factor.

LITERARY AND NONLITERARY ASPECTS OF PLAYWRITING

Since drama is often thought of as a form of literature (and is taught in departments of literature) and since many dramatic authors begin (or double) as poets or novelists, it may seem convenient to think of playwriting as primarily a literary activity. It is not. Etymology helps here: *playwright* is not *playwrite,* and writing for the theatre entails considerations not common to other literary forms. Although by homonymic coincidence the words *write* and *wright* sound alike, a "playwright" is a person who *makes* plays, just as a wheelwright is a person who makes wheels. This

distinction is particularly important, because some plays, or portions of plays, are never written at all. Improvisational plays, certain rituals, whole scenes of comic business, subtextual behaviors, and many documentary dramas are created largely or entirely in performance, or are learned simply through oral improvisation and repetition. Some are created with a tape recorder and multiple imaginations and may or may not be committed to writing after the performance is concluded. And others, although dramatic in structure, are entirely nonverbal; that is, they include no dialogue, no words, and very little that is written other than an outline of mimetic effects.

So drama is a branch of literature, but it is a special and distinctive branch. It is not merely an arrangement of words on a page; it is a conceptualization of the interactions of myriad elements in the theatrical medium: movement, speech, scenery, costume, staging, music, spectacle, and silence. It is a literature whose impact depends on a collective endeavor and whose appreciation must be, in large part, spontaneous and immediate; there can be no thought in the drama of relying purely on effects that are perceivable through solitary reading.

A play attains its finished form only in performance upon the stage: the written script is not the final play but the *blueprint* for the play, the written foundation for the production that is the play's complete realization. Some of a play's most effective writing may look very clumsy as it appears in print, as for example:

"Oh! Oh! Oh!"

Shakespeare's Othello

"Howl, howl, howl, howl!"

Shakespeare's King Lear

"No, no, the drink, the drink. O my dear Hamlet,
The drink, the drink! I am poisoned."

Shakespeare's Hamlet

These apparently unsophisticated lines of dialogue in fact provide great dramatic climaxes in an impassioned performance; they are *pretexts for great acting,* the creation of which is far more crucial than literary eloquence to the art of playwriting.

Of course some formal literary values are as important to the theatre as they are to other branches of literature: allusional complexity, descriptive precision, poetic imagery, metaphoric implication, and a careful crafting of verbal rhythms, cadences, and textures all contribute powerfully to dramatic effect. But they are effective only insofar as they are fully integrated with the whole of the theatrical medium, as they stimulate action and behavior through stage space and stage time in a way that commands audience attention and involvement. Mere literary brilliance is insufficient as theatre, as a great many successful novelists and poets have learned to their chagrin when they attempted to write plays.

PLAYWRITING AS EVENT WRITING

The core of every play is action. In contrast to other literary forms, the inner structure of a play is never a series of abstract observations or a collage of descriptions and moralizings; it is an ordering of observable, dramatizable *events.* These events are the basic building blocks of the play, regardless of its style or genre or theme.

Fundamentally, the playwright works with but two tools, both representing the externals of human behavior: dialogue and physical action. The inner story and theme of a play—the psychology of the characters, the viewpoint of the author, the impact of the social environment—must be inferred, by the audience, from outward appearances, from the play's events as the audience sees them. Whatever the playwright's intended message and whatever the playwright's perspective on the function and process of playwriting itself, the play cannot be put together until the playwright has conceived of an event—and then a series of related events—designed to be enacted on a stage. It is this series of related events that constitutes the play's scenario or, more formally, its plot.

The events of drama are, by their nature, compelling. Some are bold and unusual, such as the scene in which Prometheus—in Aeschylus' tragedy—is chained to his rock. Some are subdued, as when the military regiment in Chekhov's *The Three Sisters* leaves town at the play's end. Some are quite ordinary, as in the domestic sequences depicted in most modern realist plays. But they are always aimed at creating a memorable impression. To begin playwriting, one must first conceptualize events and envision them enacted in such a way as to hold the attention of an audience.

The events of a play can be connected to each other in a strict chronological, cause-effect continuity. This has been a goal of the realistic theatre, in which dramatic events are arranged to convey a lifelike progression of experiences in time. Such plays are said to be *continuous* in structure and *linear* in chronology, and they can be analyzed like sociological events, with the audience simply watching them unfold as it might watch a family quarrel in progress in an adjoining apartment.

Continuous linearity, however, is by no means a requirement for play construction (although it was in the days of the neoclassic "Rules"). Many plays are discontinuous and/or nonlinear. The surviving plays of ancient Greece are highly discontinuous, with odes alternating with episodes in the tragedies and a whole host of nonlinear theatrical inventions popping in and out during the comedies. Shakespeare's plays are structured in a highly complex arrangement of time shifts, place shifts, style shifts, songs and subplots ingeniously integrated around a basic theme or investigation of character. And many contemporary plays break with chronological linearity altogether, flashing instantly backward and forward through time to incorporate character memories, character fantasies, direct expressions of the playwright's social manifesto, historical exposition, comic relief, or any other ingredient the playwright can successfully work in.

Linear, point-to-point storytelling still has not disappeared from the theatre—indeed, it remains the basic architecture of most popular and serious plays—but modern (and postmodern) audiences have proven increasingly receptive to less conventional structures: the exuberance of the music hall, for instance, inspired the structuring of Joan Littlewood's *Oh, What a Lovely War!,* the minstrel show served as a structure for George C. Wolfe's *The Colored Museum,* and the didacticism of the lecture hall underlay much of the theatre of Bertolt Brecht. Nonlinear, discontinuous, and even stream-of-consciousness structures can provide powerful and sustained dramatic impact in the theatre, provided they are based in the dramatization of events that the audience can put together in some sort of meaningful and satisfying fashion.

THE QUALITIES OF A FINE PLAY

As with any art form, the qualities that make up a good play can be discussed individually, but it is only in their combination, only in their interaction—only in ways that cannot be dissected or measured—that these qualities have meaning.

Credibility and Intrigue

To say that a play must be credible is not at all to say that it has to be lifelike, for fantasy, ritual, and absurdity have all proven to be en-

duringly popular theatrical modes. The demand of credibility is an audience-imposed demand, and it has to do with the play's internal consistency: the actions must flow logically from the characters, the situation, and the theatrical context the playwright provides. In other words, we might say that credibility is the audience's demand that what happens in Act II makes sense in terms of what happened in Act I.

Credibility demands, for example, that the characters in a play appear to act out of their own individual interests, instincts, and intentions rather than serving as mere pawns for the development of theatrical plot or effect, as empty disseminators of propaganda. Credibility means that characters must maintain consistency within themselves: that their thoughts, feelings, hopes, fears, and plans must appear to flow from human needs rather than purely theatrical ones. Credibility also demands that human characters appear to act and think like human beings (even in humanly impossible situations) and not purely as thematic automatons. Credibility, in short, is the essence of a contract between author and audience, whereby the audience agrees to view the characters as "people" so long as the author abides by the agreement not to shatter that belief in order to accomplish other purposes.

Thus James Barrie's famous play *Peter Pan,* while undeniably fantastical, creates a cast of characters wholly appropriate to their highly imaginary situation and internally consistent in their actions within the context of their developing experience. All of their aspirations (including those of the dog!) are human ones, and their urgencies are so believable that when Tinker Bell steps out of the play's context to ask the audience to demonstrate its belief in fairies, the audience is willing to applaud its approval. At that moment, the world of the play becomes more credible, more "real," than that of the audience. So much for the power—and consequently the necessity—of dramatic credibility.

What's in the box? A standard thriller technique, here used in Paul Giovanni's The Crucifer of Blood, *is to intrigue the audience with mysterious locked boxes. This one, opened by a soldier's sword in India, will provoke an investigation from Sherlock Holmes on London's Baker Street. From American Conservatory Theatre. (Photo: William Ganslen.)*

Intrigue is that quality of a play which makes us curious (sometimes fervently so) to see "what happens next." Sheer plot intrigue—which is sometimes called "suspense" in that it leaves us suspended (that is, "hanging")—is one of the most powerful of dramatic approaches. Whole plays can be based on little more than artfully contrived plotting designed to keep the audience in a continual state of anticipation and wonder. Plot, however, is only one of the elements of a play that can support intrigue. Most plays that aspire to deeper insights than whodunits or farces develop intrigue in character as well, and even in theme. Most of the great plays, in fact, demand that we ask not so much "What will happen?" as "What does this mean?" Most great plays, in other words, make us care about the characters and invite us to probe the mysteries of the human condition.

Writers of tragedy tend to dispense with plot intrigue altogether. The Greek tragedies were retellings of well-known legends whose conclusions were known to the audience before they even entered the theatre. Shakespeare also used earlier works as the bases for his tragedies; on occasion—in *Romeo and Juliet,* for instance—he even reminded his audience of the play's ending in its first words. Peter Shaffer's *Equus* is a modern tragedy whose most significant incident is described early in the play in order that it may be analyzed (by characters and audience) for the balance of the play, which culminates in an enactment of the same incident. Intrigue of character depends on the author's ability first to present characters who are so fascinating that we want to understand them better— and then to devise situations and scenes that deepen our fascination with each successive revelation.

Surprise is an essential ingredient of intrigue: a play that is truly intriguing is one that leads us to expect surprises and then appropriately rewards our expectations. The plays of Harold Pinter, which are filled with abrupt, almost inexplicable transitions, intense pauses and glances, and elliptical dialogue that seems to contain innuendoes we don't fully comprehend, create an almost palpable sense of foreboding and spookiness that plunges the audience deeper and deeper into Pinteresque moods and reveries. The plays of Tom Stoppard, by contrast, race glibly through brilliant rhetorical flights of language that always manage to stay one step ahead of the audience's capability to follow, keeping the audience breathless while forcing them to remain intellectually alert.

Sometimes a playwright's theme can provide sufficient intrigue in itself to engage an audience's deepest attention. "What is the playwright getting at?" we wonder, and this question can lead us, for a while at least, to follow closely a dialogue that would hold no interest for us if overheard in a real-life situation. The mere fact that the author has seen fit to incorporate such dialogue in a play— and moreover that many people have labored to get that play to the point of production— is sufficient to confer a modicum of intrigue. But, of course, the audience must soon receive intellectual or emotional or "entertainment" reward for its attention.

Intrigue draws us into the world of a play; credibility keeps us there. In the best plays the two are sustained throughout the course of the action in a fine tension of opposites: intrigue demanding surprise, credibility demanding consistency. Combined, they generate a kind of "believable wonder," which is the fundamental state of drama. All the credibility in the world will not suffice by itself to make a play interesting, and all the intrigue that craft can contrive will fail to make an incredible play palatable. The integration of the two must be explored by the playwright in order to establish that shared ground which satisfies both human inertia and human potential, which transcends our expectations but not our credulity.

Speakability, Stageability, and Flow

The dialogue of drama is written upon the page, but it must be spoken by an actor and staged by a director. Thus the goal of the dramatist is to fabricate dialogue that is both actable and stageable and which flows in a progression leading to theatrical impact.

One of the most common faults in the work of the beginning playwright—sometimes even when that playwright is an established novelist or poet—is that the lines lack "speakability." This is not to say that play dialogue must resemble ordinary speech. No one imagines people in life speaking like characters out of the works of Aeschylus, Shakespeare, Shaw, or Giraudoux, or even like con-

PINTER AND STOPPARD

Harold Pinter and Tom Stoppard, contemporary British playwrights, exemplify sharply contrasting dramatic styles. The following samples are reasonably typical of their respective works.

From Pinter's *Silence* (1969):

BATES: (*moves to* ELLEN) Will we meet tonight?
ELLEN: I don't know. (*Pause*)
BATES: Come with me tonight.
ELLEN: Where?
BATES: Anywhere. For a walk. (*Pause*)
ELLEN: I don't want to walk.
BATES: Why not? (*Pause*)
ELLEN: I want to go somewhere else. (*Pause*)
BATES: Where?
ELLEN: I don't know. (*Pause*)
BATES: What's wrong with a walk?
ELLEN: I don't want to walk. (*Pause*)
BATES: What do you want to do?

ELLEN: I don't know. (*Pause*)
BATES: Do you want to go somewhere else?
ELLEN: Yes.
BATES: Where?
ELLEN: I don't know. (*Pause*)

From Stoppard's *Dirty Linen* (1976):

COCKLEBURY-SMYTHE: May I be the first to welcome you to Room 3B. You will find the working conditions primitive, the hours antisocial, the amenities non-existent and the catering beneath contempt. On top of that the people are for the most part very boring, with interests either so generalized as to mimic wholesale ignorance or so particular as to be lunatic obsessions. Their level of conversation would pass without comment in the lavatory of a mixed comprehensive and the lavatories, by the way, are few and far between.

Mirrored surfaces on floor and backdrop amplify the empty communication between Bates and Ellen in the Royal Shakespeare Company's 1969 production of Harold Pinter's Silence, *directed by Peter Hall. (Photo: Zoë Dominic.)*

Surprise! Steven Berkoff's dark comedy Kvetch *is filled with sudden discoveries. It was written in part out of experiences from his childhood. Odyssey Theatre Ensemble, 1986.*

temporary characters fashioned by Harold Pinter or Edward Albee. A brilliantly styled language has been a feature of most of the great plays in theatre history, and naturalness or super-realism is not, by itself, a dramatic virtue—nor is its absence a dramatic fault.

Rather, *speakability* means that a line of dialogue should be so written that it achieves its maximum impact when *spoken*. In order to accomplish this, the playwright must be closely attuned to the "audial shape" of dialogue: the rhythm of sound that creates emphasis, meaning, focus, and power. Verbal lullabies and climaxes, fast punch lines, sonorous lamentations, sparkling epigrams and devastating expletives, significant pauses and electrifying whispers—these are some of the devices of dialogue that impart audial shape to great plays written by master dramatists.

Speakability also requires that the spoken line seem to emanate from the character who utters it and that it contain, in its syntax, vocabulary, and mode of expression, the marks of that character's milieu and his or her personality. The spoken line is not merely an expression of the author's perspective; it is the

Stageability is a matter of the highest importance in farce. The dialogue for this clumsily urgent seduction scene from Feydeau's Hotel Paradiso *is of relatively little importance. Staged by director Tom Moore at American Conservatory Theatre with actors Elizabeth Huddle and Raye Birk. (Photo: William Ganslen, ACT.)*

basis from which the actor develops characterization and the acting ensemble creates a play's style. Thus the mastery of dramatic dialogue writing demands more than mere semantic skills; it requires a constant awareness of the purposes and tactics underlying human communication, as well as of the multiple psychological and aesthetic properties of language.

Stageability, of course, requires that dialogue be written so that it can be spoken effectively upon a stage, but it requires something more: dialogue must be conceived as an integral element of a particular staged situation, in which setting, physical action, and spoken dialogue are inextricably combined. *Romeo and Juliet* affords a splendid illustration of the successful integration of lyrical dramatic dialogue and physical stage behavior (together with a multitude of stage properties) into a dramatic unity that cannot be expressed outside the theatrical context itself. A stageable script is one in which staging and stage business—as well as design and the acting demands—are neither adornments for the dialogue nor sugarcoating for the writer's opinions, but are intrinsic to the very nature of the play.

Both speakability and stageability are contingent upon human limitations: those of the actors and directors as well as those of the audience. Speakability must take into account that the actor must breathe from time to time, for example, and that the audience can take in only so many metaphors in a single spoken sentence. Stageability must reckon with the forces of gravity and inertia, which both the poet and the novelist may conveniently ignore. The playwright need not simply succumb to the common denominator—all the great playwrights strive to extend the capacities of actors and audience alike—but still must not forget that the theatre is fundamentally a human event that cannot transcend human capabilities.

A speakable and stageable script flows rather than stumbles; this is true for nonlinear plays as well as for more straightforwardly structured ones. Flow consists above all in the creation of a continual stream of *information,* and a play that flows is one that is continually saying something, doing something, and meaning something to the audience. To serve this end, the playwright should address such technical problems as scene shifting, entrances and exits, and act breaks (intermissions) as early as possible in the scriptwriting process. Furthermore, in drafting scenes, the writer should be aware that needless waits, arid expositions (no matter how "necessary" to the plot), inane ramblings on the part of the characters, and incomprehensible plot developments can sink the sturdiest script in a sea of audience apathy.

The combined demands of speakability, stageability, and dramatic flow apply in some measure to the crafting of any play; hence every professional playwright necessarily develops certain skills to meet these demands. In many theatrical eras in the past, playwriting was considered so technically demanding that craft appeared to be all that was involved, and playwrights spent long in-house apprenticeships as "company men" learning their skills through continual exposure to theatrical rehearsal and performance. Even today, many playwrights come to their craft after decades of experience as actors, stage managers, or directors. But craft—which is largely an understanding of what has worked before—is not the sole determinant of the good play, and a blind reliance on craft has never led to great writing in any genre. With his *Waiting for Godot* in 1953, Samuel Beckett virtually rewrote the book on playwriting, teaching actors and directors new lessons about what is speakable and stageable and introducing audiences to a kind of dramatic flow that was radically different from anything they had ever seen before. Great playwriting always straddles the line between solid craft and brilliant innovation; it is always based in a theatre wisdom that both understands the conventional and seeks, consciously or unconsciously, to improve upon it.

Richness

Depth, subtlety, fineness, quality, wholeness, and inevitability—these are words often called into service on behalf of plays that we like. They are fundamentally subjective terms, easier to apply than to define or defend, for the fact is that when a play pleases us, when it "works," the feelings of pleasure and stimulation it affords are beyond the verbal level. Certainly *richness* is one of the qualities common to plays that leave us with this sense of satisfaction—richness of *detail* and richness of *dimension.*

A play that is rich with detail is not necessarily one that is rife with detail; it is simply one whose every detail fortifies our insight into the world of the play. For going to a play is in part a matter of paying a visit to the playwright's world, and the more vividly created that world, the greater the play's final impact. The best plays of Anton Chekhov, for example, portray in loving and incisive detail the end-of-a-century, end-of-an-era world of provincial Russia before the revolution: attending a well-mounted production of Chekhov's *The Three Sisters* is like stepping backward in time into an adventure no travel agent could possibly book. Similarly, to attend a play by Bernard Shaw is to venture into a dazzling Edwardian milieu brimming with bright rhetoric and to be caught up in a flurry of intellectual activity whose every speech gives occasion for thought or laughter—or both. And a play by Tennessee Williams is a journey into complex lives lived in steamy Southern towns, a journey into a firmer, deeper, broader set of impressions than could ever be provided by a guided tour. Each of these playwrights exhibits an extraordinary skill in the selection of meaningful detail.

Richness of detail—in movement, in language, in character outlook, in environmental features—lends a play authority, an aura of sureness. It surrounds the play's characters as a city surrounds a home and gives them a cultural context in which to exist. It lends a play specificity—the feeling that it deals with specific people engaged in specific tasks in a specific place. In short, richness of detail makes a play authentic. It also makes it informative and, therefore, memorable.

Richness is not an easy quality to develop in writing. It demands a certain richness in the resources and capabilities of the author: a gift for close observation, an uninhibited imagination, and an astute sense of what to leave out as well as what to include. One who can recollect personal experiences in great detail, who can create convincing situations, peoples, locales, and conversations when called upon to do so, and who is closely attuned to nuance can perhaps work these talents into the writing of plays. Training programs for playwrights frequently assign exercises in observation and require the writing of imaginative or evocative description. These exercises can be useful up to a point. True richness tends to be a characteristic of the work of the mature writer, and too often attempts to foster it in the young only result in counterfeit richness, a product of imitation rather than of observation and personal creativity.

Beyond question, *depth of characterization* is the single most important factor in determining a play's richness of dimension. It also presents perhaps the greatest single stumbling block for novice playwrights, who tend either to write all characters "in the same voice" (normally the author's own) or to divide them into two camps: the good ones and the bad ones. Although shallowness of characterization can sometimes be offset by strengths in other dramatic areas, a play that lacks sound character development can rarely achieve the profound embodiment of the human condition that represents theatre at its best.

Depth of characterization requires that every character possess, at least to a certain extent, an independence of intention, expression, and motivation; moreover, these characteristics must appear sensible in the light of our general knowledge of psychology and human behavior. In plays as in life, all characters must act from motives that appear reasonable *to them* (if not to those watching them, or those affected by them). Moreover, the writer should bear in mind that every character is, *to himself,* an extremely important and worthwhile person, even though he may be haunted by self-doubts or may perceive himself to be despised by others. These observations apply in even the most nonrealistic of plays. The great villains of drama—Hermes in *Prometheus,* Satan in the York cycle, and Iago in *Othello,* for example—all convey the impression that they believe in themselves and in the fundamental "rightness" of their cause; and even if we never completely understand their ultimate motivations (as we do not completely understand the motivations of historical villains like Hitler, Caligula, and John Wilkes Booth), we can sense at the bottom of their behavior a certain validity of purpose, however twisted or perverse.

Depth of characterization requires that the characters convey the complexity of real human beings and do not simply represent thematic integers in the playwright's grand design. Even in a theatre in which the psychology of characterization takes second place to the promulgation of ideas, the "ideas" that are worth exploring theatrically are concerned with people and their behavior; and if the complexity of people and the purposes for their behavior are not conveyed in the writer's work, the ideas he or she wishes to get across can only appear trivial and ill-conceived.

The realistic theatre, particularly in the turn-of-the-century domestic plays of Chekhov, Strindberg, and Maxim Gorky, has provided many works in which the psychological dimensions of the characters dominate all other aspects of the theatrical experience. By the mid-twentieth century, this approach had become equally important in the American theatre, most notably in the searching, probing dramas of Tennessee Williams, Arthur Miller, Eugene O'Neill, and William Inge. The psychiatric process itself has stood at the core of the action in several plays, including Williams's *Suddenly Last Summer,* Miller's *After the Fall,* Shaffer's *Equus,* and the 1941 American musical *Lady in the Dark,* each of which portrays a principal character undergoing analysis or psychotherapy. The psychological sophistication of modern theatre audiences has afforded playwrights an expanded opportunity to explore and dramatize their characters in greater and greater depth and has helped to make the "case study" drama a major genre of the current theatre.

Gravity and Pertinence

Gravity and pertinence are terms used to describe the importance of a play's theme and its overall relevance to the concerns of the intended audience.

To say that a play has *gravity* is to say simply that its central theme is one of serious and lasting significance in humanity's spiritual, moral, or intellectual life. All the world's major dramas—whatever their genre—are concerned fundamentally with life problems about which human beings regularly seek lucidity and enlightenment. Even comedies and farces deal with universal issues—issues such as adultery, aging, marital discord, religious and financial intimidation, personal and romantic insecurity, social ambition—and no amount of surface slapstick or badinage should obscure the fact that these issues are serious daily preoccupations of the human species.

Obviously, then, gravity does not mean somberness, which indeed often only signifies an attempt to imitate profundity. To the contrary, gravity is usually attended by a considerable release of theatrical energy, owing precisely to the universality of its appeal: when an audience truly understands and deeply identifies with the experiences set forth by the playwright, even the darkest tragedy radiates power, animation, and light.

If a play has the quality of *pertinence,* it relates in some fashion to the current personal concerns of its audience. These concerns can be timeless or ephemeral.

Plays about current political situations or personalities usually rely heavily on pertinence to attract their audiences. Writers of such plays, of course, must be aware that their work may be quickly outdated; for that reason, most producers are loath to have anything to do with any but the most promising topical plays. Indeed, many highly topical plays that do find their way into production require extensive adaptation and updating before they can be successfully revived.

More timeless concerns—such as the conflicts between passion and practicality (as in *Romeo and Juliet*) or between salvation and material well-being (as in *Waiting for Godot*)—lead to a kind of theatre that achieves pertinence without being merely topical or trendy and engages the attention of the audience without regard to the current or local scene.

If we think of the mind of the author as a wheel turning in space, and the mind of the audience as another wheel similarly turning, pertinence would be the axle that connects them and makes them turn in some sort of synchronization. If that axle is missing, if a play does not stimulate the audience to consider, in its own frame of reference, the issues the playwright raises, then the theatre has failed: it has committed the unforgivable sin of disengaging the audience.

Compression, Economy, and Intensity

Compression, economy, and intensity make up another set of related aspects of the finest plays.

Compression refers to the playwright's skill at condensing a story (which may span many days, even years, of chronological time) into a theatrical time frame; *economy* relates to her skill at eliminating or consolidating characters, events, locales, and words in the service of compression. We have seen how Shakespeare combined these skills in creating the "two-hour traffic of the stage" which is *Romeo and Juliet*. Unlike other literary or visual art forms that can be examined in private and at the leisure of the observer, a play must be structured to unfold in a public setting and at a predetermined pace. If the playwright can manage to meet these needs and at the same time to make every scene, every incident, every character, every word deliver an impact, he or she has satisfied the dramatic demand for *intensity*.

Many beginning playwrights attempt to convert a story to a play in the most obvious way: by writing a separate scene for every event described in the story (and sometimes including a different setting and supporting cast for each scene). Economy and compression, however, require that most stories be re-

Larry Gelbart's Mastergate *is a satire about American politics, specifically the Iran-Contra investigations of the late 1980s; the characters, including "Major Manley Battle" (pictured), are satiric representations of contemporary public figures. Satire's appeal is generally limited to the period of time its subject matter is relevant ("Satire is what closes Saturday night," said playwright George S. Kaufman); some satirical dramas, however, stand the test of time. From the American Repertory Theatre production directed by Michael Engler; Daniel Von Bargen is the actor. (Photo: Richard Feldman.)*

structured in order to be dramatically viable. If the play is to be basically realistic, the playwright has traditionally reworked the story so as to have all the events occur in one location, or perhaps in two locations with an act break between to allow for scenery changes. Events that are integral to the story but cannot be shown within the devised settings can simply be reported (as in Bernard Shaw's *Misalliance,* for example, in which an airplane crash occurs offstage, as the onstage characters gawk and exclaim). More common today is the use of theatricalist techniques which permit an integration of settings so that events occurring in various places can be presented on the same set without intermission. Similarly, economy and compression commonly dictate the deletion or combination of certain characters who appear in the story and the reduction of important expository passages to a line or two of dialogue.

The effects of economy and compression are both financial and aesthetic. Obviously, when scenery changes and the number of characters are held to a minimum, the costs of production are minimized as well. But beyond that, compression and economy in playwriting serve to stimulate intrigue and focus audience expectation: a tightly written play gives us the feeling that we are on the trail of something important and that our quarry is right around the next bend. In other words, economy and compression actually lead to intensity, and dramatic intensity is one of the theatre's most powerful attributes.

Dramatic intensity can take many forms. It can be harsh, abrasive, explosive, eminently physical or overtly calm. It can be ruminative, tender, or comic. But whenever intensity occurs and in whatever mood or context, it conveys to the audience an ineradicable feeling that this moment in theatre is unique and its revelations are profound.

Intensity in the theatre does not come about by happy accident, obviously, but neither can it be straightforwardly injected at the whim of the playwright. It must evolve out of a careful development of issues, through the increasing urgency of character goals and intentions and the focused actions and interactions of the plot that draw characters and their conflicts ever closer to some sort of climactic confrontation. A play must spiral inward toward its core; that is, its compression must increase, its mood must intensify, as it circles toward its dénouement. Too many tangential diversions can deflect a play from this course and render it formless and apparently devoid of purpose.

Celebration

Finally, a fine play celebrates life; it does not merely depict or analyze or criticize it.

The first plays were presented at festivals that, though perhaps haunted by angry or capricious gods, were essentially joyful celebrations. Even the darkest of the ancient Greek tragedies sought to transcend the more negative aspects of existence and to exalt the human spirit, for the whole of Greek theatre was informed by the positive (and therapeutic) elements of the Dionysian festival: spring, fertility, the gaiety and solidarity of public communion.

The theatre can never successfully venture too far from this source. A purely didactic theatre has never *in fact* satisfied the public's expectations of theatre, and the merely grim depiction of ordinary life has proved equally inadequate to this art form. Although the word *theatrical* is often debased to suggest something like "glittery" or "showy," it should instead be used to connote an accord with the theatre's most fundamental aspirations: to go beyond known experience, to illuminate life, and to raise existence to the level of an art.

This "celebration" of which drama is capable can easily be perverted. Whole eras have been dedicated to a theatre that was deemed acceptable only insofar as it was "uplifting,"

Athol Fugard's My Children! My Africa! *ends tragically; but before it does, South African township teacher Mr. M. (played here by Brock Peters) and his visiting pupil Isabel (Nancy Travis) share an exquisite moment of triumph, which makes the resulting tragedy all the more poignant and insupportable. La Jolla Playhouse production, 1990. (Photo: Micha Langer.)*

and in those times many of the greatest tragedies were drastically revised so as to include happy endings and none but the most noble sentiments. Other dramas, in our own times, have been self-consciously written in "elevated" tones, in pale imitation of the more vigorous poetry of Shakespeare or Sophocles. These dramas do not celebrate life—they try to whitewash it and to build a dramatic style that is independent of reality; to most observers these works seem but affectations.

The truest and most exciting theatre, whether played out on the tragic stage or in the music hall, in the innyard or behind the proscenium, has always been based on those dramas that were written out of a passionate, personal vision of reality and a deep devotion to the aim of extracting and expressing life's magnificence. For the theatre is fundamentally an affirmation in all of its aspects. Like the writing of plays, the acts of putting them on, performing in them, and attending them are also acts of affirmation: they attest to a desire to share and to communicate; they celebrate human existence and participation and communion. Purely bitter plays, no matter how justly based or how well grounded in experience, remain incomplete and unsatisfying as theatre, which simply is not an effective medium for the conveyance of unalloyed pessimism. Even the bleakest of modern plays radiates a persistent hopefulness—even joyousness—as represented archetypally by Samuel Beckett's two old men singing, punning, and pantomiming so engagingly in the forlorn shadow of their leafless tree as they wait for Godot.

THE PLAYWRIGHT'S PROCESS

How does one go about writing a play?

It is important that one know the elements of a play, as discussed in Chapter 2, and the characteristics of the best plays—credibility, intrigue, richness in detail and characterization, gravity, pertinence, compression, economy, intensity, and celebration—as discussed in the preceding sections. But that is not enough; one must still confront the practical task of writing.

The blank sheet of paper is the writer's nemesis. It is the accuser, the goad and critic that coldly commands action even as it threatens humiliation.

There is no consensus among writers as to where to begin. Some prefer to begin with a story line or a plot outline. Some begin with a real event and write the play to explain why that event occurred. Some begin with a real character or set of characters and develop a plot around them. Some begin with a setting and try to animate it with characters and actions. Some begin with a theatrical effect or an idea for a new form of theatrical expression. Some write entirely from personal experience. Some adapt a story or a legend, others a biography of a famous person, others a play

by an earlier playwright, and others simply expand upon a remembered dream.

"Theatre of fact" usually begins with a document, such as the transcript of a trial or a committee hearing. Other documentary forms might begin with a tape recorder and a situation contrived by the playwright. Some plays are created out of actors' improvisations or acting class exercises. Some are compilations of material written over the course of many years or collected from many sources.

The fact is, writers tend to begin with whatever works for *them* and accords with their immediate aims. Since playwrights usually work alone, at least in the initial stages, they can do as they please whenever they want: there is no norm. On the other hand, certain "steps" can be followed as introductory exercises to playwriting, and these may in fact lead to the creation of an entire play.

Dialogue

Transcription of dialogue from previous observation and experience—that is, the writing down of *remembered dialogue* from overheard conversations or from conversations in which the author has participated—is a fundamental playwriting exercise; probably most finished plays contain such scenes. Because we remem-

The best way for a writer to create credible characters is to draw them from life. Brian Friel's Dancing at Lughnasa *is an autobiographical study of the author's own sisters and his growing up in Ireland; the author actually appears as a narrator of the play. Three of "Friel's" sisters are shown here in the Alabama Shakespeare Festival's 1994 production. (Photo: Scarsbrook.)*

ber conversations only selectively and subjectively, a certain amount of fictionalizing and shading inevitably creeps into these transcriptions; and often without even meaning to do so, authors also transform people in their memory into characters in their scenes.

Writing scenes of *imagined dialogue* is the logical next step in this exercise, for all the author need do now is to extend the situation beyond its remembered reality into the area of "what might have happened." The dialogue then constructed will be essentially original, yet in keeping with the personalized "characters" developed in the earlier transcription. The characters now react and respond as dramatic figures, interacting with each other freshly and under the control of the author. Many fine plays have resulted from the author's working out, in plot and dialogue, hypothetical relations between real

Lee Blessing's A Walk in the Woods *consists wholly of an imaginary conversation between two arms negotiators: one American and the other Soviet. The play, which contains little in the way of physical action, must be carried mainly by the intensity of the acting and the brilliance of the dialogue. La Jolla Playhouse production, 1987; the actors are Lawrence Pressman and Michael Constantine. (Photo: Micha Langer.)*

people who never confronted each other in life; indeed, many plays are inspired by the author's notion of what *should* have happened among people who evaded the very confrontations she wishes them to experience. In this way, the theatre has often been used as a form of psychotherapy, with the patient-playwright simply acting out—in imagination or with words on paper—certain obligatory scenes in her life that never occurred.

Conflict

Writing scenes of *forced conflict* accelerates the exercise and becomes a third step toward the creation of a play. Scenes of separation, loss, crucial decision, rejection, or emotional breakthrough are climactic scenes in a play and usually help enormously to define its structure. If a writer can create a convincing scene of high conflict that gets inside *each* of the characters involved and not merely one of them, then there is a good chance of making that scene the core of an exciting play—especially if it incorporates some subtlety and is not dependent entirely on shouting and denunciation. What is more, such a scene will be highly actable in its own right and thus can serve as a valuable tool for demonstrating the writer's potential.

Exercises that result in scripted scenes—even if the scenes are just a page or two in length—have the advantage of allowing the writer to test his work as it progresses. For a short scene is easily producible: all it requires is a group of agreeable actors and a modest investment of time, and the playwright can quickly assess the total impact. The costs and difficulties of testing a complete play, on the other hand, may prove insurmountable for the inexperienced playwright. Moreover, the performance of a short original scene can sometimes develop such impact as to generate enthusiasm for the theatrical collaboration needed for a fuller theatrical experience. Most playwrights today see their words staged first in the form of acted original scenes, either in colleges and universities or in professional theatre laboratories or community playreading groups.

Structure

Developing a complete play demands more than stringing together a number of scenes,

of course, and at some point in the scene-writing process the playwright inevitably confronts the need for structure. Many playwrights develop outlines for their plays after writing a scene or two; some have an outline ready before any scenes are written or even thought of. Other playwrights never write down anything except dialogue and stage directions, yet find an overall structure asserting itself almost unconsciously as the writing progresses. But the beginner should bear in mind that intrigue, thematic development, compression, and even credibility depend upon a carefully built structure and that it is an axiom of theatre that most playwriting is in fact *rewriting*—rewriting aimed principally at organizing and reorganizing the play's staged actions and events.

A strong dramatic structure compels interest and attention. It creates intrigue by establishing certain expectations—both in the characters and in the audience—and then by creating new and bigger expectations out of the fulfillment of the first ones. A good dramatic structure keeps us always wanting more until the final curtain call, and at the end it leaves us with a sense of the inevitability of the play's conclusion, a sense that what happened on stage was precisely as it had to be. A great structure makes us comfortable and receptive; we feel in good hands, expertly led through whatever terrain the play may take us. And we are willing, therefore, to abandon ourselves to a celebration of vital and ineffable matters.

THE PLAYWRIGHT'S REWARDS

There always will be a need for playwrights, for the theatre never abandons its clamor for new and better dramatic works. Hundreds of producers today are so anxious to discover new authors and new scripts that they will read (or instruct an associate to read) everything that comes their way; thus a truly fine play need not go unnoticed for long. More-

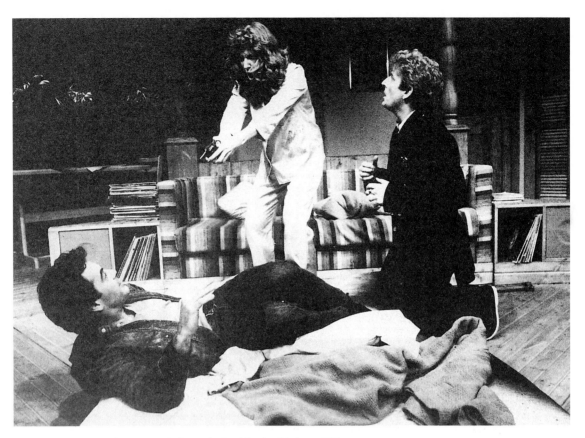

If a gun appears in the first act, it has to be fired by the third act. This tongue-in-cheek "rule" of theatre (said to be first uttered by Chekhov) implies a valid precept: exposition should lead to actions, which should lead to climax and resolution. This means a dramatic structure that can deliver an escalating momentum of excitement. The photograph is from Astronauts, *by Claudia Reilly, staged at the Humana Festival at the Actors Theatre of Louisville. On the ground is John Shepard; Peggity Price holds the gun on him. (Photo: David S. Talbott.)*

over, playwrights are the only artists in the theatre who can bring their work to the first stage of completion without any outside professional help at all; they do not need to be auditioned, interviewed, hired, cast, or contracted to an agent in order to come up with the world's greatest dramatic manuscript.

The rewards that await the successful playwright are absolutely staggering: they are the most fully celebrated artists of the theatre, for not only do they receive remuneration commensurate with their success but they also acquire enormous influence and prestige on the basis of their personal vision. The public may adore an actor and it may admire a director or designer, but it *listens* to the playwright, who in Western culture has always assumed the role of prophet. Playwriting at its best is more than a profession, and it is more than a component of the theatrical machine. It is a creative act that enlarges human experience and enriches our awe and appreciation of life.

13

Designers and Technicians

The actor and the playscript may be at the core of the theatrical experience, but they are by no means the sum of it. Indeed, in the view of many spectators and participants, the primacy of acting and playwriting is extremely debatable.

For acting and textual brilliance are not isolated components capable of full expression in and by themselves. In even the most primitive of dramas the theatrical experience always has a "look" and a "sound" and a "shape"—a visual and aural impact—that can be achieved only through *design*. And the execution of that design always entails a measure of *technology*. In many ways and at many times, the theatre has had occasion to celebrate the artistic talent of its designers and the engineering capability of its technicians, for many of the world's great aesthetic and technological innovations have been made public primarily through theatrical exploitation.

Therefore, in examining a play it is hardly sufficient to inquire merely as to what it is "about." We must also ask, How does it look? How does it sound? How is it built? How does it run? These questions bring us face to face with an army of backstage personnel: the artists and technicians who create and make possible what Aristotle called the "spectacle" of theatre, who are responsible for the overall

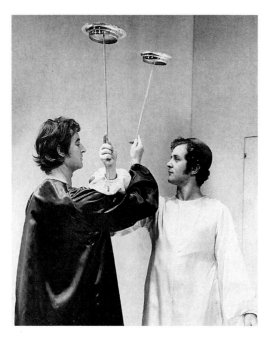

Sally Jacobs's bare white walls for this internationally celebrated 1970 production of A Midsummer Night's Dream, *directed by Peter Brook, were in stark contrast to the then-standard woody romanticism expected for this play. But the abstraction brilliantly served both the actors (who employed various circus techniques, such as the illustrated plate-twirling) and the text. (Photo: Holte Photographics.)*

appearance, orchestration, and management of the theatrical experience.

It is customary for purposes of discussion to divide design functions into a series of components—scenery, lighting, make-up, and so forth—and to a certain extent this categorization is appropriate; most productions involve separate "departments" of design, each with its own designers, assistants, and crews. Nonetheless, we must keep in mind that all the design functions of a production are interrelated—that the appearance of scenery, for example, is heavily dependent on the light that falls upon it and that the look of a costume is greatly affected by the actress's make-up and hairstyle, to say nothing of her acting and bearing. In listing the various contribut-

ing "arts" of theatrical design, therefore, we must recognize that in abstracting each of them for separate examination, we are attempting only to clarify certain traditional practices and that no single design art can be fully realized in isolation.

Similarly, the ordering of these separate arts can only be one of convenience, for no fundamental hierarchy exists among them. It is for a certain convenience, therefore, that we shall first discuss the theatre's architecture, scenery, and lighting and then deal with costuming, sound design, make-up, computer technologies in theatre design, and technical production.

THEATRE ARCHITECTURE

Despite its largely anonymous instigation, theatre architecture has long been one of the glories of the Western world. The Greek theatres, which evolved out of a pagan rite celebrated on a hillside, rank high among the magnificent relics of antiquity: the surviving theatre at Epidaurus is only one of many from the fourth century B.C. that still resound from time to time with revivals of the same great plays that thrilled audiences in the Hellenistic Age. The theatres of ancient Rome were so grandiose in conception and execution that only hyperbole, it appears, could convey their proper character. For example, can we believe Pliny's account of an 80,000-seat theatre built in three stories, one each of marble, glass, and gilt? Or of the two theatres built back to back that, filled with spectators, rotated on a pivot to join in a huge amphitheatre that was then flooded for sea battle scenes?

Later times have given us only a few names of architects, but many more fine theatres. Of Peter Street, the architect of Shakespeare's Globe and Henslowe's Fortune, history unfortunately tells us little beyond the notation that his theatres were provocative of the best in dramatic art. The Teatro Olimpico in Vicenza,

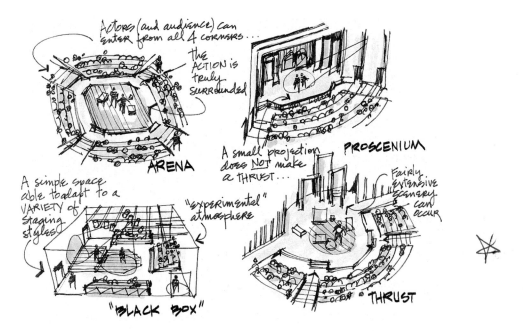

Four basic theatre spaces. The architect's first decisions are, Where is the stage? Where is the audience? The arena, proscenium, thrust, and neutral "black box" formats constitute the realm of possibilities. (Drawing: John von Szeliski.)

Italy, was designed by the famed Andrea Palladio and is the oldest extant theatre of known design and known architect—it was built in 1584, and it not only survives intact but also continues to be used for opera and dramatic presentations. Other theatres surviving from earlier eras, such as the elegant eighteenth-century court theatre at Drottningholm, Sweden, and the opulent nineteenth-century romantic structure built for the Paris Opera, are cultural landmarks as well as theatrically significant sites of contemporary production.

The last half of the twentieth century has seen an explosion of theatre construction that began just after the end of World War II. Since that time, theatres and performing arts centers have sprung up in virtually every major city in North America, Europe, and Asia. Indeed, the last half-century may well be considered a golden age of theatrical architecture, an age marked by a growing public willingness to lend financial support as well as by a greatly increased understanding of the need for extensive collaboration between theatre artists and architects in order to reconcile the needs for theatrical "tone" and atmosphere with those of practical flexibility and operational ease.

Staging Formats

The two principal types of modern theatre building are the proscenium stage design and the thrust stage design. These two basic types account for more than 95 percent of the professional theatres in Europe and America today and for the bulk of amateur stages as well.

The *proscenium* theatre is essentially a rectangular room with the audience on one side facing the stage on the other, the two separated by an arch (the proscenium arch) through which the audience peers. This creates the well-known "picture frame" stage, with the

Jo Mielziner's celebrated two-story cutaway set for Arthur Miller's Death of a Salesman, *1949. Mielziner's own rendering of the set shows Willy coming into the ground-floor dining area while his two sons sit up in their bedroom upstairs. Willy's wife is barely visible sleeping in her bed at left.*

arch serving as the frame for the action going on within. The proscenium format developed in Italy during the Renaissance as a mode of presenting elaborate court masques and other court entertainments; because it put the audience on but one side of the action, it allowed extensive "hidden" areas backstage for the scene shifting and trickery involved in creating the illusions and fantasies so admired at the time. The proscenium theatre achieved its fullest realization in the baroque era, and some of the surviving court theatres and opera houses of Europe testify eloquently to the splendor of that age. Modern proscenium theatres have proven particularly serviceable for the use of realistic scenery and for the presentation of scenic spectaculars. Virtually all Broadway theatres feature the proscenium format.

The *thrust* format, a design pioneered in North America by Tyrone Guthrie, was in fact the favored format in ancient Greece and Elizabethan England. Because it places much of the action in the midst of the audience, it is a more actor-centered than scenery-centered theatre configuration. In the thrust format the members of the audience are more aware of each other than they are in a darkened proscenium "fan," and their viewing perspectives differ radically, depending on their seating locations. When the acting platform, or thrust, has access from tunnels (*vomitoria*) that come up through the audience, the stage can be flooded by actors in a matter of seconds, creating a whirlwind of movement that is dazzling and immediate—the thrust stage's alternative to elaborate stage machinery and painted scenes. That is not at all to say that there can be no scenery on a thrust stage, but merely that major scenic pieces tend to be placed behind the action rather than surrounding it, leaving a major acting space, scenically neutral, projecting into the center of the audience.

A third theatrical configuration is the *arena format*, in which the audience surrounds the action on all sides; one American regional theatre, the Arena Stage in Washington, D.C., has presented an arena season regularly since 1950. Arena staging dispenses with all scenery except floor treatments, furniture, and out-of-the-way hanging or standing pieces, and it focuses audience attention sharply and simply on the actors. The long-standing success of the Arena Stage testifies to the viability of this format; however, since no other major theatre has followed D.C.'s example (and indeed since the Arena Stage itself has built an adjacent proscenium theatre as a second space), it would appear that arena staging is destined to remain an interesting novelty rather than to initiate a staging revolution.

A final staging alternative is afforded by the so-called *black box* theatre, a formatless space that can be adjusted to any desired arrangement and is therefore particularly useful in experimental, environmental, or academic stagings. Usually painted black (hence the name), this type of theatre consists of a bare room fitted with omniflexible overhead lighting; in this room, stages and seating can be set up in any configuration—proscenium, thrust, arena, or two-sided "center stage"—or the action can occur at selected spots interspersed throughout the room: an "environmental" staging. The black box allows the director/creator to develop a near-infinite variety of actor-audience interactions and to make use of highly unusual scenic designs and/or mechanisms. "Happenings," participatory dramas, participatory rituals, and seminar plays—all of which demand active audience involvement—are frequently best presented in these sorts of spaces.

Other Architectural Considerations

Designing a theatre involves a great deal more than choosing a staging format.

It involves creating a seating space that is suited to the requirements of the expected audience; this may mean one thing in a sophis-ticated urban area, another in a rural outpost, yet another on a college campus.

It involves providing for effective communications systems, sightlines, and stage mechanisms for the sorts of productions the theatre will handle. This means there must be adequate wiring, soundproofing, and rigging, as well as a good use of backstage and onstage spaces, both open and enclosed—and often that means calling in a consultant who specializes in ascertaining the most practical design for the widest variety of uses.

Theatre building also involves principles of acoustics, which can determine whether actors' voices will be heard, given a normal volume level, in all parts of the house, and whether singers' voices can be heard when the orchestra is playing. As a science, acoustics is maddeningly inexact so that the best results come only after much experience and testing.

Theatre architecture involves the art of lighting, for no lighting designer can possibly overcome the limitations imposed by poorly located, permanently installed lighting positions. One of the sadder aspects of many older theatres is the jungle gym of exposed pipes and lighting instruments awkwardly strapped to gilded cupids in a latter-day attempt to make up for antiquated lighting systems.

And finally, designing and building a theatre involves a love of theatre, an emotional and aesthetic understanding that a theatre is not merely a room, a hall, or an institutional building with certain features, but a permanent home for the portrayal of human concerns and a repository of twenty-five hundred years of glorious tradition. Such a place must be functional and flexible, to be sure, but it is deserving of more: it deserves to have the distinctive identity that comes from the architect's ineffable sense of purpose and passion and theatrical imagination.

SCENERY

Scenery is likely to be the first thing we think of under the general category of theatrical de-

Fire is a design medium in Peter Brook's production of The Mahabharata, *which was staged on the clay (and therefore fireproof) floor of the Bouffes du Nord theatre in Paris. (Photo: Gilles Abegg.)*

Seemingly disconnected elements are compiled in an overall theatrical effect in Robert Wilson and Tomm Kamm's setting for Wilson's the CIVIL warS, *which Wilson also directed at the American Repertory Theatre. (Photo: Richard Feldman.)*

sign; if a production is said to be "designed by Jane Jones," we may simply assume that this means the scenery was designed by Jane Jones. Scenery is usually the first thing we see of a play, either at the rise of the curtain in a traditional proscenium production or as we enter the theatre where there is no curtain.

And yet scenery, as considered apart from architecture, is a relatively new phenomenon in the theatre. It was not needed for the dithyramb, and it probably played little part in Greek tragedy or comedy save to afford entry, exit, and sometimes expanded acting space for actors; such rotating prisms, rolling platforms, and painted panels as were used in the Greek theatre probably had no representational significance. So none of these features was intended to disguise the fact that the play's action took place in a Greek theatre. The same is more or less true of the Roman theatre, the medieval theatre, and the out-

door Elizabethan theatre—apart from a few set pieces that were painted and otherwise detailed to resemble free-standing walls, trees, caves, thrones, tombs, porches, and the inevitable Hellmouth—for virtually all visual aspects of public outdoor staging prior to the seventeenth century were dictated by the architecture of the theatre structure itself.

It was the development of indoor stages, artificially illuminated, that fostered the first great phase of scene design: the period of painted, flat scenery. Working indoors out of the reach of the elements, designers of Renaissance spectacles and court masques were free for the first time to erect painted canvases and temporary wooden structures without fear of having the colors run and the supports rot out or blow away. And with the advent of controllable indoor lighting, designers could illuminate their settings and acting areas as they wished without calling attention to the

Starlight Express is never static; the roller-skating musical features an "erector-set" design by John Napier that encircles the theatre audience and includes rising and descending ramps and straightaways for the whizzing-by performers. From the 1987 Broadway production. (Photo: Martha Swope and Associates.)

permanent structures behind: they could, in short, create both realistic illusion and decorative spectacle without having to contend with bad weather, bird droppings, and extraneous architectural interference.

The result was a series of scene-design revelations that brought the names of a new class of theatre artists—designers—to public consciousness, designers such as the Italians Aristotile da Sangallo (1481–1551), Sebastiano Serlio (1475–1554), and Giacomo Torelli (1604–1678), the Englishman Inigo Jones (1573–1652), and the Frenchman Jean Berain (c. 1637–1711). By the beginning of the eighteenth century, the scene designer's art had attained a prominence equal to (or perhaps greater than) the playwright's; and for almost two hundred years thereafter, flat scenery, painted in exquisite perspective, took

on even greater sophistication under the brilliant artists of the theatre's baroque, rococo, and romantic epochs. The proscenium format, which was developed primarily to show off elegant settings, dominated theatre architecture for all that time. It was not until the beginning of the present century that scenery went into its second major phase—the modern one—which continues in various fashions today.

Modern scenery is of two basic types: realistic and abstract. Often the two types are used in combination, and often the line between them is difficult to draw. But in their separate ways, both have contributed mightily to the important position of scenery in the theatrical experience today.

Realistic settings carry on the tradition of "illusionism" established in eighteenth-century

The stunning 1994 Broadway revival of Rodgers and Hammerstein's 1945 Carousel showed what a powerful impact the "golden age" Broadway musicals can still deliver. Although elements of the script—adapted from Ferenc Molnar's Hungarian classic, Liliom—are clearly dated, brilliant design and a contemporary staging and sensitivity bring out the play's still-valid insights and premises, along with Rodgers's glorious musical score. Scenery and costumes by Bob Crowley; direction by Nicholas Hytner. (Photo: Joan Marcus.)

The garment factory in the 1994 Lincoln Center revival of Carousel. The expressionistic scenery, designed by Bob Crowley, emphasizes the routine, impersonality, and clock-domination of industrial labor. (Photo: Joan Marcus.)

painted perspective stagings; the familiar "box set" of modern realistic or naturalistic theatre is essentially a series of interconnected flats of framed canvas painted to resemble walls and ceilings, filled with real furniture and real properties taken from ordinary real-world environments. This type of set, a development of the early nineteenth century, is very much alive today and is indeed the major scenic format for contemporary domestic drama (particularly comedy) of New York's Broadway, London's West End, and most community and college theatres across America. No longer particularly voguish, the box set rarely wins design awards; but it admirably fulfills the staging requirements of a great many domestic comedies, thrillers, and serious linearly structured dramas, particularly those requir-

ing interior settings. Advances in scenic construction and technology have made the box set a marvel of lifelike appearance and detail.

Box sets and other forms of realistic painted scenery can be immensely useful in designating a play's locale. The cleverly painted wings and drops of the era of flat, perspective-painted scenery portrayed with great precision the drawing rooms, conservatories, ballrooms, reception halls, parlors, libraries, servants' quarters, professional offices, and factory yards of many a dramatist's imagination or prescription. The box set served to heighten the verisimilitude by adding three-dimensional features: suitable doors to enter through, windows to peer through, bookcases to hide revolvers in, and grandfather clocks to hide characters in. The public fasci-

A grand rococo theatre becomes the stage setting for this 1987 production of Pir-andello's metatheatrical comedy Tonight We Improvise at the Théâtre de la Ville, in Paris. The "theatre within a theatre" design is particularly Pirandel-lian. (Photo: Gilles Abegg.)

nation with realistic scenery reached its high-water mark in the ultrarealist "theatre of the fourth wall removed," in which the box set was used to such advantage that it helped to foster a uniquely architectural theory of the-atre—that it should always represent life "with one wall removed."

The most talked-about scenic design today, however, tends to be more plastic than rigid, more kinetic than stable, more symbolic and evocative than realistic and explicit. In other words, abstract scenography is distinctly gain-ing ground.

The movement toward scenic abstraction began with the theoretical (and occasionally practical) works of designers Adolphe Appia (1862–1928) and Gordon Craig (1872–1966), both of whom urged the fluid use of space,

form, and light as a fundamental principle of dramatic design. Aided by technological ad-vances in lighting and motorized scene shift-ing, the movement toward a more plastic sce-nography has inspired a great many impressive abstract stylizations. Projections, shafts and walls of light, transparent scrims, outsized graphics and photoreproductions, sculptural configurations, metals both polished and coarse, mirrored and burlaped surfaces both hard and soft, "floating" walls and rising staircases, and wholly "found" or wholly "surreal" environ-ments: all of these have become major media for many contemporary scene designers.

These more plastic and more abstract set-tings can establish locales if need be, but they are perhaps more effective in establishing moods and styles. Of course, mood and style

Ming Cho Lee's great realistic setting for Patrick Meyer's adventure drama K-2 portrays a ledge in the Himalaya Mountains. It even feels cold. (Photo: Martha Swope and Associates.)

THE HIDDEN ENERGY

A stage setting has no independent life of its own. Its emphasis is directed toward the performance. In the absence of the actor it does not exist. Strange as it may seem, this simple and fundamental principle of stage design still seems to be widely misunderstood. . . .

A scene on the stage is . . . like a mixture of chemical elements held in solution. The actor adds the one element that releases the hidden energy of the whole. Meanwhile, wanting the actor, the various elements which go into the setting remain suspended, as it were, in an indefinable tension. To create this suspense, this tension, is the essence of . . . stage designing.

Robert Edmund Jones

---

can be established to some extent by realistic scenery as well: by creating a theatrical space that is tall and airy, for example, or cramped and squat, by using or withholding color and clutter, the designer in any mode can define an environment in such a way that the action of the play takes on a highly special tone. But with the extension into nonrealistic abstraction, the designer can greatly elaborate upon tone and develop it into a highly specific sensory approach.

The dark walls and cobwebby interiors designed by Edward Gorey for the Broadway production of *Dracula* (1977), for example, were a significant factor in the play's communication of fascinating horror. The bare but shiny white walls and lacy black catwalks designed by Sally Jacobs for the 1970 Peter Brook production of *A Midsummer Night's Dream* focused all attention on the poetry of the human relationships in that famous Shakespearean revival. The remarkable "found object"—a complete nineteenth-century iron foundry—that served as the surround for Eugene Lee's basic set in the original Harold

Prince production of *Sweeney Todd* (1979) indelibly conveyed the underlying theme of industrial oppression. Designer Eiko Ishioka's soaring white ramp, arcing through a brilliant Chinese-red background, epitomized the racial conflict and the psychosexual theme of David Henry Hwang's *M. Butterfly* in 1988. And Tony Walton's boldly colorful, brashly cartoonish street scenes for the 1992 Broadway revival of *Guys and Dolls* animated the play's New York City setting with a giddy, unworldly, and unthinking nostalgia, allowing current audiences to bask in Runyon's fantasy Manhattan—while just outside the door, on real New York City streets, contemporary urban agony and despair dominated the scene.

Specifically postmodern design elements, too, have made their appearance in the theatre of the 1980s and 90s. Because the postmodern emphasizes disharmonies and associations, it travels in a somewhat different path from the departures of modernist innovators Craig and Appia; postmodern design can be recognized by the conscious disruption of "unifying" stylistic themes, replacing them with apparently random assemblages of different and unrelated styles, some "quoting" other historical periods or intellectual sources. Postmodern design often reconfigures, or refers to, the theatre facility itself, with painted scenery made to look specifically scenic, particularly in contrast to seemingly arbitrary found objects strewn about the set, and with designed units meant to comment on—and to mock—their own "theatricality." Richard Hudson's setting and costumes for David Hirson's 1990 *La Bête,* a play set in 1654, ironically juxtaposes classical, neoclassical, baroque, and contemporary images with superbly ironic, and hilarious, effect.

The best scenic design today goes far beyond mere "backing" for the action of a play; it creates a basic visual and spatial architecture of performance, an architecture that when fully realized, becomes *intrinsic to the action.* Consider, for example, the multilevel, multiroomed setting designed by Jo Mielziner for

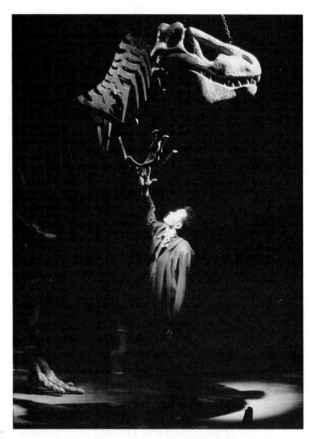

The scenic elements are central in Nicky Silver's Pterodactyls. *This funny-sad contemporary American drama concerns a dysfunctional modern American family, but poses it against a paleontological reconstruction of ancient times (and values). South Coast Repertory Theatre; scenery designed by Michael Vaughn Sims, 1994. (Photo: Cristofer Gross.)*

the original production of Arthur Miller's American classic, *Death of a Salesman.* This set, which provided a cutaway view of both floors of the salesman's house, permitting the simultaneous staging of activity in the kitchen and in the upstairs bedrooms, caused playwright Miller (and director Elia Kazan) to restructure the play so that events originally planned to evolve sequentially could be performed simultaneously, thereby tremendously

Eiko Ishioka's stunning set for David Henry Hwang's M. Butterfly *employs minimal details: soaring white ramp, black floor, glossy Chinese-red chairs, and a red surround, contrasting purity and passion in this 1987 Broadway play of East-West cultural (and male-female sexual) tensions. (Photo: Martha Swope and Associates.)*

Ocean waves create the Baltic seacoast in this 1991 Hamlet, *designed by Antony McDonald and staged by Ron Daniels at the American Repertory Theatre. The waves were handpainted on a giant canvas backdrop. (Photo: Richard Feldman.)*

Eighteenth-century Venetian playwright Carlo Gozzi blended medieval fantasy, a florid commedia dell'arte *style, and his own aristocratic sensibility to create visually spectacular productions in the late Royal era. Here, Andrei Serban's eye-popping production of* The Serpent Woman *at the American Repertory Theatre of Cambridge, Massachusetts, features scenery and costumes by Setsu Asakura and lighting by Victor En Yu Tan. (Photo: Richard Feldman.)*

increasing the intensity and impact of the action.

The many brilliant designs of Joseph Svoboda, who is certainly Europe's most celebrated "scenographer" (his own term) in the second half of this century, are nothing short of dramatic architecture in action. Svoboda has made highly imaginative use of a whole array of contemporary technologies, including laser beams, computerized slide and film projections, pneumatic mirrors, low-voltage lighting instruments, aerosol sprays, and innovative stage machinery, to create a body of scenic design unrivaled for theatrical impact and expressive dramaturgy. Speaking of "dramatic space" as "psychoplastic," Svoboda has said: "The goal of a designer can no longer be a description of a copy of actuality, but the creation of its multidimensional model." And for Svoboda—as for most contemporary designers—that multidimensional model is a dynamic one, flowing through time as well as space and responding to the inner biological and psychological rhythms of the actors and the dramatic actions.

Thus the functions of scenery design are both practical and abstract, both concrete and imaginative. Although it is a latecomer to theatre history, scenery has occasionally overwhelmed the drama itself: in the 1730s, in the "mute spectacles" of Jean-Nicholas Servandoni, whole performances were arranged with nothing but scene designs, lighting, music, and posed actors; Svoboda's *Diapolyekran* and *Lanterna Magika* have accomplished the same in more recent years (the 1960s and 70s). Scenery's place in the theatre is not inevitable—the theatre has managed in the past without it and still does so from time to time—but its future looks very secure. It has the capacity,

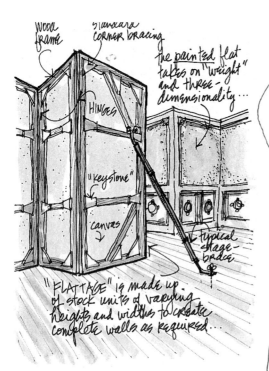

Labels on drawing:
wood frame
standard corner bracing
the painted flat takes on "weight" and three-dimensionality ...
HINGES
"keystone"
canvas
typical stage-brace
"FLATTAGE" is made up of stock units of varying heights and widths to create complete walls as required ...

The "flat" is an inexpensive way to create the illusion of an interior or exterior wall. Light, easy to move and to store, flats can be repainted almost indefinitely to create a variety of settings. (Drawing: John von Szeliski.)

when well used, to develop enormous visual, emotional, aesthetic, and dramatic impact, lending the theatre a conjunction with artistic technology that it can in no other way acquire.

The Scene Designer's Media

The traditional media of scenery design—wood, canvas, and paint—have in recent times been extended to include steel, plastics, and projected images. Designing and building scenic components from each of these sources is the first area of training for every scenic designer.

Platforms, flats, and draperies are the traditional building blocks of fixed stage scenery—and no changes in aesthetics or technology have in any way diminished their importance in the contemporary theatre.

Platforming serves the all-important function of giving the actor an elevated space from which to perform, making him or her visible over the heads of other actors and stage furniture. A stage setting that utilizes several artfully arranged platforming levels (of increasing height toward the back of the stage), together with appropriate connecting staircases and ramps or "raked" platform units, can permit dozens of actors to be seen simultaneously. Platforms can be created in any size and shape; moreover, with the growing use of steel in stage-platform construction, platform support can be fairly open, allowing huge but still "lacy" settings of great structural stability.

Flats, which are ordinarily made of canvas stretched over a wooden frame and then painted, are generally used to indicate vertical walls (realistic or abstract) and to define space. Flats can be pierced with windows, doors, and open archways; they can be adorned with moldings, paintings, hangings, bookcases, or fireplaces; they can be turned horizontally to serve as ceilings; they can be "tracked" onto the stage in grooves, as they were in the eighteenth century, or "flown" down from the overhead flies, as they often are in repertory theatres that store many settings at one time. The flat is an immensely versatile workhorse that has almost become a symbol of the theatre itself.

Drapery is the great neutral stuff of stage settings; it is often used to bridge the gap between the setting itself and the permanent features of the theatre building, and occasionally it is used in more realistic fashion as well. The stage curtain of a proscenium theatre is one form of hanging drapery—when the curtain rises or parts or is pulled diagonally upward (the "opera drape") at the beginning of a play, it signals the drama's first engagement of the audience. Another form of hanging drapery is used conventionally to mask (hide)

Sheets of plastic, corrugated plastic grating, and open steel scaffolding are some of the contemporary scene designer's media in this production of Julius Caesar *in Atlanta. (Photo: Charles M. Rafshoon.)*

the stage lighting above the set (this is called a "drapery border"), and yet another is used to mask the machinery and personnel behind the flats (the "drapery legs" or "wings").

Black drapery at the rear of the stage can provide a neutral backdrop to the action of a play, and frequently a whole set of drapery, usually black, is used as the entire setting for readings, chamber productions, and "reader's theatre" productions. Sometimes this sort of scenery is deemed suitable even for full-scale theatricalizations, and a theatre possessing such a "set of blacks" is able to present many plays with a minimal expenditure of scenery time or budget.

A final drapery found in most well-equipped theatres is the *cyclorama*, a hanging fabric stretched taut between upper and lower pipes and curved to surround the rear and sides of the stage. Colored white, gray, or gray-blue, the "cyc" can be lighted with stronger colors to represent a variety of "skyscapes" with great effectiveness; it can also be used for abstract backgrounds and projections.

In addition to the three primary components of stage settings, many productions make use of the special one-of-a-kind "set piece," which frequently becomes the focal point for an overall setting design or even for the action of a whole play. The tree in *Waiting*

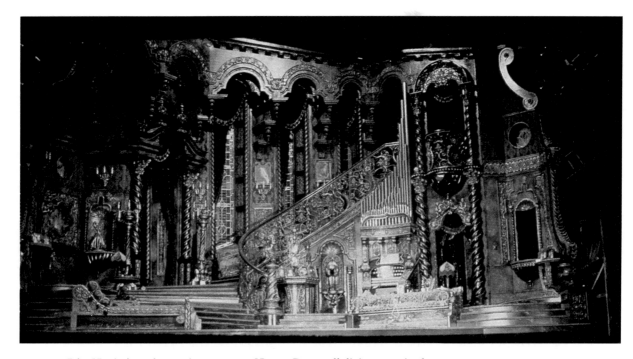

John Napier's opulent setting represents Norma Desmond's living room in the 1994 New York production of the musical Sunset Boulevard. *As sumptuous an interior as has been seen on Broadway in recent years, it—amazingly—lifts entirely off the ground during the play, the actors still aboard it, in order to permit another scene to appear below! (Photo: Joan Marcus.)*

for Godot, for example, is the primary scenic feature of that play's setting, symbolizing both life and death. The moment when Vladimir and Estragon "do the tree"—a calisthenic exercise in which each man stands on one leg and tries to assume the shape of the tree—is a profound moment of theatre in which set piece and actors coalesce in a single image, referred to in the text of the play, of the triple crucifixion on Calvary where two thieves died alongside Christ. Similarly, the massive supply wagon hauled by Mother Courage in Bertolt Brecht's epic play of that name gives rise to a powerful visual impression of struggle and travail that may last long after the words of the characters are forgotten. And what would

Prometheus Bound be without its striking set piece, Prometheus' rock and chains? No matter how stylized this element may have been in its original realization, it must have radiated to the Athenian audience a visual poetry every bit as eloquent as the verbal poetry with which Aeschylus supported it. Individual set pieces indeed tax the imagination of author, director, designer, and scene technician alike, and the masterpieces of scenic invention can long outlive their makers in the memory of the audience.

A host of modern materials and technological inventions add to the primary components and set pieces from which scenery is created.

Light as scenery, apart from the stage lighting discussed later, can create walls, images, even (with laser holography) three-dimensional visualizations. Banks of sharply focused light sent through dense atmospheres, enhanced by smoke or dust or fog, can create trenches of light that have the appearance of massive solidity and yet can be made to disappear at the flick of a switch. Carefully controlled slide projections can provide images either realistic or abstract, fixed or fluid, precise or indefinite.

Scrim, which is a loosely woven fabric that looks opaque when lit from one side and transparent when lit from the other, has been a staple of theatre "magic" for many years.

Stage machinery—turntables, elevators, hoists, rolling carts and wagons, and the like—can be used to create a veritable dance of scenic elements to accompany and support dramatic action. The ancient Greeks apparently understood the importance of mechanical devices quite well, as did Shakespeare with his winched thrones and disappearing witches. Tricks and sleight of hand (called, in the medieval theatre, "trucs" and "feynts") have always imparted a certain sparkle of mystery to the theatre and hence will always play a part in the designer's art.

Sound also must be taken into consideration by the designer, who must plan for the footfalls of the actor as well as for the visual elements behind, around, and underneath him or her. The floor of a stage designed for the production of Japanese Nō Drama, for example, has a characteristic look and produces a characteristic sound; it is meant to be stamped upon, and it must sound just so. Joseph Svoboda has designed a stage floor for *Faust* that can be either resonant or silent depending on the arrangement of certain mechanisms concealed underneath; when Faust walks upstage his steps reverberate; when he turns and walks downstage his steps are silent—and we know Mephistopheles has taken his body.

Properties and furniture, which are often handled by a separate artist working under the guidance of the scene designer, are crucial not only in establishing realism but also in enhancing mood and style. Although furniture is most often used in the theatre just as it is in life—to sit upon, lie upon, and so forth—it also has a crucial stylistic importance; often stage furniture is designed and built in highly imaginative ways to convey a special visual impact when coordinated with the setting. Properties such as ash trays, telephones, letters, and tableware are often functional in realistic plays, but they can also have aesthetic importance and are therefore carefully selected—or else specially designed. Frequently, furniture pieces or properties have considerable symbolic significance, as in the case of the thrones in Shakespeare's *Richard III* or the glass figurines in Williams's *Glass Menagerie.*

The Scene Designer at Work

The scene designer's work inevitably begins with a reading and rereading of the play, discussions with the director, and a consideration of the type of theatre in which the play is to be produced. This step is usually followed with a series of visualizations—sketches, drawings, collected illustrations (for example, clippings from magazines, notations from historical sources, color ideas, spatial concepts), or three-dimensional models. Whatever the scenic inspiration, it must ultimately be rendered in a fashion suitable to serve as a guide for construction—which ordinarily means, minimally, a full set of working drawings explaining in precise technical detail the construction practices to be used. All along the way, of course, the designer must reckon with budgetary restraints and the skills of the construction staff available to execute and install the finished design. Part architect, part engineer, part painter, part decorator, part builder, part interpretive genius, part accountant, the scene designer today is one of the theatre's premier artists/craftspeople.

Natasha Katz's intense downlighting keeps our attention on Edmund (Jonathan Fried), his sword drawn before his duel with Edgar (deep background). For the 1991 Adrian Hall production of King Lear *at the American Repertory Theatre. (Photo: Richard Feldman.)*

LIGHTING

The very word *theatre,* meaning "seeing place," implies the crucial function of light. Light is the basic condition for theatrical appearance; without light, nothing is to be seen.

The use of light for dramatic effect, as distinct from pure illumination, can be traced back to the earliest surviving plays: *Agamemnon,* by Aeschylus, was staged so that the watchman's spotting of the signal fire heralding Agamemnon's return to Argos coincided with the actual sunrise over the Athenian *skene* (stagehouse); it is also probable that the burning of Troy at the conclusion of Euripides' *The Trojan Women* was staged to coincide with the hour when sunset reddened the Attic sky. Modern plays commonly use light in metaphoric and symbolic ways: the blinking neon light that regularly reddens Blanche's quarters in Tennessee Williams's *A Streetcar Named Desire* affords one example; another is the searching followspot demanded by Samuel Beckett to train upon the hapless, trapped characters in his play entitled *Play.*

It is customary to think of theatre lighting as a relatively recent technology, dating from the invention of electricity. Nothing could be more misleading; lighting has always been a major theatrical consideration. The Greeks paid a great deal of attention to the proper orientation of their theatres to take best advantage of the sun's rays. The medieval outdoor theatre, although as dependent on sunlight as was the Greek theatre, made use of several devices to redirect sunlight, including the halos made of reflective metal that were used to surround Jesus and his disciples with a focused and intensified illumination; in one production a brightly polished metal basin was held over Jesus' head to concentrate the sun's rays—and surviving instructions tell the medieval stagehands to substitute torches for the bowl in case of cloudy skies!

It was in indoor stagings, however, that lighting technology attained its first significant sophistication—and this as early as the Middle Ages. In a 1439 production of the *Annunciation* in Florence, one thousand oil lamps were used for illumination, plus a host of candles that were lighted by a "ray of fire" that shot through the cathedral. One can imagine the spectacle. Leonardo da Vinci designed a 1490 production of *Paradise* with twinkling stars and backlit zodiac signs on colored glass; by the sixteenth century the great festival lighting of indoor theatres, located in manor houses and public halls, would serve as a symbol of the intellectual and artistic achievements of the Renaissance itself, a mark of the luxury, technical wizardry, and ostentatious, exuberant humanism of the times. People went to the theatres in those times simply to revel in light and escape the outside gloom—in rather the same way that Americans, earlier in this century, populated air-conditioned movie theatres largely to escape the heat of summer days.

The indoor stages of the Renaissance have perhaps never been equaled in terms of sheer opulence of illumination—and the entire effect was created simply from tallow, wax, and fireworks. Raphael "painted" the name of his patron, Pope Leo X, with thirteen lighted chandeliers in a 1519 dramatic production; Sebastiano Serlio placed sparkling panes of colored glass, illuminated from behind, into his flat painted scenery to create glistening and seductive scenic effects.

As the Renaissance spirit give way to the lavish Royal theatre of the age of Louis XIV, the Sun King, artificial illumination calculated to match Louis's presumed incendiary brilliance developed apace: one 1664 presentation at Versailles featured 20,000 colored lanterns, hundreds of transparent veils and bowls of colored water, and a massive display of fireworks.

It was the invention of the gaslight in the nineteenth century and the development of electricity shortly thereafter—first in carbon arc and "limelight" electrical lighting and then in incandescence—that brought stage lighting into its modern phase and made it less strictly showy and more pertinent to individual works and dramatic action. Ease and flexibility of control is the cardinal virtue of both gas and electricity. A single operator at a "gas table" could, by throwing a valve, raise or dim the intensity of any individual light or of a preselected "gang" of lights—just as we can raise or lower the fire on a gas range by turning a knob.

And, of course, with electricity—which was introduced in American theatres in 1879 and in European theatres the following year—

LIMITS OF ELECTRICITY

For all the efficiency, economy, safety, and extraordinary flexibility of electric lighting, it is by no means regarded universally as an unmixed blessing for the theatre. Gone is the "living flame" that for eight hundred years had illumined indoor theatrical performance, and gone with it the warm, mellow, flickering glow cast by gaslight and, more particularly, by candlelight. Undeniably, the very strengths of electrical lighting—its uniform beam, its whiteness, its precision—have also contributed a certain sterility, coldness, and harshness, and for this reason its nearly exclusive use in the theatre today is seen by some as a definite step in the wrong direction.

As candlelight and gaslight have returned in recent years to many restaurants, homes, and even street corners—almost always in successful conjunction with incandescent or even fluorescent lighting—so a few designers now are attempting to reintegrate the "living flame" into stage lighting. The great electrical revolution of the past hundred years need not forever define the future of stage illumination.

the great fire hazard of live flame, a danger that had plagued the theatre for centuries and claimed three buildings a year on average (including Shakespeare's Globe), was at last over. The fire crews, which had been a permanent, 24-hour staff in the employ of every major theatre in the early nineteenth century, were dismissed; and the deterioration of scenery and costumes from heat, smoke, and carbon pollution of flame lighting similarly came to a halt. Incandescent lighting also had the great advantage of being fully self-starting—it did not need to be relit or kept alive by "pilots"—and it could easily be switched off, dimmed up and down, and reganged or reconnected simply by fastening and unfasten-

Individual pools of light illuminate the parasols and costumes—and the isolation—of ladies waiting for the soldiers' return at the beginning of Much Ado About Nothing. *Indiana Repertory Theatre production, directed by Libby Appel, 1994.*

ing flexible wires. Within a few years of its introduction, electricity became the primary medium of stage lighting in the Western world, and great dynamo generators—for electricity was used in the theatre long before it was commercially available from municipal power supplies—were installed as essential equipment in the basements of theatres from Vienna to San Francisco.

Electricity provides the enormous flexibility of lighting that we know and use today. The incandescent filament is a reasonably small, reasonably cool point of light that can be focused, reflected, aimed, shaped, and col-ored by a great variety of devices invented and adapted for those purposes; and electric light can be trained in innumerable ways upon actors, scenery, audience, or combinations of these to create realistic and/or atmospheric effects, through dimensionality, focus, animation, distortion, diffusion, and overwhelming radiance. Today, thanks to the added sophistication of computer technology and microelectronics, it is not uncommon to see theatres with nearly a thousand lighting instruments all under the complete control of a single technician seated in a comfortable booth above the audience.

Modern Lighting Design

Today, the lighting for any given production is likely to have been conceived and directly supervised by a professional lighting designer, a species of theatre artist who has appeared as a principal member of the production team only in the past two or three decades.

By skillfully working with lighting instruments, hanging positions, angles, colors, shadows, and moment-to-moment adjustment of intensity and directionality, the lighting designer can illuminate a dramatic production in a great variety of subtle and complex ways. The way in which the lighting designer uses the medium to blend the more rigid design elements (architecture and scenery) with the evolving patterns of the movements of the actors, and the meanings of the play, can be a crucial factor in a production's artistic and theatrical success.

Visibility and *focus* are the primary considerations of lighting design: visibility ensures that the audience sees what they want to see, and focus ensures that they see what they are *supposed* to see without undue distraction. Visibility, then, is the passive accomplishment of lighting design and focus is its active accomplishment. The spotlight used in contemporary theatre, a development of the twentieth century, has fostered something akin to a revolution in staging, which now routinely features a darkened auditorium (a rarity prior to this century) and a deliberate effort to illuminate certain characters (or props or set pieces) more than others—in other words, to direct the audience's attention toward those visual elements that are dramatically the most significant.

Realism and *atmosphere* also are frequent goals of the lighting designer, and both can be achieved largely through the color and direction of lighting. Realistic lighting can be created to appear as if emanating from familiar sources: from the sun, for example, or from "practical" (real) lamps on the stage, or from moonlight, fire, street lights, neon signs, or the headlights of moving automobiles. Atmospheric lighting, which may or may not suggest a familiar source, can be used to evoke a mood appropriate to a play's action: sparkly, for example, or gloomy, oppressive, nightmarish, austere, verdant, smoky, funeral, or regal.

Sharp, bold lighting designs are frequently employed to create highly theatrical effects—for glittery entertainments in the Broadway musical tradition, for example, or for harsher experimental stagings like those often associated with the plays and theories of Bertolt Brecht. Brecht's concept of a "didactic" theatre suggested the lighting be bright, cold (uncolored), and specifically "unmagical"; Brecht suggested, in fact, that the lighting instruments themselves be made part of the setting, placed in full view of the audience, and this "theatricalist" use of the lighting instruments

Robert Wilson uses lighting in both subtle and flamboyant fashions. The lighting for his 1992 production of Einstein at the Beach *has the effect of seeming to magically propel a character beyond an imprisoning "jail" of steel bars. (Photo: Martha Swope and Associates/William Gibson.)*

One of the most fundamental uses of scenic and costume design is to establish the time and place in which dramatic events are presumed to take place.

Top left: Ceremonies in Dark Old Men *by the late Lonnie Elder III is set in a Depression-era Harlem apartment; as re-created in the production by the Long Wharf Theatre of New Haven. Scenery by Donald Eastman; costumes by Mary Mease Warren; lighting by Frances Aronson. (Photo: T. Charles Erickson.)*

Top right: The 1988 Actors Theatre of Louisville production of W. S. Gilbert's Engaged *takes us back to the play's Victorian setting a hundred years before. (Photo: Richard C. Trigg.)*

Middle: George S. Kaufman and Moss Hart's You Can't Take It With You, *though also set in a New York home in the 1930s, reflects a far different social world. Shown in the Utah Shakespearean Festival production (scenery by George Maxwell, costumes by Bill Black, make-up and hair by Amanda French.)*

Bottom: Glenn Close's make-up and costume define the character of Norma Desmond as living in her past, as a star of the silent screen, though the play—Broadway's 1994 production of Sunset Boulevard—*is set in much more recent times. (Photo: Joan Marcus.)*

themselves is now in widespread use even in nondidactic plays. The splashy musical, more romantically, often makes use of footlights, banks of colored border lights, onstage "tracer" lights that flash on and off in sequence, followspots, and high-voltage incandescence that makes a finale seem to burn up the stage; in fact, this traditional exploitation of light has done as much to give Broadway the name "Great White Way" as have the famous billboards and marquees that line the street.

Stylized lighting effects are often used to express radical changes of mood or event; indeed, the use of lighting alone to signal a complete change of scene is an increasingly common theatrical expedient. Merely by switching from full front to full overhead lighting, for example, a technician can throw a character into silhouette and make her or his figure appear suddenly ominous, grotesque, or isolated. The illumination of an actor with odd lighting colors, such as green, or from odd lighting positions, such as from below, can create mysterious, unsettling effects. The use of followspots can metaphorically put a character "on the spot" and convey a specific sense of unspeakable terror. Highly expressive lighting and projections, when applied to a production utilizing only a cyclorama, a set piece, sculpture, or stage mechanism and neutrally clad actors, can create an infinite variety of convincing theatrical environments for all but the most resolutely realistic of plays; it is here, in the area of stylization and expressive theatricality, that the modern lighting designer has made the most significant mark.

The Lighting Designer at Work

The lighting designer ordinarily conceives a lighting design out of a synthesis of many discrete elements: the play, the director's approach or concept, the characteristics of the theatre building (lighting positions, control facilities, and wiring system), the basic scenery design, the costumes and movements of the actors, and the available lighting instruments.

LIGHT AS MUSIC: ADOLPHE APPIA

Light and shadow in the course of the drama achieve the same significance as a musical motif which, once stated and developed, has an infinite range of variation. Tristan's agony is sufficient motivation for carrying this kind of lighting to its greatest degree of expressiveness, and the audience, overwhelmed vicariously by the spiritual tragedy of the hero and heroine, would be disturbed by any form of stage setting which did not incorporate this element of design. The audience would really suffer for lack of the kind of staging I have indicated, because it needs to get through its eyes a kind of impression which, up to a given point, can equal the unexampled emotional power of the score. Light is the only medium which can continuously create this impression and its use is motivated and justified by the score itself.

Adolphe Appia

Occasionally the availability of an experienced lighting crew must also be a consideration.

Because not all of these variables can be known from the outset—the stage movement, for example, may change from one day to the next right up to the final dress rehearsal—the lighting designer must possess a certain skill at making adjustments and must have the opportunity to exercise a certain amount of control, or at least to voice concerns with regard to areas affecting lighting problems.

Ordinarily, the two major preparations required of the lighting designer are the light plot and the cue sheet. A light plot is a plan or series of plans showing the placement of each lighting instrument; its type, wattage, and size; its wiring and connection to an appropriate dimmer; its color; and any special instruc-

Robert Wilson, who designs or codesigns (as here, with Jennifer Tipton) the light-ing for his productions, paints the stage with lights from various sources, including lasers, and coming from unusual positions, including beneath the stage. Shown here: light as scenery in his 1986 Alcestis *at the American Repertory Theatre. (Photo: Richard Feldman.)*

tions as to its use. A cue sheet is a list of the occasions, referred to by number and keyed to the script of the play (or, in final form, the more fully annotated stage manager's script), when lights change, either in intensity or in their use. These two documents—light plot and cue sheet—are developed in consultation with the director, who may take a major or minor role in the consultation depending on his or her interest and expertise. Inasmuch as some productions use hundreds of lighting instruments and require thousands of individual cues, the complexity of these documents can be extraordinary; weeks and months may go into their preparation.

The lighting designer works with a number of different sorts of lighting instruments and must know the properties of each instrument well enough to anticipate fully how it will perform when hung and focused on the stage. Few theatres have the time or space flexibility to permit much on-site experimentation in lighting design; thus most of the development of light plot and cue sheet must take place in the imagination and, where possible, in workshop or free experimentation apart from the working facility. This requirement places a premium on the designer's ability to predict instrument performance from various distances and angles and with various color elements installed; it also demands a sharp awareness of how various lights will reflect off different surfaces.

Ordinarily the lighting designer develops the plot and cue sheet gradually, over the course of regular discussions with the director and after attending some rehearsals, studying a model of the setting and perhaps some of the completed set pieces, and looking at the actual fabrics purchased for costuming. At a certain point, with the plot complete, the lights are mounted (hung) in appropriate positions, attached to the theatre's wiring system (or wired separately), "patched" to proper dimmers, focused (aimed) in the desired directions, and colored by the attachment of frames containing "gelatins" (actually thin, transparent sheets of colored plastic). Ideally, the stage setting is finished and in position when all of this occurs, but this ideal is rarely fully achieved, particularly on Broadway, where theatres are rented only a short time before the opening performance.

Once the instruments are in place and functioning, the lighting designer begins setting the intensities of each instrument for each cue, a painstaking process involving the recording of thousands of individual numerical decisions on a series of cue sheets for the precise instruction of technicians who must effect the cues. Computer technology has vastly simplified this process for those theatres able to afford "computer boards"; with or without computers, however, much time and care inevitably go into this process, which is vital to the development and execution of a fully satisfying lighting design.

Finally, the lighting designer presides over the working and timing of the cues, making certain that in actual operation the lights shift as subtly or as boldly, as grandly or as imperceptibly, as is appropriate for the play's action and for the design aesthetic.

It is out of thousands of details, most of which are pulled together in a single final week, that great lighting design springs. Gradations of light, difficult to measure in isolation, can have vastly differing impacts in the moment-to-moment focus and feel of a play. Since light is a medium rather than an object, the audience is rarely if ever directly aware of it—they are aware only of its illuminated target. Therefore, the lighting designer's work is poorly understood by the theatregoing public at large. But everyone who works professionally in the theatre, from the set and costume designer to the director to the actor, knows what a crucial role lighting plays in the success of the theatre venture. As the "Old Actor" says as he departs the stage in off-Broadway's longest running hit, *The Fantasticks:* "Remember me—in light!" The light that illuminates the theatre also glorifies it; it is a symbol of revelation—of knowledge and humanity—upon which the theatrical impulse finally rests.

COSTUME

Costume has always been a major element in the theatrical experience, a vehicle for the "dressing up" that actors and audiences alike have at all times felt to be necessary for the fullest degree of theatrical satisfaction. Costume serves both ceremonial and illustrative functions.

The Functions of Costume

The first theatrical costumes were essentially ceremonial vestments. The *himation* of the early Aeschylean actor was derived from the garment worn by the priest-chanter of the dithyramb; the comic and satyr costumes, with their use of phalluses and goatskins, were likewise derived from more primitive god-centered rites. The priests who first enacted the *Quem Queritis* trope in medieval Europe simply wore their sacred albs, hooded to indicate an outdoor scene but otherwise unaltered; the actors of the classic Japanese Nō Drama even today wear costumes that relate more to spiritual sources than to secular life.

These ancient and original uses of costuming served primarily to separate the actor from the audience, to "elevate" the actor to a quasi-divine status. The thick-soled footwear (*kothurnoi*) worn by Greek actors in the fourth century B.C. were calculated to en-

Costuming can signal a drastically reconceived production, as in the celebrated Kabuki Medea, *which was conceived, directed, and designed by Shozo Sato at the Wisdom Bridge Theatre in Chicago in 1983. The production has subsequently toured the United States, and Sato has embarked on a series of such "Kabuki-ized" ventures. (Photo: Jennifer Girard.)*

hance this ceremonial effect by greatly increasing the height of the wearers, thereby "dressing them up" both figuratively and literally.

The shift of stress in costuming from a "dressing up" of the actor to a defining of the character came about gradually in the theatre's history. In the Elizabethan theatre, the costumes often had an almost regal ceremonial quality because the acting companies frequently solicited the castoff raiment of the nobility; English theatre of this time was known throughout Europe for the splendor of its costuming, but apparently little effort was made to suit costume to characterization.

Moreover, it was not unusual in Shakespeare's time for some actors to wear contemporary garb on stage while others wore costumes expressive of the period of the play. In Renaissance Italy, costuming developed a high degree of stylization in the *commedia dell'arte*, where each of the recurring characters wore a distinctive and arresting costume that brightly and instantly signified a particular age, intelligence, and disposition. The same characters and the same costumes can be seen today in contemporary *commedia* productions, and they are still as eloquent and entertaining as they were four hundred years ago.

Modern costuming took on much of its present character in the eighteenth and nineteenth centuries, when certain realistic considerations took control of the Western theatre. These centuries witnessed a great deal of radical social change that led to, among other things, the widespread acceptance of science and its methods and a great fascination with detail and accuracy. These trends coalesced in the European (and eventually the American) theatre with a series of productions in which historical accuracy served as the guiding principle. For the first time, a massive effort was made to ensure that the design of every costume in a play (and every prop and every set piece as well) accorded with an authentic "period" source. Thus a production of *Julius Caesar* would be intensively researched to recreate the clothing worn in Rome in the first century A.D., a *Hamlet* would be designed to mirror the records of medieval Denmark, and a *Romeo and Juliet* would seek to re-create, in detail, the world of Renaissance Verona.

The movement toward historical accuracy and the devotion with which it was pursued led ultimately to a widespread change in the philosophy of costume design that persists to this day. For although historical accuracy itself is no longer the ultimate goal of costume design, stylistic consistency and overall design control have proven to be lasting principles. Costuming today stresses, in addition to an imaginative aesthetic creativity, a coordinated dramatic suitability as well; thus the influence of realism, with its attendant emphasis on historical accuracy, has fostered coherent and principled design in place of the near anarchy that once obtained.

This does not mean that costuming has lost touch with its ancient origins. On the one hand, we can still capture in the combination of bright stage lights and grotesque or exotic costumes the ceremonial magic conjured by ancient priests and modern-day shamans alike. What is more, our potential for capturing that magic is probably *enhanced* by costume consistency and control.

On the other hand, however, costuming has gained a great deal by its commitment to character definition and dramatic suitability. Costuming can provide the audience's first clues to a character's profession, wealth, class status, tastes, and self-image. More subtly, costume can symbolize human vices and virtues: sloth, vanity, benevolence, pride, generosity, for example. Some costumes are intrinsic to the characters who wear them—as are Hamlet's "inky cloak" and Harlequin's particolored tights. By judicious use of color, shape, and fabric, costume designers can imbue every character in a play with individuality. The collective costuming of a play, in addition to setting a historical period and creating an overall theatrical style, can also convey social and personal meanings supportive of the text's intent; consider, for example, Tennessee Williams's direction in *A Streetcar Named Desire* that the poker players are to wear shirts of "bright primary colors," to contrast them with Blanche du Bois's dead husband, one "Allen Grey."

The specific challenge of the costume designer, then, is to impart patterns of meaning and an aggregate theatrical excitement to what must finally be *wearable clothing for the characters*. For costume, of course, is clothing; it must be functional as well as meaningful and aesthetic. The actor does not model his costume; he wears it, walks in it, sits in it, duels in it, dances in it, tumbles downstairs in it.

COSTUME DESIGN

I see my job as a cross between camouflage and magic.

Edith Head

The costume designer thus cannot be content merely to draw pictures on paper but must also design workable, danceable, actable clothing for which cutting, stitching, fitting, and quick-changing are as important considerations as color coordination and historical context.

The costume as clothing gives rise to both ensemble and individual impressions. As one of an ensemble, the costume an actor wears contributes not only to a play's overall symbolic effects, but also to its particularized milieu, to a specific "world" in which people are seen to dress in special and perhaps unique ways. This world may portray a period out of the past, accurately rendered, or it may be modern, or it may be a world fashioned out of the purest fantasy; whatever the case, however, there is always a demand for a certain costume coherence, even in the most inventive and idiosyncratic productions. The word *costume* has the same root meaning as *custom* and *customary;* and the costumes of a particular world, theatrically created, must be seen to represent the "customary costume" (or, in the same vein, the "habitual habit") of the "inhabitants" of that world. Costume, in other words, sets style; it is the garb of choice for the general run of people in the play.

This leads us to an examination of the importance of costume for the definition of individual characters within the ensemble. A character's adherence or nonadherence to the "going dress" of the other characters in a play will always be loaded with significance. For costume is a character's way of expressing individuality and self-image: *it is the clothing he or she chooses to wear* within the context of the dress favored by his or her peers. When Ham-

Costumes play a major role in Luis Valdez's play and production of Zoot Suit, *in which the dress of 1940s Latinos living in the Los Angeles area becomes a metaphor for cultural pride and social advancement. Roberta Delgado Esparza, Daniel Valdez, Edward James Olmos, and Evelina Fernandez are featured in this Mark Taper Forum production. (Photo: Courtesy of the Mark Taper Forum.)*

let wears his "inky cloak" to the royal court, for example, it signifies his refusal to adapt to his surroundings and the expectations of his superiors. It is both a mark of his character and a significant action in the play; it says a great deal about how he perceives himself and how he wants the world to see him. When Monsieur Jourdain in Molière's *The Bourgeois Gentleman* dons his fancy suit with the upside-down flowers and, later, his Turkish gown and grotesque turban, he is proclaiming (foolishly) to his peers that he is a person of elegance and refinement. And Estragon's unlaced shoes in *Waiting for Godot* represent—pathetically to be sure—his great

wish to be unfettered, not "tied to Godot" but simply free, fed, and happy. Further, the battered bowler hats and smelly shoes that figure into that play, as well as the empty pockets in Vladimir's tattered overcoat, symbolize the fruitlessness of Gogo's and Didi's quest for salvation and at the same time suggest their reluctance to part with the familiar, the known quantity.

In Luis Valdez's *Zoot Suit,* the contemporary drama about Mexican Americans in Los Angeles during World War II, the costume of the title acquires major significance, representing both the world of the play's central characters and the struggle of individual characters to stand apart from that world. Eugène Brieux's *The Red Robe* and Paul Claudel's *Satin Slipper* illustrate similar uses of costume elements as metaphor in modern (postromantic) drama.

The Costume Designer at Work

The costume designer works primarily with fabric, which comes in a variety of materials and weaves and can be cut, shaped, stitched, colored, and draped in innumerable ways. Aside from fabric, jewels, armor, feathers, fur, hair (real or simulated), and metallic ornamentation commonly figure into costume design.

The costume designer both selects and builds costume elements, usually in combination. The costumes for some plays are assembled entirely out of items ready at hand. For contemporary plays with modern settings, the costumes are often selected from the actors' own wardrobes or from department store racks. Sometimes a costume designer will acquire clothing from thrift shops and used-clothing stores, particularly for plays set in the recent past; indeed, this is not unusual practice even for high-budget professional productions. In one celebrated instance, Louis Jouvet appealed to the citizens of Paris to donate costumes for the posthumous premiere of Jean Giraudoux's *The Madwoman of Chaillot,* and the clothing that poured into the Athénée theatre for that brilliant 1945 Parisian production signaled to the world that France had survived the scourge of Nazi Occupation with its devotion to the theatre intact.

Even in a "fully designed, fully built" production, some costume elements are usually purchased, rented, or taken from costume storage; shoes, for example, are not ordinarily built from scratch for theatrical productions. Nonetheless, it is those productions that are designed and built for a given set of performances that test the full measure of the costume designer's imagination and ability. In

---

IMPORTANCE OF SMALL DETAILS

The task of subtly distorting uniformity, without destroying the desired illusion, is a difficult one. Anton Chekhov's play *The Three Sisters* presents a case in point. The characters of the male players are clearly defined in Chekhov's writing, but because the men are all wearing military uniforms they are theoretically similar in appearance. One of the few ways in which the designer can help to differentiate between characters is by the alteration of proportion; alterations such as these, which do not show enough from the "front" to make the uniforms seem strange to the audience, can be extremely effective, as well as helpful to the actor. In a London production of *The Three Sisters,* Sir Michael Redgrave wore a coat with a collar that was too low; Sir John Gielgud one that was too high. No one in the audience was unaware of the characters' individuality, the talents of these actors being what they are, but the small details added to the scope of their performances.

Motley

---

these productions, subject only to the ultimate inspiration and control of the director, the costume designer can create a top-to-toe originality.

The comprehensive design for such a production begins with a series of sketches and material estimates—these usually proceed hand in hand—based on a thorough knowledge of the play, a clear agreement with the director on interpretation and style, research into necessary historical sources, and a firm understanding of the production monies and costume technologies available to the production organization. Generally, a separate costume sketch is made for each character, although choruses and "extras" are sometimes grouped in, or represented by, a single

Costume design does not always entail fresh construction; brilliant designs can often be a dramatic combination of existing garments and fabrics employed in unique ways. In Sam Shepard's A Lie of the Mind, *directed by Shepard, military decorations on an air corps flight jacket and an American flag ironically used as a scarf create a provocative and indelible design element in a play that probes deeply into our national culture and mythos. Costume design by Rita Ryack. (Photo: Martha Swope and Associates.)*

sketch; then, after such conferences with the director to gain full support and approval, the sketches are developed into full-color renderings. When these are approved and the material estimates are "costed out" and budgeted, fabrics are purchased and appropriate sample swatches are attached to the corner of each rendering. Construction details are frequently included on the rendering itself so that a single document conveys both the general look and specific construction of each costume.

The purchase of fabric is of course a crucial stage in costuming, for fabric is the basic medium of the costumer's art. Texture, weight, suppleness, and response to draping, dying, folding, crushing, twirling, and twisting are all considerations applied to the purchase of costume fabric. Velvet (and its synthetic substitute, velveteen), raw silk, woolens, and satin are the costumer's luxury fabrics; cottons, felt, burlap, and even painted canvas are less expensive and often appropriate for theatrical use. Coloring, "aging" (making a new fabric appear old and used), and detailing are often achieved with dyes, appliqués, and embroidery, and sometimes with paint, tie-dyes, and other special treatments (for example, the costume designers Motley—three women working under a single professional name—simulate leather by rubbing thick felt with moist yellow soap and spraying it down with brown paints). Frequently, of course, printed or embossed fabrics with designs woven in are purchased for women's costumes or for male period attire.

The cutting, fitting, and stitching of original costumes are equally important stages in costume design. Most designers insist on at least some control over these procedures, for the cutting of a fabric determines the manner in which it drapes and moves, and the fitting of a costume determines its shape and silhouette. Needless to say, a "cutter" is a full-time professional in the theatre, and the designer must work in close collaboration with the cutter to achieve the intended result. Fitting and stitching (as well as refitting, restitching, and often re-refitting and re-restitching) are part of the obligatory and time-consuming backstage process by which the costume becomes a wearable garment for the actor and the actor "grows into" the theatrically costumed characterization.

Finally, the accessories of costume can greatly affect the impact of the basic design; occasionally they may even stand out in such a way as to "make" the costume or to obliterate it. Hairstyles and headdresses, since they

Consummate costumography—with historically based but creatively exaggerated wigs, hats, gowns, and uniforms—in an avant-garde production of The Bourgeois Gentleman *at the Théâtre de l'Est in Paris. (Photo: Marc Enguerand.)*

frame the actor's face, will convey a visual message every time the actor speaks a line; they are obviously of paramount importance. Jewelry, sashes, purses, muffs, and other adornments and badges of various sorts have considerable dramatic impact insofar as they "read" from the audience—that is, insofar as the audience can see them clearly and take notice of what they may signify about the character. The lowly shoe, if unwisely chosen, can destroy the artistry of a production, either by being unsuitable for the character or style of the play or by being so badly fitted (or so unwieldy) that the actor stumbles awkwardly about the stage.

Good costuming for a play, whether arrived at through design and fabrication or through careful selection from the Army sur-plus store, creates a sense of character, period, style, and theatricality out of wearable garments. In harmony with scenery, make-up, and lighting, and with the play's interpretation and performance, costuming can have its maximum impact in a subtle way—by underlining the play's meaning and the characters' personalities—or it can scream for attention and sometimes even become the "star of the show." Not a few musicals have succeeded primarily because the audience "came out whistling the costumes," as a Shubert Alley phrase reminds us.

Certain theorists contend that costuming must at all times relegate itself to a subordinate role, and perhaps for most Western plays of the latter part of this century that has been a valid principle. But who is to say that the grand dancers of the Kabuki theatre, or the patchworked Arlecchino of the *commedia dell' arte,* or the stunningly garbed black-and-white mannequins of Cecil Beaton's creation in *My Fair Lady* represent any less a theatrical realization than their more modestly attired counterparts in other forms of theatre? Costume has always exerted a certain magical force in the theatre, lending a special magnitude to the actor's and the playwright's art. There are occasions when it seems altogether fitting and proper that this contribution should be celebrated in its own right.

SOUND DESIGN

The *sound designer* occupies a position of rapidly increasing importance in the theatre today. The sound designer's rise in prominence has been prompted by swiftly developing audio-technologies that now include computerized sampling devices, compact discs, miniaturized microphones and transmitters, and advances in electronic mixing and multiphonic sound. The influence of cinema is probably also a factor: modern audiences have become accustomed (and receptive) to near-continuous musical and sound underscoring for films and likewise for dramatic scenes in the theatre. These changes have made the sound technician's function vastly more demanding than that of the stagehand who just a few decades ago was expected to do little more than rattle a tin sheet to indicate thunder or play a scratchy record during scene changes.

As we have seen, the origins of theatre and music are intertwined (Aristotle included music as one of the six components of tragedy), and until about two hundred years ago no one even considered staging a play without music. Today the established popularity of the musical theatre, whether in the splashy Broadway format or the more socially expressive Brechtian one, exerts a continuing demand for both live and recorded sound that goes well beyond the simpler effects once required. Some sound "scores" for serious plays, such as the hoofbeats in *Equus,* the voices in *Wings,* and the offstage military band music at the end of *The Three Sisters,* are intrinsic to the text and indeed convey—often by contrast—the whole point of the actions they accompany. Finally, the amplification of live stage sound is becoming a major practice (much derided by many) in an attempt to give theatre the audible "boom-boom" punch of films, rock concerts, and certain religious revivals.

MAKE-UP

Make-up, which is essentially the design of the actor's face, occupies a curiously paradoxical position in the theatre.

In much modern production, make-up seems sorely neglected. It tends to be the last design technology to be considered; indeed, it is often applied (literally) for the first time at the final dress rehearsal—and sometimes

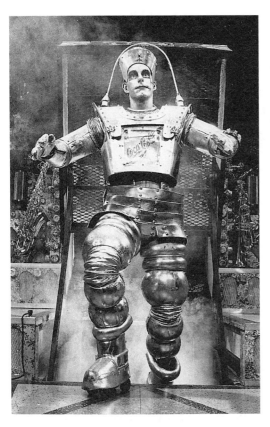

Witty irreverence and low-tech fantasy proved triumphant in the 1991 off-Broadway musical Return to the Forbidden Planet, *which was billed as "Shakespeare's forgotten rock-and-roll masterpiece." This is the futuristic costume for a robotic Ariel (from Shakespeare's* The Tempest*). (Photo: Martha Swope and Associates/Carol Rosegg.)*

Make-up and hair (the latter including facial hair) are key to the character's appearance. Beryl Reid and Bob Peck here play Lady Wishfort and Sir Wilfull Witwoud in Congreve's The Way of the World; *costumes, make-up, and hairstyling help bring them back through the centuries. (Photo: Donald Cooper.)*

not until just before the opening performance. Many directors spend little time planning for it, and rarely is an independent artist engaged to guide the make-up design of a contemporary play. Indeed, make-up is the only major design element whose planning and execution are often left entirely to the actor's decision.

And yet, ironically, make-up is one of the archetypal arts of the theatre, absolutely fundamental to the origins of drama. The earliest chanters of the dithyramb, like the spiritual leaders of primitive tribes today, invariably made themselves up in preparation for the

performance of their holy rites: their make-up in later centuries inspired the Greek tragic and comic masks that are today the universal symbols of theatre itself.

The reason for this paradox resides in the changing emphasis of theatre aims. Make-up, like costuming, serves both ceremonial and illustrative functions. The illustrative function of make-up is unquestionably the most obvious one today—so much so that we tend to forget its other use altogether.

Illustrative make-up is the means by which the actor changes his appearance to resemble that of his character—or at least the appear-

THE MAKE-UP KIT

Basic make-up consists of a foundation, color shadings, and various special applications.

The foundation is a basic color that is applied generally to the face and neck and sometimes to other parts of the body as well. Greasepaint, the traditional foundation material, is a highly opaque and relatively inexpensive skin paint that can be purchased in tube or stick form in a variety of colors. Cake make-up, or "pancake" as it is commonly known, is also used for foundations; it is less messy than greasepaint but also somewhat less flexible. Cake make-up comes in small plastic cases and is applied with a damp sponge. Most theatrical foundation colors are richer and deeper than the actor's normal skin color so as to counteract the white and blue tones of stage lights. Foundations, whether of greasepaint or cake, should be applied thinly and evenly.

Color shading defines the facial structure and exaggerates its dimensions so as to give the face a sculptured appearance from a distance; ordinarily, the least imposing characteristics of the face are put in shadow and the prominent features are highlighted. Shading colors—which are universally called "liners" for some obscure reason—come in both grease and cake form and are usually chosen to harmonize with the foundation color, as well as with the color of the actor's costume and the color of the lighting. Shadows are made with darker colors and highlights with light ones; both are applied with small brushes and blended into the foundation. Rouge, a special color application used to redden lips and cheeks, is usually applied along with the shading colors. When greasepaints are used, the make-up must be dusted with make-up powder to "set" it and prevent running.

A make-up pencil is regularly used to darken eyebrows and also to accentuate eyes and facial wrinkles.

Special applications may include false eyelashes or heavy mascara, facial hair (beards and moustaches, ordinarily made from crepe wool), nose putty and various other prosthetic materials, and various treatments for aging, wrinkling, scarring, and otherwise disfiguring the skin. A well-equipped make-up kit includes glue (spirit gum and liquid latex), solvents, synthetic hair, wax (to mask eyebrows), and hair whiteners in addition to the standard foundation and shading colors so that the actor will be prepared to create a variety of make-ups without making additional trips to the make-up retailer.

---

ance of his character as author, director, and actor imagine it. Make-up of this sort is particularly useful in helping to make a young actor look older or an old one look younger, and in making an actor of any age resemble a known historical figure or a fictitious character whose appearance is already set in the public imagination. Make-up gives Cyrano his great nose and Bardolf his red one; it turns the Caucasian Laurence Olivier into the Moorish Othello; and it makes Miss Sandy Duncan into Master Peter Pan. Make-up transformed the young Hal Holbrook into the old Mark Twain, and it permitted Cicely Tyson to portray a character's aging over an eighty-year period. Scars, deformities, bruises, beards, sunburn, frostbite, and scores of other facial embellishments, textures, and shadings can be mastered by the make-up artist's brush and can contribute significantly to realistic stagecraft when needed or desired.

A subtler use of make-up, but still within the realistic mode, is aimed at the evocation of psychological traits through physiognomic clues. For example, the modern make-up artist may try to suggest character by exaggerating or distorting the actor's natural eye placement, the size and shape of her mouth,

Cyrano's famous nose is made of putty in this American Conservatory Theatre production. The Cyrano is Ray Reinhardt. (Photo: William Ganslen, ACT.)

the angularity of her nose, or the tilt of her eyebrows. There can be no question that we do form impressions of a character's inner state on the basis of observable physical characteristics—as Caesar notices and interprets Cassius's "lean and hungry look" so do we. And the skilled make-up artist can go far in enhancing the psychological texture of a play by the imaginative use of facial shapings and shadings.

Still another use of make-up, also within the realistic and practical spectrum, seeks merely to simplify and embolden the actor's features in order to make them distinct and expressive to every member of the audience. In theatre jargon this is known as creating a face that "reads" to the house—in other words, a face that conveys its fullest expression (that "can be read like a book") over a great distance. Make-ups that read in this way do so primarily by exaggerating highlights and shadows and by sharply defining specific

features such as wrinkles, eyelashes, eyebrows, and jaw lines. Such simplified, emboldened, and subtly exaggerated make-up goes hand in hand with stage lighting and, in conjunction with it, creates an impression of realism far greater than any that could be achieved by make-up or lighting alone; in fact, a certain minimum level of make-up is thought by most actors and directors to be a necessity if only to prevent the actor from looking "washed out" in the glare of the stage lights.

Yet none of these realistic or practical uses of make-up truly touches upon its original theatrical use, which was aimed at announcing the actor as a performer and at establishing a milieu for acting that was neither realistic nor practical, but rather supernatural, mysterious, and calculatedly theatrical. For it was the white-lead make-up of Thespis and his fellows that endowed them with the same aspect of spiritual transcendence that warpaint provides for the celebrant in tribal rituals today: by making himself "up," the actor was preparing to ascend to a higher world; he was self-consciously assuming something of the power and divinity of the gods, and he was moreover offering to guide the audience on a divine adventure.

Today one still sees some obvious examples of such traditional make-up and "making up," particularly in the European and Asian theatres. The make-ups of the circus and the classic mime, two formats that developed in Europe out of the masked *commedia dell'arte* of centuries past, both use bold primary colors: white, black, and sometimes red for the mimist; these plus several more for the circus clown. Avant-garde and expressionist playwrights also frequently utilize similar sorts of abstracted make-ups, as did Jean Genet in *The Blacks,* which features black actors in clownish white-face, and Peter Handke, whose *Kaspar* featured similarly stylized facial painting. And the Japanese theatre, representative of much Asian practice, has always relied on the extreme colors and manelike wigs of the classical Nō and Kabuki now evolved into the violently expressive make-ups of the contemporary Tokyo avant-garde. The American theatre, which so far has witnessed only a small sampling of stylized make-ups, is perhaps due for an awakening to this fascinating approach to theatrical design.

But the realistic and symbolic functions of make-up are probably always combined to some extent in the theatre, for even the most stylized make-up is ultimately based on the human form, and even the most realistic make-up conveys an obvious theatricality. The theatre, after all, is never very far from human concerns, nor is it ever so immersed in the ordinary that it is completely mistaken for such. It might not be overly sentimental to suggest that when the American actor sits at a make-up table opening little bottles and tubes, moistening Chinese brushes and sharpening eyebrow pencils, more is going on than simple practical face-making: atavistic forces are at work, linking the actor not merely to the imagined physiognomy of his or her character or to the demands of facial projection in a large arena, but also, and more fundamentally, to the primitive celebrants who in ages past painted their faces to assure the world that they were leaving their temporal bodies and boldly venturing into the exalted domain of gods.

NEW COMPUTER TECHNOLOGIES IN THEATRE DESIGN

Designers—as other visual artists—have always used the technologies that were available to them: such basic drawing implements as charcoal, colored paints, rulers, squares, and drafting tables, for example, have been employed by designers for centuries. Complicated "drawing machines" came into play during the Renaissance: Leonardo da Vinci invented a "perspectograph" to help artists transform their perceived earthly realities into two-dimensional sketches and engravings in the early 1500s, and Caneletto's detailed paintings of eighteenth-century Venice were executed with the aid of a room-sized "camera obscura." The computer of today is only the most recent in a long list of technological tools used by visual artists, but it is a tool of far-reaching potential for the theatre. Becoming widespread in industry in the mid-1980s, by the 1990s computer-aided design (CAD) had become securely established as the fastest growing technology of the current stage.

What do computers do that pencil and paper don't? Computers don't think and can't create. Nor can they analyze a text, imagine an environment, suggest a costume, conceive a style, or even make an audience laugh. But what they can do is aid those artists who do. In its capacity for combining and configuring (and then reconfiguring) ideas, angles, shapes, colors, spaces, perspectives, and measurements, which designers uncover through research or create through imagination, the computer consolidates a vast realm of experimental possibilities with the technical assurance of a mathematician or an engineer. Perhaps no "machine" of any era has so successfully counterpoised reality's hard facts with the artist's free-floating imagination.

Computers are useful—and becoming invaluable—to the contemporary designer on a variety of levels.

First, they can assist with—or even replace—much of the drudgery of sheer drawing mechanics. Straight lines, angles, circles, shapes, colors, and typefaces can simply be lifted off a menu of choices and placed where desired. Moreover, all of these design elements can be reconfigured in an instant: colors can be changed, lines lengthened, walls thickened, floors raised, furniture moved, sightlines adjusted, and texts edited and resized with a few clicks of the mouse. Individual design elements can be instantly replicated: an elaborately drawn bannister post can become a dozen such posts in a matter of seconds. Indeed, whole drawings can be almost immediately rescaled, zoomed in or out on, printed and reprinted. Whole designs—or designated portions of them—can be rotated or relocated freely about the page. And working designs can be instantly sent around the world by digital electronic transmission. Instant and virtually unlimited "clean" revisions, and instantaneous communications, are the hallmarks of the computer revolution, in art as well as in text processing.

Second, computers enable designers to draw upon vast *visual data bases:* virtual libraries of art that can be found in commercial clip-art palettes or CD-ROMs, or which designers themselves may create and store for later use. These libraries give instant access to thousands of existing drawings and photos— such as "virtual catalogues" of eighteenth-century chandeliers, or Victorian drapery, or Roman statuary—which have been digitized for computer retrieval and can be, subject to legal copyright considerations, incorporated into stage designs.

Computerized data banks have already revolutionized costume management in several theatre shops and film studios, permitting designers to access pictures of, for example, hundreds of blouses currently available in various wardrobe collections. Computerized libraries are also replacing the plastic templates used by scenic and lighting designers to indicate furniture on the set, or lighting instruments on the light pipes, saving many hours of painstaking pencil and plastic copywork, particularly where multiple revisions are undertaken.

Yet far more advanced computing capabilities are now coming into the art and craft of theatre design.

Computerized cutting and pasting goes beyond retrieving art elements and actually (or virtually) combines visual forms on the screen. This can permit, for example, a costume designer to "virtually sew" the sleeves of one garment onto another without requiring a single stitch. It permits a wig designer to have an actress "virtually try on" a wig by combining a photo of the actress with a drawing of the wig—whereupon the wig colors can be changed at a whim, without having to buy a single strand of hair or call the actress in for a fitting. Actors, indeed, can be "virtually dressed" in entire costume designs long before actual fabric is purchased.

Computerized scenographic modeling supplements traditional ground-plan and elevation drawings by creating, on a computer screen, apparent three-dimensional models of the stage set that can demonstrate perspectives from any vantage: from the left, right, and center of the house, or from the "bird's-eye" position that may clarify lighting and offstage storage positions. With sufficient computing power and memory, designers, directors, and actors can then "walk through" the designed set, which at that point exists only as a "virtual reality," not as a hard construction of steel, wood, and fabric. Though computing equipment for such modeling is expensive, it is surely—in the long run— much cheaper than building and rebuilding stage scenery until "you finally get it just right."

And *integrated computer design,* which might enable a design team to design a scenic model, inhabit it with actors wearing designed costumes, and throw colored light upon the scene from precisely calibrated lighting positions, is already with us in some places and is likely to become a regular part of design conferences in many new theatres in the coming decade. The opportunity to "storyboard" scenery, costumes, and lighting—together with text and music and sound—is an extraordinary advance in the art of production planning wherever time and money are involved, as they almost always are.

Will computerized design—or computer-aided design—reduce the elements of creativity and imagination that go into the designer's art? Veteran designers often voice this concern; it was estimated in 1990 that less than 20 percent of professional designers regularly employed computers in their work, many of them expressing trepidation at the encroachment of "cold" electronics on what has been considered a romantic art of ink and paint, wood and canvas. But it is also estimated that the majority of theatrical designers will be largely computerized by the year 2000.[1] Computer adherents answer, therefore, with a thunderous "Yes!" to the computer revolution. To its professional devotees, computers are tools—superpencils, really—not ends in themselves; they provoke experimentation and innovation as well as (or even in lieu of) mere craft precision and mechanics. The computer age has, of course, long since arrived in all major areas of commerce and culture, and it already has a substantial history in the theatre; indeed, one of the first commercial uses of computing was in theatrical lighting, which has been largely computerized since at least the mid-1960s. And the theatre has been one of the testing places for many of the world's

emerging technologies, including hydraulic elevators, gas lighting, electricity, and air conditioning. It seems inevitable that the computer screen will become a principal conveyor of design creativity and communication in the immediate years to come.

TECHNICAL PRODUCTION

We shall end this chapter with a discussion of theatre technicians.

They are the true proletariat of the theatre: the worker-artists whose functions, although various, all revolve around getting the production organized, built, installed, lit, and ready to open and then seeing that it runs. They far outnumber all the others—the actors, designers, writers, and directors—put together.

Because of their numbers, theatrical technicians are ordinarily marshaled into a hierarchical structure, with stage and house managers, technical directors, and production managers at the top, and carpenters, electricians, cutters, stitchers, wigmakers, publicists, make-up artists, stagehands, light and sound operators, prompters, and various running crews at the bottom. Top to bottom, however, they all play crucial roles in each theatrical presentation—and the "stage fright" of the actor playing Hamlet is not neccessarily any greater than that of the stagehand who must pull the curtain.

The great bulk of technical work in the theatre is executed in accord with traditional practices developed over centuries of theatrical organizations and management; still, every production poses a host of problems and situations in each technical area that are new to the people asked to deal with them and, sometimes, new to the theatre itself. It is in the junction of sound knowledge of craft with creative imagination in the face of unanticipated problems that technological innovation takes place; and the technical artists of the theatre have always manifested an impressive

_____
[1]Payne, 1994, p. 158.

We all dream, but theatre designers have the opportunity to re-create their
dreams—and the dreams of playwrights and directors—as artistic realizations.
In this 1989 American Repertory Theatre production of Life is a Dream, *written*
by Spanish Renaissance author Calderón de la Barca, designers Loy Arcenas
(scenery), Catherine Zuber (costumes), and Richard Riddell (lighting)
create the highly surrealistic dream world. Anne Bogart directed. (Photo:
Richard Feldman.)

ingenuity at meeting unprecedented challenges
in creative ways.

Most theatrical crafts in the production areas are learned through apprenticeship after
little or no preliminary instruction. Each of
the shops of the theatre—the scene shop, the
costume shop, the prop shop, and the make-
up room—is a laboratory of instruction as
well as a working unit of the theatre; most of
what is learned is acquired on site and in action. Artistic components are never absent in
the technical workings of the theatre: the
painting of a set, the hanging of a lighting
instrument, the timing of a scene shift, the
sewing of a costume, and the calling of a
sound cue are services that contribute might-

ily to the overall artistry of the enterprise. The
technical crafts, therefore, are both learned
and practiced in an aesthetic context, as a central activity of the theatrical venture. And although written and unwritten "textbooks" of
stage practice can illustrate the traditional
means of building a flat, cutting a pattern, organizing a rehearsal, and painting a prop, it is
artistic sensitivity that ultimately determines
the technical quality of a production, and it
is artistic imagination that brings about the
technical and technological advances.

Many separate production crafts go into
building, promoting, managing, and running
a show, and a separate textbook would be required to describe them all. Two of them,

however, deserve special mention owing to the importance of their contribution to the growing art of stage production.

The *stage manager,* now often called the *production stage manager,* has the highly responsible position of overseeing all elements of production, coordinating all the director's work with that of the actors and the technical and design departments. At the beginning of rehearsals, he or she is involved primarily in organizational work: scheduling calls and appointments, recording the blocking of actors, anticipating technical problems of quick costume changes, set shifts, and the like, and organizing the basic "calling" of the show—that is, the system by which lighting, sound, and scene-shift cues are initiated. During performance, the stage manager actually runs the show, having final authority over the entire onstage and backstage operation; moreover, it is the stage manager who ordinarily conducts understudy and replacement rehearsals in a professional run and who assumes the functions of the director when the director is absent or no longer employed by the production.

The *technical director,* who is also sometimes called the *production manager* (sometimes both titles exist in the same production) is generally in charge of the building and operation of scenery and stage machinery and may also have charge of the lighting crews and of all technical scheduling. The technical director must oversee the moving of scenery into and out of the theatre, assure all technical departments adequate "stage time" to do their jobs, establish policies and directives for scene shifting, special effects, and "strike" (the final removal of scenery from the theatre after a run), and, most important, make certain that everything is ready on time—no small order considering the massive technical complexities of theatre today.

The influence of Bertolt Brecht, as we have seen, has brought lighting instruments into plain view even for many "non-Brechtian" productions. It has also tended to pull the backstage technician into public awareness in recent years. A popular fascination with technology, together with a diminishing interest in stage "magic" or naturalistic illusion, has led to a scenography that deliberately incorporates the activities of scene technology as a visible aesthetic component of the theatre. Given this trend and the theatre's increasing use of newer and newer technical innovations—lasers and holograms, air cushions, videotape, and computerized slide projections, to name but a few—it would appear that the theatre technician is on the verge of being widely recognized as a full-fledged theatre artist and creator as well as a craftsperson and mechanic who executes the creations of others.

14

The Director

The room is already filled with people when she enters, a bit fussily, with a bundle of books and papers under her arm. Expectation, tension, and even a hint of panic can be sensed behind the muffled greetings, loose laughter, and choked conversation that greet her arrival.

She sits, and an assistant arranges chairs. Gradually, starting at the other end of that piece of furniture which suddenly has become "her" table, the others seat themselves. An edgy silence descends. Where are they going? What experiences lie ahead? What risks, what challenges, are to be demanded? What feelings, in the coming weeks and months, are going to be stirred to poignant reality?

Only she knows—or if she doesn't, no one does. It is in this silence, tender with hope and fear, that the director breaks ground for the production. It is here that plan begins to become work and idea begins to become art. It is the peak moment of directing and of the director.

This is an idealized picture, to be sure. There are many directors who deliberately avoid invoking an impression of "mystique" and whose primary efforts are directed toward dispelling awe, dread, or any form of personal tension among their associates. Nonetheless, the picture holds a measure of truth for every theatrical production, for the art of directing

The Irish-born, Harrow-educated playwright Richard Brinsley Sheridan wrote a century after the Restoration, but his "comedies of manners" were equally witty and delightful. His 1777 masterpiece, The School for Scandal, *is shown here in Paul Marcus's audacious 1988 production, mixing traditional design elements with contemporary props at the South Coast Repertory Theatre. Scenery by Cliff Faulkner, costumes by Shigeru Yaji. (Photo: Cristofer Gross.)*

is an exercise in leadership, imagination, and control; in the director's hands, finally, rest the aspirations, neuroses, skills, and ideas of the entire theatrical company.

Directing is an art whose product is the most ambiguous, perhaps the most mysterious, in the theatre. The direction of a play is not visible like scenery or costumes; and unlike the actor's voice or the sound designer's score, it cannot be directly heard or sensed. And yet direction underlies everything we see and hear in the theatre. Utterly absorbed by the final theatrical experience, direction animates and defines that experience. A whole class of theatrical artists in our time has reached international eminence in this particular art. But what, exactly, is it?

At the *technical* level, the director is the person who organizes the production. This involves scheduling the work process and supervising the acting, designing, staging, and technical operation of the play. This is the easiest part of the directorial function.

At the more fundamental *artistic* level, the director inspires a creation of theatre with each production. He or she conceptualizes the play, gives it vision and purpose—both social and aesthetic—and inspires the company of artists to join together in collaboration.

It is in the conjunction of these levels, the technical and the artistic, that each director defines the directorial function anew. And it is with one foot in each that the director creates—through an adroit synthesis of text, materials, and available talent—a unique and vivid theatrical experience.

THE ARRIVAL OF THE DIRECTOR: A HISTORICAL OVERVIEW

Directing has been going on ever since theatre began, but there has not always been a director—that is, there has not always been an individual specifically charged solely with directorial functions and responsibilities. The evolution of the director as an independent theatre artist, less than a century ago, has had as much to do with the development of modern theatre as has any dramatic innovation. The gradual process of this evolution can be roughly divided into three phases.

Phase One: The Teacher-Directors

In the earliest days of the theatre and for some time thereafter, directing was considered a form of teaching. The Greeks called the director the *didaskalos,* which means "teacher," and in medieval times the director's designation, in all the various European languages, was "master." The underlying assumption of teaching, of course, is that a given subject is already known and understood; the teacher's task is simply to transmit what is known to persons yet unversed. The earliest directors, therefore, were simply asked to pass along the accumulated wisdom and techniques of "correct" performance within a "given" convention. Often the playwrights themselves served as directors, for who would be better qualified to "teach" a play than the person who wrote it? In one famous dramatic scene, Molière delightfully depicts himself directing one of his own plays; this is surely an effective model of the author-teacher-director for the seventeenth century and indeed for much of the theatre's history.

The teacher-director reached a pinnacle of influence, albeit anonymously, during the late Enlightenment and Victorian eras—during the eighteenth and nineteenth centuries— partly in response to the remarkable fascination of those times with science, scientific method, and humanistic research: the same dedication to rationalism that fostered a profusion of libraries, museums, and historic preservations also emphasized accuracy, consistency, and precision in the arts. The temper of the times led to major directorial changes in the theatre. For on the one hand, audiences were demanding revivals of classic plays— whose authors were no longer around to direct them—and on the other hand they were demanding that these revivals be historically edifying, that they have a museum-like authenticity. All of this required research, organization, and comprehensive coordination; in other words, it demanded an independent director.

Most of the directors of this time—virtually all of them until the latter part of the nineteenth century—received no more recognition for their efforts than the museum director who created historical dioramas. Sometimes the directing was attributed to a famous acting star, such as the Englishman Charles Kean or the American Edwin Booth, when in fact the work was done by a lesser functionary; in Booth's case, for example, one D. W. Waller was the true director, but his name was all but buried in the program and never appeared in the reviews or publicity. Nevertheless, these teacher-directors who labored largely in the shadows began the art of directing as we know it today. They organized their productions around specific concepts, independently arrived at, and they dedicated themselves to creating unified and coherent theatrical works by "directing" an ensemble of actors, designers, and technicians toward established ends.

Phase Two: The Realistic Directors

The second stage in the development of modern-day directing began toward the end of the nineteenth century and brought to the fore a group of directors who restudied the conventions of theatrical presentation and strove in various ways to make them more lifelike.

George II, Duke of Saxe-Meiningen, was the first of this breed and is generally regarded as the first modern director. The duke, who headed a provincial troupe of actors in his rural duchy, presented a series of premieres and classical revivals throughout Europe in the late 1870s and 80s that were dazzling in their harmonized acting, staging, and scenery. Although still historically "correct," the duke's productions featured an ensemble of performances rather than a hierarchy of "star, support, and supernumerary." All of his performers were vigorously rehearsed toward the development of individual, realistically conceived roles—which were then played out in highly organic, even volatile patterns of dramatic action. The stodgy line-up of spear carriers that had traditionally looked on while the star recited center stage was conspicuously absent from the Meiningen productions; so was the "super" who was customarily hired on the afternoon of performance, squeezed into a costume, and set upon the stage like so much living scenery. The totality of the Meiningen theatre aesthetic, embracing acting, interpretation, and design, was acclaimed throughout Europe: when the Meiningen troupe ceased touring in 1890, the position of a director who would organize and rehearse an entire company toward a complexly and comprehensively fashioned theatrical presentation was firmly established.

In 1887 André Antoine began a movement of greater realism in Paris with his Théâtre Libre, and Konstantin Stanislavsky initiated his even more celebrated Moscow Art Theatre in 1898. Both of these directors, amateurs like the Duke of Saxe-Meiningen at the start of their careers, went on to develop wholly innovative techniques in acting and actor-coaching based on the staging concepts of the duke; both also theorized and worked pragmatically at the organizing of theatre companies, the development of a dramatic repertory, the reeducation of theatregoing audiences, and the re-creation of an overall aesthetic of the theatre. Although both Antoine and Stanislavsky were known primarily as naturalists—somewhat to their disadvantage, perhaps, for they had many other interests as well—they were above all idealists who sought to make the theatre a powerful social and artistic instrument for the expression of truth. Their ideals and their commitment virtually forced them to expand the directorial function into an all-encompassing and inspirational art.

The importance of these directors—and of certain other pioneers of the same spirit, including Harley Granville-Barker in England, David Belasco in America, and Otto Brahm in Germany—was not merely that they fostered the developing realist and naturalist drama, but also that they opened up the theatre to the almost infinite possibilities of psychological interpretation. Once the psychology of the human individual becomes crucial to the analysis and acting of plays, directors become more than teachers: they become part analyst, part therapist, and even part mystic; their *creative* function in play production has increased substantially. The rise of realism in the theatre of the late nineteenth and early twentieth centuries, and the rise of directors capable of bringing out realistic nuances and patterning them into highly theatrical productions, brought about an irreversible theatrical renovation that in turn irrevocably established the importance of the director.

Phase Three: The Stylizing Directors

Right on the heels of the realist phase of direction came a third phase—one that brought the director to the present position of power and recognition. This phase arrived with the directors who joined forces with nonrealist playwrights to create the modern antirealistic theatre. Their forces are still growing. They are the ones who demand of directing that it aim primarily at the creation of originality, theatricality, and style. The stylizing directors are unrestrained by rigid formulas with respect to verisimilitude or realistic behavior; their goal is to create sheer theatrical brilliance, beauty, and excitement and to lead their collaborators in explorations of pure theatre and pure theatrical imagination.

Paul Fort, one of the first of these third-phase directors, launched his Théâtre d'Art in Paris in 1890 as a direct assault upon the realist principles espoused by Antoine. Similarly, Vsevolod Meyerhold, a one-time disciple of Stanislavsky, began his theatre of "biomechanical constructivism" in Moscow to combat the master's realism. The movement toward stylized directing occasioned by these innovators and others like them introduced a lyricism and symbolism, an expressive and abstract use of design, an explosive theatricality, and certain intentionally contrived methods of acting that continue to the present day to have a profound effect on the theatre and its drama.

Perhaps the most influential proponent of this third-phase position of the director, however, was not himself a director at all, but an eminent designer and theorist: Gordon Craig. In a seminal essay titled "The Art of the Theatre" (1905), Craig compared the director of a play to the captain of a ship: an absolutely indispensable leader whose rule, maintained by strict discipline, extends over every last facet of the enterprise. "Until discipline is understood in a theatre to be willing and reliant obedience to the manager [director] or captain," wrote Craig, "no supreme achievement can be accomplished." Craig's essay was aimed at a full-scale "Renaissance of the Art of the Theatre," in which a "systematic progression" of reform would overtake all the theatre arts—"acting, scenery, costuming, lighting, carpentering, singing, dancing, etc."—under the complete control and organizing genius of this newcomer to the ranks of theatrical artistry, the independent director.

The Contemporary Director

Craig's renaissance has surely arrived: this indeed is the "Age of the Director," an age in which the directorial function is fully established as the art of synthesizing script, design, and performance into a unique and splendid theatrical event that creates its own harmony and its own ineffable yet memorable distinction. If, as J. L. Styan says, "the theatre persists in communicating by a simultaneity of sensory impressions," it is above all the director who is charged with inspiring these impressions and ensuring this simultaneity.

Today, in a world of mass travel and mass communications, the exotic quickly becomes familiar and the familiar just as quickly becomes trite. Nothing is binding; the directorial function has shifted from teaching what is "proper" to creating what is stimulating and wondrous. At the beginning of a production, the director faces a blank canvas but has at hand a generous palette. At his or her disposal

Nudity, in one fashion or another, has increasingly been employed in contemporary theatre. Jerôme Savary, once a director of Parisian follies-type reviews, has in the past two decades increasingly turned his interests—and skills—to racy stagings of classic plays, as in this 1989 production of Molière's The Bourgeois Gentleman *at the Théâtre du Chaillot in Paris; Savary employs the breast-baring attendants to illustrate bourgeois society's exploitation of women and menial workers. Or is it only the audience's prurience that Savary is exploiting? (Photo: Brigitte Enguerand.)*

are not only the underlying conventions of the time, but also all those of the past, which may be revived in an instant for novel effects and stunning juxtapositions. Our conglomerate theatre of today allows Shakespeare in modern dress, Greek tragedy à la Kabuki spectacle, theatre of the absurd as vaudevillian buffoonery, and romantic melodrama as campy satire. Thus at the conception of a theatrical idea today—in the first moments of imagining a specific production—no question can be answered automatically, no style is obligatory, no interpretation is definitive. Jean-Paul Sartre has said about the whole of modern life that "man is condemned to be free"; in the theatre the director's freedom in the face of almost limitless possibilities leads to a certain existential anxiety that is both chilling and thrilling in its challenge.

Ariane Mnouchkine, artistic director of the Théâtre du Soleil, has been considered one of France's—and Europe's—greatest directors since the 1970s. She is known particularly for melding Eastern and Western theatrical forms. Her 1995 production of Molière's Tartuffe *transported the play to an Algerian setting and unmistakably referenced current French concerns over the rising tide of Islamic fundamentalism in that country and in France as well. Tartuffe was played by a Turkish actor, and Elmire by an East Indian. The setting (by Guy-Claude François) is Orgon's souk-styled courtyard. (Photo: Marc and Brigitte Enguerand.)*

DIRECTORIAL FUNCTIONS

Directing is not simply a craft; it is "directing" in the dictionary as well as in the theatrical sense: it is to lead, to supervise, to instruct, to give shape. In other words, it is to do what is necessary to make things "work." The director has final responsibility for *everything* that happens in a production, and so the "function" of a director must be, at least in part, subject to day-to-day demands and continuous improvisation.

Producer and Director

Part of what the director does in any given production will be determined by the possible existence of a *producer.* The producer is the person (or the institution) responsible for the financial support of the production: the producer may be a resident theatre, or a university theatre, or, as in Broadway or off-Broadway productions, an independent individual or partnership of individuals. In the regional theatre, the theatre's artistic director normally serves as the producer of each production in the theatre's season as well as the director of one or more plays; associate and/or freelance directors may be hired to direct other individual productions.

Where there is an active producer, separate from the director, it is the producer who is generally responsible for hiring the director, for establishing the production budget, and

One of the most crucial tasks for a director is developing—from actors who may not even know each other when rehearsals begin—a shared sense of the lifelong community their characters inhabit. Libby Appel's 1995 production of Brian Friel's Dancing at Lughnasa *at the Indiana Repertory Theatre evokes the rural eloquence of the five sisters around whom the play centers, and it all but bursts with the energy of their communal dance that climaxes (and titles) this remarkable drama. (Photo: Courtesy Indiana Repertory Theatre.)*

for determining the theatre facility and the production dates. The producer also normally plays an important role (if not *the* dominant role) in selecting the play, engaging the artistic staff (designers, technicians), and possibly even casting the actors.

As a result, functions listed below as "directorial" may in fact may be divided between the director and the producer. They remain "directorial" functions, however, inasmuch as they "direct" the artistic product that will finally appear on the stage.

Directorial Vision

Principally, the directorial function is one of *envisioning* the main lines of the production

and providing artistic *leadership* necessary to realize that vision.

Envisioning, however, does not mean plotting out every detail in advance, nor does leadership mean dictatorship or tyranny. Directing means, quite literally, "giving direction," which implies choosing a point of focus and guiding everyone to face the same way. The talents of the play director are, in this regard, not unlike those of the bank director or the director of a research team: to provide goals, establish procedures, facilitate communication, drive the schedule, monitor the progress, encourage the timid, rein in the errant, heighten the stakes, refine the objectives, build the morale, and inspire absolute excellence from all and sundry. No two individuals will fulfill each of these functions in the same way, nor to the same degree. Directing clearly involves a confident and natural way of working with other people, as well as learned directorial technique. Artistic sensitivity, interpersonal skills, and an eagerness to accept responsibility (and exercise authority) should always be expected of the professional play director.

For purposes of discussion, individual directorial functions can be viewed as so many separate steps in the process of play production. The process, in fact, takes place over a period of weeks and sometimes years and is at no time as orderly as a schematic listing might suggest. Nonetheless, such a listing can help us to see the basic architecture of the directorial process and the progression of decisions and actions that bear upon the final production.

The steps divide easily into phases: a preparatory phase, which involves play selection, concept, designer selection, designing, and casting, and an implementing phase, which involves staging, coaching, pacing, coordinating, and presenting. All of these steps are continuous rather than segmented—a director is conceptualizing the production right up to the last minute and is pacing it at the instant the play is chosen—but they are generally centered in a time frame of relatively set order and organization.

Preparatory Phase

The preparatory phase of a production may take days or months or years; it is the director's dream world, wherein ideas germinate and begin to flower. Most directors are "in preparation" for several productions at once: even as one production is in rehearsal, others are taking shape in the mind. At various times these preparatory phases move from fancy to plain and from the world of dreams to the conference room, the rehearsal hall, and the scene shop.

Play Selection   The selection of a script is unquestionably the most critical single act of any director. The play is the essential theatrical product, so to speak: it is the basic element to which the audience responds—or thinks it responds—and it is universally perceived as the core of the theatrical experience. For this reason, play selection is the one directorial decision over which the producer—the provider of a production's financial support—invariably reserves the right of review.

Three basic considerations go into play selection: the director's interest, the interest of the intended audience, and the capability of the director and producer to acquire, conceptualize, and produce the play.

The director's interest is important because no director, save by chance, can create theatrical excitement from a script he or she finds dull and uninteresting. But at the same time it is part of the director's job to seek the excitement latent in a script and to imagine its various theatrical possibilities. Often a director who can envision the improvements to be gained by script revision, adaptation, or reinterpretation can discover plays that otherwise would be ignored; indeed, one of the marks of a great director is the ability to make us recognize the brilliance or beauty of a script we have unwittingly passed over.

The audience's interest is of even greater importance. It is the audience, after all, that makes the theatre possible; and the ability to assess an audience's needs and wants is absolutely fundamental to directing, both for pragmatic reasons (to ensure that an audience turns out to see the play) and for artistic reasons (to ensure that the play is satisfying and pertinent to those who come to see it). For a director directs not only the actors and designers but the audience as well and gives direction to their feelings and perceptions by the intellectual focus provided within the production. A director who discounts or ignores the interests—and the intelligence—of the audience stands little chance of creating any genuine theatrical impact.

Play selection that considers audience interest does not necessarily mean a reliance on the "tried and true"; quite the contrary, it means providing the audience with theatrical work that is fresh, fascinating, vigorous, and exciting. For some audiences, these ingredients can be provided by musicals, thrillers, and domestic comedies, for others by works of the European avant-garde, for others by plays of social protest and reform, for still others by new plays hot from the typewriters of yet unknown authors. There is an audience for every sort of good play, and it is the director's job to find that audience and attract it to the theatre. The audience demand is to be challenged as well as to be confirmed—and, in the long run, directors who lead their audiences are far more likely to gain artistic recognition than are those who either follow the audience or ignore them completely.

The capability of the director to produce the play adequately with available resources is the final requisite for sound play selection. Can the production rights to the play be acquired? Can a cast be brought together? a production staff? a theatre? Is there enough money? Interest alone—the director's and the audience's—will not buy the scripts, rent the theatre, pay for the electricity, or perform the roles. Considerations of quality must be factored in: are the available actors experienced enough to master the play's style? Is the costume budget adequate for the size of the cast and the period of the play? And finally, does the director understand this play well enough to bring out its ideas? A realistic consideration of one's own capabilities, together with an ability to assess the potential of one's expected collaborators, must be a significant factor in the critical decisions of play selection.

Concept   More has been written in modern times about the director's role in conceptualizing a play than about any other directorial tasks; entire books have been devoted to the "directorial image," or the creation of the central concept that focuses and informs an entire production.

It is particularly with regard to those concepts that give unexpected and fresh insights into character, story, or style that the modern director has seized the imagination of the public. Like it or not (and there are many who do not), audiences and critics today are much more likely to admire (and remember) "high-concept" productions like Peter Brook's staging of *A Midsummer Night's Dream* than they are "traditional" stagings of this sixteenth-century play.[1] Although the director runs a considerable risk with this kind of undertaking—for indeed Wild West Romeos, homosexual Hamlets, and Watergate Macbeths have more often been laughable than laudable—a brilliantly appropriate concept can completely captivate an audience by focusing a play production with such pertinence and meaning that it transcends time, place, and stylistic artifice to create profound, moving, and illuminating theatricalization.

The formation of a directorial concept takes place at both the conscious and the unconscious level; it takes place, in fact, whether the director wants it to or not. There is no avoiding it: it begins when the director first hears of a certain play, and it grows and develops as she reads the play, considers producing it, imagines its effects on an audience, and mentally experiments with possible modes of staging. The directorial concept is a product not only of the director's personal intelligence and vision, but also of the director's personal experiences that relate to the matters portrayed by the play as well as personal likes and

---

[1]Indeed, what *is* a "traditional" staging of Shakespeare? We don't really know how the play was staged in Shakespeare's own time; what people call traditional staging is generally nineteenth-century staging, which is far removed from whatever Shakespeare intended. In truth, *all* stagings of Shakespeare and of other authors of his era are speculative and creative, governed by imaginative concepts as much as by historical research.

This "high-concept" production of Shakespeare's Twelfth Night *was directed, with jaundiced neoclassicism, by Andrei Serban in 1989, with scenery by Derek McLane and costumes by Catherine Zuber.*

lusts, appreciations and philosophical leanings, and desires concerning audience reaction to the final directorial product. The thought processes by which the concept develops are both deductive and inductive, and they are set in motion with the first impressions the director receives from a play.

Concepts can be expressed in many ways. Often they are social statements ("this is a play about tyranny") or philosophical ones ("this is a play about self-knowledge"). Often they involve specific interpretations ("this is a play about a man who cannot make up his mind"), and often they invoke a particular genre of theatricality ("this is a revenge melodrama"). Frequently a director will state the concept psychodramatically ("this is a primitive ritual of puberty"), and frequently the concept is predominantly historical ("a play about fratricide in the Middle Ages") or imagistic ("a play about swords, sables, and skulls") or metatheatrical ("a play about playing"). Often the conception of a play includes a basic tone ("sad," "heroic," "royal"), often a basic texture ("rich," "cerebral," "stark"). Diverse as these examples may seem, they all

fall within the range of possibility in conceptualizing a single play: indeed, any one of them could be applied to Shakespeare's *Hamlet,* and probably at one time or another every one of them has been, as have hundreds of others besides.

The concept is the director's creation, and to a certain extent it remains primarily his or her own concern. It constitutes a personal organizing focus, the means of keeping the production aimed in a *specific* direction and impervious to deflection by tempting possibilities that might come to mind over the course of a production period. Therefore the concept, expressed succinctly but comprehensive in its implications, becomes the director's starting point in choosing designers and actors, in initiating design discussions, and in setting the direction of the first rehearsals. Directing, of course, means giving *direction,* and the concept is the first and most decisive step in getting a particular production under way.

A great directorial concept has many qualities. It is specific, it is appropriate, it is evocative, it is visual, it is theatrical, it is concrete, it is original, and it is also a bit mysterious, a bit must ultimately be translated into concrete visual effects by a group of human beings of individual temperament, sensibility, and vision. The concept is the director's own creation, but its refinement and realization finally rest in the hands of collaborators, whose personal artistry and inclinations will inevitably play an enormous role in the shape and impact of the final product. Hence the selection of these individuals is by no means a mechanical or arbitrary task; it is a central directorial concern of great artistic consequence.

Director-designer teams are common in the theatre; some run for years, encompassing dozens of productions. Resident companies, whether national, regional, or community, often keep a core staff of directors and designers on the payroll year after year to facilitate continuing team relationships; most university theatre groups establish similar long-standing collaborations among faculty artists. Even the more fractious Broadway stage has its collaborations that span years and decades, although these teams work on a show-to-show basis rather than under continuing contract; Broadway directors frequently demand to work with certain designers whose work has proven sympathetic to their own in the past.

Ordinarily directors make every effort to find designers with whom they feel not only a personal compatibility but also a mutual respect and a synchrony of artistic and intellectual vision. Like all true collaborations, the most effective director-designer relationships result not in simple point-by-point agreement or master-slave autocracy, but in a give-and-take of ideas, plans, feelings, and hypotheses: a sense of sharing and complementary support.

Apart from these general considerations in designer selection, the director must look more specifically for the designers most appropriate for the play at hand: those whose abilities are best suited to the demands of the script and the director's conception of the production. Sometimes these specific considerations lead in a direction different from that generally indicated—away from the designer

amusing. It *leads* the actors and the designers; and if it is truly inspired, it leads the director as well. Doubtless some play productions manage to attain a measure of success without the benefit of much conceptualization or with concepts flying in and out of the production process like so many blackbirds, but in today's multimedia, future-shocked world, theatrical excellence increasingly requires that the director have a strong and persistent conceptual vision.

Designer Selection Although normally falling to the producer, the selection of production designers constitutes a vital step in the directorial process simply because both the playwright's script and the director's concept with whom the director feels most comfortable and toward the one who promises to be more helpful in narrowing and clarifying the director's concept. A designer's interest in a certain kind of scenic technology, for example, or in historical aestheticism or light cuing, can often help in many ways to sharpen the conceptual focus and provide insights through the design that will serve to inspire the production itself.

Designer selection, then, is a subtle and complicated process. The director chooses *people,* not colors or fabrics or instruments, and must select those people based on an estimate of their ultimate potential in the working conditions provided for them. Naturally the director will be interested in knowing something about the designer's previous work—and most designers can show prospective directors a résumé of experience and a portfolio of completed designs—but the director will also be interested in sounding out the designer's thinking and artistic sensibility. Like all decisions made in the developmental phase of production, the choice of designers will affect the entire production process; it is a choice that is difficult to retract, and the moment it is made it automatically closes certain directorial options and opens others that could prove either brilliant or catastrophic.

Designing   The design phase of production marks the first step toward transforming vision into actuality: at this stage people turn ideas into concrete visual realizations.

The director's work in designing a production is generally suggestive and corrective; how well he or she succeeds in this delicate task is highly dependent on the personalities and predilections of the individuals involved. In theory, the director's and designer's goals in this phase are identical: actable space, wearable costumes, and an evocative, memorable, and meaningful appearance of the whole. In practice, each of the principals will have an independent perspective on what is actable, what is memorable, and what is

evocative; moreover, each may have a different sense of the importance of sometimes contradictory values. A costume designer, for example, may place a higher value on the appearance of a garment than will the director, who may be more concerned with the actor's ability to move in it. A lighting designer may be greatly interested in the aesthetics of murkiness whereas a director may be more anxious that an actor's face be clearly seen at a particular moment. These are the sorts of artistic perspectives that must be reconciled in the design phase, which is essentially a collaboration in which the decisions are acknowledged to be subjective rather than "right" or "wrong"; it is a phase that demands qualities of leadership and artistic inspiration that are as sensitive as any the director may ever be called upon to exercise.

The design phase normally takes place in a series of personal conferences between director and designers, sometimes on a one-to-one basis and sometimes in group meetings. These are give-and-take affairs, for the most part, with the director doing most of the giving at the beginning and the designers taking over shortly thereafter. Often the first step is a collective meeting—the "first design conference"—at which the director discusses his or her concept in detail and suggests some possibilities for its visual realization: colors, images, spaces, textures, and technological implementations. Occasionally the director deliberately usurps a large measure of the designer's role, suggesting (or mandating) specific ground plans, sets, fabrics, and light colors and intensities, and proffering sketches of the finished work. Obviously, however, directors who so invade the designer's creative function risk losing precisely what they are trying to cultivate: the designer's talent and imagination. For this reason most professional directors seek primarily to stimulate, not stultify, the minds and abilities of the designers with whom they have chosen to work.

In the ensuing conferences, which are often conducted one on one and sometimes on an

The multihued sky in Robert Wilson's 1988 production of The Forest *silhouettes human, animal, and mythical creatures in an eerie arboreal setting. (Photo: Martha Swope and Associates/Rebecca Lesher.)*

ad hoc basis, designers normally present their own conceptions and eventually provide the director with a progressive series of concrete visualizations: sketches (roughs), drawings, renderings, models, ground plans, working drawings, fabrics, technical details, and devices. During these conferences the design evolves through a collaborative sharing, in which the director's involvement may range from minimal to maximal depending on how well the initial concept and the developing design seem to be cohering. Periodically—whenever the overall design effort reaches a stage requiring coordinated planning—full design conferences are called to review and compare current plans for scenery, costume, lighting, and property areas; these conferences afford opportunities for the designers to collaborate with each other instead of simply with the director.

The director's function at this stage of design is to approve or reject, as well as to suggest. As the person who sits at the top of the artistic hierarchy, the director has the last word on design matters, but that does not mean she or he can simply command the show into being: theatre design, like any creative process, cannot be summoned forth like an obedient servant. Moreover, wholesale rejection of a designer's work after the initial stages inevitably involves serious time loss and budgetary waste—not to mention the probability of some important staff resignations. For these reasons, the directorial effort must be committed from the outset to sound collaborative principles. Once under way, the

Warner Shook's casting for The Kentucky Cycle *had to serve the nine different plays of the cycle; each actor had to play several roles, of varying ages, over many generations. Typecasting is useless in this situation: Katherine Hiler and Scott MacDonald play a young couple in this photo; later they play their aged descendants. (Photo: Jay Thompson.)*

director-designer collaboration must take the form of shared responsibility in a developing enterprise, not confrontation between warring artists attempting to seize the reins of aesthetic control.

Casting The cliché "Casting is 90 percent of directing" undeniably contains more than a germ of truth.

The people in a play—the actors—not only attract more audience attention than any other aspect of the play, but they also represent what the audience *cares* about and will remember the next day. They garner about 90 percent of all the interest an audience expends on a play, and if they squander that interest they can destroy the effectiveness of any theatrical presentation.

When you look at theatre as a medium, you see many individual elements that are standardized and predictable: flats are made according to formula, lighting instruments are factory-calibrated to conform to precise specifications, color media are mathematically measured and numbered, and one theatre's black velours are identical to those of another. The one unique ingredient of the theatre—as the audience sees it—is the actor. Actors are people, and as people they are exquisitely individual; moreover the audience, being human itself, is particularly attuned to the actor's human and idiosyncratic uniqueness. We would never mistake the Hamlet of Kevin Kline with the Hamlets of Kenneth Branagh, Ralph Fiennes, Roger Rees, Mel Gibson, or Val Kilmer. The actor's personality, physical and vocal characteristics, technical abilities, and sheer talent and "presence" weigh mightily in the final realization of every individual performance and in every ensemble of performances. A miscast or untalented or untrained actor can mar the effectiveness of any production even in a minor role; in a major role a poor performance simply ruins the play. Casting may not, in the end, account for 90 percent of the director's contribution, but there can be no doubt that bad casting renders all other efforts immaterial.

Most casting takes place in auditions, where the actor can be seen and heard by the director and associates either in a "cold" reading of material from the play to be produced or in a prepared presentation of previously developed material not necessarily related to the production at hand. Although "star" performers are often cast apart from auditions owing to their known ability to attract audiences to any production, most veteran professional actors regularly submit to auditioning; and the director's ability to detect an incipiently brilliant performance in the contrived audition format is a critical factor in effective casting.

The director looks for many things in an audition. Depending on the specific demands of the play and the rehearsal situation, the director may pay special attention to any or all of the following characteristics: the actor's training and experience, physical characteristics and vocal technique, suitability for the style of the play, perceived ability to impersonate a specific character in the play, personality traits that seem fitted to the material at hand, ability to understand the play and its milieu, personal liveliness and apparent stage "presence," past record of achievement, general deportment and attitude, apparent cooperativeness and "directability" in the context of an ensemble of actors in a collaborative enterprise, and overall attractiveness as a person with whom one must work closely over the next four to ten weeks. And the director might well be looking for a great many other things besides.

What is ultimately astonishing about the casting process is that most of the decisions based on these complex criteria are made not in agonizing conferences but in two- to four-minute "cold" auditions among perfect strangers! Indeed, this practice is often looked upon as a regrettable theatrical fact, but its very persistence indicates that a great many valid casting judgments can be made in a very short time—provided that time is used with wisdom and sensitivity.

Most of the decisions that are made that quickly—in the two- to four-minute initial audition—are "no" decisions; that is, those actors who are immediately perceived as wrong for the play, wrong for the part, or lacking in the desired level of proficiency are winnowed out. Others may be winnowed out on the subjective ground of apparent attitude—a dangerous ground because the director might mistake shyness for hostility or "audition jitters" for an exaggerated reserve.

Actors who survive the first audition are then "read" again, sometimes several times, and at this stage the director is involved more and more in the audition process, often coaching the actors to determine how rapidly they can acquire the qualities needed. Such "callbacks" can go on for days and even weeks in the professional theatre, limited only by the union requirement that actors receive pay for the fifth and ensuing calls; the frequency with which such payments are made amply attests to the care that attends final casting decisions in the professional theatre.

There is good casting and bad casting, of course, and there is also inspired casting. Many of the greatest performances in theatre history have been achieved by actors who at first glance might appear oddly suited to their roles: by Bert Lahr as Estragon in *Waiting for Godot*, for example, or by Laurence Olivier as the title character in John Osborne's *The Entertainer*. Franco Zeffirelli's casting of two inexperienced teenagers in his Royal Shakespeare Company production of *Romeo and Juliet*, much derided at the time, proved to be the spark of genius that made that celebrated production, and the film later adapted from it, two of the most memorable interpretations of the Shakespearean canon. And surely one of the finest King Lears in the American theatre was the late Michael O'Sullivan, who at the time he was cast in the role was still in his twenties and an unknown actor with the San Francisco Actor's Workshop. The ability to perceive an actor's unique and unexpected relationship to a specific role—and to chance that casting in place of a "safer" and more traditional choice—has always been the mark of the most daring and most successful film and play directors.

Implementation Phase

With the play selected and conceptualized, with the designers chosen and the designs under way, and with the actors auditioned and cast, the production moves from its preparatory phase to its implementation. It is here that the meeting described at the beginning of this chapter occurs; it is here in the silence between the completion of a plan and its execution that the blood begins to flow in a *cor-*

Staging battle scenes requires precise choreography: the fight must look dangerous but actually be safe. Usually a specialist—a fight choreographer—is assigned. Acting intensity, the use of real (if blunted) spears, throbbing music, and stage smoke make the battle scene exciting, but strict directorial control is required. JoAnne Akalaitis directed this 1989 production of Cymbeline *at the New York Shakespeare Festival. (Photo: © George E. Joseph.)*

pus dramaticus that heretofore lived only in the form of conversation and ink on paper.

The time structure of a production is a variable affair, but its direction is inevitably toward greater and greater tautness; that is, time becomes more and more precious as the play draws nearer and nearer to its opening performance. At the juncture between a production's developmental phase and its implementation, a major jump to a tighter time schedule takes place; what could conceivably be leisurely at the conceptual stage now becomes accelerated and intense. Now, because more and more must be done in less and less time, pressure becomes inevitable. Now the director's ability to maintain both leadership and creative inspiration under pressure—always an important element of professional skill—becomes crucial.

From the time of that first company meeting, the director controls the focus and consciousness of the entire cast and staff. As head of an ambitious and emotionally consuming enterprise, the director will be the repository of the company's collective artistic hopes—the focal point for the company's collective frustration, its anxiety, and, on occasion, its despair. The company's shield against the intrusions of an outside world, the director is also the spokesperson for the enterprise to which the company has collectively dedicated itself. Directorial power or influence will not be substantially altered by any attempt the director may make to cultivate or repudiate it—it simply comes with the job and with the need for every theatrical company to have a head, a focus, a direction. The manner in which the director uses that power, and the sensitivity with which he or she now brings the production into being, determines the nature of each director's individual brand of artistry.

Staging Staging—which essentially involves positioning actors on the set and moving them about in a theatrically effective manner—is certainly the most obvious of directorial functions. It is the one thing directors are always expected to do and to do well, and it is the one they are most often *seen* doing; it is no wonder that traditional textbooks on directing tend to be largely devoted to this function.

The medium of staging is the actor in space and time—with the space defined by the acting area and the settings, and the time defined by the duration of the theatrical event and the dynamics of its dramatic structure. The goals of staging are multiple and complementary: to create focus for the play's themes, to lend credibility to the play's characters, to generate interest in the play's action, to impart an aesthetic wholeness to the play's appearance, to provoke suspenseful involvement in the play's events, and, in general, to stimulate a fulfilling theatricality for the entire production.

The basic architecture of staging is called "blocking," which refers to the timing and placement of a character's entrances, exits, rises, crosses, embraces, and other major movements of all sorts. The "blocking pattern" that results from the interaction of characters in motion provides the framework of an overall staging; it is also the physical foundation of the actors' performance—and many actors have difficulty memorizing their lines until they know the blocking that will be associated with them.

The director may block a play either by preplanning the movements ("preblocking") on paper or by allowing the actors to improvise movement on a rehearsal set and then "fixing" the blocking sometime before the first performance. Often a combination of these methods is employed, with the director

favoring one method or the other depending on the specific demands of the play, the rehearsal schedule, rapport with the acting company, or the director's own stage of preparation: complex or stylized plays and settings and short rehearsal periods usually dictate a great deal of preblocking; simple domestic plays and experienced acting ensembles are often accorded more room for improvisation. Each method can produce highly commendable results in the right hands and at the right time; both can present serious problems if misapplied or ineptly handled.

For the most part, the blocking of a play is "hidden" in the play's action; it tends to be effective insofar as it is *not* noticed and insofar as it simply brings other values into play and focuses the audience's attention on significant aspects of the drama. By providing a physical enhancement of the dramatic action and lending variety to the play's visual presentation, a good blocking pattern can play a large role in creating theatrical life and excitement.

But beyond this, there are moments when inspired blocking choices can create astonishing theatrical effects—effects that are not "hidden" at all but are so surprising and shocking that they compel intense consideration of specific dramatic moments and their implications. Such a *coup de théâtre* was achieved, for example, by director Peter Brook in his celebrated 1962 production of *King Lear,* when Paul Scofield, as Lear, suddenly rose and, with one violent sweep of his arm, overturned the huge oaken dining table at which he had been seated and sent pewter mugs crashing to the floor as he raged at his daughter Goneril's treachery. This stunning action led to a reevaluation of the character of both Lear and Goneril and of the relationship between this tempestuous and sporadically vulgar father and his socially ambitious daughter.

Some plays require specialized blocking for certain scenes—for duels, for example, or dances. Such scenes demand more than nuts-and-bolts blocking and are frequently directed by specialists, such as dueling masters

Acting "business" creates mood and atmosphere as well as subtle characterization. Here, Trish Hawkins and Judd Hirsch smoke cigarettes in a production of Lanford Wilson's Talley's Folly *at the Mark Taper Forum Theatre of Los Angeles. The manner in which the actor holds the cigarette, inhales or puffs smoke, and flicks ashes gives clues to the character's personality. (Photo: Courtesy of the Mark Taper Forum.)*

trances and crosses and exits. Mixing a cocktail, answering a telephone, adjusting a tie, shaking hands, fiddling with a pencil, winking an eye, and drumming on a tabletop are all "bits of business" that can lend a character credibility, depth, and fascination. Much of the stage business in a performance is originated by the actor—usually spontaneously in the course of rehearsal—although it may be stimulated by a directorial suggestion or command. The director ultimately must select from among the rehearsal inventions and determine what business will become a part of the finished performance; when this determination is made, bits of business become part of the blocking plan.

Staging, then, in the largest sense, includes both hidden and bold blocking effects, specialized movements and small idiosyncratic behaviors, all combined into a complex pattern that creates meaning, impact, and style. Skillful staging unites the design elements of a production with the acting, creating an omnidynamic spatial interaction between actors, costumes, scenery, and audience, infusing the stage with life. Getting a play "on its feet," as the theatrical jargon puts it, is usually the first step in making it breathe; and the best staging is that which gives the actors the chance to breathe the air of the playwright's world and to awaken to the true vitality of the playwright's characters.

or choreographers, working in concert with the director. These specialized situations are not at all rare in the theatre—almost every play that was written before the last century includes a duel or a dance or both—and the ability to stage an effective fight scene or choreographic interlude (or at least to supervise the staging of one) is certainly a requisite for any director who aspires to work beyond the strictly realistic theatre.

"Business" is a theatre term that refers to small-scale movement—that which a character performs within the larger pattern of en-

Actor-Coaching The director is the actor's coach, and in practice the director is likely to spend the largest share of her or his time exercising this particular function. The coaching begins at the first meeting with the cast.

Initially, it is the director who conveys the direction the production is expected to take: the concept, the interpretation, the intended "look" and style of the theatrical product. It is also the director who determines the schedule and process of work that will lead up to that final product. The director is the rehearsal leader and decides what activities—discussions, improvisations, games, exercises, lectures, research, blocking, or polishing—will occupy each rehearsal period; the director leads such activities with an eye to their ultimate goal.

Further, like the manager of an athletic team, the director is responsible for stimulating the best efforts of the cast and for instilling in them a high regard for teamwork (which in the theatre is called "ensemble") as well as for individual craft excellence and artistry. And, because the work of the theatre inevitably demands of the actor a good measure of emotional, psychological, even irrational investment, the director has an opportunity (if not an obligation) to provide an atmosphere in which actors can feel free to liberate their powers of sensitivity and creativity. Good directors lead their cast; great directors inspire them.

The ways in which directors go about coaching actors are various and probably more dependent on personality than on planning. Some directors are largely passive; they either "block and run," in the jargon of commercial theatre, or function primarily as a sounding board for actors' decisions about intention, action, or business. Conversely, there are directors closer to the popular stereotype, mercurial directors whose approaches at times verge on the despotic: they cajole, bully, plead, storm, and rage at their actors, involve themselves in every detail of motive and characterization, and turn every rehearsal into a mixture of acting class, group therapy session, and religious experience. Both methods, as experience teaches, can produce theatrical wizardry, and both can fail utterly; probably the determining factors either way are the strength of the director's ideas and the extent to which the cast is willing to accept his or her directorial authority.

Too little direction, of course, can be as stultifying to an actor as too much; the passive director runs the risk of defeating an actor's performance by failing to confirm it, that is, by withholding constructive response. Similarly, the extremely active director may, in a whirlwind of passion, overwhelm the actor's own creativity and squelch his efforts to build a sensitive performance, thereby condemning the production to oppressive dullness. For these and other reasons, most directors today strive to find a middle ground, somewhere between task mastery and suggestion, from which they can provide the actor with both a goal and a disciplined path toward it while maintaining an atmosphere of creative freedom.

Directors need not be actors themselves, but they must understand the paradoxes and ambiguities inherent in that art if they are to help the actor fashion a solid and powerful performance. The greatest acting braves the unknown and flirts continuously with danger (the danger of exposure, of failure, of transparency, of artifice); the director must give the actor a careful balance of freedom and guidance in order to foster the confidence which leads to that kind of acting. Directors who are insensitive to this requirement—no matter how colorful their stormings and coaxings or how rational their discussions of the playwright's vision—are virtually certain to forfeit the performance rewards that arise from the great actor-director collaborations.

"THIS IS HOW IT'S DONE!"

Publicity photographs taken in rehearsal frequently show a director on stage with a few actors, demonstrating a bit of business and "showing them how it's done." This kind of publicity has probably fostered a certain misunderstanding of the director's role among the general public, for demonstration is only a part of directing, and a distinctly small part at that. Indeed, some directors scrupulously avoid it altogether.

Demonstration as a way of teaching an actor a role has a long history in the theatre and was a particularly common practice in those periods when directing was carried out chiefly by retired actors. Even today, young actors rehearsing for classical plays at the Comédie Française (founded in 1680) are expected to learn their parts by mimicking the performance of their elders down to the last detail of inflection, tone, gesture, and timing. And,

of course, many contemporary American directors occasionally give "line readings" to an actor or demonstrate the precise manner of gesturing, moving, sitting, or handling a prop, if they perceive that a specific desired behavior might not come naturally from the actor himself.

But demonstration as an *exclusive* method of coaching an actor in his role is very much a thing of the past. Most contemporary directors make far greater use of discussion, suggestion, and improvisation. These methods seek to address the inner actor and to encourage him to distill his performance out of self-motivated passions and enthusiasms. Because they know that a purely imitative performance is all too likely to be a mechanical performance, today's directors tend to rely on more creative methods than "getting up there and showing how it's done."

Pacing Despite all the director's responsibilities, pace is perhaps the only aspect of a theatrical production for which general audiences and theatre critics alike are certain to hold the director accountable. Frequently, newspaper reviews of productions devote whole paragraphs of praise or blame to the actors and designers and evaluate the director's contribution solely in terms of the play's pace: "well paced" and "well directed" are almost interchangeable plaudits in the theatre critic's lexicon; and when a critic pronounces a play "slow" or "dragging," everyone understands he or she is firing a barrage at the director.

To the novice director (or critic), pace appears to be primarily a function of the rate at which lines are said; hence a great many beginning directors attempt to make their productions more lively simply by instructing everyone to speak and move at a lively clip:

"More energy!" and "Make it happen faster!" are somewhat generalized expressions of a director's suspicion that the production somehow lacks the proper pace.

But pace is fundamentally determined by a complex and composite time structure that must be developed to accommodate many variables, such as credibility, suspense, mood, style, and the natural rhythms of life: heartbeat, respiration, the duration of a spontaneous sob and an unexpected laugh. How much time is properly consumed, for example, by a moment of panic? a pregnant pause? a flash of remembrance? an agonized glance? a quick retort? These are the ingredients of pace and are not subject to the generalized "hurry-up" of the director who has not first discovered the pattern of rhythms inherent in a play.

The pace of a play should be determined largely by the quantity and quality of the information it conveys to the audience, and the director must decide how much time the audience requires to assimilate that information. In a farce, of course, the audience needs almost no time to synthesize information—therefore, farce generally is propelled rapidly, with the audience virtually assaulted with information coming as fast as the actors can get it out. A psychological drama, on the other hand, may require of the audience a deeper understanding of its characters and issues; sympathy is engendered as we have an opportunity to compare the characters' lives with our own, to put ourselves in their situations, and to engage in introspection even as we observe the action on stage. Similarly, political drama commonly demands of us a critical inquiry into our own societies and our own lives as part of our understanding of what is happening on stage; this form, too, demands time to linger over certain perfectly poised questions—and the pace of a production must give us that time.

As a symphony is composed of several movements, so a well-paced theatrical production will inevitably have its adagio, andante, and allegro tempos. Faster tempos tend to excite, to bedazzle, and to sharpen audience attention; slower ones give the audience a chance to consider and to augment the play's actions and ideas with their own reflections. Often directors speak in terms of "setting up" an audience with a rapid pace and then delivering a "payoff" with a powerful, more deliberately paced dramatic catharsis. The sheer mechanics of theatrical pacing demand the greatest skill and concentration on the part of both actor and director, and for both the perfection of dramatic timing (and most notably comic timing) is a mark of great theatrical artistry.

Directors vary in their manner of pacing plays, of course. Some wait until final rehearsals and then, martinet-like, stamp out rhythms on the stage floor with a stick or clap their hands in the back of the house. Some work out intricate timing patterns in the early rehearsals and explore them in great detail with the actors as to motivation, inner monologue, and interpersonal effect. Directorial intervention of some sort is almost always present in the achievement of an excellent dramatic pace; it rarely occurs spontaneously. Actors trained to the realist manner often tend to work through material slowly and to savor certain moments all out of proportion to the information they convey; actors trained in a more technical manner just as often are "off to the races" with dialogue, leaving the audience somewhat at sea about the meaning or importance of the matters at hand. And when a variety of actors, trained in different schools, come together in production for the first time, they can create such an arrhythmic pace that the play becomes unintelligible until the director steps in to guide and control the tempo.

Coordinating   In the final rehearsals the director's responsibility becomes more and more one of coordination: of bringing together the concept and the designs, the acting and the staging, the pace and the performance. Now all the production elements that were developed separately must be judged, adjusted, polished, and perfected in their fuller context. Costumes must be seen under lights, staging must be seen against scenery, pacing must include the shifting of sets, acting must coalesce with sound amplification, and the original concept must be reexamined in light of its emerging realization. Is the theme coming across? Are the actions coming across? Can the voices be heard and understood? Do the costumes read? Is the play focused? Is the play interesting? Do we care about the characters? about the themes? about anything? Does the production seem to *work?*

Timing and wholeness are governing concepts in this final coordinating phase of production. In assessing the play's overall timing, the director must be prepared to judge the play's effectiveness against its duration and to modify or even eliminate those parts of the production that overextend the play's potential for communicating information, feelings, or ideas. Last-minute cutting is always a painful process—much labor and creative spirit have gone into those parts that will be cut—but many a production has been vastly improved by judicious pruning at this time. And in the interest of providing wholeness—that quality which unifies a play and gives it the stamp of taste and aesthetic assurance—the best and bravest directors are willing in these final moments to eliminate those elements that fail to cohere with the play's overall appearance and significance. Often these elements hold a special meaning for the director; they may even have figured into his or her earliest conception of the production. But now, in the cold light of disciplined analysis, they look painfully like directorial indulgence or extraneous showing off. The best directors are those who can be most rigorous with themselves at this stage, for they are the ones who are capable not only of generating ideas but also of refining and focusing artistic form.

In the final rehearsals—the "technical rehearsals" when scenery, lighting, and sound are added, and the "dress rehearsals" when the actors don costumes and make-up for the first time—the director arrives at a crossroads: although remaining fundamentally responsible for every final decision about the timing and balance of theatrical elements, he or she must now "give over" the production to the actors and technicians who will execute it. Beyond this junction the director will be consumed by the production and will disappear within it in a matter of days: it will reflect the director's personal conceptions and directorial skills without reflecting the director's own persona. After contributing to everything that appears upon the stage and initiating much of it, the director must accept the fact that he or she will not be recognized in any single moment, any single act, any single costume or lighting cue. In these final rehearsals the director's presence normally becomes more a force for organization than a source of in-spiration—clipboard in hand, he or she delivers hundreds of last-minute notes to actors, technicians, and stage managers in an effort to give the production that extra finesse which distinguishes the outstanding from the mediocre.

What an extraordinary exchange of power has taken place between the first meeting of the cast and director and these final days! Whereas earlier the entire production was in the director's head and the cast waited in awe and expectation, now the actors hold the play in their heads and everyone confronts the unknowns of the play's reception. The actors have a new master now: the audience. It is in these days that even the most experienced actors confront their fundamental nakedness in performance: they must face the audience, and they must do it without benefit of directorial protection, with nothing to shield them save their costumes, characters, and lines. At these times the actor comes to see the director as no longer leader but partner, no longer parent but friend. Actors may indeed experience a certain feeling of betrayal; the director, after all, has abandoned them to face the audience alone, just as Good Deeds accompanied Everyman only to the brink of the grave. But then acting, like death, is a trial that cannot be shared.

Presenting   It is an axiom of the theatre that nobody is more useless on opening night than the director. If all has progressed without major catastrophe and the production has successfully been "given over" to those who will run it and perform in it, the director's task on opening night consists chiefly in seeing and evaluating the production and gauging the audience response. This night may, of course, prove to be nothing but a calm between storms, and in the professional theatre it may simply be the first of a series of opening nights, one calculated to serve as a guide to future rehearsals, rewritings, and rethinkings. Still, at this time the major work has reached a stopping point, and the director must shift perspectives accordingly.

The director in this last phase sometimes takes on certain responsibilities of a para-theatrical nature, such as writing directorial notes for use in newspaper stories and interviews and overseeing the house management, the dress of the ushers, the lobby decorations, the concession stands, or the "dressing of the house" (the spacing of spectators in a less than full house). The director may also play an active role as audience member by greeting patrons, chatting with critics, or leading the laughter and applause—although all of these activities are more common in community theatres than in professional ones.

More central to the directorial function in this final stage is the director's continuing evaluation of every production element in an effort to improve the audience impact. This may lead to changes at any time during the run of a play. In the professional theatre, new productions commonly go through a tryout period of two weeks or more—up to a year in a few cases—when the play is rehearsed and re-rehearsed daily between performances and material is deleted, revised, restaged, and freshly created in response to audience reception. Some quite famous plays have succeeded only because of such "doctoring" during tryout periods, and it is not at all uncommon in the contemporary commercial theatre for a director to be replaced during this phase in order to accelerate revision.

Even after the final opening, however, and throughout the run of a play, most directors attend performances periodically and follow up their visits with notes to the actors—either to encourage them to maintain spontaneity or to discourage them from revising the original directorial plan. One perhaps apocryphal show-business story has it that the American director George Abbott once posted a rehearsal call late in a play's run in order to "take out the improvements."

Just as the actor might feel alone and somewhat betrayed in those empty moments prior to opening performance, so might the director feel a twinge of apartness at the ova-

Cheryl West's Jar the Floor, *shown here in a South Coast Repertory Theatre production directed by Benny Sato Ambush (1994), portrays the generational conflict across four generations of black women in Illinois. (Photo: Cristofer Gross.)*

tion that follows the first performance. For it is in that curtain-call ovation that the audience takes over the director's critic-mentor function and the director is consigned to anonymity. The actors, heady with the applause, suddenly remember that it is they who provide the essential ingredient of theatre, while the director, cheering the ensemble from the back of the house, suddenly realizes he or she is now just one of the crowd, one witness among many to the realization of his or her own intangible and now remote plans and ideas. In the professional theatre, it is at this moment that the director's contract expires—

a fitting reminder of the "giving over" that occurs in the direction of all plays. Only those directors who can derive genuine satisfaction from creating out of the medium of others' performance will thrive and prosper in directorial pursuits; those who aspire to public acclaim and adulation will most likely face perpetual frustration as practitioners of this all-encompassing and yet all-consuming art.

THE TRAINING OF A DIRECTOR

Traditionally, directors have come to their craft from a great many areas, usually after achieving distinction in another theatrical discipline: for example, Elia Kazan was first an actor, Gower Champion was a choreographer, Harold Prince was a producer, Peter Hunt was a lighting designer, Franco Zeffirelli was a scene designer, Robert Brustein was a drama critic, Harold Pinter was a playwright, Mike Nichols was an improvisational comedian, and Robert Wilson was an architectural student. Still, in addition to a specialty, most of these directors have brought to their art a comprehensive knowledge of the theatre in its various aspects. Having distinction in one field is important chiefly insofar as it gives directors a certain confidence and authority—and it gives others a confidence in their exercise of that authority. But it is comprehensive knowledge that enables directors to collaborate successfully with actors, designers, managers, playwrights, and technicians with facility and enthusiasm.

New directors entering the profession today are more likely than not to have been trained in a dramatic graduate program or conservatory—and often they have supplemented this training with an apprenticeship at a repertory theatre. One of the most remarkable recent developments in the American theatre has been the emergence of a cadre of expertly trained directors: men and women with a broad understanding of the theatre and a disciplined approach to directorial creativity.

Well-trained directors will possess, in addition to the craft mastery of staging, actor-coaching, pacing, and production coordinating, a strong literary imagination and an ability to conceptualize intellectually and visually. They will be sensitive to interpersonal relationships, which will play an important role in both the onstage and offstage activities under their control. They will have a sound working knowledge of the history of the theatre, the various styles and masterworks of dramatic literature, the potential of various theatre technologies, and the design possibilities inherent in the use of theatrical space. They will have at their command resources in music, art, literature, and history; they will be able to research plays and investigate production possibilities without starting at absolute zero; and they will be able to base ideas and conceptions on sound social, psychological, and aesthetic understandings.

All of these advanced skills can be effectively taught in a first-rate drama program, and for that reason today's top-flight theatre directors, more than any other group of stage artists, are likely to have studied in one or another of the rigorous drama programs now in place across the country. The accomplished director is perhaps the one all-around "expert" of the theatre; this is not to deride the director's function as a creative and imaginative force, but to emphasize her or his responsibility over a broad and highly complex enterprise. Nothing is truly irrelevant to the training of a director, for virtually every field of knowledge can be brought to bear upon theatre production. The distinctiveness of any production of the contemporary theatre is largely a reflection of the unique but comprehensive training of its *director*, who is responsible not only for the overall initiative and corrective authority that infuse the production, but also for the personal vision that inspires its singular *direction*.

15

The Critic

....

It is eleven o'clock; the lights fade a final time, the curtain falls, the audience applauds, and the play is over. The actors go back to their dressing rooms, take off their make-up, and depart. The audience disperses into the night.

But the theatrical experience is not over; in important ways, it is just beginning.

A play does not begin and end its life on a stage. A play begins in the mind of its creator, and its final repository is in the minds and memories of its audiences. The stage is simply a focal point where the transmission takes place—in the form of communication we know as theatrical performance.

After the performance is over, the play's impact remains. It is something to think about, talk about, fantasize about, and live with for hours, days, and years to come. Some plays we remember all our lives: plays whose characters are as indelible in our memories as the real beings who populate our personal world, plays whose settings are more deeply experienced than are most of the locales of our growing up, and plays whose themes abide as major object lessons behind our decision making. Should we take up arms against a sea of troubles? Can we depend on the kindness of strangers? What's in a name? Shall we be as defiant as Prometheus, as determined as Oedipus, as passionate as Romeo, as accepting as Winnie, as noble as Hecuba? What is

The Humana New Play Festival at the Actors Theatre of Louisville generates a national gathering of critics, who have a chance to review several important new American plays from around the country in a single long weekend. Shown here, Marisol, by José Rivera, which was featured at the 1992 Humana festival; critical response was so favorable that Rivera's play was accepted for production by several other theatres around the country in 1993–94. (Photo: Richard C. Trigg.)

Hecuba to us, or we to Hecuba? We talk about these matters with our friends.

And we also talk about the production, about the acting, the costumes, the scenery, the sound effects. Were we convinced? impressed? moved? transported? changed? Did the production hold our attention throughout? Did our involvement with the action increase during the play, or did we feel a letdown after the intermission? Did we accept the actors as the characters they were playing, or were we uncomfortably aware that they were simply "acting" their parts rather than embodying their roles?

The formalization of postplay thinking and conversation is known as dramatic criticism. When it is formalized into writing it can take many forms: production reviews in newspapers or periodicals, essays about plays or play productions written as academic assignments, commentaries in theatre programs or theatre journals, magazine feature articles on theatre artists, or scholarly articles or books on dramatic literature, history, or theory. All of these and more are in the realm of dramatic criticism, which is nothing other than an informed, articulate, and communicative response to what the critic has seen in the theatre or read in the theatre's vast literature.

CRITICAL PERSPECTIVES

What makes a play particularly successful? What gives a theatrical production significance and impact, and what makes it unforgettable? What should we be looking for when we read a play or see a dramatic production? We have, of course, complete freedom

---

IS IT ART . . . OR TRASH?

The theatre critic spends most of his time with trash. But the trash is as much a part of his subject as the non-trash. . . . Part of his function is to make sure that false messiahs and peddlers and charlatans are shown as such. Hope—non-delusionary, non-inflationary, non-self-aggrandizing hope—is the core of the critic's being: hope that good work will recurrently arrive, hope that (partly by identifying trash) he may help it to arrive, hope that he may have the excitement and privilege of helping to connect that good work with its audience.

Stanley Kauffman

---

in making up our minds, for response, by definition, can never be dictated: the price of theatrical admission carries with it the privilege of thinking what we wish and responding as we will. But five perspectives can be particularly useful in helping us focus our response to any individual theatrical event. These perspectives relate to a play's social significance, its human or personal significance, its artistic quality, its theatrical expression, and its capacity to entertain.

A Play's Relation to Society

Theatre, as we have seen in the preceding pages, is always tied to its culture. Many theatres have been directly created or sustained by governments and ruling elites: the Greek theatre of the fifth century B.C. was a creation of the state; the medieval theatre was generated by the Church, the township, and the municipal craft guilds; and the Royal theatre was a direct extension of a monarchical reign. Even in modern times, government often serves as sponsor or cosponsor or silent benefactor of the theatre. But the intellectual ties between a theatre and its culture extend well beyond merely political concerns: thematically, the theatre has at one time or another served as an arena for the discussion of every social issue imaginable. In modern times, for example, we have seen such issues as alcoholism, homosexuality, venereal disease, prostitution, public education, racial prejudice, capital punishment, thought control, prison reform, character assassination, civil equality, political corruption, and military excess examined repeatedly in theatrical productions, and from different points of view. The best of these productions have presented the issues in all of their complexity and have proffered solutions not as dogma but as food for thought—for great theatre has never sought to purvey pure propaganda.

The playwright is not necessarily brighter than the audience, nor even better informed:

Realism, by "making real" the personal consequences of public policy, often develops a genuine political impact. American policy was certainly influenced during the Vietnam War by a series of realistic dramas portraying the human dimensions of the conflict, including this powerful 1972 production of David Rabe's The Basic Training of Pavlo Hummel at the New York Public Theatre. (Photo: © George E. Joseph.)

he and his collaborators however, may be able to focus public debate, stimulate dialogue, and turn public attention and compassion toward social injustices, inconsistencies, and irregularities. The theatre artist traditionally is something of a nonconformist; her point of view is generally to the left or right of the social mainstream, and her perspective is of necessity somewhat unusual. Therefore, the theatre is in a strong position to force and focus public confrontation with social issues, and at its best it succeeds in bringing the audience into touch with its own thoughts and feelings about those issues.

South African dramatist Athol Fugard's passionate advocacy for racial justice undeniably hastened the ending of apartheid in his country. Fugard's outspoken plays, which date from the 1950s, are not mere political tracts, however, but lively and affecting portrayals of courage and compassion. Playland, *set in a provincial South African amusement park, depicts a chance encounter between a night watchman and a park patron, black and white respectively, who share their dreams—and their deeply harbored guilts—over the course of a long evening together. South Coast Repertory Theatre, 1993. (Photo: Cristofer Gross.)*

A Play's Relation to the Individual

The theatre is a highly personal art, in part because it stems from the unique (and often oblique) perspectives of the playwrights who initiate it and the theatre artists who execute it, and in part because its audiences all through history have decreed that it be so.

The greatest plays transcend the social and political to confront the hopes, concerns, and conflicts faced by all humankind: personal identity, courage, compassion, fantasy versus practicality, kindness versus self-serving, love versus exploitation, and the inescapable problems of growing up and growing old, of wasting and dying. These are some of the basic themes of the finest of plays and of our own stray thoughts as well: the best plays simply link up with our deepest musings and help us to put our random ideas into some sort of order or philosophy. The theatre is a medium in which we of the audience invariably see reflections of ourselves, and in the theatre's best achievements those reflections lead to certain discoveries and evaluations concerning our own individual personalities and perplexities.

The Actors Theatre of Louisville also sponsors an annual "Classics in Concert" series, which serves to reinvest past theatrical styles with both historical research and a contemporary sensibility. Jon Jory's production of Carlos Goldoni's The Three Cuckolds *breathed fresh life into the play's venerable* commedia dell'arte *format in 1990.*

G. W. Mercier's fanciful costume is part of the delight in John Milligan's performance as Launce, in the 1991 Alabama Shakespeare Festival production of The Two Gentlemen of Verona, *directed by Festival artistic director Kent Thompson.*

A Play's Relation to Art

The theatre is an art of such distinctive form that even with the briefest exposure we can begin to develop certain aesthetic notions as to what that form should be. We quickly come to know—or think we know—honesty on stage, for without being experts we feel we can recognize false notes in acting, in playwriting, and even in design.

Beyond that, we can ask a number of questions of ourselves. Does the play excite our emotions? Does it stimulate the intellect? Does it surprise us? Does it thrill us? Does it seem complete and all of a piece? Are the characters credible? Are the actors convincing? enchanting? electrifying? Does the play seem alive or dead? Does it seem in any way original? Is it logically sound? Is the action purposeful, or is it gratuitous? Are we transported, or are we simply waiting for the final curtain? In the last analysis, does the play fit our idea of what a play should be—or, even better, does it force us, by its sheer luster and power, to rewrite our standards of theatre?

Aesthetic judgments of this sort are neces-

Costume designs are normally drawn on paper or canvas before being built, and they are often annotated by the designer with construction details or actual fabric swatches. Many such drawings have come down to us through history, though the costumes (and swatches) have long disappeared. Jean Bérain (1637–1711) has left us many colorful renderings, including this costume for the character of Pluton in the 1680 "lyrical tragedy" (what we would today call an opera) of Proserpine *by Jean-Baptiste Lully.*

sarily comparative, and they are subjective as well. What seems original to one member of the audience may be old hat to another; what seems an obvious gimmick to a veteran theatregoer can seem brilliantly innovative to a less jaded appetite. None of this should intimidate us. An audience does not bring absolute standards into the theatre—and certainly such standards as it brings are not shared absolutely. The theatrical response is a composite of many individual reactions. But each of us has an aesthetic sensibility and an aesthetic response. We appreciate colors, sights, sounds, words, actions, behaviors, and people that please us. We appreciate constructions that seem to us balanced, harmonic, expressive, and assured. We appreciate designs, ideas, and performances that exceed our expectations, that reveal patterns and viewpoints we didn't know existed. We take great pleasure in sensing underlying *structure:* a symphony of ideas, a sturdy architecture of integrated style and action.

A Play's Relation to Theatre

As we've already discussed, plays are not simply things that happen "in" the theatre, but they "are" theatre—which is to say that each play or play production redefines the theatre itself and makes us reconsider, at least to a certain extent, the value and possibilities of the theatre itself.

In some cases the playwright makes this reconsideration mandatory, by dealing with theatrical matters in the play itself. Some plays are set in theatres where plays are going on (Luigi Pirandello's *Six Characters in Search of an Author,* Michael Frayn's *Noises Off,* Richard Nelson's *Two Shakespearean Actors*); other plays are about actors (Jean-Paul Sartre's *Kean*) or about dramatic characters (Tom Stoppard's *Rosencrantz and Guildenstern Are Dead*); still other plays contain plays within themselves (Anton Chekhov's *The Seagull,* William Shakespeare's *Hamlet*) or the rehearsals of such plays (Shakespeare's *A Midsummer Night's Dream,* Molière's *The Versailles Rehearsals,* Jean Anouilh's *The Rehearsal*). We use the term *metatheatre* or *metadrama* to describe those plays that specifically refer back to themselves in this manner, but in fact all plays and play productions can be analyzed and evaluated on the way they use the theatrical format to best advantage and the way they make us rethink the nature of theatrical production.

For all plays stand within the spectrum of a history of theatre, and a history of theatrical convention (see Chapter 2). All plays and pro-

Jean-Paul Sartre's powerful Kean *is about English actor Edmund Kean; Sartre's play is therefore about acting as well as about the life that acting represents. In this Tampere Theatre production, Finnish actor Tapani Perttu plays Kean (in black-face) playing Othello, and Sartre exploits the "meta-theatrical" (theatre-about-theatre) possibilities of this situation.*

A Play as Entertainment

Finally, we look upon all theatre as entertainment.

Great theatre is never less than pleasing. Even tragedy delights. People go to see *Hamlet* not for purpose of self-flagellation or to wallow in despair, but to revel in the tragic form and to experience the liberating catharsis of the play's murderous finale. Hamlet himself knows the thrill of staged tragedy:

HAMLET: What players are they?
ROSENCRANTZ: Even those you were wont to take such delight in, the tragedians . . .

What is this entertainment value that all plays possess? Most obviously the word *entertainment* suggests "amusement," and so we think immediately of the hilarity of comedy

ductions can be studied, often with illuminating results, from the perspective of how they adopt or reject prevailing theatrical conventions, how they fit into or deviate from prevailing dramatic genres, and how they echo various elements of past plays or productions—and what may be the theatrical effects, good and bad, of such historical resonances.

Arvin Brown's production of George Bernard Shaw's Misalliance *is meant to be—as its author fully intended—entertaining, but it captures the audience with brilliant social ideas as well as farcical pratfalls and complications. In this Long Wharf Theatre production, Frank Converse and Pamela Payton-Wright (as the Tarletons) find themselves in a panic over visitors who have just crash-landed their airplane in the conservatory. (Photo: T. Charles Erickson.)*

and farce; indeed, most of the literature regarding theatrical entertainment concentrates on the pratfalls and gags that have been part of the comic theatre throughout its history. But entertainment goes far beyond humor. Another definition for *entertainment* is "that which holds the attention." This definition casts more light on our question. It means that entertainment includes the enchantment of romance, which stimulates our curiosity about our own emotions and longings. It takes in the dazzle of brilliant debate, witty epigram, and biting repartee; the exotic appeal of the foreign and the grotesque; the beauty and grandeur of spectacle; the nuance and crescendo of a musical or rhythmic line. It accommodates suspense and adventure, the magic of sex appeal and the splendor of sheer

talent. Finally, of course, it includes any form of drama that profoundly stirs our feelings and heightens our awareness of the human condition. It is no wonder that Hamlet delights in the performance of tragedians—and that we delight in *Hamlet*—for the concatenation of ideas, language, poetry, feelings, and actions that constitute great tragedy confers one of life's sublime entertainment experiences.

Indeed, the theatre is a storehouse of pleasures, not only for the emotional, intellectual, spiritual, and aesthetic stimulation it provides, but also for its intrinsic social excitement. It is a favored public meeting place for people who care about each other; "two on the aisle" implies more than a choice seating location: it implies companionship in the best theatrical experience. For the theatre is a place to commune in an especially satisfying way with strangers. When in the course of a dramatic performance we are gripped by a staging of romantic passion, or stunned by a brilliantly articulated argument, or moved by a touching denouement, the thrill is enhanced a hundredfold by the certainty that we are not alone in these feelings, that possibly every member of the audience has been stirred to the same response. Theatre, in its essence, serves to rescue humankind from an intellectual and emotional aloneness; and therein lies its most profound "entertainment" value.

CRITICAL FOCUS

These five perspectives on the theatre experience—on its social, personal, artistic, theatrical, and entertainment values—are all implicit in the responses of any audience, regardless of its training or theatrical sophistication. These are the five angles from which we view and judge plays—and judge them we do, for our involvement with a play naturally generates a series of comparisons: the play vis-à-vis other plays, the play vis-à-vis our personal experiences, the play vis-à-vis other things we might have done that evening. Judging plays and performances, which has been done formally since ancient Greek times and continues today through the well-publicized Tony and Obie Awards, Pulitzer Prizes, and Critics Circle citations, is one of the fundamental aspects of theatrical participation—and yet it is a participation open to amateur and professional alike.

Professional Criticism

Professional criticism takes the basic form of production reviews and scholarly books and articles written, for the most part, by persons who specialize in this activity, often for an entire career.

Arthur Miller has been tracking American values— and the world's guilt—since World War II. In his latest play, Broken Glass, *he examines the psychological effect of Nazi storm troopers in the 1930s on a distressed American Jewish couple, played here by Amy Irving and Ron Rifkin, at the Long Wharf Theatre's premiere production in 1994. (Photo: T. Charles Erickson.)*

A CRITIC'S TASTES

Somebody recently wrote one of my editors to the effect that I had no sense whatever of the tastes of my readers or the public at large. He was, unintentionally, paying me a great tribute which I can only hope I deserve. For it is extremely hard not to be influenced by the tastes of one's milieu; yet resisting them is precisely the critic's duty. It is only in being uncompromisingly himself that a critic performs a true service, and as a man of taste (not infallible taste, for there can be no such thing), goes down in history, or as a man of no taste, goes down the drain.

John Simon

The Liberation of Skopje, *by the Zagreb Theatre Company of Croatia, previewed the war and devastation that has since overwhelmed much of the former Yugoslavia. Shown in the World Theatre Festival production in Denver, 1985.*

Newspaper reviews of play productions are common throughout the theatre world; indeed, the box-office success of most theatres depends on receiving favorable press coverage. In the commercial Broadway theatre, favorable reviews—particularly from the influential *New York Times*—are all but absolutely necessary in order to guarantee a successful run. Where theatre audiences are generated by subscriptions and where institu-

tional financing secures the production funds, newspaper reviews play a less crucial short-term role, but they still bear weightily in a theatre's ultimate success or failure.

In New York, newspaper reviews have traditionally been written immediately following the opening-night performance and are published the following morning; actors and producers gather after opening night at Sardi's restaurant, in the Broadway theatre district, awaiting the first edition of the next morning's *Times* to see how their show fared with the current critic. This is "instant criticism," and the journalist who tackles these assignments has to be very fluid at articulating his or her immediate impressions. Outside of New York, newspaper critics frequently take two or three days to review a production, allowing themselves the luxury of considered opinions and more polished essays. Some New York newspaper critics have recently begun to emulate this practice; though their reviews are still published the day after opening night, they have actually attended a preview performance two or three days earlier and have had the opportunity to write their review at some leisure.

Still, the journalist's review must be limited to a brief, immediate, reaction rather than to a detailed or exhaustive study. It provides a firsthand, audience-oriented response to the production, often vigorously and wittily expressed, and may serve as a useful consumer guide for the local theatregoing public. Writing skill rather than dramatic expertise is often the newspaper critic's principal job qualification, and at many smaller papers, staff reporters with little dramatic background are assigned to the theatre desk. But many fine newspaper critics throughout the years—New York's Walter Kerr and Boston's Elliot Norton, for example—have proven extremely subtle and skillful at transcending the limitations of their particular profession and have written highly intelligent dramatic criticism that remains pertinent long after its consumer-oriented function has run its course.

More scholarly critics, writing without the deadlines or strict column-inch (space) restrictions of journalists, are able to analyze plays and productions within detailed, comprehensive, and rigorously researched critical contexts. They are therefore able to understand and evaluate, in a more complex way, the achievements of playwrights and theatre artists, within any or all of the five perspectives we have discussed. Scholarly critics (and by

scholarly we mean only "one who studies") seek to uncover hidden aspects of a play's structure, to analyze its deep relationships to social or philosophical issues, to probe its various meanings and dramatic possibilities, to define its place in cultural history, to amplify its resonance of earlier works of art, to shape its future theatrical presentations, and to theorize about larger issues of dramaturgy, art, and human understanding. Such criticism is itself a literary art, and the great examples of dramatic criticism have included brilliantly styled essays which have outlasted the theatrical works that were their presumed subjects: Aristotle, Goethe, Shaw, and Nietzsche are among the drama critics who, simply through their analyses of drama, have helped shape our vision of life itself.

The scholarly critic is ordinarily distinguished by his or her broad intellectual background and exhaustive research, and writes with a comprehensive knowledge of the specific subject—a knowledge that includes the work of all important previous scholars who have studied the same materials. The professional scholar is not content to repeat the opinions or discoveries of others, but seeks to make fresh insights from the body of literature (playtexts and productions, production records, previous scholarship) that constitutes the field of study.

Scholarly critics tend to work within accepted methodologies, which develop and change rapidly in contemporary academic life. Traditional methodologies include historical and biographical approaches ("the man and his work"), thematic and rhetorical analyses, studies of character and plot, examinations of staging and theatrical styles, and detailed exegeses of meaning, or *explication de texte*. More contemporary methodologies include systems and theories developed since the 1970s, particularly structuralist, semiotic, and deconstructive approaches; these bypass traditional questions of history, biography, character, theme, and meaning and focus instead on the internal relationships of various dra-

CONTRASTING REVIEWS

Play reviewers have their individual styles; they also write for different audiences. Compare, for example, these two reviews—each by a celebrated veteran reviewer—of the 1992 New York premiere of Wendy Wasserstein's *The Sisters Rosensweig*. Mel Gussow, in the high-brow *New York Times*, provides a sensitive and balanced analysis of the text and production. Doug Watt, writing for the *Daily News*, a popular tabloid, gives a more succinct description focusing on the play's entertainment values. Neither is *the* way to write a review; each is responsive to the writer's interest and the expectations of his readers.

Wasserstein: Comedy, Character, Reflection

By Mel Gussow

"The Sisters Rosensweig" is Wendy Wasserstein's captivating look at three uncommon women and their quest for love, self-definition and fulfillment. Unified by their sisterhood, they are as different as only sisters (or brothers) can be, as each tries to live up to an image imposed by her family. At the same time, each performs her own act of rebellion— or is it penitence? Because of their disparities, they are heroines to one another.

Ms. Wasserstein's generous group portrait (at the Mitzi E. Newhouse Theater) is not only a comedy but also a play of character and shared reflection as the author confronts the question of why the sisters behave as they do. The immediate answer is that they are Rosensweigs and are only doing what is expected of them. The play offers sharp truths about what can divide relatives and what can draw them together.

The oldest sister is Sara (Jan Alexander), an overachiever, the only woman ever to head an international Hong Kong bank. She is an expatriate in England who is, we are told, "assimilated beyond her wildest dreams." Second is Gorgeous (Madeline Kahn), a triple threat as "housewife, mother and radio personality" in Newton, Mass. The youngest is Pfeni, née Penny (Frances McDormand), a globe-trotting journalist who lives her life as if she were on "an extended junior year abroad."

The three come together in London for Sara's 54th birthday. One of the show's surprises is that in a play essentially about women, the sisters are subtly upstaged by two of the men in their lives, characters enhanced in performance by Robert Klein and John Vickery.

The play is steeped in Jewish culture and humor, but the emotional subtext is broader. None of the sisters can find happiness; they have all been nurtured in a family in which heartbreak has been confused with heartburn. With effort, the women arrive at a new understanding. Bonding as siblings, they can anticipate a more promising future.

With Sara, additional hope comes from a most unlikely source: a wealthy New York furrier (Mr. Klein) who in politically correct parlance manufactures "synthetic animal protective covering." In dealing with social and cultural paradoxes, Ms. Wasserstein is, as always, the most astute of commentators. Along the way, she shatters the myth that Jewish men don't drink ("a myth made up by our mothers to persuade innocent women that Jewish men make superior husbands") as well as national patterns of speech (when an Englishman praises a stew as "brilliant," Mr. Klein adds, "the chicken was very bright, too"). But underlying the comedy is an empathetic concern for the characters and for the prospects of women today.

At the same time, the play has its imperfections. There are gratuitous remarks and irrelevancies. Both Ms. Wasserstein and her director, Daniel Sullivan, should have been more judicious in their editing, especially in dealing with the author's penchant for labeling characters and offering information in the guise of conversation. There is no need, for example, to keep saying that Sara is so intelligent; the character and the actress should speak for themselves. In addition, two stock characters represent the polarities of English society: an upper-class snob and a young radical with incredible gaps in his knowledge (and too many easy jokes made at his expense).

These flaws do not substantially detract from a play with wit as well as acumen. "The Sisters Rosensweig" grows naturally out of the author's previous work. With its Jewish themes and reference to a mother's strong influence on her adult daughters, it looks back to "Isn't It Romantic?" In contrast to the title character in "The Heidi Chronicles," each sister is focused on her life to an obsessive degree. But as with Heidi, each has difficulty with men. Those they meet seldom seem worthy of the Rosensweigs. It is in this area that the play is at its funniest and most observant, with Mr. Klein's faux furrier and Mr. Vickery as a flamboyant theater director. Both roles could lead actors into excess, but the pitfalls are assiduously avoided.

Acting as armchair counselor, the furrier sees through Sara's protective screen. As written, and as played by Mr. Klein, he is an unpretentious wise man who forces Sara to see herself as he sees her. Shrewdly, the actor plays the role straight, eradicating all thought of his background as a stand-up comic. Mr. Vickery's character is Pfeni's man of many moments, who is unable to commit himself either in love or in art. Evidently a serious man of the theater, he has made his reputation by staging an Andrew Lloyd Webber-like musical of "The Scarlet Pimpernel," from which we hear exuberant excerpts. Mr. Vickery is both dashing and self-mocking, winning laughs with looks and pauses as well as with Ms. Wasserstein's lines.

The women also rise above stereotype. As the expatriate, Ms. Alexander assumes an artful Englishness. Despite her admission of being humorless, she wryly observes her post-marital situation: because her second husband has been married so many times, his wives, past and present, could form a club with "branches in Chicago, New York, London and Tokyo." In the course of the play, Ms. Alexander reveals a vulnerability beneath the ladylike veneer.

For Ms. Kahn, Dr. Gorgeous (who advises everyone including her sisters) is the choicest of the roles. Restlessly changing her costumes

and interrupting conversations, she is a delirious combination of extravagant plumage and native intuition.

Of the three, Pfeni is the most problematic, and the problem is in the character as well as the performance. Given Pfeni's eccentric life style, one would have imagined a more vivid, Auntie Mame-ish personality instead of someone overshadowed by her sisters and by her suitor.

Although Rex Robbins is miscast as the English snob, Patrick Fitzgerald manages to invest the young radical with a certain zeal; and Julie Dretzin, in her professional stage debut (as Ms. Alexander's daughter), easily holds her own with her more experienced colleagues. On John Lee Beatty's tasteful townhouse set, Mr. Sullivan leads the actors to play scenes for their reality rather than for their comic effect. As he did with his production of Herb Gardner's "Conversations With My Father," the director reveals his expertise in dealing with a Jewish milieu.

Overlooking the play is the symbolic figure of Anton Chekhov, smiling. Although the characters do not

directly parallel those in "The Three Sisters," the comparison is intentional. The Rosensweigs have their own dreams of reclamation by romance, of escaping to a metaphorical Moscow. Ms. Wasserstein does not overstate the connection but uses it like background music while diverting her attention to other cultural matters, as in Mr. Vickery's statement that he would like to make a film entitled, "Three Days That Shook the Rosensweigs." For the two acts, the Rosensweigs (and friends) are entertaining company.

As the characters in Ms. Wasserstein's plays have become older, moving on from college to New York careers to the international setting of the current work, the author has remained keenly aware of the changes in her society and of the new roles that women play. In her writing, she continues to be reflexively in touch with her times. Drawing upon his strength as a nurturer of plays and playwrights, André Bishop has made an auspicious debut as artistic director of Lincoln Center Theater.

—The New York Times, Oct. 23, 1992

Wasserstein Pens a Pointed Drawing-Room Comedy

By Doug Watt

HERE'S A PLAY that sparkles like the autumn air. "The Sisters Rosensweig," ideally in Lincoln Center's cozy Newhouse, finds author Wendy Wasserstein at the top of her game, or very near it.

A smart drawing-room comedy, it calls to mind Philip Barry, as filtered thorough S.N. Behrman.

The play, about upper middle-class Jewish manners, is set in the John Lee Beatty-designed London townhouse of the twice-married and divorced Sara Goode (Jane Alexander). It is her 54th birthday.

There to celebrate are her two sisters Pfeni (Frances McDormand), a travel writer in her 40s eager to wed and have children by the campy, bisexual Geoffrey (John Vickery), the British director of a splashy "Scarlet Pimpernel"; and Gorgeous, a Newton, Mass., wife and radio talk-show personality,

the only halfway devout Jew of the three. It is a role in which Madeline Kahn is at her hilarious best.

The sexually repressed Sara, international rep of a Hong Kong bank, has a one-night affair (a somewhat quick quickie) with a drop-by American, Mervyn Kant (Robert Klein), a successful "furrier" dealing in synthetic animal outerwear. And in the end, the gabby, fluttery Gorgeous has a sad confession to make, after which the three sisters, Chekhovian only in their emotional losses, lovingly embrace to the strains of "Shine On, Harvest Moon."

The time is late August 1991, when the Soviet Union is breaking up.

Several supporting players, who include Sara's near-radicalized daughter, Tess (Julie Dretzin), drift through this warm, humorous, witty play—the author's most sustained piece of writing.

It is superbly directed by Daniel Sullivan.

—Daily News, Oct. 30, 1992

CRITICAL PERVERSITY

The critical voice in its ever-changing moods sometimes effects reversals that seem exceptionally perverse. In an article titled "The Curious Case of *Time* and Tennessee Williams," *Esquire* magazine demonstrated the way in which *Time* continued to accord the celebrated playwright negative notices right up to the moment it chose to call him America's greatest living dramatic author.

> The play [*A Streetcar Named Desire*] could stand more discipline; along with an absence of formulas there is sometimes an absence of form. And it could stand more variety: only the clash between Blanche and Stanley . . . gets real emotion and drama into the play.
> —December 15, 1947

> *Summer and Smoke* . . . is all too plainly—but not too happily—by the author of *The Glass Menagerie* and *A Streetcar Named Desire*. What stamps, and sometimes rubberstamps, it as his is the nature of the story and the style of the storytelling; far too often missing is the talent of the storyteller.
> —October 18, 1948

> [In] *The Rose Tattoo* . . . Williams has never seemed so blatantly himself. . . . Often the play . . . is lush, garish, operatic, decadently primitive, a salt breeze in a swamp, a Banana Truck Named Desire.
> —February 12, 1951

> Camino Real is perhaps excessively pessimistic in reaction against Williams' previous *Rose Tattoo*, with its factitious "affirmation." But very excessive it is—and not only excessively black, but excessively purple. *Camino Real* lacks philosophic or dramatic progression (on that score, it might claim the dead-endedness of a wasteland), but it also lacks all discipline and measure, so that the wasteland becomes a swamp. What makes the play ultimately unacceptable is not that it is often dull and even more often arty, but that it exposes decadence with decadent means.
> —March 30, 1953

> [T]he play [*Cat on a Hot Tin Roof*], closing on a lame, stagy note, lacks stature. Perhaps there is a little too much of everything: Williams is not only lavish of suffering, but voluble in articulating it. There might well be less emotionalism and should certainly be fewer words, particularly profane ones: the profanity often seems to relieve Williams' own feelings rather than his characters'. But more important, *Cat* never quite defines itself as chiefly a play about a marriage, about a family, or about a man. . . . It needs sharper form, greater unity, a sense of something far more deeply interfused.
> —April 4, 1955

> Unhappily, Williams' story [*Garden District*] dies with his telling it, for though he weaves a spell he cannot validate a vision. It matters less that noisomely misanthropic symbols keep recurring in his work than that they nowhere seem purgative.
> —January 20, 1958

matic ingredients and their particular combination in a self-referential dramaturgic system. Contemporary methodologies, which draw heavily from the fields of philosophy, linguistics, anthropology, and critical theory, are intellectually demanding and difficult to master; they provide, however, stunning insights to those properly initiated.

Student Criticism

One does not expect of beginning theatre students a thoroughly comprehensive background in the subject; indeed, students writing class papers are likely to be looking seriously at the subject for the first time in their life. Naturally, different standards apply.

In *Period of Adjustment,* which opened last week at Miami's Coconut Grove Playhouse, Playwright Tennessee Williams repaired no cracking masonry in his familiar dramatic neighborhood, but at least he slapped on a coat of whitewash. Billed as a "Serious Comedy," *Period* sounds more like a mad Gothic anecdote.

—January 12, 1959

Sweet Bird of Youth . . . is very close to parody, but the wonder is that Williams should be so inept at imitating himself. The sex violence, the perfumed decay, the hacking domestic quarrels, the dirge of fear and self-pity, the characters who dangle in neurotic limbo—all are present—but only like so many dramatic dead cats on a cold tin roof.

—March 23, 1959

Many serious, liberal-minded intellectuals worry profoundly about the unattractive impression the U.S. often makes abroad, blaming everyone from unimaginative ambassadors to loud tourists with star-spangled sport shirts. But few would ever admit that some of their own heroes—for example, Playwright Tennessee Williams—can be the worst ambassadors of all. Last week two Williams plays, presented by a free-lance theatrical troupe called the New York Repertory Company (which claimed association with Manhattan's Actors Studio) had left a fairly indelible stain in Rio de Janeiro.

—September 1, 1961

Summer and Smoke. . . . Playwright Tennessee Williams often writes like an arrested adolescent who disarmingly imagines that he will attain stature if (as short boys are advised in Dixie) he loads enough manure in his shoes. In his most famous plays, he has hallucinated a vast but specious pageant of depravity in which fantasies of incest, cannibalism, murder, rape, sodomy and drug addiction constitute the canon of reality. . . . Nevertheless, the film conspicuously possesses Playwright Williams' characteristic virtue: a pathetic-romantic atmosphere that lingers from scene to scene like an ineffable sachet of self-pity.

—December 1, 1961

The fact is that Tennessee Williams . . . is a consummate master of theatre. His plays beat with the heart's blood of the drama: passion. He is the greatest U.S. playwright since Eugene O'Neill, and, barring the aged Sean O'Casey, the greatest living playwright anywhere. . . . Williams has peopled the U.S. stage with characters whose vibrantly durable presences stalk the corridors of a playgoer's memory: . . . Williams' dialogue sings with a lilting eloquence far from the drab, disjunctive patterns of everyday talk. And for monologues, the theatre has not seen his like since the god of playwrights, William Shakespeare.

—March 9, 1962

Such beginning students will characteristically analyze plays from any of the five perspectives cited earlier, but without the need for a very sophisticated or advanced methodology. Some simple but effective methodologies, for writing both class essays and production reviews for local or school newspapers, are provided in the appendix to this book.

WE ARE THE CRITICS

Whether we are professional writers, students, or just plain theatregoers, we are all the critics of the theatre. We the audience are a party to the theatrical experience, not a mere passive receptacle for its contrived effects. The theatre is a forum of *communication,* and communication demands *mutual* and *active* participation.

To be an *observant* critic, one need only go to the theatre with an open mind and sharply tuned senses. Unfettered thinking should be a part of every theatrical experience, and provocative discussion should be its aftermath.

To be an *informed* critic, one needs sufficient background to provide a context for opinion and evaluation. A play may be moving, but is it as moving as *The Three Sisters?* as passionate as *The Trojan Women?* as romantic as *Romeo and Juliet?* as funny as *The Bourgeois Gentleman?* as intriguing as *Happy Days?* An actor's voice may be thrillingly resonant, but how does it compare with the voice of Laurence Olivier? If our opinions are to have weight and distinction, they may do so only against a background of knowledge and experience. If we are going to place a performance on a scale of one to ten, our friends (or readers) must know just what is our "one" and what is our "ten."

To be a *sensitive* critic, one must be receptive to life and to artistic experience. The most sensitive criticism comes from a compassionate approach to life, to humankind, and to artistic expression; this approach elicits and provokes a *personalized* response to dramatic works. Sensitive criticism admits the critic's *needs:* it begins from the view that life is difficult and problematical and that relationships are demanding. Sensitive critics are questing, not smug; humane, not self-absorbed; eternally eager for personal discovery and the opportunity to share it. They recognize that we are all groping in the dark, hoping to encounter helping hands along the way in the adventure of life—that this indeed is the hope of theatre artists too.

To be a *demanding* critic is to hold the theatre to the highest standards of which it is capable. For, paradoxically, in the theatre's capacity to entertain, to supply immediate gratification, lies the seed of its own destruction. As we have seen so often in the preceding pages, the theatre wants to be liked. It has tried from its very beginning to assimilate what is likable in the other arts. Almost scavengerlike, it has appropriated for itself in every era the most popular music and dance forms, the most trendy arguments, vocabularies, philosophies, and fashions in dress. In the process, alas, it often panders to tastelessness and propagates the meanest and most shallow values of its time. And here the drama critic in each of us can play a crucial role. The very need of the theatre to please its patrons tends to beget a crass insecurity: a tendency to resort to simple sensationalism in exchange for immediate approval. Cogent, fair-minded, penetrating criticism keeps the theatre mindful of its own artistic ideals and its essential responsibility to communicate. It prevents the theatre from either selling out completely to the current whim or bolting the other way into a hopelessly abstract and arcane self-absorption.

To be an *articulate* critic is to express one's thoughts with precision, clarity, and grace. "I loved it" or "I hated it" is not criticism, but rather a crude expression of opinion and a wholly general opinion at that. Articulation means the careful building of ideas, through a presentation of evidence, logical argument, the use of helpful analogy and example, and a style of expression neither pedantically turgid nor idiosyncratically anarchic. Good criticism should be a pleasure to write, a pleasure to read; it should make us want to go deeper into the mysteries of the theatre and not suffocate us with the prejudices or egotistical displays of the critic.

In sum, the presence of a critical focus in the audience—observant, informed, sensitive, demanding, and articulate—keeps the theatre honest. It *inspires* the theatre to reach its highest goals. It ascribes *importance* to the theatrical act. It telegraphs the expectations of the audience to producer, playwright, director, and actor alike, saying "We are out here, we are watching, we are listening, we are hoping, we *care:* we want your best—and then we want you to be better yet.'' The theatre needs such demands from its audience. The theatre and its audience need to be worthy coparticipants in a collective experience that enlarges life as well as art.

If we are to be critics of the theatre, then, we must be knowledgeable, fair, and open-minded; receptive to stimulation and excitement; open to wisdom and love. We must also admit that we have human needs.

In exchange, the theatre must enable us to see ourselves in the characters of the drama and in the performers of the theatre. We must see our situations in the situations of plays, and our hopes and possibilities in the behavior staged before us. We must be drawn to understand the theatre from the *inside* and to participate in thought and emotion in a play's performance.

Thus do we become critics, audience, and participants in one. The theatre is then no longer simply a remote subject encountered in a book, or in a class, or in the entertainment columns of the world press; the theatre is part of us.

It is *our* theatre.

Appendix

Writing
on Theatre

If you study theatre in an academic setting, sooner or later you probably will be required to write a critical paper on a play (or plays) that you read or see. "Critical" is used here not in the everyday sense of "finding fault with," but in the scholarly sense of "examining closely."

Writing such a paper is, of course, a test of your perception, but it is also much more than that: it is an opportunity to organize and focus your thoughts, to investigate drama with a specific purpose, and to communicate your considered opinion to someone else. The act of writing is an act of clarification, for the author as well as for the reader. You usually will learn much more by writing a paper than by reading one.

You will also *remember* the subject of your paper long after the course is over. This is because the acts of researching a topic, and of organizing, clarifying, and writing up your ideas, will make the subject an important part of your own life. And although you will ultimately "give" the paper to the instructor, the ideas in it will remain yours: they will represent your contribution to the literature of drama.

Your instructor will give you a specific assignment for your paper, often including its proper length and an acceptable range of topics. The instructor will also usually guide you on appropriate procedures, some of which may differ markedly from the suggestions that follow. Absent instructions to the contrary, however, the advice given here may serve as a general guide to writing an undergraduate paper.

YOUR PURPOSE

Your purpose in writing a paper is to demonstrate something to someone: to present a clear point of view about your topic that leads to some conclusions about it.

"Demonstration" involves more than merely citing facts or opinions: it requires the arrangement of these facts and opinions in a careful and persuasive way.

"Conclusions" are what the paper is finally all about; your paper should end by persuading its readers that your point of view is, if not the definitive truth, at least worthy of further consideration. A coherent set of conclusions is usually called your paper's "thesis" (which is not to be confused with a formal paper required for certain graduate degrees such as a master's thesis).

"Clear" is simply the quality of good writing, plus good rewriting. A clear paper requires a good structure and an uncluttered use of language. A good paper is clear; a fine paper is both clear and convincing; an excellent paper is clear, convincing, and original.

YOUR AUDIENCE

The actual readership of your paper is usually limited to your instructor (and perhaps a reader or teaching assistant). But you should remember that the assigned paper is an exercise, and, as with an acting exercise, you should write the paper "as if" the readership were a more general one, including the theatre students in your class, theatre students and teachers at other institutions, theatre art-

ists, and theatre enthusiasts in and out of the academic world.

Your assumption of a general audience will prevent your paper from becoming merely a letter to the instructor. At the same time, the assumption that your audience already possesses a basic theatre background means that you can use theatrical terms and cite major dramatists without detailed preamble. Your readers already know what a proscenium is and who Anton Chekhov is; you don't have to define the former or identify the latter unless it serves your purpose to do so. You can also assume that your readership is interested in the basic subject: you do not have to "sell them" on the notion that drama is a worthwhile artistic form.

YOUR WORKING METHOD

Generally, the writing of a paper consists of six steps: choosing a topic, conducting research, developing a thesis, organizing the argument, writing the draft, and revising the draft. In practice, these steps do not always proceed neatly or in this order: the topic is often chosen during the research phase, and the thesis is developed (and refined) continually throughout the process.

Choosing Your Topic

Often, this is the single most difficult part of writing a paper; certainly it is the one most subject to procrastination and deferral. You have read or seen a play, but what then? What is there to say about it?

What you might not realize is that your reading or viewing of a play, even when shared with a class or an audience, is a unique experience. What you receive from a play is a combination of two things—the play and you—and the uniqueness of either your reading or viewing comes from your contribution to the experience: your social background, your personal preoccupations, your particular hopes and fears, your unique perspective on human behavior. Your individuality gives you a view of the play that no one else has: if you can develop that view in an intelligent manner, you already have begun the search for a topic without knowing it.

It might be best, in hunting for a topic, to discuss a play that interests you with fellow students. How do they see the play differently from you? What do you see (or focus on) that they don't? What important aspect of the play have they missed? What has the instructor missed? What has the director of the play, or the editor of the play anthology, missed?

There are six general topic approaches that you should consider as well; most good papers fall into one of these:

1. *The contextual analysis.* This sort of paper analyzes one or more plays according to their historical, social, and/or philosophical context: for example, *Hamlet* as a Renaissance tragedy; *Happy Days* as a masterpiece of the twentieth-century avant-garde. Such essays are often seen as the introductory matter in play anthologies or as director's or dramaturge's notes in production programs. Beware, however: this is ordinarily the *least* interesting sort of paper you can write, for unless the assignment is purely to create a "research paper" or unless you are particularly passionate about the specified context, you might try something a little more adventurous.

The contextual paper must be marked with thorough research, which includes at least one source of recent scholarship; be certain that you are at least aware of current thinking on your topic, even if you disagree with it. Also, try to focus the contextual approach toward some sort of conclusion and evaluation so that something is finally demonstrated: it is not very interesting to say that *Hamlet* is a Renaissance tragedy, which we already know, but it might be important to understand why that does (or doesn't) make *Hamlet* a fine play or why it does (or doesn't) make Hamlet revenge his father in Act V rather than in Act III.

2. *The comparative analysis.* Comparisons are the most basic building blocks of learning: if you can understand similarities and differences at the deepest levels, you can discover untold fields of wisdom. It was Newton's comparison of the fall of an apple and the motions of the planets that led to the theory of gravity and its consequent application to rocket travel; it was Pasteur's comparison of the incidence of disease and the incidence of hygienic procedures that led to the discovery of bacterial infection and the development of rubber gloves. In the same way, the study of literature is basically the study of similarities (which define genres and styles) and differences (which define creative departures and imaginative leaps).

Comparative papers might demonstrate the similarities and differences between two or more plays or authors—or between one or more plays and a nondramatic idea. Plays by Tennessee Williams and Arthur Miller could be compared, for example, or Aristophanes' attitudes toward war could be compared to the antiwar movement of ancient Athens.

The comparative paper is not, however, merely a mechanical listing of observed similarities and differences; your comparison should point up possible influences, conscious or unconscious; or, alternatively, it might demonstrate how both compared subjects were subject to the same influences. Mere coincidental similarities are of no importance—although if you probe deeply enough, you might find the coincidences are, in fact, not coincidences at all.

A comparison is worth investigating when you discover an interesting similarity. This can be as simple as recognizing that Williams and Miller are both midcentury American playwrights, that they both write a form of poetic realism, that they both have dealt with problems of modern urban life, that they both have written autobiographical plays dealing with themselves as young writers working in impersonal surroundings, and that they both had successful Broadway hits in the same decade. Or, more originally, perhaps you read Hamlet's

> And you, my sinews, be not instant old,
> But bear me stiffly up,

and it makes you think of the line from *Henry V:*

> Stiffen the sinews, summon up the blood.

What do stiff sinews have in common, and why did Shakespeare use the same expression in these two plays? Are there any other similarities between Prince Hamlet and King Henry? Entire books have been written stemming from what were initially curiosities like this one.

3. *A problem investigation.* Often you will read or see a play and, while liking it, find yourself bothered by something. Perhaps the story seems faulty, or the characters unlikable, or you don't understand what the playwright was driving at. You ask one or two classmates, and they have the same problems with the play, although they, perhaps, are not so preoccupied with them as you. You may have found fertile ground for an investigation.

Why, for example, does Othello suspect Desdemona of unfaithfulness, when there has not been time for her to be alone with Cassio? Some eighteenth-century critics dismissed *Othello* out of hand because of this and similar problems; it might bother you too. You could work on this problem itself, for although you would not be the first to do so, there is no definitive answer. But there are an infinite number of such problems in the world's dramatic literature to investigate; and though the answers are not, so to speak, in the back of the book (final answers don't exist for most liter-

ary problems), your work on the subject may prove illuminating for both you and what will be your readership.

Problem investigations provide good opportunities for research into specialized critical literature. A reference librarian can help you find articles on your topic, and related ones, that will help guide you deeper and deeper into the subject.

4. *An observed peculiarity in a play.* "Tragedy in *Hamlet*" is not a good title, but "Comedy in *Hamlet*" is better. Everyone knows that *Hamlet* is a tragedy, but there is also a peculiarly heavy dose of comedy in the play, right up to the last act, unlike *Macbeth, King Lear,* and even *Romeo and Juliet,* where the comedy is limited to the first half of the play or so. Why is this? What does it do to the tragic conclusion of the play? Why might Shakespeare have written *Hamlet* this way? Was it a mistake? Why not?

5. *A confrontation with higher authority.* Ordinarily you will turn to critical literature for facts and for expert opinion on subjects that interest you, but there may also be times when you feel that experts, no matter how well recognized, are wrong in their opinions or evaluations. If you can back up an interesting though contrary point of view, you might have a chance at rewriting critical opinion. Of course this is a dangerous field; you will be matching wits with scholars of wide literary background and proven critical judgment. Still, in the final analysis, the best opinion will out, and it might very well be yours. All opinions are ultimately reversed, refined, or revoked anyway; there is no reason not to try to "set the matter straight."

A confrontational paper, if you have the heart for it, can draw from you your most dedicated research, persuasive writing, and passionate attention to detail; it can also give you a confidence in your ideas unattainable simply by quoting learned authority. It is certainly worth a try—when you find yourself in considered disagreement with a published expert.

6. *A discovered pattern.* Perhaps, through a series of comparisons, contextual analyses, and investigations into observed problems, you will discover some fundamental pattern of writing in an author (or directing in a director or designing in a designer). This is not usually the sort of thing one finds in an undergraduate paper—rather, it is more often the subject of a book-length Ph.D. dissertation—but it is the deepest goal of writing on the theatre or on any other scholarly subject. Discovering aesthetic or dramaturgical patterns in individual dramatic works not only makes clear the nature of the works considered, but also throws light on the art of theatre itself. Such discoveries require, of course, a broad background in theatre studies, plus a sustained intellectual investigation. Still, several such papers, on limited topics, are written by undergraduate students every year.

Limiting Your Topic

After making the initial choice of a topic, be careful to limit it to what you can realistically cover in the time allotted and what you can, in all good conscience, write about in the paper. To deal with more than one or two plays in a six-to-eight-page paper is probably a mistake, and such a paper should have only one principal topic and no more than two or three subordinate ones.

Conducting Your Research

Having initially selected your topic (and remember, you will continually refine the topic as you work), reread everything that pertained to your having selected the topic in the first place, noting everything in your reread-ing that might be relevant to the topic you have chosen. If the material that generated the topic is a play you have seen, get a copy of the play. (If it is an unpublished play, go to the theatre office, explain your purpose, and see if you can borrow a script copy.)

Make notes any way you choose, but be sure that they will be easily retrievable. Many students collect notes on handy three-by-five-inch cards, which can then be arranged in any order you like. If you have access to a personal computer, there are appropriate programs for collecting and arranging material like this.

Understand your basic material in as much detail as possible. Look up words and references that you don't know, using historical dictionaries (such as the *Oxford English Dictionary*) and well-annotated editions (such as the Arden Shakespeare) where necessary to study the meanings of older words and obsolete allusions.

Then, expand your reading to include material that might be related: other plays by the same playwright(s), essays on the play(s) by the playwright(s), and essays on the play and related subjects by scholars, critics, and editors. Get help from the reference librarian at your school library to ferret out pertinent books and essays that will help you probe deeper into your analysis, investigation, and/ or comparison. Write down important facts and interesting and/or well-expressed opinions of others, being careful to write down such opinions in their exact words, putting quotation marks around them. Such *citations,* as they are called, should be identified in your notes by their source (book or article and page reference) so that you don't have to hunt up that information all over again when writing your footnotes.

Research need not take place only in your school library, of course. There are specialized libraries containing theatre works, including one-of-a-kind production books and manuscripts, that might be useful. You may also wish to correspond with living authors, directors, designers, or actors if such communications could prove useful to your subject. Seeing one or more of the plays under consideration and talking about it afterward with the director or dramaturge could certainly prove an invaluable aid to your developing investigation.

Developing Your Thesis

Somewhere in this process—probably starting at the point where you initially selected the topic—you will be arriving at a conclusion about your research, in terms of both what it seems to indicate about the subject and why your conclusion might be important. Where does your research lead? What observations are you drawing from your study? Are the experts right? Have they missed something? Are they ignoring the most important part?

A thesis need not be earth-shattering (for example, "Shakespeare's plays were really written by Queen Elizabeth"), but it should have at least some element of surprise, some conclusion the average reader or viewer would not arrive at on his or her own. This will follow easily and naturally if you have responded to the play yourself, with your own unique set of attributes, and have not simply tried to "find" your thesis in existing essays.

Organizing Your Argument

All papers are organized in the form of an *argument,* which does not mean a quarrel, but rather a logical series of suppositions, elaborations, demonstrations, proofs, and conclusions that argues your position coherently, perhaps even convincingly. Some form of outline is usually helpful in creating this organization. Perhaps the outline will have an order something like this, which includes some headings that may usually be omitted for student papers (and are so identified) but which are fundamental to advanced critical writing:

I. Initial statement of the topic (problem, peculiarity, subjects of comparison)
   A. Major questions posed by topic
   B. Indications of why these questions have attracted your attention
II. General review of earlier scholarly attempts to deal with the topic (ordinarily omitted in undergraduate paper)
III. General review of the limitation of these earlier scholarly attempts (ordinarily omitted in undergraduate paper)
IV. Presentation of specific material to be critically considered
   A. Citations of primary materials (the texts considered)
   B. Citations of secondary analyses (historical sources, critical interpretations, reference materials)
V. Drawing of proofs and conclusions
VI. Final statement of thesis

The outline, bald as it is, provides a starting point for arranging your paper and presenting your ideas as a structured argument rather than as a random collection of unrelated notions that, however brilliant, can never lead to new discoveries.

When the outline is done, you can rearrange your notes according to the outline's structure—which will be your paper's structure as well.

Writing Your First Draft

The first draft is more than a fleshing out of the outline: it is the test of your ability to articulate, on paper, what is by now buzzing about in your head and organized in your outline.

Writing is a skill, and you learn it from the time you begin to speak and understand English. There are hundreds of ways of saying the same thing, each with its own slight variation:

These are the times that try men's souls.
These times are trying to men.

Men have a trying time of it these days.
Men's souls are sorely tried by modern
  times.
These are trying times to the soul of man.

And so forth. All of these sentences have probably been uttered at one time or another, but only Tom Paine's, the first one, has entered the history books.

No essay is going to teach you to be a good writer, but the advice from here is that the more strongly you want to demonstrate something, the more cogently and persuasively you will write. Good writing is not an end in itself; good writing serves your argument, your thesis, your point of view. If you want to develop your writing, write essays (or letters) trying to explain to somebody else something that is important to you; if what you're trying to explain is the subject of your paper, you are in good shape for this assignment.

A well-written paper is always divided into paragraphs, each having its own central point—usually broached in the opening sentence, sometimes called a "topic sentence." Look at the first sentence of the paragraph above, or of this one. The remainder of the paragraph develops and explains the topic idea. When the author thinks the idea is satisfactorily expressed and communicated, the paragraph is brought to a close, often with a slight shift in tone that signals closure and gives the reader a little breathing space. Such as "entered the history books," two paragraphs above. Or such as this short sentence fragment.

Cite all quoted material inside quotation marks, always, and identify all quoted material by author and published source. This is for two reasons: (1) you don't want to be accused of stealing another author's direct ideas, which is a serious academic crime (plagiarism), and (2) you want to direct the reader to the original author, who probably has more to say on the subject. Your instructor might have specific instructions on footnoting; if not, you can follow any of several standard formats, such as those used in any scholarly journal or textbook. Footnotes should always include page references, except for well-known classic plays from which lines can usually be cited, directly in the text of your paper, by act, scene, and line reference (an initial footnote should identify the edition used).

When should you cite an outside authority? There are basically four situations where this is useful: (1) where you want to establish a standard critical opinion on something that provides a background to your argument, (2) where you want to state facts you haven't directly uncovered yourself, (3) where you want to disagree with the outside authority, and (4) where you want to support your first steps toward your conclusion. It is in number 4 where you must be careful, because you cannot use an outside authority to state your conclusion or even to support your final finding. The final finding must be yours alone: if you are going to end up at the same place as a leading critic, then why should I read *your* essay?

Revising the Paper

Revising does *not* mean turning all the simple words into fancy ones or turning to the thesaurus. Indeed, you should think of revising not as a fancying up but as a paring down. Read each sentence—aloud if that helps—and ask yourself: "Am I saying that as clearly as possible?" "Am I being persuasive, or am I just filling in blanks?"

You should know that authors rewrite everything, and rewrite many times. Leo Tolstoy wrote out the 1,800 pages of *War and Peace* seven times—in longhand. (Actually, his wife did most of the writing out.) And he was a professional writer with great experience at the time. I've written this section five times—at least. So you mustn't be embarrassed to rewrite, nor be so cocky as to think you've said things perfectly the first time around. "These times are sure trying for men's souls." It's okay, but don't you think you could make it better?

Word-processing computer software has enormously eased the technical burden of rewriting in the past decade; if you have not already done so, and if you expect to do a substantial amount of paper writing in the next few years, consider buying or gaining access to a personal computer. Most writers who have made the switch from typewriters to computers will never go back.

SOME FINAL THOUGHTS

Writing a paper is a creative task, not a duty. (Answering essay questions on exams, by contrast, is pretty much a duty.) You choose the topic, you choose the method of investigation, you dig into the material and into the relevant research field as deeply as you have time and inclination. Perspicacity, organizational skill, writing ability, and stick-to-itiveness are all required, but so is imagination and originality. Fine papers explore new ground, and you can always be sure that if you really dig into yourself, as well as into the material at hand, you will be very much on that new ground. Nobody else could ever go precisely where you go—that is a fundamental principle. Consequently, the potential results, for someone interested in pursuing scholarship, are substantial. You really can uncover things your instructors haven't and that the world of outside experts hasn't. Undergraduate essays, particularly those that thoroughly and creatively address specific comparisons, problems, patterns, or peculiarities, are published in scholarly literature each year; the present author's writing career began with just such an undergraduate paper. And, apart from publication, the excitement of treading where no scholar or critic has ever tread before may prove to be one of the highlights of your many years of higher education.

Glossary

Terms within the definitions which are themselves defined in this glossary are in *italic*.

absurd The notion that the world is meaningless. Derives from an essay, "The Myth of Sisyphus," by Albert Camus, which suggests that man has an unquenchable desire to understand, but that the world is eternally unknowable. The resulting conflict puts man in an "absurd" position, like Sisyphus, who, according to Greek myth, was condemned for eternity to push a rock up a mountain, only to have it always fall down to the other side. The philosophical term gave the name to a principal postwar dramatic genre: theatre of the absurd.

act (verb) To perform in a play. (noun) A division of a play. Acts in modern plays are bounded by an intermission or by the beginning or end of the play on each side. Full-length modern plays are customarily divided into two acts, sometimes three. Roman, Elizabethan, and neoclassic plays were usually printed in five acts, but these were not necessarily divided by intermissions, only stage clearings.

ad lib A line improvised by an actor during a performance, usually because the actor has forgotten his or her line or because there has been an accident on stage. Sometimes an author directs the actors to ad lib, as in crowd scenes where individual words could not be distinguished by the audience.

aesthetic distance The theoretical separation between the created artifice of a play and the "real life" the play appears to represent.

agon Action, in Greek. Refers to the major struggles and interactions of Greek tragedies. The root word of our "agony."

alienation effect A technique by which the actor deliberately presents rather than represents his or her character and "illustrates" the character without trying to embody the role fully, as naturalistic acting technique demands. This may be accomplished by "stepping out of character"—as to sing a song or to address the audience directly—and by developing a highly objective and "didactic" mode of expression. Developed by German playwright Bertolt Brecht (1898–1956). The actor is alienated from the role ("estranged" and "distanced" are perhaps better terms—all translations of the German word *verfremdungs*) in order to make the audience more directly aware of current political issues. Highly influential today, particularly in Europe.

amphitheatre In Rome, a large elliptical outdoor theatre, originally used for gladiatorial contests. Today the term is often used to designate a large outdoor theatre of any type.

anagnorisis Recognition, in Greek. Aristotle claimed every fine tragedy had a recognition scene, in which the *protagonist* discovered either some fact unknown to her or him or some moral flaw in her or his character. Scholars disagree as to which of these precise meanings Aristotle had in mind. See *hamartia.*

Apollonian That which is beautiful, wise, and serene, in the theories of Friedrich Nietzsche, who believed drama sprang from the junction of Apollonian and *Dionysian* forces in Greek culture.

apron That part of the stage in front of the *proscenium;* the forwardmost portion of the stage. Used extensively in the English Restoration period, from whence the term comes. Today, usually called the *forestage.*

aragoto The flamboyant and exaggerated masculine style of acting employed in certain *Kabuki* roles.

arena stage A stage with the audience arranged on all sides. Also known as "theatre-in-the-round." A famous such stage is in Washington, D.C. (The Arena Stage). The term is Latin (where it means "sand") and originally referred to the dirt circle in the midst of an *amphitheatre.*

arras A curtain, often at the rear of the stage. Polonius is stabbed hiding behind one in Shakespeare's *Hamlet.*

aside A short line in a play delivered directly to the audience; by dramatic convention, the other characters on stage are presumed not to hear it. Popular in Shakespeare and in the Restoration, the aside has made a comeback in recent years and is used to good effect, in conjunction with the longer *direct address,* by contemporary American playwrights such as Lanford Wilson and Neil Simon.

audition The process whereby actors are seen and heard by directors or casting directors during the casting of a play or a season of plays. Actors can audition both by presenting rehearsed monologues or scenes or by reading from the text of the play being presented.

avant-garde The "advance-guard" of an army goes beyond the front lines to break new ground; in theatre, the avant-garde are those theatre artists who abandon the conventional models and create works that are in the forefront of new theatrical movements and styles. The term has had wide currency in the twentieth-century theatre, particularly in France.

backstage The offstage area that is hidden from the audience. Used for scenery storage, for actors preparing to make entrances, and for stage technicians running the show. "Backstage plays," such as *The Torchbearers* and *Noises Off,* "turn the set around" and exploit the furious backstage activity that takes place during a play production.

beat The smallest unit of action in a scene, according to acting theorist and teacher *Konstantin Stanislavsky* (1863–1938).

biomechanics An experimental acting system, characterized by expressive physicalization and bold gesticulation, developed by Russian play director Vsevolod Meyerhold in the 1920s.

blackout The sudden extinguishing of all stage lights, leaving the theatre in blackness. As contrasted to a fade-out, which is a gradual fading of the lights.

blackout sketch In *vaudeville* and vaudeville-inspired plays: a short farcical scene, culminating in a punch line that is followed by a blackout.

blocking The specific staging of a play's movements, ordinarily by the director. "Blocking" refers to the precise indications of where actors are to move, moment by moment, during the performance. Often this is worked out ("blocked out") on graph paper by the director beforehand.

book In a musical play, the dialogue text, apart from the music and song lyrics.

border A piece of flat scenery, often black velour but sometimes a *flat*, which is placed horizontally above the set, usually to *mask* the lighting instruments. Often used with side *wings*, in which combination the scenery system is known as "wing and border."

box set A stage set consisting of hard scenic pieces representing the walls and ceiling of a room, with one wall left out for the audience to peer into. Developed in the nineteenth century and still very much in use in realistic plays.

Broadway The major commercial theatre district in New York, bordered by Broadway and Eighth Avenue; 44th Street and 52nd Street.

Bunraku A Japanese puppet theatre, founded in the seventeenth century and still performed today.

burlesque Literally, a parody or mockery, from an Italian amusement form. Today used to imply broad, coarse humor in farce, particularly in parodies and vaudeville-type presentations.

business The minute physical behavior of the actor, as in fiddling with a tie, sipping a drink, drumming the fingers, lighting a cigarette, and so forth. Sometimes this is controlled to a high degree by the actor and/or the director for precise dramatic effect; at other times the business is improvised in order to convey a naturalistic verisimilitude.

callback After initial auditions, the director or casting director will "call back" for additional readings those actors who seem most promising; this is the "callback audition," of which there may be many. Rules of the actors' unions require payment to actors for callbacks after a certain minimum number have been held.

caricature A character portrayed very broadly and in a stereotypical fashion. Ordinarily objectionable in realistic dramas. See *character*.

catharsis In Aristotle's *Poetics*, the "purging" or "cleansing" of terror and pity which the audience develops during the climax of a *tragedy*.

character A "person" in a play, as performed by an actor. Hamlet, Oedipus, and Willy Loman are "characters." Characters may or may not be based on real people.

character actor An actor particularly noted for playing roles with pronounced characteristics, such as old age, a comical appearance, a foreign accent, and so on.

chorus (1) In classic Greek plays, an ensemble of characters representing the general public of the play, such as the women of Argos or the elders of Thebes. Originally, the chorus numbered fifty; Aeschylus is said to have reduced it to twelve, and Sophocles to have increased it to fifteen. More recent playwrights, including Shakespeare and Jean Anouilh, have occasionally employed a single actor (or small group of actors) as "Chorus," to provide narration between the scenes. (2) In musical plays, an ensemble of characters who sing and/or dance together (in contrast to soloists who sing and/ or dance independently).

classical drama Technically, plays from classical Greece or Rome. Now used frequently (if incorrectly) to refer to masterpieces of the early and late Renaissance (Elizabethan, Jacobean, French neoclassical, etc.).

climax The point of highest tension in a play, when the conflicts of the play are at their fullest expression.

comedy Popularly, a funny play; classically, a play that ends happily; metaphorically, a play with some humor that celebrates the eternal ironies of human existence ("divine comedy").

comedy of humours In Elizabethan England, a comedy based on character types, which in turn were thought to be based on chemical imbalances in the bodily fluids. An imbalance of blood made one character "sanguine," an imbalance of bile made another "bilious," and an imbalance of phlegm made another "phlegmatic," for example. Ben Jonson's *Every Man in His Humour* (1598) is the exemplar of this type of play.

comedy of manners A comedy that exploits the foibles and follies of contemporary social behavior. The comedy of manners perhaps originated with Molière's *The Precious Ladies* (1658) and reached its peak shortly thereafter with the playwrights of the English Restoration (1660–1700), particularly William Congreve and William Wycherley.

comic relief In a tragedy, a short comic scene that releases some of the built-up tension of the play—giving the audience a momentary "relief" before the tension mounts higher. The "porter scene" in Shakespeare's *Macbeth* is an often-cited example; following the murder of Duncan, a porter jocularly addresses the audience as to the effect of drinking on sexual behavior. In the best tragedies, comic relief also provides an ironic counterpoint to the tragic action.

commedia dell'arte A form of largely improvised, masked street theatre that began in northern Italy in the late sixteenth century and still can be seen today. The principal characters—Arlecchino, Pantalone, Columbine, Dottore, and Scapino among them—appear over and over in thousands of commedia stories.

constructivism A twentieth-century design style, marked by large structural pieces and abstract, geometric regularity, which flourished in Europe, particularly in Russia after the revolution.

continental seating An arrangement of audience seating without a center aisle.

convention A theatrical custom that the audience accepts without thinking, such as "when the curtain comes down, the play is over." Each period develops its own dramatic conventions, which playwrights may either accept or violate.

cue The last word of one speech, which then becomes the "cue" for the following speech. Actors are frequently admonished to speak "on cue" or to "pick up their cues," both of which mean to begin speaking precisely at the moment the other actor finishes.

cycle plays In medieval England, a series of *mystery plays* that, performed in series, relate the story of religion, from the *Creation of the Universe* to *Adam and Eve* to *The Crucifixion* to *Doomsday*. The York Cycle includes forty-eight such plays.

cyclorama In a proscenium theatre, a large piece of curved scenery that wraps around the rear of the stage and is illuminated to resemble the sky or to serve as an abstract neutral background. Usually made of fabric stretched between curved pipes; sometimes made permanently with concrete and plaster.

denouement The final scene or scenes in a play, devoted to tying up the loose ends after the climax (although the word originally meant "the untying").

deus ex machina In Greek tragedies, the resolution of the plot by the device of a god (*deus*) arriving onstage by means of a crane (*machina*) and solving all the characters' problems. Today, any such contrived play ending, such as the discovery of a will. Considered clumsy by Aristotle and virtually all succeeding critics; occasionally used ironically in the modern theatre, as by Bertolt Brecht in *The Threepenny Opera*.

dialogue The speeches—delivered to each other—of the characters in a play. Contrasted to *monologue*.

diction One of the six important features of a drama, according to Aristotle, who meant by the term the intelligence and appropriateness of the play's speeches. Today, refers primarily to the actor's need for articulate speech and clear pronunciation.

didactic drama Drama dedicated to teaching lessons or provoking intellectual debate beyond the confines of the play. The dramatic form espoused by Bertolt Brecht. See *alienation effect*.

dimmer In lighting, the electrical device, technically known as a potentiometer, which regulates the current passing through the bulb filaments and, thereby, the amount of light emitted from the lighting instruments.

dim out To fade the lights gradually to blackness.

Dionysia Or Great Dionysia or City Dionysia. The week-long Athenian springtime festival in honor of Dionysus, which was, after 534 B.C., the major play-producing festival of the Greek year.

Dionysian Passionate revelry, uninhibited pleasure-seeking. The opposite of *Apollonian*, according to Nietzsche, who considered drama a merger of these two primary impulses in the Greek character.

Dionysus The Greek god of drama; also the god of drinking and fertility. Bacchus in Rome.

direct address A character's speech delivered directly to the audience. Common in Greek Old Comedy (see *parabasis*), in Shakespeare (see *soliloquy*), in *epic theatre*, and in some otherwise realistic modern plays (such as Neil Simon's *Broadway Bound*).

discovery A character who appears on stage without making an entrance, as when a curtain opens. Ferdinand and Miranda are "discovered" playing chess in Shakespeare's *The Tempest* when Prospero pulls away a curtain that had been hiding them from view.

dithyramb A Greek religious rite in which a chorus of fifty men, dressed in goatskins, chanted and danced; the precursor, according to Aristotle, of Greek tragedy.

documentary drama Drama that presents historical facts in a nonfictionalized, or only slightly fictionalized, manner.

domestic tragedy A tragedy about ordinary people at home.

double (1) An actor who plays more than one role is said to "double" in the second and following roles. Ordinarily the actor will seek, through a costume change, to disguise the fact of the doubling; occasionally, however, a production with a *theatricalist* staging may make it clear that the actor doubles in many roles. (2) To Antonin Artaud, the life that drama reflects, as discussed in his book, *The Theatre and Its Double*. See *theatre of cruelty*.

downstage That part of the stage closest to the audience. The term derives from the eighteenth century, when the stage was *raked* so that the front part was literally below the back (or *upstage*) portion.

drama The art of the theatre. Plays, playmaking, and the whole body of literature of and for the stage.

dramatic Plays, scenes, and events that are high in conflict and believability and that would command attention if staged in the theatre.

dramatic irony The situation when the audience knows something the characters don't, as in Shakespeare's *Macbeth* when King Duncan remarks on his inability to judge character—while warmly greeting the man (Macbeth) we already know plans to assassinate him.

dramaturge A specialist on dramatic construction and the body of dramatic literature; a scientist of the art of drama. Dramaturges are frequently engaged by professional and academic theatres to assist in choosing and analyzing plays, develop production concepts, research topics pertinent to historic period or play production style, and write program essays. The dramaturge has been a mainstay of the German theatre since the eighteenth century and is becoming increasingly popular in the English-speaking world. Sometimes identified by the German spelling *dramaturg*.

dramaturgy The science of drama; the art of play construction. Sometimes used to refer to play structure itself.

dress rehearsal A rehearsal, perhaps one of several, in full costume; usually also with full scenery, properties, lighting, sound, and technical effects. Ordinarily the last rehearsal(s) prior to the first actual performance before an outside audience.

drop A flat piece of scenery hung from the *fly gallery*, which can "drop" into place by a *flying system*.

eccyclema (Also *ekkyklema*.) A Greek stage machine, possibly a rolling platform that could be pushed through a stage door. Often used to bear corpses, as in Aeschylus' *Libation Bearers*, when the bodies of Aegisthus and Clytemnestra are so displayed.

empathy Audience identification with dramatic characters and their consequent shared feelings with the plights and fortunes of those characters. One of the principal effects of good drama.

ensemble Literally, the group of actors (and sometimes directors and designers) who put a play together; metaphorically, the rapport and shared sense of purpose that bind such a group into a unified artistic entity.

environmental theatre Plays produced not on a conventional stage, but in an area where the actors and the audience are intermixed in the same "environment" and where there is no precise line distinguishing stage space from audience space.

epic theatre As popularized by Bertolt Brecht, a style of theatre where the play presents a series of semi-isolated episodes, intermixed with songs and other forms of *direct address*, all leading to a general moral conclusion or set of integrated moral questions. Brecht's *Mother Courage* is a celebrated example. See also *alienation*.

epilogue In Greek tragedy, a short concluding scene of certain plays, generally involving a substantial shift of tone or a *deus ex machina*. Today, a concluding scene set substantially beyond the time frame of the rest of the play, in which characters, now somewhat older, reflect on the preceding events.

existential drama A play based on the philosophical notions of existentialism, particularly as developed by Jean-Paul Sartre (1905–1980). Existentialism, basically, preaches that "you are your acts, and nothing else," and that people must be held fully accountable for their own behavior. *No Exit* contains Sartre's most concise expression of this idea.

exodos In Greek tragedy, the departure of the chorus at the end of the play.

exposition In play construction, the conveyance, through dialogue, of story events that have occurred before the play begins. The difficulty in writing effective expository dialogue is in making such discussions of the past appear to be natural and uncontrived.

expressionism An artistic style that greatly exaggerates perceived reality in order to express inner truths directly. Popular mainly in Germany between the world wars, expressionism in the theatre is notable for its gutty dialogue, piercing sounds, bright lighting and coloring, bold scenery, and shocking, vivid imagery.

farce Highly comic, light-hearted, gleefully contrived drama, usually involving stock situations (such as mistaken identity or discovered lovers' trysts), punctuated with broad physical stunts and pratfalls.

flat Fabric, stretched over a wooden frame and painted, often to resemble a wall or portion of a wall. A traditional staple of stage scenery, particularly in the realistic theatre, since it is exceptionally lightweight, may be combined with other flats in various ways, and may be repainted and reused many times over several years.

fly (verb) To raise a piece of scenery (or an actor) out of sight, by a system of ropes and/or wires. Used in the theatre at least since ancient Greek times (see *deus ex machina*).

fly gallery The operating area for flying scenery, where fly ropes are tied off (on a pinrail) or where ropes in a counterweight system are clamped in a fixed position.

flying system The specific mechanics of flying scenery, usually either rope pulleys or, more commonly, a counterweight system. Electric motorized systems are sometimes used.

footlights In a proscenium theatre, a row of lights across the front of the stage, used to light the actors' faces from below and to add light and color to the setting. Used universally in previous centuries, but employed only on special occasions today.

forestage A modern term for *apron*. The small portion of the stage forward of the *proscenium*.

full house All audience seats are filled. See *house*.

genre Literally, "kind" (French). A term used in dramatic theory to signify a distinctive class or category of play, such as tragedy, comedy, farce, and so on.

geza The stage right, semi-enclosed musicians' box in *Kabuki* theatre. Also, the music from this box.

gidayu The traditional style of chanting in *Kabuki* and *Bunraku* theatre.

greenroom A room near the stage where actors may sit comfortably before and after the show, or during scenes in which they do not appear. This room is traditionally painted green; the custom arose in England, where the color was thought to be soothing.

gridiron The open framework well above the stage, where the pulleys of the *flying system* are anchored. The "grid," as it is usually called, should be at least three times as high as the *proscenium* and should have at least six to ten feet of clearance above it, so as to permit technicians to walk freely about.

ground plan A schematic drawing of the stage setting, as seen from above, indicating the location of stage-scenery pieces and furniture on (and sometimes above) the floor. A vital working document for directors in rehearsal, as well as for technicians in the installation of scenery.

ground row A low horizontal piece of stage scenery, often used to hide lighting instruments and to indicate a horizon. Originally the term was used for the low-lying lighting instruments themselves.

hamartia In Aristotle's *Poetics,* the "tragic flaw" of the *protagonist*. Scholars differ as to whether Aristotle was referring primarily to a character's ignorance of certain facts or to a character's moral defect.

hanamichi In the *Kabuki* theatre, a long narrow gangway leading from the stage to a door at the back of the auditorium. Used for highly theatrical entrances and exits right through the audience.

Hellenistic theatre Ancient Greek theatre during the fourth and third centuries B.C. The surviving stone theatres of Athens and Epidaurus date from the Hellenistic period, which began well after the great fifth-century tragedies and comedies were written. The Hellenistic period did produce an important form of comedy (*New Comedy*), however, and Alexandrian scholars during this period collected, edited, and preserved the masterpieces of the Golden Age.

high comedy A comedy of verbal wit and visual elegance, usually peopled with upper-class characters. The Restoration comedies of William Congreve and the Victorian comedies of Oscar Wilde are often cited as examples.

hikimaku The traditional striped curtain of the *Kabuki* theatre.

himation The gown-like basic costume of the Greek tragic actor.

house The audience portion of the theatre building.

house out In lighting, a direction to take the lights out in the audience portion of the theatre.

hubris In Greek, an excess of pride. The most common character defect (one interpretation of the Greek *hamartia*) of the *protagonist* in Greek tragedy. "Pride goeth before a fall" is an Elizabethan expression of this foundation of tragedy.

improvisation Dialogue and/or stage business invented by the actor, often during the performance itself. Some plays are wholly improvised, even to the extent that the audience may suggest situations that the actors must then create. More often, improvisation is used to "fill in the gaps" between more traditionally memorized and rehearsed scenes.

inciting action In play construction, the single action that initiates the major conflict of the play.

ingenue The young, pretty, and innocent girl role in certain plays; also used to denote an actress capable of playing such roles.

interlude A scene or staged event in a play not specifically tied to the plot. Also, in medieval England, a short moral play, usually comic, that could be presented at a court banquet amid other activities.

intermission (In England, *interval*.) A pause in the action, marked by a fall of the curtain or a fade-out of the stage lights, during which the audience may leave their seats for a short time, usually ten or fifteen minutes. Intermissions divide the play into separate *acts*.

Kabuki One of the national theatres of Japan. Dating from the seventeenth century, the Kabuki features magnificent flowing costumes; highly stylized scenery, acting, and make-up; and elaborately styled choreography.

kakegoe Traditional shouts that *Kabuki* enthusiasts in the audience cry out to their favorite actors during the play.

koken Black-garbed and hooded stage assistants in the *Kabuki* theatre.

lazzo A physical joke, refined into traditional business and inserted into a play, in the *commedia dell'arte*. "Eating the fly" is a famous *lazzo*.

Lenaea The winter dramatic festival in ancient Athens. Because there were fewer foreigners in town in the winter, comedies that might embarrass the Athenians were often performed at this festival rather than at the springtime *Dionysia*.

liturgical drama Dramatic material that was written into the official Catholic Church liturgy and staged as part of regular church services in the medieval period, mainly in the tenth through twelfth centuries.

low comedy Comic actions based on broad physical humor, scatology, crude punning, and the argumentative behavior of ignorant and lower-class characters. Despite the pejorative connotation of its name, low comedy can be inspired, as in the "mechanicals" scenes of Shakespeare's *A Midsummer Night's Dream*. Good plays, such as this one, can mix low comedy with high comedy in a highly sophisticated pattern.

mask (noun) A covering of the face, used conventionally by actors in many periods, including Greek, Roman, *commedia dell'arte*. Also used in other sorts of plays for certain occasions, such as the masked balls in Shakespeare's *Romeo and Juliet* and *Much Ado About Nothing*. Also, a symbol of the theatre; particularly the two classic masks of Comedy and Tragedy. (verb) To hide backstage storage or activity by placing, in front of it, neutrally colored *flats* or drapery (which then become "masking pieces").

masque A minor dramatic form combining dance, music, a short allegorical text, and elegant scenery and costuming; often presented at court, as in the royal masques written by Ben Jonson, with scenery designed by Inigo Jones, during the Stuart era (early seventeenth century).

melodrama Originally a term for musical theatre, by the nineteenth century this became the designation of a suspenseful, plot-oriented drama featuring all-good heroes, all-bad villains, simplistic dialogue, soaring moral conclusions, and bravura acting.

metaphor A literary term designating a figure of speech that implies a comparison or identity of one thing with something else. It permits concise communication of a complex idea by use of associative imagery, as with Shakespeare's "morn in russet mantle clad."

metatheatre Literally, "beyond theatre"; plays or theatrical acts that are self-consciously theatrical; that refer back to the art of the theatre and call attention to their own theatricality. Developed by many authors, including Shakespeare (in plays-within-plays in *Hamlet* and *A Midsummer Night's Dream*) and particularly by the twentieth-century Italian playwright Luigi Pirandello (*Six Characters in Search of an Author, Tonight We Improvise*), thus leading to the term "Pirandellian" (meaning "metatheatrical"). See *play-within-the-play*.

mie A sudden tableau in *Kabuki* theatre, with the actor frozen in a tense and symbolic pose.

mime A stylized art of acting without words. Probably derived from the *commedia dell'arte*, mime was revived in France during the mid-twentieth century and is now popular again in the theatre and in street performances in Europe and the United States. Mime performers traditionally employ white-face make-up to stylize and exaggerate their features and expressions.

mise-en-scène The staging of a play; literally, the "putting [a play] into the scenery."

modern classic A term used to designate a play of the past hundred years that has nonetheless passed the test of time and seems as if it will last into the century or centuries beyond, such as the major works of Chekhov, Shaw, and Samuel Beckett. See *classical drama*.

monologue A long unbroken speech in a play, often delivered directly to the audience (when it is more technically called a *soliloquy*).

morality play An allegorical medieval play form, in which the characters represent abstractions (Good Deeds, Death, etc.) and the overall impact of the play is moral instruction. *Everyman* (fifteenth century) is the most famous of these plays in English; the name of the author is not known.

motivation That which can be construed to have determined a person's (or character's) behavior. Since *Stanislavsky*, actors have been encouraged to study the possible motivations of their characters' actions. See *objective*.

musical A generic name for a play with a large number of songs, particularly when there is also dancing and/or a chorus.

mystery play A term describing medieval plays that developed from *liturgical drama* and treated biblical stories and themes. Unlike liturgical dra-

mas, which were in Latin, mystery plays are in the vernacular (English, French, German, Italian, Spanish, and Russian versions exist) and were staged outside the church. The exact origin and original meaning of the term is unclear. See *cycle plays*.

naturalism An extreme form of realism. Its proponents, active in the late nineteenth and early twentieth century, sought to dispense with all theatrical convention in the search for complete verisimilitude to life: a "slice of life," as the naturalists would say. Probably attainable only in theory, naturalism has nonetheless had a major impact on the theatrical arts, particularly on film acting and film writing.

neoclassicism Literally, "new classicism," or a renewed interest in the literary and artistic theories of ancient Greece and Rome and an attempt to reformulate them for the current day. A dominant force in seventeenth-century France, neoclassicism promoted restrained passion, balance, artistic consistency, and formalism in all art forms; it reached its dramatic pinnacle with the tragedies of Jean Racine.

New Comedy Greek comic dramas—almost all of which are now lost—of the late fourth to the second centuries B.C. Considerably more realistic than the Old Comedy of Aristophanes, New Comedy employs stock characters and domestic scenes; it strongly influenced Roman author Plautus and, through him, Renaissance comedy.

Nō Drama The classical dance-drama of Japan. Performed on a bare wooden stage of fixed construction and dimension and accompanied by traditional music, the Nō is the aristocratic forebear of the more popular *Kabuki* and remains generally unchanged since its fourteenth-century beginnings.

objective The basic "goal" of a character. Also called "intention" or "victory." Since *Stanislavsky,* the actor has been urged to discover his or her character's objectives and, by way of "living the life of his/her character," to pursue that character's objective during the course of the play.

off-Broadway The New York professional theatre located outside the *Broadway* district; principally in Greenwich Village and around the upper East and West sides. Developed in the 1950s, when it was considered highly experimental, the off-Broadway theatre is now more of a scaled-down version of the Broadway theatre, featuring musicals and commercial revivals as much as (or more than) original works.

off-off-Broadway A term designating certain theatre activity in New York City, usually non-professional (although with professional artists involved) and usually experimental and avant-garde in nature. Developed in the 1970s as a supplement to the commercialism of both Broadway and, increasingly, off-Broadway.

onnagata Women roles in *Kabuki,* as played by men.

open the house A direction to admit the audience. See *house.*

orchestra (1) In the ancient Greek or Roman theatre, the circular (in Rome, semicircular) ground-level acting area in front of the stagehouse, or *skene.* It was used primarily by the chorus. (2) In modern theatre buildings, the main ground-level section of the audience, which usually slopes upward at the rear. Distinct from the mezzanine and balconies and ordinarily containing the more expensive seats.

parabasis A "coming-forward" of a character in Old Greek Comedy, who then gives a *direct address* to the audience in the middle of the play. In Aristophanes, the parabasis is often given in the author's name and may have been spoken by Aristophanes himself. The parabasis was often unrelated to the plot and dealt with the author's immediate political or social concerns.

parados In the ancient Greek theatre, one of two passageways between the stagehouse (*skene*) and the audience area (*theatron*), employed primarily for the entrance and exit of the chorus.

parody Dramatic material that makes fun of a dramatic genre or mode or of specific literary works. A form of theatre that is often highly entertaining but rarely has lasting value.

pathos Passion, in Greek; also suffering. The word refers to the depths of feeling evoked by tragedy; it is at the root of our words "sympathy" and "empathy," which also describe the effect of drama on audience emotions.

peripeteia (In the Anglicized form, *peripety.*) The reversal of the protagonist's fortunes that, according to Aristotle, is part of the climax of a tragedy.

pièce-bien-fait See *well-made play.*

play-within-the-play A play that is "presented" by characters who are already in a play; as "The Murder of Gonzago," which is presented by "players" in *Hamlet.* Many plays are in part about actors and plays and contain such plays-within-plays; these include Chekhov's *The Seagull,* Anouilh's *The Rehearsal,* and Shakespeare's *A Midsummer Night's Dream* and *The Taming of the Shrew.*

plot The events of the play, expressed as a series of linked dramatic actions. More generally, and in common terms, the story of the play. The most important aspect of play construction, according to Aristotle.

practical In stage terminology, a property that works on stage the way it does in life. For example, a "practical" stove, in a stage setting, is one on which the characters can actually cook. A "nonpractical" stove, by contrast, is something that only looks like a stove (and may in fact be a stove without insides).

problem play A realistic play that deals, often narrowly, with a specific social problem. George Bernard Shaw's *Mrs. Warren's Profession,* for example, is virtually a dramatic tract on prostitution; Henri Becque's *The Vultures* deals quite single-mindedly with the need for husbands to write wills that protect their widows from unscrupulous lawyers. The term was most popular around the beginning of the present century; today it is mostly descriptive of certain movies for television.

producer (1) In America, the person responsible for assembling the ingredients of a play production: financing, staff, theatre, publicity, and management. Not ordinarily involved in the day-to-day artistic direction of the production, the American producer nonetheless controls the artistic process through his or her authority over personnel selection and budgeting. (2) In the English theatre, the term refers to what Americans call the director.

prologue In Greek tragedy, a speech or brief scene preceding the entrance of the chorus and the main action of the play, usually spoken by a god or gods. Subsequently, the term has referred to a speech or brief scene that introduces the play, as by an actor in certain Elizabethan plays (often called the *chorus*) and in the Restoration. Rarely used in the modern theatre.

properties Or *props.* The furniture and hand-held objects (hand props) used in play productions. These are often real items (chairs, telephones, books, etc.) that can be purchased, rented, borrowed, or brought up from theatre storage; they may also, particularly in period or stylized plays, be designed and built in a property shop.

proscenium The arch separating the audience area from the main stage area, in a theatre so designed. The term derives from the Roman playhouse, in which the proscenium (literally, *pro skene*, or "in front of the stage") was the facing wall of the stage. Modern thrust and arena stages have no proscenium.

proscenium theatre A theatre equipped with a proscenium. First popular in the late seventeenth century, and reaching its apogee in the late nineteenth and early twentieth centuries. Still the basic theatre architecture of America's Broadway and of major European theatre companies.

protagonist In Greek tragedy, and subsequently in any drama, the principal character. Often opposed by an *antagonist*.

raked stage A sloped stage, angled so that the rear (*upstage*) area is higher than the forward (*downstage*) area. Standard theatre architecture in the seventeenth century; often used today in scene design, but rarely in a theatre's permanent architecture.

realism The general principle that the stage should portray, in a reasonable facsimile, ordinary people in ordinary circumstances and that actors should behave, as much as possible, as real people do in life. Though there are roots that go back to Euripides, realism developed as a deliberate contrast to the florid romanticism that swept the European theatre in the mid-nineteenth century. See also *naturalism*, which is an extreme version of realism.

recognition See *anagnorisis*.

rehearsal The gathering of actors and director to put a play into production; the period in which the director stages the play and the actors develop and repeat their dialogue and actions. Etymologically, a "reharrowing," or repeated digging into. In French, the comparable term is *repetition*.

repertory The plays a theatre company produces. A company's current repertory consists of those plays available for production at any time.

Restoration In England, the period following the restoration of the monarchy in 1660. In the theatre, the period is particularly noted for witty and salacious comedies, through to William Congreve's brilliant *The Way of the World* in 1700.

rising action In dramatic structure, the escalating conflict; events and actions that follow the inciting action.

ritual A traditional cultural practice, usually religious, involving precise movements, music, spoken text, and/or gestures, that serves to communicate with deities. Often incorporated into plays, either as conventions of the theatre or as specific dramatized actions.

romanticism A nineteenth-century European movement away from neoclassic formalism and toward outsized passions, exotic and grotesque stories, florid writing, and all-encompassing world views. Supplanted in the late century by *realism*, romanticism survives today primarily in grand opera.

rotating repertory The scheduling of a series of plays in nightly rotation. This is customary in most European theatres and in many American Shakespeare festivals; it is otherwise rare in America. See *repertory*.

samisen The three-stringed banjo-like instrument used in *Kabuki* and *Bunraku* theatre.

satire A play or other literary work that ridicules social follies, beliefs, religions, or human vices, almost always in a lighthearted vein. Not usually a lasting theatre form, as summed up by dramatist George S. Kaufmann's classic definition: "Satire is what closes on Saturday night."

satyr A mythological Greek creature, half man and half goat, who attended Dionysus and represented male sexuality and drunken revelry. Satyrs served as the *chorus* of the *satyr play*.

satyr play The fourth play in a Greek *tetralogy*. Satyr plays were short bawdy farces that parodied the events of the tragedies that preceded them.

scene (1) The period of a stage time, now usually marked either by the rise or fall of a curtain or by the raising or lowering of lights, but in the past often marked simply by a stage clearing, where the stage represents a single space over a continuous period of time. Often the subdivision of an *act*. (2) The locale where the events of the play are presumed to take place, as represented by *scenery*. As "the scene is the Parson's living room." (3) Of scenery, as "scene design."

scenery The physical constructions that provide the specific acting environment for a play and that often indicate, by representation, the locale where a scene is set. The physical setting for a scene or play.

scenography Scene design, particularly as it fits into the moving pattern of a play or series of plays. Scene design in four dimensions (three physical dimensions plus time).

scrim A theatrical fabric woven so finely that when lit from the front it appears opaque, and when lit from behind it becomes transparent. Often used for surprise effects or to create a mysterious mood.

script A play's text as used in and prior to play production, usually in manuscript or typescript rather than in a published version.

semiotics The study of signs, as they may be perceived in literary works, including plays. A contemporary tool of dramaturgical analysis, which offers the possibility of identifying all the ingredients of drama (staging as well as language) and determining the precise conjunctions between them.

setting Or *set*. The fixed (stable) stage scenery.

shite The principal character in *Nō Drama*.

skene The Greek stagehouse (and root word of our "scene"). The skene evolved from a small changing room behind the *orchestra* to a larger structure with a raised stage and a back wall during the Greek period.

slapstick Literally, a prop bat made up of two hinged sticks that slap sharply together when the bat is used to hit someone; a staple gag of the *commedia dell'arte*. More generally, any sort of very broad physical stage humor.

slice-of-life Pure naturalism: stage action that merely represents an ordinary and arbitrary "slice" of the daily activity of the people portrayed.

soliloquy A monologue delivered by a single actor with no one else onstage. Sometimes played as the character "thinking aloud" and sometimes as a seeming dialogue with the (silent) audience.

spine In *Stanislavsky*, the through-line of a character's actions in a play.

stage business See *business*.

stage directions Scene descriptions, blocking instructions, and general directorial comments written, usually by the playwright, in the script.

stage left Left, from the actor's point of view.

stage right Right, from the actor's point of view.

Stanislavsky, Konstantin The great Russian director, acting teacher, and acting theorist (1863–1938) whose most noted dictum was "live the life of your character on the stage."

stock character A character recognizable mainly for his or her conformity to a standard ("stock") dramatic stereotype: the wily servant, the braggart soldier, the innocent virgin, and so on. Most date from at least Roman times.

stock situation One of a number of basic plot situations, such as the lover hiding in the closet, twins mistaken for each other, and so on, which, like stock characters, have been used in the theatre since Plautus and before.

style The specific manner in which a play is shaped, as determined by its genre, its historical period, the sort of impact the director wishes to convey to the audience, and the skill of the artists involved. The term generally refers to these aspects inasmuch as they differ from naturalism, although it could also be said that naturalism, too, is a style.

stylize To deliberately shape a play (or a setting, or a costume, etc.) in a specifically non-naturalistic manner.

subplot A secondary plot in a play, usually related to the main plot by play's end. The Gloucester plot in *King Lear* and the Laertes plot in *Hamlet* are examples.

subtext In *Stanislavsky*, the deeper and usually unexpressed "real" meanings of a character's spoken lines. Of particular importance in the acting of realistic plays, such as those of Chekhov, where the action is often as much between the lines as in them.

superobjective In *Stanislavsky*, the character's long-range *objective*, pursued throughout the play.

surrealism An art movement of the early twentieth century, in which the artist sought to go beyond realism into super-realism (of which surrealism is a contraction).

symbolism The first major antirealistic movement in the arts and in the theatre; emphasizing the symbolic nature of theatrical presentation and the abstract possibilities of drama. Flourished as a significant movement from the late nineteenth century to the early twentieth, when it broke into various submovements: expressionism, surrealism, theatricalism, and so on.

tableau A "frozen moment" onstage, with the actors immobile. Usually employed at the end of a scene, as the curtain falls or the lights dim.

teaser A neutral front *border* specifically used to hide lighting instruments.

tetralogy Four plays performed together in sequence. In ancient Greek theatre, this was the basic pattern for the tragic playwrights, who presented a *trilogy* of tragedies, followed by a *satyr play.*

text A playscript. Sometimes used to indicate the spoken words of the play only, as apart from the stage directions and other material in the script.

theatre-in-the-round See *arena stage.*

theatre of cruelty A notion of theatre developed by the French theorist, Antonin Artaud (1896–1948). Artaud's goal was to employ language more for its sound than for its meaning and to create a shocking stream of sensations rather than a coherent plot and cast of characters. Although Artaud's practical achievement was slight, his theories have proven extraordinarily influential.

theatre of the absurd See *absurd.*

theatre of alienation See *alienation effect, epic theatre.*

theatrical Something that "works" in the theatre; a play that is highly entertaining, showy, and marked by virtuoso skills. Generally not used to describe naturalistic plays or performances and occasionally pejorative when so used.

theatricalist A style of contemporary theatre that boldly exploits the theatre itself and calls attention to the theatrical contexts of the play being performed. Often used to describe plays about the theatre that employ *play-within-the-play.*

theatron "Seeing place," in Greek; the original Greek theatre.

thespian Actor. After Thespis, the first Greek actor.

tormentor In a proscenium theatre, one of two large vertical flats, painted black or a neutral color, placed at the far downstage left and right of the stage to *mask* the area between the proscenium and the first piece of stage scenery.

tragedy The word comes from the Greek "goat song" and originally meant a serious play. Refined by Greek playwrights (Thespis being the first) and subsequently the philosopher Aristotle into the most celebrated of dramatic genres: a play that treats, at the most uncompromising level, human suffering. The reason for the name is unclear; a goat may have been the prize, and/or the chorus may have worn goatskins.

tragicomedy A play that begins as a tragedy, but includes comic elements and ends happily. A popular genre in the eighteenth century, but rarely employed, at least under that name, in the modern theatre.

tragic flaw See *hamartia.*

traveler A curtain that, instead of flying out (see *fly*), moves horizontally and is usually opened by dividing from the center outward.

trilogy Three plays performed in sequence. The basic pattern of ancient Greek tragedies, of which one—Aeschylus' *The Oresteia* (*Agamemnon, The Libation Bearers,* and *The Eumenides*)—is still extant.

trope A written text, usually in dialogue form, incorporated into the Catholic Church service. In the tenth century A.D. these became the first *liturgical dramas.*

unities The unity of place, unity of time, and unity of action were the three "unities" that neoclassic critics of the seventeenth century claimed to derive from Aristotle; plays said to "observe the unities" were required to take place in one locale, to have a duration of no more than one day (in an extreme interpretation, in no more time than the duration of the play itself), and could concern themselves with no more than one single action. Aristotle made no such demands on playwrights, however, and very few authors have ever been able to make such observances with success.

unit set A set that, by the moving on or off of a few simple pieces and perhaps with a change of lights, can represent all the scenes from a play. A fluid and economical staging device; particularly useful for Shakespeare.

upstage (noun) In a *proscenium theatre,* that part of the stage farthest from the audience; the rear of the stage. So called because it was in fact raised ("up") in the days of the *raked stage.* (verb) To stand upstage of another actor. Often considered rude, inasmuch as it forces the downstage actor to face upstage (and away from the audience) in order to look at the actor to whom she or he is supposed to be speaking. Figuratively, the term may be used to describe any sort of acting behavior that calls unwarranted attention to the "upstaging" actor and away from the "upstaged" one.

vaudeville A stage variety show, with singing, dancing, comedy skits, and animal acts; highly popular in America from the late 1880s to the 1930s, when it lost out to the competition from movies, radio, and subsequently television.

waki The secondary character in *Nō Drama*.

well-made play In the nineteenth century, a superbly plotted play, particularly by such gifted French playwrights as Eugène Scribe and Victorien Sardou. Today, generally used pejoratively, as to describe a play that has a workable plot but shallow characterization and trivial ideas.

West End The commercial theatre district of London, England.

wings In a *proscenium theatre,* the vertical pieces of *scenery* to the left and right of the stage, usually parallel with the footlights.

Selected Bibliography

This bibliography first lists works of general scope and then cites studies particularly pertinent to discussions in this book.

HISTORICAL SURVEYS OF THEATRE AND DRAMA

Banham, Martin, ed. *The Cambridge Guide to Theatre.* Cambridge: Cambridge University Press, 1995.

Brockett, Oscar G. *History of the Theatre.* 7th ed. Boston: Allyn & Bacon, 1995.

Duerr, Edwin. *The Length and Depth of Acting.* New York: Holt, Rinehart & Winston, 1962.

Dukore, Bernard F., ed. *Dramatic Theory and Criticism: Greeks to Grotowski.* New York: Holt, Rinehart & Winston, 1974.

Gassner, John. *Masters of the Drama.* 3d ed. New York: Dover, 1954.

Hartnoll, Phyllis, ed. *The Oxford Companion to the Theatre.* 4th ed. New York: Oxford University Press, 1983.

Hill, Errol. *The Theatre of Black Americans.* New York: Applause Books, 1987.

Kanellos, Nicolás, ed. *Hispanic Theatre in the United States.* Houston: Arte Público Press, 1984.

————. *Mexican American Theater: Legacy and Reality.* Pittsburgh: Latin American Literary Review Press, 1987.

Leacroft, Richard, and Helen Leacroft. *Theatre and Playhouse.* London: Methuen, 1984.

Nagler, Alois M. *Sources of Theatrical History.* New York: Dover, 1952.

Nicoll, Allardyce. *World Drama from Aeschylus to Anouilh.* Rev. ed. London: Harrap, 1976.

Pottlitzer, Joanne. *Hispanic Theater in the United States and Puerto Rico.* New York: Ford Foundation, 1988.

The Revels History of Drama in English. 8 vols. London: Methuen, 1975–1983.

Sanders, Leslie C. *The Development of Black Theater in America*. Baton Rouge: Louisiana State University Press, 1988.

GENERAL STUDIES OF THEATRE AND DRAMA

Barry, Jackson G. *Dramatic Structure: The Shaping of Experience*. Berkeley: University of California Press, 1970.

Beckerman, Bernard. *Dynamics of Drama: Theory and Method of Analysis*. New York: Knopf, 1970.

――――. *Theatrical Presentation: Performer, Audience, and Act,* ed. by Gloria Brim Beckerman and William Coco. New York: Routledge, 1990.

Bentley, Eric. *The Life of the Drama*. New York: Atheneum, 1964.

Blau, Herbert. *To All Appearances: Ideology and Performance*. New York: Routledge, 1992.

Chinoy, Helen, and Linda Jenkins, eds. *Women in American Theatre*. New York: Crown, 1981.

Esslin, Martin. *An Anatomy of Drama*. New York: Hill & Wang, 1976.

Fergusson, Francis. *The Idea of a Theater*. Princeton, N.J.: Princeton University Press, 1949.

Granville-Barker, Harley. *On Dramatic Method*. New York: Hill & Wang, 1956.

Hayman, Ronald. *How to Read a Play*. New York: Grove Press, 1977.

Heffner, Hubert. *The Nature of Drama*. Boston: Houghton Mifflin, 1959.

Kilgore, Emile S., ed. *Contemporary Plays by Women*. Englewood Cliffs, N.J.: Prentice-Hall, 1991.

Laughlin, Karen, and Catherine Schuler, eds. *Theatre and Feminist Aesthetics*. Madison, Wis.: Fairleigh Dickenson University Press, 1995.

Schechner, Richard. *Environmental Theatre*. 2d ed. New York: Applause Books, 1994.

Schechner, Richard, and Willa Appel, eds. *By Means of Performance: Intercultural Studies of Theatre and Ritual*. Cambridge: Cambridge University Press, 1990.

Styan, J. L. *The Elements of Drama*. New York: Cambridge University Press, 1960.

――――. *Drama, Stage, and Audience*. New York: Cambridge University Press, 1975.

SPECIALIZED STUDIES

Greek and Roman Theatre

The oldest extant archeological remains of Greek theatres date from a century following the classical period; therefore, all reconstructions of earlier times are based solely on fragmentary written evidence and stylized vase paintings, which themselves are often of later periods as well. The existence of a raised stage as part of the *skene* is disputed, as is the shape of the stage. Peter Arnott and Clifford Ashby survey the controversies in detail.

Arnott, Peter D. *Greek Scenic Conventions in the Fifth Century B.C.* New York: Oxford University Press, 1962.

――――. *Public and Performance in the Greek Theatre*. New York: Routledge, 1989.

――――. *The Ancient Greek and Roman Theatre*. 2d ed. Princeton, N.J.: Princeton University Press, 1961.

Ashby, Clifford. "The Case for the Rectangular/Trapezoidal Orchestra," *Theatre Research International* 13:1 (Spring 1988), 1–20.

――――. "The Siting of Greek Theatres," *Theatre Research International* 16:3 (Autumn 1991), 181–201.

――――. "Where Was the Altar?" *Theatre Survey* 32:1 (May 1991), 3–21.

Burkert, Walter. *Greek Religion*. Oxford: Basil Blackwell, 1985.

――――. "Greek Tragedy and Sacrificial Ritual," *Greek, Roman and Byzantine Studies* 7 (1966), 87–121.

Butler, James H. *The Theatre and Drama of Greece and Rome*. San Francisco: Chandler, 1972.

Else, Gerald F. *The Origin and Early Form of Greek Tragedy*. Cambridge, Mass.: Harvard University Press, 1965.

Flickinger, Roy C. *The Greek Theatre and Its Drama*. 4th ed. Chicago: University of Chicago Press, 1960.

Kitto, H. D. F. *Greek Tragedy*. 3d ed. London: Methuen, 1961.

Padel, Ruth. "Making Space Speak," in John Winkler and Froma I. Zeitlin, eds., *Nothing to Do With Dionysos?* Princeton, N.J.: Princeton University Press, 1990.

Pickard-Cambridge, A. W. *Dithyramb, Tragedy, and Comedy*. 2d ed., rev. by T. B. L. Webster. Oxford: Clarendon Press, 1962.

――――. *The Dramatic Festivals of Athens*. 2d ed., rev. by John Gould and D. M. Lewis. Oxford: Clarendon Press, 1968.

Taplin, Oliver. *Greek Tragedy in Action*. Berkeley: University of California Press, 1978.

――――. *The Stagecraft of Aeschylus*. New York: Oxford University Press, 1977.

Toepfer, Karl. *Theatre, Aristocracy, and Pornocracy: The Orgy Calculus*. New York: PAJ Publications, 1991.

Winnington-Ingram, R. P., "The Origins of Tragedy," in P. E. Easterling and B. M. W. Knox, eds., *The Cambridge History of Classical Literature*. Vol. 1, *Greek Literature*, pp. 258–63. Cambridge: Cambridge University Press, 1985.

Zimmerman, Bernhard. *Greek Tragedy: An Introduction*. Trans. by Thomas Marier. Baltimore: Johns Hopkins Press, 1991.

Medieval Theatre

"Perhaps the most difficult period of Western theatrical history," according to historian Dunbar Ogden in *Theatre*

Survey, May 1978. The idea of processional staging of the cycle plays has come under strong attack, primarily from Nelson, Tydeman, and Nagler, all of whom favor the position that the procession was of *tableaux vivants* only, with the full performance held either indoors (Nelson) or at the last station. Our reconstruction, however, is consistent with the available records from the period, which were published in 1979 (Johnston and Rogerson); and the traditional view, which we espouse, is still widely supported, as, for example, by Clifford Davidson: "The evidence of the records . . . does appear to prove conclusively that the Corpus Christi play was performed at various stations through the city. . . . While it remains an attractive theory to suggest that the pageants grew out of tableaux vivants, . . . we can no longer seriously defend, I believe, Alan H. Nelson's revisionist theories about the staging of the York cycle indoors" (*Comparative Drama,* Spring 1980, pp. 79–80).

Chambers, E. K. *The Medieval Stage.* 2 vols. Oxford: Clarendon Press, 1903.

Collier, Richard J. *Poetry and Drama in the York Corpus Christi Play.* New York: Archon, 1978.

Haridson, O. B. *Christian Rite and Christian Drama in the Middle Ages: Essays in the Origin and Early History of Modern Drama.* Baltimore: Johns Hopkins Press, 1965.

Johnston, Alexandra F., and Margaret Rogerson. *Records of Early English Drama: York.* Toronto: University of Toronto Press, 1979.

Kolve, V. A. *The Play Called Corpus Christi.* Stanford, Calif.: Stanford University Press, 1966.

Muir, Lynette R. *The Biblical Drama of Medieval Europe.* Cambridge: Cambridge University Press, 1995.

Nagler, A. M. *The Medieval Religious Stage: Shapes and Phantoms.* New Haven, Conn.: Yale University Press, 1976.

Nelson, Alan H. *The Medieval English Stage: Corpus Christi Pageants and Plays.* Chicago: University of Chicago Press, 1974.

Nicoll, Allardyce. *Masks, Mimes, and Miracles.* New York: Harcourt Brace, 1931.

Southern, Richard. *The Medieval Theatre in the Round.* London: Faber & Faber, 1957.

Tydeman, W. *The Theatre in the Middle Ages.* New York: Cambridge University Press, 1979.

Wickham, Glynne. *Early English Stages, 1300–1660.* 2 vols. New York: Columbia University Press, 1959.

———. *The Medieval Theatre.* London: St. Martin's Press, 1974.

Woolf, Rosemary. *The English Mystery Play.* Berkeley: University of California Press, 1972.

Shakespearean Theatre

The literature on Shakespeare is voluminous, and the attempts to reconstruct a Shakespearean theatre have yielded varied interpretations. Our reconstruction is based largely on the original evidence, particularly Hodges's reading of it; nothing uncovered in the recent excavations (reported in Gurr and Orrell) changes the speculations presented in the drawings in this chapter. The list below is highly selective.

Adams, John. *The Globe Playhouse: Its Design and Equipment.* 2d ed. New York: Barnes & Noble, 1961.

Baldwin, T. W. *The Organization and Personnel of the Shakespearean Company.* Princeton, N.J.: Princeton University Press, 1927.

Beckerman, Bernard. *Shakespeare at the Globe, 1599–1609.* New York: Macmillan, 1962.

Bentley, Gerald E. *The Profession of Dramatist in Shakespeare's Time, 1590–1642.* Princeton, N.J.: Princeton University Press, 1971.

———. *The Jacobean and Caroline Stage.* 8 vols. New York: Oxford University Press, 1941–68.

Chambers, E. K. *The Elizabethan Stage.* 4 vols. London: Oxford University Press, 1923.

Dash, Irene G. *Wooing, Wedding and Power: Women in Shakespeare's Plays.* New York: Columbia University Press, 1981.

David, Richard. *Shakespeare in the Theatre.* New York: Cambridge University Press, 1978.

Gurr, Andrew, "A First Doorway into the Globe," *Shakespeare Quarterly,* Spring 1990, 95–100.

Harbage, Alfred. *Shakespeare's Audience.* New York: Columbia University Press, 1941.

Hildy, Franklin J., ed. *New Issues in the Reconstruction of Shakespeare's Theatre.* New York: Peter Lang, 1990.

Hodges, C. Walter. *The Globe Restored.* 2d ed. New York: Oxford University Press, 1968.

———. *Shakespeare's Second Globe.* New York: Oxford University Press, 1973.

Hotson, Leslie. *Shakespeare's Wooden O.* New York: Macmillan, 1960.

Kahn, Coppélia. *Man's Estate: Masculine Identity in Shakespeare.* Berkeley: University of California Press, 1981.

Mann, David. *The Elizabethan Player.* New York: Routledge, 1991.

Nagler, A. M. *Shakespeare's Stage.* New Haven, Conn.: Yale University Press, 1958.

Neely, Carol T. *Broken Nuptials in Shakespeare's Plays.* New Haven: Yale University Press, 1985.

Orrell, John, and Andrew Gurr. "What the Rose Can Tell Us," *Antiquity* 63 (1989), 421–29.

Southern, Richard. *The Staging of Plays Before Shakespeare.* New York: Theatre Arts Books, 1973.

Speaight, Robert. *Shakespeare on the Stage.* New York: William Collins Sons, 1972.

Thompson, Ann. "The Warrent of Womanhood: Shakespeare and Feminist Criticism," in Graham Holderness, ed., *The Shakespeare Myth.* Manchester, England: Manchester University Press, 1988.

Asian Theatre

English-language scholarship in Asian theatre is growing rapidly; the following are representative texts, largely oriented toward the Japanese theatre.

Benegal, Som. *A Panorama of Theatre in India*. Bombay: Popular Prakashan, 1968.

Cavaye, Ronald. *Kabuki: A Pocket Guide*. Tokyo: Tuttle, 1993.

Dunn, Charles J., and Bunzoh Torigoe. *The Actors' Analects*. New York: Columbia University Press, 1969.

Ernst, Earle. *The Kabuki Theatre*. New York: Grove Press, 1956.

Gunji, Masakatsu. *Kabuki*. Tokyo: Kodansha International, 1988.

Hansen, Kathryn. *Grounds for Play: The Nautanki Theatre of North India*. Berkeley: University of California Press, 1992.

Immoos, Thomas. *Japanese Theatre*. Trans. by Hugh Young. Photographs by Fred Mayer. London: Studio Vista, 1977.

Keene, Donald. *Nō and Bunraku: Two Forms of Japanese Theatre*. New York: Columbia University Press, 1970.

Kenny, Don. *On Stage in Japan*. Tokyo: Shufunotomo Co., Ltd., 1974.

Lee, Meewon. *Kamyonguk: The Mask-dance Theatre of Korea*. Ann Arbor, Mich.: UMI Dissertation Information Service, 1989.

Leiter, Samuel L. *The Art of Kabuki*. Berkeley: University of California Press, 1979.

Maruoka, Daiji, and Tatsuo Yoshikoshi. *Noh*. Trans. by Don Kenny. Osaka: Hoikusha Publishing Co., 1992.

Miettinen, Jukka O. *Classical Dance and Theatre in South-East Asia*. Oxford: Oxford University Press, 1992.

Nakamura, Matazo. *Kabuki, Backstage, Onstage: An Actor's Life*. Trans. by Mark Oshima. Tokyo: Kodansha International, 1990.

Ortolani, Benito. *The Japanese Theatre: From Shamanistic Ritual to Contemporary Pluralism*. Leiden: E. J. Brill, 1990.

Pronko, Leonard. *Theatre East and West: Perspectives Toward a Total Theatre*. Berkeley: University of California Press, 1967.

Scott, A. C. *The Classical Theatre of China*. London: Simson Shand Ltd., 1957.

———. *The Theatre in Asia*. London: Weidenfeld and Nicholson, 1972.

Shindo, Shigero. *Kunisada* (The Kabuki actor portraits). Tokyo: Graphic-sha Publishing Co., 1993.

Toita, Yasuji, and Chiaki Yoshida. *Kabuki*. Trans. by Don Kenny. Osaka: Hoikusha Publishing Co., 1992.

Van Erven, Eugène. *The Playful Revolution: Theatre and Liberation in Asia*. Bloomington: Indiana University Press, 1992.

Royal Theatre

Deierkauf-Holsboer, Wilma. *Histoire de la Mise-en-scène dans le Théâtre Française à Paris de 1600 à 1673*. Paris: Nizet, 1960.

Holland, Peter. *The Ornament of Action: Text and Performance in Restoration Comedy*. New York: Cambridge University Press, 1979.

Lancaster, H. C. *A History of French Dramatic Literature in the Seventeenth Century*. 5 vols. Baltimore: Johns Hopkins Press, 1929–42.

Lawrenson, T. E. *The French Stage in the XVIIth Century*. Manchester: Manchester University Press, 1957.

McBride, Robert. *Aspects of 17th Century French Drama and Thought*. Totowa, N.J.: Rowman & Littlefield, 1980.

Nicoll, Allardyce. *History of English Drama, 1660–1900*. 6 vols. London: Cambridge University Press, 1955–59.

Wiley, W. L. *The Early Public Theatre in France*. Cambridge, Mass.: Harvard University Press, 1960.

Modern and Postmodern Theatre

Antoine, André. *Memories of the Théâtre Libre*. Trans. by Marvin Carlson. Coral Gables, Fla.: University of Miami Press, 1964.

Artaud, Antonin. *The Theatre and Its Double*. Trans. by Mary C. Richards. New York: Grove Press, 1958.

Bentley, Eric. *The Playwright as Thinker*. New York: Reynal, 1946.

Bigsby, C. W. E. *A Critical Introduction to Twentieth-Century American Drama*. 3 vols. Cambridge: Cambridge University Press, 1985.

Birringer, Johannes H. *Theatre, Theory, Postmodernism*. Bloomington: Indiana University Press, 1991.

Bordman, Gerald. *American Musical Theatre*. New York: Oxford University Press, 1978.

Bradby, David. *Modern French Drama 1940–1980*. Cambridge: Cambridge University Press, 1984.

Brecht, Bertolt. *Brecht on Theatre*. Trans. by John Willett. New York: Hill & Wang, 1965.

Brook, Peter. *The Empty Space*. New York: Atheneum, 1968.

Brown-Guillory, Elizabeth. *Their Place on the Stage: Black Women Playwrights in America*. New York: Greenwood Press, 1988.

Brustein, Robert. *The Theatre of Revolt: An Approach to Modern Drama*. Boston: Little, Brown, 1964.

Craig, Edward Gordon. *On the Art of the Theatre*. 2d ed. Boston: Small, Maynard, 1924.

Croyden, Margaret. *Lunatics, Lovers and Poets: The Contemporary Experimental Theatre*. New York: McGraw-Hill, 1974.

de Jongh, Nicholas. *Not in Front of the Audience: Homosexuality on Stage*. London: Routledge, 1992.

Derrida, Jacques. "The Theatre of Cruelty and the Closure of Representation." In *Writing and Difference*, trans. Alan Bass. Chicago: University of Chicago Press, 1978.

Esslin, Martin. *Brecht: The Man and His Work.* New York: Doubleday, 1960.

———. *The Theatre of the Absurd.* Rev. ed. New York: Doubleday, 1969.

Gaggi, Silvio. *Modern/Postmodern.* Philadelphia: University of Pennsylvania Press, 1989.

Gassner, John. *Form and Idea in the Modern Theatre.* New York: Holt, Rinehart & Winston, 1956.

Geis, Deborah R. *Postmodern Theatri(k)s: Monologue in Contemporary American Drama.* Ann Arbor: University of Michigan Press, 1993.

Gordon, Mel. *Dada Performance.* New York: PAJ Publications, 1987.

Grotowski, Jerzy. *Towards a Poor Theatre.* New York: Simon & Schuster, 1968.

Guicharnaud, Jacques. *Modern French Theatre from Giraudoux to Beckett.* New Haven, Conn.: Yale University Press, 1961.

Harris, Andre B. *Broadway Theatre.* London: Routledge, 1994.

Houghton, Norris. *Moscow Rehearsals.* New York: Harcourt Brace, 1936.

Innes, Christopher. *Modern German Drama: A Study in Form.* New York: Cambridge University Press, 1979.

Kerensky, Oleg. *The New British Drama: Fourteen Playwrights Since Osborne and Pinter.* New York: Taplinger, 1979.

Kirby, Michael, ed. *The New Theatre: Performance Documentation.* New York: New York University Press, 1974.

Marranca, Bonnie, and Gautam Dasgupta. *American Playwrights: A Critical Survey.* New York: Drama Book Specialists, 1981.

Marranca, Bonnie, and Gautam Dasgupta, eds. *Interculturalism and Performance.* New York: PAJ Publications, 1991.

Matlaw, Myron. *Modern World Drama: An Encyclopedia.* New York: E. P. Dutton, 1972.

Natalle, Elizabeth J. *Feminist Theatre: A Study in Persuasion.* Metuchen, N.J.: Scarecrow Press, 1985.

Roose-Evans, James. *Experimental Theatre: From Stanislavski to Peter Brook.* New York: Universe Books, 1984.

———. *Experimental Theatre: From Stanislavski to Today.* Rev. ed. New York: Universe Books, 1973.

Seltzer, Daniel, ed. *The Modern Theatre: Readings and Documents.* Boston: Little, Brown, 1967.

Shaw, George Bernard. *The Quintessence of Ibsenism.* London: Constable, 1913.

Trachtenberg, Stanley, ed. *The Postmodern Moment.* Westport, Conn.: Greenwood Press, 1985.

Vanden Heuvel, Michael. *Performing Drama/Dramatizing Performance.* Ann Arbor: University of Michigan Press, 1991.

Völker, Klaus. *Brecht: A Biography.* New York: Seabury Press, 1978.

Willett, John. *The Theatre of Bertolt Brecht.* New York: New Directions, 1959.

Williams, Mance. *Black Theatre in the 1960s and 1970s.* Westport, Conn.: Greenwood Press, 1985.

Ziegler, Joseph. *Regional Theatre.* New York: Da Capo Press, 1973.

Acting and Directing

Barish, Jonas. *The Anti-Theatrical Prejudice.* Berkeley: University of California Press, 1981.

Barrault, Jean-Louis. *Reflections on the Theatre.* London: Salisbury Square, 1951.

Benedetti, Robert L. *The Actor at Work.* 5th ed. Englewood Cliffs, N.J.: Prentice-Hall, 1990.

Berry, Cecily. *Voice and the Actor.* London: Harrap, 1973.

Boleslavski, Richard. *Acting: The First Six Lessons.* New York: Theatre Arts Books, 1933.

Brook, Peter. *The Shifting Point.* New York: Harper & Row, 1987.

———. *There Are No Secrets.* London: Methuen, 1993.

Chaikin, Joseph. *The Presence of the Actor.* New York: Atheneum, 1972.

Chekhov, Michael. *To the Actor.* New York: Harper & Row, 1953.

Cohen, Robert. *Acting Power.* Palo Alto, Calif.: Mayfield, 1978.

———. *Acting Professionally.* 4th ed. Mountain View, Calif.: Mayfield, 1990.

Cohen, Robert, and John Harrop. *Creative Play Direction.* 2d ed. Englewood Cliffs, N.J.: Prentice-Hall, 1984.

Cole, Toby, and Helen K. Chinoy, eds. *Actors on Acting.* Rev. ed. New York: Crown, 1970.

———. *Directors on Directing.* Rev. ed. Indianapolis: Bobbs-Merrill, 1963.

Dean, Alexander. *Fundamentals of Play Directing.* 4th ed., rev. by Lawrence Carra. New York: Holt, Rinehart & Winston, 1980.

Diderot, Denis. "The Paradox of Acting," in William Archer, *Masks or Faces?* New York: Hill & Wang, 1957.

Goldman, Michael. *The Actor's Freedom.* New York: Viking, 1975.

Guthrie, Tyrone. *Tyrone Guthrie on Acting.* New York: Viking, 1971.

Hagen, Uta. *Respect for Acting.* New York: Macmillan, 1973.

Hethmon, Robert. *Strasberg at the Actors Studio.* New York: Viking, 1965.

Hodge, Francis. *Play Directing: Analysis, Communication, and Style.* Englewood Cliffs, N.J.: Prentice-Hall, 1971.

Lewis, Robert. *Method or Madness.* London: Heinemann, 1960.

———. *Advice to the Players.* New York: Harper & Row, 1980.

Linklatter, Kristin. *Freeing the Natural Voice.* New York: DBS Publications, 1976.

Marowitz, Charles. *The Act of Being: Toward A New Theory of Acting.* New York: Taplinger, 1978.

McGaw, Charles J. *Acting Is Believing.* 4th ed. New York: Holt, Rinehart & Winston, 1980.

Roach, Joseph R. *The Player's Passion: Studies in the Science of Acting.* Newark: University of Delaware Press, 1985.

Spolin, Viola. *Improvisation for the Theatre.* Evanston, Ill.: Northwestern University Press, 1963.

Stanislavski, Konstantin. *An Actor Prepares.* Trans. by Elizabeth Reynolds Hapgood. New York: Theatre Arts Books, 1936.

Design

Aronson, Arnold. *American Set Design.* New York: Theatre Communications Group, 1985.

Bablet, Denis. *Revolutions of Stage Design in the Twentieth Century.* New York: L. Amiel, 1976.

Barton, Lucy. *Historic Costume for the Stage.* Boston: Baker's Plays, 1935.

Bay, Howard. *Stage Design.* New York: DBS Publications, 1974.

Bellman, Willard F. *Scenography and Stage Technology: An Introduction.* New York: Harper & Row, 1977.

Bergman, Gosta M. *Lighting in the Theatre.* Totowa, N.J.: Rowman & Littlefield, 1977.

Burdick, Elizabeth B., et al., eds. *Contemporary Stage Design.* Middletown, Conn.: Wesleyan University Press, 1975.

Burris-Meyer, Harold, and Edward C. Cole. *Scenery for the Theatre.* 2d rev. ed. Boston: Little, Brown, 1972.

Corson, Richard. *Stage Make-up.* 5th ed. New York: Appleton-Century-Crofts, 1975.

Izenour, George C. *Theatre Design.* New York: McGraw-Hill, 1977.

Jones, Robert Edmund. *The Dramatic Imagination.* New York: Meredith, 1941.

Mielziner, Jo. *Designing for the Theatre.* New York: Atheneum, 1965.

Motley. *Designing and Making Stage Costumes.* London: Studio Vista, 1964.

————. *Theatre Props.* New York: DBS Publications, 1976.

Oenslager, Donald. *Stage Design: Four Centuries of Scenic Invention.* New York: Viking, 1975.

Payne, Darwin Reid. *Computer Scenographics.* Carbondale: Southern Illinois University Press, 1994.

Pilbrow, Richard. *Stage Lighting.* New York: DBS Publications, 1979.

Russell, Douglas. *Stage Costume Design.* New York: Appleton-Century-Crofts, 1973.

TEXT CREDITS

Page 76 From *The Ancient Greek and Roman Theatre* by Peter D. Arnott. Copyright © by Random House, Inc. Reprinted by permission.

Page 78 From *The Acharnians,* translated by Douglass Parker, edited by William Arrowsmith. Copyright © 1961 by William Arrowsmith. The New American Library, Inc. Reprinted by permission.

Page 80 Reprinted from Aeschylus, *Prometheus Bound,* translated by David Grene by permission of The University of Chicago Press. Copyright © 1956 by The University of Chicago Press.

Page 88 Selections are reprinted from *Oedipus Tyrannus,* Sophocles. Translation copyright © by Luci Berkowitz and Theodore F. Brunner, editors. A Norton Critical Edition, with the permission of W. W. Norton & Company, Inc. Copyright © 1970 by W. W. Norton & Company, Inc.

Page 95 From "Oedipus: Tragedy of Self-Knowledge" by Laslo Verseny, by permission of *Arion.*

Page 112 York Cycle Plays. Modern adaptation by Robert Cohen.

Page 126 From *Theatre & Propaganda* by George H. Szanto, published by the University of Texas Press. Copyright © 1978 by the University of Texas Press.

Page 135 From *Masters of the Drama,* by John Gassner. (Dover Publications, Inc., 1954.)

Page 153 From *Journey to the Center of the Theatre* by Walter Kerr. Reprinted by permission of the author.

Page 195 From *One-Act Comedies of Molière,* translated by Albert Bermel by permission of Frederick Ungar Publishing Co., Inc. Copyright © 1962, 1963, 1964, 1975 by Albert Bermel.

Page 199 Molière, *The Bourgeois Gentleman.* Translation and added stage directions by Robert Cohen.

Pages 243, 376 From *Strasberg at the Actors Studio* by Robert Hethman. Copyright © 1965 by Robert Hethman. Reprinted by permission of Penguin USA.

Page 254 From *Seven Plays* by Strindberg, translated by Arvin Paulson. Copyright © 1960 by Bantam Books, Inc. From *Six Plays of Strindberg,* translated by Elizabeth Sprigge. Reprinted by permission of Curtis Brown, Ltd. Copyright © 1955 by Elizabeth Sprigge.

Page 258 *Ubu Roi* by Alfred Jarry, from *Modern French Theatre: The Avant-Garde, Dada and Surrealism* by Michael Benedikt and George E. Wellwarth. Play translation copyright © 1964 by Michael Benedikt and George E. Wellwarth. Reprinted by permission of Georges Borchardt, Inc. for the translators.

Page 262 From *The Hairy Ape* by Eugene O'Neill, Random House, 1972. Copyright © 1920 by Eugene O'Neill. Reprinted by permission.

Page 266 From *Six Characters in Search of An Author* by Luigi Pirandello, *Naked Masks: Five Plays by Luigi Pirandello,* translated by Edward Storer, edited by Eric Bentley. Copyright © 1922 by E. P. Dutton, renewed 1950 in the names of Stefano, Fausto, Lietta Pirandello. Used by permission of Dutton Signet, a division of Penguin Books USA Inc.

Page 268 *Jet of Blood* by Antonin Artaud, from *Modern French Theatre: The Avant-Garde, Dada and Surrealism* by Michael Benedikt and George E. Wellwarth. Play translation copyright © 1966 by George E. Wellwarth. Reprinted by permission of Georges Borchardt, Inc. for the translators.

Page 269 Selection by Jean-Paul Sartre from *Theatre Arts,* July 1946. Reprinted by permission of Mrs. W. A. Bradley.

Page 276 Selections from *Happy Days* by Samuel Beckett. Reprinted by permission of Grove Press, Inc. Copyright © 1961 by Grove Press, Inc.

Page 277 First published in *The Hudson Review,* Vol. XIV, No. 4 (Winter, 1961–62). Reprinted by permission of the author.

Page 289 From *The Good Person of Sezuan* by Bertolt Brecht, *The Good Person of Sezuan, Mother Courage and Her Children* and *Fear and Misery in the Third Reich, Vol. 2,* translated by John Willett, Arcade Publishing 1993. Copyright © 1943 by Bertolt Brecht. Reprinted by permission.

Page 297 From *Rockaby* by Samuel Beckett, *Rockaby and Other Short Pieces,* Grove/Atlantic, 1981. Copyright © 1981 by Samuel Beckett. Reprinted by permission.

Page 396 From *Silence* by Harold Pinter. Copyright © 1969 by Harold Pinter Limited; from *Dirty Linen* by Tom Stoppard. Copyright © 1976 by Tom Stoppard. Used by permission of Grove/Atlantic, Inc.

Page 420 From *The Dramatic Imagination* by Robert Edmund Jones. Reprinted with the permission of the publishers, Theatre Arts Books, 29 West 35 Street, New York, New York 10001.

Page 439 From *Designing and Making Stage Costumes* by Motley. Copyright © 1964 by Elizabeth Montgomery, Sophie Devine and Margaret Harris. Reprinted by permission of Watson-Guptill Publications.

Page 461 From *The Empty Space* by Peter Brook by permission of Atheneum Publishers, Inc.

Pages 486, 487 From *Wasserstein: Comedy, Character, Reflection* by Mel Gussow, *The New York Times,* October 23, 1992. Copyright © 1992 by The New York Times Co.; *Wasserstein Pens a Pointed Drawing-Room Comedy* by Doug Watt, *New York Daily News,* October 30, 1992. Copyright © 1992 New York Daily News L.P. Reprinted with permission.

Index

Note: *f* indicates figure; *q* indicates quotation.